BRITAIN DISCOVERED

BRITAIN DISCOVERED

A pictorial atlas of our land and heritage

General consultant: Arthur Marwick
Professor of History & Dean of Arts, The Open University

ARTISTS HOUSE

Executive editor Robert Saxton
Executive art editor Val Hobson
Editors Roslin Mair
Margaret Mulvihill
with assistance from:
Jane Crawley
Lesley Ellis
Ken Hewis
Nicholas Law
Michele Staple
Designers Jacquie Gulliver
Ruth Levy
Picture research Meg Price Whitlock
Gazetteer research Catherine Jackson
Cartographer Eugene Fleury
Illustration Gillie Newman
Production Barry Baker
Historical geography consultants Professor R.A. Butlin
Dr R.A. Dodgshon

Britain Discovered was produced from a concept by Stan Remington

Britain Discovered
Edited and designed by
Mitchell Beazley International Ltd,
London W1

ISBN 0 86134 122 8

Originated by Gilchrist Bros Ltd, Leeds
Typeset by Servis Filmsetting Ltd, Manchester
Printed and bound in Portugal by Printer Portuguesa Lda.

CONTENTS

Buildings & places

Transport & communications

The arts

THE CONTRIBUTORS

Detailed credits are given on page 327

P.J. Banyard
Professor S.H. Beaver
Professor E.G. Bowen
Professor Eric Brown
Professor R.A. Butlin
Hugh Canning
Dr Neil Cossons
Dr Robert A. Dodgshon
Sarah Eldridge
Judith Evans
Shula Fury
John Glaves-Smith
E.H.M. Harris
Jeanette A. Harris
R.I. Hodgson
the late Dr Alan J. Lee
Professor Donal McCartney
Michael March
Professor Arthur Marwick
Dr Richard Pestell
Colin Read
John A. Roberts
Martin Shreeves
Frank Sowerby
L.A. Spong
Dr J. Stevenson
Dr Michael Tracey
Geoffrey Trease
Dr B.J. Turton
Dr John Waller
Dr J.R. Walton
Dr Mark Wise

HOW TO USE THIS BOOK

Connections

In the *Rand McNally Pictorial Atlas of Britain,* all the themes interconnect. There are innumerable points of contact between the different kinds of human activity described in the book (political, military, commercial, agricultural, industrial, creative, and so on), and between these and the physical environment in which they take place. To help the reader trace these links there is a CONNECTIONS box (printed in gray) for each subject covered. The cross-references these boxes contain are charts for exploratory voyages within the book.

Each entry in the CONNECTIONS boxes is organized as follows: first (in bold type) the subject on which you may wish to find more information; then a reference to the essay(s) in which this subject is further explored. The latter part of the cross-reference is a page reference, followed by the title of the essay in question (in italics).

Themes & places

No one would want merely to read about Britain when the island itself is waiting to be explored. Part of the purpose of the *Rand McNally Pictorial Atlas of Britain* is to satisfy the curiosity of the traveller, who is provided with detailed guidance at the back of the book in the form of a thematic gazetteer—'Themes & places'.

This section is designed to cater to particular enthusiasms. It is organized into 34 themes, arranged alphabetically from Aviation to Windmills (there is a complete list of subjects on page 304). Each theme is subdivided into 11 regions, and within each region the organization is alphabetical. (The map on page 304 shows the regional divisions, as well as counties and major towns.)

Although the gazetteer is selective, it is intended to cover all the main sites within a given field of interest, and to say briefly what the visitor can expect to find at each. Cross-references are provided where appropriate.

INTRODUCTION

by Professor Arthur Marwick,
The Open University, Milton Keynes

The theme of this book is nothing less than the character of Britain (past and present) in all its manifestations. The approach is refreshingly interdisciplinary: too often history is set apart from geography, economics from art, and so on.

Within its small compass Britain contains an astonishing topographical diversity, which has played a major role in its development as a nation. Different types of landscape have assumed a special importance at different periods. The wealth of medieval England was founded on sheep farming; that of industrial Britain on upland streams in the early period (to provide water-power), and on rich deposits of coal and iron ore in the later phase of industrialization.

The various landscapes of Britain bear the imprint of the movements of ancient peoples and of the great events and upheavals of history. Romans, Anglo-Saxons, Vikings and Normans came, conquered, were absorbed. After the Norman conquest the mode of land tenure and the structures of local life were systematized. Efficient Norman rule left its mark in a scattering of robust castles, many of which still survive. With the growth of commerce in the Middle Ages, towns flourished; and as important new social groups became prosperous in the 16th and 17th centuries, they used their wealth to build fine country mansions in the Tudor and Jacobean styles. Changes in agriculture, culminating in the 'agricultural revolution' of the 18th century, altered the look of the land, as medieval strips gave place to enclosed fields. Political stability and the spoils of commerce and foreign wars formed the basis both for elegant architecture in the neoclassical style and for the 'industrial revolution'. Industrialization caused profound changes in British life, affecting the work habits and dwelling places of the people. The coming of the railways (from the 1820s onwards) fostered urban and suburban growth and bequeathed magnificent engineering landmarks, such as the Menai and Forth bridges.

Today the British are scarcely a deeply religious people. However, the Christian religion (Catholic until the Reformation of Henry VIII, in many forms thereafter) has been a central influence in history. Its importance can be appreciated in the immense variety of parish churches in local styles, as well as in great cathedrals such as Lincoln. Educational institutions were originally religious in inspiration, but from the Middle Ages many foundations were splendidly secular in intention and appearance.

The living symbol of secular and ecclesiastical wealth is London, whose story is told here in detail. This book avoids too metropolitan a bias, however. It also speaks of such important cities as Edinburgh and Manchester and of the varieties of ports, spas, mining towns, villages, farms, monasteries and other types of community which have evolved through the ages.

One special feature which has shaped Britain's modern history was the emergence very early on of a coherent, and increasingly confident, working class. An aristocracy or upper class has been in almost continual existence, and there is also a variegated middle class of more recent origin. The special British mix of social groups, and of religious, ethnic and national groups, has determined many aspects of life – voting habits, the quality of education, the nature of artistic patronage, the physical layout of towns and cities.

In modern times, geography has again strikingly impacted upon history, in that economic and social patterns have been affected by the exploitation of North Sea oil. Britain's economic performance from the 1970s onwards has not been as convincing as might have been expected from the pace-setter of the industrial revolution. Yet Britain continues to be the world's greatest exporter, and across the country an enormous variety of trades and crafts and new technologies are carried on, influenced by history and themselves shaping the present and the future. Political institutions, too, are dynamic, gradually yielding to evolutionary change.

The concluding section of the book (although it is not by any means an endpoint) is about the arts. Creative artists have offered special insights into the development of Britain. A Wordsworth, a D.H. Lawrence or a Turner can also affect the way we perceive a landscape, whether man-made or natural. Landscapes, it will soon be seen, are one of the central concerns of this book, for their human ramifications are inexhaustible, spilling into art, industry, architecture, everything. The book begins, though, by looking at the landscape as a physical entity. Nature too has its history – its great events and gradual evolutions.

Arthur Marwick

Nature & the landscape

The landscapes of Britain: the plural is appropriate because of the prodigious variety of the island's scenery. The following pages look at many of the forces that have gone into Britain's making, including ice movements, geological upheavals, worrying by weather and the sea, and human interference. Ecological issues – landscape as a habitat for flora and fauna – are also glanced at.

Britain's climate

Northerly latitudes are associated with cold climates, but winter temperatures in Britain are moderated by air warmed up over the North Atlantic Drift – a sea current whose warmth is ultimately equatorial in origin. The seas around Britain are warmer by about eight degrees than those of Labrador, at roughly the same latitude. The difference is largely caused by the Drift in combination with the prevailing winds, which are south-westerlies. As they move over the warm currents, they pick up heat and bring mild winter weather. In summer, when the land warms up, the effect is overturned and cool winds come off the sea.

The movement of air masses

Weather is affected by air masses from different regions, depending on wind direction. Balmy summer days, with a possibility of rain, are the product of subtropical air masses borne by the south-westerlies. Hot, dry spells in summer are caused by what meteorologists call 'continental tropical' air, ultimately from the Sahara.

In winter it is common for cold, dry air to be brought across the North Sea by north-easterlies, absorbing moisture *en route* and producing snow showers along the east coast. The harshest winter weather in Scotland is linked with cold, moist arctic air, which leads to snow, but in England and Wales snow is provoked by warm air trying to advance after a cold spell. 'Maritime polar' air gives heavy showers at all times of the year – over the mountains in winter, farther inland in summer. It also brings invigorating off-sea winds. South-westerlies in winter bring milder weather.

Depressions and anticyclones

For much of the year, Britain is affected by a series of wet spells of variable duration whose origin lies in the interaction of air masses over the Atlantic. A distortion on the boundaries between cold and warm air masses leads to an area of low pressure and rising air, known as a depression. Winds blow anticlockwise round the centre of low pressure. The advancing boundary is called a 'warm front', and the wall of cold air that follows is a 'cold front'. At the warm front, whose approach is heralded by lower cloud bases, the rising air expands and cools to give clouds and rain. At the cold front, the heavier cold air undercuts and pushes the warm air in front of it, again causing rainclouds.

Patches of high pressure (anticyclones) cause uniform conditions over large areas. The weather

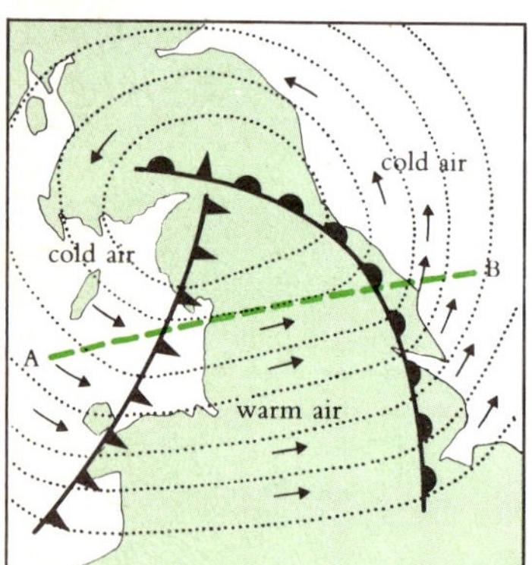

CLOUDSCAPE OVER THE RIDGEWAY, IN THE SOUTH OF ENGLAND (***above***). *Rain pours down from an evil-looking cumulonimbus, or thunder, cloud.*

ANATOMY OF A DEPRESSION (***left and below***). *On weather maps a depression is plotted using thick lines to indicate the fronts. The spiked line is a cold front, with the spikes showing the direction of movement. Semicircles are used along the line of the warm front.*

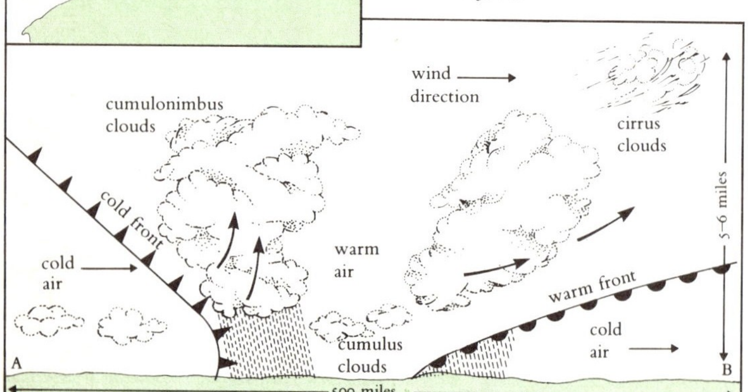

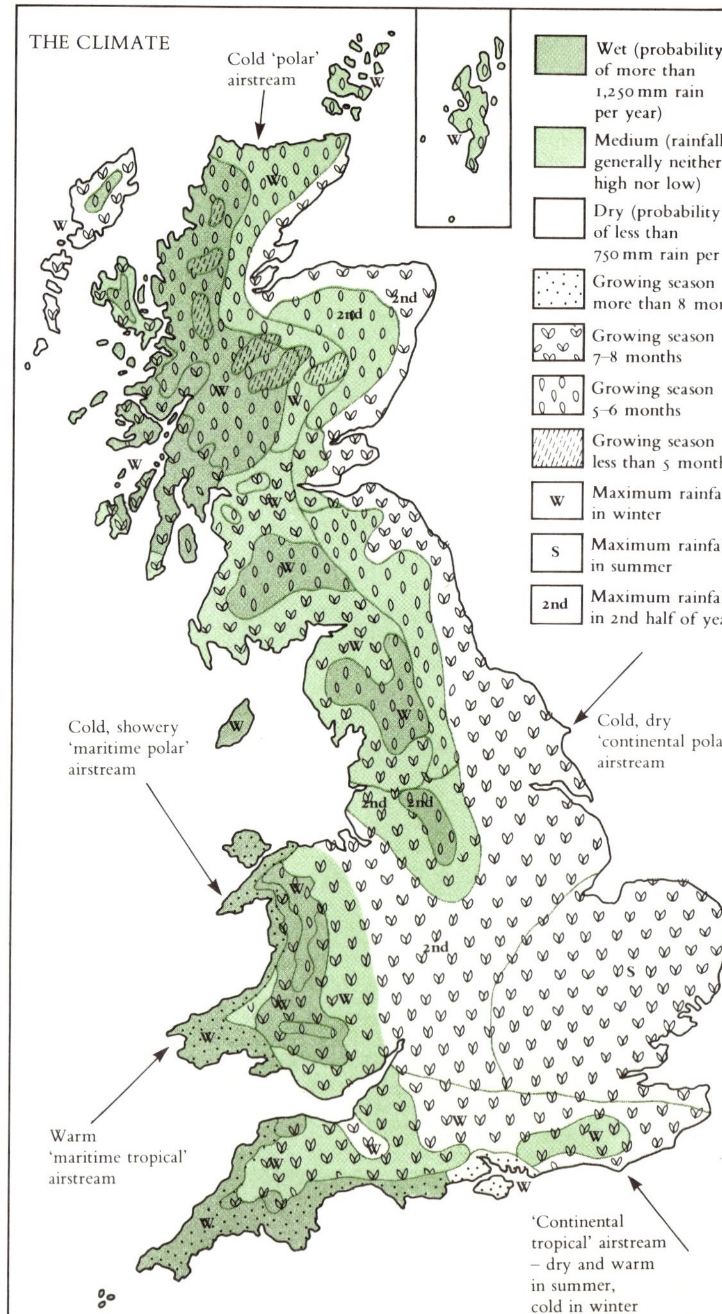

After Prof. S. Gregory, University of Sheffield

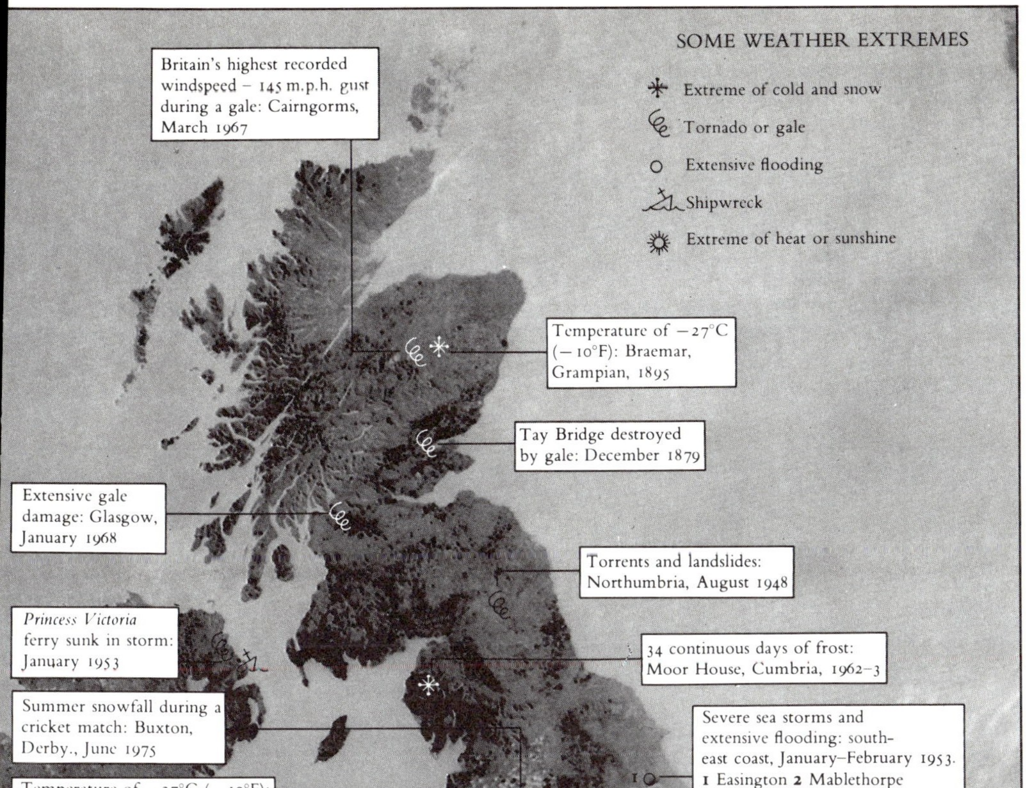

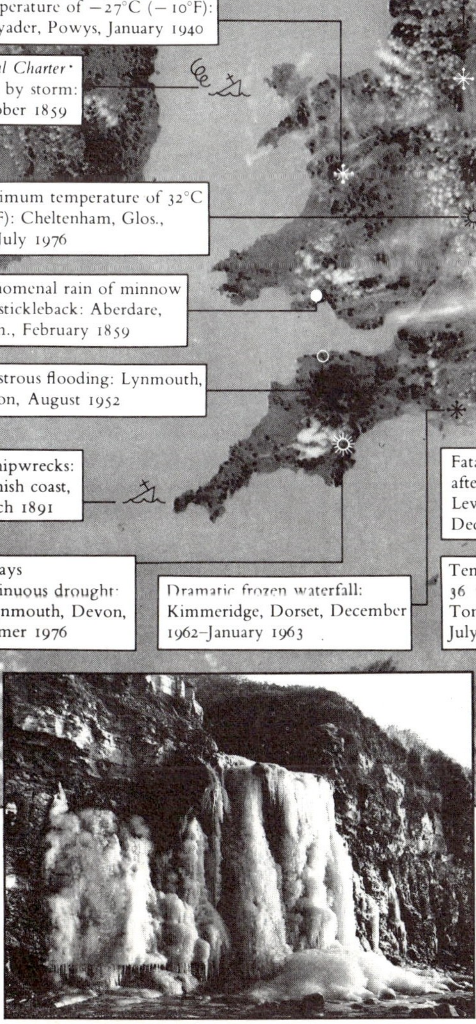

FROZEN WATERFALL AT KIMMERIDGE, DORSET (*left*). *This extraordinary photograph was taken in the Great Frost of 1962–63, when near-arctic conditions prevailed. The January was the coldest since 1795. The ground froze to a depth of a metre or more, interrupting piped water supplies and freezing sewers. Winter conditions as spectacular as these are seen very seldom.*

may be dull or sunny, but it will always be dry. At the centres of anticyclones, light winds always blow. A clear anticyclone in summer gives hot weather and in winter leads to fog at night.

Weather variations

The keynote of Britain's weather is variability. Mini-climates are created by local variations dependent on longitude, latitude and topography. Averaged out over the year, the north and east are the coldest regions. However the highest summer temperatures are found in the south-east. Because this region is farthest from maritime influences, the average annual temperature *range* is about twice that of the Western Isles of Scotland.

Regional weather differences are often expressed in terms of the growing season for plants. This is

THE CHELSEA RESERVOIR, WALTON-ON-THAMES, LONDON, IN THE DROUGHT OF 1976. *The clay bottom has dried out to form shrunken mud-plates.*

defined as the number of months with a mean temperature above 6°C (43°F). When temperatures rise to this point, and remain above it, the growth of many crops is triggered off and maintained. In England this may happen any time from mid-February to late March, but Scotland tends to lag behind. In addition to latitude, the growing season is also affected by altitude.

Rainfall varies quite dramatically according to locality. The Thames estuary has an annual average of less than 510 mm (20 in), whereas in parts of Snowdonia, the Lake District and Western Scotland, 5,000 mm (197 in) or more is common. It is topography that largely accounts for such disparities. Moist winds from the west are forced upwards by the western mountains. The air rises and cools rapidly, clouds form and rainfall is heavy on the windward slopes.

Local variations are often surprisingly dramatic over short distances. Deep valley bottoms, for example, have their own weather systems: on calm, clear nights, cold air rolls down the slopes, frosts occur and, if the air is moist, condensation takes place and a valley fog develops.

CONNECTIONS
Lowland rainfall: 138–9 *Modern agriculture*
The Thames flood barrier: 174–5 *Engineering*
Tropical plants: 216–19 *Gardens*
The water cycle: 28–9 *Rivers and lakes*

Beneath the landscape

Britain is a geologist's paradise and boasts a great variety of rocks of different ages which elsewhere are found spread monotonously across thousands of miles.

The study of geology requires an active imagination. Because the geological periods embrace tens of millions of years – and Britain in its present shape has only existed for about one two-thousandth of its geological history – we have to imagine the processes that shaped the landscape around us happening and re-happening, interacting, and indeed continuing, over aeons of time. We have to dismiss our normal visualization of the island and follow geology out beyond the coastline and under the sea. We must have an image in our minds of a Britain that buckled and bent, was crumpled and split, submerged, frozen and melted as it lurched from one geological era to the next.

The rocks themselves are divided into three groups: igneous, sedimentary and metamorphic. Igneous rocks were formed by the cooling of molten magma after violent volcanic activity. The sedimentary rocks are composed of the weathered or eroded fragments of older rocks and the remains of living organisms, either plants or animals. Metamorphic rocks have been formed by the melting or compression of older rocks through heat or subterranean forces.

Igneous rocks

There are two types of igneous rock – *extrusive* and *intrusive*. Extrusive igneous rocks, such as the basalt columns of Fingal's Cave on the Hebridean island of Staffa, cooled and solidified on the surface of the Earth. Granite, the most abundant igneous rock, is intrusive; that is, it cooled and solidified underground. This might seem a surprising origin for a rock that we associate with the heights of Arran or the great glistening tors of Dartmoor, but these granites were formed from molten rock in the roots of great mountains that have long since been eroded by the powerful forces of nature.

Sedimentary rocks

The sedimentary rocks came into being by gentler means. Erosion, transportation and deposition processes all had a part to play. When a rock is exposed it can be worn down by wind, rivers, glaciation, and even chemicals in water. The eroded particles of old rocks in combination with other materials form the sedimentary rocks. Thus, a riverside boulder yields fragments to the water that become round pebbles, then gravel, and then perhaps the sandy bottom of the sea. When such debris is sandwiched together by the pressure of overlying material, including the bones of dead sea animals, the typically layered sedimentary rocks are formed. Many of them contain fossils, which provide fascinating evidence of prehistoric life.

Most British limestones were formed in ancient shallow seas and are predominantly composed of vast numbers of sea creatures and shells. The dazzling white cliffs of Dover are made of a particularly pure form of limestone, chalk, which contains a tiny percentage of sand or mud. The nodules of flint that can be found embedded in such cliffs are thought to be the fossilized remains of ancient shoals of primitive sponges. The coalfields

THE GEOLOGICAL SUBSTRUCTURE

Sedimentary rocks are classified in the key according to age, igneous rocks according to their formation. A selection of fossils is depicted around the map.

Hoplites auritus
Cretaceous. Variety of ammonite, common fossil seashell, sometimes about a metre in diameter

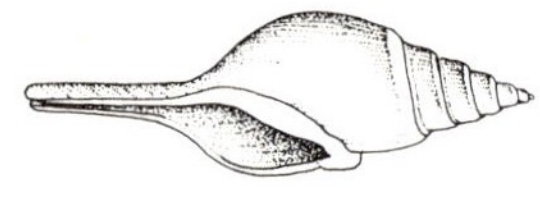

Clavilithes longaevus
Tertiary. Fossilized mollusc, relic of a subtropical sea that covered south-east England

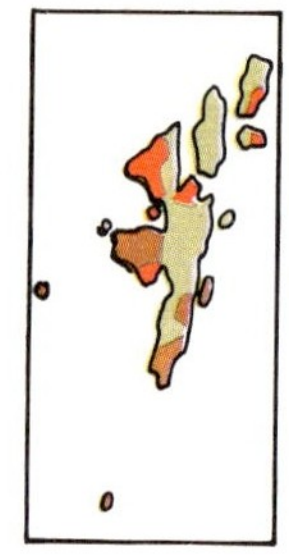

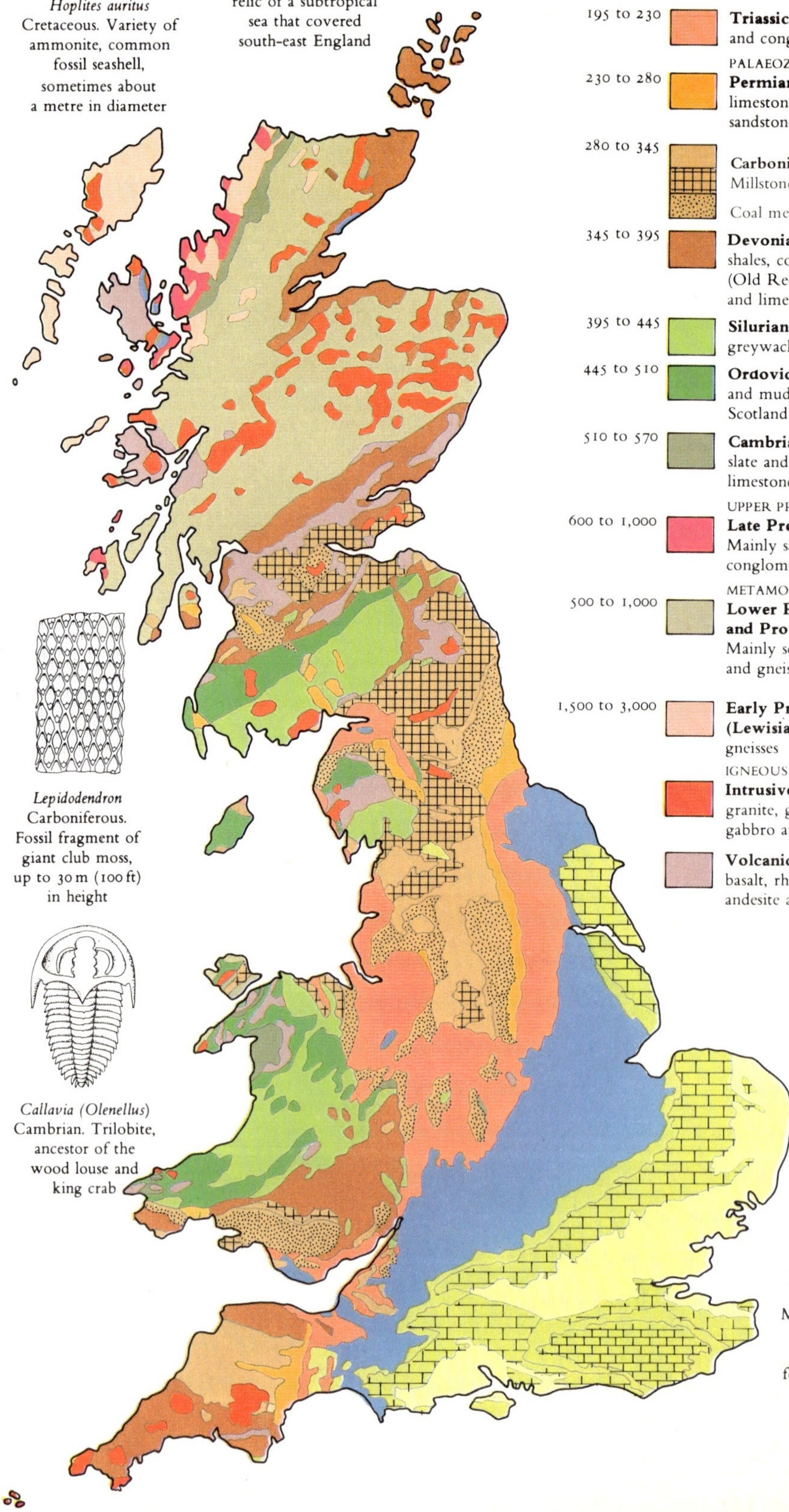

Lepidodendron
Carboniferous. Fossil fragment of giant club moss, up to 30 m (100 ft) in height

Callavia (Olenellus)
Cambrian. Trilobite, ancestor of the wood louse and king crab

Didymograptus
Ordovician. Marine organism whose tiny skeleton is found imprinted on shales

AGE (shown in millions of years)

CENOZOIC
- up to 65 — **Tertiary and marine Pleistocene** *Mainly clays and sands*

MESOZOIC
- 65 to 140 — **Cretaceous** Chalk; Gault clay and greensand; Wealden clay
- 140 to 195 — **Jurassic** Mainly limestones and clays
- 195 to 230 — **Triassic** Marls, sandstones and conglomerates

PALAEOZOIC
- 230 to 280 — **Permian** Mainly magnesian limestones, marls and sandstones
- 280 to 345 — **Carboniferous** Limestone; Millstone grit and culm measures; Coal measures
- 345 to 395 — **Devonian** Sandstones, shales, conglomerates (Old Red Sandstone); slates and limestones
- 395 to 445 — **Silurian** Shales, mudstones, greywacke; some limestones
- 445 to 510 — **Ordovician** Mainly shales and mudstones; limestone in Scotland
- 510 to 570 — **Cambrian** Mainly shales, slate and sandstones; limestone in Scotland

UPPER PROTEROZOIC
- 600 to 1,000 — **Late Precambrian** Mainly sandstones, conglomerates and siltstones

METAMORPHIC ROCKS
- 500 to 1,000 — **Lower Palaeozoic and Proterozoic** Mainly schists and gneisses
- 1,500 to 3,000 — **Early Precambrian (Lewisian)** Mainly gneisses

IGNEOUS ROCKS
- **Intrusive** Mainly granite, granodiorite, gabbro and dolerite
- **Volcanic** Mainly basalt, rhyolite, andesite and tuffs

of Britain are due to another sedimentary rock-making process, this time acting upon plant debris. Dead and decaying trees from the dense swampy forests of the Carboniferous era gradually accumulated to form vast thicknesses of peat, and after millions of years of burial under a deep layer of rock the peat was transformed by heat and pressure into coal.

Sedimentary rocks have proved immensely valuable to man because they contain oil, natural gas and coal. Limestones yield a fine building stone, but unfortunately this is vulnerable to erosion: rainwater made acidic by modern pollution has turned many a finely sculpted nose into a blob, just as the waves mould chalky cliffs with their ceaseless battering.

HIGH CUP NICK, CUMBRIA (***left***). *Tough and erosion-resistant dolerite, an intrusive igneous rock, caps the sides of this limestone valley.*

FINGAL'S CAVE, STAFFA (***below***). *These hexagonal basalt columns were produced by the rapid cooling of a lava flow in Tertiary times. The gaps between them are exploited by wave action with symphonic effect. This is the basis of the cave's Gaelic name,* Uamh Bhinn *('the cave of sweet music').*

Metamorphic rocks

Metamorphosis means change: the metamorphic rocks are formed when igneous or sedimentary rocks are changed in character by heat or pressure. Granite can be metamorphosed into gneiss, while mudstone becomes slate. Exceptionally pure limestone, composed predominantly of calcium carbonate (that is, the shelly remains of animals), is metamorphosed into a white, sugary looking true marble.

Because they contain relatively few minerals and no oil, metamorphic rocks are not so useful as sedimentary rocks, but they are esteemed for decorative purposes, while slate from the quarries of north Wales provides an attractive and functional roofing material.

A rock serves as a popular metaphor for permanence and stability. Yet all rocks, not just metamorphic ones, are in fact transient links in a long chain of geological evolution.

BRITAIN'S BONES (***below***). *A selection of rocks, including one mineral, Blue John (from the French* blue-jaune*), which is mined at Castleton, Derbys. Most rocks contain quantities of crystalline minerals built from chemical elements.*

Limestone

Sandstone

Granite

Gneiss

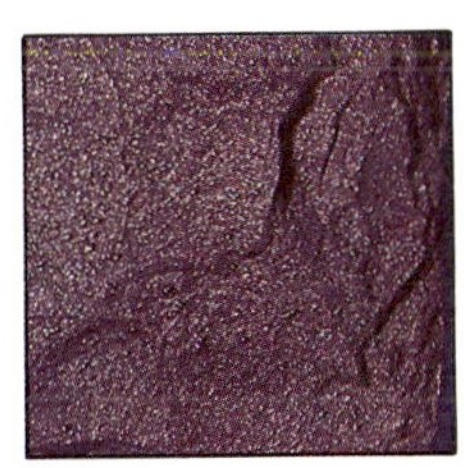

Basalt

Blue John

A SLICE THROUGH ENGLAND AND WALES

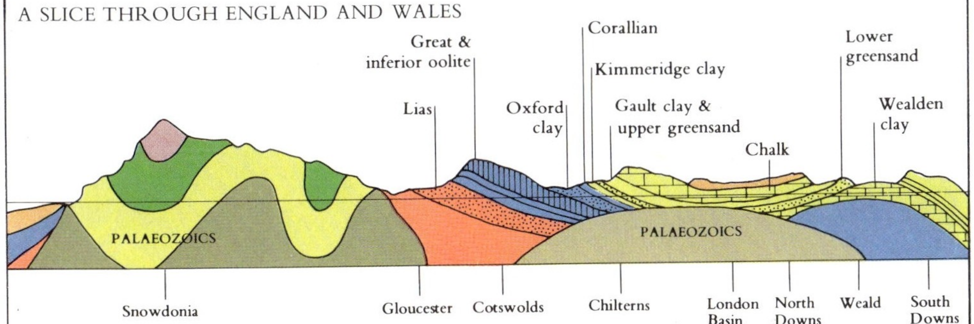

This geological X-ray reveals the rock structure of a part of Britain. The young clays and sands of the London Basin and the Midlands, which rest on a basement of old and harder rocks, give way as one journeys westwards to the ancient metamorphic formations of Wales, which were once also buried by younger rocks.

CONNECTIONS
Building materials: 170–71 *Building*
Folds and faults: 16–17 *The making of an island*
Mining: 150–51 *Coal;* **152–5** *The bowels of the earth*

The making of an island

The technical term for the study of how various processes act upon different kinds of rock to make landscapes is 'geomorphology'.

The land surface of Britain reflects the nature of its underlying rocks. A simple distinction between highlands and lowlands, separated by a line drawn between the mouths of the Rivers Exe and Tees, is useful in evaluating the development of the island. Highland rocks are old and hard; many are crystalline, all were originally molten. They are more resistant to erosion than those of the sedimentary lowlands.

Rivers and ice sheets

While rock type controls the main outlines of Britain's relief, it is to four groups of processes that we owe its precise form. The first is water action: rain falling on soil or bare rock dislodges particles and transports them to a river. The flow of rivers removes even more of the land surface and eventually deposits it in flood plains, estuaries and on the sea bed. The continuous action of water over the past sixty-five million years has accounted for the secondary outlines of Britain's relief. The valleys of the Weald (32 on the map below), for example, are underlain by floodplain deposits up to sixty metres (197 ft) deep. This simple situation is complicated by a further three factors, which, although they have acted discontinuously over time, have left a substantial legacy.

The first of these is the effect of ice sheets, which, over the past two million years, have advanced and retreated over the landscape of Britain north of a line joining the estuaries of the Severn and Thames. The impact of the moving ice, and the arctic conditions prevailing around their edges, resulted in the deepening of existing valleys and the creation of new drainage patterns by the breaching of watersheds in highland Britain, as well as the deposition of vast amounts of glacial clays, sands and gravels in the lowlands.

A related element in the shaping of Britain is the sea level, which has been steadily falling for two million years. An indicator of higher levels in the past is the great spread of marine, estuarine and alluvial deposits in the lower parts of river valleys. The Fens of Cambridgeshire (22 on the map) and the Somerset Levels (34) are the best places to study these. After the ice melted, the pressure on the land was relieved and it rose in response.

Folds, faults and subsidence

The shape of Britain's mountains and valleys was formed by the impact of folds and faults. To understand the mechanics of this, it is necessary to appreciate the principles of 'plate tectonics'. The Earth's surface is divided up into a series of interlocking plates upon which the continents of the world ride, and which move relative to one another. Thick piles of sedimentary rocks, com-

THE PHYSICAL REGIONS
The map shows the original drainage pattern, before the ice ages changed it.

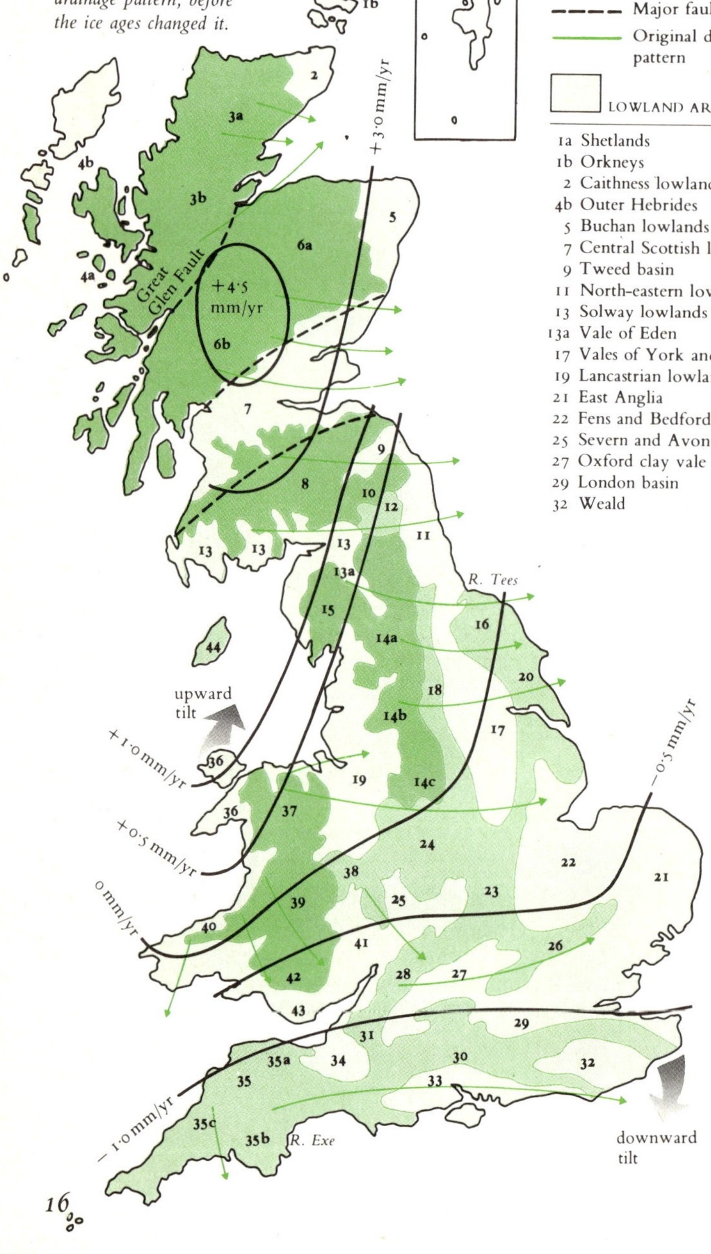

—— Line of equal 'tilt' (giving annual rise or fall in mm)
– – – Major fault
—— Original drainage pattern

LOWLAND AREAS
- 1a Shetlands
- 1b Orkneys
- 2 Caithness lowlands
- 4b Outer Hebrides
- 5 Buchan lowlands
- 7 Central Scottish lowlands
- 9 Tweed basin
- 11 North-eastern lowlands
- 13 Solway lowlands
- 13a Vale of Eden
- 17 Vales of York and Trent
- 19 Lancastrian lowlands
- 21 East Anglia
- 22 Fens and Bedford lowlands
- 25 Severn and Avon valleys
- 27 Oxford clay vale
- 29 London basin
- 32 Weald
- 33 Hampshire basin
- 34 Somerset plain
- 36 North Wales coastal lowlands and Anglesey
- 40 West Wales coastal lowlands
- 41 Lower Wye basin
- 43 South Wales coastal lowlands

UPLAND AREAS
- 12 Northumbrian Fells
- 16 North York Moors
- 18 Foothills of the eastern Pennines
- 20 East Yorks. and Lincs. scarps and vales
- 23 East Midland plateaux
- 24 West Midland plateaux
- 26 Chilterns
- 28 Cotswolds
- 30 Wessex Downs (includes Salisbury Plain and White Horse Hills)
- 31 Mendips
- 35 The south-western peninsula
- 35a Exmoor
- 35b Dartmoor
- 35c Bodmin Moor

MOUNTAIN AREAS
- 3a North-west Highlands (Northern)
- 3b North-west Highlands (Southern)
- 4a Inner Hebrides
- 4b Outer Hebrides
- 6a Grampians (North-eastern)
- 6b Grampians (South-western)
- 8 Southern uplands
- 10 Cheviots
- 14a Northern Pennines
- 14b Central Pennines
- 14c Southern Pennines
- 15 Lake District (Cumbria)
- 37 North Wales mountains
- 39 Dissected plateau of central Wales
- 42 Dissected plateau and mountains of south Wales

BRITAIN BEFORE MAN: A CHRONOLOGY

Episode		Main characteristics
ANTHROPOGENIC	0 years before present	Temperate interglacial climate. Human influence on the landscape prominent, e.g. in forest clearance, soil erosion, urbanization.
BOREAL	5,000	Rising sea level. Forest cover developed inland. Stable soils.
DEVENSIAN	10,250	Last glaciation. Ice covered Ireland and all England north of a line joining the Severn to the Thames estuary. Severe frost climate south of this line. Low sea level.
MIDDLE PLEISTOCENE	118,000	Succession of temperate interglacial and arctic glacial periods. First record of man 140,000 years ago.
EARLY PLEISTOCENE	600,000	Earlier glaciations. Valleys incised. Sea level falling.
TERTIARY	1,200,000	Subtropical climate. Folding produced the main uplands of southern Britain. Rivers and the sea cut the extensive upland plateaux.
MESOZOIC	65,000,000	Mainly tropical climate. The North Atlantic ocean created by the drifting apart of the American and European plates.
PALAEOZOIC	240,000,000	Living creatures emerged from the sea and colonized the land. Forests grew.

SCOTLAND'S GREAT GLEN. *This huge valley separates the north-west Highlands from the Grampian Mountains. It has been carved out by ice and rivers along a 100-mile wrench (tear) fault.*

STAIR HOLE, DORSET (***below***). *The sea has breached a block of Portland limestone (to the right) and has eroded Wealden clays and sands to reveal intensely folded strata of Purbeck limestone.*

posed of alternating layers of weak rock, such as clays, and resistant rocks, such as cemented sandstones and limestones, are tilted, folded and faulted when they are subjected to such mountain-building movements. Subsequent erosion then produces characteristic landforms.

A tilted sheeting of resistant rock forms a *cuesta*, which is a steep slope (scarp) backed by a gentle slope, as exemplified by the Downs, the Cotswolds and the Chilterns. An upfold, or anticline, may make a dome, but this may be breached by erosion to create inward-facing scarps, as in the Weald. A downfold, or syncline, may form a valley such as the London basin, but erosion can remove the surrounding rocks to leave a synclinal mountain, such as Snowdon.

Fault patterns are predominantly vertical. If the blocks are moving apart, one side will drop down along a normal fault. If the blocks are pushed together, one may ride up over the other along a thrust fault. If the movement is horizontal, then the blocks may move along a wrench, or tear fault, such as the seventy-mile-long Great Glen of Scotland; the small earthquake shocks still recorded at Inverness demonstrate that this fault is more than a geomorphological abstraction.

Lowland Britain is affected by subsidence more than by faulting. The North Sea basin is slowly sinking under the weight of sediments deposited by rivers such as the Thames and Humber, and, on the continent of Europe, the Rhine. This sinking evokes a sympathetic response in lowland Britain, which means that the south and east are subsiding obliquely. This warping is the cause of many of the drowned river valleys in eastern England, and has contributed to recent flooding.

CONNECTIONS
Erosion and deposition: 26–7 *The changing shoreline*
Geology: 14–15 *Beneath the landscape*
Glaciation: 18–19 *The legacy of the ice ages*

FOLDS AND FAULTS

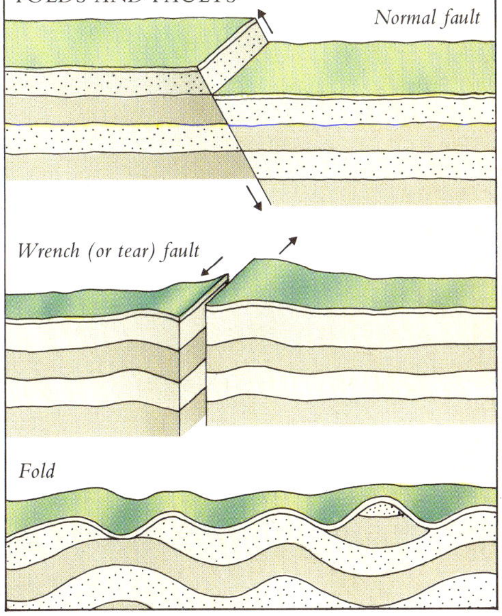

The legacy of the ice ages

Over the last two million years there have probably been about twelve ice ages, separated by periods of temperate climate known as interglacials – such as we live in today. The ultimate causes of such climatic changes remain obscure. What we do know is that a worldwide drop in temperature, of perhaps only a few degrees, stimulated rapid ice formation at the polar ice caps and on mountain tops. The ice sheets continued to advance until the temperature rose again.

Glaciation and the landscape

The immediate effect of widespread ice accumulation was a lowering of the sea level, because land ice took up water from the oceans. The impact of this change has been most remarkable in river valleys, which acquired multiple terraces as they cut downwards, and on the coast, where parts of the former sea bed were left stranded as raised beaches (notably on the west coast of Scotland). Some of these coastal areas, which were covered in trees during an interglacial, have since subsided into the sea again: hence the submerged forests that are sometimes visible along the seashore; there is a good example at Borth, west Wales.

The ice itself created many major landforms in Britain by erosion and deposition. The origins of such landforms have been discovered by analogy with present freezing environments. For example, active glaciers in the Alps are forming moraines (long, low hills of material deposited at the sides and in front of the ice); these are comparable to the deposits found in Britain's glaciated valleys. Similarly, the corries (or cirques) of the Scottish and Welsh mountains – rock-cut 'amphitheatres' produced by glacial erosion – are the final results of a process which is still taking place in the Himalayas.

Glacial features can reveal many clues as to what happened in the ice ages. The rocky sides of a glaciated river valley are marked by cracks and scratches (striations), which indicate the direction of ice movement. As the valleys were being deepened by glaciers, small tributary valleys along their sides remained at the same level, and after the melt were left as the 'hanging valleys' we find today, from which streams drop sheerly down into the main valley below. Ice journeys can also be mapped by studying erratics – rocks carried by ice and left as alien lumps far distant from their origin.

The erosional effect of glaciation in the lowlands is difficult to assess. That it took place is clearly reflected in the shaping of hard outcrops of stone into well-polished mounds (*roches moutonnées*) whose form can reveal the direction of ice flow. Most lowland glacial forms are, however, depositional. For instance, eskers and drumlins are mounds of sediment which accumulated beneath an ice sheet. More widespread are the moraines, and the extensive glacial meltwater deposits exemplified by the vast mantle of boulder clay covering East Anglia – the product of several ice ages and intermediary melts.

Ice did not penetrate south of a line joining the Severn and the Thames estuaries. But this region still bears the scars of intense cold and of higher-flowing rivers as ice melted farther north in summer. The freezing of the ground gave rise to pingos (see diagram), regularly patterned land, and deep ice-formed cracks. The effect of ice on drainage was substantial. For example, the lower Thames, which formerly flowed north-eastwards, was dammed by a lobe of ice and diverted to its present course. Streams pouring into the area now occupied by the Vale of Pickering in Yorkshire were blocked by ice to form a lake – and a new exit channel was cut to the south-west through the Kirkham Abbey Gorge.

Another ice age?

If there is another ice age, when will it come? By comparing the length of the present interglacial (10,000 years to date) with those of former interglacials (an average of 120,000 years), it would seem we have a long time to go. Some experts think a worldwide heat loss will not occur if we continue to pollute our atmosphere. Other theorists, though, believe that Britain could be in the grip of another freeze within ten years.

DRUMLIN IN SCOTLAND. *Drumlins are usually covered in sand and sometimes occur in droves. Their precise origins are still a puzzle.*

GLACIATED VALLEY, CUMBRIA. *Glacial valleys, which are U-shaped, are created where a glacier has slid through a V-shaped valley. The ice slices through spurs on the valley sides (formed between tributary streams) and leaves steep walls. It scratches the rocks, leaves moraines and scoops out channels, in which lakes may form such as Windermere (in the background of the photograph).*

THE FORMATION OF PINGOS

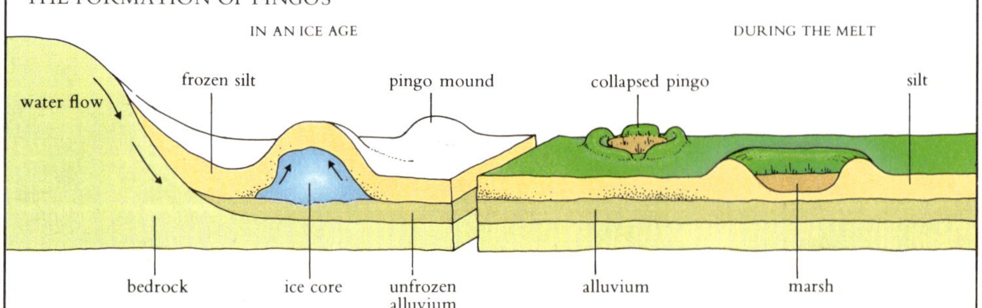

Often during an ice age, water flowing down a slope would freeze when it accumulated at lower levels. The result was a pingo – a hillock over a core of underground ice. The soil on top of the pingo would eventually slip away and the ice core melt, leaving small mounds around a surface depression. Pingo scars have even been found beneath the surface of London.

BRITAIN UNDER ICE

Major erosional and depositional features left by the ice are shown, as well as secondary features. Arrows show the approximate direction of ice movements.

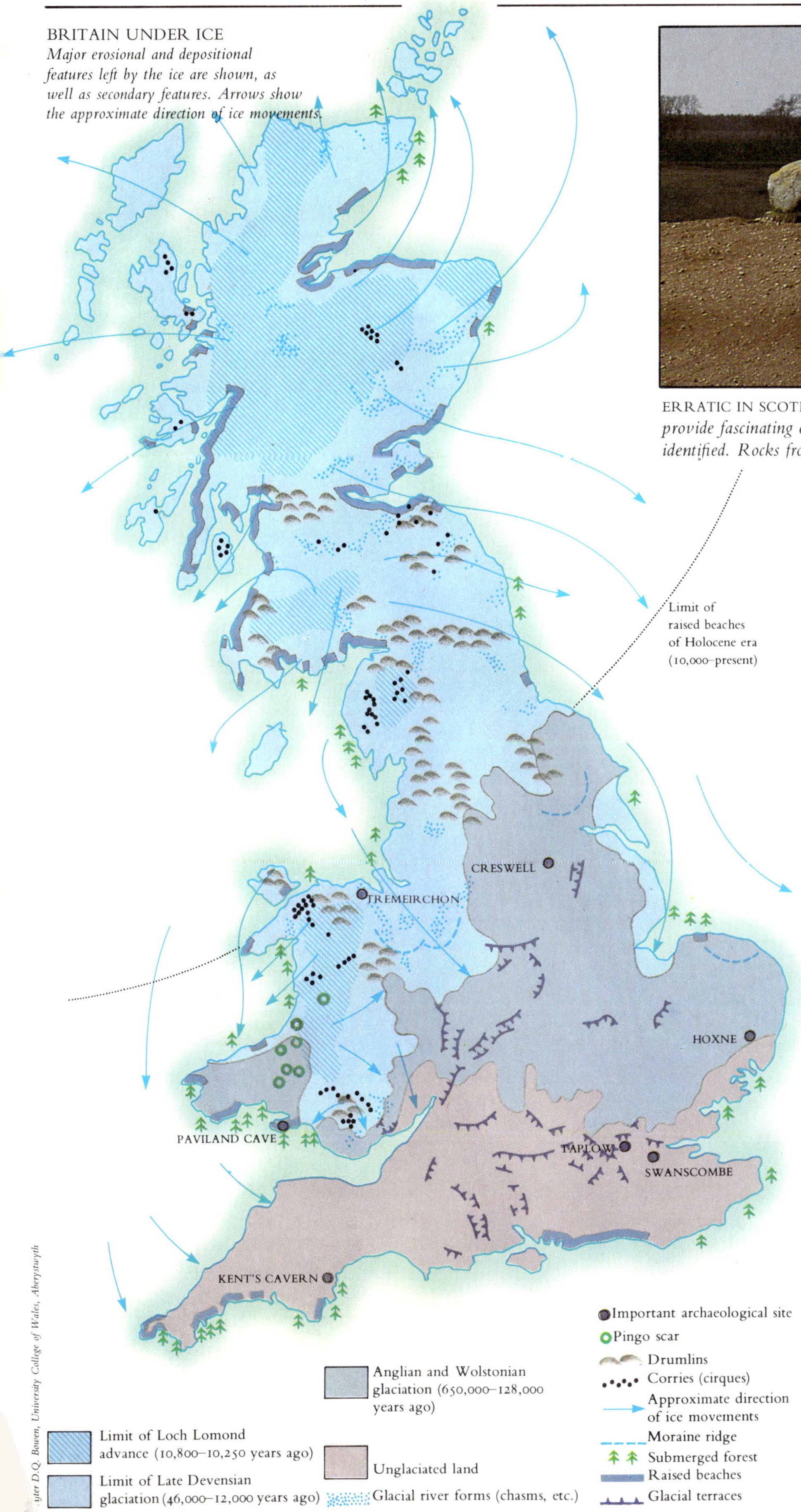

After D.Q. Bowen, University College of Wales, Aberystwyth

ERRATIC IN SCOTLAND. *Stranded after its ice-borne journey, an erratic can provide fascinating evidence of ice movement if the rock can be precisely identified. Rocks from as far away as Oslo have been carried to Britain.*

PATTERNED GROUND, CAMBS. *Patterned ground is a relic of ice-age disturbances in the soil. Cracking by frost, or desiccation, has resulted in bands of stony material. In this way, stripes, networks, circles and polygons have formed.*

Glacial archaeology

Remains of animals and plants of the interglacial periods, preserved in glacial deposits, have enabled us to work out a relative chronology of the climatic pendulum of the ice ages. For example, organic deposits found on the site of a glacial lake at Hoxne in Suffolk have been shown to derive from a temperate climate that preceded an early glaciation. A number of ice-age fauna have been preserved, such as the mammoth whose remains were discovered in river terrace gravels at Taplow, Buckinghamshire. At several sites the artefacts of ice-age man have come to light, for example at Kent's Cavern, Somerset, where hand-axes were found. Fairly accurate dating has been achieved by fluoride and radiometric methods; by such means the human skull fragment found at Swanscombe, Kent, has been dated to about 140,000 years ago.

CONNECTIONS

Glacial deposits: 20–21 *The lowlands*

Glacial valleys: 24–5 *The highlands*

The sea-level: 26–7 *The changing coastline*

The lowlands

Early prehistoric man looked upon a lowland panorama of tree-clad vales and marshy plains, a no-man's-land today so thoroughly transformed that its origins are all but concealed. These regions, which have ultimately proved the most hospitable, were the product of the softest rocks – the ones most easily worn down by weather, rivers and ice long before man began to clear the forests and drain the swamps.

Most lowlands have been made by a continuous process of erosion and deposition. Beneath the Lancashire lowlands, for example, is a basin of soft Triassic marls which was eroded by rivers, scoured by glaciation, then clothed again in a mixture of sands and gravels deposited by the melting ice. In the south, bands and basins of clay proved just as susceptible to the slow wearing action of water and wind. Deep subterranean forces have also sometimes come into play. The chalk foundation of East Anglia is much lower than the same rock farther west because of the 'downwarping' of the earth's crust in this region, which has caused the land to tilt into the North Sea. In Scotland, coal-bearing rocks have been faulted down in a rift between the Highlands and the Southern Uplands to create the Central Lowlands.

Few of the lowlands are consistent in relief or composition. Hard rocks, such as the volcanic intrusions in central Scotland, form hills in the midst of softer valleys, and a variety of surface deposits complicate the flattest of plains. Sometimes glaciers on the move have left small hump-backed knolls (drumlins) or long banks (moraines). Elsewhere, expanses of glacial sands and pebbly rubble have formed bleak heaths in the heart of fertile farmland: an example is the sandy Breckland of Norfolk. Even the wind has played strange tricks, whisking off topsoil in one place and abandoning it in another – placing drifts of brick sand, for instance, over the clay of the eastern London basin.

The contrast between upland heights and lowland spaces has been sharpened immeasurably by modern man, above all where the lowland has yielded farmland and ground for settlement. Today the largest expanses of farming country, which are also the richest, are based on thick sheets of glacial soils, as in the Vale of York and East Anglia. With new kinds of husbandry, lighter soils have also proved very productive.

The lesser valleys also offer fertile land, largely the fruit of an age-old process: the flooding which

EAST SUSSEX FARMLAND (**right**). *In the lee of the grassy chalk South Downs, a string of small villages presides over the Wealden farmland. Flints washed out of the chalk are found in deep beds on the clay.*

NORTH UIST, OUTER HEBRIDES. *The lowland islands of Scotland, worn down by rivers, waves and ice, have poor soil cover and offer little more than crofting farmland. But the climate, warmed by the Gulf Stream, is less severe than in the neighbouring Highlands. Oats, barley, potatoes and grass flourish.*

BRICKWORKS NEAR BEDFORD. *Near Bedford and Peterborough the brickmaking factories feed on the Oxford clay and sprout tall, narrow chimneys, visible for miles around in flat countryside. These chimneys, with the cathedral towers and spires of the medieval 'island' towns (notably Ely), are the greatest landmarks on the plain. Nearby claypits, once abandoned, are now reclaimed for agricultural land or converted into artificial lakes for recreational purposes.*

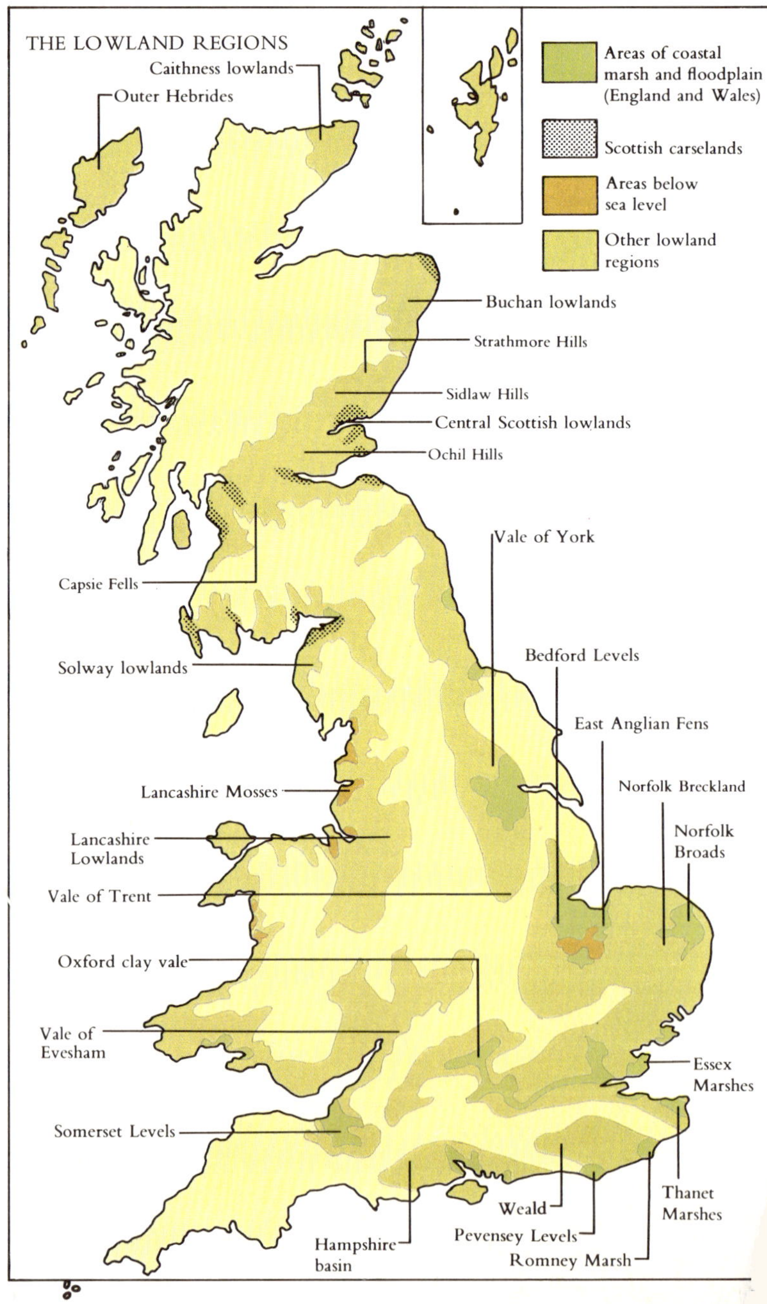

spreads alluvium over the plains on each side of a mature river. Eroding downwards, the river deepens the valley and leaves a series of steps or terraces at higher levels.

Coastal lowlands

At the mouths of many rivers, a combination of river-borne silts and deposits made by the sea created marshes such as the Somerset Levels and, in the east, the Fens. These have been built up from silts and peats over the last 5,000 years, and now form great plains, partly below sea level. A few carefully preserved nature reserves, still undrained, allow a backward glance in time to a terrain which could repel all but the most determined invaders. The name of Sedgemoor in the Somerset Levels evokes the reed beds and swampy wastes where huddled lake villages were once built. Now, as with the Fens, little remains of the old wilderness, and drainage ditches enclose new farmland.

Other coastal lands, built up by the sea but threatened by it, have been gradually reclaimed by drainage, sometimes with the aid of sea walls, as at Romney Marsh. Some, though, have evaded man, notably on the west coast, where marshes tend to be sandier and less rewarding to the farmer.

The Scottish 'carselands', which emerged from the sea as Scotland rebounded from the load of the ice, have provided another type of lowland. This, once drained and fertilized, also provides good farmland. Carselands are found on both coasts of the central lowland, but farther north only on the eastern side. The precious stretches of fertile land in the north-west are restricted to narrow valleys and to the strips of sand-covered peat around the Western Isles – the machair. Behind the small farmlands, the ill-drained acid soils overlying the granite maintain only wild peat moors.

Competing for the land

Agriculture still fills surprisingly extensive spaces, but urban activity and the major routes of communication – roads, railways and canals – have also naturally concentrated on the plains and in the valleys. Though most geological resources are found in the uplands and mountains (with the exception of the hidden coal seams of Kent, the salts of Cheshire and Teeside and the brick making clays of the south Midlands), industry has increasingly developed in the lowlands, both in the free coastal margins and around towns and cities. In the valleys of south Wales, for example, extractive industry, together with towns and farmland, has almost swallowed up the available land, imposing a pattern which all but conceals the geological foundation. Exploitation in the past has evolved new landscapes, such as the lake-land of the Norfolk Broads, made by peat-cutting in the Middle Ages. Other strange scenes will probably form as man makes further marks on the lowlands.

CONNECTIONS
Brickmaking: 170–71 *Building*
Coastal lowlands: 26–7 *The changing shoreline*
Farming: 138–9 *Modern agriculture*
River terraces: 28–9 *Rivers and lakes*
Windmills: 148–9 *Wind, water and steam*

THE DRAINING OF THE FENS

The Fenland basin is a huge clay lowland drained by the rivers Ouse, Nene, Welland and Witham and lapped by the Wash, an inlet formed after the rivers breached a chalk ridge which had previously held back the sea. The rivers then deposited silt at their mouths to create the silt fen. Farther inland, poor drainage favoured the growth of peat swamps. The silt fen was settled from Roman times and islands of higher ground, as at Ely and March, became sites for villages and towns. The peat fen, originally the home of wild fowlers, fishermen and sedge-cutters, was re-created as farming land from the 17th century, initially by the Dutchman Cornelius Vermuyden. Lowland peat (the concentrated remains of ancient deciduous forest vegetation) gives a rich black soil when drained. First windmills, then steam, diesel and electric pumps, were used to pump the water drained from the peat into dykes and thence into the rivers.

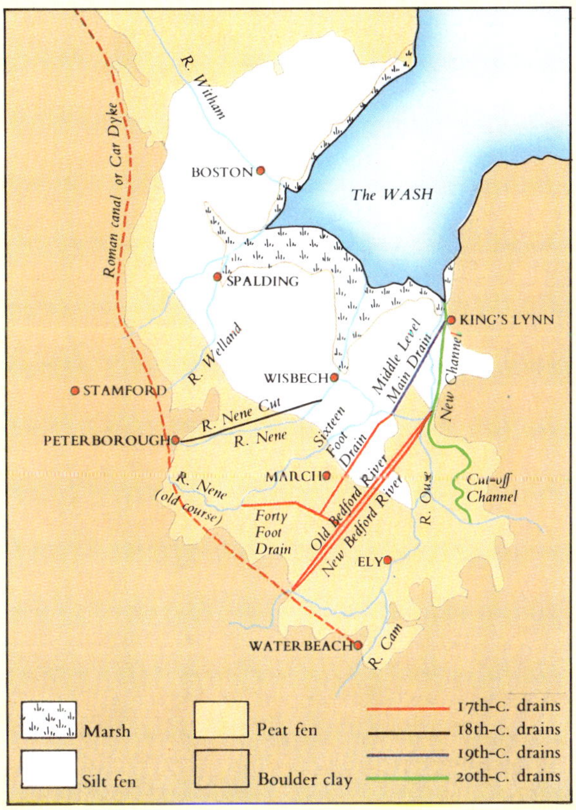

DRAINAGE WINDMILL AT WICKEN FEN, CAMBS. *This is a carefully preserved historical relic. Drainage at Wicken Fen has for some time been halted, and a high water table is maintained in order to preserve the sedge fen as a nature reserve.*

DRAINAGE DYKES, CAMBS. (***right***). *Shrinkage of the peat owing to drainage has lifted the waterways and demanded the building of strong banks and dykes.*

The uplands

Britain's uplands may be broadly defined as the hilly areas that are not quite high enough to qualify as mountains. They were mainly formed through folding since Cretaceous times, and most of them are composed of sedimentary rocks – limestone, sandstone and chalk – which have offered relatively little resistance to erosion.

The limestone scarplands

The geologist makes connections that can seem untenable to eyes trained to look more readily for 'superficial' cultural similarities. We would resist the contention that the desolate upland moors of north-east Yorkshire are an extension of the cosier Cotswolds, because their common geological heritage is not immediately apparent. In fact, both regions belong to an upland ridge of limestone that stretches south from the Cotswolds into Dorset and north as far as Yorkshire. The whole area is punctuated with asymmetrical hills, with a gentle slope on one side and a steep scarp, sometimes crowned by the hardest limestones, on the other.

The North York Moors, immortalized by Emily Brontë's *Wuthering Heights*, harbour few towns, and little ground is cultivated. These uplands are made of shales, ironstones, grits and limestones, and there is a great variety of soil and landform. Indeed, few other uplands present such contrasts of colour or sustain such a variety of wild plants and creatures. Hemmed in between the Yorkshire uplands are the dales – deep and narrow valleys where the prominence of sheep farming reminds us of the Cotswold connection.

The chalk uplands

All the chalk uplands are also asymmetrically escarped and, again, they have a wide distribution. They ring the Weald and radiate north-eastwards to take in the Marlborough Downs, the Berkshire Downs, the Chilterns and the Lincolnshire and Yorkshire Wolds, as well as sending out smaller branches into Wiltshire, Dorset, Somerset and

SWALEDALE, NORTH YORKS. *The sheep-filled dales are treeless but grassy limestone valleys, wedged in between the high and inhospitable moorland plateaux.*

THE WESTBURY HORSE, WILTS. (***below***). *An 18th-century 'vandal' created this elegant horse, startlingly incised in the soft white chalk of an upland slope.*

even the Isle of Wight. Perhaps because we have a 'model' chalk uplands in our heads, based on the Downs, we are surprised by the fact that they extend so far north. This model features rolling grassy slopes gashed now and then to reveal white chalk, which is in fact an exceptionally pure form of limestone. Because chalk (like limestone) is very porous, water seeps through the ground, leaving a dry surface. Typically, only beech trees, which send their long roots down in search of water in pockets of clay-with-flint deposits, can grow on these relatively treeless uplands.

But there are many variations on this chalkland theme. Certain level summits of the Chilterns and the North Downs, for example, sport denser mixed woodlands because of their damp brown soils, which were spared by the ice caps and have been weathered over millions of years. In the Lincolnshire Wolds, on the other hand, ice-deposited clay, sand and gravel give rise to soil conditions and agricultural patterns quite different from those of the bare chalk southern uplands, whose thin soils support little more than grassland for sheep (although the better, more sheltered soils were reclaimed from waste by 17th- and 18th-century farmers using variations of the Norfolk four-course and sheep folding system). Again, to deviate from the southern model, the Yorkshire Wolds, because the chalk is harder, look more like limestone uplands with their bony silhouettes and stark cliffs.

Prehistoric Britons on the move would not have needed a geologist to delineate the chalk upland system. In an epoch when the lowlands were covered with dense forests, travellers preferred the more penetrable undergrowth-free beechwoods of the hilltops. Stonehenge in Salisbury Plain is accessible from a series of routes following the dry and relatively open uplands, and many of these ancient trackways are marked by the remains of strategic scarp-top camps, burial mounds visible for miles around, and flint mines.

The igneous uplands

Most of the other uplands in Britain consist of volcanic rocks. In the south-west, masses of intrusive granite form the upland plateaux of Dartmoor and Bodmin Moor, but Exmoor is formed of sandstone. The agricultural potential of Exmoor, for so long given over to sheep and rugged ponies, was demonstrated in the 19th century when an enterprising farmer drained, ploughed and limed a part of it to create fine pastureland. The round peat-covered slopes of the lonely Cheviots on the Scottish–English border are underlain by granite but include no impressive peaks.

CONNECTIONS
Cotswold cottages: 220–21 *Cottages and rural homes*
Emily Brontë: 296–9 *Writers and places*
Prehistoric Britain: 192–3 *Marks on the landscape*
Upland farming: 134–5 *The agricultural revolution*
Wool: 142–3 *The wool trade*

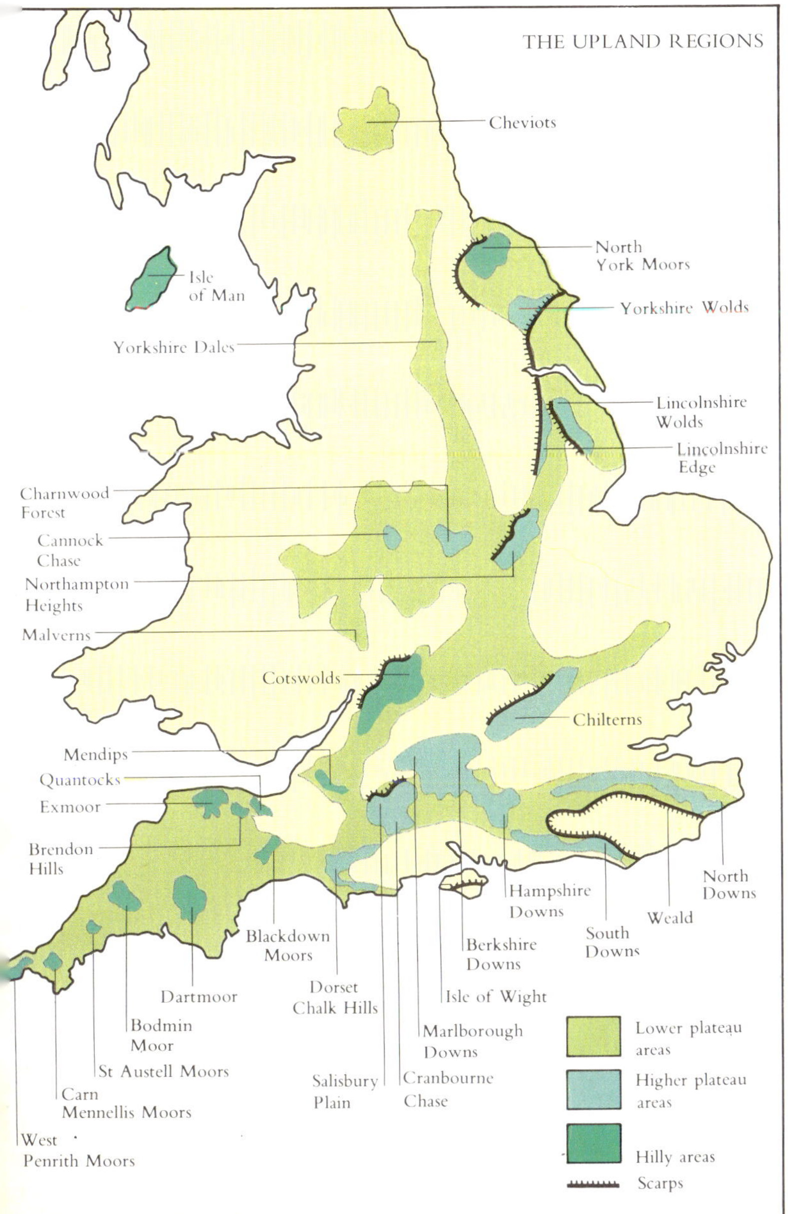

HAYTOR, DEVON. *This is one of the many granite tors that crown Dartmoor. Sculpted by weather, such tors are the remnants of old plateaux.*

THE COTSWOLDS (***below***). *Like the drystone walls dividing them, the Cotswolds are made of a light-coloured limestone that weathers attractively.*

The highlands

Britain's mountains, though obviously not as thrilling as, say, the Andes or the Rockies, nevertheless in places approach the sublime. There are four major groups: the Scottish Highlands and Grampians, the Lake District (Cumbrian) mountains, the Pennines and the Cambrian range of Wales. Almost all the peaks were sculpted into their present form by glaciers. Highland regions are magnets for climbers and tourists seeking breathtaking scenery, sometimes scarcely touched by human influences, though often cloaked in dense afforestation.

The highland regions

The Scottish mountains comprise great ranges of jagged ice-moulded peaks and massive, smooth rock domes. The northern part is separated from the Grampians by the hundred-mile-long trench of the Great Glen. Both areas are underlain by ancient metamorphic rocks, broken in places by granite intrusions to form peaks such as Ben Nevis. Torridonian sandstone in the north forms steep-sided domes, while in the Tertiary era volcanoes were active in the Western Isles. On Skye, volcanic cones and craters are still to be seen in the Cuillin Hills. The resistance of the harder rocks to erosion is the main cause of their superior height, but they have also been buckled by periods of folding, creating the distinctive Caledonian fold structure along a line from south-west to north-east.

The Lake District is a huge dome made up of both volcanic and sedimentary rocks, both folded. The most spectacular mountains, such as Scafell Pike, are the result of ancient lava flows, but Skiddaw, an upfold of Ordovician slates, is a notable exception.

The geology of the Pennines is dominated by a mixture of Carboniferous limestones, coal-bearing sandstones, and grits. The limestones in particular, permeable and vulnerable to erosion, have produced a strange and varied 'karst' landscape, with gorges, interrupted drainage patterns, rock pavements and cave systems. The grits, such as millstone grit, are tough, and where they outcrop at the surface, as in the Peak District of Derbyshire, they may take the form of sharply outlined ridges, or 'edges'. The sombre moorlands of the millstone grit region of the central Pennines contrast sharply with the green, rolling limestone hills to the south.

The Welsh massif mainly comprises metamorphosed Ordovician and Silurian sediments, more than 400 million years old. Here again, the Cal-

LIMESTONE GORGES AND PAVEMENTS

GORDALE, NEAR MALHAM, NORTH YORKS. *The gorge is probably a cavern whose roof has fallen in. Numerous limestone pavements are evident on the plateaux to either side. Here and there, clumps of ash grow.*

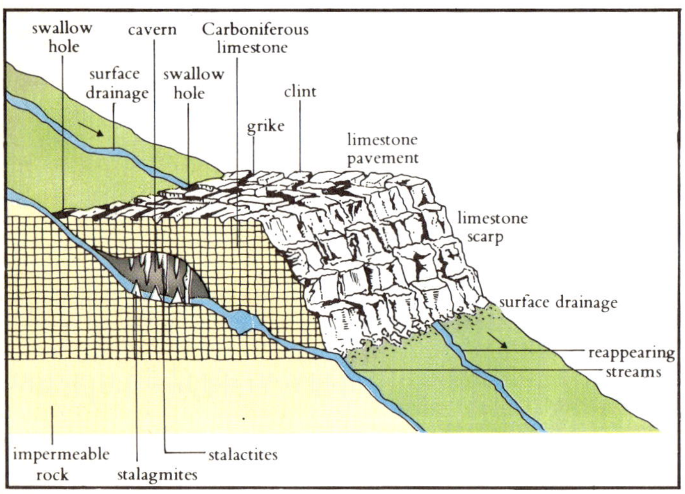

Limestone, being soluble, is highly susceptible to chemical weathering: rainwater, containing carbon dioxide, can dissolve the limestone surface on which it falls, producing a 'pavement' patterned with chasms (grikes) and blocks (clints).

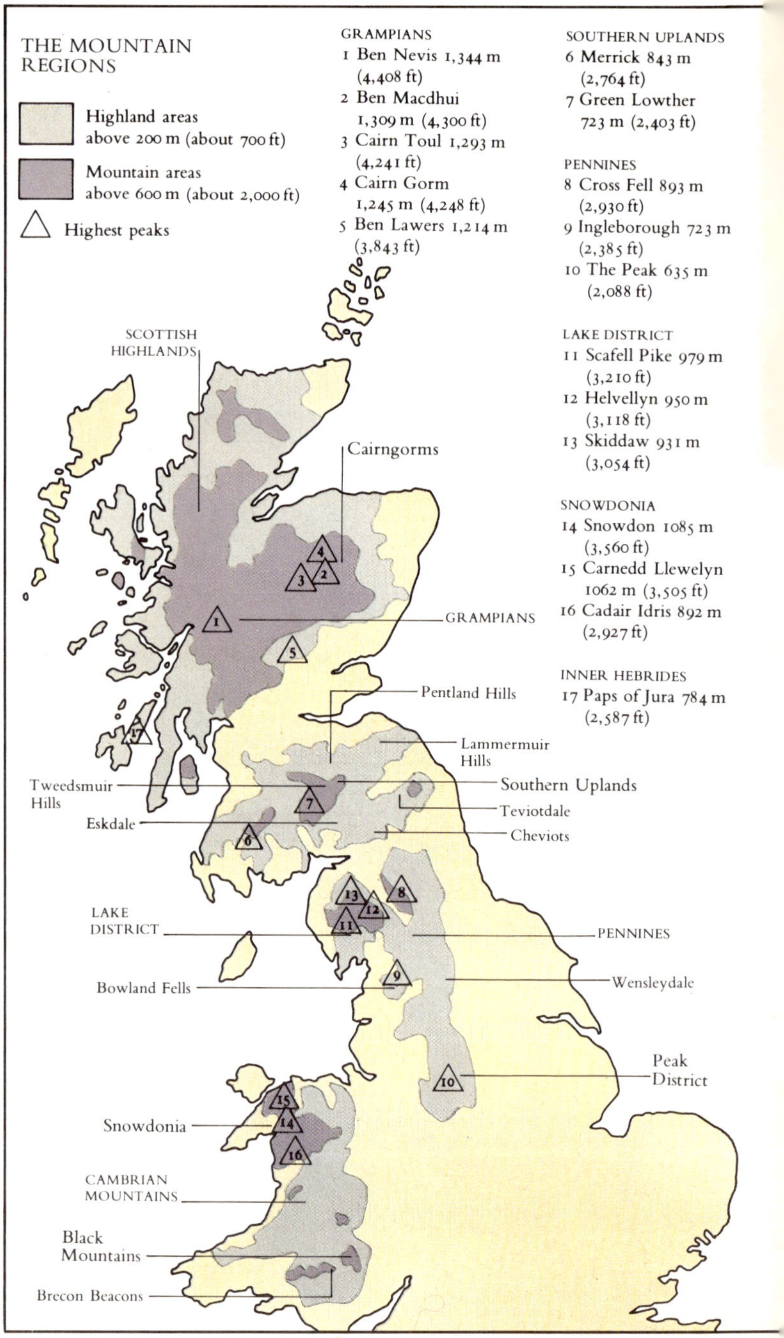

THE MOUNTAINS AROUND HAWESWATER, CUMBRIA. *In the middle distance to the right are two water-filled corries, marking the former sites of small glaciers. The* U*-shaped profile of the valley (middle ground) is an unmistakable sign of glacial formation.*

THE GRAMPIANS AROUND BEN NEVIS (***left***). *The steep slope in the left foreground is covered with scree – the result of 'frost-shattering'.*

edonian fold structure is evident. Inland of Harlech is a dome of Cambrian sediments containing the oldest fossils in Britain. In the south, coal-measure sandstones are folded up on to the older plateau to create the Black Mountains.

Water in the mountains

A glacially formed mountain lake, such as Haweswater in the Lake District or Vrynwy in Wales, can be vital to the lowlands in times of drought, when mountains are the only places where substantial amounts of water collect. Carboniferous limestone regions, however, are not so useful in this respect, as their rocks are permeable, and most of their drainage is underground. Water flowing over millstone grit may disappear into the ground (sometimes dramatically down a 'swallow hole') when it meets a bed of limestone, and dissolve rock beneath to excavate a system of caverns, such as those in the Ingleborough district of North Yorkshire. Where water drips from the roof of a cave, it evaporates to leave icicle-like limestone stalactites. Water reaching the cavern floor builds up to form stumpier stalagmites. When an underground stream reaches another layer of impermeable rock, it reappears as a spring.

Settlement, farming and mining

Despite their begrudging opportunities for settlement, the mountainous areas have witnessed a human presence since the start of the Mesolithic era (*c.* 8300 BC), when a sharp amelioration of climate freed them from the tyranny of the ice. Human occupation at the end of the Iron Age (about the 1st century AD) is indicated by a diverse range of settlement types and field systems. A spectacular testimony to the tenacity of these early settlers in a hostile terrain is the hill fort that crowns Tre'r Ceiri in north Wales.

Left relatively undisturbed by both Romans and Anglo-Saxons, the essentially Celtic culture of these areas survived intact. Only in the Lake District was it seriously diluted, with the intrusion of a strong Norse element during the 10th century. While it is right to stress the antiquity and conservatism of culture in these remote mountain fastnesses, it is also true that they have experienced profound social and economic changes over the last four or five hundred years. Rapid population growth from the 16th to the early 19th century produced a landscape and economy dominated by smallholdings. Their emergence in the west Highlands was condoned by clan chiefs, who saw a numerous and loyal tenantry as a source of political strength, even though it meant the cultivation of waterlogged and stone-ridden soils.

Conditions in Wales and the Pennines differed. Here, an abundance of common waste and an absence of strong lordship left large areas open to squatting. The living eked out from smallholdings and cottage-allotments in such regions was often a supplement to other activities, for these mountain areas had more to offer than just land. Minerals, and building materials such as slate, were extensively mined or quarried during the 18th and 19th centuries. The coal mines of the south Wales valleys, the lead and zinc mines of the Pennines and mid-Wales and the slate quarries of north-west Wales and Argyll were all foci for sprawling settlements, with not only company-built cottages but also batteries of smallholdings.

The high population carried by these areas around 1800 proved impossible to sustain in the long term. Mining and quarrying increasingly declined. More important, the rising urban–industrial markets of the lowlands raised the demand for livestock and attached new values to the extensive pastures of the north and west. Estates became less willing to approve the formation of small subsistence holdings. The declining opportunities forced many to leave the countryside, with whole new areas of marginal land becoming slowly depopulated, as at Mynydd Bach in west Wales. In Scotland, the shift from cattle to sheep and the great expansion of livestock farming from the late 18th century onwards led to many Highland tenants being evicted to make way for large, commercial sheep runs.

CONNECTIONS
Glacial features: 18–19 *The legacy of the ice ages*
Hydro-electricity: 166–7 *Electricity*
Mining: 152–5 *The bowels of the earth*
Mountains in art: 294–5 *Artists and places*
Mountains in literature: 296–9 *Writers and places*

The changing shoreline

The highly indented coastline of Britain is, on a geological time-scale, very young indeed. It was only about 5,000 years ago, after the last ice age, that the sea rose to its present level. As it crept forward, resistant rocks formed headlands and cliffs, softer rocks were eroded by wave action into bays, and the lower ends of river valleys were drowned to create estuaries such as those of the Thames and Severn. Where these drowned valleys are steep-sided, like Plymouth Sound and Milford Haven, they are called rias. The sea lochs of Scotland, formed like the Norwegian fiords, are submerged U-shaped *glacial* valleys.

Rocky coasts

The shape of a cliff is largely determined by some of the most aggressive of natural forces: wave action at the foot and weathering, which causes landslips, on the rest of the face. Storm waves, compressing air into the fissures in a rock, are so powerful that they can eventually burst it asunder. At the same time, alternate dousing and drying out between high and low tides induces chemical breakdown and the enlargement of the fissures. Blowholes are formed when air is forced up through the roof of a sea-cave.

Where the rocks are soft, the undercutting and

LULWORTH COVE, DORSET. *A strip of Purbeck and Portland limestones along the shore has been breached by the sea, which has etched a cove into the softer clays and sandstones behind.*

ST GOVAN'S HEAD, DYFED. *Vertical cliffs of Carboniferous limestone have been eroded along vertical planes of weakness to isolate a stack and create a natural arch.*

LONGSHORE DRIFT

Waves breaking obliquely to a beach push sand and shingle upslope in the direction in which they are travelling. But the backwash runs down at right angles to the shore. Thus, sediment is moved along in a zigzag, in a continuous process of erosion and deposition known as longshore drift. In some places a beach has been extended out to sea to form a spit, as at Holderness, Yorks., where the spit has been 'recurved' by waves from other directions.

GROYNES, EASTBOURNE, SUSSEX. *Seven maids with seven mops could not in a lifetime rival the effects of the sweeping waves. To protect the beach from longshore drift, wooden barriers (groynes) have been built.*

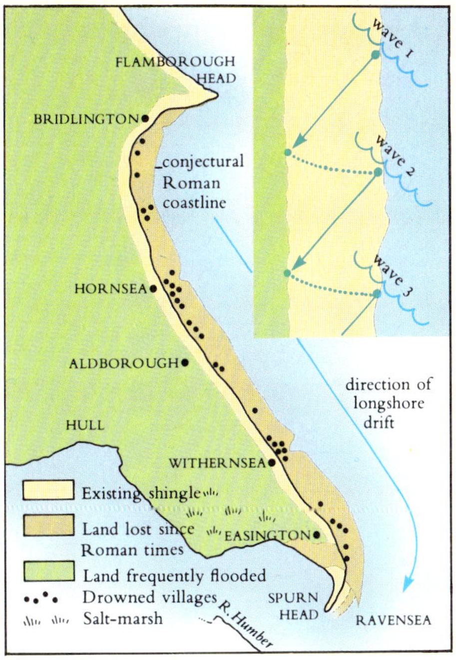

consequent landslipping can put the cliffs into a rapid retreat of up to two metres ($6\frac{1}{2}$ ft) annually, sometimes swallowing up farmland and villages as they go. The cliffs of glacial boulder clay on the east coast of England are especially vulnerable to this robbery of the land. The seashore can be defended against nature by cliff-foot barriers. But this is costly, and will often cause erosion farther along the coast.

A cliff in retreat leaves behind it a wave-cut platform, exposed at low tides. This is often covered by a veneer of sediment, which wears it smooth as the material is jostled by the waves.

Low coasts

Low seashores are the product of deposition. On balance, more land is built up by deposition than is lost by erosion. The tendency is towards a smoother coastline: as headlands are being demolished, bays are being filled in. The latter process often consists, first of sketching in the outline of a new coastline, then of proceeding to a more radical redrawing. Deposition may close off a bay with a spit. This will sometimes build up right across a bay to form a bar (as at Slapton Sands, Devon) or link up with an offshore island to form a tombolo (such as Portland Bill, Dorset).

The lagoons trapped behind spits and bars are gradually clogged with mud-flats and marsh. Deposition of mud is facilitated by the growth of salt-marsh vegetation in the complex branchings of tidal creeks. In time, what was sea becomes land, which drainage can turn into an extremely fertile farming belt, such as Romney Marsh in Kent.

Bars are also formed offshore, below low-tide level, by the action of waves and currents. They are evident at low water as a line of breaking waves. Every few hundred metres or so, the bar is broken by a rip channel, through which the retreating tide surges. In summer, at the high-tide mark, it is common to see a low ridge (berm), picked out by an accumulation of seaweed and shells. In winter storms, the berm is destroyed and a winter ridge is built still higher up the beach. On a shingle beach there may be several such ridges, one behind the other, marking successive shorelines formed as the coast has shifted seaward. The depressions between the ridges are known as swales; in wet weather they often contain small lakes.

Sandy bays backed by wind-blown dunes are found particularly on the east coast of Scotland. At Culbin Sands, on the south shore of the Moray Firth, the dunes have invaded farming land and conifers have had to be planted to anchor them.

CONNECTIONS

Man and the coastline: 230–31 *Ports*
Man and the sea: 140–41 *Fishing*
The seaside: 238–9 *Spas and seaside resorts*
Submerged forests: 18–19 *The legacy of the ice ages*

SEVEN SISTERS, SUSSEX (***below***). *The dip slope of this chalk outcrop, furrowed by parallel dry valleys, has been cut back by the sea. At low tide a wave-cut platform is exposed. The cliffs end in the spectacular headland of Beachy Head.*

Rivers and lakes

Water, the most versatile of natural resources, has satisfied an increasing number of thirsts as Britain has progressed. An early need for defence and for communication meant that rivers played a major role in the siting of settlements along their lower and middle reaches. They have also been the lifeblood of farming. The upper reaches of rivers became significant in the 18th century, when fast-flowing streams were used to power textile mills. Increasingly after the Second World War, reservoirs were created in the highland regions, many of them crucial as a source of hydroelectric power as well as of water.

River patterns

Rivers form complex patterns on the land. They often follow circuitous routes which it is one of the tasks of geomorphologists to explain. Ancient drainage patterns formed after geological upheavals were subsequently modified further by the ice ages, and by the process known as river capture – the impingement of a powerfully erosive stream onto a weaker river system, so that the latter's water is 'stolen' (the Yorkshire Ouse, for example, has captured the Nidd, Ure and Swale). In some parts of Britain, the pre-glacial direction of rivers has not been much altered. For example, the courses of the Tweed, lower Tyne and Tees still reflect the ancient drainage eastwards towards the North Sea. One river which has been radically modified by ice blocking its path is the Severn, which once flowed north to join the River Dee. The Thames had a more northerly course before glaciation; its mouth was where the Wash is now.

Rivers in close-up

River action is one of the most powerful of the forces that mould the landscape. In its upper course, a river is shallow and turbulent. As it erodes vertically downwards, the valley slopes thus created are worn down by weathering to a V-shaped profile. A waterfall forms when the river crosses a hard band of rock and then comes to softer rock beyond. The soft rock is swiftly eroded, a deep 'plunge pool' is drilled out at the base, and spray helps to undermine weaker rocks beneath the

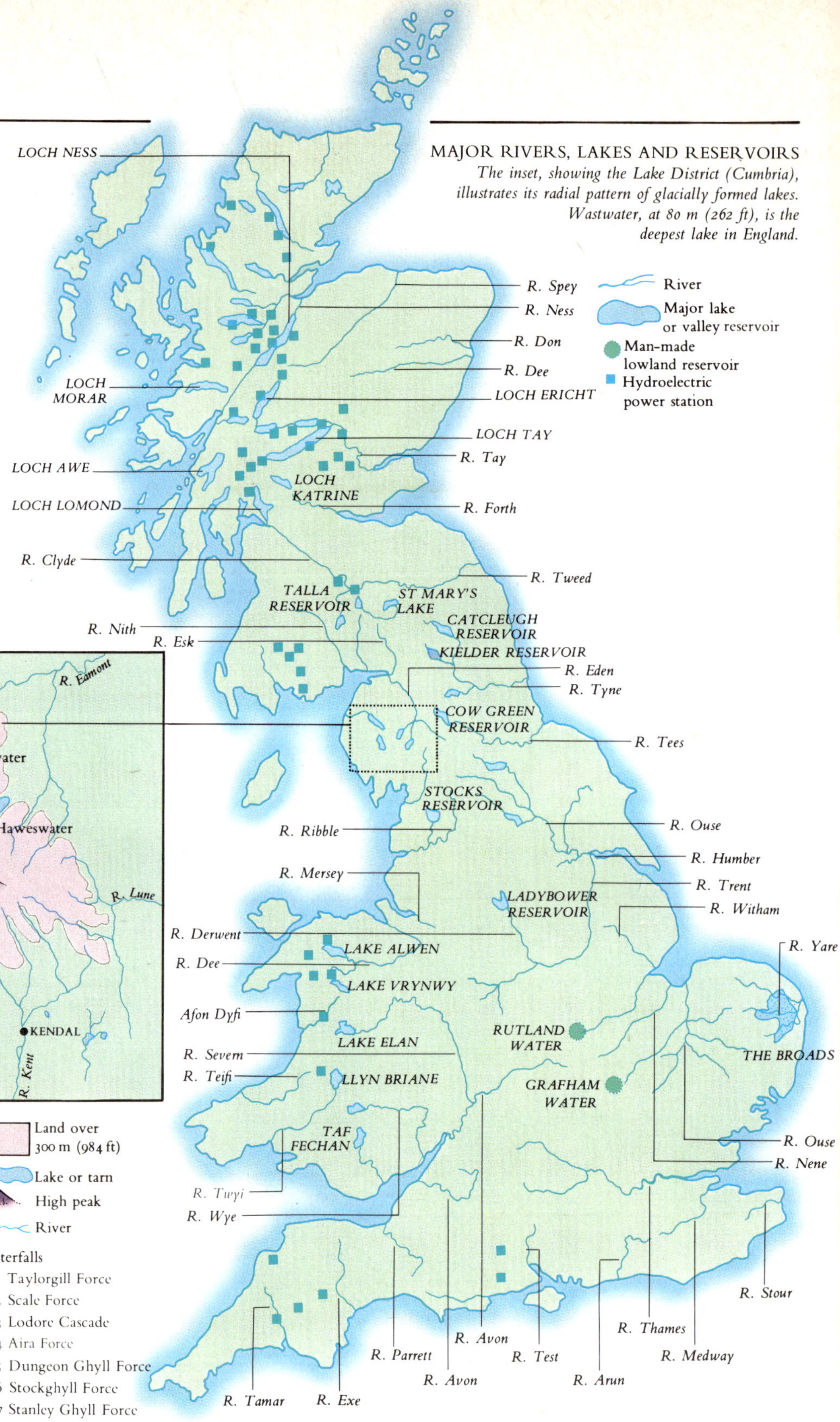

MAJOR RIVERS, LAKES AND RESERVOIRS
The inset, showing the Lake District (Cumbria), illustrates its radial pattern of glacially formed lakes. Wastwater, at 80 m (262 ft), is the deepest lake in England.

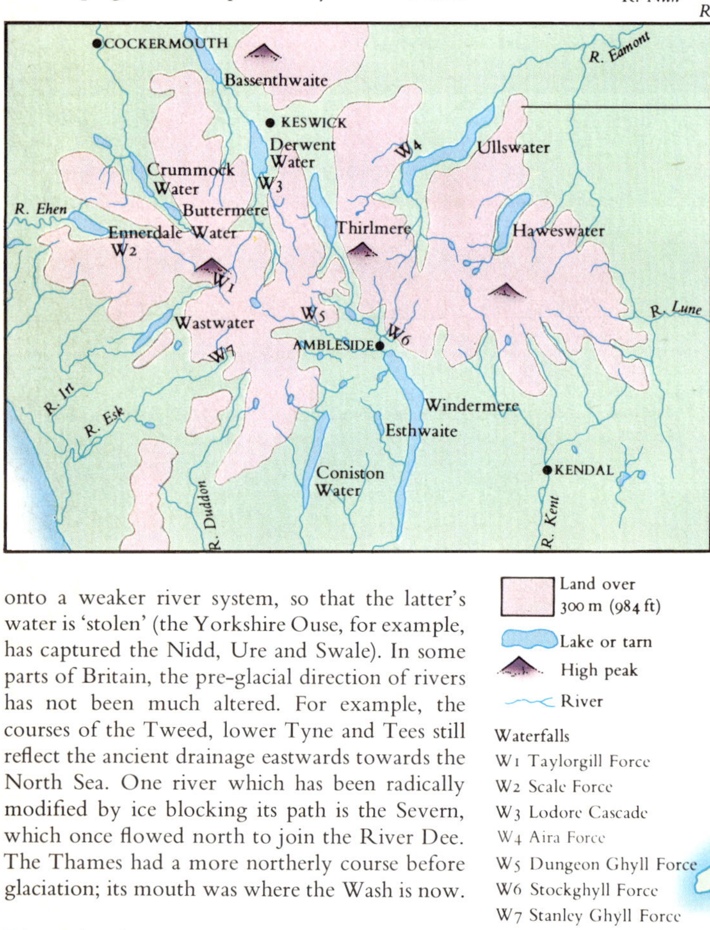

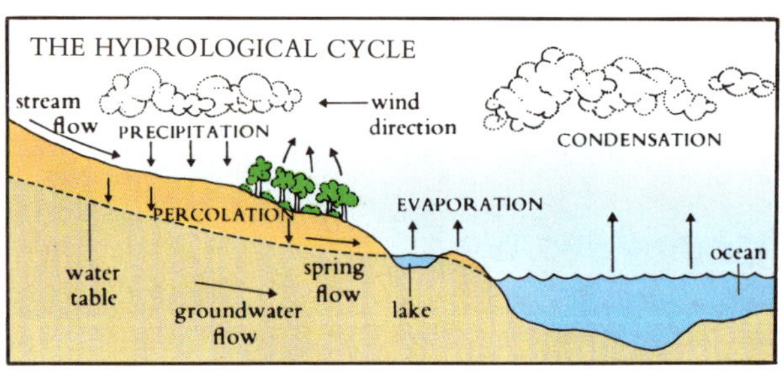

WHERE WATER COMES FROM (**left**). *As water evaporates from the oceans it becomes part of the atmosphere and eventually returns to the earth as precipitation (rain, snow, etc.). It may then be absorbed by plants, or evaporate, or join streams and rivers, or penetrate the ground. The wheel comes full circle when rainwater reaches the sea again.*

ESTHWAITE, CUMBRIA. *The hills above Esthwaite, where Beatrix Potter wrought her charming animal tales, were once deep under ice, which created numerous ribbon lakes such as this one. Many of the lakes are studded with islands and deltas formed by river silt and glacial deposits.*

WATERFALL AT THE HUNT POT, NEAR HULLPORT, YORKS. *There are numerous falls in the upland dales of the Pennines, where beds of resistant grit alternate with softer rocks.*

resistant band, whose face gradually crumbles. Thus the waterfall inches backwards, leaving a gorge in its trail.

In the middle course of a river, the channel is deeper and wider, and gentler in profile. The valley now contains a floodplain, over which the river meanders. If the sea level has fallen, a river has sometimes cut down below its former floodplain turning a meander into a prominent knoll, such as Durham is built on, on the Wear.

A floodplain flanked by terraces (also the result of the sea level falling) is a feature of the lower course of some rivers. After heavy rain, the whole floodplain may be temporarily covered by floodwater, which drains away to leave a fertile alluvium. When a river in flood bursts its banks, the heavier material in its load is deposited first, so that in time a natural embankment (levee) is created.

Industrial effluence (as in the Thames and Irwell), and farmers' pesticides, have wreaked havoc in the waterways. Untreated sewage contains tiny organisms that steal oxygen from other life forms. Even solid particles that pour into a river from mines have a harmful effect, for they block out sunlight essential to the ecosystem. A crusade against pollution is being waged in the Thames, where fish now thrive again, and in the Clyde.

THE MEANDERING RIVER SPEY, NORTH-EAST SCOTLAND. *On a lowland plain a river tends to swing from side to side. The curves of the bank take the force of the current, which carves away material from the outside of a curve, to form a river bluff, and deposits it on the inside. A loop so-formed (meander) may be short-circuited to create an ox-bow lake.*

Lakes and reservoirs

Lowland lakes in Britain have been formed in various ways: for example, by subsidence (which has created the Cheshire meres) or by the melting of ice (Lock Leven, Tayside). In highland Britain, glaciation is the primary cause. For example, in the dome-shaped Lake District, glaciers have swept from the mountainous centre, overdeepening river valleys and creating a radial pattern of lakes. The mountains here and in north Wales are dotted with water-filled corries, known as tarns (or in Welsh, llyns). 'Barrier lakes' also occur in highland Britain, where rivers have been dammed by terminal moraines, marking the limit of a glacier or a temporary halt in its retreat.

Lakes can be ephemeral features in the landscape. Rivers draining into them are slowed down, and drop their loads to produce deposits which creep down the lake and eventually fill the basin. At Keswick in the Lake District, deltas formed by two rivers have coalesced and now separate Derwent Water and Bassenthwaite Lake.

Among the earliest reservoirs were the 'hammer ponds' in the Surrey and Sussex Weald, made to provide power for the iron industry of the south-east, which peaked in the 17th century. The Elan Valley complex in central Wales, which supplies Birmingham, is one of the most impressive examples of a modern reservoir. Among the advantages of the Welsh mountains as reservoir sites are the high rainfall and the narrow, easily dammed valleys.

CONNECTIONS
Lake dwellings: 192–3 *Marks on the landscape*
Water and power: 144–5 *The birth of industry*
Water and transport: 260–61 *The canals*
Waterwheels: 148–9 *Wind, water and steam*

Woodlands and forests

British woodlands today are composed mainly of broadleaved deciduous trees in the lowlands and evergreen conifers in the uplands. Nowhere in Britain can trees grow at high altitudes, as they cannot abide exposure to windy conditions. The limit is about 610 metres (2,000 ft), whereas in Switzerland, where the terrain is less exposed, they are found up to about 2,400 metres (8,000 ft).

Woodland history: shrinkage and regeneration

The retreat of the ice about 12,000 years ago left Britain a treeless waste. Then the tundra landscape was slowly colonized by trees, at first birch and willow, followed by aspen, juniper and sea buckthorn. Later, Scots pine and hazel predominated. After the land connection with Europe was broken and Britain became an island warmed by the North Atlantic Drift, the main species were oak, alder and lime. About two thirds of Britain was heavily wooded by the time man progressed from a nomadic to a settled existence. Trees were hacked down, or cleared by burning, to create farmland. This exploitation, combined with the gathering of firewood and timber, resulted in the gradual shrinkage of the woodlands. From the Domesday survey of 1086 we know that only 20 per cent of England was wooded at that time.

Today we usually associate forests with vast, regimented plantations of conifers, but the forests of Norman England were much more open and parklike. New growth in the clearings was inhibited by animals grazing on the saplings. Some areas – the royal forests – were preserved for the king's hunting, and within them commoners' rights were strictly controlled. The creation of the New Forest by William the Conqueror in 1079 was said to have necessitated the levelling of many farms and some villages. The royal forests reached their apogee in the reign of Henry II, when they probably covered as much as a third of the country. Added to these were the forests in baronial hands.

SILVER BIRCHES AT THETFORD CHASE, NORFOLK. *The softwood plantation in the background is dominated by Corsican pine.*

In Tudor times royal forests became an important timber resource: it has been calculated that about 2,000 oaks went into the construction of an Elizabethan galleon.

The process of clearance was relentless. By the 16th century wood was being used increasingly to make charcoal for iron smelting (for cannons and anchors), as well as for the manufacture of bricks, glass and gunpowder. The 'Great Rebuilding' also created a vast appetite for timber for houses. Encouraged by John Evelyn, a plantation movement developed in the late 17th century in an attempt to stem the despoliation. Species were also imported from abroad, but to begin with this was mostly for ornamental purposes. One of the earliest introductions was the sycamore, which now commonly gives shelter to upland farms. The first species brought in to supply timber, in the 16th and early 17th centuries, were the Norway

CHARCOAL BURNING BY THE TRADITIONAL METHOD. *The fuel was produced in the forest by partial burning of wood in an oxygen-starved earth kiln. As the process needed long supervision, the charcoal-burner lived in a hut nearby.*

BEECHWOOD, NEW FOREST, HANTS (***right***). *Beech leaves are tough and slow to rot, and form a deep autumn 'litter'.*

POLLARDING AND COPPICING

Coppicing is a form of woodland management used for centuries to supply thin, pliable poles for charcoal burning, for wattle fences and walls and for firewood. The technique is to cut off the stem at ground level so that a number of new stems rise from the same root system. Because the roots are already established, the new growth is vigorous, and crops can be cut every twelve to fifteen years. All broadleaved trees will coppice but the most suitable are hazel and sweet chestnut. The latter is still used in Kent and Sussex for wattle hurdles.

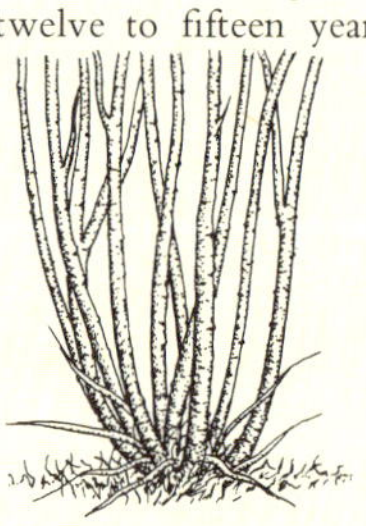

Coppice

Pollarding was a similar method, but the tree was cut at about 2.5 metres (8 ft) above the ground, so that the new shoots would be above reach of grazing cattle and deer. The leafy foliage thus produced was used for cattle feed in times of shortage and the multiple branches lopped periodically for timber and firewood. Beech and oak in particular were treated in this way.

WILLOW POLLARDS. *Each tree has thin branches fanning out from a 'bolling' (stump).*

SIX BRITISH TREES

ENGLISH OAK (**left**). *The dominant tree on loams and clays. Also known as the pedunculate oak, as its acorns sprout from peduncles (stalks). Huge veterans commonest in the Midlands.*

HEDGEROW ELM (**right**). *Increases from suckers which run along hedgerows. Now almost extinct in most English counties, owing to Dutch elm disease.*

HORSE CHESTNUT (**left**). *A native of Albania and Greece. Introduced into Britain in early 17th century, as a parkland tree. Abundant flowers.*

ASH (**right**). *Thrives in limestone regions. Sooty buds and grey, olive-tinted bark. Distinctive bunches of winged seeds ('keys'). Timber useful for furniture.*

SCOTS PINE (**left**). *This, and the yew, are Britain's only native woodland conifers. In the wild, now grows only in Scotland. Semi-wild examples in the New Forest and elsewhere.*

SYCAMORE (**right**). *Introduced in 15th or 16th century into Scotland, where it is still often called a 'plane', owing to similarity of leaf shape. Now naturalized in most of Britain.*

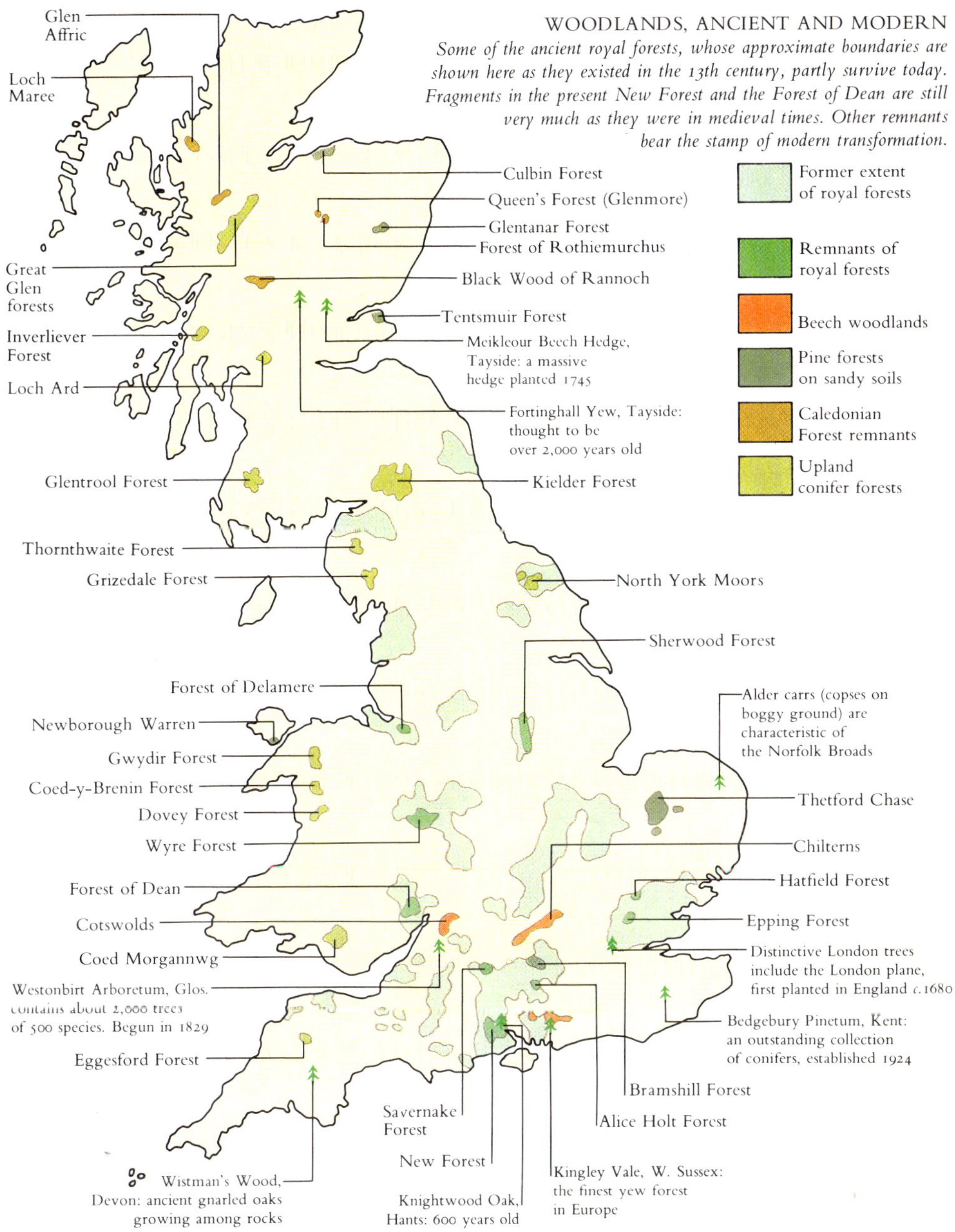

WOODLANDS, ANCIENT AND MODERN

Some of the ancient royal forests, whose approximate boundaries are shown here as they existed in the 13th century, partly survive today. Fragments in the present New Forest and the Forest of Dean are still very much as they were in medieval times. Other remnants bear the stamp of modern transformation.

spruce, European larch and European silver fir – harbingers of a whole wave of coniferous timber trees, many of which came from the north-west seaboard of America.

In spite of new planting, the woodlands continued to diminish. The industrial revolution meant that timber was needed for pit props, telegraph poles and many other uses, though coal replaced wood as the staple fuel and iron was now used for ships. The First World War saw the destruction of millions of acres of trees, and the forests dwindled to an all-time low of 4 per cent of the land cover. To replenish reserves, the Forestry Commission was set up in 1919, and at once began large-scale planting of conifers, at Eggesford (Devon) and elsewhere. Its efforts have been complemented valiantly over the years by conservation bodies such as the Woodland Trust and the National Trust, as well as by numerous commercial companies.

Contrasts of old and new

British woodlands today cover about 8 per cent of the land surface. Some deciduous woods, particularly oakwoods, occupy sites which have always been wooded, but they have been exploited and managed for centuries, and are no longer in a truly natural state. The most natural forests remaining are the remnants of the once extensive Caledonian Forest (Scots pine and birch) in the Scottish Highlands. These still have an air of wilderness, although they have been severely plundered for timber.

We cannot be so sure about the origin of the beechwoods on the Chilterns, Cotswolds and South Downs. But almost certainly there was more oak in them in the past, and they have been intensively managed. They always have a natural appearance, however, as beech is one of the few forest trees in Britain that regenerates by a process of natural seeding.

In dramatic contrast to the beechwoods are the commercial conifer plantations established over the last sixty years in much of upland Britain. They produce valuable timber much more quickly than beech or oak on sites where the latter would often grow only as scrub. In youth these forests are uniform in character and do not blend easily into the landscape. As they age and are thinned out, letting in more light, they become more hospitable to wildlife, until felling and regeneration for the next crop break the monotony and provide a variety of habitats.

CONNECTIONS
Charcoal-burning: 86–7 *Vanishing skills*
The shrinkage of the woodland: 178–9 *Shipbuilding*
Timber as a fuel: 144–5 *The birth of industry;* **158–9** *Iron and steel*
Timbered architecture: 170–71 *Building*

Nature conservation

PROTECTED BRITAIN

The finest landscapes and most precious wildlife in Britain are protected in special areas. Scotland's Scenic Areas are not yet under the same control as the National Parks (England and Wales). The map shows a selection of outstanding nature reserves. It does not include sites with no public access or restricted visiting, or the numerous county naturalists' trust and National Trust reserves.

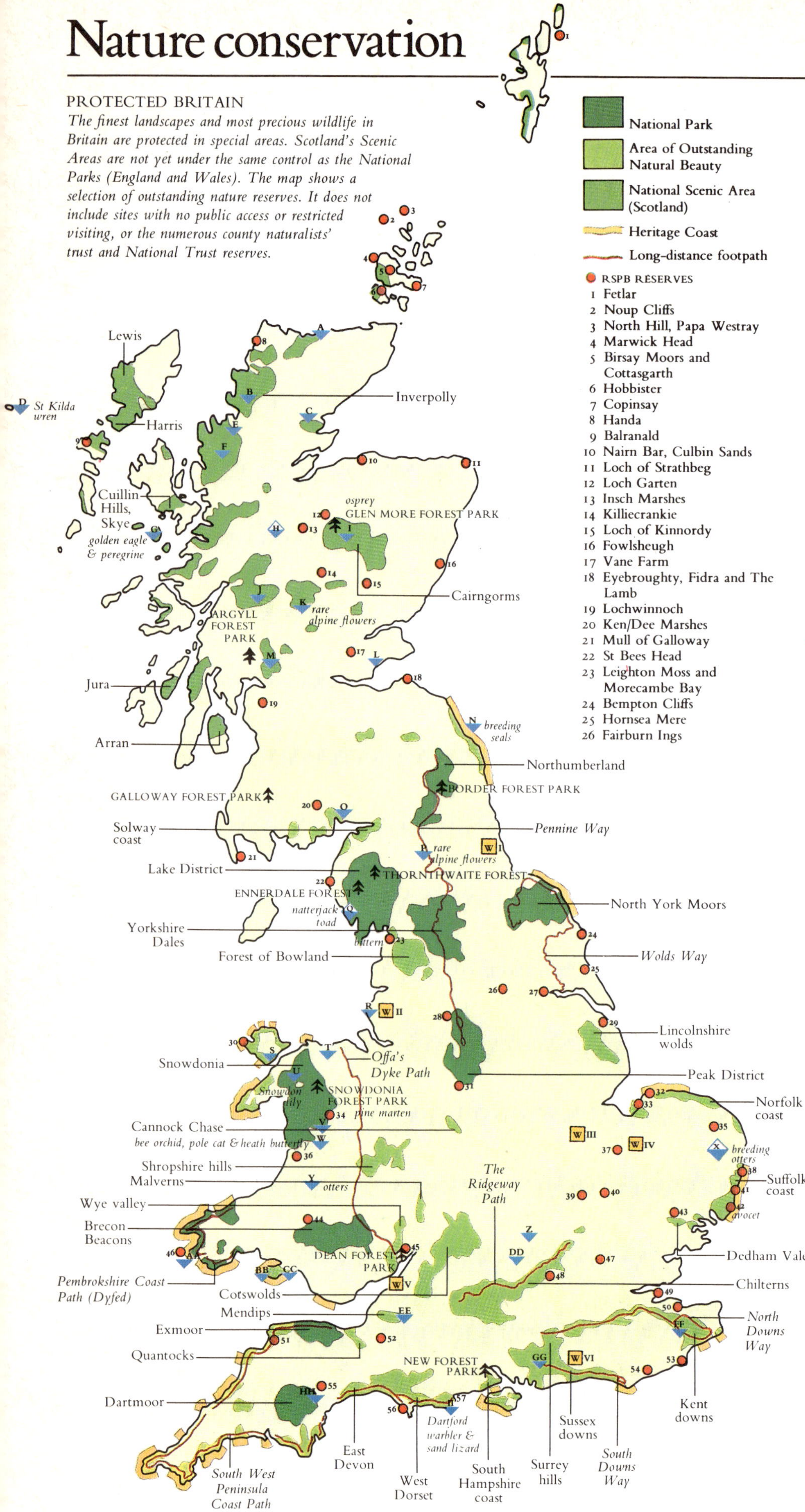

National Park
Area of Outstanding Natural Beauty
National Scenic Area (Scotland)
Heritage Coast
Long-distance footpath

RSPB RESERVES

1 Fetlar
2 Noup Cliffs
3 North Hill, Papa Westray
4 Marwick Head
5 Birsay Moors and Cottasgarth
6 Hobbister
7 Copinsay
8 Handa
9 Balranald
10 Nairn Bar, Culbin Sands
11 Loch of Strathbeg
12 Loch Garten
13 Insch Marshes
14 Killiecrankie
15 Loch of Kinnordy
16 Fowlsheugh
17 Vane Farm
18 Eyebroughty, Fidra and The Lamb
19 Lochwinnoch
20 Ken/Dee Marshes
21 Mull of Galloway
22 St Bees Head
23 Leighton Moss and Morecambe Bay
24 Bempton Cliffs
25 Hornsea Mere
26 Fairburn Ings
27 Blacktoft Sands
28 Eastwood
29 Tetney Marshes
30 South Stack Cliffs
31 Coombes Valley and Rough Knipe
32 Titchwell
33 Snettisham
34 Lake Vyrnwy
35 Strumpshaw Fen
36 Dyfi
37 Ouse Washes
38 Minsmere
39 The Lodge and Sutton Fen
40 Fowlmere
41 North Warren
42 Havergate Island
43 Wolves Wood
44 Gwenffrwd and Dinas
45 Nagshead
46 Grassholm
47 Rye House Marsh
48 Church Wood
49 Northward Hill
50 Elmsley Marshes
51 Chapel Wood
52 West Sedgemoor
53 Dungeness
54 Fore Wood
55 Aysleb eare Common
56 Radipole Lake
57 Arne

G Rhum
H Kincraig: Highland Wildlife Park (independent)
I Cairngorms
J Rannoch Moor
K Ben Lawers
L Loch Leven
M Loch Lomond
N Lindisfarne
O Caerlaverock
P Upper Teesdale
Q Ravenglass (independent)
R Ainsdale Sand Dunes
S Newborough Warren-ynys-Llanddwyn
T Coedydd Aber
UY Wyddfa-Snowdon
V Cader Idris
W Dyfi
X Norfolk Wildlife Zoo (independent)
Y Cors Caron
Z Tring reservoirs
AA Skomer
BB Gower Coast
CC Oxwich
DD Aston Rowant
EE Ebbor Gorge
FF Wye
GG Kingley Vale
HH Yarner Wood
II Studland Heath

MAJOR NATURE RESERVES

A Invernaver
B Inverpolly
C Mound Alderwoods
D St Kilda
E Corrieshalloch
F Beinn Eighe

WILDLIFE TRUST RESERVES

WI Washington
WII Martin Mere
WIII Peakirk
WIV Welney Refuge
WV Slimbridge
WVI Arundel

THE HUNTER'S PRIZE. *Deer have been 'conserved' in private parks for centuries, to preserve the pleasures of the chase. Man alone controls the deer population, as the bear and wolf have disappeared.*

Few of us now fail to appreciate the precious stretches of unspoilt countryside in Britain: grassy cliff tops shimmering with windswept flowers, or miles of mountain landscape with breathtaking views of peaks and valleys. Much of what we can still enjoy we owe to a long campaign to foster public interest in the preservation of our countryside and its wildlife, and to the dedication of the conservationists.

The origins of conservation

The conservation movement could be said to have been launched by poets and painters – great Romantic writers like Wordsworth and his contemporaries, and artists such as Constable and Turner. Their love of natural beauty encouraged others to value what had previously been taken for

PROTECTED LAND. *In the Yorkshire Dales, paths such as the Pennine Way and other, gentler routes offer glorious views of unspoilt countryside. National Park authorities safeguard the character of the land, with its rolling green sward, stone-built cottages and drystone walls, whilst also providing facilities for visitors.*

SAVED. *Brilliantly feathered and famous for its courtship display, the great crested grebe was almost annihilated in the 19th century, as a result of the fashion for fine plumed hats.*

granted. Ironically, their paeons of praise accompanied the dawn of the most destructive era. The land-hunger of the industrial revolution, with its dramatic population explosion, caused a serious loss of open space and animal habitats after the early 19th century. Another threat, in Victorian times, was the passion for collecting specimens and the practice of displaying stuffed dead creatures in glass cases. Many game parks were created, where certain species, such as hawks and polecats, were regarded as vermin and were almost made extinct. By the mid-19th century, growing concern stimulated a reform movement, and voluntary societies were formed whose aims were to protect wildlife and to curb the rapid swallowing-up of the land.

The first positive steps were small – for example, the launching of the Commons Preservation Society in 1865 – but they were followed by more significant developments. Most notable of these was the foundation of the National Trust in 1894, and its gradual acquisition of large areas of land, of both natural beauty and historic interest. The Royal Society for the Protection of Birds (RSPB) was founded in 1899, and the Society for the Promotion of Nature Reserves (now Royal Society for Nature Conservation) appeared in 1912.

More dramatic progress, however, was dependent upon government support. In the 1930s the government backed the first of the Land Utilization Surveys, which brought a fully informed awareness of the dangers inherent in city growth and the loss of agricultural land.

Patches of unspoilt nature

The National Parks Commission (now the Countryside Commission) was founded in 1949. Ten parks – extensive areas of unmolested scenery in England and Wales – were designated by Act of Parliament, to preserve them for public enjoyment while maintaining established farming use. These National Parks are predominantly in the north and west, in upland areas such as the Peak District (the first park to be formed) and the much-loved Lake District (which a Manchester man had campaigned to 'nationalize' in the late 19th century). Much of the land remains in private hands. Some areas are now owned by the Forestry Commission and are designated Forest Parks. Others are controlled as National Nature Reserves (there are sixteen of these within Snowdonia's great park). Five National Parks were recommended for Scotland, but instead the less firmly protected National Park Direction Areas were established. Scotland's National Scenic Areas were announced in 1978.

Smaller stretches of countryside in England and Wales, less wild but still of high landscape value, were designated Areas of Outstanding Natural Beauty in 1949. Another category of special landscape, safeguarded by the Nature Conservancy, is a group of Sites of Special Scientific Interest, covering small areas with outstanding features – zoological, botanical, geological or physiographical. There are now almost 4,000 of these, but their number is constantly changing, with new acquisitions and alarming losses.

By the Countryside Act of 1968 the National Parks Commission was given powers to create long-distance footpaths by negotiation with landowners and to single out parts of the coastline as Heritage Coasts, where some control over unsightly developments could be maintained.

Wildlife legislation

The emergence of positive and comprehensive law to protect wildlife has stemmed from relatively recent activity. It was a capital offence to kill a kite in London in the 15th century, but this was because the birds helped to clean the streets of carrion. The Sea Birds Preservation Act of 1869 reflected the growth of a more humane concern, restricting the practice of slaughtering these birds for their plumage. The first general Bird Protection Act, in 1880, established a closed season (during which the shooting of game birds is prohibited), and gave special, fuller protection to over eighty named species, including the great crested grebe, which was saved from extinction. A number of other laws followed, culminating in the Protection of Birds Act (1954–67) that is currently in force. Plants, and animals other than birds, grey seals, badgers and game animals, gained protection for the first time only in 1975, in the Wild Creatures and Wild Plants Act. It is now an offence to uproot wildflowers without the permission of the landowner concerned, and it is illegal to pick any of the rare plants that are scheduled by the Act for maximum protection. A further Wildlife and Countryside Bill, currently under debate, seeks to give better safeguards to habitats, and to strengthen the legal protection of endangered species. *cont'd.*

THE RESULTS OF OVER-USE. *Increasing numbers of hill walkers have eroded footpaths, particularly in the Lake District and Snowdonia. Mats and raised walkways are put down to protect plant cover.*

Nature conservation

The efforts of wildlife conservation often have to be concentrated on the most threatened species and their habitats. Britain is distinguished by remarkably diverse conditions of geology and weather, resulting in a wide range of habitats with many highly specialist species. Among the most important categories of habitat are mountainous land, lakes and rivers, large marshes, primary woodland, and coastal areas (dunes, cliffs and salt marsh). In addition, farmers have gradually forged a whole new category in the form of rough grazing ground, cultivated fields, and hedges. The most drastically reduced habitats this century have been heaths in southern England, and wetland marshes, but all areas have been severely affected by industrial and urban growth, by the pollution of the atmosphere and waterways, or by the intensification of farming methods.

The list of species already lost is substantial. Birds, flowers and insects have been particularly vulnerable. No species of mammal has become extinct in the last century, but overall numbers and distribution have diminished.

THE PATTERN OF LAND USE IN BRITAIN
Land used by man has for long supported a rich range of flora and fauna. Agricultural areas, covering the greater part of the countryside, are particularly important wildlife habitats; rapid changes in farming practice threaten many species.

- Nature reserves
- Urban areas
- Arable land
- Inland waters
- Broadleaved woodland
- Coniferous woodland
- Permanent grassland
- Rough grazing

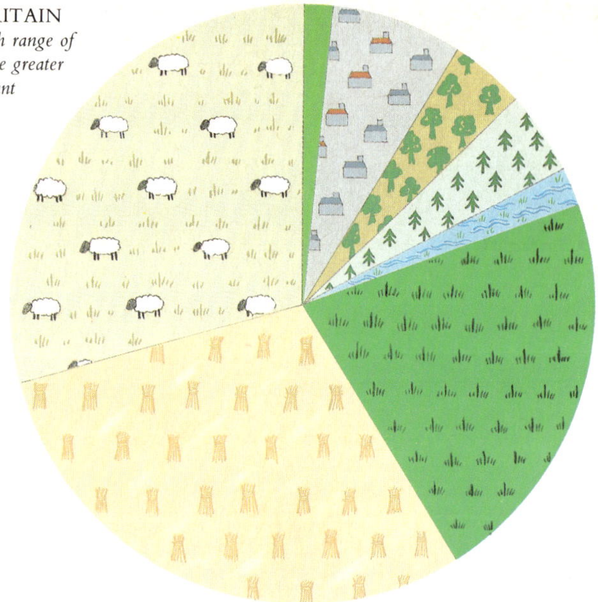

FARMING AND CONSERVATION

Award schemes have been founded recently to encourage farmers to save the most important habitats on their land. The rural landscape of the past included permanent pasture and meadows, hayfields, hedges and copses, small marshes and bogs, farm ponds and moorland. The specialized farmland wildlife included the corncrake, once a denizen of the old-fashioned hayfield but now a rarity, and the snakeshead fritillary, which once covered wet meadows in several English counties. Drainage to improve farmland has had a ruinous effect on such ancient wildlife habitats as the East Anglian Fens and the Somerset Levels, provoking conservationists' protests. The highly toxic pesticides and herbicides, which came into general use in the 1960s, have caused almost irreparable damage, killing not only weeds and pests but also creatures whose food is thus poisoned, such as the partridge. Chemical treatment and ploughing have destroyed acres of downland, and the conversion of heath land and scrub land has imperilled several species – notably the shy Dartford warbler. Such practices have produced a bleak monoculture in some areas. Removal of hedges has resulted in almost prairie-like vistas in East Anglia (approximately half this region's hedges have been uprooted since the Second World War). Surveys have also indicated a severe reduction in the number of farm ponds. However, some farmers are now alert to the dangers and are restoring ponds and hedges to safeguard farmland wildlife. They are also building nest boxes and otter havens, planting small woods, and reinforcing old copses with new trees.

GRASSLAND ORCHIDS. *Fragile and slow to establish themselves, orchids are highly vulnerable to changes in grassland management.*

THE CORNCOCKLE. *Cornfield weeds have become rare owing to the use of modern clean seed mixtures and crop-spraying.*

AVOCET, *at Havergate nature reserve, Suffolk. The avocet returned to England in the 1940s, after drained coastal areas were flooded to prevent German landings and thus reverted to their natural state.*

HEDGEROW HAVENS. *Hedges are ideal homes for flowers, small mammals and woodland birds. They protect small creatures from predators, provide berries to feed them, and act as corridors between woods.*

Nature reserves

The conservation of some individual species and their habitats has been effectively achieved so far by segregating them in reserves. The first formal reserves were founded in the late 19th century, and the total number is now about 2,000, a figure swollen by the foundations of numerous voluntary and charitable organizations – the RSPB, the Wildfowl Trust, local county naturalists' trusts, and others. The National Trust owns acres of wild scenery that are effectively wildlife reserves. The sanctuaries range from tiny areas to vast tracts comprising several different categories of habitat. A lone thorn tree in Norfolk, a pond of rare fringed waterlilies in the Gower peninsula (Glamorgan) and a ruined manor in Gloucestershire with an extraordinary colony of rare greater horseshoe bats, have each merited protection. The Nature Conservancy, founded in 1949, has created large-scale National Nature Reserves (NNRs), which covered nearly 800,000 acres (131,850 ha) by 1980. Those within the National Parks are particularly popular, but others are less easily accessible.

HARVEST MOUSE. *Weighing less than a gram, and only a few centimetres long, this mouse was once feared to have suffered from the onslaught of combine harvesters on its field habitat. New studies, however, have found no good evidence of a decline in its numbers or distribution. The mouse is so small that machinery can pass over it without crushing it, and grassy motorway verges have given it another home.*

DARTFORD WARBLER. *Loss of its heathland habitat, and a series of very cold winters in the 1960s, have brought this warbler to the brink of extinction.*

'COMMON' OTTER. *The decline of the otter has been rapid. Several factors are responsible: the pollution of rivers (killing fish, the otter's food), disturbance of waterways, and loss of riverside cover.*

Successes and hazards

Several species have already been successfully re-established. The osprey, which returned to Britain in 1954 for the first time in decades, was almost instantly given vigilant protection by the RSPB at its nesting site, Loch Garten in the Highlands. It has since been a constant resident. An earlier triumph distinguishes a reserve at Havergate in Suffolk, which was created, in 1947, to protect a small colony of avocets that were found breeding there (after an absence of nearly a century). To preserve their wetland habitat it has been necessary to maintain the water-level artificially by means of a series of sluices. Problems of similar magnitude were encountered at Minsmere in Norfolk, a reserve founded in 1948, which covers heathland, oakwood, reedswamp and salt marsh. Reeds, which shelter the rare marsh harrier, have to be harvested periodically (to prevent takeover by willow carr), and lagoons are maintained by dredging. Downland and wet meadows may even require seasonal grazing to maintain their original character. A constant problem in all reserves is disturbance by visitors, including enthusiastic birdwatchers.

Individual species depend for their survival on complex chains of interdependence. The decline of rabbits in the 1940s owing to myxomatosis caused widespread harm to flowers and insects that could only flourish on rabbit-grazed turf. The spread of Dutch elm disease in recent years has devastated dependants of the elm – notably the white letter hairstreak butterfly.

Changing nature

Some species, however, have been able to meet the challenge presented by recent changes in habitat. Foxes, for example, have moved into town suburbs, and modern conditions have favoured several species of birds – such as the black-headed gull – which have multiplied so much that they have become pests. The grey squirrel, the coypu and the mink, all relatively recently introduced in this country, have been quick to establish themselves. Colonizing birds from the Continent now include the firecrest, the redwing and two types of marshland warbler. 'New' habitats have favoured certain threatened animals; polecats, wild cats and pine martens have regained their numbers in new homes – the Forestry Commission plantations. Disused quarries, motorway verges and even wasteland near nuclear reactors have developed their own groups of flora and fauna. Flooded sand pits, reservoirs and sewage works have attracted splendid colonies of waterbirds.

Nevertheless, the harmful effect of many recent environmental changes cannot be underestimated. Reduction of pollution and of the use of toxic treatments in farming are essential, but some responsibility must rest with the individual, to help conservationists preserve the natural heritage.

CONNECTIONS
Fox-hunting: 36–7 *Man and the landscape*
Hedgerows: 138–9 *Modern agriculture*
Hunting game: 92–3 *Landownership*
The woodland habitat: 30–31 *Woodlands and forests*

Man and the landscape

Today, hardly any part of the British landscape is free of the imprint of human agency. The countless influences that have operated over the centuries include the clearing and planting of trees, drainage schemes (especially in the Fens), complex patterns of cultivation and livestock rearing, webs of communication between settlements, and the business of extracting useful materials from the land. There are always fascinating connections between such factors, and links with broader historical trends – the growth of the population, the balance of wealth and power, and so on. All this is the concern of the relatively young discipline of landscape history.

Among the earliest human traces left in considerable numbers on the landscape are the lynchets (cultivation terraces) of Celtic fields on the grassy downlands of south-east England. Elsewhere, signs of Celtic farming have been obscured by later cultivation. The ridges and furrows of Saxon and medieval times are still discernible in parts of the Midlands, though here too much has been obliterated by the modern plough. Early industries have also left their imprints on today's landscape, one of the most impressive relics being the pitted terrain at Grimes Graves, near Thetford, Norfolk – evidence of flint-mining over 4,000 years ago.

Other ancient marks on the land include the effects of two basic impulses of a civilized society – to travel and to make boundaries. Old boundary banks, many of them dating back to Saxon times, are of great interest to the landscape detective. More conspicuous are prehistoric trackways such as the Ridgeway (along the Berkshire Downs) and the Icknield Way (over the Cotswolds); like the old drovers' roads used for driving sheep and cattle from upland pastures to markets, they cross miles of lonely countryside, which the human impact has altered but not scarred.

Two of the most momentous themes of landscape history are the clearing of the wildwood and the enclosure of the fields (by either hedges or stone walls). The latter trend has in one sense been reversed in recent years with unfortunate consequences for the integrity of the landscape. In the

THE CORNISH ALPS. *The spoil heaps of the china clay industry, which dates from the 18th century, make an eyesore of the landscape near St Austell.*

BRICK CLAY PITS, *Peterborough. An example of land reclamation and ingenious waste disposal. The pits left by clay extraction have been filled with pulverized furnace ash from Trent valley power stations, and the surface then covered with sugar beet washings. The area is now being returned to agriculture.*

LEAD-MINING COUNTRY. *Lead output in the northern Pennines dwindled after reaching a climax in the 18th century. The landscape is still dotted with old smelters and with spoil heaps that look like the result of geological upheavals. Lines of former workings can be traced in trench-like 'rakes' across the moors.*

BARTON BROAD, NORFOLK: *a man-made landscape that looks natural. The Broads were created by medieval peat-diggers. A rise in sea-level in the 13th century flooded the workings. In 1287 water rose right above the altar of St Benet's Priory, which collected the revenues of the industry in many local parishes.*

interests of profitability, fields are getting larger and hedgerows are being lost. Vandalism of this kind, however, takes place against a chorus of public protest. The new atmosphere of environmental concern has resulted in ambitious landscaping projects by various industries to prevent desolate pockets of spoil heaps and industrial clutter. Such schemes recall Capability Brown's creation of artificial parkland scenery in the 18th century. Brown's imitators produced too many uninspired variations on the theme of tamed nature. One danger today is that landscape cosmetics will similarly settle into a cliché.

MEDIEVAL RIDGES AND FURROWS (*left*), *Crimscote, Warwickshire. This well-preserved field system owes its survival to the fact that it was converted to pasture at a later period, rather than reploughed. But scrub has now started to invade.*

CONNECTIONS
'Capability' Brown: 216–19 *Gardens*
The impact of farming: 134–5 *The agricultural revolution;* **138–9** *Modern agriculture*
The impact of mining: 150–51 *Coal;* **152–5** *The bowels of the earth*

RURAL LEICESTERSHIRE: THE HOME OF THE HUNT

The agricultural landscape of east Leicestershire owes much of its present appearance to the parliamentary enclosures of the late 18th and early 19th centuries, when its grassy open spaces were parcelled up into regular 10-acre fields – the most economic size for grazing cattle. Before enclosure, this was perfect fox-hunting country. Ancient hedges broke up the countryside along parish boundaries, but there were not enough of them to interfere with long, exhilarating gallops in pursuit of the quarry.

Fox-hunting in Leicestershire developed in its modern form, as an organized sport, in the 1770s. By the late 17th century the deer, regarded as the noblest victim of the hunt, had become relatively scarce. Much of its woodland habitat had been destroyed to create new farmland and to supply timber for houses and ships. In the absence of deer, the sporting aristocracy turned increasingly to foxes. In the early days, the action was slow: foxes were walked to death soon after dawn, hampered by a full meal inside them (they feed at night). Hounds were valued for their nose, not for their speed. However, fast gallops became part of the enjoyment after the mid-morning start was introduced by Hugo Meynell, master of the Quorn Hunt from 1753 to 1800.

After the momentum of enclosure had got under way, fox-hunting landlords were naturally reluctant to put up an obstacle-course of hedges that would spell the end of their pleasure. Some of them delayed in implementing the changes, but the economic rationale of enclosure eventually triumphed. In the event it was found that jumping four-foot hedges gave added spice to the sport.

The tree cover in Leicestershire was drastically reduced by the time of the enclosures. Many of the trees that remained went into the making of railed fences used to protect the newly planted thorn hedges, which took twenty years to mature. This continued plunder of the woodland, together with the conversion of gorse-scattered heaths and commons into good arable land, deprived the foxes of cover. The hunters therefore planted artificial covers, or 'coverts', of thorn or blackthorn, so that their prey would have more of a chance to breed. Such coverts, sometimes with picturesque names like Botany Bay Covert and Fox Holes Spinneys (both near Houghton-on-the-Hill), have made a minor but highly distinctive contribution to the attractive rural landscape of 'High Leicestershire', the land of the Quorn.

THE HUNTING SCENE. *A portrait of Lord Lonsdale and his wife. Hugh Lonsdale was master of two famous hunts, the Quorn (1893–8) and the Cottesmore (1907–11).*

THE QUORN COUNTRY, *from the air. Much of the pasture was ploughed up in the First and Second World Wars, but since the 1940s there has been some reconversion to grass. The large patch of woodland at the bottom of the photograph is Botany Bay Covert, named in the late 18th century after the Australian penal settlement, because of its remoteness.*

The shaping of the present

History need be no more unreal or academic a subject than our childhood: it is a dimension of our lives in Britain today. Battles, invasions, Acts of Parliament, riots, speeches, epidemics, every selfish or selfless act in the public sphere, have had repercussions on the present moment. These pages bring alive the historical dimension by looking at it thematically, and by tracing the connections with what we see around us.

The growth of population

THE BLACK DEATH. *In the late 14th century, bubonic plagues took a dramatic toll of life, especially in towns. Current estimates suggest that Britain lost an average of 40–50% of her population, and as much as 70% in some areas, to the Black Death.*

THE REVEREND THOMAS MALTHUS *(1766–1834)* (***right***) *believed that Britain's population was growing too fast in the late 18th century, partly because such natural checks as plagues – 'nature's auditing with a red pencil' – had waned. He was unduly pessimistic, however, and after 1815 population and employment grew together.*

Today's level of population – 54.1 million in 1981 – reflects three centuries of rapid growth in which the introduction of new foods, such as the acre-economizing and nutritious potato, the development of towns, the industrial revolution and advances in public health and preventive medicine all played a part.

The first national census was taken in 1801, and thereafter decennially. New questions were asked and old ones were revised in the course of the 19th century, as more information was sought about the rate of increase and its nature – for example, the population's age-structure. Before 1801 we have to make do with intelligent guesswork based on a wide variety of direct and indirect sources, such as tax lists, parish registers, apprenticeship records, bills of mortality and local census material.

Plague and famine

At the time of the Domesday Survey (1086) the population of England has been estimated to have been between 1.1 and 1.2 million (Scotland and Wales were not covered by the operation). By 1300 there were about 6 million Britons, but this considerable rate of increase was slowed down by the ravages of the Black Death, which struck Britain first in 1348–9 and then repeatedly until 1377. The Black Death was a bubonic plague that spread from China and central Asia into southern and then western Europe. Other major epidemics and infectious diseases – dysentery, typhus, famine-sickness, tuberculosis, diphtheria, measles, smallpox and various virulent pneumonic and bubonic plagues – also took their toll.

Other notable causes of death included the crises of harvest failure or famine. In Scotland, food shortages created a susceptibility to epidemic diseases. However, in England plagues mainly ravaged the towns rather than the countryside, and were not eradicated until the late 17th century.

POPULATION DISTRIBUTION, 1701–1801 (***below***). *It is evident that by 1801 the rapidly industrializing areas, such as Lancashire, were recording the highest population densities.*

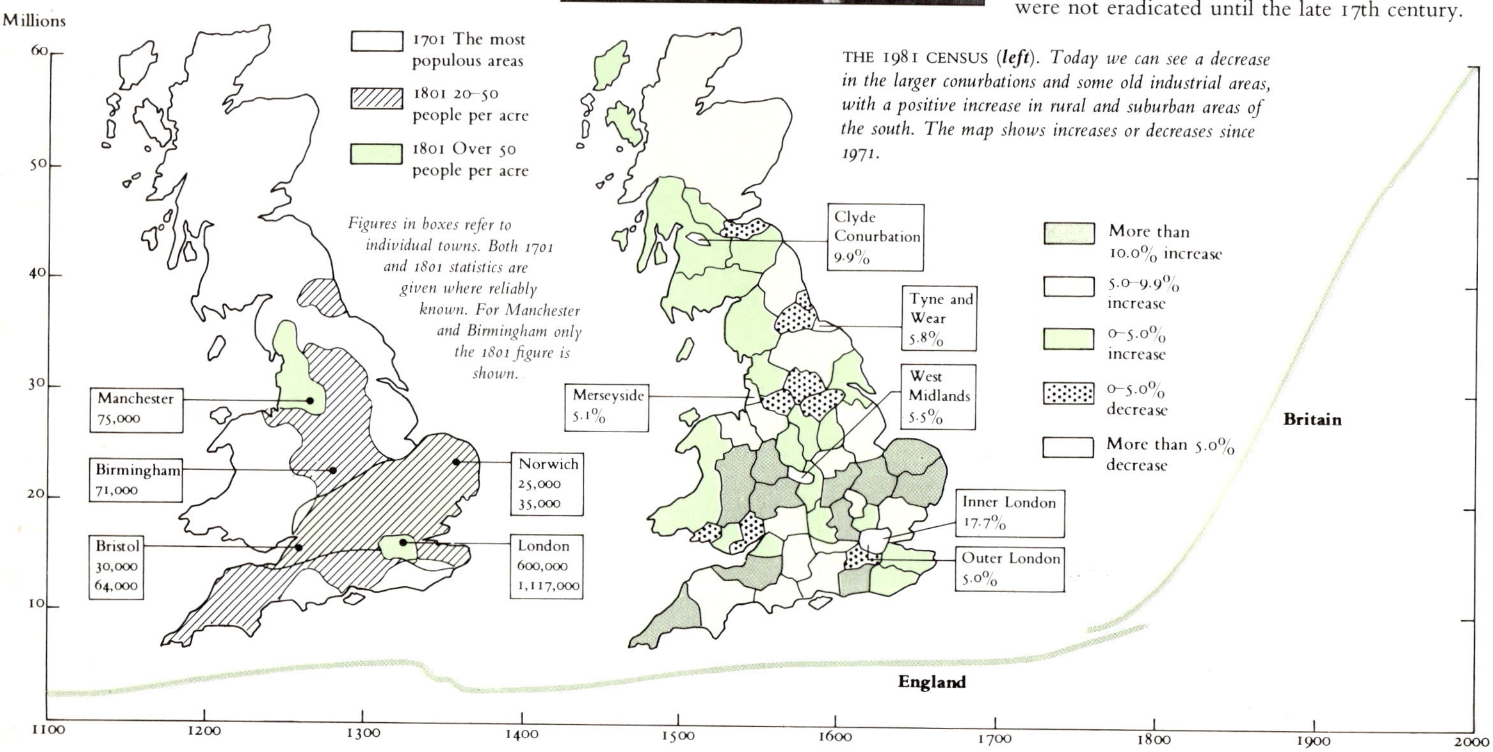

THE 1981 CENSUS (***left***). *Today we can see a decrease in the larger conurbations and some old industrial areas, with a positive increase in rural and suburban areas of the south. The map shows increases or decreases since 1971.*

The population of England was reduced to 2.25–2.75 million by the early 16th century, but notwithstanding the tempering influence of plague and famine, it had crept up to around 6 million again by 1750. The populations of medieval Scotland and Wales are almost impossible to calculate but there seems to have been a growth in the 12th and 13th centuries, and in the 16th century, with a standstill or decline in between.

The hidden mechanisms of change

In analysing the influences that lie behind population trends, demographers have to take many factors into account. These include not only natural disasters but also attitudes connected with employment opportunities, availability of contraception, health and hygiene, and so on.

The design of houses, the mood of epitaphs in old churchyards, children's rhymes, old wives' tales and contemporary literature can flesh out the demographer's abstractions. When a medieval couple christened their first three children with the same name, we can tell that, realistically, they probably expected only one of them to live. A rich man with a large farm might marry several times (his first wife dying in childbirth perhaps) in order to have as many children as possible and guarantee one surviving male heir. If fewer female than male births were recorded, it did not necessarily mean that fewer occurred, but possibly that they were not considered important.

When children were unquestionably an economic asset, especially on the land, large families were desirable. But a late Victorian middle-class couple had to educate and rear their children as dependants for a relatively longer time. The statistics show that middle-class families were smaller in the late 19th century, and we can guess that late marrying and restraint within marriage were the means to this end.

The population explosion

The major and most spectacular growth in Britain's population occurred in the 18th and 19th centuries. After 1750 the growth rates were: 1751–1801, 45.4%; 1801–1851, 98.2%; 1851–1901, 77.7%. Some 'natural' checks on population growth had been removed by this time, and many Victorians, informed by the teachings of Thomas Malthus, were alarmed at the consequent increase, especially among the improvident lower orders. The New Poor Law of 1834 institutionalized this fear by cruelly separating pauper couples in the workhouses. What the Victorians could not appreciate, and we can with hindsight, was that their modernizing economy needed a large reserve of cheap labour.

This was a period of great internal change in the distribution of population, with distinct tendencies towards concentration and growth in major industrial and coalfield areas and a general increase in the urban population. The starving rural labourer from Wiltshire, or the evicted Irish small farmer, left for the factories, and their daughters went into service with town families. In 1801 only 30 per cent of the population lived in urban areas, but by 1851 the figure was over 50 per cent and by 1901 had risen to nearly 80 per cent.

In our own times

The 20th century has seen a drop in the rate of population growth, and the overall trend has been one of stability. The loss of large numbers of young men during the First World War strongly affected marriage rates and this, together with the Depression of the 1930s, led to a much slower rate of increase. After the Second World War, however, there was a rise in the birth-rate, a lowering of the age of marriage and a general increase in the number of marriages, all leading to a larger population. This trend was reinforced by decreasing mortality – more people now live to be old – and more migration from overseas.

The 1970s saw very little growth, but overall generalizations like this conceal significant variations. Scotland's population declined by more than 100,000 in that decade, while that of England increased by 100,000 and that of Wales by 60,000. Regional variations for this period have been partly influenced by migration, and include significant gains in population for the English south-west, East Anglia and the east Midlands, with slower growth in the west Midlands and south-east, and loss of population from the north and north-west. Large cities on the whole have dwindled, with Greater London experiencing a 10 per cent loss and recording its smallest population total since the beginning of the century. The cause of the dramatic slow-down was the mysteriously low birth-rate for the period 1973–8, which started to rise again after 1978. Projections of future trends suggest a slight increase to the end of the 20th century for Britain as a whole, with a continued loss of population for Scotland.

FAMILY SIZE. *Efficient and widely available contraception has a lot to do with today's smaller families (**above**). The prosperous late Victorian couple (**top**) could afford to rear numerous children as dependants, while their more impoverished contemporaries might have seen a big family as insurance for their pensionless old age or as early contributors to the family income.*

CONNECTIONS
The fight against disease: 110–11 *Health and medicine*
The growth of Victorian London: 248–9 *London*
Size of families: 90–91 *Women and the family*
Urbanization: 144–5 *The birth of industry;* **236–7** *Factory towns*

The movement of peoples/*From Celts to Normans*

MAIDEN CASTLE. *This Dorset landmark has a long history. Celtic Britons built a hill fort on the site of an even earlier Neolithic camp. It was subjected to a fierce assault in* AD *43 by Romans, who then refurbished it for themselves.*

UP-HELLY-A' (***below***). *Shetlanders celebrate their seafaring ancestors, but the image of the Vikings as marauders detracts from their more positive traits.*

When the Romans conquered the southern half of Britain, it was occupied mainly by the various Celtic peoples who, since about 650 BC, had come from Europe in successive waves. For over 300 years (AD 43–407) Britain was a Roman province. Under civil rule native Britons lived peacably and enjoyed many advantages of the Roman lifestyle: the new towns such as Lincoln, the roads built for administrative and military convenience, and some of the new religions, among them Christianity. But after 407 the Romans withdrew and, undefended by the legions, Britain was subjected to pressure in the east and south-east from Anglo-Saxons (that is, Angles, Saxons and Jutes from the west Germanic regions) and in the north from the Irish and the Picts.

Tradition has it that the first Anglo-Saxons landed on the Kent coast in 449, but their presence as hired mercenaries and pirates had been felt before the Romans left. Over the next century or so further bands of invaders crossed the North Sea to penetrate deep into the heart of England via rivers such as the Thames, or the Great Ouse and the Welland which feed into the Wash. The Angles established themselves in East Anglia, the northern Midlands, Yorkshire and Northumberland; the Saxons in Essex, Middlesex, Wessex and the Hampshire Basin; and the Jutes in Kent. By 800 the Anglo-Saxons had pushed down into south-west England, westwards as far as Offa's Dyke (which divided Wales and Mercia), and across the Pennines.

The old idea of the Anglo-Saxon conquest as a large scale folk movement, with massive numbers of peasant families displacing older British communities, is now no longer accepted. Some British kingdoms even managed to survive after the coming of the Anglo-Saxons. Elmet, a British kingdom occupying the area around Leeds, maintained its independence up to the early 7th century. It now seems likely that the Anglo-Saxon ascendency over England was achieved not by weight of numbers but by a warrior aristocracy who took over the reins of lordship and imposed their culture. Some Anglo-Saxon sunken huts have been reconstructed at West Stow, Suffolk.

The Vikings

The Danes (who are generally grouped together with the Norse as Vikings) began raiding England for plunder and slaves during the 8th century. By the second half of the 9th century, their intentions changed and they began settling in eastern England. As with the Anglo-Saxons, their settlement did not involve a massive movement of peoples. The Danish 'Great Army' divided up the land and began to farm it. In the regions where they settled in large numbers they imparted a distinctly freer character to local society. Eastern England became the Danelaw, an area where Danish criminal law and inheritance customs held sway until the early 11th century.

While the Danes were colonizing eastern England, the Norse (Norwegians) were establishing a foothold in northern Britain. Commencing around 800, they overwhelmed the northern isles, then spread southwards via the Hebrides to Ireland and the Isle of Man. Given their command over the Irish Sea, it was not surprising that the Norse should eventually cross into the coastal lowlands of Cheshire and Lancashire and into the Lake District. They even pushed eastwards over the watershed into the upper reaches of the Yorkshire Dales. The emigration of the Norse was decidedly a folk movement, motivated by land-hunger. Indeed, Orkney and Shetland remained in Norse hands, and were shaped in their cultural evolution by Norse language and custom, until 1469.

Because of their early raids, particularly on rich monasteries (notably on Lindisfarne in 793), the pagan Vikings received a bad press from contemporary chroniclers, who were, of course, the monks who had suffered most from the onslaughts. But the Scandinavians later made many positive contributions to British life. Agricultural settlements, for example in the Lake District and Pennines, derived from their pioneering efforts, and latterly we have begun to appreciate their vital role as organizers of trade. With their seamanship and wide-flung contacts, they were well-placed to exploit the potential of long-distance trade: towns like York and Ipswich became key centres.

THE SUTTON HOO HELMET *was found, along with many domestic utensils and much jewellery, in an Anglo-Saxon king's burial-ship (c.625).*

PATTERNS OF SETTLEMENT

PLACE-NAMES are often clues to the movements of different peoples:
Celtic *bre* (hill) as in Breedon-on-the-Hill, Leics.
Roman *castra* (fort) as in Chester, Cheshire.
Gaelic *baile* (farmstead, village) as in Ballasalla, Tayside.
Anglo-Saxon *ham* (estate, village) as in Amersham, Bucks.
Later Anglo-Saxon *ton* (village) as in Taunton, Somerset.
Norse and Danish *by* (farmstead, village) as in Grimsby, Humber.

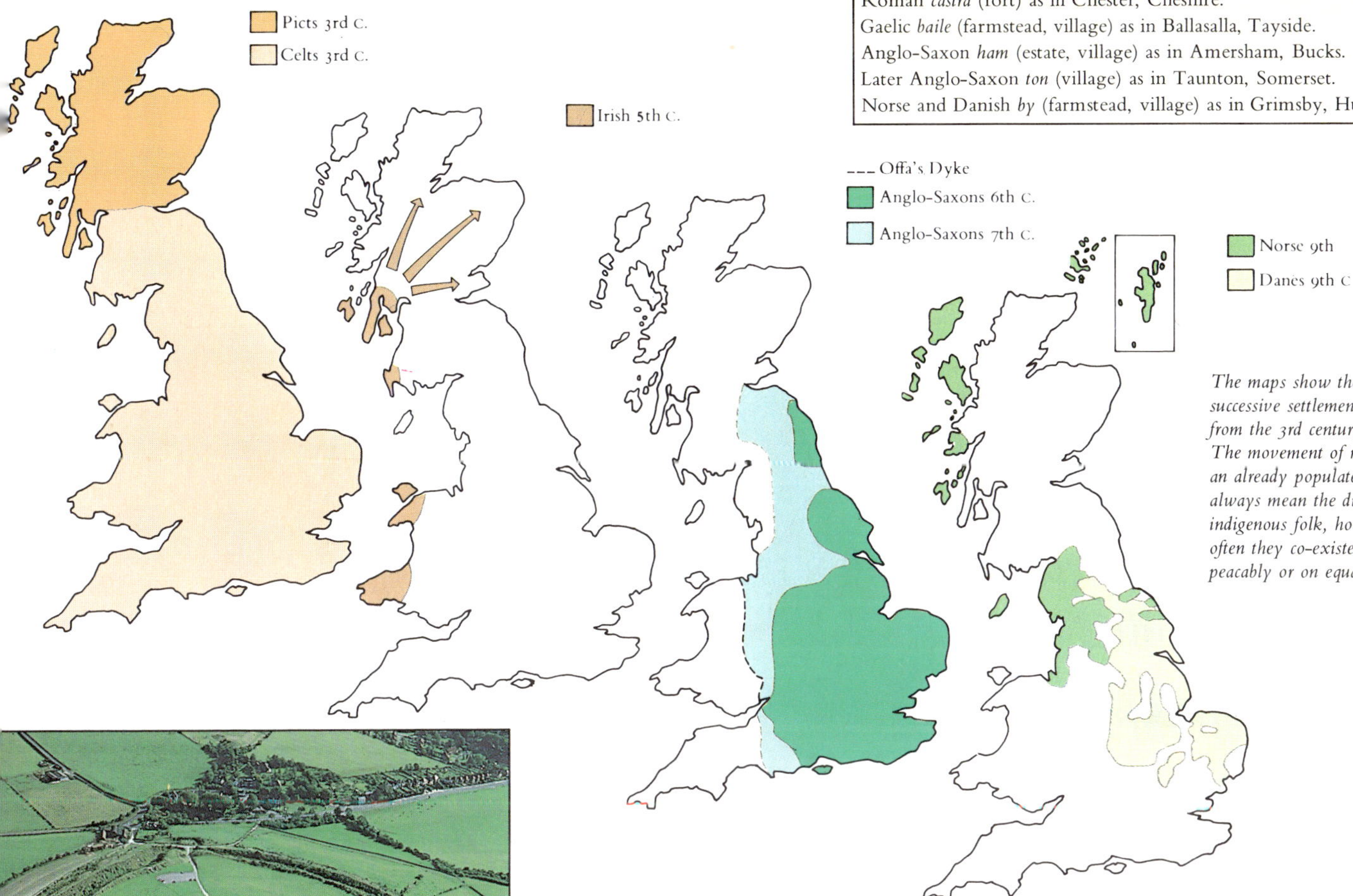

The maps show the extent of the successive settlements of Britain from the 3rd century to the 10th. The movement of new settlers into an already populated area did not always mean the displacement of indigenous folk, however. More often they co-existed, if not always peacably or on equal terms.

OLD SARUM *had been an Iron Age and then a Saxon settlement before the Normans built a town and the first Salisbury cathedral in the 12th century.*

The Irish invasions

The immediate post-Roman period also saw the invasion of various parts of Britain by the Irish. The main Irish colonization involved a movement of Ulster 'Scots' into the south-west Highlands and islands after 450, where they formed the kingdom of Dalriada and introduced the Gaelic language. By a union with the Picts, a Scottish king, Kenneth mac Alpin (d.858), became ruler of all the Highlands. Traces of further Irish settlement during the 5th and 6th centuries have been uncovered in south-west Scotland, Cumbria, north-west Wales and south-west Wales. In the latter area, the Irish ruled Dyfed and established Irish as the spoken tongue of the area. Only in the 8th century did Welsh kingship and language re-assert themselves.

The Norman conquest

The last successful invasion of Britain was by the Normans. With William the Conqueror's victory over Harold at the battle of Hastings in 1066, the whole of England was opened to a land-grab by Norman lords and knights. Nor did the conquest stop at England: by the end of the 11th century, the Normans had pushed deep into Wales and established vast Marcher lordships such as Brecon and Clun, as well as taking control of the southern coastal lowlands as far west as Pembrokeshire. Their penetration of Scotland took a different course. With the accession of David I (1124–53), many Anglo-Normans were invited to settle there. Slowly but surely, the whole of southern Scotland and eastern Scotland as far as Moray acquired a significant Anglo-Norman presence.

The Normans brought with them a complex feudal hierarchy of landholding, with the king and the great barons at its apex and the ordinary peasants at its base. The conquest had little effect on the peasantry, but the Anglo-Saxon nobles lost much land and status.

ROBERT, DUKE OF NORMANDY. *Even in effigy (at Gloucester Cathedral) William I's eldest son (d.1134) has a conquering sword at the ready. The leading Norman families did not regard England, a lucrative colony, as 'home' and for 300 years Norman French was spoken by the English nobility.*

CONNECTIONS
Anglo-Saxon art: **280–81** *The artist's eye*
The impact of the Romans: **194–5** *Roman Britain*
Irish missionaries: **46–7** *The coming of Christianity*
Later immigration: **44–5** *Foreign settlers*
Norman churches: **200–201** *The springtime of church architecture*

Foreign settlers

The last invaders of Britain were the Normans, but since the 11th century there have been waves of more peaceful migration, which have often made an important contribution to British life. An outstanding example, and the first of the large-scale, non-military migrations, was the arrival of the Huguenots (French Protestants) who had been expelled from France by Louis XIV in 1685. They fled from persecution to Protestant states such as England, where they settled mainly in Norwich and in London, taking over the areas of Soho, St Giles and Spitalfields. Many of them were silk weavers and dyers, and Spitalfields became the centre of a silk industry whose craftsmen were the finest in Europe. At a time when manufacturing skills were highly prized national assets, and were treated as closely guarded secrets, the Huguenot weavers' techniques for making the 'new draperies' brought them great esteem.

The Jews

The first Jewish settlers in Britain came with William the Conqueror, who invited a number of Rouen Jews to accompany him and help to finance the conquest. Jews and finance were inseparably linked in medieval Europe, because of the limitations on their employment in a Christian world, and their exemption from the laws forbidding usury. This association with money and profit

ANTI-SEMITISM *plagued the Jewish communities of the Middle Ages. Jews were often accused of ritual murder: there was a famous case in Lincoln in 1255.*

fuelled the phobias of a populace trained by medieval Christianity to treat the Jews as scapegoats for their woes, and the Jewish communities that grew up in many British towns were regularly intimidated. Punishing taxes were extorted from the Jews by Henry III, and in 1290, no longer capable of contributing to the royal coffers, they were expelled from the country by Edward I.

In 1656 Oliver Cromwell re-opened the doors to Jewish settlers, and by the early 18th century a flourishing community had established itself in London, around the Bevis Marks synagogue (opened 1701). Large-scale Jewish immigration, however, was a phenomenon of the late 19th century: refugees from the pogroms of eastern Europe travelled far afield in search of new homes.

The new Jewish arrivals settled mainly in areas of Manchester, Newcastle, Hull and, above all, the East End of London. With their considerable business acumen and the support of close-knit street communities, they set up tailoring, shoemaking and cabinet-making enterprises, supplying the new multiple shops and chain stores with their cheap goods. The business started by one Jewish immigrant, Montague Burton, soon became synonymous with the working man's 'Sunday best' suit.

The Irish

At the beginning of the 19th century, seasonal migration from Ireland became customary among poor farmers, who worked on the building sites and big farms of the 'mainland' in the summer, and returned to dig their own spring-sown crops in the autumn. The famine of the 1840s was a catalyst that stimulated the arrival of permanent Irish settlers in Britain (and in far greater numbers in America). Thereafter, emigration was made a significant feature of Irish life by two factors: the chain process, whereby those already abroad enabled

ENLARGING THE CRYSTAL PALACE, *1854. Massive construction undertakings of this kind depended heavily on immigrant Irish labour.*

WAVES OF SETTLEMENT
*The map (**below**) shows waves of immigration since the 17th century.*

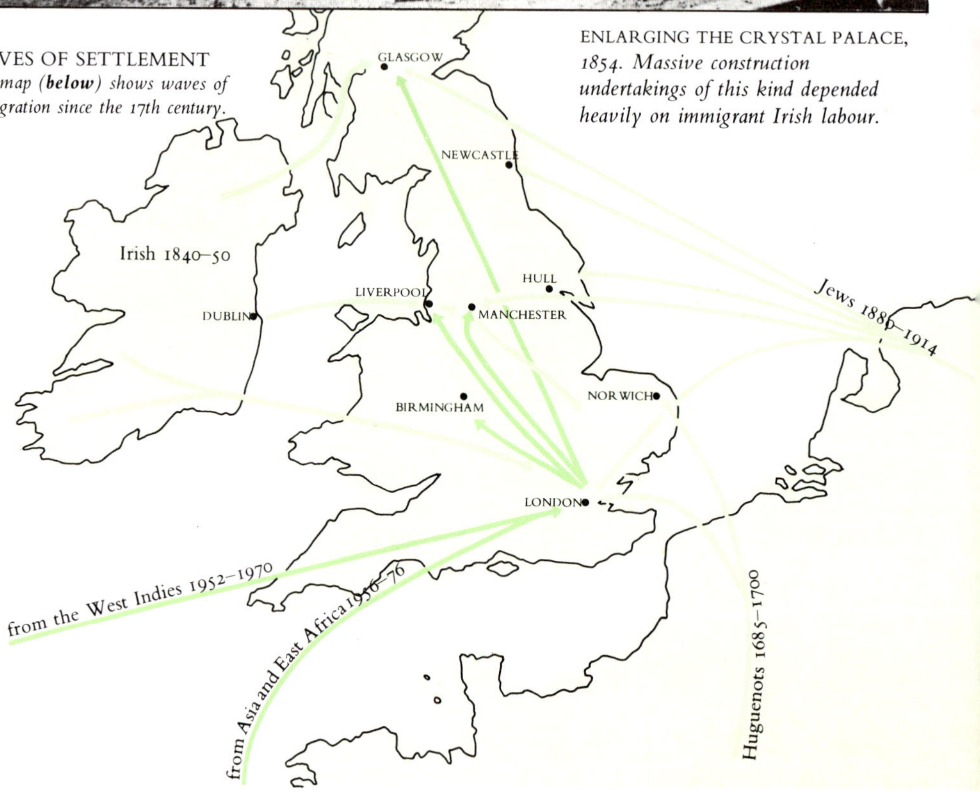

A CHAMELEON PLACE OF WORSHIP. *This Brick Lane building has a complex history. It was built in 1742 as a Huguenot church, but in 1809 became a Methodist chapel. In 1879 it was purchased by a Jewish society and renamed the Spitalfields Great Synagogue. Since this photograph was taken it has become a mosque, serving the religious needs of the latest immigrants to this part of London.*

A SHOPPING PARTNERSHIP (***right***) *on the East End's Mile End Road.*

IMMIGRANTS AND THE EAST END

From the 17th century onwards, London's East End has harboured successive waves of foreign immigrants. The Huguenots in the 17th century were followed by the Irish in the 18th and 19th, and between 1870 and 1914 the area received large numbers of Jewish settlers in flight from eastern Europe.

As early as 1850 a Jewish ghetto had become established around Petticoat Lane, its occupants competing with the Irish in the cut and thrust of street-selling. After 1881 refugees from Russian pogroms swelled the quarter, and it expanded farther east. The industrious Jewish East Enders worked in the 'sweated' trades, and especially the rag trade. In 1889 the social investigator Charles Booth observed of them: 'They live and crowd together and work and meet their fate independent of the great stream of London life surging around them.' For many, however, America was the ultimate destiny. In 1887, for example, Victor Adler left England with his drama troupe, which had played to East End audiences, and helped to found the great Yiddish theatre tradition in New York.

The black and Asian immigrants who have settled in the East End in modern times echo, in their different ways, the Jewish experience. Revivalist chapels sustain the religious and cultural identity of the West Indians in a way that recalls the old East End synagogues; and the Asians, like the Jews, have taken to the mass production of cheap clothing in small factories.

CHINESE MEMORIALS *at Everton testify to a tradition of Chinese settlement in Merseyside. Most Chinese in Britain are from Hong Kong.*

their relatives to join them; and the custom by which a farm was inherited by only one son, instead of being subdivided among numerous children into uneconomically sized holdings.

Irish muscle-power was welcome to Britain's industrialists. The first mass incursions of Irish 'navvies', whose agricultural background enabled them to do unskilled but arduous jobs better than the native workforce, coincided with the development of the railways. In 1851, one Mancunian in ten and one Liverpudlian in six was Irish-born. For large numbers of Irish, Britain was a half-way house for the voyage across the Atlantic, but many of them stayed, and some made a notable contribution to the rise of the British labour movement.

Commonwealth immigrants

As Britain gradually divested itself of empire in the present century, increasing numbers of immigrants came from the former colonies. Encouraged to think of Britain as the 'motherland', they emigrated in search of prosperity, or in flight from new, unsympathetic regimes. It was the latter reason that brought over waves of Kenyan Asians in the late 1960s and Ugandan Asians in the 1970s.

The West Indians came to Britain because they were encouraged to, after the Second World War: London Transport advertised in the Caribbean for drivers and conductors, and West Indians were also encouraged to emigrate in order to take up jobs in British hospitals. The West Indians tended to make their homes in areas that had been settled originally by the Irish.

Asian immigrants seeking economic opportunity have tended to find it in the clothing trade, in the Midlands and the north as well as in London. Many have taken advantage of the collapse of Britain's small shops, and in place of the old specialized shops of the high streets, they have developed urban versions of the village store.

For some immigrants, particularly those who have met with racial prejudice or language difficulties, or who have found some aspects of Western society unacceptable for religious reasons, life in Britain has been fraught with difficulties. Immigration laws of 1961, 1968 and 1971 made a crude attempt to create a better-adjusted society by severely restricting the flow. More constructive steps, such as the Race Relations Bill of 1968, have concentrated on promoting racial harmony.

CONNECTIONS
Commonwealth history: 98–9 *The imperial experience*
Irish Catholicism: 50–51 *Catholics and Protestants*
Irish history: 66–7 *Ireland and Britain*

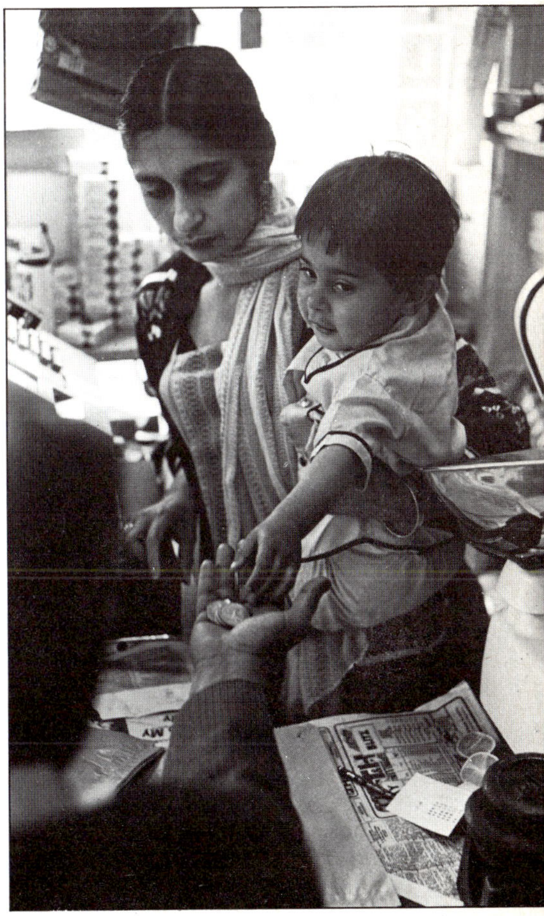

ASIAN LADY WITH CHILD, *in Coventry. In many major towns, the corner shops run by Asian settlers – usually involving the whole family – perform a valuable, personalized service.*

The coming of Christianity

The first mention of Christians in Britain occurs as early as the close of the 2nd century in the writings of Tertullian, a North African Christian. Apart from saying that Christianity was present in parts of Britain inaccessible to the Romans, he gives no information as to where exactly it was located, nor any indication of its strength, nor indeed exactly when or by whom it was introduced. Legend and tradition are rife, and even involve leading characters in the New Testament: St Paul, St Philip and St Joseph of Arimathea figure prominently. King Caractacus and his family, who had been carried off to Rome, were sometimes assumed to have brought Christianity back to Britain with them.

LULLINGSTONE PIETY. *The prosperous occupants of this 4th-century Romano-British villa in Kent were Christian. This praying figure, his arms outstretched in the* orans *position that is a common posture in early Christian art in Mediterranean countries, belonged to the frieze decorating the house-chapel's west wall. It has been painstakingly reconstructed from plaster fragments found on the site.*

Present authorities tend to think that the transmission of Christianity to Britain was not an isolated fact of history but occurred within the framework of continuous contact between the eastern territories of the Roman Empire and Britain, which was one of its remote provinces in the north-west. These contacts were established largely by merchants and by private soldiers in the army of occupation. In fact, the first Christian in Britain whose name we know was a soldier – Albanus – in the Roman city of Verulamium (now St Albans). He was martyred there probably as early as the year AD 209. Likewise, Julius and Aaron, martyred at Caerleon-on-Usk (a legionary fortress in south-east Wales), were probably in the Roman army.

Wine, oil and ideas

Traders were particularly active along the western sea routes of early Britain, and there is strong archaeological evidence to suggest that the ports of the west coast were in direct touch with the islands and shores of the eastern Mediterranean. If wine and oil could travel this way, so too could pilgrims to and from the Holy Land, refugees, books and, most certainly, ideas. This is how the elements of the Christian faith arrived, reinforced *en route* by similar trade relations with Gaul.

Modern archaeological evidence shows that once Christianity had become the official religion of the Roman Empire in the 4th century, Christian activity in Britain was located in two major zones: first, in the thoroughly Romanized south-east; and also in a northern frontier area contained by a line running from the River Humber north-westwards to Hadrian's Wall. Both areas had Roman towns, and in the rural areas there were many large villas. The villas often have small house-like churches; the well-known villa at Lullingstone in Kent contains one of the earliest types, as well as a chapel.

In the 5th and 6th centuries the Roman Empire was overrun by pagan hordes, and Angles, Jutes and Saxons invaded Britain. They were later united under the Christian leadership of King Alfred (871–99), but not before the work of Christianization had to be undertaken anew. This was partly the work of St Augustine (died 604). He was sent by Pope Gregory the Great, who had succeeded in re-establishing the power of Rome on a Christian basis. It was Gregory's dream of a Christian Empire based on Rome that lay behind his sending of Augustine to England. The missionary party landed in Kent in 597. The pagan king of Kent, Ethelbert, received them cautiously, and in due course he and his court were converted. In 601 Augustine received his *pallium* (mantle of office) from the Pope and became Archbishop of Canterbury. But Christianization of the pagan Saxons was no easy task and the mission suffered many setbacks. Indeed, for many decades after Augustine's death the Roman brand of Christianity was confined to a small bridgehead in Kent.

Meanwhile, the 'Celtic Church' had come into being. In the eastern Mediterranean, northern Egypt and Africa, many Christians had withdrawn to the deserts and lived there as hermits or holy men, denying themselves all wealth and practising all manner of privations to allay the sins of the flesh. The idea spread along the mercantile routes to southern Gaul, western Britain and southern Ireland, where it took root and considerably modified the more orthodox Christianity that had survived in these parts, possibly from late Roman times. Individuals lived in solitude, or gathered together in small monastic settlements.

IONA (***below***). *In 563 St Columba left Ireland and founded a monastery on this tiny island, which became the centre of Celtic Christianity in Britain.*

SPHERES OF INFLUENCE

Christianity returned to Britain in the late 6th century in a two-pronged movement. The Celtic Church, with its Irish traditions of individualist ascetism and mysticism, spread down from Columba's Iona; while St Augustine's Canterbury was the centre of the Inner Province, where the intellectual and doctrinal rigour of Rome prevailed. (See the map, ***left***.)

Iona and Canterbury

While Britain lapsed into heathen ways, this monastic culture flowered among the Irish, who had been spared the 'barbarian' invasions and had remained Christian since the mission of St Patrick

ST BRYNACH'S CROSS (***right***) *at Nevern in Dyfed is a 10th- or 11th-century example of the beautifully carved Celtic high crosses that acted as symbols of Christianity and sometimes as the centres of preaching before churches were constructed.*

ST MARTIN'S CHURCH, CANTERBURY (***bottom right***). *Probably the oldest-established church in England. The pagan king of Kent, Ethelbert, allowed St Augustine to use it as his headquarters because his wife, already a believer, worshipped there.*

THE VENERABLE BEDE (c.673–735) (***below***) *wrote the history of the Church in England at a time when it was firmly established. Writing at Jarrow, in his native kingdom of Northumbria, he regarded the Celtic tradition with some suspicion, although he acknowledged the greatness of its major figures, notably St Columba at Iona and St Aidan of Lindisfarne.*

in 444. In 563 St Columba left Ireland for the island of Iona, and from this base Pictish Scotland was Christianized. The inspiration for the movement of this Celtic Church into Northumbria came from St Oswald, who had fled to Iona (and became a Christian there) when the heathen King Edwin seized his kingdom. When Oswald returned to reclaim Northumbria in 633, he naturally looked north for Christian aid to Iona, rather than south to Canterbury. St Aidan, who set up his church on Lindisfarne (Holy Island), was sent to Oswald to rescue his people from paganism.

By feats of arms and great resourcefulness Oswald eventually became overlord of Mercia, East Anglia and Wessex, all of which were drawn within the orbit of the Celtic Church in the early 7th century.

Monasticism was also an important part of the Church structure established by St Augustine at Canterbury. The two Churches were not so far apart that unification was impossible, though the

Roman Church was more firmly controlled. The inevitable conflict was settled when the Synod of Whitby (664) decided for Rome. Monasticism grew rapidly under such great enthusiasts as St Benedict Biscop, St Wilfred and Coelfrith. But by the time of St Dunstan (d. 988) English religious life had been severely shaken by the fierce onslaught of the Viking raids. It was he who was largely responsible for its reorganization. When the Normans arrived in 1066, the Anglo-Saxon bishops had been comfortably settled in their dioceses for some time.

CONNECTIONS

Celtic and Saxon art: 280–81 *The artist's eye*

Early churches: 200–201 *The springtime of church architecture*

Medieval traditions: 52–3 *Medieval saints and shrines*

Roman influences: 194–5 *Roman Britain*

Church and State/*From William I to the Reformation*

WILLIAM THE CONQUEROR. *His invasion of England in 1066 was in part a crusade, with papal backing, aimed at reforming the English Church and bringing it into line with the Continent.*

Throughout the Middle Ages the Church in Europe was closely bound to and supported by the secular powers. However, in the 11th and 12th centuries the popes and the ecclesiastical leaders of Europe were determined to assert the independence of the Church from State control. The stage was set for a series of conflicts that lasted right until the Reformation.

A BIBULOUS MONK. *Such images of monastic good living, though frequently exaggerated, helped Henry VIII and Thomas Cromwell to discredit the monasteries in the early 16th century.*

Church reform and championship

William I was friendly to the idea of Church reform, although he became increasingly alarmed at the growing power of the Papacy. In 1070 he appointed to the Primacy (that is, to the Archbishopric of Canterbury) a scholarly monk named Lanfranc, who made a determined assault on the laxity of the Church (notably clerical marriages and the sale of ecclesiastical offices). He succeeded in reorganizing the English dioceses, and in establishing Church courts which were independent of the civil legal system.

William's successor William Rufus was not so enlightened. To this king the Church was just another feudal barony, and he abused it with impunity. He kept Church appointments vacant and enjoyed their revenues, ignoring papal threats. For four years there was no replacement for Lanfranc. However, during a serious illness Rufus relented and appointed Anselm of Bec, one of the greatest theologians of the age. Anselm refused to receive the symbols of his office – the ring and pastoral staff – from the hands of the King and insisted on papal confirmation of his appointment. Further disagreements led to Anselm's voluntary exile in Rome.

The battle for Church independence continued in the 12th century, and became a highly charged issue after Henry II appointed to the Primacy his friend and Chancellor Thomas à Becket, in the hope that by combining the two offices he could arrest the growth of ecclesiastical power. But Becket resigned the Chancellorship and devoted all his energies to the Church. He infuriated Henry by opposing his attempts to establish State control over the punishment of members of the clergy who had committed serious crimes. Becket eventually met retribution for his rebelliousness when he was murdered in his own cathedral by four knights in 1170.

In the following century the struggle was resumed when King John refused to accept a papal candidate for the Primacy. England was consequently placed under an Interdict (1208–14) – the churches were closed and no masses, marriages or funerals were conducted – and the King himself was excommunicated. Eventually John had to surrender his kingdom to the Pope and receive it back as a papal fief.

Corruption in the Church

By the 14th century the papal bureaucracy was vast and Rome demanded increasingly onerous financial support throughout Europe. From the 1350s Parliament enacted statutes against papal powers, but the tendency was towards compromise rather than entrenchment.

A feeling that the spirit of official Christianity had become too political and authoritarian increased when the Great Schism divided the Papacy in 1378. There was also a widespread belief that abuses in the Church were gaining ground. Bishops were seen as nothing more than royal servants, and the monasteries were criticized for inordinate wealth. Ignorance and pluralism (the practice of holding more than one benefice) were rife among the priesthood. The poets Chaucer and Langland expressed popular opinion by depicting priests, monks and friars (the latter first appeared in the early 13th century) as money-grabbing gluttons and drunkards.

The anti-clerical doctrines of the Lollards, who took their ideas from John Wycliffe, faintly foreshadowed the Reformation. Wycliffe believed in the self-sufficiency of the scriptures, which led him to criticize the whole structure of the Church. His views were declared heretical in 1382, and Lollardy declined in popularity after an uprising of 1414.

The Reformation

The final break with Rome was provoked by Henry VIII's failure to obtain an annulment of his first marriage, though the ease with which he established himself as head of the Church of England and Wales reflects a broad base of support. The Act of Supremacy (1534) was followed by the cataclysmic dissolution of the monasteries, whose possessions were redistributed by sales and grants. The monks and nuns were pensioned off, their buildings pulled down, the stone and lead put up for sale, and monastic gold and silver either sold or melted down to augment the wealth of the Crown. Thomas Cromwell, the King's chief minister, was awarded the earldom of Essex for his part in the dissolution. In Lincolnshire, Yorkshire and the northern counties Robert Aske led an unsuccessful rebellion in defence of the monasteries – the Pilgrimage of Grace.

THE MURDER OF THOMAS À BECKET, *1170. After Becket's martyrdom, Henry II was genuinely repentant. The cult of St Thomas gathered strength right up to the Reformation, when Henry VIII attempted to stamp it out.*

The Scottish Reformation, influenced by the preachings of John Knox, came somewhat later than the English one. Papal authority was denied and masses abolished in 1560, but the consolidation of Protestantism in Scotland was delayed by the Catholic beliefs of Queen Mary.

CONNECTIONS
Thomas à Becket: 52–3 *Medieval saints and shrines*
The Counter-Reformation: 50–51 *Catholics and Protestants*
Medieval church music: 300–301 *Music and song*
Monasticism: 206–7 *Monasteries*

SECULAR CANON (*above left*). *Secular canons served cathedrals or collegiate churches. Unlike monks, they could own personal property.*

CLUNIAC MONK (*left*). *The Cluniac Order followed the reformed Benedictine Rule that had been established at Cluny in France.*

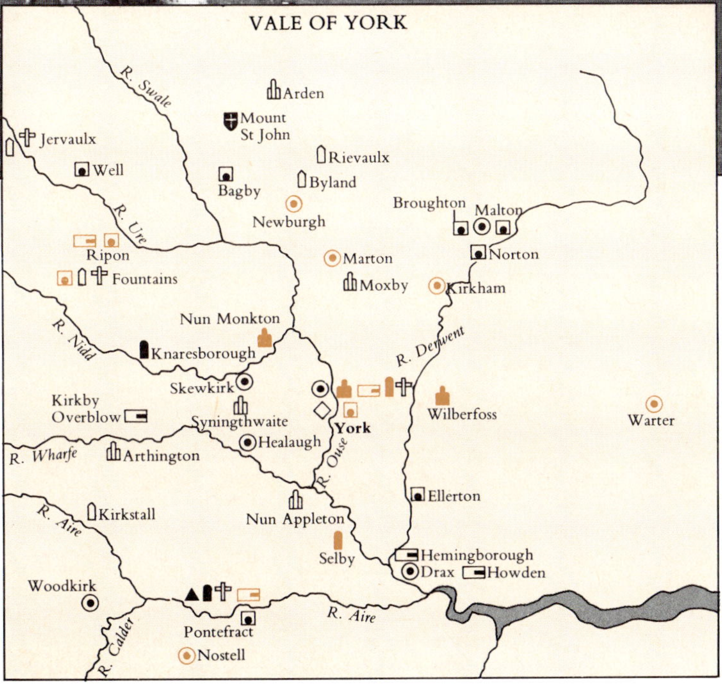

RELIGIOUS HOUSES IN MEDIEVAL YORKSHIRE

In the 12th century large tracts of land in Yorkshire were given to the monastic Orders – to the Cluniacs and, above all, to the Cistercians. The Cistercian monasteries of Jervaulx, Rievaulx and Fountains (all ruined at the dissolution) became extraordinarily rich, for the monks were sheep farmers and amassed huge profits from the wool trade. At Fountains (*above*) a huge cellarium was built in which wool was stored. York itself supported the magnificent Benedictine abbey of St Mary's, whose church had exceptionally fine sculpture. There were many communities of regular canons (priests following monastic rule), for example at Nostell Priory; and houses of secular canons served the cathedrals of Ripon and York. Most towns and many rural monasteries had hospitals attached, which catered for the destitute and the incurable (including lepers) rather than for the treatment of the curably sick.

When the agents of Thomas Cromwell visited Yorkshire they found 'manifest sin, vicious, carnal and abominable living' among the religious communities. After the dissolution of the smaller monasteries, several abbots who supported the risings known as the Pilgrimage of Grace (1536) were put to death.

- Greater house of Canons Regular
- Lesser house of Canons Regular
- Greater nunnery
- Lesser nunnery
- Greater secular college
- Lesser secular college
- Benedictine monastery
- Cluniac monastery
- Cistercian monastery
- Monastery whose abbot was executed during the dissolution
- City with several friaries
- Single community of friars
- Greater hospital or hospice
- Lesser hospital or hospice
- House of Knights Templar

Catholics and Protestants

MARTYRDOM UNDER MARY I. *The Protestants Hugh Latimer and Nicholas Ridley receiving merciless treatment at Oxford.*

THE LANDING OF WILLIAM OF ORANGE, *1688. The following year, Parliament passed the Toleration Act, giving freedom of worship to Nonconformists, but not to Catholics.*

THE PILGRIM FATHERS *in 1620 set sail from Plymouth for New England in the* Mayflower, *in flight from the tyrannical Church of England.*

COLLECTING THE OFFERTORY IN A SCOTTISH KIRK, *1855, by John Phillip. The reputation of the Presbyterian Church for dour joylessness is belied by this cheerful 19th-century view. The Established Church in Scotland has been Presbyterian since the 17th century.*

Henry VIII, 'the majestic lord who broke the bonds of Rome', undermined the Catholic Church in England and Wales, but he was not in fact a Protestant. Throughout his reign he shunned the more radical ideas of Martin Luther, and persecuted those few who adhered to them in his own country. Only after his death, during the minority of Edward VI (1547–53), were the laws against these 'heretics' relaxed and the Latin Mass replaced by Thomas Cranmer's Prayer Book. The reign of 'Bloody Mary' (1553–8) was a brief respite for the Catholics, but in the long term the outrage over the martyrdom of over 300 Protestants (including Cranmer) only strengthened the power of the reformed Church.

Puritans and Calvinists

Elizabeth I sought the middle way of Anglicanism, between Catholicism and incipient Puritanism. A group of missionary Catholic priests attempted to bring England back into the papal fold in a wave of Counter-Reformation zeal. The Jesuit Edmund Campion was a notable martyr in this cause. The Catholics at this time suffered from the Recusancy Laws, which punished those who failed to attend Church of England services. But in the same period, 'Puritan' came into use as a term of ridicule, applied to a growing group of Protestant extremists, who were distinguished by their severe dress and radical aims. Many Puritans wished to abolish all bishops and the official Prayer Book, and they banned images, candles and rich vestments in their churches. Such ungodly pleasures as theatre-going were anathema to them. Most of the ideas of the Puritans were strongly influenced by the theology of the Frenchman John Calvin, who believed that only the elect were destined for salvation.

Neither James I nor Charles I sought to return the Established Church to Rome, but both believed in a hierarchical Church, and were disliked for their autocratic rule. The parliamentary protests in Charles's reign were strongly supported by Puritans. Similarly, in Scotland, the Covenanters who protested against Charles's attempts to foist a revised Prayer Book on them gradually became identified with an anti-royalist movement. Despite severe repression, they maintained an underground Church in south-west Scotland, Fife and Easter Ross.

Persecution of the Catholics

In 1688 the Glorious Revolution brought the Protestant William of Orange and his wife Mary to the throne. Laws of the 17th century denying civil rights to the Catholics were maintained in the 18th century. Nonconformists were also seen as a danger to the Established Church, especially during the High Tory years in the reign of Queen Anne (1702–14). There was a gradual growth of toleration in the reign of George I, but popular reactions to the Jacobites in 1715 and 1745, and the anti-Catholic Gordon Riots in 1780, revealed the frightening militancy of Protestant feeling. In Scotland, adherents of the Episcopal Church, many of whom supported the Jacobite cause, were vigorously persecuted. Henry Dundas, when he tried to support a Bill relieving Scottish Catholics of some of their disabilities, provoked a storm of indignation.

Revival and reform

Emancipation for Catholics was finally secured in the 19th century. The Roman Catholic Relief Act of 1829 removed the antiquated penalties and, following the Irish potato famine of the 1840s, a flood of Irish immigrants swelled the Catholic percentage of the population (particularly in Lancashire and Scotland). The Catholic hierarchy was restored in England and Wales in 1850 and in Scotland in 1878. The socially conscious Cardinal Manning, Primate from 1865 to 1892, was particularly active in moving the British Catholic Church closer to Rome. Establishment and expansion were gloriously reflected in the vast new building of Westminster Cathedral, whose foundation stone was laid in 1894.

At the same time, Nonconformism was being radically affected by the Evangelical Revival. The Clapham Sect and the British and Foreign Bible Society made considerable impact. The general social conscience was quickened, and philanthropic fervour succeeded in abolishing the slave trade and improving factory conditions in Britain. In contrast, the Oxford Movement (led by Edward Pusey, John Keble and John Henry Newman) wished to restore the ideals of the pre-Reformation Church, and concerned itself with order and beauty in worship. Ritualism and Anglo-Catholicism in the mid-19th century pushed the Established Church further from the Nonconformists.

In spite of the stereotyped view of the Victorian period as an age of piety, atheism was surprisingly rife. The Religious Census of 1851 revealed that many of the new working classes were untouched by religion. Faith was greatly shaken, moreover, by the theory of evolution propounded by Charles Darwin in his *Origin of Species* (1859).

Religion in modern society

At the turn of this century, despite such currents of unbelief, British society was still basically devout, and church-going commonly dominated Sundays. The Edwardian period saw relaxations in the Victorian code, but it was the First World War that really struck at the roots of the Christian faith. The anguish evoked by the war inspired a National Mission for Repentance and Hope in 1916.

Following the war, attempts were made to update both the Church of England and the Church of Scotland through legislation. The two main Presbyterian Churches of Scotland were united in 1929. Two prominent Anglican leaders, H.R.L. Sheppard and William Temple, were active in promoting social concern.

The Second World War brought new ferment, and inspired fresh ideals. The British Council of Churches, founded in 1942, has become a strong ecumenical force, pulling together the Catholic and Protestant Churches for more effective Christian action – for example, through Christian Aid. There have been considerable changes in both Catholic and Protestant patterns of worship, including reform of liturgy (for instance, the Catholics' introduction of an English-language mass) and of service books and the scriptures (producing, most notably, the New English Bible).

CONNECTIONS

Catholics against Protestants: 108–9 *Riot and revolution;* 72–3 *The Civil War*

Henry VIII and the Reformation: 48–9 *Church and State*

The Irish situation: 66–7 *Ireland and Britain*

The Jacobites: 60–61 *Scotland and England*

HENRY EDWARD MANNING

As Archbishop of Westminster (1865–92) and as a Cardinal from 1875, Manning led the Roman Catholic Church in late 19th-century Britain. He was portrayed in his glorious Cardinal's robes by G.F. Watts in 1888 (***right***). As a young man he was a member of the Oxford Movement, and, like Newman, he was soon converted to the Catholic faith. One of his chief ambitions was to raise the standards of the Catholic priesthood, which, partly owing to shortage of funds, were considerably lower than those of the Anglican clergy. Manning was an active social reformer, campaigning for temperance and supporting the National Agricultural Labourers' Union at its foundation in 1872. He was concerned with the plight of the poor and underprivileged. At a fund-raising meeting for London's Westminster Cathedral, he asked his colleagues, 'Could I leave 20,000 children without education, and drain my friends and my flock to pile up stones and bricks?' The great new Cathedral was begun after his death.

A BISHOP'S ENTHRONEMENT *in Liverpool's Anglican Cathedral. Much of the ceremony derives from medieval ritual.*

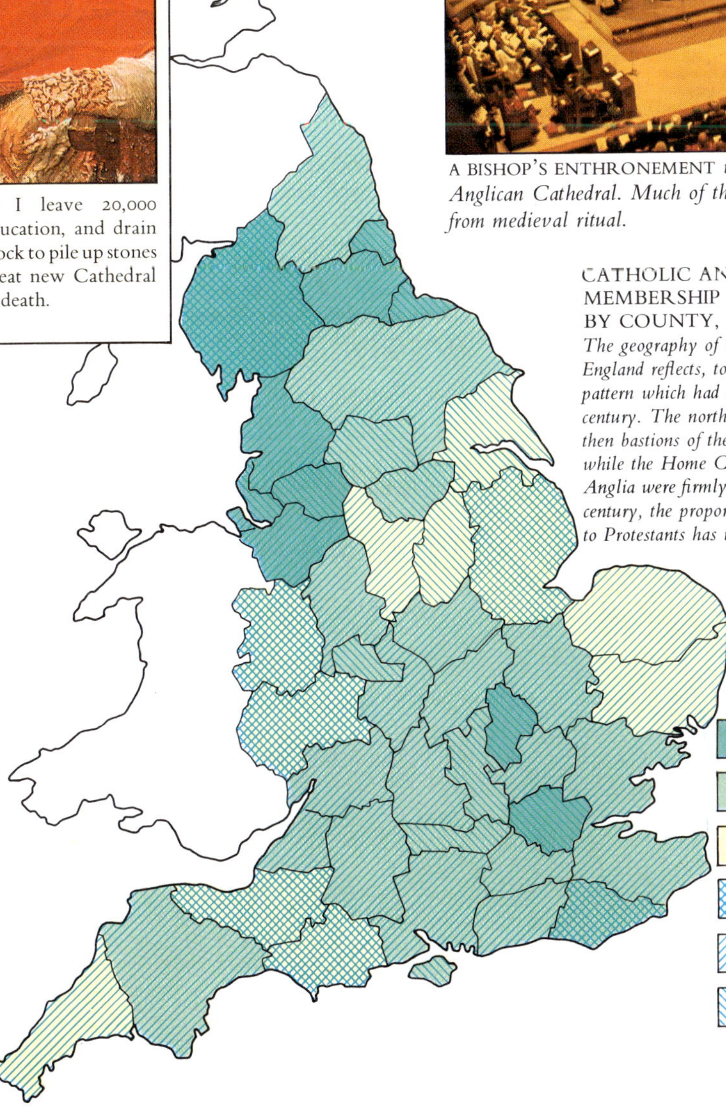

CATHOLIC AND ANGLICAN MEMBERSHIP IN ENGLAND, BY COUNTY, 1980

The geography of Church affiliation in England reflects, to a large extent, a pattern which had emerged in the 17th century. The northern counties were then bastions of the Catholic faith, while the Home Counties and East Anglia were firmly Protestant. During this century, the proportion of Catholics to Protestants has increased.

Medieval saints and shrines

The medieval universe was peopled by a multitude of saints, and their celebration in the vicinity of their relics or in places associated with their lives was one of the dominant themes of religion. Britain's medieval pantheon of saints, which accommodated the warrior George and the simple Celtic maiden Winifred alongside great political prelates like Thomas à Becket and intellectuals like the Venerable Bede, presented an extraordinary diversity of human types. Every human ailment or predicament was associated with a saintly figure who had the power to intervene favourably.

From the early Christian period, the Virgin Mary, the Apostles and the Evangelists were considered to be saints by popular consent. Before long, the appellation was attached to early martyrs who died for the faith in times of persecution. After Christianity had become established there were fewer martyrs, and sainthood was now conferred upon individuals who lived exemplary lives involving heroic self-sacrifice in the name of God. A saint was assured of a good, and probably influential, place in heaven. It was therefore logical to suppose that he or she, if appealed to in the right way, might alleviate the sufferings of those left languishing in the Vale of Tears.

A Christian of steadfast virtue naturally inspired the respect, and possibly the veneration, of witnessing contemporaries. A local bishop might ratify the saintly status of such a person, sometimes in

ST DUNSTAN. *A gifted composer, craftsman and prelate of the 10th century, Dunstan (**above left** and **above right**) was renowned for his steadfast godliness, alleged to have enabled him on one occasion to seize the Devil with his tongs.* ST CUTHBERT *(c.634–87), shown here (**bottom right**) being offered the Bishopric of Hexham by King Egfrith of Northumbria, was a saint in the earlier, less worldly, Celtic mould.*

AN ENGLISH MECCA (***below***) *Each spring for more than three centuries, all roads to Canterbury were thronged with pilgrims – on foot, on horseback and in carriages – bound for the shrine of Thomas à Becket. Geoffrey Chaucer (1345–1400) probably based the characters of his* Canterbury Tales *(some shown here around the map) on the people he met while on pilgrimage himself.*

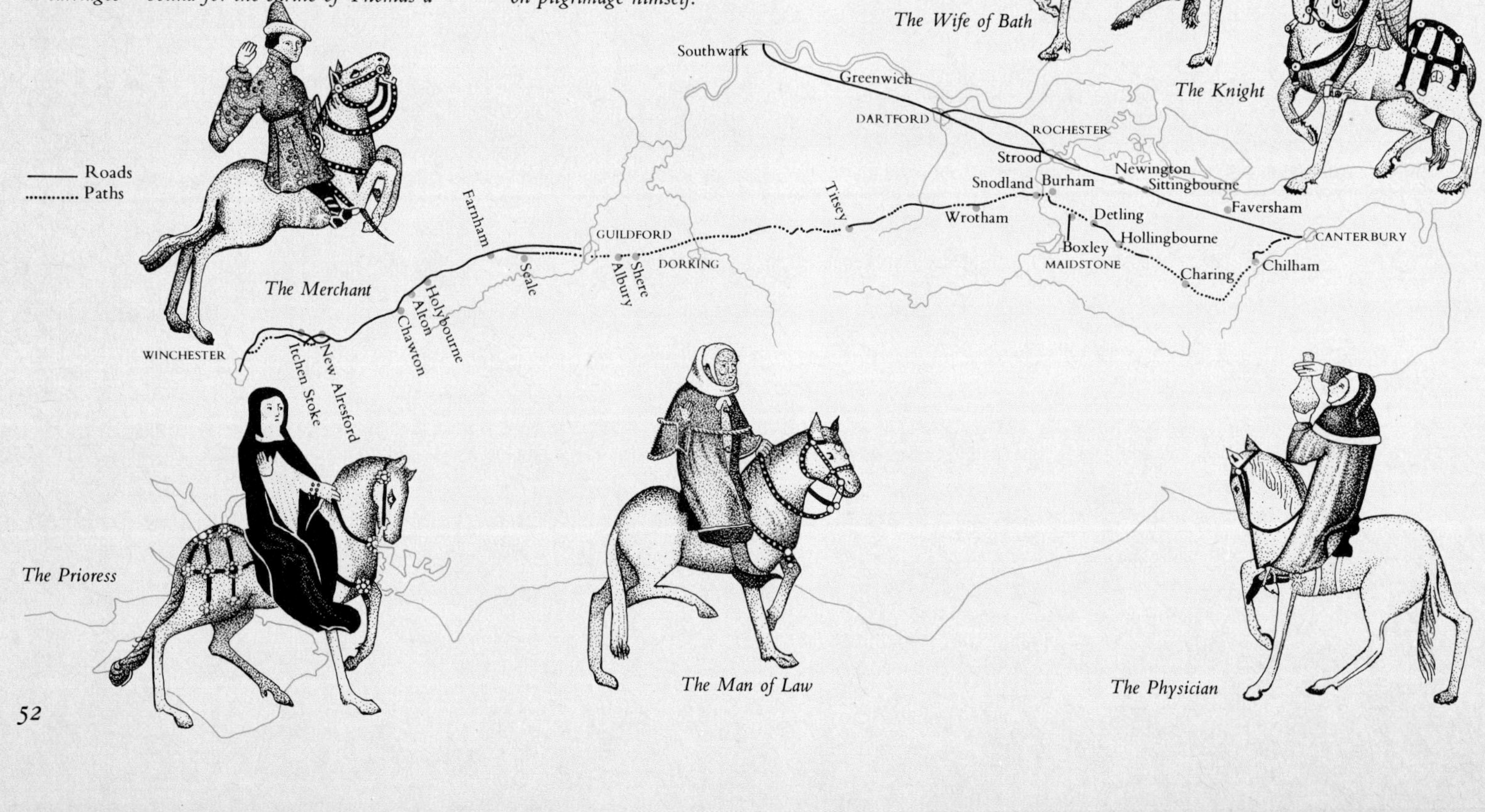

response to pressure of popular opinion. However, from the time of Pope Alexander (d.1187), canonization was tightened up. There was still room for local initiative, but gradually the making of saints became a more formal and Rome-based process. A candidate for sainthood had to undergo a strict examination into his or her life and miracles; this was a costly, lengthy routine, and the requisite support from wealthy and influential backers prepared to go to Rome could not always be commanded.

RUINED WALSINGHAM (***right***). *A remnant of England's most famous Marian shrine. In its 15th-century heyday it was second only to Canterbury. In 1538 Walsingham fell to the dissolution.*

A PILGRIM'S SOUVENIR (***below left***). *Such lead badges of Thomas à Becket were probably given to pilgrims as they left London for Canterbury.*

ST EDWARD'S SHRINE, WESTMINSTER (***below right***). *The niches around the tomb of this saintly English king (c.1002–66) afforded pilgrims direct contact with the stone that held the actual relics. This was considered holier than any outer structure.*

BONE OF ST THOMAS CANTILUPE. *This richly decorated relic of an aristocratic 13th-century saint, who was Bishop of Hereford, is one of the few to have survived the Reformation.*

Miracles and relics

Canonization, even so, was often a mere formality, because most people had a more practical attitude to the status of their saints. The most immediate proof of a person's sanctity and glory in the eyes of God was the ability to work miracles, either while alive or posthumously.

Many people today are sceptical about tales of pilgrims who walked away from shrines cured of blindness, paralysis or leprosy (in the Middle Ages this term covered a variety of skin disorders). But such reports have to be seen in the light of our awareness of the potency of psychosomatic factors in relation to health. Clearly, intensity of belief in a faithful pilgrim could in many cases bring on a cure. Environmental factors may also have been significant. For example, eye diseases caused by vitamin-deficient diets would probably clear up as the quality and quantity of food improved during the spring and summer pilgrimage season.

In the Middle Ages, the bones of saints, or objects associated with them, were as mobile as they were miraculously curative. Holy relics were bought, sold, stolen, counterfeited and hoarded, and they were frequently moved (or 'translated') to different shrines. No relic was dismissed out of hand as bogus, or its powers as suspect, in an age of such passionate belief. Medieval Britain boasted many girdles of the Blessed Virgin Mary, innumerable heads of John the Baptist, and enough fragments of the True Cross to build a ship.

The more pilgrims who visited a shrine, the greater the shrine's reputation, and consequently its wealth. For the monks at Gloucester, the bones of the ignoble Edward II, who acquired sanctity through being murdered and through the persuasiveness of his son, proved a veritable goldmine. The nave of Hereford Cathedral was enlarged thanks to the donations from pilgrims supplicating at the shrine of St Cantilupe. When a small, impecunious Cluniac foundation at Bromholm in Norfolk acquired a piece of the True Cross in the 13th century, it was launched from obscurity to fantastic popularity. The monasteries, often subsidized by pilgrims' offerings, lodged and fed *all* travellers, not just the pilgrims themselves: cults of sainthood in this way paid for a valuable social service of the Middle Ages.

Glastonbury, Walsingham and Canterbury

A pilgrimage was more than a religious exercise, it could also have the character of a festival. Sometimes, the sheer weight of numbers at a shrine created a holiday atmosphere. Huge crowds converged upon Walsingham in Norfolk, where the 11th-century vision of a gentlewoman was celebrated around a replica of the home of the Virgin Mary. Canterbury, after the murder of Thomas à Becket in 1170, became a magnet for pilgrims throughout the whole of Europe. To St Thomas's golden and bejewelled memorial, one of the greatest concentrations of wealth in medieval England, came lepers, blind people, cripples and lunatics, as well as the healthy in search of spiritual succour. But the destination with the most complex and romantic associations was Glastonbury, linked with St Joseph of Arimathea, who brought there the Holy Grail (the chalice used at the Last Supper) and a staff cut from the thorn bush from which Christ's crown of thorns was made.

Today, the divine aura emanating from the remains of an undisputed saint is harder for us to appreciate. Yet the prominent place that saints occupied in the medieval mind is still reflected in popular lore. The spluttering 'catherine wheels' of Guy Fawkes' night are a reminder of an early virgin's martyrdom. The weather on the feast day of St Swithin (d.862) is said to hold good or bad for forty days thereafter, demonstrating saintly influences over rain clouds. And a popular child's toy – the jack-in-the-box – commemorates an unofficial Buckinghamshire saint, Sir John Schorne (d.1308), who conjured the Devil into a boot.

CONNECTIONS

Thomas à Becket: 48–9 *Church and State*
Glastonbury: 56–7 *Lore and legend*
Medieval medicine: 110–11 *Health and medicine*
Royal saints: 280–81 *The artist's eye*

Christian minorities

The establishment of the Church of England caused immense difficulties for numerous groups of believers who practised their own, irregular versions of deeply felt faith. In the late 16th century, for example, there was some alarm at the growth of the Independents, or Congregationalists, who believed that every congregation should be self-governing. Another group of separatists was the Baptists, who originated when some Puritan exiles in Holland encouraged their followers to enter the faith with a positive act of will – adult baptism. One of the Baptists, Thomas Helwys, returned to establish a church at Pinners Hall in London in 1612.

Also beyond the pale were the Quakers (or Society of Friends), a group organized by George Fox in the 1660s, although they had existed in a more amorphous form since the 1640s. They rejected dogma, sacraments and formal ministry, and believed passionately in the 'indwelling light'. At first notorious and widely persecuted for their outrageously unconventional behaviour, they eventually became known for a more sober piety, tinged with tolerance and compassion.

Presbyterianism, which was to become the orthodoxy in Scotland, was also potent in England. During the Civil War the Presbyterian system of Church government by 'presbyteries' of ministers and elders was briefly adopted, but the re-establishment of the Church of England in 1660 thwarted the Presbyterians' ambitions.

A QUAKER MEETING *in the 17th century. Quakers were harassed by the authorities for their outspoken disregard of rank or title.*

Old and New Dissent

The Restoration began a period of legislative harassment for all these dissenting minorities. The new religious settlement in England was embodied in the Clarendon Code of the 1660s – a series of Acts severely restricting freedom of worship. Further disabilities, involving disqualification from public office, were imposed by the Test Act of 1673. The Toleration Act (1689) gave some relief by permitting services in licensed meeting houses and the maintenance of teachers and preachers; it did not apply, however, to the Unitarians, who disbelieved in the Trinity.

In the 18th century the Old Dissenters declined, but a new and vastly popular type of Nonconformity was in the making. This was Methodism, a movement shaped by John Wesley (1703–91) and his brother Charles, whose tireless evangelical missions among the poor inspired a multitude of conversions. Methodism stayed within the Established Church, however uneasily, during John Wesley's lifetime. It also remained impressively disciplined and unified, thanks to 'Pope John's' iron control. A few years after his death it became a separate denomination, and subsequently broke into divergent groups, the first of which were the New Connexion (1797), the Independent Methodists (1805) and the working-class Primitive Methodists (1810). Calvinistic Methodism, meanwhile, had taken root in Wales.

Subversion and salvation

In the atmosphere of panic created by the French Revolution, some types of Nonconformity were regarded as highly subversive. William Cobbett wrote of the New Dissenters with the Methodists particularly in mind: 'They are as much like the dissenters of old times as horse dung is like an apple . . . as a body I know of none so decidedly hostile to public liberty.' However, the Methodists' devotion to hard work meant that they were highly valued by employers.

Nonconformists were enabled to play a fuller part in national life by measures such as the repeal of the Test and Corporation Acts in 1828. They were admitted to the universities of Oxford and Cambridge, in 1854 as undergraduates, in 1871 as dons. Figures such as the Quaker John Bright and the Unitarian Joseph Chamberlain became important in Liberal politics, and the organizational experience of prominent Methodists was later to be turned to advantage in the labour movement.

Victorian Nonconformity, though predominantly middle-class and commercially prosperous, remained committed to bringing the Gospel to the poor, but it alienated many by its censorious attitude to drink and to frivolous pursuits on Sundays. William Booth's Salvation Army aroused the violent hostility that no form of religious enthusiasm seemed able to avoid. However, by 1883 its journal *War Cry* had a weekly circula-

JOHN WESLEY AND THE BIRTH OF METHODISM

In 1708 Samuel Wesley, after failing to rescue his 5½-year-old son John from a fire at Epworth Rectory (***above right***), prayed for his deliverance, and the boy was saved by other onlookers. At Oxford, John and his brother Charles formed a 'Holy Club', which was disparagingly labelled by some as 'methodistical'. Wesley was ordained an Anglican priest, and in 1738 had a profound religious experience in which his heart was 'strangely warmed'. He dedicated his remaining 53 years to the task of passing on to others his belief in personal salvation through Christ, concentrating his mission in areas neglected by the Established Church – parish churches were adequate in rural areas but failed to serve the needs of a growing industrial urban population. In all he delivered over 40,000 sermons, many of them outdoors, and his peregrinations have been estimated to have covered about a quarter of a million miles.

By 1784 there were already 356 Methodist chapels, but private houses were also used for meetings. The illustration (***above left***) shows Wesley preaching to a sexually segregated congregation in a specially adapted house in Nottingham. The emotional impact of such meetings was intensified by the singing of hymns, most of which were written by Charles Wesley, who is said to have composed over 6,500.

THE BETHEL CALVINIST METHODIST CHAPEL, MEIDRIM, DYFED, *built in 1903. Calvinist Methodism originated when George Whitefield (1714–70), with the patronage of the Countess of Huntingdon, broke away from John Wesley and preached a variety of Methodism that embraced John Calvin's belief in predestination. It has always been most popular in Wales.*

NONCONFORMITY IN 1851
The 1851 religious census provides a clear view of the pattern of Nonconformity throughout Britain. This map, based on the census, works in two ways. The tint shows the strongest Nonconformist denomination in each county (and in the case of the Wesleyan Methodists and the English Baptists, hatching is used to indicate the most numerous sect within the denomination). The function of the symbols is to denote whether the denomination or sect in question had greater or fewer members than the Established Church (that is, the Church of England in England and Wales, the Presbyterian 'Kirk' in Scotland).

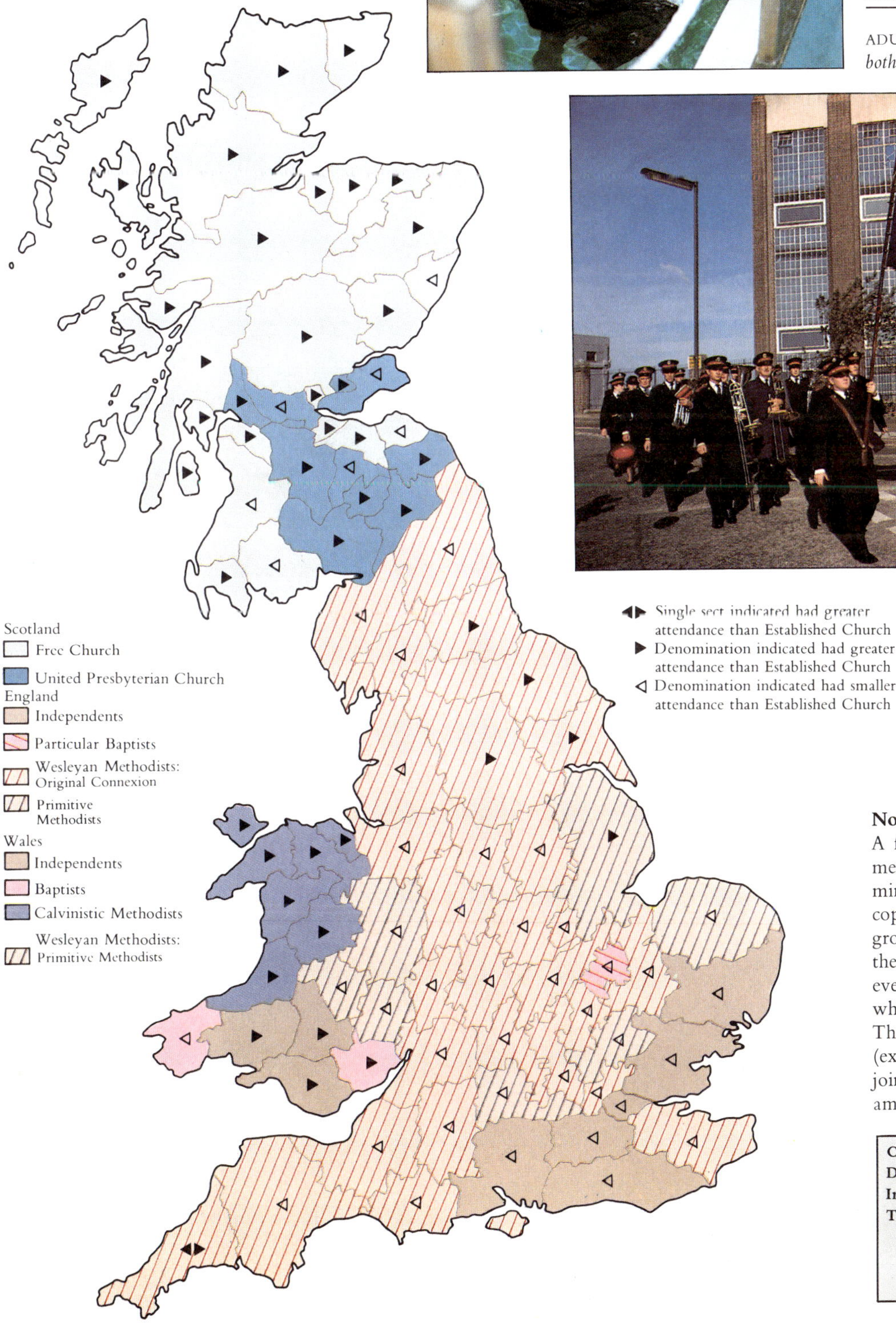

ADULT BAPTISM *by total immersion is practised by both the Baptists (**left**) and the Plymouth Brethren.*

tion of 350,000. After 1890, when its emphasis shifted to social welfare, it brought relief to countless victims of urban poverty.

Lloyd George, in 1916, became the first Nonconformist Prime Minister. Against a background of declining membership, the main developments from this period onwards were the creation of the United Methodist Church of Great Britain in 1932, the union of the Congregationalists and the English Presbyterians to create the United Reformed Church (1972), and the emergence of a vigorous transatlantic influence (notably in the missions of the Pentecostalists and Mormons).

A SALVATION ARMY BAND. *William Booth began his evangelicalism as a Wesleyan Methodist in Nottingham in the 1840s. In 1865 he and his wife founded a Christian Mission in Whitechapel, London, and this grew into the Salvation Army. The famous brass bands lifted hearts to God, but in the early days they also drowned hostile voices.*

Nonconformity in Scotland

A fully Presbyterian system of Church government was adopted in Scotland in 1690. Various minorities were excluded, most notably the Episcopalians. In the mid-18th century numerous groups of Presbyterian dissenters broke away from the Established Church. More significant, however, was the Disruption of 1843—a secession which created the Free Church, brilliantly led by Thomas Chalmers. In 1900 the Free Church (except for the minority known as the 'Wee Frees') joined the United Presbyterian Church, which amalgamated with the Church of Scotland in 1929.

CONNECTIONS
Dissenting academies: 114–15 *Higher education*
Immigrant religions: 44–5 *Foreign settlers*
The Protestants in Ireland: 66–7 *Ireland and Britain*

Lore and legend

The great legends of early Britain expose us to a form of expression that once played a vital role in the cultural life of society. Often it is their sheer antiquity, no less than their imagery, that impresses. The oral tradition surrounding many of them has been so continuous and faithful that only in modern times have they been written down.

Ancient tales of magic

Amongst the best of early legends are those preserved in the *Mabinogion*, a medieval collection of eleven Welsh stories which mix the earthly with the fantastic. One of the most striking themes is the legend of Culhwch and his beloved Olwen, daughter of Ysbaddaden Chief Giant, whom he wins by performing almost Herculean feats, such as sowing and harvesting the food for the wedding feast on the same day. The plot features monsters

THE MARSHFIELD MUMMERS, GLOS. *With costumes made of strips of paper, the mummers enact ancient dramas, sometimes symbolizing human sacrifices made in pagan times.*

and – typically for a Celtic legend – shape-shifters, such as Gwrhyr the Interpreter of Tongues, who could change into a bird.

As deeply cloaked in the mists of time are the myths of Scotland (and Ireland) that tell of Ossian and his father Fingal, magical figures preserved in Gaelic tradition. They were popularized by the 18th-century poet James Macpherson in his famous forgery the 'Ossianic fragments', and for many travellers they give added romance to the Scottish landscape.

Arthur, the hero king

The most intriguing legends are those that blend fact and fiction, the one deriving heightened drama from the other. The life of King Arthur, in popular myth, is steeped in romance and chivalry. He supposedly dwelt with his beautiful queen Guinevere at Camelot in the mysterious region of Avalon. There, the Knights of the Round Table devoted themselves to deeds of honour and bravery, and thence they set out on their quest for the Holy Grail, the chalice used at the Last Supper. Arthur was supported by his invincible sword Excalibur and by the wise wizard Merlin.

This courtly image of Arthur was imaginatively treated in the 15th century by the poet Sir Thomas Malory. It was later revived and Victorianized by Tennyson and in the luxurious, doleful images of the Pre-Raphaelite painters. The historical facts, however, are both stark and sparse. Arthur was in fact a Dark Age chieftain who lived in the late 5th to early 6th century. He may indeed, as popular belief has it, have been the leader of the Britons in their victory over the Saxons at Badon around AD 500. Some say that he was an utterly provincial figure, living in the Kingdom of Rheged, in Scotland. But a much stronger claim can be made for south-west England as his area of activity. He was reputedly born at Tintagel, and, more convincingly, the hill-fort at Cadbury (Somerset) has been identified with Camelot.

Freebooting heroes

Legend has endowed a number of notorious bandits with heroic stature. No matter how flimsy the evidence for their existence, they are anchored in time and space to a remarkably exact degree. Robin Hood, who robbed the rich to give to the poor, is thought to have lived in Sherwood Forest, in Nottinghamshire, in the 12th century, possibly as a contemporary of Richard I. His rivalry with the Sheriff of Nottingham, his marriage to Maid Marian, and his fight with Friar Tuck at Fountain Dale, are well-known elements of the story.

The existence of Rob Roy Macgregor is beyond doubt. Born in the mid-17th century, he spent most of his early life on the east bank of Loch Lomond. His enmity with the Duke of Montrose turned him more and more into a bandit, stealing cattle from nearby lowland farms and demanding a ransom for their return. His audacity and cunning made him no less popular a hero than the selfless Robin Hood.

Pagan and holy rites

The farming calendar is naturally rich in traditional lore and legend. Many rites are linked with the fertility of the soil and the quality of the harvest. The bonfires lit on Twelfth Night, May 1st (the Celtic festival of Beltane) and at Hallowe'en (the Celtic festival of Samhain) were designed to propitiate the sun-god, Bran or Lugh. As late as the 18th century, Highland farmers were even known to drive barren cattle between two fires as a cure. Other customs, such as the ceremony of the pace-egg (prototype of the Easter egg), or dancing round the maypole, were also meant to ensure fertility, for couples as well as for the land. Embroidered around epic tales like that of St George and the Dragon were complex rituals symbolizing springtime regeneration. Some of the deeper myths about the countryside were embodied, and still are, in the simple stories enacted by mummers or jolly boys.

Another recurrent theme in the folk culture of many regions is the veneration of wells. Although their significance was originally pagan, many holy wells were sanctified by the early Church in order to assert the dominance of Christianity. The strange marriage of pagan cult and Christian ceremony is a telling witness of the deep-rooted strength of ancient tradition.

WELL CEREMONIES

The belief in water as a mystical source of life gave wells a central place in ancient religions. This importance is demonstrated by votive offerings found at attested early wells like that at Carrawburgh, Northumberland. Some wells were thought to be curative, often with regard to specific complaints such as rheumatism or bad eyesight. Others were the focus of May Day gatherings when young people drank sugared water and celebrated life with a carnival, or even an orgy. The successors to these ancient ceremonies are the annual well-dressings which take place today most notably in Derbyshire, for example at Buxton (***below***). The well is given an embellishment of biblical or other scenes, made from thousands of petals pressed into clay.

The 5 wells at Tissington are dressed on Ascension Day, in April or May; the well-dressing ceremonies at Castleton and Wirksworth are held in May; and the others take place in June or August.

DRAGON LORE. *Dragons, serpents or 'worms' are still commemorated in songs, mummers' plays and place names. Folk tales in over 70 villages and towns have kept alive a local tradition of a dragon.*

ROB ROY. *Born at Balquhidder, Argyll, the legendary cattle rustler was immortalized in the novel Rob Roy by Sir Walter Scott.*

LA MORT D'ARTHUR. *Malory's moving account of Arthur's last moments inspired this romantic Victorian painting by James Archer. The King is tended by Queen Guinevere, Morgan le Fay and the Lady of the Lake. The barge coming ashore behind them will bear him to Avalon. The legend promises that 'the once and future king' will one day return.*

THE HERO OF MEDIEVAL BALLADS. *Robin Hood is said to have made his home in Sherwood Forest. There he gathered round him his 'merrie men': Little John, Friar Tuck and a host of minor characters, fictitious perhaps, but still, like Robin, taking pride of place in local folklore. Robin tested each of his men in combat, and together they plagued the rascally figures of the surrounding region, the Sheriff of Nottingham, and various greedy prelates.*

CONNECTIONS
Curative wells: 238–9 *Spas and seaside resorts*
Legends of saints: 52–3 *Medieval saints and shrines*
Stone circles: 192–3 *Marks on the landscape*

GLASTONBURY TOR, SOMERSET (***right***). *This curious mound is reputedly Avalon, which in Celtic pagan myth is a vestibule to Annwn, the Otherworld. The tower on the summit contains a secret chamber: anyone who chances to find it will go mad.*

Monarchy and display

The monarchy, which has its origins in the 9th century, is the oldest secular institution in Britain, preceding Parliament by 400 years. Throughout its history, ritual, pageantry and grand display have played a major role in announcing and buttressing the monarch's authority.

The earliest coronation was that of Edgar, great-grandson of Alfred the Great, in 973. The basic elements of the service, performed by the Archbishop of Canterbury St Dunstan, included oath-taking, anointment, investiture with ring, sword, crown, sceptre and rod, and enthronement. The coronation regalia that can be seen today at the Tower of London are mostly those made by Robert Vyner for Charles II, as the older jewels had been defaced by the Cromwellians and turned into coin.

The Stone of Destiny, in Scone Abbey (near Perth), played a part in the consecration of Scottish kings until it was brought south by Edward I, who commandeered it for his own consecration in 1308. It can still be seen at Westminster Abbey.

Pomp and patronage

Precious jewellery and lavish costume were once used not only on ceremonial occasions such as coronations, but also as part of a daily curriculum of royal ostentation. For example, Elizabeth I's huge wardrobe is legendary. In 1600 the ageing

THE ROYAL PROGRESS OF KENT AND EAST SUSSEX, 1573

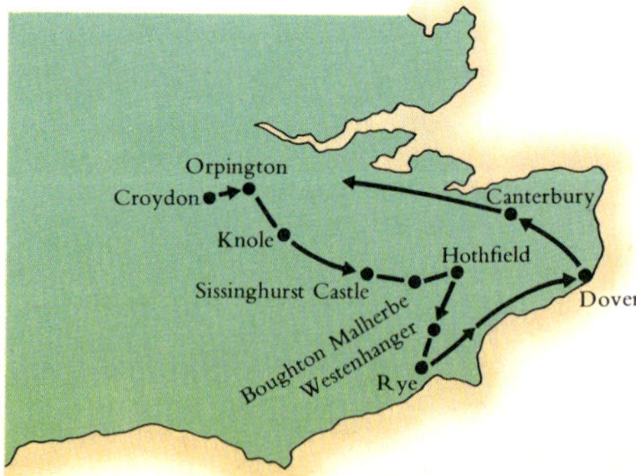

GLORIANA ON TOUR. *Elizabeth I kept in touch with her subjects by going on royal 'progresses' in summer – lavish expeditions that involved an army of courtiers and servants.*

queen possessed 102 'French gowns', 100 loose gowns and 125 petticoats. Some of the kings, too, notably Edward II and Richard II, were arrayed like peacocks. Richard, like Charles I and George IV long afterwards, was sensitive to the arts, and this interest gave the royal lifestyle a dimension that we have reason to be grateful for today. Among those he patronized was Geoffrey Chaucer, and he was the first English monarch to sit for his portrait in the modern sense of the word.

A BOY KING. *Under a gold canopy Edward VI processes in triumph from the Tower to Westminster on the eve of his coronation.*

Etiquette

Etiquette grew stiffer with the years. The Plantagenets and Tudors, though ever conscious of their own majesty, allowed their courtiers to behave with reasonable freedom. James I, indeed, permitted extremes of drunken debauchery – odd, since this intellectual, theologically minded ruler emphasized the divine right whereby he reigned. His son, Charles I, reacted violently. Impressed in his youth by the staid protocol of the Spanish court, he introduced even greater rigidity at Whitehall. Written rules hung in every room to ensure decorum. At dinner the king and queen had to be served on bended knee, and not even the noblest courtier could sit at table with them.

Later, under the Hanoverian Georges, there was the same inhumane punctilio. Even ladies had to stand for hours in the royal presence until given leave to retire, a practice which was frequently exhausting and sometimes acutely embarrassing. Today the rules are more sensible and the few old conventions that remain are based on respect without obsequiousness.

MODERN MAJESTY. *Pietro Annigoni's 1954 portrait of Elizabeth II in Garter robes. Although queenly she is a recognizable individual, in contrast with the stylized hauteur of the first Elizabeth's image.*

THE ROYAL WEDDING, 1981 (***left***). *The marriage of the Prince and Princess of Wales was an occasion for national celebration and pageantry, but royal weddings were once private family affairs.*

CONNECTIONS
Monarchy and patronage: 280–3 *The artist's eye;* **290–93** *Great art collections*
Monarchy and the Church: 48–9 *Church and State*
Palaces: 214–15 *Royal retreats*
Revenues of the Crown: 94–5 *Money and finance*

Scotland and England

ALEXANDER III *(1241–86), an illustration from the 15th-century* Scotichronicon. *This king's fatal fall from his horse one stormy night led to war with Edward I of England, who claimed the Scottish throne.*

In the 6th century, the people who lived in the Scottish Borders had little sense of a clear division between England and Scotland. The Angles, occupying the Kingdom of Northumbria, held sway in the border hills and in what is now south-east Scotland. There was the vaguest of frontiers between these Teutonic invaders and, to the north, the Celtic peoples of the Highlands in the Kingdom of Scotia.

England: the 'auld enemy'

The southward shift of this border followed two key events. In 1018 Malcolm II, King of the Scots, defeated the Northumbrians and pushed the south-eastern frontier down to the Tweed. In the same year his grandson Duncan (later killed in battle by the much-maligned King Macbeth) acquired the Kingdom of Strathclyde to the south-west by marriage. With Duncan's accession to his grandfather's throne (1034), the Anglo-Scottish border became approximately what we know today.

Relationships between England and Scotland remained strained throughout the medieval period, though there were a few intervals of peace, and an Anglo-Norman nobility succeeded in settling in the Scottish lowlands. After the death of Alexander III in 1286, there were thirteen claimants to the throne. The mightiest of these was Edward I of England, the Hammer of the Scots. He invaded in 1296, initiating a profound and bitter conflict that was to last discontinuously until 1371.

DRYBURGH ABBEY. *One result of the scarring of the border regions by intermittent warfare was the destruction of abbeys at Dryburgh, Melrose, Kelso and Jedburgh.*

The Wars of Independence provoked a spirit of Scottish unity and patriotism, embodied in individuals such as William Wallace and Robert Bruce. Both were heroes of the resistance, the former in defeat at Falkirk (1297), the latter in victory – against superior numbers – at Bannockburn (1314). The 'Declaration of Arbroath', addressed to Pope John XXII by the Scottish barons in 1320, made clear the new determination: 'We shall never . . . submit to the rule of the English for it is not for glory we fight . . . but for freedom alone.'

The House of Stuart

In 1371 the Scottish crown passed to Robert Bruce's grandson, and a new dynasty was launched that survived for nearly 350 years. Their first century was dogged by disaster. James I was imprisoned by the English at the age of eleven; James II was six when he was killed by a bursting cannon at Roxburgh; and James III was nine when he was thrown from his horse at Sauchieburn. Yet by the 16th century the Stuarts were achieving some measure of peace.

Conflict flared again when James IV invaded England in August 1513. The Scottish defeat, barely a month later, on the battlefield of Flodden just south of the Tweed, was one of Scotland's most traumatic experiences. A new wave of strife broke not long afterwards. When the Earl of Hertford raided deep into the eastern Scottish borderland in 1544 and 1545, he reputedly ravaged and burnt hundreds of farms and townships in what is called the 'Rough Wooing'. In reaction, grim fortified tower-houses were built by the wealthy landowners, while burghers and farmers built 'bastle houses' in which the ground floor could be sealed off in an attack.

Unification

It was almost by genealogical accident that in 1603 James VI of Scotland succeeded to the throne of England, as James I. His mother, Mary Queen of Scots, had had pretensions to the English throne, but she had been less than canny in attempts to supplant her rival Elizabeth I.

Once the two crowns had been united, and the border pacified, full political union was only a matter of time. It was facilitated by the economic contrast between the countries. Scotland was racked by chronic inflation, low productivity and food shortages. The Union of Parliaments in 1707 was seen by many Scots more as a door opened on English markets than as a loss of political free-will.

The Jacobite rebellion

With the death of the last Stuart king and the accession of the Protestant William of Orange in 1689, the loyalties of many Highlanders were directed towards the exiled James II (James VII of Scotland) and, later, his son James Edward Stuart and grandson Charles Edward. Attempts were made to assert the Catholic Stuart (that is, Jacobite) claim to the English and Scottish throne in 1708, 1715, 1719 and 1745.

It was the '45 that evoked the greatest emotions. Jacobite aspirations became fixed on the magnetic figure of the young Charles Edward (Bonnie Prince Charlie), who sailed from France to Scotland in July. With support from the Macdonalds and other Highland clans, he advanced on Edinburgh and captured it. However, his subsequent

JAMES VI AND I *(1566–1625)* ***(below)***. *The English regarded James as a shrewd politician, but they intensely disliked his character.*

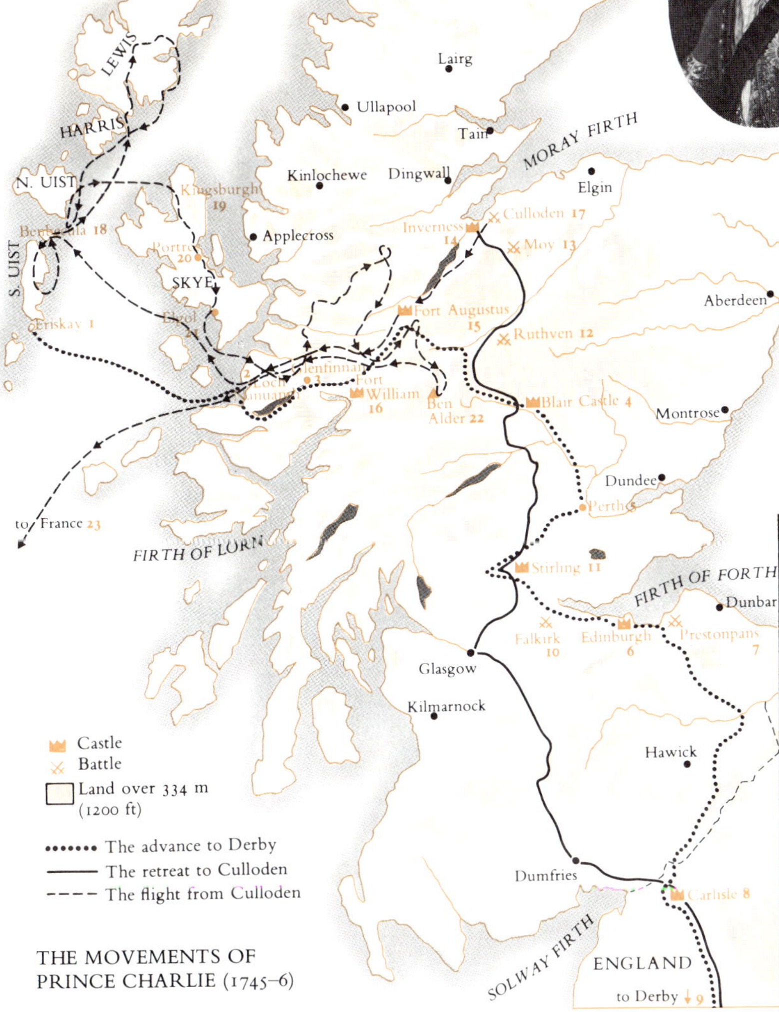

THE MOVEMENTS OF PRINCE CHARLIE (1745–6)

1 July 23 *1745* Charles lands on Eriskay with only 7 men
2 July 25 He reaches mainland Scotland
3 August 19 He proclaims his father King James VIII and III
4 late August He halts at Blair on his unopposed journey to Perth
5 September 4 He captures Perth and continues southwards
6 September 17 He enters Edinburgh and is cheered by crowds
7 September 21 Jacobites beat government troops at Prestonpans
8 November 15 Carlisle surrenders after 5 days' siege
9 December 6 Charles reaches Derby, but then retreats north
10 January 8 *1746* Falkirk falls to Jacobites but castle remains intact
11 January 17 Government troops suffer second defeat
12 February 10 Charles and Jacobites capture Ruthren barracks
13 February 16 At Moy a few Highlanders hold off 1,500 redcoats
14 February 20 Charles overcomes all resistance at Inverness
15 March 6 Fort Augustus falls to Jacobites
16 mid-March Jacobites unsuccessfully lay siege to Fort William
17 April 16 Prince and his Highlanders are routed at Culloden
18 June 28 Flora Macdonald accompanies fugitive Charles to Skye
19 June 29 Flora's relatives hide Charles
20 June 30 Charles takes leave of the faithful Flora
21 July 4 He makes his last venture on mainland Scotland
22 September 5–13 Charles sheltered by the Macphersons
23 September 19 The escape back to France

THE BATTLE OF CULLODEN, *16 April 1746. The 'Butcher' Cumberland here presides over the massacre of Prince Charles's Highlanders near Inverness. The English victory was followed by savage repression.*

GENERAL WADE'S BRIDGE, ABERFELDY *(1733–35), Tayside* (***below***). *For military penetration of rebel territory, Wade built a series of roads and bridges.*

determined march on England exhausted his army, which dispiritedly retreated north and was routed in a fierce battle at Culloden.

The Prince and other survivors were pursued through the Highlands by the English. The Jacobite chiefs' estates were ravaged, and the Disarming Act removed the means for further rebellion. Culloden was a turning point: the old political role of the Highland chiefs was destroyed. But Scotland retained its independent institutional framework – notably in law, education and religion. And the spirit of independence was to rise again in the emergence in 1927 of the Scottish Nationalist Party, which amalgamated with the more right-wing Scottish Party in 1934 and rose to prominence in the late 1960s. The Nationalists had eleven seats in Parliament by October 1974, but lost nine of them in the 1979 election.

CONNECTIONS
The Highlanders: 62–3 *Scottish clans and tartans*
Scots against English: 70–71 *Battles*
The Scottish capital: 256–7 *Edinburgh*
Scottish strongholds: 196–9 *Castles*
Scotland in literature: 296–9 *Writers and places*

Scottish clans and tartans

CLANS OF SCOTLAND

1 Macaulays
2 Macleods of Harris
3 Clan Donald
4 Macdonalds of Clanranald
5 Macneils
6 Macqueen
7 Macleods of Lewis
8 Mackinnons
9 Macdonells of Glengarry
10 Munroes
11 Mclennans or Logans
12 Macraes
13 Macgillivrays, Davidsons
14 Brodies
15 Dunbars
16 Leslies
17 Forbeses
18 Hays
19 Keiths
20 Skenes
21 Burnetts, Irvines
22 Arbuthnotts
23 Barclays
24 Grahams
25 Maules
26 Moncrieffs
27 Earl of Gowrie
28 Menzies
29 Mackintoshes of Glentilt
30 Murrays
31 Macdonells of Keppoch
32 Macdonells of Glencoe
33 Stewarts of Appin
34 Magregors
35 Macintyres
36 Macdougals
37 Macnaughtons
38 Stewarts of Balquhidder
39 Macfarlanes
40 Maclarens
41 Colquhouns
42 Galbraiths
43 Stewarts of Bute
44 Malcolms

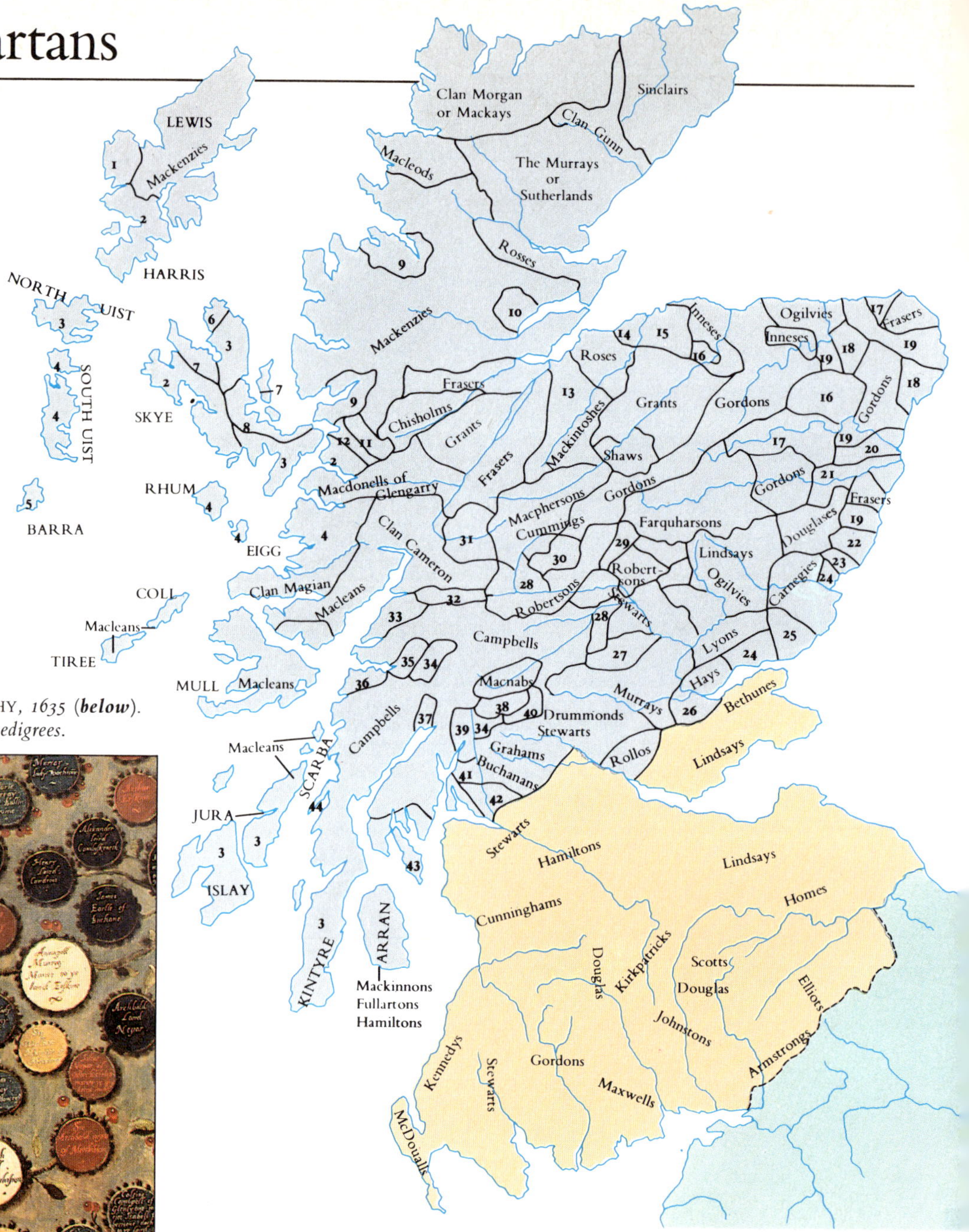

THE GENEALOGY OF THE CAMPBELLS OF GLENORCHY, *1635* (***below***). *Painted trees like this were made to immortalize clan pedigrees.*

THE MACKENZIE STRONGHOLD, *Eilean Donan. Kintail in the western Highlands, where this grim fortress guards access to the sea, is the territory of the Mackenzie clan. The castle was built by Alexander II in the 13th century.*

The first clans of the Scottish Highlands and islands emerged in the 12th and 13th centuries. By the 14th century the Highlanders had achieved a reputation for wildness and wickedness; they were later criticized by King James VI and I as 'utterly barbarous, without any sort or show of civility'. But they could scarcely be ignored, for the changing and conflicting fortunes of the clans dominated the Highlands for many centuries. The names of certain chieftains, such as the Wolf of Badenoch and Black Douglas, still conjure up images from an unruly past.

The clan system

Central to the idea of a clan (the Gaelic word *clann* means children) was a feeling of common ancestry and kinship. The more senior clans trace their descent back to the great Irish and Norse kings of the Hebrides and west Highlands, but their pedigrees were often more presumed than proven. The true extent of a clan's membership, similarly, was sometimes exaggerated: common surnames did not always denote family ties, as it was not unusual for a tenant to take the name of his landlord. A chief of the Frasers of Lovat is said to have offered a boll of meal to anyone who took his name.

The early clans had a political as well as a social and economic role. Over large areas, a clan would control the operation of law, as well as determining the leasing of land. Those families allied to the Scottish Crown, such as the Campbells of Argyll, saw themselves as representing royal authority. But other clans were a rule unto themselves. From the 13th century until 1493 the Lords of the Isles remained absolutely detached from the Scottish Crown. The Highlanders' support for the Jacobite cause in the early 18th century was the supreme demonstration of their traditional independence of spirit.

The Lordship of the Isles illustrates how complex the clan system could be. Its senior family was the Donalds (later Macdonalds) of Islay. Like all great clans, this one was divided into a hierarchy of septs and cadet branches. Allied to the Donalds were other major families like the MacLeans, MacLeods and Mackinnons. The function of a minor clan in this system was often to perform some special service: for example, the Macfies of Colonsay kept the records of the Lordship, while the MacCrimmons were hereditary bagpipers to the MacLeods.

Traditionally, clansmen were called to arms by the sign of a burning branch, or 'fiery cross'. Inter-clan fighting was a major and bloody theme in Highland history. The most notorious incident was the massacre of the chief and thirty-seven of the Macdonalds of Glencoe in 1692 by soldiers under the command of a Campbell of Glenlyon (though this was the result of a government order).

The Borders also had their clans – some, such as the Homes and the Douglases, were well entrenched as early as the 13th century. Particularly infamous for their lawlessness were the Elliots of upper Liddesdale and the Armstrongs of lower Liddesdale. In 1530 Johnnie Armstrong of Gilnockie was summarily hanged by James V at Langholm, during a visit designed to restore waning royal authority to the area.

HIGHLAND DRESS

One of the earliest authentic pictures of Highland dress is from a German broadside of about 1630 (***left***), showing men of Mackay's regiment, who were mercenaries to the Swedish kings. They wear the traditional belted plaid. Purple and blue were then the favourite shades, but today red and green are predominant. The attempt to regularize the tartans in the early 19th century produced two categories of dress: Hunting and Ancient. The Stewarts also had a special royal tartan. Stewart tartans are shown (***below***) in the following order: Dress, Hunting Royal, Royal.

HIGHLAND DANCERS. *In the late summer, Highland Games are held in several Scottish towns and villages, notably in Braemar (Grampian). Events include dancing, caber-tossing, hammer-throwing and bagpiping contests.*

Clans and land ownership

It was tongue-twistingly said in the Highlands that a clan without land was a broken clan, just as a man without a clan was a broken man. A clan needed land in order to thrive. Many of the problems that beset the clan Macgregor, who were outlawed on a number of occasions, sprang from the gradual loss of their lands around the head of Loch Awe (Argyll), mainly to the Campbells of Breadalbane. By contrast, the Campbells of Argyll and the Mackenzies rose to importance as a result of the multiplication of their estates. The Kerrs and Scotts in the Borders were relatively insignificant until the 16th century, when windfalls of land (including ex-monastic property) provided them with scope for expansion.

The tartan armies

The tartan has become the most vivid expression of the clan system. However, as an emblem of clan identity, woven to a fixed pattern (or sett), the tartan's emergence was relatively late. A Frenchman visiting Scotland in the 16th century observed that the Highlanders wore 'no clothes except their dyed shirts and a sort of woollen covering of several colours'. A wide variety of shades and setts was worn within a single clan, but group uniformity seems to have been gaining ground by the 17th century.

In the same period, a loose arrangement of pleats around the waist developed into the kilt (although some say that kilts were invented by an Englishman who lived at Glengarry during the early 18th century).

After the Jacobite defeat at Culloden in 1746, tartans were banned. However, within a century the idea had been revived for its romantic associations. The old tartans were regularized, and many new ones were devised (by Queen Victoria among others). They became fashionable in France and America. The Highland Games were also revived and numerous clan societies were formed, some in Commonwealth countries; these still enjoy passionate support. The Gathering of the Clans in Edinburgh in 1951 was the apotheosis of this romantic devotion to a colourful and evocative aspect of Scottish history.

CONNECTIONS
The Highland clearances: 136–7 *The impact of the new farming*
Rob Roy MacGregor: 56–7 *Lore and legend*
Scots against English: 61–2 *Scotland and England*

Wales and England

LLYWELYN'S WALES

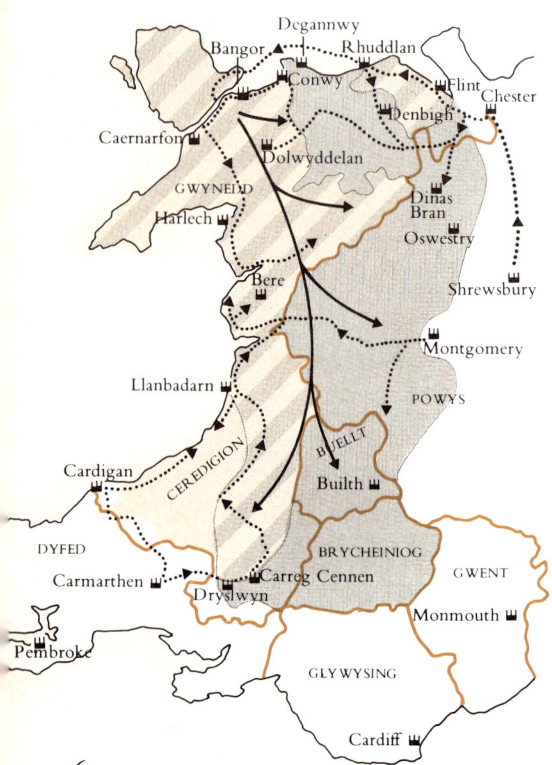

LLYWELYN THE LAST: *a Victorian view.*

CONWY CASTLE, GWYNEDD, *built mainly in the 1280s, is a powerful symbol of Edward I's conquest. It is one of a series of bastides (fortified towns) created by the English in west and north-west Wales at this period. Edward was besieged here in 1294.*

The emergence of Wales as a distinct territorial unit and a separate nation can be dated to the early Middle Ages. From the 5th century the attacks of the Irish, the Picts and, later, the Saxons increasingly reduced and fragmented the lands of the Britons (or Celts) in western Britain. By the 7th century the Celtic peoples were concentrated in a series of disconnected blocks of land, one of which was Wales. Its distinct geographical identity was given material expression in AD 778–96 in the building of Offa's Dyke, an official boundary between the Welsh to the west and the Saxons of Mercia to the east. However, it was still very far from being a unified nation.

The Welsh kingdoms

Since the withdrawal of the Romans, Wales had been distinguished by the number of its petty kingdoms and chiefdoms. Tradition relates that a certain Cunedda and his sons came from southern Scotland to Wales to help drive out the Irish, who had begun to settle there. The sons and their descendants are said to have established a network of dynasties which assumed kingship over existing tribes and left their mark in the creation of local kingdoms such as Ceredigion and Meirionydd. Other kingdoms, however, evolved directly of the tribes that had flourished during the Roman period: Powys, for example, was probably Cornovii territory, while Dyfed emerged from the lands of the Demetae. By the 7th century, a process of coalescence had reduced the number of territorial units to eight.

The prospect of a fully unified Wales was first

THE INTERNATIONAL MUSICAL EISTEDDFOD *at Llangollen (Clwyd): the annual festival of Welsh folk music and dance, held in July.*

CARDIFF, *whose city hall of 1905* ***(right)*** *is part of an impressive civic centre, was confirmed as the official capital city in 1955.*

brought into view by Rhodri Mawr (844–78), a ruler of Gwynedd who extended his power to both Powys and Seisyllwg (which by this time had absorbed Ceredigion). The division of this domain after his death reversed for a while the trend towards unity, but his grandson Hywel Dda (*c.*900–950) succeeded in knitting together the whole of west and north Wales. His honoured place in Welsh history is also due to his codification of Welsh law – a potent factor in the shaping of Welsh consciousness.

No sooner had the unity of Wales been asserted than it was challenged by the Anglo-Normans. Before 1100 these alien land-grabbers had established themselves in the Welsh Borderland and had pushed westwards along the coasts of north and south Wales. Stern opposition contained the invaders' expansion, but they carved out considerable estates, notably the extensive Marcher Lordships (such as Brecon and Usk), within which they were conceded wide-ranging powers over justice and administration by the English King.

In some areas of the Marcher Lordships, known as the 'Englishries', Norman culture made a lasting impact, while Welsh law, customs and language remained in the ascendant in the 'Welshries'. Today, a former lordship such as the Gower still bears the impact of this dichotomy, with Welsh place-names prevailing mainly in the north.

The principality

Relations between the Welsh lords and the Anglo-Normans were fraught, and broke out into full-scale warfare in the 13th century. By then, the acknowledged leader of the independent Welsh princes was Llywelyn the Great (1173–1240), ruler of Gwynedd. The princes pushed Welsh lordship southwards and eastwards, to Carmarthen and Montgomery. The climax of this movement towards independence came with Llywelyn the Last, who assumed the title 'Prince of Wales' and was recognized as such by Henry III of England. However, the overmightiness of Llywelyn's lords provoked the English into war (1276), and the army of Edward I pushed the Welsh forces back to Gwynedd. By the Treaty of Conwy (1277), Llywelyn was recognized as prince of Gwynedd alone. In 1282, during another Welsh revolt, he was slain at Cilmeri, near Builth.

Llywelyn was the last native prince to assert his kingship over Wales, but he was not the last of the great Welsh freedom fighters. This title must be reserved for Owain Glyndwr (anglicized as Owen Glendower), who became a national hero when he rebelled against foreign rule in 1400, and even established a Welsh parliament. The tide turned against him in 1409, and the revolt came to nothing.

The political situation took on a different complexion when the first Tudor, Henry VII (r. 1485–1507), took up the English throne. He was descended on his father's side from an Anglesey family, and there was widespread support for him within Wales. His accession paved the way for the full Act of Union (1536), which extended English styles of administration and law to all of Wales.

Welsh identity

In the centuries that followed, the decay of the Welsh language symptomized a decline in national culture which was accelerated by industrialization. The growth of new mining and industrial communities along the valleys of south Wales brought further English influence in its wake and weakened traditional ties. It also encouraged the depopulation of the countryside, where Welsh culture had been strongest.

Today, the proportion of Welsh speakers in the industrial valleys, south Pembrokeshire and the borders is less than 50 per cent, but it is higher than 70 per cent in parts of Dyfed and Gwynedd. The revival of the language is one of the focal points of the modern nationalist movement.

CONNECTIONS
Chapel-going: 54–5 *Christian minorities*
Mining in Wales: 150–51 *Coal;* 152–5 *The bowels of the earth;* 234–5 *Coal mining towns*
Strongholds of Edward I: 196–9 *Castles*
Welsh poetry: 296–9 *Writers and places*

THE COAL MINING COMMUNITIES *of south Wales were crucial to English industrialization, and traditional Welsh culture, which was pre-eminently rural, did not flourish there. In time, however, a distinctively Welsh lifestyle emerged in which the chapel played an important part.*

Ireland and Britain

The distinctive language, literature, laws and political institutions of Celtic Ireland were left undisturbed by Roman conquest or, for centuries, by any other foreign invasion. After the Irish were Christianized in the 5th century AD, Celtic and Christian cultures merged happily to produce a golden age. Viking raids in the 8th and 9th centuries marked the end of this tranquil period.

With the Anglo-Norman invasion of 1169, there began that close and uneasy link between Britain and Ireland which has lasted to our own time. From the reign of Henry II, the kings of England claimed overlordship, although allegiance was not always forthcoming. While the Anglo-Normans were sufficiently strong to disrupt native Irish political development, they were never powerful enough to effect a complete conquest.

The real conquest begins

The conquest of Ireland began in earnest under the Tudors. Initially, the territory had the status of a feudal lordship. Henry VIII was proclaimed King of Ireland in 1541. From that date, Ireland and England were ruled by the same sovereign, and the centralized government of Ireland was controlled from the English court. After Henry VIII's break with Rome, the attempt to subjugate Catholic Ireland began to take on a religious aspect. To ensure Irish conformity with English religious practices, it was necessary to achieve a more general cultural conquest. At the same time, the policy of systematic confiscation and colonization ('plantation') replaced native landlords with more amenable subjects from England and Scotland.

The conquest, which occupied much of the attention of the Tudors and Stuarts and of Oliver Cromwell, was not completed until after William III defeated James VII and II's Irish and French army at the Battle of the Boyne in 1690. There followed the period of Protestant ascendancy, during which the colonists, with the backing of the English government, dominated the Catholic majority. Penal laws deprived the Catholics of political power, denying them the right to sit in parliament, vote in elections or hold government office. Catholic worship was restricted, Catholic schools forbidden and religious Orders banished. Catholics were also denied the right to purchase land. These and other prohibitions ensured that by the end of the 18th century only about five per cent of the land was in Catholic hands.

By this time, however, the Irish Protestant ascendancy, feeling itself more secure and less dependent on England, became more liberal. Influenced by the revolt of the American colonists, the Protestant Irish also became more patriotic, demanding and winning (in 1782) legislative independence for their own parliament in Dublin. Before long, the statesman Henry Grattan's ideal of a sisterly relationship between the two kingdoms had been realized.

The threat posed by the French Revolution and

THE MARRIAGE OF AOIFE AND STRONGBOW *in 1170: a Victorian painting. Dermot MacMurrough, traditionally the 'Judas' of Irish history, sealed his alliance with the Anglo-Norman invaders by giving his daughter Aoife in marriage to their leader, Strongbow, and making him heir to his kingdom of Leinster in defiance of Irish rules of succession.*

CAPTAIN THOMAS LEE *(d. 1601): an English colonist in hunting costume.*

THE IRISH HOUSE OF COMMONS, *1790 (**below**). In this painting by Francis Wheatley, Henry Grattan (standing on the right) addresses the independent legislative assembly.*

THE EASTER RISING (***left*** *and* ***below***). *On Easter Monday 1916, republican and socialist nationalists seized key buildings in Dublin and rose in revolt against British rule. Much of the city was gutted by fire in the short time the conflict lasted. The rising was not as effective militarily as it was politically: when its leaders were executed by the British, many southern Irish were won over to the cause.*

the Revolutionary Wars destroyed the delicate constitution of Grattan's parliament. Under the spell of French revolutionary ideals, Protestant radicals such as Wolfe Tone aimed to unite Catholics, Protestants and Dissenters in Ireland, and by breaking the connection with England altogether to establish an independent Irish republic on the French model. The French attempted a number of invasions of Ireland to aid their allies the United Irishmen. The bloody insurrection of 1798 showed how serious the threat had become.

The 19th and 20th centuries

The Prime Minister William Pitt, supported by frightened conservatives in the Irish administration, proposed the elimination of the separate Irish parliament and the union of the two kingdoms. The Act of Union was passed in 1801 and remained in force until 1922. Wiser statesmanship might have made it more palatable to the Catholic majority.

In the 1820s the continued disadvantages suffered by the Catholics prompted a massive civil rights campaign organized by Daniel O'Connell. The pressure it exerted led to the abolition of the last of the penal laws in 1829. In the 1840s, O'Connell channelled his supporters' energies to agitate for the repeal of the Act of Union. The Great Famine of the 1840s was held in the folk memory as abundant proof of maladministration by the English. Irish nationalists in the late 19th century either campaigned by constitutional means for 'home rule' (that is, 'devolved' rather than separate government) or chose extra-parliamentary tactics to further the cause of republican separatism.

Liberal governments, seeking to pacify Ireland, introduced Home Rule bills in 1886, 1893 and 1912. The third one was passed in 1914. Unionist opposition was especially bitter in the north-east, where Belfast had become a thriving industrial and commercial city, closely linked with English trade. Home rule was 'frozen' by the outbreak of the First World War. In 1916 the Irish Republican Brotherhood proclaimed the Irish Republic during the Easter Rising in Dublin.

Following the general election of 1918, the victorious Sinn Fein republican party constituted itself as *Dáil Éireann* (the Irish Parliament) and proceeded to govern the country without any reference to England. The War of Independence (1919–1921), characterized by ambushes on the one side and reprisals on the other, seriously embittered Anglo-Irish relations. In December 1921 the Anglo-Irish Treaty was signed. It was essentially a compromise, conceding dominion status to twenty-six of the thirty-two counties.

Meanwhile, under the Government of Ireland Act (1920), the six counties of Ulster had been given their own domestic parliament. While this arrangement suited one million Protestant Unionists, it was not acceptable to the half-million Catholic nationalists in the area. The tensions between the two communities in Northern Ireland eventually came to the boil in the late 1960s. A solution to the problem continues to elude the best-intentioned efforts of all concerned, whether in Ulster, in the Republic or in Britain.

IRISH LINEN. *Linen was once made all over Ireland, but in the 19th century a factory-based linen industry developed in the north-east of Ulster. Along with shipbuilding, linen manufacture became one of this area's most important activities, underpinning an economic development parallel with that of Victorian Britain. This relationship strengthened resistance in Ulster to the cause of home rule.*

CONNECTIONS
Early peoples: 42–3 *The movement of peoples*
Irish immigration: 44–5 *Foreign settlers*
Religious history: 46–7 *The coming of Christianity;* **48–9** *Church and State;* **50–51** *Catholics and Protestants*

Parliament/*The beginnings*

During the early Middle Ages it was believed that the monarchy was a divinely sanctioned institution, and that the king's actions represented the workings of God's will on Earth. Moral restraints were laid down in the Coronation Oath, but they did not proscribe an autocratic style of government. Inevitably, royal policies and exactions sometimes aroused opposition, but resistance was usually of a fragmentary nature. Generally rulers tried to operate with the consent of the most powerful groups in the land, notably the barons and the Church. Successful kings such as Henry II took counsel with their leading barons, though there is little evidence that at this stage the advisers sought to institutionalize their role.

Tightening the reins

The rule of King John (1199–1216) saw the beginnings of a limited movement to circumscribe royal power. The main complaints were against excessive taxation and an unsuccessful foreign war – grievances that were articulated by the barons as a demand for a greater share in government. As a result of their concerted pressure the King was forced to sign Magna Carta (the Great Charter) in 1215 on the island of Runnymede in the Thames. Although viewed in subsequent ages as the foundation of constitutional liberties in Britain (and in North America), the Charter was in fact very much a product of its time – as much a statement of vested interests as of civil liberties. However, an important precedent had been set: the King was now obliged to consult the chief men of the realm in all important matters, and to be bound by law. In addition, the privileges of the Church and of the towns were confirmed, and provision was made

EDWARD I IN PARLIAMENT, *with the kings of Wales and Scotland (although they never in fact attended together). Archbishops sit next to the head of the assembly, with barons and bishops along the sides. In the centre are the judges, the councillors and the legal advisers of the Crown. The Commons and the proctors of the clergy (only the front row is depicted) are at the back of the hall facing the King.*

THE KING AND HIS COUNCIL (***below***) *in the 11th century: a primitive stage in the evolution of English government. The main function of the Council was judicial.*

A SEAL OF SIMON DE MONTFORT, *who was an early believer in corporate government.*

for regular baronial assemblies, or 'parliaments', at which royal abuses could be checked.

In the troubled reign of John's successor, Henry III (r. 1216–72), the barons resented the increasing influence of foreigners from Poitou, Provence and Savoy, especially after the King's marriage to Eleanor of Provence. They campaigned for a direct share in government and in the appointment of royal councillors and ministers. In 1258 the Provisions of Oxford were drawn up, creating a limited monarchy regulated by a council of fifteen advisers, who were to consult with the barons at triennial parliaments. After Henry washed his hands of the Provisions three years later, Simon de Montfort, Earl of Leicester, led a movement to enforce them, which led to outright war and the Earl's death at the Battle of Evesham in 1265.

Between 1258 and 1300 seventy parliaments were convoked, but most of them were attended only by the great magnates. In the reign of Edward I, however, it became customary for knights of the shire and burgesses from the towns to be called. The main reason for this broadening of the parliamentary base was the need to ensure widespread consent to taxation, particularly (in the 14th century) during the Hundred Years' War with France. Parliament's function was also to advise, and occasionally it was called upon to give consent to legislation. It served too as an important channel for the presentation of grievances for redress, both from the community and from individuals.

A hereditary parliamentary peerage emerged by the 15th century. The House of Lords, where the peers sat, was an extension of the great Council suggested in Magna Carta. In contrast, the House of Commons had evolved as a separate body by the 14th century. By 1370 statutes had to be promulgated by the king in Parliament, and the kind of business on which the assembly legislated had meanwhile broadened in scope. For example, the Statute of Labourers (1351) arose from petitions by landowners to Parliament to control labourers' wages. In 1376 the office of the Speaker came into existence, his task initially being to represent the opinions of the Commons to the Crown and the Lords. The Speaker's role became more important as the Commons grew stronger, but declined with the development of the 'cabinet' system.

The Tudors and after

Under Henry VII, when taxation was not such a pressing need, Parliament was summoned with declining frequency – there was only one session in the last twelve years of his rule. The main parliamentary function remained one of giving approval rather than of taking initiatives. However, in the reign of Henry VIII its importance was reinforced. The Reformation, the royal divorce and the dissolution of the monasteries were carried through almost without opposition under the skilful direction of the King's advisers: but what was significant in this was the precedent set for full parliamentary involvement in important acts of sovereign power. Under Mary Tudor Parliament showed a measure of independence in its unwillingness to consent to some aspects of religious legislation, such as the return of Church lands.

Although the House of Lords came increasingly under the royal thumb, the Commons became a more powerful force in its own right in the late Tudor period. Representation was extended to Wales, and more boroughs were included in the system. Under Elizabeth I the Commons demanded freedom of speech on matters such as religion, the Queen's marriage and the succession. Some Puritan MPs such as Peter Wentworth ended up in the Tower as a result of their bluntly phrased insistence on the right to discuss religion freely. Wentworth objected to the way in which MPs were too easily intimidated by the Queen's Privy Counsellors who sat in the Commons. By the end of Elizabeth's reign only her own tact and personal charisma had staved off major clashes with Parliament.

A complex history of Crown-Commons antagonism dominates the Stuart period, initiated by James I's insistence on the 'royal prerogative'. By the end of the 17th century Parliament emerged with permanent ascendancy at last.

CONNECTIONS

Crown and Commons: 72–3 *The Civil War*
The House of Lords: 104–5 *Courts of the land*
Parliamentary reform: 76–7 *Parliament/Abuse and reform*
Reporting on Parliament: 120–21 *The Press*

WESTMINSTER: THE CHAPTER HOUSE. *This was where the Commons first sat separately from the Lords in the 'Good Parliament' of 1376, which was led by the earliest known Speaker (Sir Peter de la Mare) and took a hard line on taxation. Parliaments sat here until the mid-16th century.*

WESTMINSTER, *drawn by W. Hollar in 1647 (**below**). The scene had changed little since the 14th century. St Stephen's Chapel (on the left) in 1549 became the home of the Commons, which until then had usually met in Westminster Abbey (right).*

Battles

HASTINGS. *The Bayeux Tapestry (c.1080) records the battle. The Saxons were tired, having defeated the Norsemen at Stamford Bridge 19 days earlier.*

Myths can be as compelling as realities, but we must be wary of the claims of some local patriots when it comes to the location of ancient battlefields. For example, no one knows positively where the Britons, under King Arthur, fought the pagan Saxons at 'Badon', although a number of authorities suggest a ridgeway near Swindon (Wiltshire) as the most probable site. King Alfred's first victory over the Danes at Ashdown is also uncertain in location, but we are on surer ground with Maldon on the Essex coast, where the Norsemen triumphed in 991, and at Stamford Bridge (Humberside), where they were defeated by Harold in 1066.

Medieval engagements

If we ignore sieges and innumerable raids and skirmishes, battles in the Middle Ages can be grouped under four main headings: the Barons' War, the Wars of Henry IV, the Anglo-Scottish conflict and the Wars of the Roses.

The Barons' War was a struggle between Henry III and, principally, Simon de Montfort, who tried to obtain for the barons a share in government. The King was captured at Lewes (Sussex), but the young Prince Edward turned the tables at Evesham, near Worcester. The Evesham campaign (1265) revealed the future Edward I as a gifted tactician. He split his army into three effective units, which cornered the enemy within a meander of the River Severn.

Henry IV, a king by conquest and election but not by heredity, faced a formidable alliance of the rebellious Percies of Northumberland with the Scots and Welsh under Owen Glendower. The struggle culminated in the King's victory at Battlefield three miles from Shrewsbury in the summer of 1403. Battlefield Church was founded by Henry in commemoration of the fallen.

The climaxes of England's wars with Scotland were Robert Bruce's triumph at Bannockburn (1314) and James IV's defeat at Flodden.

Battles in the extremely bloody Wars of the Roses featured the typically English formation of

THE WARS OF THE ROSES

The wars over rival Yorkist and Lancastrian claims to the throne, waged from 1455 to 1485, were so called after the respective emblems of each house: a white rose for York, a red one for Lancaster.

After a skirmish at St Albans, the principal battle in the initial phase was Wakefield, when Richard the Duke of York was defeated and killed. York's son continued the cause, was crowned Edward IV by his chief ally the Earl of Warwick, and triumphed in a battle at Towton. In 1470, Warwick, later known as the 'Kingmaker', joined the Lancastrians, who were efficiently led by Henry's redoubtable queen, Margaret of Anjou. At Tewkesbury the Queen's forces were routed. Her son, Prince Edward, was slain and shortly afterwards Henry himself was despatched in the Tower of London.

After Edward IV died in 1483 his two young sons were murdered and his brother took the throne as Richard III. Henry Tudor then rallied the Lancastrians and defeated Richard at Bosworth. As Henry VII, the Tudor victor married Margaret of York and the unification of the two factions was symbolized in the composite Tudor rose.

TEWKESBURY. *Edward IV (left) wears a crown. The Lancastrian Prince Edward is beheaded as he falls.*

THE DEFEAT OF THE SPANISH ARMADA

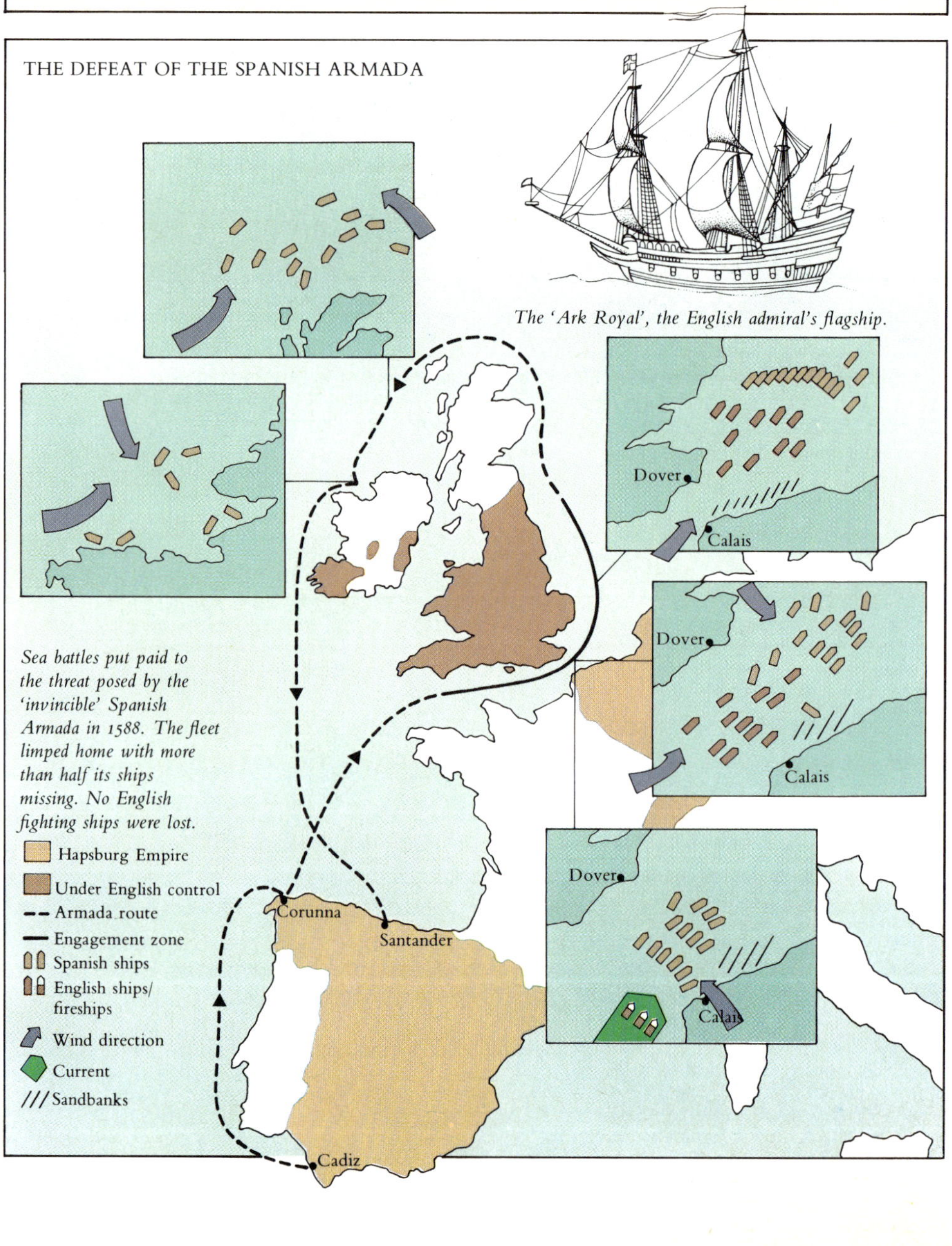

The 'Ark Royal', the English admiral's flagship.

Sea battles put paid to the threat posed by the 'invincible' Spanish Armada in 1588. The fleet limped home with more than half its ships missing. No English fighting ships were lost.

'PIKEMEN' IN A CIVIL WAR BATTLE. *A re-enactment at Warwick by costumed members of the Sealed Knot society.*

dismounted men-at-arms flanked by archers. At the start of a battle, each side would send out showers of arrows, and then move in for hand-to-hand fighting. The Yorkist King Edward IV emerged as a thoughtful military leader at Tewkesbury and elsewhere. One of his greatest skills was in the planning of well-timed marches. The magnificent abbey at Tewkesbury, to which the nobler Lancastrian prisoners were taken, has a brass plate commemorating the killing of the Prince Edward, son of Queen Margaret, by the Yorkists. This was in 1471. Fourteen exhausting years later the Wars ended, at Bosworth Field.

The Civil War and after

After Bosworth, a century and a half elapsed before the English countryside was tainted again by the blood of battles. Field guns, muskets and pistols now supplemented bows and edged weapons. Armour, apart from helmets and breastplates, was now obsolete. Drillbooks produced before the Civil War recommended that the cavalry should advance until the enemy was just within their line of pistol fire, discharge, then trot back to reload. At Edgehill, Prince Rupert, on the Royalist side, introduced the Swedish technique of Gustavus Adolphus: instead of trotting back, the cavalry charged. The last decisive battle of the war was Naseby, in Northamptonshire (1645), where both armies were drawn up in a double line of foot regiments, each comprising a central block of pikemen with two wings of musketeers; field guns were deployed in the gaps between the regiments.

When warfare was resumed after the King's execution, the main battles were at Dunbar, where Cromwell defeated the Scots, and Worcester, where Charles II was put to flight. Since then, there have been only two important battles in Britain – Sedgemoor (Somerset), where the Duke of Monmouth's rebels were routed on a foggy July night in 1685, and Culloden Moor near Inverness, where the Jacobites were crushed in 1746.

CONNECTIONS
The army: 122–3 *The armed forces*
Battles of the 17th century: 72–3 *The Civil War*
Battles of the 18th century: 60–61 *Scotland and England*
Insurrections: 108–9 *Riot and revolution*
Modern warfare: 124–5 *The First World War;* **126–7** *The Second World War*

MAJOR BATTLES IN BRITAIN

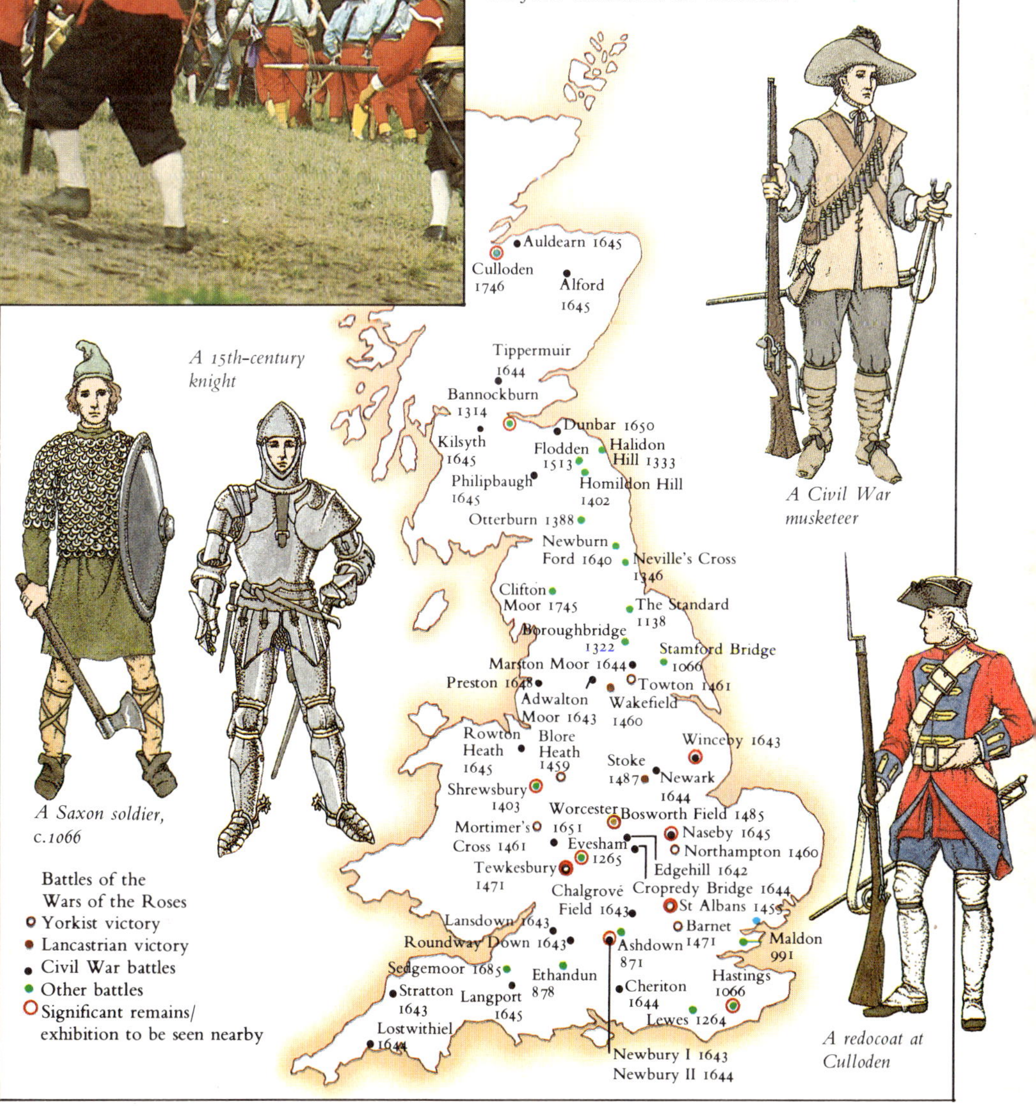

A 15th-century knight

A Saxon soldier, c.1066

A Civil War musketeer

A redcoat at Culloden

Battles of the Wars of the Roses
Yorkist victory
Lancastrian victory
Civil War battles
Other battles
Significant remains/exhibition to be seen nearby

The Civil War

OLIVER CROMWELL. *He is portrayed here with typical Puritanical honesty, 'warts and all'.*

Initially, the Royalist strongholds were in the north, the west and Wales. The Parliamentarians held London, and south-east England was predominantly for them. They also had supporters isolated in Royalist territory, especially in mercantilist seaports such as Plymouth and Hull.

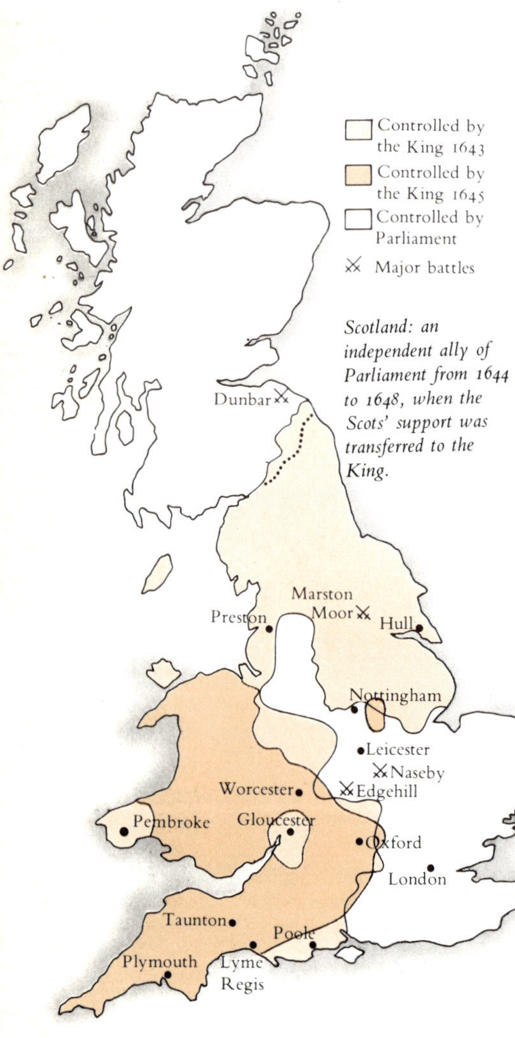

CROMWELL'S DISMISSAL OF THE COMMONS, 1653. *This 'Rump' Parliament was already a reduced assembly from which opposition had been purged. From now on, Cromwell ruled as a dictator.*

'DIGGERS' AT WORK. *The Diggers' community at George Hill in Surrey, here re-created in the film* Winstanley, *was crushed in 1650, as were other popular democratic experiments in this period.*

England's Civil War (1642–46 and 1648) differed from the Wars of the Roses in that it was fought over religious and political ideals, and reflected the stresses of a society in which new social groups, such as the commercial classes, were growing in strength. The autocratic Charles I had managed to dispense with his Parliament for eleven years until 1640. In that year, he convened the so-called Long Parliament, because he needed money to buy off the rebellious Presbyterian Scots, who had overrun Northumberland and Durham. But this assembly passed measures that restricted his power and reinforced his financial dependence upon it. The House of Commons was unanimous in wanting to put reins on a would-be absolutist monarch, but on other issues it divided into rival parties. The Royalists (cavaliers) were soon arrayed against the Parliamentarians (roundheads), who were anxious for religious and political reforms. In 1642, after an unsuccessful attempt to arrest the most militant Parliamentarians, Charles had to flee London. After a short propaganda war, the Civil War began.

The course of the war

Between 1642 and the King's decisive defeat at Naseby in 1645, followed by his surrender to the Scots at Newark in 1646, the war ebbed and flowed in a complicated way. By 1643 Charles was broadly in control of the north and west, while Parliament held the south-east and the City of London, both areas in which much of the country's wealth was concentrated. After getting slightly the best of the fight at Edgehill the King marched on London to re-occupy his capital, but had to fall

PRINCE RUPERT. *Charles's dashing nephew was the Royalists' brilliant cavalry commander. He had served on the Continent during the Thirty Years War, and was well versed in the latest tactics.*

back in the face of resistance and make his headquarters at Oxford. The next year there was some hope of recovering London as his northern army was sweeping south in apparent triumph, but this chance was lost, and in 1644 the Scots came over the border again, helping to destroy the northern cavaliers at Marston Moor. The Scots, who owed allegiance to the King but none to his English parliament, had kept aloof at first. They then became an independent ally of Parliament's, but after the end of the first phase of conflict they were seduced by Charles. In 1650, when they refused to reorganize the Commonwealth after Charles's execution, they took a harsh beating from Cromwell at Dunbar.

The rise of Cromwell

Oliver Cromwell's outstanding personal qualities had soon brought him to the fore. First, as a soldier, he introduced new standards of discipline and efficiency. The crucial factor in winning the war was the creation of the New Model Army in 1644, based on Cromwell's own fighting force, the Ironsides, and commanded by Sir Thomas Fairfax. As a political leader, Cromwell was resolute and ruthless in doing what he felt was right. After the King had shown himself to be completely untrustworthy by allying with the Scots, a special Parliament purged of Royalist sympathies ordered his execution in January 1649. Cromwell, now secure in his position of power, struck left and right against opposition. Some of the men who fought in the Parliamentary army had done so in the hope of a new democratic order. The Levellers, for example, believed that 'the poorest hee that is in England hath a right to live as the greatest hee', and they wanted all men to have a vote. Cromwell was as ruthless towards these elements as he was in crushing the sporadic Royalist uprisings which lasted until his defeat of the young Charles II at Worcester in September 1651. Thereafter, as Lord Protector, he was unchallenged. In 1653 he dismissed Parliament and continued to rule, without recalling it, until his death in 1658.

Under Cromwell, England was an extremely undemocratic republic, albeit one that allowed a great degree of religious freedom, except to Catholics, and went to great lengths to protect and encourage the nation's trade. By May 1660 an era of great experiment and upheaval ended, for Charles II was invited to return from exile as King. The monarchy, though, was never quite the same again. Charles I would have abhorred the controlled kingship accepted by his son, and the changes released by the Civil War were confirmed and extended in the Glorious Revolution of 1688.

CHARLES I. *Van Dyck's portraits convey the King's dapper elegance. The contrast, on canvas, between the gracious Charles and the blunt Cromwell reinforces a popular image: debonair cavaliers on one side, uncouth roundheads on the other. In fact, both sides dressed similarly.*

CONNECTIONS
Armed engagements: 71–2 *Battles*
The Glorious Revolution: 108–9 *Riot and revolution*
Parliamentary history: 68–9 *Parliament/The beginnings*
The religious aspect: 50–51 *Catholics and Protestants*
Sieges: 196–9 *Castles*

Class in Britain

Human societies tend to divide into groups possessing different degrees of power and wealth. At one extreme there are nobles with special privileges; and at the other, serfs with few rights or slaves with none. Archaeological evidence reveals rigid social distinctions within the tribes of Celtic Britain: the warrior aristocracy (who were buried with silver vessels and other fine possessions); the free cultivators of the land; the serfs (who were tied to the land); and the slaves (whose manacles and chains have survived at many sites).

NURSERIES OF NOBILITY. *Medieval lords were often waited upon by attendants of gentle birth, who saw this service as part of their education as nobles.*

TOWN AND COUNTRY. *From the 18th century onwards, upper-class families regularly travelled in private coaches (**above**) between their country homes and the capital. A town house was necessary while Parliament sat and while the 'season' was in full swing. A gentleman's club, such as Brooks's of St James's Street (**right**), was an important component in the luxury of London life.*

The Romans brought with them a more sophisticated social hierarchy. Below the highest, senatorial class was the lesser equestrian order. There was also a basic distinction between the privileged *honestiores* and the low-born *humiliores*, who were subject to torture and frequent exaction of the death penalty. More importantly, Roman Britain witnessed the gradual growth of a prosperous, town-based commercial class.

In Anglo-Saxon times, the commercial class disappeared. Social gradations were reflected most clearly in the different rates of *wergild* – the compensation paid by a murderer to the victim's family. The ordinary farmer, or *ceorl*, was rated at 100 shillings in early Kentish law, while a nobleman was rated at 300 shillings; the various lower orders, possibly including freed slaves or subject Britons, had *wergilds* of 80, 60 or 40 shillings.

The rise of the commercial classes

Some forms of feudalism (the holding of land in return for services) were already apparent in England before the Norman conquest, but William I introduced a more rigorous land-based social hierarchy. No sooner had the structure become established, however, than its symmetry was challenged by the emergence of new social groups. A common phenomenon in medieval society was the struggle within the towns between the richer citizens and the 'commonality'. Townspeople were often divided, on the basis of property owned, into *potentiores, mediocres* and *inferiores*. Control of the towns tended to remain in the hands of the *potentiores*, who steadily became important figures in a national, as well as a local, context.

Those who amassed great commercial fortunes bought their way into the landed class. The upheavals of the Tudor period, and particularly the dissolution of the monasteries, greatly accelerated this development, and many of Britain's great aristocratic families – for example, the Russells and the Cecils – were essentially the products of Elizabethan commerce and politics.

Class in industrial society

The word 'class', as opposed to 'rank' or 'order', came into popular use only in the early 19th century. Under the impact of the industrial revolution and of political reform, a new society came into existence in which the social groups were more unified within themselves than ever before, even though explicit *legal* distinctions had been levelled out.

In the early 19th century the landed aristocracy and gentry were still the most powerful political force in the country. The unreformed parliamentary system excluded most of the middle classes, although the organized agitation associated with the Reform Bill demonstrated their strength. At the same time the growth of trade unionism and Chartism demonstrated that a new working class was also coming into existence.

In the later 19th century, the upper class took a distinctive shape as an amalgam of the older aristocracy with new recruits from commerce, industry, government and the professions. The middle classes had not risen to power as a group (though individuals had), but seemed content to continue to be ruled by the upper class. They did, however, enjoy a status and standard of living that meant that even the most prosperous members of the working class were sharply cut off from them. In the 1870s, for example, class differences could be physically gauged: owing to dietary and other differences, eleven- to twelve-year-old boys from the public schools were on average over twelve centimetres taller than boys of the same age from industrial schools, and throughout their teens they remained seven centimetres taller than the sons of artisans.

High-born or wealthy middle-class Victorians with servants – this too was a good index of status – accepted a class society as 'natural' and right. Their confidence in this is well expressed in a verse from the popular hymn, 'All Things Bright and Beautiful': 'The rich man in his castle, The poor man at his gate, God made them, high or lowly, And order'd their estate.'

Beneath the servant-keeping group were the lower middle-class families – those of shopkeepers, clerks and other 'clean-handed' workers – who were very conscious of being, by culture and status (though not by income), a 'cut above' the manual workers.

Among the workers, too, there was considerable internal stratification. The skilled 'aristocrats of labour' (with their gold watches and pianos) were distinguished from the semi-skilled and unskilled workers, who in turn were above the outcast poor, known to many Victorians as the 'residuum' and to some modern sociologists as the 'under class'. The growth of the Labour Party ensured that the special interests of the working people were advanced. After 1945 they occupied a position in the community similar to that of the middle class after the 1832 Reform Act.

Although we no longer have some of the more offensive trappings of a class society, class distinctions remain sharper in modern Britain than in most other countries of western Europe, and have perhaps contributed to economic stagnation. Even so, there has been remarkably little open class conflict in British history, and to some extent class divisions are now overlaid by still more deeply felt divisions of race, nation and even, with the rise of the feminist movement, of gender.

CONNECTIONS
Class and democracy: 76–7 *Parliament/Abuse and reform*
Class in education: 112–13 *Learning and the people*, 114–15 *Higher education*
Landed wealth: 92–3 *Landownership*
The workers' struggle: 82–3 *Democracy and the franchise*; 84–5 *Workers' movements*

STAN AND HILDA (***below***) – *the names themselves, like the milkbottle on the table, have class overtones – are characters in the TV series* Coronation Street, *set in a working-class community in Lancashire. Hilda is seldom seen without her curlers.*

PUBLIC SCHOOLS

The public schools occupy a special position in the British class system. A few, including King's School, Canterbury (*c.* AD 598), are of considerable antiquity, but the great lay foundations, such as Winchester (1382) and Eton (1442), date from the 14th, 15th and 16th centuries. The basic function of the earlier schools was to train men for the Church, but after the Reformation both old and new foundations were directed more towards training for service in the State.

In the 1820s, Thomas Arnold at Rugby began the reform movement that converted these schools into centres for inculcating the sons of the Victorian upper class (that is, the business and professional élites, as well as the aristocracy) with the principles of leadership and gentlemanly manners.

THE PUBLIC SCHOOL ETHOS *was started by Thomas Arnold at Rugby* (***above***). *Its Victorian origins are reflected in the dress of these modern Etonians* (***left***).

Parliament/*Abuse and reform*

Britain emerged from the constitutional and religious upheavals of the 17th century as a limited monarchy in which political power was shared with Parliament. While the monarch could choose his own ministers, Parliament had to approve the passing of legislation and controlled finance.

Anomalies and anachronisms

The system was a long way from being truly representative, however, for by the 18th century Parliament reflected primarily the power and influence of the landed classes. The House of Lords was composed of hereditary peers, and the House of Commons consisted overwhelmingly of landowners, many of whom were the younger sons of peers, with a few merchants and professional men representing some of the long-established commercial communities such as Bristol and the City of London. High property qualifications restricted entry into Parliament to a wealthy élite, and the passing of the Septennial Act in 1716 reduced the frequency of elections from three to seven years. Only one in twenty of the population was entitled to vote at elections, and in many places the number of electors was so small that seats in Parliament were entirely subject to the control of the major landowners.

CANVASSING FOR VOTERS. *William Hogarth's depiction of 18th-century electioneering. Voters are being bribed, and encouraged to eat and drink at the candidate's expense. With an open ballot it was possible to ensure that those 'canvassed' would vote as expected.*

JOHN WILKES (***below***). *His political career was synonymous with the cause of parliamentary reform in the late 18th century. Outspoken in his criticism of the government, he was repeatedly expelled from the House of Commons, re-elected and imprisoned amongst huge public controversy.*

These 'pocket' or 'rotten' boroughs were manipulated by politicians to serve their own interests, so that patronage and influence played a much greater role in the shaping of governments than the wishes of the population as a whole. A seat in Parliament was often regarded as an adjunct to social status, or as a passport to a lucrative career, rather than as a serious responsibility.

The growth and movement of the population during the industrial revolution, and changes in the nature of the economy, highlighted the flaws of this system. Many manufacturing centres, such as Leeds and Manchester, were unrepresented, while ports and market towns that had been important in the past retained the right to send two members to Parliament. Parliamentary representation was concentrated in the agricultural counties of southern England, while Wales, Scotland and the north were grossly under-represented in relation to their population. Elections, moreover, were frequently accompanied by corruption.

The beginnings of reform

From the end of the 18th century the middle classes and the emerging working class attacked the corruption of Parliament and demanded reform. The Catholic Emancipation Act of 1829, which removed the ban prohibiting Roman Catholics from being Members of Parliament, was a hint of change, but the first major step forward was the 1832 First Reform Act. Although it increased the electorate and redistributed seats to give greater representation to the new industrial areas and disenfranchise rotten boroughs, this Act was not a radical measure. The qualification for voting rights was still property.

This cautious attempt at reform was initially rejected by the House of Lords, causing widespread unrest, and riots in Derby, Nottingham and Bristol. But under threat of being flooded by a host of reform-minded new peers (King William IV had been induced to guarantee their creation), the Lords backed down. (The primacy of the elected assembly – the House of Commons – was not to be established until 1911 when, because of its resistance to Lloyd George's 'People's Budget', the upper chamber's power to veto legislation was curbed by legislation. A bill now becomes law even when it is vetoed by the Lords, if it is passed three times by the Commons.)

The 1832 Act, although it cured certain anomalies of the old electoral system and set a precedent for further change, was a bitter disappointment to many. The new Parliament fairly represented the well-to-do landowning and business classes but it resisted the Chartist campaigns for a package of radical reforms that included secret ballots, payment of MPs and universal manhood suffrage. The stability of Britain's political system was reflected, however, in the fact that, unlike their revolutionary equivalents on the Continent, the Chartists respected Parliament and wished to carry out the transformations they desired by first achieving a majority in the House of Commons.

The later Reform Acts of 1867 and 1884, and the Redistribution Act of 1885, gradually provided a more equitable distribution of parliamentary seats as well as extending the franchise to a majority of the adult male population. Only in 1928, however, when women achieved equal voting rights with men, was full adult suffrage attained.

The parliamentary system today

By the end of the Second World War, Parliament had achieved its present shape. Over 600 members are elected at general elections, which must take

LORD JOHN RUSSELL *skilfully piloted the 1832 Reform Bill through the Commons.*

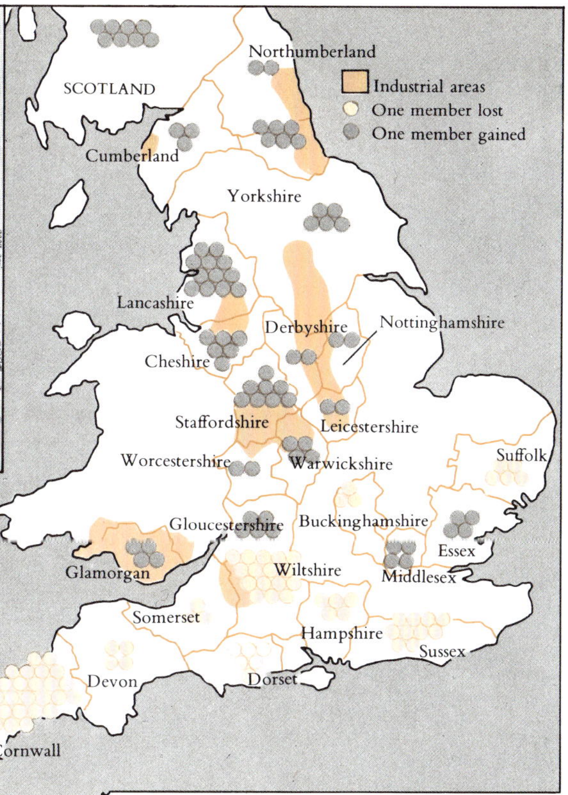

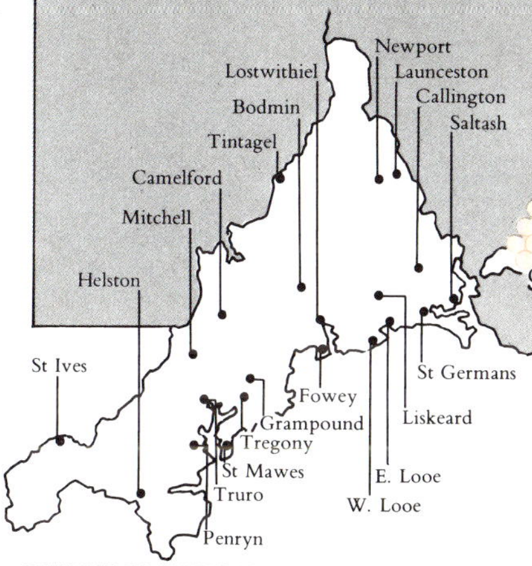

CORNISH POCKET BOROUGHS

THE GREAT REFORM ACT *of 1832. In the process of removing anomalies, areas such as Cornwall, which was notoriously over-represented, with a high density of rotten boroughs, lost many seats. The 143 seats made available by the reform were allocated to the larger counties, the larger towns and to Scotland and Ireland. The Act removed 56 rotten boroughs, and took away a member from another 30. (In addition, the electorate was enlarged by about 300,000.)*

DISRAELI WINS THE RACE *for reform in 1867. The Act transferred some seats from small boroughs to the expanding towns, and almost doubled the electorate. The newly enfranchised urban workers were not grateful, however, and voted in the Liberals in 1868.*

A POSTER OF 1909 ***(below)****, showing the clash between the hereditary Lords and elected Commons over Lloyd George's 'People's Budget'.*

place at least every five years, and vacancies caused by death or resignation are filled at by-elections. Members are elected to the House of Commons for single-member constituencies on a simple majority system. Today, effective political power is almost entirely vested in the House of Commons. Since 1945 the House of Lords has contained life peers (who are nominated by governments and whose titles may not be inherited) as well as hereditary peers. Its role is to act as a forum for discussion of legislation before it becomes law.

Members of Parliament have been paid since 1911, and there are no longer any property qualifications restricting membership of Parliament to the well-to-do. Sittings occupy only about half the year and sessions do not begin until the afternoon, although they can last late into the night. Although modern MPs are generally elected to serve under a particular party label, they are in theory representatives of all their constituents, whatever their political affiliation. Members of Parliament customarily hold 'surgeries' in their constituencies, where members of the public can discuss their problems, and most MPs carry on an extensive correspondence with constituents.

In recent years the tendency has been for the work of Parliament and of MPs to become more complicated, and it has become increasingly difficult for MPs to keep an adequate check upon the actions of the government and the administration. The position of Ombudsman, or Parliamentary Commissioner for Administration, was created in 1967 to counteract this tendency by investigating complaints passed on by MPs concerning the actions of government departments. Although there remain many criticisms of the ability of 'back-bench' MPs to play an effective role, an important recent initiative has been the creation of all-party select committees to investigate crucial areas of government policy.

Recently, a further constitutional change has been discussed: the possibility of introducing a new voting system – proportional representation (PR) – whereby a closer relation would be achieved between total votes cast for a particular party and the number of MPs from that party elected to Parliament. The present system, with single-member constituencies, discriminates against minority parties, and PR systems have already been adopted by many other democratic countries.

CONNECTIONS
Agitation for reform: 108–9 *Riot and revolution*
The birth of Parliament: 68–9 *Parliament/The beginnings*
Discrimination on religious grounds: 54–5 *Christian minorities*
Political parties: 78–9 *Party politics*
The right to vote: 82–3 *Democracy and the franchise*

Party politics

The growing importance of Parliament in British government led from the end of the 17th century to the formation of factions, or 'parties', which reflected significant bodies of opinion both inside and outside Westminster. Initially, parties were loose groupings of members who met in London clubs (while Parliament was in session) or in the great country houses of influential landed magnates. With the extension of the franchise and the growth of a better-informed electorate, parties became more formalized, seeking to obtain the election of their candidates to Parliament through centrally run, national organizations.

Whigs and Tories

The Whig Party emerged as early as the reign of Charles II when the Earl of Shaftesbury and his followers in the Green Ribbon Club attempted to exclude Charles's Catholic brother, later James II, from the succession. As a result, they became associated with the cause of the Dissenters and the defence of the liberties of subject and Parliament against the threat of monarchical absolutism. The term 'Whig', from 'whiggamore' (cattle-drover), began as a term of abuse used by opponents.

Although led by the nobility, the Whigs appealed to the interests of commerce and the professions. On the other side, the Tory Party emerged as staunch supporters of the Crown and the Church of England. 'Tory' also was initially a derogatory nickname, meaning an Irish bandit. In the aftermath of James II's unsuccessful reign (1685–8) and the Glorious Revolution of 1688 when William and Mary were placed on the throne, the two groups battled against each other, often very acrimoniously, for positions of influence.

Violent party conflict in the reign of Queen Anne (1702–14) over religion, the succession and foreign policy led to bitter election contests, and propaganda warfare between partisan writers such as Jonathan Swift and Joseph Addison.

The Tories, many of whom continued to profess their allegiance to the Jacobite line, were virtually excluded from power after the Hanoverian succession of 1714 and the failed Jacobite rising of 1715. Under Sir Robert Walpole (the King's first minister, 1721–42), a quieter period of Whig dominance began that lasted for much of the 18th century. However, with the accession of George III (1760–1820) the Tories gradually regained respectability as a party who were, above all else, loyal to the monarchy and the Church. Under Pitt the Younger, a new Tory party rose to dominance in Parliament, where they were opposed by the Whigs under the erratic leadership of Charles James Fox.

The 19th century

During the 19th century, the Whig and Tory parties gradually widened their appeal to tap the support of the growing middle and working classes. Under leaders such as Sir Robert Peel (1788–1850), the Tory Party became associated with 'Conservatism' – the cautious adjustment of government and society to accommodate the pressures for change which surfaced in the campaign for parliamentary reform and the repeal of the Corn Laws (which had unfairly favoured the landowners). Peel is often considered the founder

WILLIAM PITT THE YOUNGER *(1759–1806). Pitt became Prime Minister at 24, despite the hostility of most prominent Whigs. Pitt was a Whig himself but his government acquired the old name 'Tory', to distinguish it from the opposition.*

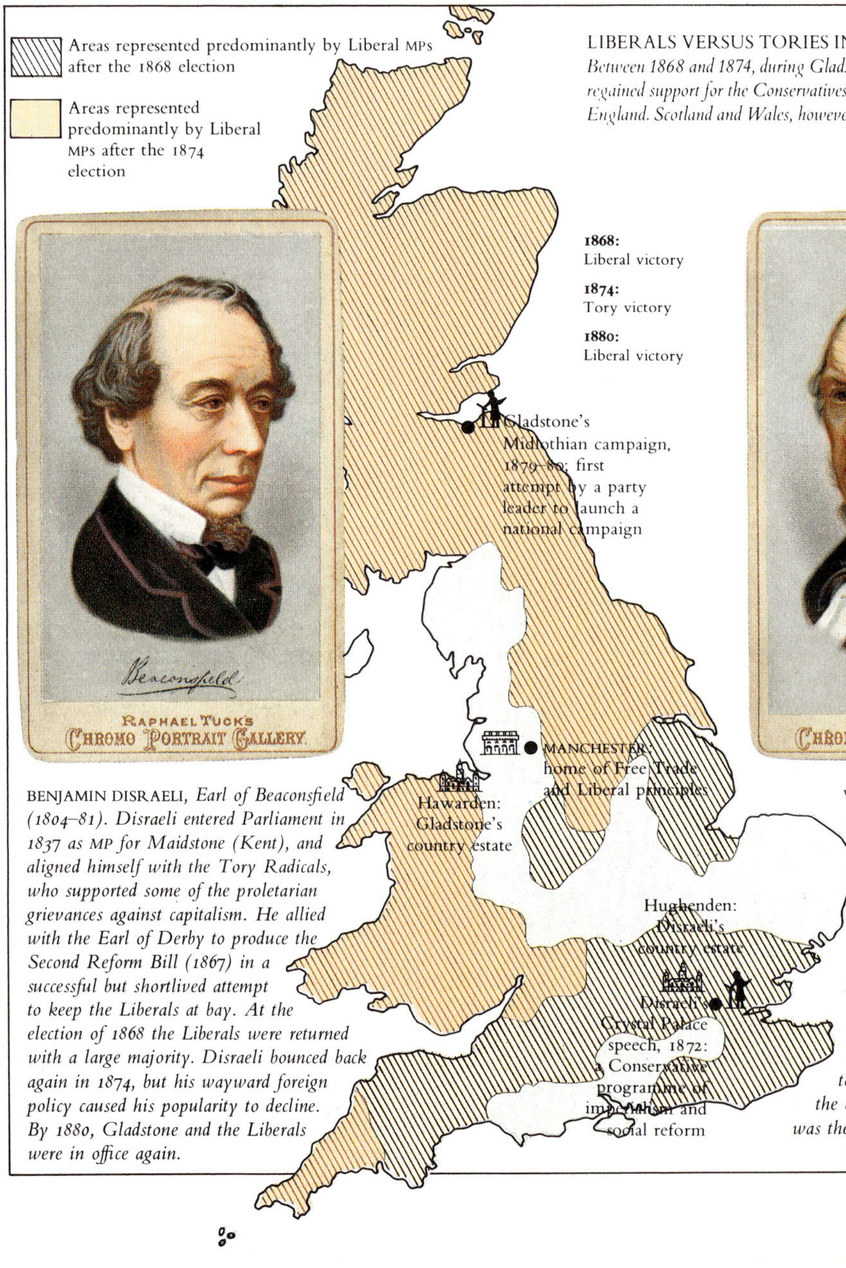

LIBERALS VERSUS TORIES IN VICTORIAN BRITAIN
Between 1868 and 1874, during Gladstone's premiership, Disraeli regained support for the Conservatives in southern and midland England. Scotland and Wales, however, remained staunchly Liberal.

BENJAMIN DISRAELI, *Earl of Beaconsfield (1804–81). Disraeli entered Parliament in 1837 as MP for Maidstone (Kent), and aligned himself with the Tory Radicals, who supported some of the proletarian grievances against capitalism. He allied with the Earl of Derby to produce the Second Reform Bill (1867) in a successful but shortlived attempt to keep the Liberals at bay. At the election of 1868 the Liberals were returned with a large majority. Disraeli bounced back again in 1874, but his wayward foreign policy caused his popularity to decline. By 1880, Gladstone and the Liberals were in office again.*

WILLIAM EWART GLADSTONE *(1809–98) entered Parliament as MP for Grantham (Lincs.). As Palmerston's Chancellor he cut back on government spending and advanced the cause of Free Trade, one of the principal planks of the Liberal platform. His first and greatest ministry after the Liberal victory of 1868 was brought down over an attempt to reform Irish education. After the comeback of 1880 a main issue was the Irish crisis: Gladstone was a keen advocate of Home Rule.*

COALITIONS

'England does not love coalitions,' said Disraeli. Yet joint governments have intermittently played a part in British politics, especially in wartime. The three most important were:

May 1915–November 1922
Wartime coalition begun under Herbert Asquith. It continued under a Liberal – David Lloyd George – even after the Conservatives had won a clear majority in December 1918.

August 1931–November 1935
National Government set up by Ramsay MacDonald (Labour) to combat the effects of the Depression.

May 1940–May 1945
Wartime coalition under Churchill. Again, the Conservatives had a clear majority.

ELECTION POSTER, *1929. Labour secured a brief minority government, but the Depression proved too much for it. The party lost 226* MPs *in 1931, but in 1935 made a recovery under Clement Attlee.*

CONSERVATIVE PARTY CONFERENCE, *1978. The optimism was justified. In the 1979 election the Tories under Margaret Thatcher, the first woman Prime Minister, won the day.*

THE SOCIAL DEMOCRATIC PARTY, *1981* (**below**)*: the leadership. All four leaders – Roy Jenkins, David Owen, William Rodgers and Shirley Williams – were formerly Labour Cabinet Ministers.*

of the modern Conservative Party, but his work was greatly consolidated by Benjamin Disraeli, who sought to appeal to middle- and working-class voters in his promotion of social reform and imperialism.

The Whigs, led by Earl Grey, developed an aristocratic attachment to the notion of reform. They passed the Great Reform Act of 1832 and in the mid-19th century drew increasingly upon the support of other groups than the old Whig landed families. Disenchanted Tories, Nonconformists, working men and many supporters from the 'Celtic fringe' came together with the old Whigs to form the Liberal Party in 1859. Under their great leader, William Ewart Gladstone, the Liberals promoted Free Trade, undertook major administrative reforms in the Army, the Civil Service and the universities, and championed the cause of Irish Home Rule.

By the end of the 19th century, both major political parties had become organized on a nationwide basis, with election agents, constituency organizations and a London headquarters. In Parliament, the two-party system which had been emerging from the end of the 18th century was given formal acknowledgement when the House of Commons was rebuilt after a fire destroyed the old one in 1834. A new chamber was provided with two sets of benches, one for an administration party, one for an opposition party.

Party proliferations

The growth of socialist ideas and the rise of trade unionism led to growing disenchantment amongst working men with the existing political parties. Keir Hardie set up the Independent Labour Party in 1893, and this was followed in 1900 by the creation of the Labour Representation Committee, which was formally constituted into the Labour Party in 1906. Between the wars the Labour Party grew to supplant the Liberals as the major opposition to the Conservatives; they formed minority governments in 1923 and 1929–31, and came to power under Clement Attlee in the landslide victory of 1945, when they gained 394 seats against the Conservatives' 213.

The inter-war years also saw the establishment of the Communist Party of Great Britain (1920), the Welsh Nationalist Party (1925), the Scottish Nationalists (1928) and the British Union of Fascists (created by Sir Oswald Mosley in 1932). After 1945 further minority parties were born, such as the anti-immigrant National Front and British Movement, the conservationist Ecology Party, and, in 1981, the Social Democratic Party led by defecting Labour members.

A political party today is a complex and sophisticated organization, with elaborate machinery for fund-raising and obtaining support in local and national elections. The main focus for the discussion of policy and the preparation of manifestos to be submitted to the electorate is the annual party conference. Most parties continue to depend heavily for their finances and day-to-day activities upon voluntary help from members, though there are other, more substantial sources of support: big business plays an important role in the finances of the Conservative Party, while the trade unions heavily back Labour. A system of government funding for political parties in proportion to their electoral support has recently been mooted, but the issue remains unresolved.

Increasingly, in the age of mass media, popular attention has come to focus on the personalities of party leaders. At the same time, there has been a decline in active membership of the major parties. Some observers find a causal connection here, and claim that the role of local parties is giving way to a national, TV-orientated political arena.

CONNECTIONS
Dissenters: 54–5 *Christian minorities*
The Labour Party: 84–5 *Workers' movements*
The parliamentary system: 68–9 *Parliament/The beginnings;* **76–7** *Parliament/Abuse and reform*
Politics and the media: 120–21 *The Press;* **276–7** *Radio and television*

Local government and the Civil Service

INSPECTING WEIGHTS AND MEASURES: *a 16th-century woodcut. Such inspections are an ancient duty of local authorities. The medieval Exchequer sent standard weights and measures to all towns.*

Changes in the structure of local government in Britain have tended to be evolutionary rather than revolutionary. The major reforms have taken place since the 19th century. Names of traditional units of local administration (such as the borough and the shire) and of ancient officials (such as the sheriff and the bailiff) are still familiar to us; however, the precise meanings behind the names have altered considerably since medieval times.

The smallest unit of local administration has for centuries been the parish. Initially an ecclesiastical organization, it gradually took on secular functions, and played an important role in local government with the passing of the Elizabethan Poor Laws, under which it was entrusted with catering for the destitute. Parish officers – the churchwarden, overseer and constable – were responsible for a variety of maintenance matters (including the upkeep of bridges and footpaths and the care of straying animals). In the 18th century the range of the parish's functions was gradually whittled away: roads and welfare matters were put into the hands of special trusts (such as the turnpike trusts) under central control. The largest units of the ancient system were the shires (equivalent to the counties of later times); these were subdivided into hundreds, each with its own local court.

In each English county there was a sheriff (or 'shire reeve'), who acted as the direct agent of the Crown. Initially, sheriffs were appointed from the great feudal magnates, but by the later Middle Ages, after their powers had diminished, they were elected annually from among the local gentry. Their role was now overshadowed by that of the lords-lieutenant.

In 1361 local landowners in England were appointed as justices of the peace to maintain law and order. The justices gained extra responsibilities from the 16th century onwards, until in the early years of the 17th century their quarter sessions became the most important assemblies of local administration. The quarter sessions continued until 1888, but as the justices' duties became more onerous, standards of competence gradually fell.

A major urban unit, from an early date, was the borough – originally a town which had a royal charter granting privileges and self-government. By the later medieval period, each borough had an elected mayor who was supported by his aldermen. All boroughs acquired the right to elect their own justices, and London was also granted the power to appoint its own sheriff.

SANITARY SERVICES (***below***): *refuse collection in Manchester. It was the 1866 Sanitary Act that first compelled local authorities to supply adequate waste disposal facilities.*

Local government reform

It was not until the 1830s that substantial changes were made to the old structure. These reforms were largely called for by the demands of expanding towns, but were also a response to confusion and corruption. Change came earliest in Scotland, where the old system of self-elected burgh councils was overhauled in 1833. In England the Municipal Corporations Act of 1835 revised the constitution of boroughs, providing a democratic system whereby town councils were elected by male ratepayers. After this measure was passed, some of the new corporations began to construct proper sewage and water systems and introduced street-cleaning, but it was only by degrees that such responsibilities were enforced by law.

The next radical reform came with the Local Government Act (1888), which improved representation in rural areas by the creation of elected

THE TOWN HALL. *This one at Abingdon (Berks.), built in 1677–80, was one of the finest of the new civic centres which replaced the medieval guild halls and market halls. After the functions of municipal authorities were expanded by the Municipal Corporations Act (1835), the provincial towns acquired still grander town halls, such as those of Leeds (1858) and Bradford (1873).*

A PARISH COUNCIL *in 1951. Such bodies today can play an important part in controlling changes in the local environment.*

THE LADY MAYOR OF SHEFFIELD, *giving her inaugural address in 1981. A mayor is the chairman of a borough or town council. The prefix 'lord' or 'lady' is applied when a town has county status.*

SIR STAFFORD NORTHCOTE *(1818–87)* ***(left)****, with Charles Trevelyan, insisted on radical reforms in the Civil Service in the report of 1854.*

WHITEHALL, *London: the traditional centre of the Civil Service. It was transformed in Victoria's reign by massive new buildings, including Sir George Gilbert Scott's Foreign Office (1873).*

county councils, and granted sixty-one towns the status of county boroughs. London became a separate county. There was also a Scottish re-organization in 1889. In 1894, the English structure was rationalized further by the establishment of urban and rural district councils and of nearly 7,000 parish councils.

In modern times, the balance between local and central powers has shifted. Since 1902, education has remained essentially in the hands of local authorities, but many other important functions have been centralized. After the Second World War it was realized that further reform was needed to make local government more rational. A solution for London was found in 1965, when the London County Council was transformed into the larger Greater London Council. On a wider scale, the 1972 Local Government Act (effective in 1974) introduced a two-tier system, which broke up England into thirty-nine counties and thirty-six metropolitan districts (the latter grouped into six metropolitan counties). Many of the old counties (such as Rutland) disappeared. Scotland was similarly re-grouped in 1973.

The dangers of excessive centralized control are obvious but are offset, to some degree, by the existence of neighbourhood councils and by the role of the local ombudsman.

The Civil Service

The ultimate origin of the British Civil Service – the administrative establishment responsible for carrying on the work of government – is the personal household of the medieval monarch. However, it was not until the late 18th century that the modern service began to take shape. By a series of Acts, the holding of a non-ministerial, salaried office became incompatible with having a seat in parliament. At the same time, the sheer volume of parliamentary business became too onerous for ministers to concern themselves with both policy-making and day-to-day administration. The Treasury acquired its first permanent secretary in 1805, and a permanent official was appointed to the Colonial Office in 1825.

Recruitment, in the early period of the Civil Service, was by patronage, and the number of sinecures was notorious. In 1854, the Northcote-Trevelyan report analysed the chaotic situation and put forward proposals for reform. It recommended a more unified structure in which recruitment and promotion were to depend on merit: examinations were to be conducted by a single body, independently of the departments. Senior posts were to be filled by those with university degrees. The principles of the report were not effectively adopted until 1870, and not applied to the Foreign Service until 1943.

In the 20th century, continued accusations of élitism and amateurishness culminated in the Fulton report of 1968, which proposed a single, unitary staffing structure (abandoning the old administrative, executive and clerical grades), easier promotion routes, and the recruitment of more specialists. An interesting aspect of the modern Civil Service is the degree of its influence on ministerial decisions.

CONNECTIONS
Education: 112–13 *Learning and the people*
Local courts: 104–5 *Courts of the land*
Public health: 110–11 *Health and medicine*
Taxation: 94–5 *Money and finance*
Welfare: 88–9 *The growth of the Welfare State*

Democracy and the franchise

TOM PAINE *(1737–1809) advanced cogent arguments for democracy in Britain.*

The word 'franchise' means freedom, particularly the freedom to vote at elections. Voting in the past was not regarded as the universal right of every citizen, but was limited to special groups according to a variety of different rules. On the eve of the industrial revolution voting in the counties rested with the forty-shilling freeholder: the franchise was therefore restricted to the gentry and most prosperous merchants. In the boroughs, electoral rights varied enormously. In some places almost every householder was entitled to vote, while elsewhere voting was restricted to the freemen of the borough, or even just to the Mayor and the members of the Corporation. The result was a corrupt and undemocratic system.

The number of voters in many places was so small that elections could be swayed by the local landowners or manufacturers; intimidation was common and voters often expected simply to sell their vote to the highest bidder. In some of the famous elections of the unreformed Parliament candidates spent a fortune bribing and treating electors. At the Yorkshire county election in 1807, for example, an estimated £100,000 was spent; while at the Westminster election in 1796 it was recorded that hogsheads of beer were broached for the electors to scoop up from the gutters.

As early as the 17th century, the Levellers had maintained that the franchise should be extended to all adult males, since it was the Englishman's 'birthright' to have a say in his own government. In the 18th century, these ideas were championed by men such as Major John Cartwright (a Lincolnshire gentleman and writer on the Constitution) and the popular radical John Wilkes. Wilkes's election for Middlesex in 1768, and his battle to retain his seat when excluded by the House of Commons, helped to focus attention on the need for parliamentary reform.

The rights of men

The American and the French revolutions gave a fresh impetus to democratic ideas. Tom Paine (1737–1809) was the apostle of 18th-century democracy and republicanism in Britain. His book *The Rights of Man* reached a wide audience and led groups such as the London Corresponding Society (formed in 1792) to adopt a programme of universal manhood suffrage and annually elected parliaments. By the early 19th century the movement towards a more democratic system included both working-class and middle-class reformers. Writers such as William Cobbett set out to link the economic distress of the early 19th century with the need for parliamentary reform and a wider franchise. The reformers organized mass meetings that were attended by thousands of working men and women. One of the most famous was at St Peter's Fields in Manchester in August 1819: the gathering was broken up by troops with the loss of eleven lives, and the phrase 'Peterloo Massacre' gained a prominent place in the history books.

In the reform crisis of 1831–2, Britain appeared to be on the brink of revolution. Riots in Nottingham, Bristol and elsewhere, and mass meetings in London and towns such as Birmingham, forced reform through against the bitter opposition of the House of Lords. But the 1832 Reform Act granted only a limited extension of the franchise, mainly to the propertied classes. In disgust the working-class reformers continued to campaign in the Chartist movement of the late 1830s and 1840s for a charter of radical constitutional changes. Universal male suffrage was one of their five principal aims.

The Chartists presented massive petitions to Parliament in 1839, 1842 and 1848, but their movement was defeated by internal divisions and by the firm response of the government. In 1867, however, after demonstrations in London, the Second Reform Act was passed, granting the vote to the better-paid workmen in the towns. A further Act in 1884 extended the franchise to working men in the country. Almost three in every five adult males now had the vote. Bribery and other forms of persuasion were also reduced by the introduction of the secret ballot in 1872 and the Corrupt Practices Act of 1883.

CHARTIST SHOW-DOWN AT KENNINGTON, *1848. Despite large meetings and three mass petitions, the Chartists could not succeed while democracy remained synonymous with social revolution.*

ENFRANCHISED FARM WORKERS, *1884. The introduction of the secret ballot (1872) was important in rural communities, where farmers were in a position to monitor how their workers voted.*

The rights of women

A few women in possession of particular property rights had been able to vote in the 18th century, but the Reform Acts of the 19th century made it clear that votes were to be confined strictly to men. Mary Wollstonecraft's *Vindication of the Rights of Women* (1792), which applied the logic of the French Revolution to the status of women, marked the beginning of the women's movement in Britain. Then, in 1866, John Stuart Mill's parliamentary motion in favour of votes for women marked the beginning of the female suffrage movement, and around this time a number of suffrage bodies was founded.

In 1896 the various local societies formed them-

SYLVIA PANKHURST ORATING, *1912* (***right***). *She differed from her mother and her sister Christabel in linking the struggle for votes for women with wider social and economic issues.*

A MOTHER VOTING (***below***). *It was only after much agitation and the experience of the First World War that respectable matrons like this were awarded the right to vote.*

THE SWELLING ELECTORATE

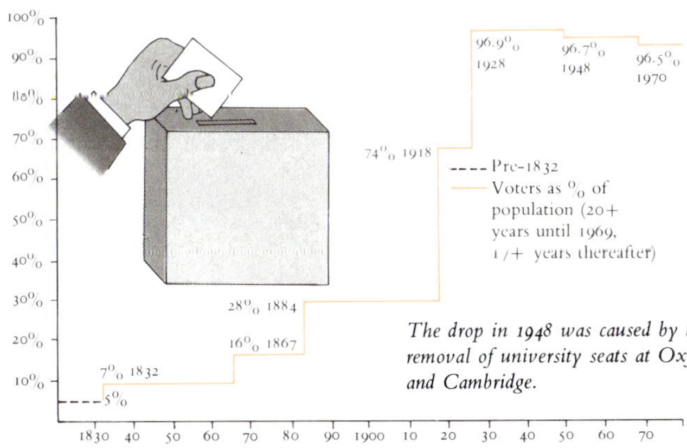

The drop in 1948 was caused by the removal of university seats at Oxford and Cambridge.

FLAPPERS VOTING, *1928. Twenty-one-year-old, newly enfranchised women at the polls.*

THE PERSONAL TOUCH. *Last-minute canvassing in the Orpington by-election of March 1962.*

selves into the National Union of Women's Suffrage Societies under the presidency of Millicent Fawcett. These – the suffragists – advocated votes for women by constitutional means. Votes were, in fact, conceded to women in local elections, and women could also serve on local councils. But no progress was made at parliamentary level, and in 1903 Emmeline Pankhurst founded the Women's Social and Political Union.

Towards the end of the decade, it became clear that the Liberal government was not going to give a lead in introducing women's suffrage. Emmeline Pankhurst, and her daughter Christabel, began to lead the increasingly violent activities that characterized the group christened the 'suffragettes' by the *Daily Mail*. The suffragettes' campaign was in many ways a heroic one, and it can be said that it focused attention on a problem which, though much talked about, was not being effectively dealt with. At the same time, their more violent exploits antagonized many people.

The crucial and versatile role of women in the First World War effort made it obviously anachronistic for them to be vote-less, but the 1918 Reform Act, which gave some women (and men who had been previously excluded) the vote for the first time, held a sting in its tail – only women over thirty years of age were eligible to vote. It was not until the 'flapper vote' Act of 1928 that women, like men, could vote at twenty-one years of age. In our own time the franchise has widened again. The lowering of the voting age to eighteen in 1969 reflected the increasing education and affluence of young adults.

CONNECTIONS
Agitation for reform: 108–9 *Riot and revolution*
Democracy: 76–7 *Parliament/Abuse and reform*
Discrimination on religious grounds: 54–5 *Christian minorities*
The woman's role: 90–91 *Women and the family*

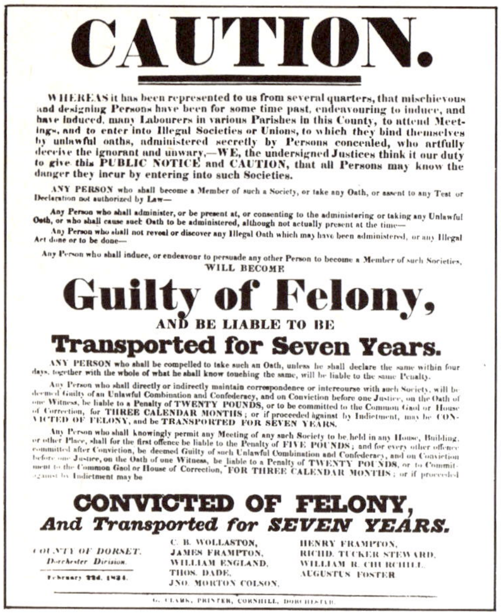
CAUTION.

WHEREAS it has been represented to us from several quarters, that mischievous and designing Persons have been for some time past, endeavouring to induce, and have induced, many Labourers in various Parishes in this County, to attend Meetings, and to enter into Illegal Societies or Unions, to which they bind themselves by unlawful oaths, administered secretly by Persons concealed, who artfully deceive the ignorant and unwary,—WE, the undersigned Justices think it our duty to give this PUBLIC NOTICE and CAUTION, that all Persons may know the danger they incur by entering into such Societies.

ANY PERSON who shall become a Member of such a Society, or take any Oath, or assent to any Test or Declaration not authorized by Law—

Any Person who shall administer, or be present at, or consenting to the administering or taking any Unlawful Oath, or who shall cause such Oath to be administered, although not actually present at the time—

Any Person who shall not reveal or discover any Illegal Oath which may have been administered, or any Illegal Act done or to be done—

Any Person who shall induce, or endeavour to persuade any other Person to become a Member of such Societies,

WILL BECOME

Guilty of Felony,

AND BE LIABLE TO BE

Transported for Seven Years.

ANY PERSON who shall be compelled to take such an Oath, unless he shall declare the same within four days, together with the whole of what he shall know touching the same, will be liable to the same Penalty.

Any Person who shall directly or indirectly maintain correspondence or intercourse with such Society, will be deemed Guilty of an Unlawful Combination and Confederacy, and on Conviction before one Justice, on the Oath of one Witness, be liable to a Penalty of TWENTY POUNDS, or to be committed to the Common Gaol or House of Correction, for THREE CALENDAR MONTHS; or if proceeded against by Indictment, may be CONVICTED OF FELONY, and be TRANSPORTED FOR SEVEN YEARS.

Any Person who shall knowingly permit any Meeting of any such Society to be held in any House, Building, or other Place, shall for the first offence be liable to the Penalty of FIVE POUNDS; and for every other offence committed after Conviction, be deemed Guilty of such Unlawful Combination and Confederacy, and on Conviction before one Justice, on the Oath of one Witness, be liable to a Penalty of TWENTY POUNDS, or to Commitment to the Common Gaol or House of Correction, FOR THREE CALENDAR MONTHS; or if proceeded against by Indictment may be

CONVICTED OF FELONY,

And Transported for SEVEN YEARS.

COUNTY OF DORSET.
Dorchester Division.
February 22d, 1834.

C. B. WOLLASTON,
JAMES FRAMPTON,
WILLIAM ENGLAND,
THOS. DADE,
JNO. MORTON COLSON,

HENRY FRAMPTON,
RICHD. TUCKER STEWARD,
WILLIAM R. CHURCHILL,
AUGUSTUS FOSTER

G. CLARK, PRINTER, CORNHILL, DORCHESTER.

THE TOLPUDDLE MARTYRS. *In 1834 six Dorset farm labourers were transported for organizing a union. As a result of the massive protest campaign that followed, their sentences were remitted in 1836.*

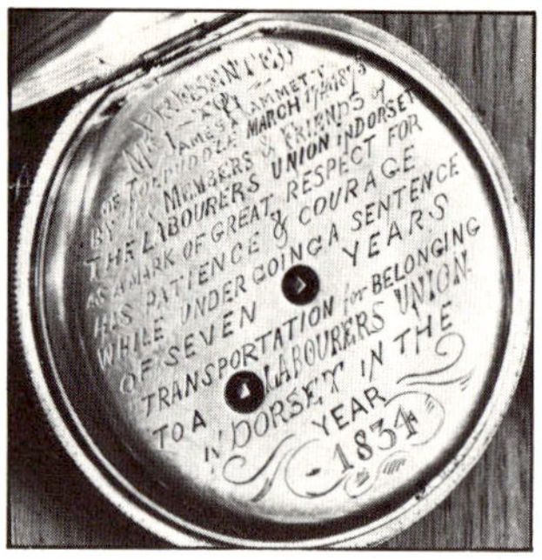

A HERO'S RETURN. *A watch presented to a Tolpuddle martyr.*

KEIR HARDIE (1856–1915)

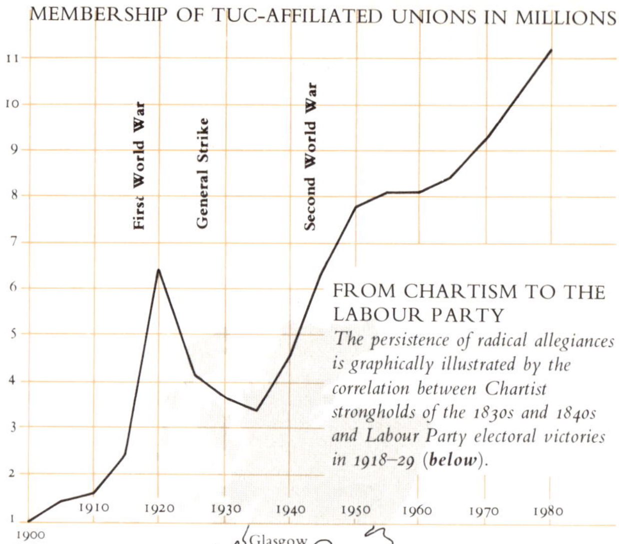

FROM CHARTISM TO THE LABOUR PARTY
*The persistence of radical allegiances is graphically illustrated by the correlation between Chartist strongholds of the 1830s and 1840s and Labour Party electoral victories in 1918–29 (**below**).*

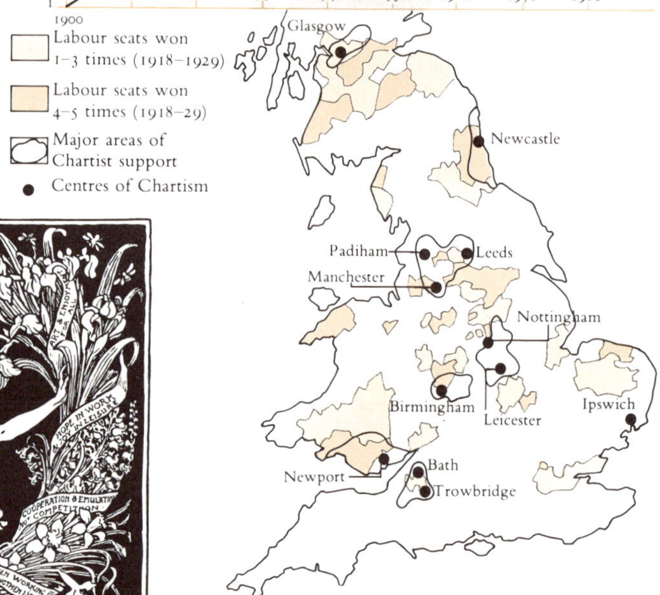

A 19TH-CENTURY UNION BANNER. *'Aristocrats of labour', the craft-proud engineers were conscious of their centrality in the Victorian economy.*

A MAY DAY GARLAND. *Walter Crane's design features the labour movement's aims in 1895.*

The first workers' organizations were the medieval guilds that regulated apprenticeship, wages and the quality of workmanship amongst urban craftsmen. These were the precursors of the trade societies formed by skilled workers such as shipwrights, printers and tailors in pre- and early industrial Britain. The Friendly Societies Act in 1793 allowed some of them to establish benefit clubs through which they could collect funds from their members and insure them against loss of earnings from sickness and accident.

Such funds could also be used, however, to sustain members on strike. When the first political organizations of working men were formed under the stimulus of the French Revolution, fears of subversion led the government to react with a series of repressive measures. The Combination Acts of 1799 and 1800 outlawed workmen who combined together in trade unions or went on strike. Trade societies continued to exist, but many were forced underground.

Formative experiences

In the early 19th century the 'Luddite' outbreaks (1810–12) convulsed the north and Midlands, as groups of workers suffering from high prices and unemployment smashed the new machines that were seen as threats to their livelihood. Others looked to extension of the franchise as the answer; inspired by radical journalists such as William Cobbett, they organized political clubs and reform meetings. In 1824, Francis Place, a former London tailor, led a successful campaign to repeal the Combination laws, and trade unions started to grow more freely among newer occupational groups such as the mill-workers and coalminers. Under the influence of Robert Owen (1771–1858), the enlightened cotton master of New Lanark, the vision of a society based on co-operation instead of competition began to emerge.

The Chartist campaigns of the 1830s and 1840s brought together the different strands in the workers' movement: the demand for votes, opposition to the new Poor Law of 1834 (especially the workhouses), free trade unionism, utopian socialist ideals and the movement for self-help through co-operative ventures.

The rise of the labour movement

Although Chartism failed to achieve its programme of radical constitutional reform, it marked a growing awareness among working people of the need to combine unity with pragmatism in the struggle for reasonable living standards and political democracy. As economic conditions improved after 1850, new 'model' unions were set up among the skilled workers, particularly the engineers, based upon high subscriptions, central headquarters (often in London) and a strategy of peaceful negotiation with employers from a position of strength. In 1868 the first Trades Union Congress (TUC) met at Manchester, to provide a forum for trade union opinion. At the same time violent incidents directed at non-union members in Sheffield – the 'Sheffield outrages' – resulted in a Royal Commission investigation of trade unions, which led to laws in 1871 and 1875 that fully legalized trade unions, allowing them to have more control over their funds and carry out peaceful picketing.

By the end of the 19th century, unskilled workers (including women) were being drawn into the unions. Joseph Arch founded the Agricultural Workers Union in the 1870s, and in 1889 the London dockers mounted a prolonged and successful strike. The spread of socialist ideas led to the founding in 1893 of the Independent Labour Party. Then in 1900, a resolution of Keir Hardie's (his cloth cap became emblematic of the movement) called for 'a distinct Labour group in Parliament who shall have their own whips and agree upon their policy'. This led to the formation of the Labour Representation Committee (renamed the Labour Party in 1906). Keir Hardie was among the first Labour MPs and played an indispensable role in creating the Party.

In the years of the 'labour unrest', just before the First World War, increasing trade union militancy was expressed in an unprecedented number of strikes. These reflected rising prices and stagnating wages, as well as the influence, at least among the workers' leaders, of the 'syndicalist' idea that a general strike of all workers could destroy capitalism altogether.

The Russian Revolution (1917) gave a further fillip to socialist ideas within the labour movement and the success of collectivism influenced the flavour of the constitution adopted by the young Labour Party in 1918. By 1922 the Labour Party was the second largest in Parliament, forming a brief minority government (under Ramsay MacDonald) in 1924, and a slightly longer one in 1929–31. In 1926 came the trauma of the nine-day General Strike, which was originally called in support of the miners, upon whom savage wage cuts were being imposed. It collapsed because the moderate trade union leaders were afraid of taking any action that might be termed 'unconstitutional'.

Following the financial and political crisis of 1931, Labour suffered a heavy defeat at the polls; nowadays, however, historians stress how remarkably working-class loyalty to the party held up in the most adverse circumstances.

The Second World War restored the position of the labour movement. The trade unions had been considered crucial in the winning of the 'people's war', while the Labour Party won a landslide electoral victory in 1945 and became firmly established as one of the 'natural governing parties'. Since 1945 the trade unions have multiplied their ranks. Because of their mass membership, large funds and institutional links with the Labour Party, they now form one of the great estates of the realm. However, restrictive practices such as the closed shop (the exclusion of non-members from a unionized workplace), and what some see as the excessive power of the unions, have led to calls for reform and tighter controls. Advocates of workers' control have proposed an alternative idea: a system of industrial democracy whereby workers would have a greater say in management.

UNEMPLOYMENT DEMONSTRATION, LIVERPOOL, *1980. The diversity of banners reflects union growth beyond traditional areas.*

CONNECTIONS
Guilds: 86–7 *Vanishing skills*
The Labour Party: 78–9 *Party politics*
The Luddites: 108–9 *Riot and revolution*
Unemployment: 88–9 *The growth of the Welfare State*
The workers' environment: 226–7 *Town houses;* **236–7** *Factory towns*

Vanishing skills

THE GUILDS

Guilds were originally simple religious and social fraternities, but by the 13th and 14th centuries they had become exclusive bodies of craftsmen or traders, and were highly organized and very powerful. They could effectively operate closed shops and fix the level of wages, and they maintained strict quality control over their members. However, by the 16th century much of their influence had been eroded by legislation, and they were further weakened in the 19th century by the decline of apprenticeship. Of the 84 Livery Companies (descendants of the craft guilds) that still exist in London, a few (such as the Goldsmiths) are still active in controlling standards, though others are merely clubs, with only a tenuous relation to working life.

A GUILD WARDEN. *A 15th-century manuscript illustration of the vital moment when a mason and a carpenter were set to prove their skills to a warden. Apprenticeships were arduous, but guild membership was a great reward.*

A WELSH FARMWIFE MAKING BUTTER, *in the 19th century. One of many domestic crafts that are now vanishing. The painstaking process of butter-making is vividly described by Thomas Hardy in* Tess of the D'Urbevilles *(1891).*

A WHEELWRIGHT'S SHOP (**below**): *a reconstruction in the City Museum of St Albans (Herts.). The craftsman is fitting a new section (felloe) to the wheel and is drawing the spokes together with a specialized tool known as a spoke-dog. In the days of wagons, coaches and carts, wheelwrights were in great demand.*

JOHN VINE, THE KENT AND SURREY MOLECATCHER. *Molecatchers were employed by farmers to prevent moles causing damage to pasture land. Since moles are extremely shy, great cunning was required. The skins of the prey were used for clothing, as well as by plumbers for smoothing soldered material.*

Many of the crafts that are practised in Britain today have a venerable history. Baskets miraculously preserved from the Stone Age display patterns still in use in a few rural areas. Although basket-making still flourishes, most skills of this kind would soon be lost to us forever were it not for the efforts of those who are concerned to preserve our craft heritage.

Before the coming of industry, communities were often entirely self-sufficient and relied on numerous craft workshops. In addition to domestic activities such as butter- and cheese-making, many more specialized skills flourished, including furniture-making, hand-forging and milling. In the late 19th century William Morris championed the ideals of honest manual labour, and a number of new craft guilds emerged. This conservationist attitude is continued today in the work of the Arts and Crafts Council and other bodies. A widespread fascination with these aspects of the past is reflected in the popularity of craft demonstrations.

BASKET-MAKING IN GLOUCESTERSHIRE (***below***), *using the traditional 'lap board'. The twigs, known as withies, are grown by the River Severn. There is a particularly long-lived basket industry in the Sedgemoor district of Somerset, using local willow. Some types of basket are peculiar to particular regions.*

CLOG-MAKING. *Before the Second World War, clogging gangs were a common sight all over Britain, but especially in the woodlands of south Wales and the Border counties. Alder and sycamore were the favourite materials. Clogs were at one time standard dress in the industrial north.*

THE BLACKSMITH AT HIS FORGE, C. 1900 (***below***). *The village blacksmith was also often a farrier. After the first quarter of the 20th century, the craft declined with the growth of motor transport, but there is still a limited demand for the blacksmith's services. Forges remain in use for farriery, for repairing farm tools and for making wrought-iron articles.*

CONNECTIONS

The Arts and Crafts Movement: 286–7 *The artist's eye*
Early trade unions: 84–5 *Workers' movements*
Rural communities: 222–3 *Villages and hamlets;* 224–5 *Market towns*
Spinning: 142–3 *The wool trade*
Thatching: 170–71 *Building*

The growth of the Welfare State

For centuries in Britain, responsibility for the care of the poor, the sick and the elderly rested entirely on the Church and on charitable individuals. Only in modern times has the State developed a comprehensive system of social welfare.

Charity, Church and State

The Synod of Aix in 816 decreed the foundation of special houses to cater for the poor and the sick, as well as for travellers. Many later foundations were originally lazar (that is, leper) houses, but as the disease gradually disappeared from Britain, they too turned their attention to other types of illness and to the elderly. Almshouses remained almost exclusively ecclesiastical in foundation, endowment and administration until the middle of the 16th century. Many of them survive today near abbeys or churches.

In the Tudor period the prosperity of the wool trade increased the temptation for landowners to enclose arable land for sheep pasturage, with the result that many labourers lost their livelihoods. At the same time, gold and silver shipped from South America lowered the value of money, and poverty and vagrancy increased. The dissolution of the monasteries at the Reformation destroyed many almshouses, and further aggravated the hardships of the poor. Eventually, however, the State began to offer an alternative form of poor relief.

Elizabeth I's government passed the first pauper Act in 1563, imposing a compulsory levy to raise money for State charity. In 1598, Overseers of the Poor were appointed in each parish and empowered to collect and redistribute 'poor rates'. Houses of correction for idle vagrants and poor houses for the sick were established three years later. Fears that parish resources would be swamped led to the Act of Settlement (1662), which limited poor relief to working residents of the parish.

In the early days of the industrial revolution, rapid population growth and the steady drift of people to the towns in search of jobs exacerbated urban unemployment and poverty. London parishes occasionally resorted to exportation of large numbers of orphans and illegitimate children to a grim life of factory work in the Midlands and the north. As the industrial towns increased in size, parish-based relief became totally inadequate to meet the needs of thousands of families whose wage-earners had been thrown out of work by trade depression. Poverty was also widespread in rural areas. Rising food prices in the 1790s, partly due to bad harvests and the war with France, obliged the magistrates of Speen in Berkshire to introduce a system of subsidising farm labourers' wages from the poor rates. This 'Speenhamland system', widely adopted in southern England, was exploited by employers to depress wage levels.

THE ST NICHOLAS HOSPITAL *for lepers at Harbledown near Canterbury, founded c. 1084 by Archbishop Lanfranc. The sloping floor in the church facilitated cleaning after the leper services.*

THE MARYLEBONE WORKHOUSE, LONDON (***below***): *a ward for the homeless poor (1867). Life in a workhouse was deliberately harsher than the lot of the lowest-paid labourer.*

The Victorian social conscience

Traditional methods of poor relief were radically altered in 1834 by the Poor Law Amendment Act, which introduced the workhouse as a deterrent to idleness. Vagrants and paupers were treated with equal harshness. Tasks – often of a futile nature – were imposed, and strict discipline was enforced by corporal punishment. The workhouse system, in an improved form, continued to operate well into the 20th century.

The equation of unemployment with idleness was gradually discarded as more people realized that the workhouse system treated the symptoms rather than the causes of urban misery. Appalling living conditions among the poor in the booming industrial cities inspired the foundation of the first modern hospitals. Church-sponsored societies and enlightened individuals took on specific problems – Lord Ashley (later Lord Shaftesbury), for example, campaigned on behalf of young boys employed as chimney sweeps. Factory Acts regulated some of the worst abuses of child and female labour, and Sir Edwin Chadwick, who had been chief architect of the Poor Law Amendment Act, set up a general board of health in 1848. Chadwick's change of policy reflects a new emphasis on public health reform and correction of the attendant ills of the industrial age. The first local medical health officers were appointed to combat cholera and other diseases that thrived in industrial squalor, and the increasing use of smallpox vaccinations, combined with agricultural advances which combated malnutrition, greatly improved the health of the nation.

These advances were consolidated when a series of public health Acts created national sanitary authorities responsible for sewage, drainage, street cleaning and the water supply. The Artisans Dwellings Act of 1875 authorized councils to clear slums (though the houses built to replace them often had such high rents that their intended occupants were unable to move in). The expansion of State education also accelerated in this period.

The Welfare State is born

By the beginning of the 20th century it was widely accepted that more public money should be spent on the provision of welfare. The Liberal governments of Edwardian Britain, under the influence of reform-minded politicians such as Lloyd George, introduced Old Age Pensions (1908) and, three years later, a system of national insurance against sickness, accident and unemployment. Although slum clearance was a major theme of the inter-war years, the brightest hopes of continued social reform were dashed by Sir Eric Geddes's cutbacks (1921–2) and by the discriminatory Means Test (1931). Enduring poverty and ill health, and the rather haphazard pattern of welfare services, focused attention on the need for a more radical welfare programme.

The climate of concerted endeavour induced by the Second World War gave shape to this idea. In 1942 the Beveridge Report proposed generous benefits from the cradle to the grave, to be paid for out of an extended system of national insurance. Child allowances were established by the Conservative 'caretaker' government at the end of the war. A universal national insurance scheme and a new free, comprehensive National Health Service were instituted by the post-war Labour government, both passed in 1946 and put into effect in 1948.

The destruction of housing in the war stimulated a massive rebuilding programme. Slums were demolished, and new council estates and blocks of high-rise flats sprang up. In the first decade after the end of the war, three-quarters of all new dwellings built were council houses.

The welfare services have grown enormously since 1945, reaching further into local communities and answering specialized social needs.

CONNECTIONS
Housing: 226–7 *Town houses*
Public health: 110–11 *Health and medicine*
State education: 112–13 *Learning and the people;* **114–15** *Higher education*
Welfare services: 80–81 *Local government and the Civil Service*

PRIVATE CHARITY. *Many wealthy Victorians, out of a growing sense of civic duty, visited the poor regularly and gave donations.*

CONDEMNED HOUSING, LIVERPOOL (***right***). *Slum clearance is still not complete, but the worst housing had gone by the mid-1950s.*

SIR WILLIAM BEVERIDGE (*1879–1963*). *His report of 1942 recommended a national insurance system, with benefits payable on 'interruption of earnings' through illness, unemployment, retirement or widowhood. Beveridge also pressed for child allowances. He believed that want was 'only one of the five giants on the road . . . of social progress': the others were idleness, squalor, ignorance and disease. The latter was tackled in the 1940s by Aneurin Bevin, who set up the National Health Service.*

HELP FOR THE JOBLESS

After the National Insurance Act of 1911 Labour Exchanges came into their own as offices at which jobless workers could call to obtain information about vacancies, and as centres for the payment of benefits – seven shillings a week for a maximum of 15 weeks. Initially, however, only the construction, shipbuilding and engineering trades were covered. The thinking behind the scheme was largely that of Lloyd George, who had closely studied the German system. Thirty years later unemployed claimants still referred colloquially to 'being on Lloyd George'.

An Act of 1946, based on the Beveridge Report, extended and improved the system. In 1966 benefits became wage-related: the weekly payments were scaled in relation to the applicant's usual income.

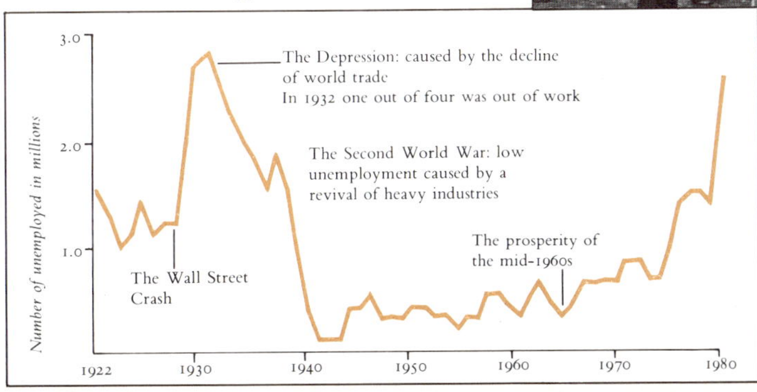

A DOLE QUEUE, *1979. The crisis of the Depression led to the introduction of dole – extra payments to commence from the time when an unemployed person's basic entitlement ran out. The term now has a wider sense.*

UNEMPLOYMENT, *1922–1982* (***left***). *The graph shows the trends in British unemployment since the aftermath of the First World War.*

Women and the family

A MEDIEVAL MARRIAGE. *Then, as now, an important element in the wedding ceremony was the moment when the groom presented his bride with a ceremonial ring.*

The family is the basic unit in human society and throughout European history men, formally at least, have occupied the dominant roles within it. Yet, whatever law and custom have decreed, women have always had an important and far from passive part to play in social development. From the Anglo-Saxon period right through the Middle Ages, there are accounts of abbesses, widows and women landowners actively participating in their own right in local and national affairs. Both Queen Mathilda (1102–67) and Queen Isabella (1298–1358) were prominent in medieval politics, and the contribution of Elizabeth I needs no elaboration. Still, the odds were heavily stacked against the majority of women.

Ill-nourished and racked by illness, most medieval people led a hard life, but for women it was especially hard. They took a full part in the routine of backbreaking toil, but because of their inferior social status their work was valued less than that of men. The normal age of first conception (at around twenty-six) was relatively high, that of the last (in the early thirties) relatively low. In between there were many infant deaths, and the primitive state of obstetrics meant that childbirth was a mortal hazard. There was little room for romantic love, or even sexual passion, and despite the demonstrable bonds between parents and *adult* offspring, attitudes towards children were correspondingly harsh.

THE HAY MONTH *(14th century). The women gather the hay with forks, while the men wield heavy scythes. This division of labour in haymaking lasted until the coming of machines in the 19th century.*

A CHILDHOOD WEDDING, 1642. *Mary Stuart (aged 10) with her spouse, William II of Orange (aged 15). Strategic marriages between aristocratic children were not uncommon in the 17th century.*

The marriage market

Upper-class daughters, more often than not, were goods in the matrimonial market. Obviously, the more wealth a family possessed, the less freedom its female members had in their choice of the partners who would share or augment that wealth. A woman could always improve her social position through marriage, and the institution remained a gambit in this game until the 20th century. The significance of such resorts as Bath, Cheltenham, Buxton and Tunbridge Wells in the later 18th century partly lay in the fact that their assembly rooms were essentially marriage markets. However, an era of romanticism had dawned by this time and marriage was seen as involving love and true companionship, as well as convenience. This ambivalent attitude is brilliantly fictionalized in the novels of Jane Austen.

Women and ladies

The industrial revolution changed the lives of most British women. In the days of a primarily agricultural economy, women had worked with the rest of the family to produce the household livelihood. A cottier's wife, for example, might have kept poultry and spun with her children at home; while the wives of craftsmen in the towns often managed their husbands' accounts and ran their shops. By the 19th century workplaces had become separated from homes, and women with children had no choice but to go out in search of paid employment or stay at home: the housewife was born.

Typically, women who were not housewives did unskilled factory jobs or entered domestic service. Able-bodied female servants were needed in aristocratic and middle-class households presided over by 'ladies' who, by definition, did not work themselves. For the latter category of women, the industrial revolution and the cultural changes of the early 19th century, particularly the stress on women as ornamental status symbols and the rise of evangelical piety, may have actually worsened

GETTING ABOVE THEMSELVES, 1809 (***below***). *This caricature ridicules the pretensions of well-off farmers who were educating their daughters to be accomplished, marriageable 'young ladies'.*

MANY HAPPY RETURNS OF THE DAY, 1856. *In compensation for their otherwise suffocatingly prim lives, middle-class Victorian women had relatively affectionate relations with their children.*

same time, there was a widespread revolt of youth. It might have seemed that the family was now menaced. Yet if the divorce rate has accelerated, so also have the marriage and re-marriage rates. Although its patriarchal aspects have been modified and motherhood is no longer synonymous with complete dependence on the 'breadwinner', the family is such a resilient human institution that its future survival, in one form or another, seems beyond doubt.

FAMILY SOLIDARITY, 1889. *Meal-time for the wives and children of striking London dockers.*

their circumstances. Certainly a double moral standard prevailed, whereby conduct that would have been condoned or even admired in a male could spell ruin for a respectable female.

A widening sphere

Because of Victorian notions about a lady's proper place in society, the genteel spinster without means – that unfortunate of the period – had few options when it came to selecting a job in which she would not lose her status; underpaid governessing was one of them. But as educational opportunities increased in the last quarter of the 19th century, more single women could become elementary school teachers. This was also the time at which the clerical, secretarial and commercial jobs were creating crucially significant new openings for women, and female infiltration of the prestigious higher professions had begun.

Much controversy rages over the exact significance of the First World War in confirming these trends. It is certainly true that, because of the onset of unemployment in the 1920s, many of the social and economic gains made by women during the war were nullified. But the overall tendency, resumed in the Second World War and never reversed thereafter, was of more and more women finding employment outside the home.

The family now

The modern women's movement emerged from the great cultural upheavals of the 1960s, although, in Britain, it did not get going seriously until the next decade. Important reforms of the late 1960s were the Abortion Act, the Family Planning Act, the Divorce Act and the Equal Pay Act. At the

THE NEW WOMEN. *The women scheduled to speak at this 1908 demonstration in favour of votes for women were very different from their mothers and grandmothers. As forthright and independent individuals they rejected the Victorian notion of the home as woman's only proper sphere and demanded a full role in public life. For such women the vote was a major step towards equality.*

CONNECTIONS
Jobs for women: 124–5 *The First World War*
Miners' wives: 234–5 *Coal mining towns*
Sexual segregation: 210–11 *Rooms in country houses*
Votes for women: 76–7 *Parliament/Abuse and reform;*
82–3 *Democracy and the franchise*
Women's education: 114–15 *Higher education*

Landownership

SQUIRES AND POACHERS

Private hunting has for centuries been one of the primary pleasures associated with the ownership of certain types of land. In the Middle Ages the Crown reserved the right to hunt in the royal forests, but awarded subsidiary hunting rights to an élite of loyal subjects, who were also sometimes granted the right to 'empark' – to build walls around part of a chase or forest.

Game laws have given fierce protection to the privileges of landlords, especially during the Restoration – the age when the squirearchy began to acquire great power in the House of Commons. In 1671 a law was passed that prevented any freeholder of less than £100 per year (or any leaseholder of under £150 per year) from killing game, even on his own property. This law penalized the yeoman farmer, who had previously tended to bag any partridge that happened to wander on to his farm from the neighbouring estates belonging to game preservers.

In 1831 the property qualification on the shooting of game was finally abolished. The ban on dealing in game, and the inconvenient system whereby only a squire or a squire's son could kill game, were also ended. Attitudes to poaching, however, remained harsh. Springs and mantraps, which were commonly used to protect pheasant reserves, were prohibited in 1827, but in the following year the Night Poaching Act was passed, which made armed gangs of three or more night poachers liable to a sentence of 7 years' transportation to Botany Bay.

A POACHER CAUGHT IN A MANTRAP: *a late 18th-century illustration. Mantraps like this were humane in comparison with spring-guns, which fired at anyone who triggered off the mechanism. Since it was illegal for anyone to buy or sell game, poaching could be very lucrative.*

A GROUSE SHOOTER *takes aim. The presence of red grouse on the heather-covered hills of Scotland and northern England has made shooting rights over the moors an important commercial asset. Since Edwardian times, estates have been increasingly let to syndicates.*

PRIDE IN PROPERTY (***below***): *a painting (by Arthur Devis, 1763) of Francis Vincent and his family in the grounds of their home, Weddington Hall in Warwickshire. The genre has a recent equivalent: the aerial photos of house and garden that hang over many a modern mantelpiece.*

A GREAT ESTATE (***below** and **right***): *a view of Blenheim Palace, Oxfordshire, and an 18th-century plan of the surrounding park. The estate was originally a royal manor, but in 1704 was granted to John Churchill, Duke of Marlborough, as a reward for his victory over the French at Blenheim. The park (by 'Capability' Brown) dates from the 1760s.*

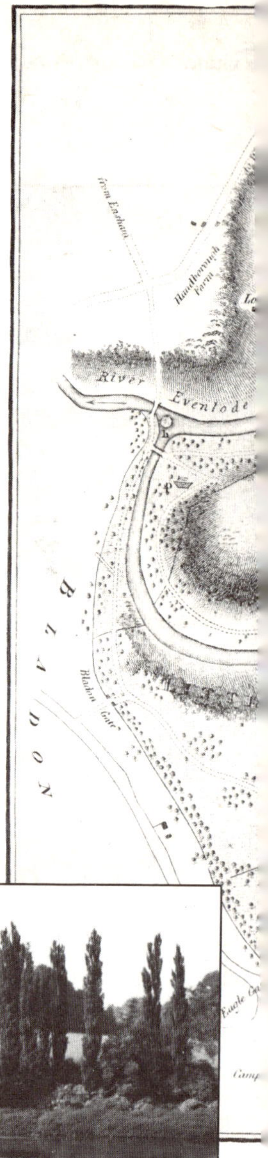

An individual's entitlement to a piece of land has taken various forms throughout history. In the feudal period, which properly began when William I amply rewarded his followers by grants of property seized from the Anglo-Saxons, all land was held directly or indirectly from the Crown. Today, the plots of many freeholders are ultimately owned by the building societies that have provided the capital. However, there have been many individuals and families whose direct ownership of one or more estates has been the basis of great wealth and status. The times have occasionally favoured the tenant more than the landlord – for example, in the 15th century, when hired labour was expensive and it was difficult to let farms. But more often, land has been greatly coveted as the key to multiple benefits, not the least of which was political power.

Landlords and holdings

During the Middle Ages, the Church owned vast tracts of land and grew wealthy on a steady income from rents. The bequests of pious laymen swelled ecclesiastical landholdings, and some of the religious orders made handsome profits from their extensive farmlands. Even before the Reformation, laws were passed that prevented the bequeathing of land to the Church. With the dissolution of the monasteries and the seizure of monastic property, the Church ceased to be such a major landowner. Although the monarchy had the initial title to what was confiscated, the greater part was sold off by Henry VIII to pay for wars with France. One result of this was that the Crown was not an outstandingly important landholder in the Tudor and Stuart period; this led to many of the financial difficulties that contributed to conflict between Crown and Parliament in the 17th century.

The 16th century was a period of land hunger. At a time when labour was readily available and demand for produce was high, it made economic sense to increase the size of one's holding. This was an early phase in the evolution of progressively larger estates – a process that culminated in the reign of George III. The heyday of the small squire,

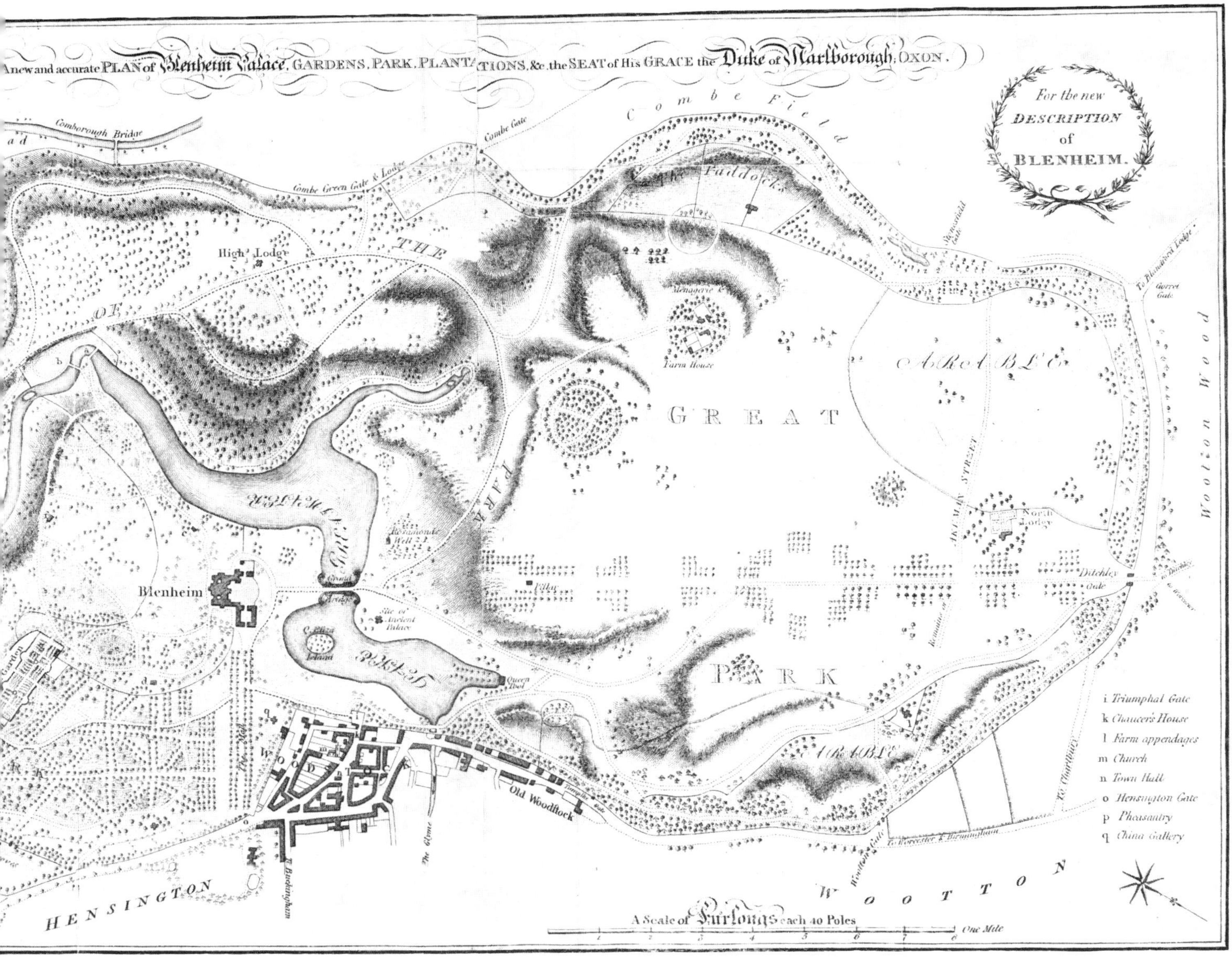

A PATCHWORK OF PLOTS. *Privately owned inter-war housing at Chislehurst, south-east of London. The size of the gardens is well above the British national average.*

by this time, had come to an end, for the capital required to keep up with advances in agricultural technology was more than he could muster, and the only alternative was to sell. Those who could afford to buy good farming land seldom hesitated, because British farming was highly favoured by the Corn Laws.

Agriculture was one way in which land could generate money, but it was not the only way. Many ambitious landed families also sought to exploit the mineral resources of their estates. Others, such as the Duke of Portland, built up great fortunes from the development of urban estates in the capital and elsewhere.

There was also a long-standing tradition of merchants and financiers buying land to establish their place in the social hierarchy. With the coming of industrialization, manufacturers sought to acquire status by the same means, and there was considerable intermarriage between landed and manufactured wealth.

The landed interest retained a large measure of power and influence even after the passage of parliamentary reform and the transformation of Britain into an urban, industrial society. However, the agricultural depression of the late 19th century adversely affected many landowners, especially the smaller gentry. The break-up of estates was hastened by the introduction of death duties, which were raised to punishing levels during the First World War.

In recent decades the difficulties of many landowners have been greatly increased by inflation and estate duties. Many estates depend for their survival on revenues derived from opening the houses and grounds to the public. However, banks and pension funds still treat land as a valuable commodity for investment.

CONNECTIONS
The dissolution of the monasteries: 48–9 *Church and State;* **206–7** *Monasteries*
Fox-hunting: 36–7 *Man and the landscape*
Royal forests: 30–31 *Woodlands and forests*
Secular estates: 208–9 *The great country houses*
Urban landowners: 228–9 *Town planning*

Money and finance

ANGLO-SAXON COINAGE. *Each Anglo-Saxon kingdom had its mint, producing coins stamped with the ruler's mark. The London Mint, set up in the 7th century, came to issue the dies for all other mints.*

A nation with a sophisticated commercial and economic life depends fundamentally upon currency and a refined system of credit. Britain first began to enjoy the benefits of a sound coinage under the settled administration of the Romans. There was something of a monetary collapse after their departure, but in the 8th century King Offa of Mercia produced a silver penny which remained in circulation in England until the reign of Henry III.

Under the later Anglo-Saxon kings more than sixty royal mints, in London, Canterbury, Southampton, Exeter and elsewhere, made high-quality coins which were strictly regulated by royal control. The Normans took over the Anglo-Saxon system and turned it to their own ends. Royal mints were maintained, and the famous Domesday survey was conducted to investigate the taxable value of each shire.

In Henry I's reign the Exchequer superseded the Chamber as the financial and auditing department of the government; it recorded the Crown income from each shire in documents known as 'pipe rolls'. A more adaptable instrument of finance, the Wardrobe, emerged in response to the need to subsidize royal military campaigns. Further subsidies for war were provided by sales of charters for markets and fairs, grants from Parliament and the Church and the imposition of customs duties. But despite these devices, the monarchy often had to resort to borrowing: Edward III, for example, drew upon the banking services of the Lombard family (who were consequently ruined).

Under the Tudors and Stuarts the question of royal finance loomed large in the clashes with Parliament. A wave of inflation throughout Europe exacerbated the problem. By the 17th century the monarchy could barely make ends meet, and the 'illegal' money-raising methods of Charles I contributed to the coming of the Civil War. Only after the Glorious Revolution of 1688, when Crown and Parliament entered a more stable relationship, could a more regular system of finance be established.

Banking

In 1694, the Bank of England was founded as a private company to fund William of Orange in his struggle against France. It was a joint-stock venture, which meant that shares were put on sale to the general public. The joint-stock Bank of Scotland, founded the following year, later became the first bank to issue £1 notes (1704).

In 1698 the need for further war subsidies led to the creation of the 'national debt', comprising loans from private lenders secured against revenue. This debt was administered by the Bank of England from 1751.

By 1800 there were about 470 private banks in London and the provinces, and their numbers were later swollen by the emergence of specialist merchant banks. Like their predecessors the London goldsmiths of the 17th century, they issued their own banknotes. The smaller 'country' banks were vulnerable to 'runs' – sudden calls by investors on their savings, provoked by financial panics. But during the first half of the 19th century the system was strengthened by basing all note issue in England on the Bank of England, and by the setting up of other joint-stock banks (at first allowed only outside a 65-mile radius of London). Scottish banks could still issue their own notes.

From 1890 the Bank of England handled foreign exchange and held the country's gold reserves (the gold standard, which meant that sterling was fully convertible into gold, was adopted in 1816). It also came to dictate the general rate of interest and support other banks in times of crisis, becoming the touchstone of financial security for the country as a whole. It was nationalized in 1946. The smaller banks, meanwhile, had amalgamated, reducing the number to only forty by 1914.

THE SOUTH SEA BUBBLE (***right***), *a cartoon of 1720. Massive investment in South Sea Company stock was followed by the bursting of the 'bubble', and the ruin of several banks.*

JOHN BULL AT HIS STUDIES (***below right***), *a cartoon of 1799. The nation was constitutionally averse to taxation. The first income tax (1790s) provoked an uproar of protest.*

INSURANCE: THE BEGINNINGS

The earliest insurance companies in Britain were those protecting private householders from the risks of fire and merchants from losses at sea. Underwriters in marine insurance met at Lloyd's coffee house in London in the late 17th century. Lloyd's became, and remains, a dominant power in the insurance world. The early fire insurance companies, such as the Sun, the Royal and the Alliance, date from the 18th century. They had their own fire brigades and issued moulded lead 'marks' (***above***) which were displayed on the front walls of 'protected' houses. There is an excellent collection of fire marks in the museum of local history at Huntly House in Edinburgh.

THE BANK OF ENGLAND (***below***), *rebuilt by Sir John Soane (from 1788) and again between 1925 and 1939. Its stock, and the celebrated Consols (government securities), were the mainstay of the Victorian investor. The Bank's Governor and a crowd of investors are portrayed in* Dividend Day *(**above**), 1859, painted by G.E. Hicks.*

JOHN MAYNARD KEYNES (***below***). *Keynes's advocacy of government control of the economy revolutionized economic thinking in the 1930s.*

THE STOCK EXCHANGE (***right***) *in the City of London. Stock Exchange prices are the barometer of the financial climate. Big investors now include the insurance companies, the banks, the building societies, the pension funds and overseas governments.*

Investment and credit

Investment, no less than banking, has played an important part in the commercial and industrial development of Britain. An early commercial institution was London's Royal Exchange (built in the reign of Elizabeth I), where dealers and merchants congregated for business. In the 17th and 18th centuries frantic financial speculation, often inspired by the emergence of new markets overseas, led at times to spectacular collapses, such as the failure of the South Sea Company in 1721, which ruined thousands of investors. Brokers did not gain respectability until the creation in 1773 of the City of London Stock Exchange, which gave financiers and industrialists an organized framework for raising money for investment. The formation of 'limited liability' companies after 1855 encouraged investment by reducing the shareholders' financial responsibility.

British finance today is founded increasingly upon credit. Even the currency is based on trust: the gold standard was abandoned in 1931, and the real value of coins has been progressively reduced. The credit card society has immensely simplified transactions, yet increasing financial sophistication has done nothing to solve the major problem of rampant inflation, which is likely to bedevil the country for many years to come. The country's financial difficulties are so complex that they have not been convincingly analysed, let alone solved.

Taxation in the modern age

Until the 19th century the Land Tax and customs and excise duties provided the principal source of government revenue. However, the need to subsidize the Napoleonic Wars brought about the introduction of income tax. Abandoned in 1816, it was reimposed by Sir Robert Peel in 1842 and gradually became a major source of revenue, particularly after the two World Wars, when rates of income tax were greatly increased.

Excise duties on tobacco and alcohol have also played a major part in the economy, while most sales and services, since 1971, have been subject to Value Added Tax. There is now a formidable range of revenue-raising taxes, including estate or 'death' duties, Corporation Tax and Capital Gains Tax, all of which are subject to readjustment in government budgets disclosed by the Chancellor of the Exchequer. These annual (more recently, biennial) financial statements are almost traditionally the object of nation-wide complaint.

CONNECTIONS
Commerce: 100–101 *Britain in the world marketplace*
Conspicuous consumption: 96–7 *Wealth*
Retailing: 102–3 *Reaching the consumer*
Taxation and royal wealth: 72–3 *The Civil War*

GILT-ETCHED ARMOUR (*c. 1600*): *a symbol of aristocratic wealth and power. The armour was made for Thomas Sackville, Lord Buckhurst.*

WEALTH IN STONE: *Hardwick Hall, Derbys., an Elizabethan mansion built for Bess of Hardwick, Countess of Shrewsbury. Her monogram,* ES, *is prominent on the parapets.*

THE RITZ HOTEL, *Piccadilly, London, in the 1930s: a lady inspects the luncheon list. Among those who kept suites in the hotel at this period were the Aga Khan and the Earl of Carnarvon (for whom the Ritz was a luxurious London home for over 50 years).*

A 'COMING OUT' BALL (***left***). *Society débutantes were once presented at court during the 'season'. Only the very rich can now meet the cost of a début.*

For much of Britain's history, land was the most important source of wealth. The estates of the great landed magnates provided large incomes in the form of rents and from the sale of produce. Property ownership was the basis of political power and local reputation.

Another source of profit was commerce. Merchants filled positions of local authority (such as mayor and alderman) and frequently channelled some of their resources into the endowment of

WEALTH AND ILLUSION. *What looks like a room in a Victorian neo-Jacobean mansion is in fact a lounge in a* P & O *cruising yacht, the* Viceroy of India, *launched in 1928.*

WEALTH AT THE SPIN OF A WHEEL, *in a London casino. British gambling is strictly controlled by law.*

ELTON JOHN IN SPLENDOUR (***below***): *money from music. The clichés of wealth – including furs and a pampered pet – are here treated half-ironically.*

important public buildings such as almshouses, guildhalls and churches. From the earliest times there was some intermarriage between merchant and landed families: the one provided wealth, while the other furnished social prestige which wealth alone could never entirely command.

From Tudor times onwards, city merchants, wealthy financiers and successful royal officials often translated wealth into status by the acquisition of broad acres. However, the sources of landed wealth were relatively static, whereas the possibilities in domestic and external trade were growing at a rapid rate.

In the late 18th century there were between 500 and 600 families (mostly landowners, merchants and bankers) with incomes of more than £2,500 per year. Their ranks were swollen by 'nabobs' of the East India Company, and by the West Indian sugar planters and slave traders. But it was the industrial revolution which brought a radical shift in the balance of British wealth. Many of the wealthy entrepreneurs of the textile, coal and iron industries were men of humble origin. Spectacular examples of financial gain came particularly with the railway boom of the mid-19th century. Thomas Brassey, who built railways both in Britain and abroad, left a fortune of £5 million when he died in 1870. By the end of the 19th century, the servicing of existing wealth through banking, finance and investment was also generating riches (for example, for the Rothschilds).

ART AS INVESTMENT: *a scene at Christie's auction rooms, March 1981. The painting, by Sir Lawrence Alma-Tadema, sold for £110,000.*

During the 20th century, the base of wealth has broadened still further. One of the richest men in the early part of the century was William Morris (Lord Nuffield), the motor car manufacturer. Family fortunes have also been founded in the consumer industries and in property.

Before the Great War, 5 per cent of the population held about 50 per cent of all wealth. Even in 1975 the latter figure was still 35 per cent. Although personal fortunes are still plentiful (many of them inherited), the most substantial owners are corporate (for example, banks and building societies), and millions of small savers and investors participate in a complex system in which wealth is managed and circulated.

CONNECTIONS

Royal wealth: 58–9 *Monarchy and display;* **214–15** *Royal retreats*
Wealth and land: 92–3 *Landownership*
Wealth and politics: 76–7 *Parliament/Abuse and reform*
Wealth and property: 208–9 *The great country houses*
Wealth and wool: 142–3 *The wool trade*

The imperial experience

THE TAKING OF QUEBEC, *1959. In the 18th century, power meant wealth. When the daring British general James Wolfe wrested Quebec from the French, Canada's fur, fish and timber were secured for Britain.*

Britain's policy of overseas expansion began with the seafaring and trading activities of the Tudors. In the reign of Henry VII, two explorers who were searching for a western passage to the Far East – John and Sebastian Cabot – discovered instead the valuable cod-fishing grounds of Newfoundland. Under Elizabeth I merchants began to explore new and distant markets, while adventurers such as Sir Francis Drake, Sir Martin Frobisher and Sir Walter Raleigh made sallies against the imperial power of Spain and Portugal. Although no successful colonies were founded in the Elizabethan period, Sir Humphrey Gilbert made attempts in Newfoundland and Raleigh in Virginia. Concerted colonization began in the 17th century when groups of merchants, such as the Virginia Company and Massachusetts Bay Company, financed and organized emigration to North America, with the object of creating overseas markets for British goods and of importing from the New World products that could be re-exported in Europe.

Religious persecution was also one of the reasons behind emigration. The Pilgrim Fathers' embarkation in the *Mayflower* in 1620 was only one episode in a movement that carried almost 100,000 settlers to New England and Virginia in the years before the Civil War. The West Indies also began to be settled, by a mixture of ambitious emigrants of all classes, indentured servants and increasing numbers of negro slaves brought from Africa in British and other ships. In the East, the East India Company, founded in 1600, obtained a monopoly for trade with the East Indies, but soon shifted its attention to the Indian mainland, where it ran a private army to defend its commercial interests.

The first British Empire

During the long series of naval wars with the Dutch under Oliver Cromwell and Charles II, and then against the French and the Spanish, Britain gradually acquired an increasing share of the lucrative Atlantic and Eastern trades, and with it more and more overseas possessions. By the Treaty of Utrecht (1713) Gibraltar was taken from Spain, and became an important British naval base. By this time Britain had gained most of the eastern seaboard of North America, as well as Jamaica (seized from the Spanish in 1665). Following the Seven Years' War (1756–63) virtually the whole of Canada was wrested from the French, and French power in India was also destroyed. This 'first British Empire', already of vast extent, brought great fortunes to the nabobs of the East India Company, the West Indian sugar planters and the slave traders who served the plantations of the West Indies and the southern colonies of America.

However, a major setback came in the 1760s, when the thirteen colonies of North America voiced objections to being taxed by a parliament 3,000 miles away to pay for an army whose purpose (defence against the French) seemed to have been eliminated. Raising the cry of 'no taxation without representation', in 1775 they began the war that led to the granting of independence (1783). The loss of these colonies had a profound effect upon Britain's colonial policy. In India the East India Company was brought under tighter control, but the general feeling was that it was wisest to avoid the responsibility of founding further settlements. In Canada the Durham Report of 1839 laid the basis for eventual self-rule.

Ruling the waves

Such imperialistic caution was relatively short-lived. Britain emerged from the Napoleonic wars (1803–1815) as the strongest naval and colonial power in the world. In spite of the emergence of the doctrine of Free Trade, which might have discouraged imperialism, expansion continued, with the acquisition of further trading concessions and of possessions such as Aden (1839) and Hong Kong (1842), which became important as telegraph and coaling stations. Australia and New Zealand, claimed for Britain by Captain Cook in 1770, gradually developed from penal colonies into fully fledged settlements, to which emigration was accelerated after the discovery of gold in New South Wales and Victoria in 1851.

The centrepiece of the Victorian Empire was India, whose vast population provided a vital market for British manufactured goods. The British soon began to westernize the subcontinent, stamping out Indian customs (often with great insensitivity) and introducing, during Lord Dalhousie's term as Governor-General (1848–56), a cheap postal service and telegraphs, as well as a network of roads and railways. The Indian Mutiny of 1857–8 among native troops (sepoys) resulted in the final destruction of the power of the East India Company, but left India even more firmly part of the Empire. Its role was confirmed in 1876 when Victoria assumed the title Empress of India.

The late 19th century was the era of the 'scramble for Africa', fired partly by missionary and civilizing zeal, as well as by the explorers' appetite for adventure and by the discovery of gold and diamonds. Britain extended its territories in Egypt, the Sudan and the north-east and made new gains in south and west Africa. Native powers such as those of the Ashanti and the Zulus were broken, and revolts, such as that led by the Mahdi in the Sudan, put down. In 1899 Britain found itself engaged in a war against the independent Dutch settlers of south Africa – the Boers. Initial disasters exposed the weakness of Britain's military machine, but by 1902 the Boers were defeated and their territories taken over.

The return of the Orange Free State and the Transvaal to the Boers in 1906, and their subsequent incorporation into the self-governing Union of South Africa, were part of a general movement towards decolonization. By the First World War the major 'white' colonies had been granted Dominion status (that is, virtual self-rule). By this time there were already the first stirrings of nationalist movements in India and Africa. The Second World War undermined the British presence in the Far East, and the eventual relegation of Britain to a second-rate power led inevitably to the transformation of most of the Empire into a Commonwealth of independent states. India

THE EMIGRANTS' FAREWELL, *1853. The far-flung colonies, in this case Australia, offered many opportunities for British emigrants.*

ROBERT CLIVE OF INDIA, *at this stage (1765) the real ruler of Bengal, is authorized to collect land revenue by Shah Alam.*

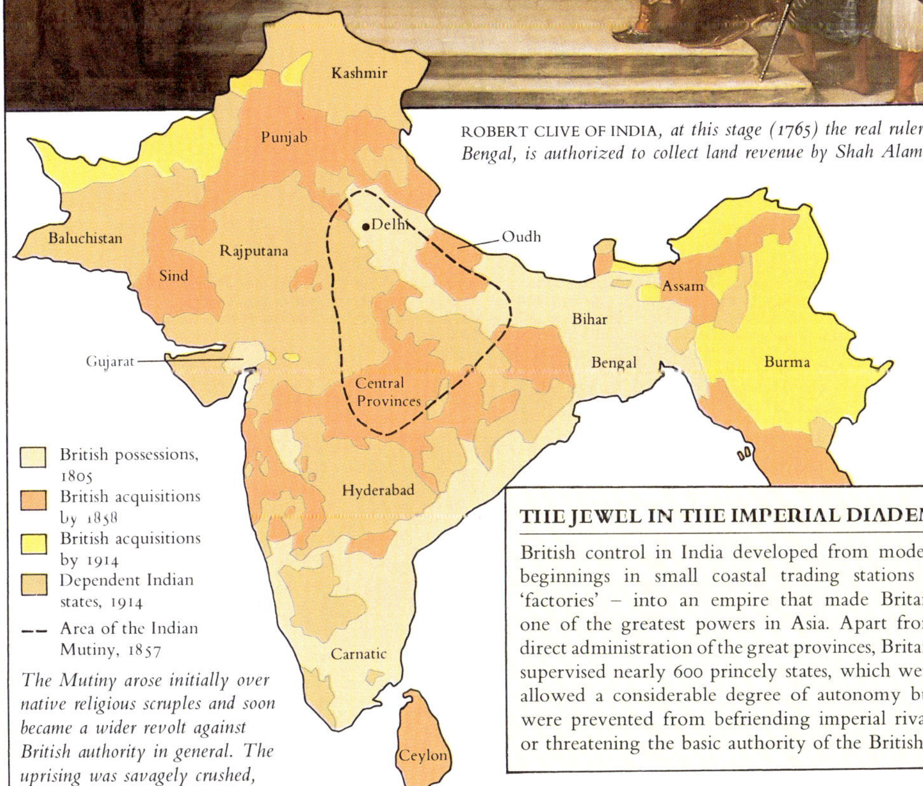

The Mutiny arose initially over native religious scruples and soon became a wider revolt against British authority in general. The uprising was savagely crushed, but afterwards British administrative policy took more account of Indian feelings.

THE JEWEL IN THE IMPERIAL DIADEM

British control in India developed from modest beginnings in small coastal trading stations – 'factories' – into an empire that made Britain one of the greatest powers in Asia. Apart from direct administration of the great provinces, Britain supervised nearly 600 princely states, which were allowed a considerable degree of autonomy but were prevented from befriending imperial rivals or threatening the basic authority of the British.

THE BRITISH EMPIRE, *on which the sun never set, was approaching its height in 1914 (**below**). (The map does not show the small island possessions.)*

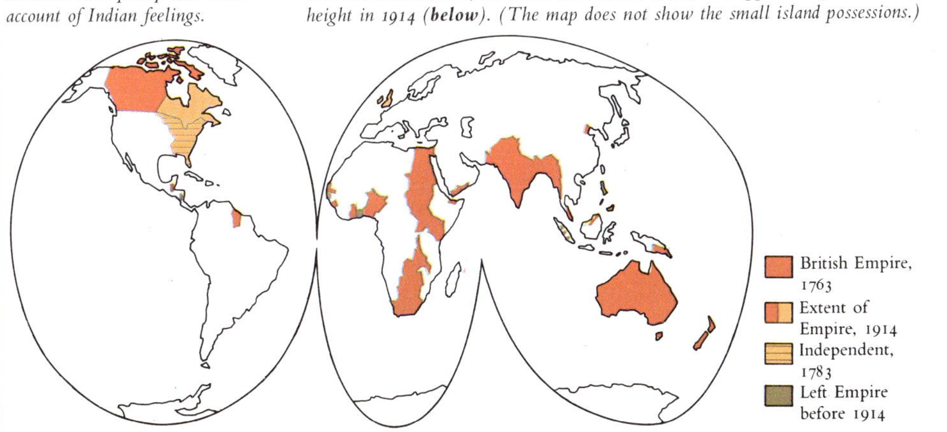

THE ZULU WAR, *1879. Of all the wars fought against Bantu peoples in Africa, the one against the Zulus was hardest. This painting shows the Zulu victory at Isandhlwana (Natal).*

achieved independence in 1947, becoming two nations – India and Pakistan.

There were only four independent states in Africa in 1945 but the 'wind of change' – in Harold Macmillan's phrase – soon began to blow, liberating first Ghana (1957), then Nigeria (1960). When Britain made a last imperial sortie in Egypt in 1956 after the nationalization of the Suez Canal, it provoked almost total international disapproval. The imperial heyday was now long past.

INDEPENDENCE CEREMONY IN KENYA. *Jomo Kenyatta, here reviewing a guard of honour, was prominent in Kenya's independence struggle and became his country's first president (1964).*

CONNECTIONS
Empire and trade: 100–101 *Britain in the world marketplace*
Imperial imports: 160–63 *Cotton*
Maritime Britain: 178–9 *Shipbuilding*
The Royal Navy: 122–3 *The armed forces*

Britain in the world marketplace

Britain has a long and prosperous history as a trading nation. Even before the coming of the Romans, Phoenician traders bought tin and other minerals from Cornwall, bringing Britain into the European network of commerce. As a province of the Roman Empire, the southern part of Britain became a source of precious metals, tin, corn and other products, and in turn imported Mediterranean wine, oil, pottery and glass. Similar contacts were maintained after the Anglo-Saxon and Viking invasions. With the Norman conquest trade relations became more heavily orientated towards France and the Low Countries. England's principal export, sold in exchange for wine and finished cloth, was raw wool, which in later centuries was overshadowed by woollen cloth as the mainstay of trade with the Continent.

Merchant adventurers and trade wars

English merchants, from the 15th century onwards, played an important role in opening up new markets overseas. Increasingly, their ships ranged the oceans of the world from the Americas to the Far East, in fierce rivalry with traders from Holland, Spain, Portugal and France. The Merchant Adventurers (a company chartered in 1407) controlled much of England's overseas trade up to the mid-16th century, but there was plenty of scope for privateers attracted by the prospect of easy riches across the Atlantic – gold and silver in America, tobacco and rum in the West Indies.

The so-called 'commercial revolution' came in the 17th century, the age of the great trading companies. Prominent among these were the Levant Company (1581), which took cloth to the east Mediterranean and returned with cotton, currants, figs and spices, and the East India Company (1600), which exchanged gold for cotton and spices. The position of the British traders was threatened, however, by the Dutch, who were making a handsome profit carrying goods to and from England. To remedy this situation, the Navigation Acts (1651, 1660 and 1663) reserved colonial trade to English shipping and demanded that imports from Europe had to be transported in English ships or ships of their country of origin. These measures prompted a series of naval wars with the Dutch, which resulted in the capture of the lucrative carrying trade of the Baltic and north Europe. War with the Spanish in 1653–9 extended the British colonies in the Americas and gave Britain control of the sugar market. Such colonial products were now beginning to play a crucial part in the British economy.

The 18th and 19th centuries

By the mid-18th century one of the most important sources of commercial wealth for Britain was the 'triangular trade' between the coasts of Africa and the colonies of the West Indies and America. In return for African slaves British ships were loaded with sugar, tobacco and cotton which were sold throughout Europe. Another profitable triangular route was followed by ships bearing Cheshire salt to Newfoundland, where they bought cod which was taken to be sold in the plantation colonies.

After the Americans achieved independence in 1776, Britain's interests turned more strongly towards India and the Far East. New trading-post colonies were established (in Singapore and Hong Kong) and the closed market of China was subjected to determined assaults. However, the United States proved to have a great appetite for British exports, and the West Indies remained a profitable colonial possession.

Britain's naval supremacy, confirmed by victory in the Napoleonic Wars (1803–1815), gave her virtual dominance in the world marketplace of the

SIR THOMAS SMYTHE, *1616. A leading entrepreneur in his time, Smythe promoted trading expeditions to America and Russia and became the first Governor of the East India Company (1600–20).*

ANGLO-DUTCH WARRING IN THE MEDWAY (**below**), *1667. The Dutch were zealous rivals to British traders in the American colonies and in the Baltic, until their defeat in a series of naval battles.*

THE EXPORT OF WOOL *played a crucial role in England's economy in the Middle Ages. The trade was often carried by foreign merchant ships but, from the 14th century, it was increasingly controlled by the English Company of the Staple.*

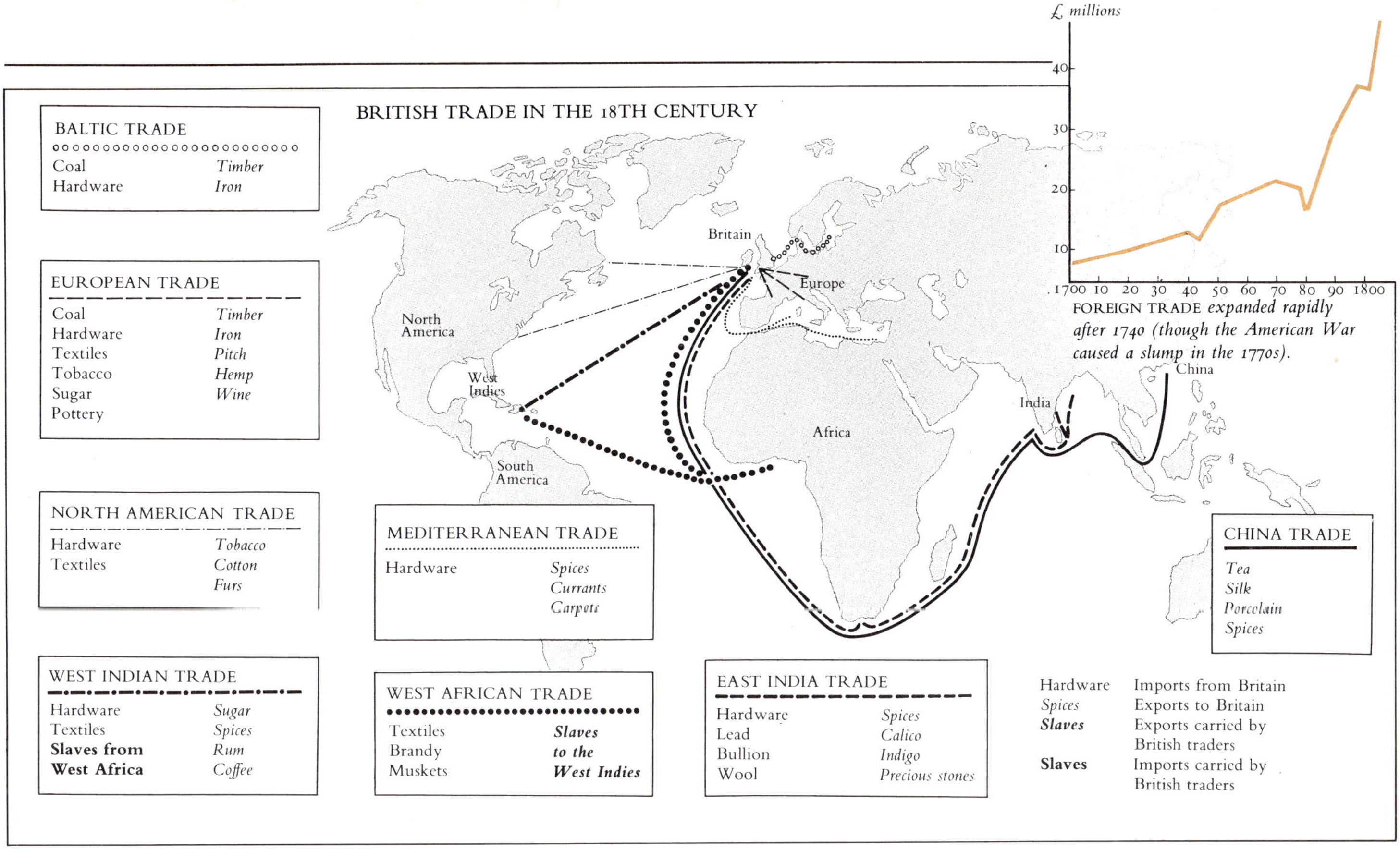

FOREIGN TRADE *expanded rapidly after 1740 (though the American War caused a slump in the 1770s).*

THE SLAVE TRADE

The slave traders, setting forth from Liverpool, Bristol and Glasgow to Africa and the West Indies, reaped huge rewards. Over 50 years the cost of a slave escalated from about £15 to £40. The trade was eventually made illegal in 1807, after a long campaign.

574. Kingston, July 11, 1788.
For Sale,
On TUESDAY the 22d INST
ON BOARD THE SHIP
COMMERCE,
Robert Brown, Master,
FROM GOLD COAST,
162 SLAVES,
By A. LINDO.

SLAVES FOR SALE *in Jamaica.*

BRANDING SLAVES, *a 19th-century engraving.*

BRITAIN ENTERS EUROPE, *1973. As Prime Minister, Edward Heath brought Britain into one of the world's most powerful trading blocs.*

19th century. The industrial revolution meant that a vast range of manufactured goods, such as cotton fabrics, iron and steel and hardware, could be produced very rapidly to supply needs that could not be met by any other country. It was this exporting success that lay beneath the mid-Victorian faith in Free Trade, which was reflected in the repeal of the Corn Laws of 1846 (that is, the lifting of heavy import duties on foreign corn) and in an Anglo-French Free Trade treaty.

By 1870 Britain had a third of the world trade in manufactured goods, although foreign rivals such as the United States and Germany were beginning to industrialize and to give more serious competition. This share had diminished to about a seventh by 1914, but the vast empire still provided an assurance of prosperity, and banking and insurance overseas brought in substantial 'invisible' earnings. London remained the commercial and financial capital of the world.

The European trade bloc

The First World War was a crushing set-back to British commerce, owing to the loss of overseas markets and the debility of industry. Old established export trades such as cotton and shipbuilding collapsed in the economic depression of the 1930s, and the process of adjustment to new industries – for example, motor vehicles, artificial fibres, aircraft and electronics – was painfully slow.

The next war brought further difficulties. By 1945 the country was virtually bankrupt; there was a massive export drive and considerable austerity at home. In the event, rapid growth of international trade caused an improvement, and by joining with European trade blocs – EFTA (the European Free Trade Area) in the 1960s and the EEC (European Economic Community) in 1973 – Britain found a compensation for the loss of empire and the collapse of her industrial supremacy.

CONNECTIONS
The dockyards: 230–31 *Ports*
The Empire: 98–9 *The imperial experience*
Textiles: 142–3 *The wool trade;* **160–61** *Cotton*
Trade at home: 102–3 *Reaching the consumer*

Reaching the consumer

The modern term 'marketing' suggests an almost scientific process of matching goods to consumers' needs and to current preferences. It is, however, a development of relatively recent date. For centuries, most of the population depended on their domestic resources for most of their daily needs, using markets or annual fairs (such as the famous one at St Ives) to sell surplus produce or buy luxury goods. In many rural areas, the travelling pedlar or 'chapman' provided the main source of items which could not be produced locally.

The growth of shops

The first shops appeared in the 14th century, and usually took the form of a room on the ground floor of a house, with a workshop attached. Goods were sold through the front window, whose lowered shutter served as a counter during the daytime. Gradually, the medieval-style shops gave way in London, Brighton, Bath and other towns to glass-fronted establishments designed to attract the wealthy passer-by. Fancy goods, drapery, hats and tobacco were retailed in this way, but everyday foodstuffs were supplied largely from the marketplace and by house-to-house tradesmen.

The mass-production techniques of the industrial revolution, the vast array of goods which now became available and the increased spending-power of wage-earners added up to a retailing boom which made shopkeepers better off than craftsmen. An important 19th-century development was the birth of the Co-operative movement, whose first store was founded in Rochdale in 1844: the principle was to benefit the working classes by diverting profits to the customers in proportion to the money spent.

The entrance of big business into the world of

A VICTORIAN BUTCHER'S SHOP (***right***), *reconstructed at the Blists Hill Open-Air Museum in the Ironbridge Gorge (Salop).*

A MARKET CROSS. *The fine example at Chichester, W. Sussex, is one of many that still survive today, as testimony to a formerly thriving marketplace.*

ADVERTISING OF THE VICTORIAN PERIOD. *Many early posters have a period charm that is irresistibly appealing to modern collectors.*

W.H. SMITH & SON: THE ORIGINS

William Henry Smith (with his brother Henry Edward) took over his father's news vendor's concern in London in 1816, and organized a rapid country delivery service that put the traditional mail coach service to shame. Smith's son, also W.H., bought the bookstall rights offered by the London & North-Western Railway in 1848. The first WHS bookstall was on Euston Station. Before long the market had been captured on other lines. By 1935 there were 1,115 bookstalls, and meanwhile the firm had embarked on a successful policy of diversification.

THE BOOKSTALLS OF W.H. SMITH, *such as this one in London's Liverpool Street Station (**left**, in 1921), sold papers and books (and even, in the mid-19th century, candles and rugs) to the railway-travelling public. The firm has also developed newspaper distribution houses and lending libraries. Today, the high street bookshops (**above**) are just one aspect of a multi-faceted operation.*

THE COVERED MARKET, CARDIFF (*left*). *Many early markets have survived in an altered form. Even markets that are housed in permanent buildings often have a pleasing ambience of barter, neighbourliness and local colour.*

FREEMAN'S MAIL-ORDER CATALOGUE, *1912. The mail order concept has a late 19th-century origin.*

DOOR-TO-DOOR *in the 1950s. Delivery services are now threatened by the supermarkets. Even the early morning milk round cannot be taken for granted.*

THE MODERN DEPARTMENT STORE: *the John Lewis branch at Milton Keynes. Lifts and escalators ensure an efficient movement of shoppers from one floor to another.*

shopping was heralded by the coming of the chain store. The pioneer of the grocery chain store was Thomas Lipton, whose first shop opened in Glasgow in 1872. Apart from tea, his specialities were cheap bacon and ham, supplied by his own pig stockyards in Chicago. By 1898 he had 245 branches throughout Britain.

The later 19th century was also the period of the earliest department stores, beginning with Whiteley's in London in 1863. The concept of providing a wide range of goods under one roof for a largely middle-class clientele rapidly spread all over Britain. The department stores often employed legions of assistants: Harrods, for example, had a staff of 4,000 by 1908.

Advertising and credit

One of the earliest forms of advertising, apart from signboards, was the distribution of engraved 'shop bills', which could be handed to customers. By the early 18th century, local newspapers carried advertisements for shops and particular products, but it was not until the latter part of the 19th century that advertising was practised on a large scale. Much use was made of eye-catching handbills and hoardings, whose claims for a product could be wildly hyperbolic. Custom was also boosted by gimmicks: for example, the opening of branches of Boots the chemists in the Nottingham area in the 1880s and 1890s was celebrated by brass bands and colourful parades. Competition for the customer inspired every conceivable device to achieve extra sales. New techniques included mail order, successfully operated by the department stores, and hire purchase, promoted in the 1860s by the manufacturers of sewing machines.

The new consumers

Even during the depressed inter-war years, retailing enjoyed a dynamic rate of growth. Between 1918 and 1939 almost a thousand new stores were built, and chain stores began to appear on every high street. The replacement of horse-drawn carts by motorized delivery vehicles was of immense benefit to the industry. Britain's first self-service supermarket opened in London in 1950, and five years later advertising opportunities were enormously increased by the introduction of commercial television. Other features of the post-war shopping scene have been the disappearance of many small shops, the spread of covered shopping precincts, and the proliferation of credit systems.

CONNECTIONS
The British diet: 184–5 *Food in Britain*
The impact of the railways: 264–5 *The railway revolution*
Markets: 224–5 *Market towns*
Roads: 268–9 *The road network*

Courts of the land

There are two distinct systems of law in Britain: one governing England and Wales (with local variations in the Isle of Man), and one governing Scotland. In contrast to the English tradition, which is based on a body of precedents, Scottish law owes much to the codification of abstract principles.

Both systems have their own court structures, but they are alike in having separate courts to administer criminal law and civil law. Broadly speaking, criminal law is concerned with wrongs against the Crown, civil law with disputes between private individuals.

The sanction of the criminal courts is to punish, while that of the civil courts is to award compensation. However, this distinction is blurred, as the same assault could give rise both to civil proceedings for damages and to criminal proceedings, which may result in a fine or imprisonment. Criminal courts, moreover, can now award compensation to the victim.

THE COURT OF THE KING'S BENCH, *Westminster Hall, in the 14th century. The five judges are each wearing a coif (white linen cap): it was not until the 17th century that wigs were introduced.*

The criminal courts

Some 97 per cent of all criminal cases in the English system are dealt with in the 900 or so magistrates' courts. Generally, these are less serious crimes, but in weightier cases such as rape or murder the magistrates hold a preliminary 'commital' hearing to determine whether there is sufficient evidence to justify sending the accused to the Crown court for trial by judge and jury.

The vast majority of magistrates (also known as justices of the peace, or JPs) are unpaid and without legal qualifications, but in some of the larger urban areas there are professional 'stipendiary' magistrates; the first of these was probably the novelist Henry Fielding (1704–54), appointed to Bow Street in 1748. Stipendaries usually sit alone, whereas lay magistrates sit as a bench of three.

THE OLD BAILEY: *a murder trial in progress, in the early 20th century. London's Old Bailey, built on the site of the old Newgate prison, is the chief criminal court for Greater London and parts of Surrey, Kent and Essex.*

SOLICITORS AND BARRISTERS. *The distinction dates back to 1292, when Edward I ordered the judges to appoint 'apprentices' and 'advocates'. The solicitor (**above**, in a Victorian painting) has many functions, including advising clients on legal matters, drawing up documents and preparing cases for barristers. A major role of a barrister is to present cases in the higher courts (**right**).*

The origins of the magistrates' court probably lie in the Anglo-Saxon 'moot courts'. 'Knights of the Peace' were first appointed in 1195 and 'Keepers of the Peace' in 1264, but their duties were largely those of administrators and police officers. In the 14th century, however, the judicial function came to predominate. The office of JP in its modern sense began with the Justice of the Peace Act of 1361.

The more serious transgressions of criminal law are the concern of the Crown courts, which also handle appeals against magistrates' decisions. The 90 or so Crown courts in the English system were established as recently as 1971, replacing the old assizes and quarter sessions whose history stretched back to Norman times. In 1166 the Assize of Clarendon ordered travelling judges to enquire into murder, robbery, larceny and the harbouring of criminals, and thereafter the Assizes had an uninterrupted history of eight centuries.

On a plea of not guilty, a case in a Crown court will be heard by a judge, whose function is to interpret and explain the law and pass the sentence. But the guilt or innocence of the accused is decided not by the judge but by the jury. The beginnings of the jury system pre-date the Norman conquest. Originally called to testify to their members' local knowledge, juries developed along modern lines in the 13th century to replace earlier forms of trial by battle and ordeal. From the 16th to the 18th centuries, prisoners who refused to face trial would be forced to plead by the torture of 'pressing with weights' (*peine forte et dure*). Not until the very end of Victoria's reign was the defendant allowed to give evidence. In 1968, the need for a unanimous verdict was modified: with the leave of the judge, a majority of at least 10–2 may now be accepted.

The civil courts

There are about 330 county courts. Although their remote origins are pre-conquest, they date in their modern form from 1846, when they were established to deal relatively quickly and cheaply with smaller claims (the financial limit has recently been raised to £5,000). A major proportion of their work is now concerned with the law of landlord-tenant relations and with undefended

SCOTTISH JUDGES, *on their way to Parliament House, Edinburgh, in the annual procession to mark the new term of the Court of Session and the High Court of the Justiciary. The robes are of ancient design.*

THE SCOTTISH SYSTEM

Scotland's independence, hostility to England and consequent alliance with various European powers contributed to the establishment of a legal system that was greatly influenced by Continental and Roman law. The emphasis was on abstract principle, in contrast to the English tradition. The systematization of Scots law was largely the work of Viscount Stair, in the 1680s. When the Act of Union drew England and Scotland under one Crown in 1707, the separate identity of the Scottish courts was confirmed for all time.

The supreme criminal court in Scotland is the High Court of Justiciary, created in 1672. This is both an appeal court, with three or more judges presiding, and a trial court, with judge and jury. The inferior criminal court is the sheriff court, which has its origins in the early 12th century. Here, procedure is either 'solemn' (that is, with a jury) or 'summary' (without a jury), and one peculiarity of a summary conviction (which has occasioned criticism) is that there can be no appeal to a higher court except in a question of law.

Scottish juries have 15 members, and a bare majority can convict. In England and Wales, most prosecutions are brought by the police, but the Scottish procedure differs radically from this in that the responsibility rests with the Lord Advocate and the Crown Office (in Edinburgh), and at a local level the Procurator Fiscal, who receives complaints from the police.

The Court of Session, which was established in 1532, is the supreme Scottish civil court. It is divided into two parts: the Inner House, concerned mostly with appeals, and the Outer House, which hears trials. Since 1712, in civil proceedings (but not in criminal cases) there has been a right of appeal to the House of Lords. The lower civil court is, again, the sheriff court.

Among the various specialized courts of the Scottish system is the land court, which deals primarily with agricultural tenancies, particularly in the Highlands.

divorce (and related financial and property disputes). Cases are usually decided by a judge alone but small claims are settled by a registrar.

The history of the superior civil courts is extremely complex, for until the 19th century there were various courts competing for the same jurisdiction. The present structure was created by the Judicature Acts of 1873–5. There are now three divisions of the High Court: the Family Division, dealing with matrimonial, adoption, wardship and guardianship cases; the Chancery Division, concerned with trusts, estates and mortgages; and the Queen's Bench Division, which handles most other litigation. Until 1857 matrimonial and probate cases (that is, cases involving the authenticity of wills) were under the aegis of the Church courts. Before 1854 a jury always sat in civil cases, but now this happens only rarely – for example, in libel and slander cases.

THE ROYAL COURTS OF JUSTICE, *The Strand, London (**right**). The buildings, designed by G.E. Street and opened in 1882, house all the divisions of the High Court of Justice.*

Appeals

The Court of Appeal was founded in 1873 to replace a muddled system whereby appeals could be taken to the House of Lords, the Privy Council or the Court of Appeal in Chancery. Three judges usually sit in the Court of Appeal, and may include the Lord Chancellor, the Lord Chief Justice or the Master of the Rolls – offices that all have their origins in the Middle Ages.

The final court of appeal in both civil and criminal cases is the House of Lords, whose function in this respect rests on a long tradition of parliamentary involvement in the dispensation of justice. Until the end of the 19th century the entire House could sit in judgment, but since then cases have been heard by a committee (usually five in number) of trained lawyers. The House is now almost exclusively an appeals court, but until 1948 a peer had the right, enshrined in Magna Carta, to a trial by his fellows.

Other courts

Ancient English legal history is crowded with a fascinating array of small local courts. Most of these (such as the piepowder courts – literally, the courts of the dusty feet – dealing with local market disputes) are now obsolete, but there are others (for example, the New Forest Verderers' Court, controlling forest law) which still meet.

Among the ancient judicial bodies still in existence today is the coroner's court. As well as investigating suspicious deaths the coroner, whose office dates back to the 12th century, is also concerned with treasure trove, and in London can look into the outbreak of fires.

CONNECTIONS
Forest law: 30–31 *Woodlands and forests*
The House of Lords: 68–9 *Parliament/The beginnings*
Justices of the Peace: 80–81 *Local government and the Civil Service*
Law enforcement: 106–7 *Crime and punishment*
Mining law: 152–5 *The bowels of the earth*

Crime and punishment

A TREADWHEEL *in a Victorian prison. There is one at Beaumaris Gaol, Anglesey (now a museum).*

A SPELL IN THE PILLORY, *1812* (***left***). *The effect was arbitrary, as the victim might be harmlessly pelted with fruit, or stoned to death.*

Crime in Britain is as old as the earliest communities. The first law codes date from the early Anglo-Saxon kingdoms and contain a system of punishments – usually in the form of money compensation – for murder, theft and other offences. After the Conquest and the organization of England into a more unified nation-state, major and minor justice was administered by manorial courts, local justices of the peace, and Assize Judges who travelled in six (and later eight) 'circuits' of the country. Felonies – the more serious crimes – were usually punished by death, while minor offences – misdemeanours – could be dealt with by fines, whipping, or a spell in the stocks or pillory.

Some attempt was made to fit the punishment to the crime: a thief would often lose a hand, while the penalty for slandering a neighbour was to have the tongue cut out. Witches and heretics were executed with manic cruelty, by being burned at the stake, or hanged, drawn and quartered.

The 18th and 19th centuries

During the 18th century, crime was the occupation of multitudes. Horace Walpole said of London, that 'one is forced to travel even at noon as if one were going into battle'. The severity of the problem led to a great increase in the number of offences for which the death sentence could be exacted. By 1815 it was estimated that there were over 200 'capital' offences on the statute book, ranging down to minor thefts of property worth only a few shillings. For lower levels of crime, the pillory and stocks remained in use until the early 19th century, and whippings continued.

Transportation was practised as early as the 17th century, when Cromwell deported thousands of Irish rebels to the West Indies. From the late 18th century thousands of convicts were sent to penal settlements in Australia and other far-flung colonies. Prison hulks in the Thames estuary and other moorings were also used to house convicted criminals, especially those awaiting transportation.

Growing revulsion at the harshness of the penal system, and particularly at conditions in local gaols, gradually led to reforms. The idea of long-term imprisonment in modernized gaols was championed by humanitarians such as Jeremy Bentham, John Howard and Elizabeth Fry, whose premise was that incarceration might be curative. The old gaols, such as Newgate in London, which was notorious for its stench, were often appallingly unhealthy, ill run and riddled with corruption. Wardens extorted money from their prisoners, and all classes of inmate were mixed together, without regard to age or sex. Prisons were not exempt from window tax (levied from 1696 to 1851), with the result that insufficient windows were provided and the prisoners lived in perpetual gloom.

The spirit of reform led to new government-run prisons (or penitentiaries), of which the first was Millbank in London (opened in 1816). They were designed to prevent communication between inmates, who even in chapel were prevented from seeing each other by wooden screens which allowed them to look only forwards. At exercise

ELIZABETH FRY READING TO PRISONERS (***right***). *Fry's interest in prison welfare dated from 1813, when a fellow Quaker described to her the wretchedness at Newgate. She organized a prison school there and began women's sewing classes. Her reforming ideas were highly influential.*

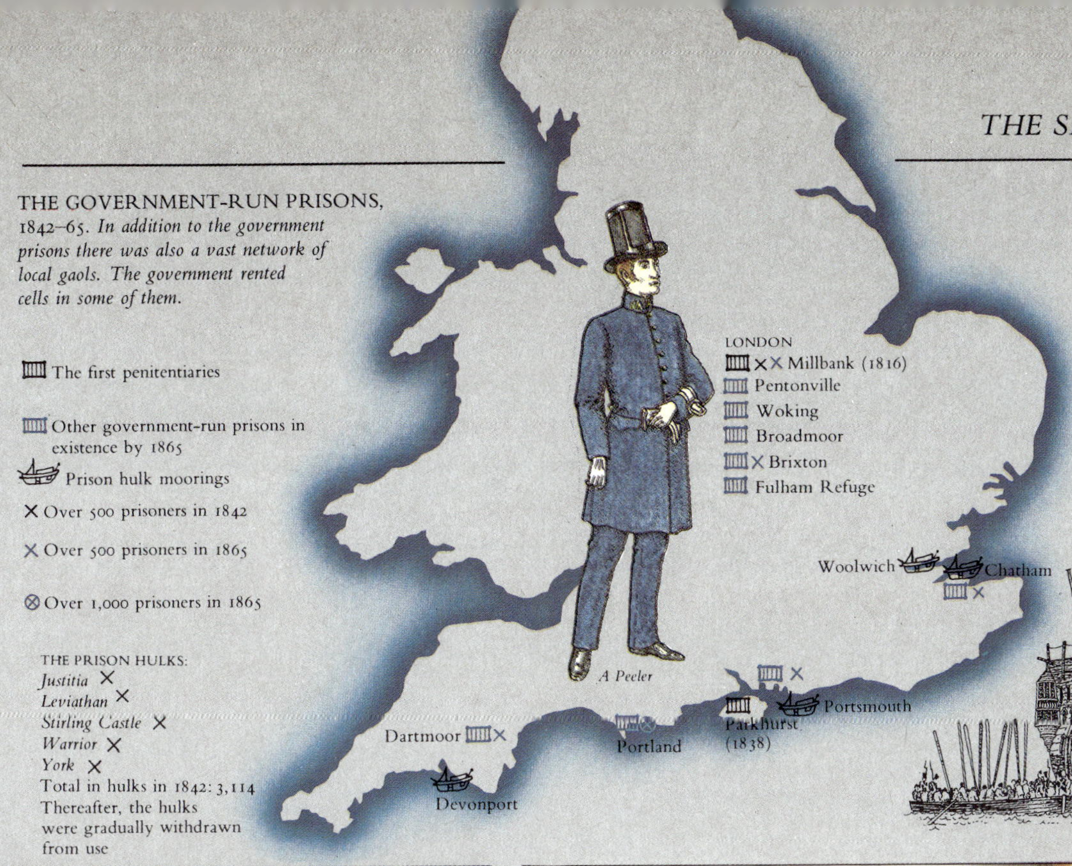

THE GOVERNMENT-RUN PRISONS, 1842–65. *In addition to the government prisons there was also a vast network of local gaols. The government rented cells in some of them.*

A PRISON HULK *at Portsmouth* (***below***). *The hulks were brought into use in 1776, initially as an emergency measure after the American Revolution closed off the penal colonies in Maryland and Virginia. They were used as a base for hard labour, and from time to time shifted their moorings.*

DARTMOOR PRISON, *Devon, originated as a gaol for French prisoners of war in 1809. It was rebuilt for convicts in 1850. The radiating plan was typical of the new Victorian prisons.*

STRANGEWAYS PRISON, MANCHESTER (***left*** *and* ***above***) *as it is today. The building was completed in 1868. The new liberalism suggested by the generous skylight was only part of the story.*

they had to wear masks. Reformation was encouraged through work and strict discipline. Treadmills were often part of prison routine; they were sometimes put to useful purposes such as pumping water or grinding grain, but were mostly merely punitive. In the new context of reform, transportation was obsolete; the last shipload of 451 convicts set sail for Western Australia in 1867, though the prison at Gibraltar had British inmates until 1875.

Law enforcement in the 18th century was haphazard. The traditional means – aged watchmen, unpaid parish constables and a network of informants – were inadequate for the growing towns of the industrial revolution. A first step towards a more disciplined method of crime control came with the creation of the Bow Street Runners in London in the 1740s by Henry Fielding. In 1829 Sir Robert Peel created a corps of civil police in London – 3,000 'Bobbies' or 'Peelers', armed with wooden truncheons. By 1856 every county and borough had to employ a similar force.

Peel also turned his attention to injustices in the Penal Code, which allocated the death penalty to over 200 offences, including sheep stealing. Peel argued that this encouraged offenders to commit murder to escape detection, and succeeded in pressing Parliament to reduce the number of capital offences.

The 20th century

During this century, penal policy has become more liberal in spite of a rise in the amount of crime. Corporal punishment was abolished in 1948, and capital punishment has been discontinued since 1967 (except on the Isle of Man). Borstal and special detention centres now deal with juveniles; and for many lesser offences, probation and community service have replaced imprisonment. Prison conditions have also been liberalized, though Britain retains many obsolete and overcrowded prisons dating from the 19th century.

The modern police force has also become increasingly professionalized and well-equipped, but crime shows no sign of abating. A particularly worrying trend has been the rise of violent crime. Although the police remain unarmed in normal circumstances, all police are now trained to use firearms, and some special squads are armed as a matter of routine. Police-community relations are now considered an important issue, particularly in controlling juvenile crime.

CONNECTIONS
Civil unrest: 108–9 *Riot and revolution*
Justice: 104–5 *Courts of the land*
The London 'rookeries': 248–9 *London*

Riot and revolution

The development of Britain's political character has been relatively peaceful. Nevertheless, various groups have resorted to violence, or had to defend themselves against violent opposition, in order to articulate grievances, put a check on arbitrary rule, or substitute one ruler for another. No less significant were the risings of the common people against injustice or hardship. Most disturbances were highly localized, but the 'mob' was feared, and the leaders of popular revolts often managed to achieve a surprising degree of organization.

THE PEASANTS JOIN FORCES *in the revolt of 1381. Both groups show the royal standard, as they had no wish to be disloyal to the Crown. The State's vengeance was merciful compared with reaction to revolts elsewhere in Europe.*

The great uprisings

The most famous medieval rebellion was the Peasants' Revolt in southern England in 1381, against excessive taxes. The rebels extracted from Richard II an agreement to abolish serfdom, but after their leader Wat Tyler was murdered, fresh disturbances were put down and the main rebels were tried and executed.

In Tudor times, the most serious uprising was the Pilgrimage of Grace, which expressed Catholic opposition in the north to the dissolution of the monasteries. The Catholic-Protestant conflict was to be a leitmotif of British unrest for the next century and a half. Elizabeth I suppressed a Catholic revolt in 1569, and Guy Fawkes's plot to blow up Parliament in 1605 was only one of many such conspiracies. During the Civil War opposed factions were too absorbed in the struggle to worry about the neutral populace, and in Dorset, Wiltshire and Somerset, farmers and labourers rebelled against the exactions of both sides in the so-called 'Clubmen's Revolt'.

A bizarre incident in Catholic-Protestant relations was the Popish Plot of 1678 – a complete fiction retailed to Charles II by Titus Oates, whose claim was that leading Catholics planned to kill the King and put his brother James (later James VII and II) in his place. This was widely believed, and London was stricken with anti-Catholic hysteria. On Charles's death (from a stroke), James took up an uncertain throne, fearing the imminence of rebellion. It came within a year, and was led by the Duke of Monmouth, illegitimate son of Charles II. Monmouth's defeat at Sedgemoor was the last major battle on English soil.

In 1688 James's queen gave birth to a son. The prospect of a Catholic successor led English Protestants to invite the Protestant leader William of Orange to seize power. When he landed in England, James fled to France. The 'Glorious Revolution', which brought William and his wife Mary (James's Protestant daughter) to the throne, was hailed as bloodless, although there were violent repercussions in Ireland and Scotland.

The people's grievances

There were no major rebellions in Britain after the defeat of the Jacobites. However, local disorders and riots were frequent over food prices, agricultural enclosure, recruiting and other issues. The London mob rioted against the Excise Bill (1733) and in support of John Wilkes, radical champion of civil liberties, in the 1760s.

The main themes of disorder in the early 19th century were the demands for parliamentary reform and for the release of the labouring classes from poverty and distress. The close of the Napoleonic Wars did nothing to alleviate the hardship, and the government, haunted by the memory of the French Revolution, chose severity rather than concessions.

THE GORDON RIOTS, *London, 1780 (**below**), were provoked by Lord George Gordon's mass demonstration against the Catholic Relief Act. Distilleries were sacked and prisons opened.*

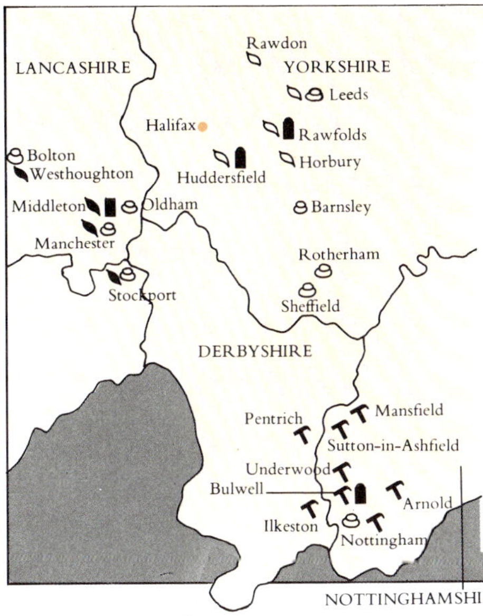

THE LUDDITES, 1811–12

Over 10,000 troops were deployed against the Luddite machine-breakers. The underlying causes of discontent were rising food prices, low wages, precarious employment and class antagonism. The attackers had various aims. In the East Midlands, where the first incident broke out at Arnold (Notts.) in March 1811, stocking-frame knitters struck against employers who were threatening their livelihoods by using old machines in new ways. Further north, in 1812, weavers and finishers attacked new power looms, shearing frames and gig frames.

Main attacks by hosiers on wide frames
Main attacks by cloth-finishers on gig frames and shearing frames
Main attacks by weavers on power looms
Food riots
Incident causing one or more deaths

THE PETERLOO MASSACRE, *Manchester, 1819, named in mocking memory of Waterloo. An orderly reform meeting, gathered to hear 'Orator' Hunt speak at St Peter's Fields, was broken up by cavalry. Eleven died and 400 were wounded after a confused attempt by yeomanry to arrest Hunt.*

DISTURBANCE AT ATLANTIC ROAD, BRIXTON, *south London, 1981 (**right**), against a background of youth unemployment and racial tensions. There were similar outbreaks at Toxteth (Liverpool) and elsewhere.*

FASCIST RALLY, *1932. Growing violence at meetings of Oswald Mosley's 'Blackshirts' led in 1936 to the Public Order Act, empowering the authorities to ban demonstrations.*

Violence during the Reform Bill struggle, when Nottingham Castle was burned down, continued into the Chartist era: John Frost led a rising at Newport in 1839; and the workers of south Lancashire took part in the 'Plug-plot' riots (1842), pulling the plugs from steam boilers in factories to enforce a general strike for the Charter. Instability also reigned in the countryside. In the early 1830s in southern England, protesters against low wages broke up threshing machines and set fire to ricks in the 'Captain Swing' riots. Agrarian unrest broke out in south-west Wales (1839–44) over toll charges and turnpike roads (the 'Rebecca' riots), and in Scotland over the eviction of crofters.

In the 1860s the Fenians (a group of Irish nationalists) brought terrorism to London. Further troubles in the capital in the later 19th century were caused over reform and unemployment.

Before the First World War a new militancy emerged in the workers' movement. At a strike at Tonypandy in south Wales in 1910 two men were killed by troops. A general strike was averted by war, but militancy continued after the Armistice. Tanks were deployed against strikers in Glasgow (1919), and troops dealt with rioting in Liverpool during the police strike of the same year.

By 1912 the suffragettes were using violence to draw attention to their cause. Members of the radical women's movement smashed shop windows, burned down buildings, cut telephone wires and slashed paintings in the National Gallery.

The depression of the inter-war years led to further unrest among the unemployed. Most famous of the consequent 'hunger marches' was the Jarrow Crusade of 1936, but earlier marches were less peaceful. Feelings in the 1930s also ran high over Oswald Mosley's British Union of Fascists. Civil disturbance is still a frightening possibility in any British town. The most recent incidents have been connected with racial tensions, unemployment and the bomb campaigns of Irish and Middle Eastern terrorists.

CONNECTIONS
Agrarian unrest: 136–7 *The impact of the new farming*
Chartism: 76–7 *Parliament/Abuse and reform*
Ireland: 66–7 *Ireland and Britain*
The Jacobite rebellion: 60–61 *Scotland and England*
Religious conflict: 50–51 *Catholics and Protestants*

Health and medicine

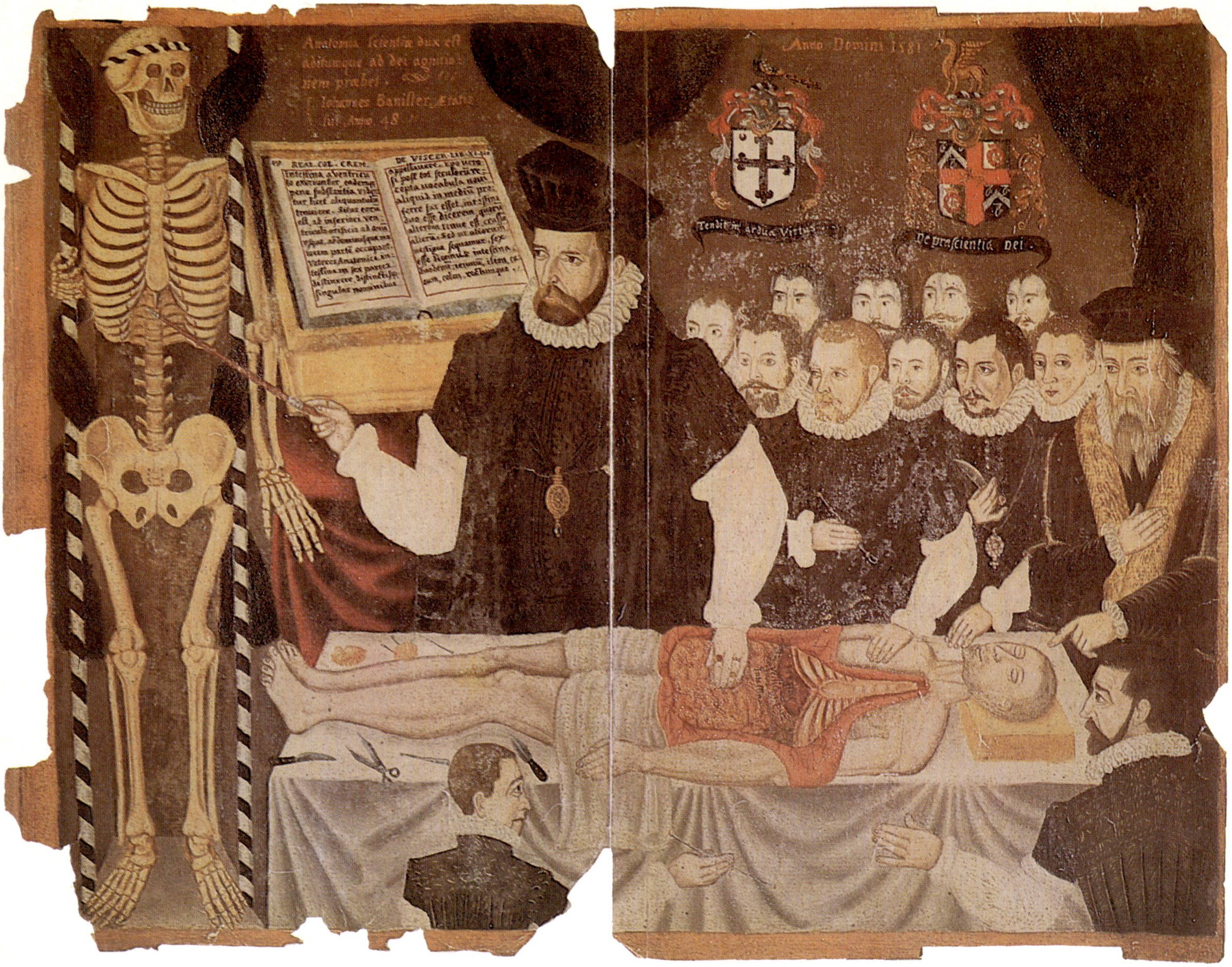

ANATOMY LECTURE *in 1581, at the Barber-Surgeons' Hall, London. The barber-surgeons were annually entitled to the corpses of two executed criminals for study.*

The Romans brought good health and hygiene to Britain, but standards fell suddenly after their departure. In the Middle Ages, knowledge of medical matters was extremely unsophisticated and clouded by superstition. Prayer and fasting were thought to be the best cure for illness. When pestilence struck, the people were helpless. The Black Death, carried by black rats and transmitted to humans by fleas, made its first assault at Melcombe Regis on the Dorset coast in the summer of 1348, and by the end of the following year had killed almost half the population of Britain. Special notoriety has also attached to the Great Plague of London, which began in April 1665 and caused around 100,000 deaths. But London had already suffered from worse outbreaks in 1563, 1603 and 1625, and other towns had a similar history of appalling epidemics.

The fight against disease

The Renaissance emphasis on rational thought and empirical study yielded important medical advances: for example, in the 1620s, William Harvey discovered the circulation of the blood. In 1651 the Royal College of Physicians was founded. Such developments had little immediate effect on the treatment of patients, but gradually great steps forward were made in medicine, surgery and obstetrics. Philanthropists such as the bookseller Thomas Guy founded new hospitals, and a major medical school was well established at Edinburgh by the mid-18th century.

Smallpox replaced the plague as the scourge of the human race. It was known as early as the 17th century that inoculation could be effective, but the substance used was smallpox itself, and often

SURGEON'S CERTIFICATE (***right***) *from St Bartholomew's Hospital, London, 1776. This was the oldest hospital in Britain (1123). The precinct shown on the certificate was begun in the 1730s.*

THE MONSTROSITY OF VACCINATION: *a cartoon published by the Anti-Vaccine Society in 1802. It was widely believed that patients inoculated with cowpox serum for the treatment of smallpox would develop a cow's features.*

THE ASIATIC PERIL

By May 1831 Asiatic cholera reached the ports of the Baltic and the North Sea and began to pose a threat to Britain. The disease struck at Tyneside and from there spread throughout the country. Further epidemics broke out in 1848, 1853 and 1866. Only in 1854 was it found, by a doctor in London's Soho, that cholera was transmitted by the drinking of contaminated water.

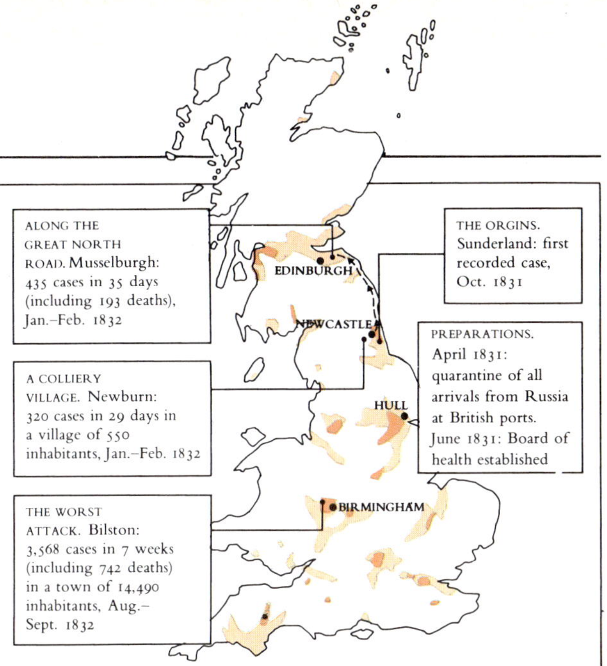

LISTER AND THE ANTISEPTIC REVOLUTION

To eliminate post-operative infection, Joseph Lister, Professor of Surgery at Glasgow, decided in 1847 to use carbolic acid as a disinfectant. His first experiment was unsuccessful, as the acid damaged the patient's skin. In subsequent cases he applied a solution of carbolic acid to his hands and instruments and to the wounds and dressings, and disinfected the atmosphere with a spray (***right***). Lister's ideas were adopted in America and Germany long before they won acceptance in Britain.

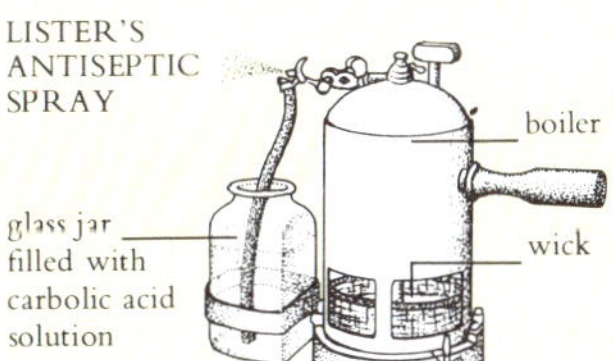

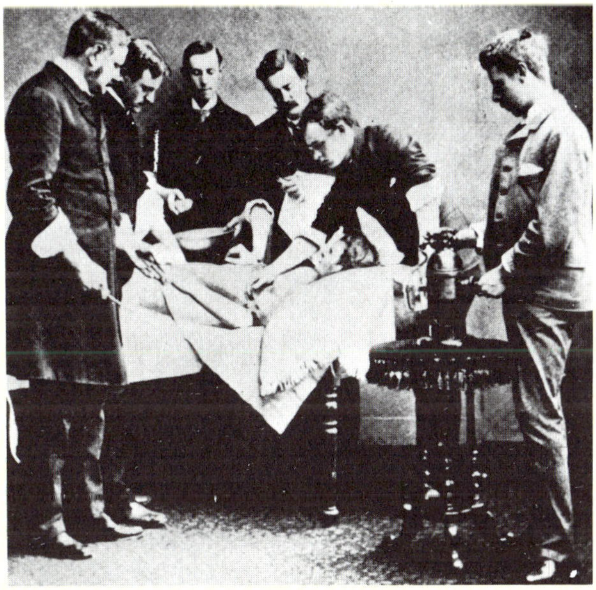

NURSES ON DUTY *at St Thomas's Hospital, London, c. 1905. The first properly trained and professional nurses came from this hospital.*

HEART TRANSPLANT EQUIPMENT (***below***) *at Papworth Hospital, Cambs. The techniques of heart transplants are still in their infancy.*

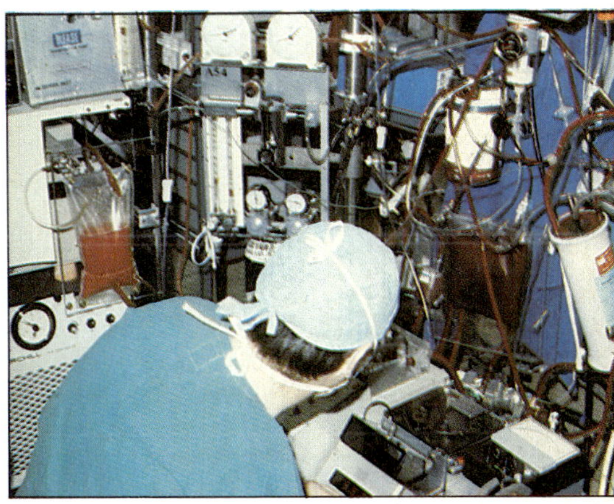

brought death. In 1796 the Gloucestershire doctor Edward Jenner substituted the milder cowpox and made an important breakthrough in preventive medicine. By this time, the industrial revolution had begun to re-create on a larger scale the insanitary horrors of urban life in the Middle Ages. Tuberculosis, typhoid and typhus were rampant, and in 1831 came the first of a series of terrible cholera attacks.

The threat of cholera stimulated action. Sir Edwin Chadwick's Sanitary Report (1842) led to the Public Health Act of 1848, which set up a national Board of Health with Chadwick in charge. A further Act of 1875 imposed upon the local authorities the onus of responsibility for sanitation and health. Social reform alone, though, was not enough: science was needed too. In 1846, Robert Liston was the first British surgeon to use ether (while amputating a leg), and in the following year James Simpson took anaesthetics a stage further with chloroform, which Queen Victoria permitted to assist her in the birth of two children.

Surgery at this period was extremely hazardous. Too often the outcome was: 'Operation successful, patient subsequently died.' However, under the influence of Louis Pasteur's germ theory of disease, Joseph Lister, in Glasgow, instituted the use of carbolic acid as an antiseptic, and the importance of cleanliness in the operating theatre gradually became a commonplace.

In the early decades of the 20th century voluntary and local authority hospitals competed in an absurd and damaging rivalry. This situation was radically changed when Aneurin Bevan set up the National Health Service (NHS) in 1948: it was open to all and was entirely free. The demand for medicines, dentures and spectacles proved to be enormous, but controls were placed on it in 1951 and 1952 with the introduction of limited charges.

Some advances were fostered by the two World Wars, notably blood transfusion by the First and plastic surgery by the Second (just as nursing had been stimulated by the Crimean War). Penicillin was discovered in the inter-war years, but was only fully exploited in response to wartime needs. Since then, a major and controversial episode in medical history has been the development of transplant and spare-part surgery.

CONNECTIONS
The Great Plague: 244–5 *London*
Hazards of maternity: 90–91 *Women and the family*
Mortality: 40–41 *The growth of population*
Public health: 88–9 *The growth of the Welfare State*
Water cures: 238–9 *Spas and seaside resorts*

Learning and the people

In the Middle Ages literacy tended to be found only among clerics, and the Church, which maintained libraries and organized the training of the clergy as well as of court officials, was the main source of learning. However, the great changes associated with the Renaissance, the Reformation and the growth of commerce stimulated secular initiatives in education, bringing an end to the Church's monopoly. In 1382 the seed of the public school system was planted when William of Wykeham founded a college at Winchester.

The Tudor and Stuart reigns saw the creation of a large number of 'grammar schools', usually set up as charitable bequests to provide education for boys in Latin grammar and a smattering of other subjects. However, it was the religious fervour of the 17th century and after that stimulated an interest in mass literacy, because the study of the Bible was considered to be a very important aspect of the Protestant faith.

IGNORANT AND YE INSTRUCTED US, *reads one motto on this notice for a collection for poor children. But the charitable were more often motivated by the need to 'moralize' than to educate the lower orders.*

ELISABETH RAMSAY'S SAMPLER (***right***), *1815. The literacy of this ten-year-old girl is demonstrated in combination with skill in needlework. Sewing expertise was a vital part of every girl's education.*

Moralizing the poor

Religion continued to be a major theme in education. The charity schools which began to multiply in the early 18th century concentrated on scripture, but also taught reading and writing. In the 1780s the first Sunday schools were set up by reformers who sought to shake the new industrial working class out of their godlessness – and sometimes to school them in habits of deference. An ex-army chaplain, Andrew Bell, and a Quaker, Joseph Lancaster, simultaneously set up rival elementary schools in London in 1798 to give Christian instruction to pauper children. Both men were short of funds and of competent teachers, so

THE MONITORIAL SYSTEM (***left***), *1839. Huge classes were run on the lines of a military operation, with older pupils passing on to the younger ones what they learned from the teacher. With ten younger children per monitor, a schoolteacher could handle 100 pupils.*

A BOARD SCHOOL (***right***), *c.1890. Gaunt redbrick schools (this one is Hackney's Bonner Street School, opened by the London School Board in 1876) are still a familiar sight.*

SCHOOLDAYS AT GRANGE HILL (***below***): *a classroom scene from the BBC television series about the lives of pupils and teachers at a modern comprehensive school.*

they ran huge classes by using older children as pupil-teachers, or monitors. The methods of Bell and Lancaster were taken up on a national scale by two Church societies: the Church of England National Society for the Education of the Poor (1811) and the British and Foreign Schools Society (1814), which was run by dissenters.

The spread of education suffered from sectarianism, ignorance and illiteracy being considered preferable by many to the risk of infection by the wrong denomination. The country's industrial take-off happened without the benefit of a national system of education: the cotton magnate Richard Arkwright proved that fortunes could be made without the aid of good grammar, and the incidence of signed marriage certificates shows that levels of literacy were conspicuously low among new occupational groups such as the millworkers.

The spread of the three Rs

In contrast with Scotland, where Acts of 1616 and 1696 resulted in the setting up of a primary school in each parish, England and Wales had no state system of elementary education for most of the 19th century. A tentative step towards state support for teaching was the Factory Act of 1833, which provided for the rudimentary education of young factory hands. In 1839 it was enhanced by a larger grant for educational expenditure. However, serious government interest in education for the masses was frustrated by two factors. One was the persistence of rivalry among the different Christian denominations about who should control state-assisted schools; the other was the British tradition of self-help and free enterprise, which valued knowledge gained by experience rather than by tuition.

England and Wales acquired a state system of primary education – basically, reading, writing and arithmetic – in 1870. The first Education Act made locally elected school boards responsible for the provision of primary education which was state-assisted, though not yet free. This measure was motivated by the continuance of large pockets of illiteracy, which had not been eradicated by the expansion of voluntary educational establishments in the 1850s and 1860s. In addition, after the 1867 extension of the franchise, there was a powerful incentive to educate the working class, 'our future masters'. In 1880 compulsory education was brought in for children up to the age of ten, and mass literacy became a real possibility.

Secondary education had been available to the better-off for many years, through the perversely termed public schools. In the mid-19th century, after Thomas Arnold had reformed the system at Rugby, the curriculum of the public schools was modernized, and scholarships were introduced. Such improvements, however, affected only a tiny minority, and in 1902 local education authorities were set up to provide limited secondary education for more people. Although the school leaving age was raised to fourteen in 1918, financial constraints made further progress difficult between the wars. After the Butler Education Act of 1944 (engineered by R.A. Butler) local authorities used the '11-plus' examination to decide which children would benefit from a free grammar school education. The more practically minded pupils were sent instead to 'secondary modern' or 'technical' schools, where the curriculum was less academic. The school leaving age was set at fifteen in 1947.

The coming of comprehensives

During the post-war years, dissatisfaction with the selectiveness of this system was voiced. An alternative idea was that of 'comprehensive' schools, which would take children of all abilities without an examination. The Labour governments of 1964–70 made the implementation of comprehensive education a major plank of their platform and by the end of the 1970s it had largely been accomplished. Many traditional grammar schools were absorbed into comprehensive schemes or became sixth-form colleges, while others chose to become independent, joining the still flourishing private sector. The leaving age was further raised, to sixteen, in 1973.

The last twenty years have been a period of continuous debate on educational organization and methods. One of the most prominent issues has been the question of 'mixed ability' teaching, while to many educationalists the crucial argument is whether private schools should be abolished. Considerable attention has also been given to nursery schools and to the provision of specialist education for handicapped and disabled people.

CONNECTIONS
Learning from the media: 276–7 *Radio and television*
Public schools: 74–5 *Class in Britain*
The universities and vocational training: 114–15 *Higher education*

THE LEEDS MECHANICS' INSTITUTE *(now the School of Art). Mechanics' Institutes had appeared in every sizeable British town by the 1840s.*

The two oldest universities in Britain – Oxford and Cambridge – were founded as part of a religious and intellectual revival in medieval Europe. Initially, their principal role was to educate trainee clerics in theology and Church law, but a general foundation course in the liberal arts preceded the study for a higher degree. The idea of a layman completing his education at university without any vocational aim in view took root only after the Reformation had struck at the predominance of the clergy.

The rise of professional training

Apart from the legal training given by the Inns of Court, the universities were for centuries the only independent institutions providing professional training. The growth of further establishments in which a vocation could be learned awaited the stimulus of the industrial revolution.

From about 1823 Mechanics' Institutes were set up in Britain, giving working-class adults new opportunities to improve their prospects, and disseminating up-to-date information on engineering advances. The rise in status of the banker and the accountant also inspired teaching institutions, notably the Institute of Chartered Accountants. Other new establishments included the medical schools and teaching hospitals and, from about 1805, the first teacher training colleges.

By the second half of the 19th century the threatening position of Britain's industrial competitors had contributed to a full recognition of the importance of technical education. Prince Albert, Lyon Playfair and the biologist Thomas Huxley did much to stimulate further advances, and between them successfully encouraged the foundation of London's Imperial College. Meanwhile, fired by a strong evangelical Christianity, Quintin Hogg progressed from teaching at evening classes (from 1864) to the creation of the Polytechnic in Regent Street, London, in 1882. It was an immediate success, and by 1897 nine polytechnics were in operation, funded by local authorities.

University expansion

At the beginning of the 19th century there were only two universities in England, none in Wales, and four in Scotland. During the 18th century the Scottish universities had nurtured a great blossom-

THE UNIVERSITIES

MERTON COLLEGE LIBRARY, OXFORD, *built in the 1370s and still functioning, ranks as the oldest library in England.*

STUDENTS OF ST ANDREWS *maintaining the tradition of the Sunday pier walk. The university was established in 1411, partly to combat heresy.*

ing of philosophical, scientific and literary talent, but the general picture in England was one of decline. Dissenters in England were barred from Oxford and Cambridge and if they wanted further education they had to go to one of the excellent 'dissenting academies' or to a university in Scotland or abroad. The first serious attempt to destroy the restrictive system in England was made with the foundation in 1828 of London's University College by Jeremy Bentham. There were no religious or residential qualifications and the curriculum offered was broader than that of the 'Oxbridge' colleges. The Church felt it necessary to combat this new 'godless institution' by the foundation of the rival King's College in 1831. Five years later the two colleges entered a new relationship to become the University of London.

The 19th and early 20th centuries were an extraordinarily active period in the creation of new universities. Durham was founded in 1832, and several 'redbrick' universities were established in the major cities of the Midlands and the north. They offered a broad range of subjects, but became especially respected for work in science, engineering and medicine. Moreover, in contrast to Oxford and Cambridge which continued to be dominated by ex-public school pupils, they drew students from a wide range of backgrounds. This new spirit of modernization led, in the 1850s, to extensive reform in the old universities: degree examinations were introduced and new courses set up, especially in the sciences. A number of University Extension Colleges were opened – for example, at Exeter and Nottingham – and these eventually became universities in their own right.

A great barrier was breached when the first women's colleges were started (Bedford College, London, in 1860, and Girton College, Cambridge, in 1869), and after many years of struggle women won the right of entry to all courses. London was the first university to confer degrees on women (in 1878), followed by the Scottish universities, the redbricks and finally by Oxford (1920) and Cambridge (1948). The disabilities of the Nonconformists were also removed, by a series of measures in the later 19th century.

CAMPUS BUILDINGS *at the University of Sussex, near Brighton. A campus is a self-contained student community, with libraries, lecture halls and residential blocks. Like the other seven universities founded in 1961, Sussex has been free to develop its own courses and teaching methods.*

The 20th century

By the close of the 19th century attention had turned again to adult and worker education. Two important working men's colleges appeared in 1899: Toynbee Hall in London and Ruskin College in Oxford. In 1903 the Workers' Educational Association was founded to provide a network of classes given by university lecturers to mature students. But in spite of such developments, the total number of students in Britain remained small in comparison with some other European countries such as Germany.

Increasing awareness of the educational needs of a complex and technological society led to the celebrated Robbins Report of 1963, which urged a major expansion of higher education. The aim was to provide an opportunity for a university or equivalent place to everyone who could benefit from it. Seven new universities were created. In addition, a number of Colleges of Advanced Technology (CATs) gained university status. Some thirty polytechnics were founded in England and Wales, as well as fourteen 'central institutions' in Scotland. A system of local authority grants and a generous proportion of lecturers to students brought great renown to British education.

A major initiative in adult education in 1969 was the inauguration of the Open University, providing part-time, home-based degree courses, partly through radio and television programmes.

The period of rapid expansion in higher education has lately been reversed by a reduction of government grants.

MIDDLESEX POLYTECHNIC. *Many of the polytechnics were originally colleges of technology, commerce, art or education. Courses still tend to be more vocationally orientated than in the universities. Since the 1960s several polytechnics have been granted university charters.*

CONNECTIONS
The college system: 254–5 *Oxford and Cambridge*
Dissenters: 54–5 *Christian minorities*
Schools: 112–13 *Learning and the people*

Science/*The age of discovery*

AN ALCHEMIST PREPARING COLOURS: *a 15th-century illustration. Experiments by alchemists were based on the common medieval belief that all matter was composed of four elements – earth, water, fire and air.*

In medieval Britain, as elsewhere in Europe, scientific advance was severely constrained by the strength of religion and superstition. Astronomy, arithmetic and geometry were studied at the universities, but theology was regarded as the highest academic discipline, although Aristotelian logic challenged its primacy by asserting that reason was the basis of all knowledge. A particularly popular pseudo-scientific pursuit was alchemy – the attempt to transmute base metals into gold. But the promotion of pure science awaited the dawning of the Renaissance.

THE ORIGINAL 'ORRERY', *1716: a clockwork model of the solar system, invented by George Graham and improved by John Rowley. It was used to demonstrate the movements of the planets.*

The scientific Renaissance

In England the most important pioneer of scientific thought before the great discoveries of the late 17th century was the statesman and philosopher Sir Francis Bacon (1561–1626). He was the champion of the empirical, deductive method – the practice of testing and proving scientific theories by controlled experiments – and the ideas he put forward in *The Advancement of Learning* (1605) and *Novum Organum* (1620) inspired the creation of the Royal Society. This, one of the earliest scientific societies in Europe, met informally from the middle of the century onwards, but did not come fully into the limelight until it was granted a royal charter by Charles II in 1662. Its members were determined to accumulate experimental evidence on a wide range of scientific subjects, including medicine.

SIR FRANCIS BACON (***right***) *was the Renaissance polymath* par excellence*: he was a literary figure of the first rank, as well as the first scientific thinker to make the decisive break with Aristotelian logic. His work was an inspiration to those 'divers worthy persons, inquisitive into natural philosophy and other parts of human learning' who held regular meetings in London from 1645, and finally formed the Royal Society (1662). An allegory of the Society (**below**),* c. *1667, shows Bacon (right) and the Society's first president, Lord Brouckner (left), beside the bust of Charles II.*

The most distinguished member of the Royal Society, and one of the greatest scientists that has ever lived, was Sir Isaac Newton (1642–1727). He developed the three laws of motion and through his studies of planetary rotation arrived, in the 1660s, at what was to become known as the 'law of universal gravitation'. When the astronomer Edmund Halley visited Newton at Cambridge in 1684, he was amazed to find that the problems under debate in London had been solved. The Royal Society persuaded Newton to set out his theories in his famous *Principia* (or *Mathematical Principles of Natural Philosophy*).

Newton was the founder of modern physics. A similar title in respect of chemistry could well be claimed for his near-contemporary Robert Boyle (1627–91), whose book *The Sceptical Chymist* (1661) made a decisive break with the alchemists.

The 18th century

In the 18th century, the inventor-manufacturer acquired an increasing importance. Science was advanced not only by physicists and chemists but also by the manufacturers and merchants of the new middle classes. One of the earliest inventions of the century, the brainchild of Thomas Newcomen, a blacksmith and ironmonger from Devon, was the atmospheric steam pump used to pump water from mines, particularly those of Cornwall. Fierce commercial competition stimulated many industrial developments. New methods of producing high-quality steel were invented and improved between about 1710 and 1750, and some were closely guarded secrets – such as Benjamin Huntsman's method of producing crucible steel, which is said to have been stolen by a rival manufacturer, Samuel Walker of Sheffield, who disguised himself as a tramp.

Technical innovations were responsible not only for industrial development, but also for an extraordinary growth of knowledge in this period. The refinement of the telescope by Sir William Herschel allowed further astronomical discoveries, including the discovery of Uranus in 1781. The invention of the sextant, the orrery and the marine chronometer revolutionized maritime navigation and aided the discoveries of the great explorers, notably Captain James Cook, who charted vast, previously unknown areas of the Pacific and contributed greatly to European knowledge of natural history and Oceanic cultures.

In Scotland outstanding contributions were made by Joseph Black, who formulated a theory of latent heat, by the engineer Thomas Telford and, above all, by James Watt (1736–1819), the inventor of the first truly efficient steam engine.

THE GENIUS OF NEWTON

Isaac Newton made some of his greatest discoveries during an 18-month retreat at Woolsthorpe in Lincolnshire in 1667–8, when Cambridge University had been temporarily closed because of the great plague. The young Newton lived, as he said later, in the prime age of invention. The discovery of the force of gravity (occasioned by the fall of an apple) demonstrated for the first time how a single mathematical law could account for a wide range of previously mysterious phenomena: gravity explained the structure of the solar system, as well as the tides and the motion of objects on earth. It became possible to estimate the path and orbit of a comet, and – with more practical implications – to plot with great accuracy the path of the Moon. Longitude could be estimated by studying the relation of the Moon to the stars, and navigators benefited enormously from this. After leaving Cambridge for London in 1693, Newton soon became President of the Royal Society. He produced a fundamental study of the nature of light in his treatise *Opticks* (1704), which described the composition of the spectrum.

THE FIRST REFLECTING TELESCOPE (***left***, *in facsimile*) *was perfected by Newton in 1668. The eyepiece is just below the top of the instrument, and a mirror inside reflects the focal object. With the aid of the telescope, astronomers at the Royal Observatory at Greenwich* (***below***), *founded in 1675 and built by Christopher Wren, proceeded to catalogue the stars. Greenwich was a major observatory until 1946. (Observation is now carried out at Herstmonceux Castle, Sussex.)*

AN EXPERIMENT WITH THE AIR PUMP (***left***), *1768, painted by Joseph Wright of Derby. The invention of an efficient air pump in the early 18th century led to fascinating experiments with static electricity.*

Science in the industrial age

The marriage of the sciences with industrial endeavours was fully realized in the late 18th century, in the 'classic' period of the industrial revolution. The spirit of enterprise in the manufacturing towns was promoted by the famous Lunar Society of Birmingham, which was responsive to the latest advances, such as Benjamin Franklin's experiments with electricity. Joseph Priestley (1733–1804), a leading 'Lunatic', succeeded in isolating 'dephlogisticated air' (that is, oxygen) from other gases – and invented carbonated drinks. Another prominent provincial scientist was the Lancashire Nonconformist John Dalton, progenitor of the atomic theory.

The provinces, though, could not completely eclipse London in the advancement of science. It was at the Royal Institution (founded in 1799) that Sir Humphry Davy and later Michael Faraday propounded the basic principles of electrochemistry. It was many years before electricity was properly understood and usefully exploited, but by now the lesson that science could be harnessed in the service of society had been fully absorbed.

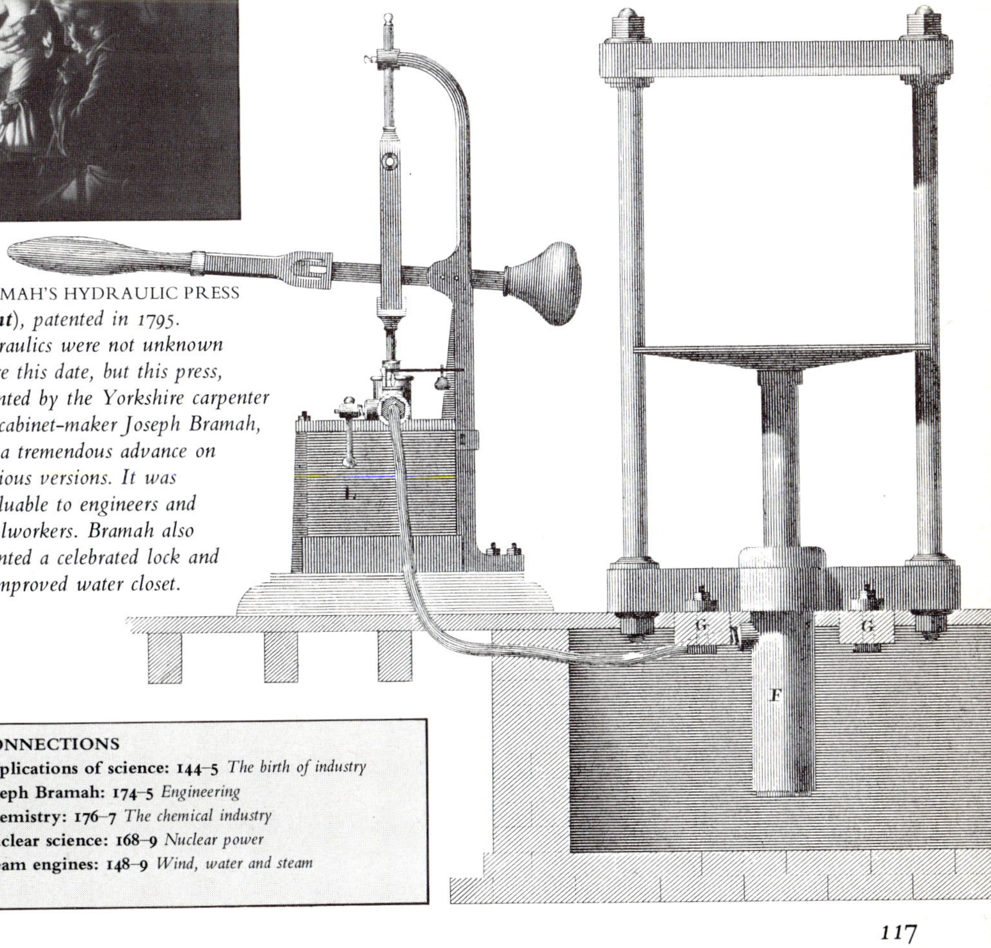

BRAMAH'S HYDRAULIC PRESS (***right***), *patented in 1795. Hydraulics were not unknown before this date, but this press, invented by the Yorkshire carpenter and cabinet-maker Joseph Bramah, was a tremendous advance on previous versions. It was invaluable to engineers and metalworkers. Bramah also invented a celebrated lock and an improved water closet.*

CONNECTIONS
Applications of science: 144–5 *The birth of industry*
Joseph Bramah: 174–5 *Engineering*
Chemistry: 176–7 *The chemical industry*
Nuclear science: 168–9 *Nuclear power*
Steam engines: 148–9 *Wind, water and steam*

Sporting Britain

We know of medieval sport largely through royal attempts to suppress it in favour of the practice of that necessary military art, archery. Although life was hard, holy days (holidays) abounded, and whenever they could get away with it medieval workers added a 'St Monday' and a 'St Tuesday' to Sunday. On such days running, wrestling, skating and bat-and-ball games all took place, while cock-fighting and bear-baiting provided sport of a more vicarious kind. Football, usually played with a pig's bladder encased in leather, was a popular game for larger numbers.

The first ball game to emerge with clear rules – real tennis – was exclusive to royal and aristocratic circles (the 'real' comes from the old French word for 'royal'). It came to Tudor England from the Continent, where it was first played in the 12th or 13th century. The ingenious hazards of the special indoor court were apparently derived from the buttresses and galleries of monastic cloisters. Not until the middle of Queen Victoria's reign did a popular outdoor variant emerge. In 1873 a Major Wingfield produced a set of lawn tennis rules with simple scoring in single points up to fifteen, and in 1875 the All-England Croquet Club at Wimbledon decided to take up the game. When they established the first Wimbledon Championship in 1877, the ancient scoring method of real tennis was re-adopted.

Aristocratic sponsorship and mass sport

Towards the end of the 16th century a sort of cricket had emerged on the grasslands of the Kentish and east Sussex Weald. It was established by the early 18th century in a clear pattern: a game run by noblemen, in which one aristocrat pitted his team against another. For about thirty years, until the early 1790s, the village of Hambledon (near Portsmouth) fielded the finest team in the country. In 1787 Thomas Lord founded the Marylebone Cricket Club (MCC), which named its famous London ground after him. Somewhat reluctantly, but typically of the way in which the major British sports developed through the initiative of private individuals and clubs, the MCC became responsible for establishing the code of rules for the game.

The beginning of the 19th century was a time of corruption and decline in cricket, and a hiatus in British sport generally. But a new era for cricket dawned with the formation of the first county clubs, Sussex (1839) and Surrey (1845). The first tour of English cricketers to Australia took place in 1861, although it was another sixteen years before the first Test Match at Melbourne. By this time the County Championship had been established.

Boxing was another essentially 18th-century sport. The first prize-fighting champion was James Figg, who defended his title in 1727 before a distinguished audience that included the writers Swift and Pope. The continuation of aristocratic patronage was demonstrated in 1867 when the Marquess of Queensberry gave his name to the rules for glove-fighting.

Golf began among shepherds (and remained relatively democratic in its Scottish homeland) and rowing among professional watermen, but both sports took rather similar courses in becoming enmeshed with English wealth and privilege. The first Oxford and Cambridge Boat Race took place in 1829, and the first Henley Regatta in 1839.

The varieties of football

The evolution of perhaps the most widely played games of our modern era, the various types of football, was indebted to the Victorian faith in the value of organized games and the need in the industrial cities for some form of mass relaxation, once trade unionists and reformers had achieved the Saturday half-day holiday.

At Cambridge University, students who had previously played at their various public schools agreed to a set of common football rules in 1849. Ten clubs, all from London and the Home Counties, formed the Football Association in 1863 with rules that banned tripping and hacking but permitted handling (confined to the goalkeeper after 1871).

As the game grew in popularity, more clubs were formed with a working-class basis, in the north of England, and the best of them entered the FA Cup competition (started 1871). However, the growth of professionalism (legitimized in 1885) led to the setting up of regular Football League matches (from 1888) as a preferable alternative to the rather haphazard Cup games. League football steadily expanded to take in clubs from the south, eventually overcoming the initial hostility of the FA.

Many prestigious clubs had continued, meanwhile, to play a handling game, and in Wales in particular this form of the sport was deep-rooted. Established in 1871, the Rugby Union in 1895 set its face against payment of players to compensate for 'broken time' at work, but some northern clubs objected to this restriction and seceded to form the basis of the professional Rugby League, whose rules were devised to attract more spectators.

A COCK FIGHT *in the early 19th century. This cruel sport was declared illegal in 1849, but it lingered on in remoter country areas.*

REAL TENNIS, *17th century. Long-handled rackets, strung with sheep's gut, replaced solid wooden bats around 1500.*

THE WINNER OF THE MATCH, *1864. This was the year, coincidentally, of the first publication of* Wisden's Almanack, *the cricketers' vade-mecum, and of the introduction of overarm bowling. Cricket was becoming increasingly professionalized, but the amateur spirit remained strong.*

MODERN SPORT: THE ORIGINS

The development of transport, mass media and settled urban communities in the 19th century gave rise to mass spectator sports, organized on a national basis.

THEY'RE OFF! *Horse-racing has been popular in Britain since Tudor times, and perhaps even earlier. Starting stalls were first used in 1965, at Newmarket.*

MANCHESTER UNITED FANS. *During the season, attendances at Football League matches total around 30 million; many more watch on television.*

RUGBY UNION AT TWICKENHAM, *London. The first rubgy match at this famous ground was a victory by the Harlequins over Richmond in October 1909.*

Sport today

There have been many thrilling achievements this century to satisfy the countless amateur historians of British sport. These range from Roger Bannister's running of a mile in under 4 minutes in 1954 to the England football team's victory against West Germany in the 1966 World Cup. A great many sports have become accessible as never before – a trend towards democratization that has been encouraged in recent years by the growth of multi-purpose sports centres where squash, badminton, swimming, Japanese martial arts and other activities can be pursued.

CONNECTIONS
Fox-hunting: 36–7 *Man and the landscape*
Gamesmanship: 74–5 *Class in Britain*
Royal hunts: 30–31 *Woodlands and forests*
Shooting game: 92–3 *Landownership*

The Press

The history of the Press is inextricable from political history. Its dominant theme is the growth of an institution that eventually became a power in its own right – 'the fourth estate'. This process began when rumour, gossip and letters first gave way to printed news in the politically turbulent 17th century. The first English-language newspapers and journals came to Britain from Europe in the 1620s. They had to be printed abroad so as to avoid government censorship. This operated as a crude licensing system whereby an English printer rash enough to print material that was unlicensed (that is, critical of and therefore intolerable to the State) was liable to arrest and imprisonment. However, in the age spanning the Civil War, Cromwell's Protectorate and the Restoration, sections of the population were hungry for information, and within the fluctuating limits of government control, newspapers mushroomed.

AN ENGLISH PRINT SHOP, *1619. 'In serving others, we are worn away,' reads the motto. But English printers at this time could not risk printing any home news for fear of the government reaction.*

The adolescent Press

The licensing system had lapsed by 1695. By the early 18th century, there were twenty newspapers in London, appearing once, twice or three times a week and, in one case, daily, while the first of the provincial weeklies were being published in some major towns, such as Norwich and Worcester. Unwilling to accustom itself to an independent Press as a permanent feature of life, the government attempted to take control again with the first Stamp Act of 1712, which imposed a punitive tax on newspapers. This measure crippled many newspapers, but not all: some survived by paying the stamp duty with revenue from advertising, and by exploiting loopholes provided by the Act's conveniently rigid definition of a newspaper.

Soon the State's grip weakened again. From 1736 the *Gentleman's Magazine* published parliamentary reports, and the incorrigible John Wilkes (1727–97), with the support of public opinion, triumphed in the bitter clashes over his anti-government journal, the *North Briton*.

The 'unstamped' and the 'respectable' Press

Just as events in the 17th century had stimulated the demand for news, so the American and French revolutions of the late 18th century gave an impetus to the expansion of a radical Press. Accordingly, fiscal controls were tightened once more, and in the 1820s and 1830s the government waged war on 'subversive', unstamped newspapers, which had a far higher circulation than 'respectable', stamped ones. The battle to remove all the 'taxes on knowledge' was won only in the mid-century, and then by middle-class reform groups in an atmosphere of political quietude. The way was now opened for a government-free Press, as market forces and public opinion began to take over as arbiters of Press behaviour.

THE POWER OF A FREE PRESS. *This symbolic celebration of 1829 incorporates a Stanhope printing press, the first all-metal press, invented around 1800 by the Earl of that name.*

The success of the Victorian Press was based on the prosperity of the 1850s and 1860s, increasing literacy, and technical progress, as well as cheaper paper. Steam and rotary presses were followed in the 1860s by machines using continuous 'webbs' of paper, and in the 1870s by mechanical composition. Each of these developments speeded up production. Already, the railways had reduced the time taken to distribute newspapers, and the telegraphs the time taken to collect the news itself. The nationalization of the telegraphs in 1870 made them cheaper and encouraged the development of news agencies, which had begun with Reuters (1851) and the Press Association (1868). The Press was now respectable; and after being considered a low, demagogic hack, the journalist was now a well-regarded, even a formidable figure, with a duty to 'arouse the nation or be damned'.

The new journalism

In the 1890s the great proprietors, among them Alfred Harmsworth (later Lord Northcliffe) and his brother Harold (Lord Rothermere), banded together in order to introduce labour-saving linotype composition. The cost of such new machinery helped to ensure that the ownership of the Press developed in the hands of men of great capital, and also started off the pressure to go 'down market' in search of the large circulations that were increasingly vital for a commercially profitable newspaper.

In the 1870s the halfpenny evening papers began to supersede the provincial penny mornings. In the next decade W. T. Stead helped to introduce the livelier 'new journalism' from America in the London evening *Pall Mall Gazette*. Credit is usually given, however, to Alfred Harmsworth for

WAITING FOR 'THE TIMES'. *By 1851 the 'Thunderer', marshal of Victorian middle-class opinion, was selling three times as many copies as all the other London dailies put together.*

THE RACE FOR READERS

In 1937 Colonel Lawson of the *Daily Telegraph*, himself responsible for many ingenious circulation-boosting stunts (***opposite right***), was heard to remark: 'Newspapers, I think, resemble fashionable ladies of the West End, in that they are more concerned with their figures than their morals.' From the time of Lord Northcliffe's *Daily Mail* (founded 1896), which overtook the *Telegraph* (1855) as market-leader soon after its launch, this emphasis on figures has been crucial to the Press. Newspapers need high circulations in order to keep prices low – this is itself a condition of mass readership – and the more readers they have, the more paying advertisers they attract.

The *Daily Mirror* (1903) was the first daily to hit the million mark. Along with most other national dailies, it enjoyed a further mushrooming of circulation in the 1930s, followed by a general boom period for the Press that lasted up to 1950. Since then there has been a decline in newspaper circulations, partly due to a combination of labour problems within the industry and competition from newer media such as television.

The provincial papers suffered from the nationals' expansion, but those that survived, for example the *Glasgow Herald* (1783), have remained strong. One provincial, the *Manchester Guardian* (1821), expanded to achieve a national readership.

Popular Sundays, such as the *News of the World* (1843), have always captured the greatest number of readers, while the 'quality' Sundays, such as the *Observer* (1791), have enjoyed a more modest success. Today the Sunday colour magazine supplement, so crammed with advertisements that it often resembles a mail-order catalogue, is an important competitive weapon.

The quality daily newspapers, among them the illustrious *Times* (1785), have always had smaller circulations than the popular dailies, and recent owners of *The Times* have been prepared to underwrite its losses in return for the great prestige attached to being its proprietor.

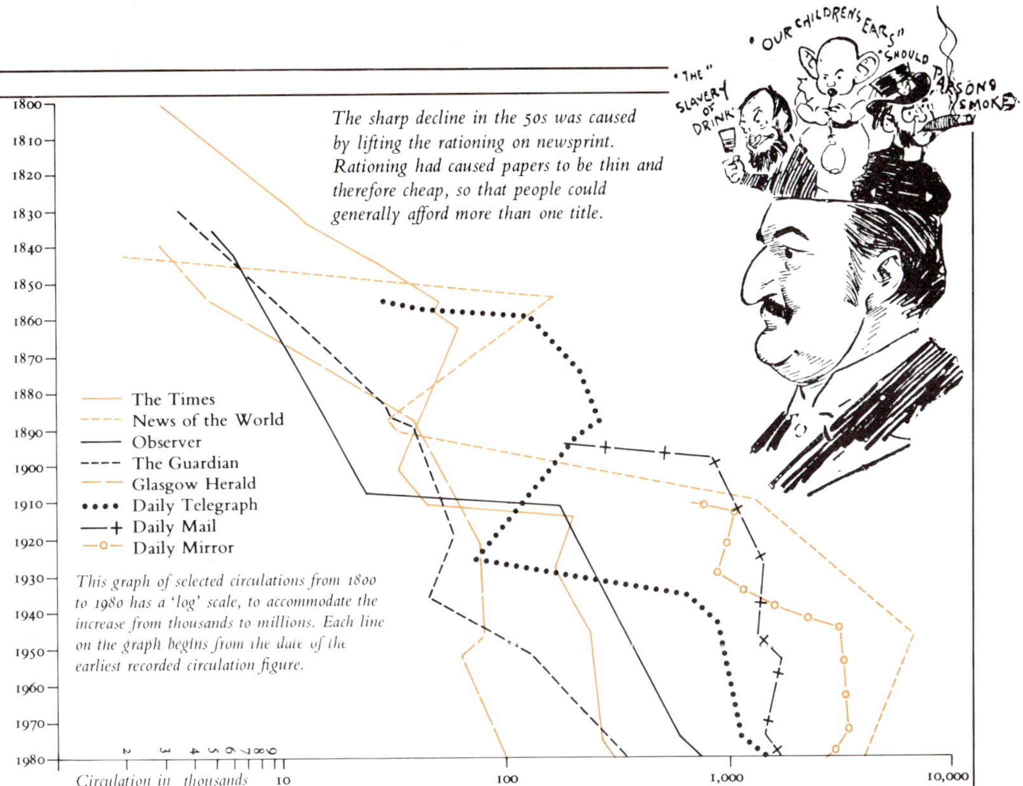

The sharp decline in the 50s was caused by lifting the rationing on newsprint. Rationing had caused papers to be thin and therefore cheap, so that people could generally afford more than one title.

This graph of selected circulations from 1800 to 1980 has a 'log' scale, to accommodate the increase from thousands to millions. Each line on the graph begins from the date of the earliest recorded circulation figure.

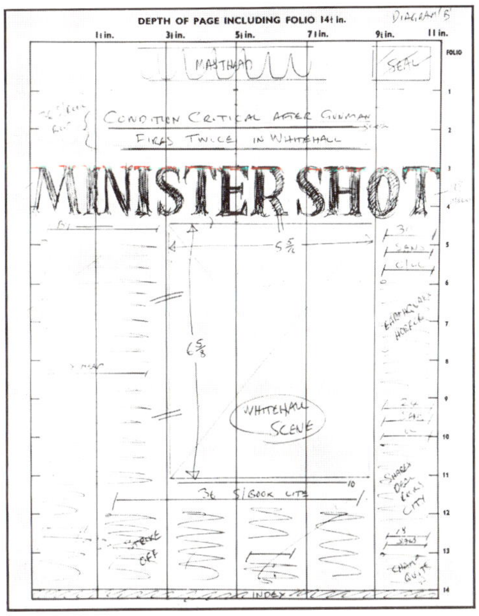

THE FRONT PAGE (***right***). *In the race for readers an eye-catching front page is essential. This design layout for the* Daily Mail, *with its 'banner headline' and 'lead story', reflects the sensationalism of today's popular tabloids.*

THE NEW TECHNOLOGY (***far right***). *Newspaper production has always been labour-intensive, but today it is also capital-intensive. New equipment threatens many of the craft traditions that have evolved over the last century. The unions are complaining fiercely about the consequent loss of jobs. It remains to be seen whether a satisfactory compromise between the craft pride of the Press and modern technology can be reached.*

being the innovator who most successfully tapped a mass readership with a new formula. His *Daily Mail* (founded 1896) regaled its readers with striking headlines, short, crisp news items, lavish sports coverage, a regular women's column and a daily story.

In the 1900s pictures became a major aspect of the competitive response of the Press to the silent cinema. *The Illustrated London News* (founded 1843) and the *Daily Mirror* were quick to make use of photography. But it was the circulation wars of the 1930s between the *Daily Mail*, *Daily Express* and the *Daily Herald* that effectively created the mass circulation popular press by buying readers with gimmicks such as gifts and free insurance schemes. The war was accompanied by the tabloid revolution, as designers such as Arthur Christiansen of the *Express* and Guy Bartholemew of the *Mirror* borrowed from American newspaper styles, using banner headlines and exploiting photography with great flair and originality.

Mergers and closures

The nationals expanded at the expense of the provincials, however, and by 1980 only eighteen provincial mornings existed in Britain, as against forty-one in 1921. Alarm about the reduction of titles before the Second World War led to the establishment of the Royal Commission on the Press (1949), and this prompted the industry to found the Press Council (1953). Nevertheless, the increased costs of labour-saving technology (which led to a new Royal Commission in 1977), as well as competition from radio and television, continued to lead to mergers and closures. The total number of newspaper titles has contracted. Yet by international standards Britain retains a very high circulation of newspapers in proportion to the population: about 83 per cent of British adults still read a daily newspaper.

CONNECTIONS
Advertisements: 102–3 *Reaching the consumer*
Broadcasting: 276–7 *Radio and television*
Literacy: 112–13 *Learning and the people*
Politics in the 17th century: 72–3 *The Civil War*

The armed forces

The first of Britain's three armed services to be regularly established as a standing national force was the Royal Navy. Its origins, like those of the Army, substantially predate its actual establishment. Alfred the Great, King of Wessex, mobilized a royal navy to counter the aggressive seafaring forces of the Danes. But for most of the Middle Ages the organization of the fleet was haphazard, and for centuries maritime defence – particularly necessary during the protracted quarrels with the French – was the responsibility of the Cinque Ports – five (later seven) harbours in Sussex and Kent.

For landed militia the kings of feudal England relied on their vassals' forces (which owed only limited service) and on a small permanent military class of thegns or knights. Armies were raised only for specific purposes. England's first permanently gathered land force was that of the Yeomen of the Guard, founded by Henry VII in 1485 – a small London-based body that served as a protection against the possibility of a sudden coup.

The Senior Service

The firm establishment of the Royal Navy as the principal British maritime corps occurred, though hesitantly, under the Tudor kings. Henry VII was too careful with his money to build up a large personal force, but he had Britain's first dry dock constructed at Deptford, London. His son Henry VIII was far more belligerent, and raised a force of specially designed battleships with 'broadside guns' (cannons mounted in a low line along the deck); this was the beginning of a long-enduring type of naval tactic. Henry VIII's other lasting achievement was to create the administrative machinery of the Admiralty. The Elizabethan victory over the Spanish Armada fleet in 1588, under Sir Francis Drake, owed much to Henry's groundwork, though few of the English ships were owned entirely by the Crown.

ENGLISH ARCHERS IN THE 14TH CENTURY *(**above**). In the Middle Ages archery practice was enjoined on the country by law. The longbow was then an unequalled long-range weapon.*

JOHN CHURCHILL, 1ST DUKE OF MARLBOROUGH *(**above right**)* c. 1706. *Marlborough was one of the greatest commanders in English history. He outmanoeuvred the French enemy in a series of huge battles, notably at Blenheim – a victory that won him fame, royal favour and a dukedom.*

VISCOUNT HORATIO NELSON *(**right**) was mortally wounded at Trafalgar when his flagship* Victory *closed with an enemy vessel. Nevertheless Nelson had effectively destroyed French naval power. The* Victory *now lies preserved at Portsmouth (**above**).*

The Rifle Regiment, 1809: sergeant's dress

THE REAR GUARD *by J.P. Beadle. Brigadier-General Craufurd and the Rifle Brigade are remembered for their well-disciplined endurance during this retreat from Napoleon's forces in Portugal (1809).*

The Rifle Brigade, 1825: officer's court dress

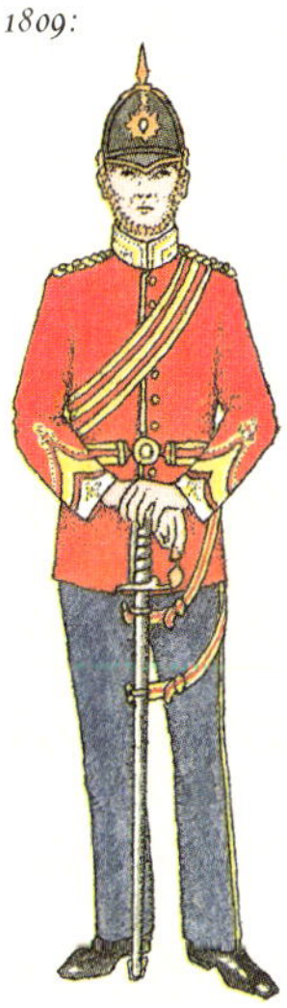

Oxfordshire Light Infantry, 1894: officer's dress

Royal Green Jackets, 1970: officer's dress

THE REGIMENTAL SYSTEM

In the regular British Army, loyalty to the regiment has been and still is a strong factor in maintaining morale and motivation. Its focus, binding a man's heart to his comrades, is in many cases the regimental colours – that mystic embodiment of the life of the regiment. The Royal Green Jackets lack colours, but wear their battle honours in their cap badges and prize the traditions of the numerous groups (examples, (***left***) from which they were formed. They are reminded of their history by the roll of Regimental Battle Honours, by the celebration of regimental birthdays and parades commemorating past victories, and by paintings and trophies in their regimental museum at Winchester.

The Royal Navy flourished under the early Stuart kings, though the 'ship money' tax raised to pay for it was the cause of a celebrated quarrel between Crown and Parliament. In the reign of Charles II shortage of funds led to a lack of stores and munitions and men, and consequent rough treatment from the Dutch in a series of sea battles.

By the 18th century the Navy began to emerge, however, as the most powerful in the world. But it was controlled by an often arbitrary and brutal discipline. The behaviour of the Admiralty was exemplified at its most tyrannical when it had Admiral John Byng shot in 1757 for lack of success. The famous mutinies of Spithead and Nore (1797) were the desperate reactions of enslaved seamen. This harsh regime still characterized the British Navy when it won undisputed world dominion at the Battle of Trafalgar in 1805.

Technical advances of the 19th and 20th centuries kept the Navy abreast of its rivals, but it struggled through the Second World War with depleted resources. Since the withdrawal of the last battleship in 1955 the fleet has been progressively reduced.

The regular Army

It was not until the Restoration of the monarchy in 1660 that soldiers were permanently maintained: General Monck's troops avoided the disbandment accorded to the rest of Cromwell's Model Army (and, earlier, the Royalist troops) and were formed into the Coldstream Guards. Other regiments were swiftly added, both as Household troops and to serve standing military commitments such as the manning of the garrison of Tangier, and, by the 18th century, those of the expanding Empire.

Between 1704 and 1714 the Duke of Marlborough's wars in northern and central Europe established Britain as a great military power. This period saw the emergence of the red coats, a style of dress that became traditional with British regiments. The infantry took to the field equipped not with pikes, as before, but with muskets and bayonets. After Marlborough's fall from favour the Army's efficiency declined, principally because the new Tory government disliked large armies – small units were quartered all over the country, and training in the complicated mass manoeuvres of the day was impossible. In contrast to the Navy in the same period, whose officers were predominantly English, the Army recruited whole regiments of Highlanders and numerous Irishmen, as well as sizeable contingents of Germans. Discipline was ferocious, but it is probable that miscreants were executed more rarely (though they were flogged more frequently) than in the contemporary French army.

The Army's lack of training proved a great handicap at the outbreak of the Napoleonic Wars in 1803. However, the Peninsular and Waterloo campaigns under the Duke of Wellington moulded a highly efficient service. During the rest of the 19th century this standard deteriorated and the Army became specially tailored to its colonial responsibilities. It was too small and under-equipped in artillery for the mass conflict it faced in 1914. Conscription was introduced in both the World Wars but it was abandoned in 1960.

SERGEANT BAKER OF THE QUEEN'S BODYGUARD, 1955. *The Yeomen of the Guard still protect the sovereign on occasion, uniformed much as they were in Henry VII's day.*

The Royal Air Force

The youngest of the services was formed in 1918 by the fusion of the Royal Flying Corps and the Royal Naval Air Service. Between the wars, less starved of funds than its sister services, the RAF developed its aircraft enormously, and was able to win the vital Battle of Britain in 1940. Military air power has transformed the concept of war at sea as well as ground tactics, and, since the 1950s, it has played an important part in the British nuclear deterrent force.

CONNECTIONS

Cromwell's New Model Army: 72–3 *The Civil War*
Military tactics: 70–71 *Battles*
Modern weaponry: 124–5 *The First World War;* **126–7** *The Second World War;* **180–81** *The plane-makers*
The Royal Navy: 178–9 *Shipbuilding*

The First World War

Edwardian Britain, before 1914, was in a deceptive state of social and political conflict. The Labour movement was yearly becoming more organized and less docile, the suffragettes resorted to violence in their fight for women's rights, and the shadow of Irish Home Rule at times seemed to threaten civil war. Yet by contrast with the turmoils that followed, this seemed in retrospect like a golden epoch, a period of confidence and stability.

For King and country

The declaration of war on Germany on 4 August 1914 proved that patriotism and the fighting spirit were capable of triumphing over disunity. The German invasion of neutral Belgium, which Britain was treaty-bound to defend, was felt to be an outrage and an insult. Jingoism came to the fore, as wildly enthusiastic crowds cheered the soldiers departing for the front. Britain had been the supreme world power for almost a century, and any notion of catastrophe or defeat was not contemplated. 'Now God be thanked who has matched us with this hour,' wrote the young poet Rupert Brooke.

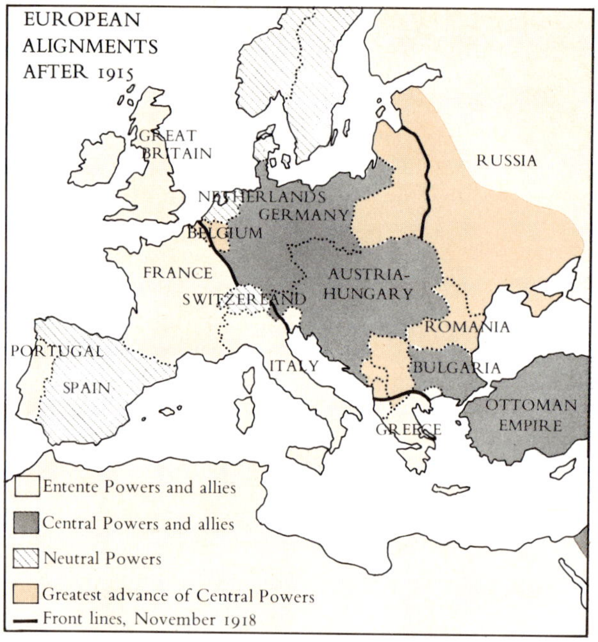

THE CALL TO ARMS. *The campaign begun by Lord Kitchener, who is depicted on this famous poster, drew 3 million volunteers. The government promoted the idea that it was every man's bounden duty to offer himself for service.*

WOMEN AT WORK *in an aeroplane factory. The crucial role of women in the war – as workers, nurses and in the new women's sections of the forces – improved their status.*

The first wounded to return from France and Belgium were given heroes' welcomes. But soon the welcomes contained a note of anguish, as trainloads of maimed men arrived all too frequently and the lists of dead became terrifyingly long. There had been a widespread belief that the war would be over by Christmas – the slogan 'Christmas in Berlin' was scrawled on troop trains leaving Victoria station. But at the end of 1914 there was stalemate on the western front, with opposing armies dug into long lines of trenches, bombarding each other almost ceaselessly.

Because the regular Army was too small, the War Minister, Lord Kitchener, called for volunteers to form a new force, keeping the Territorial reserves for home defence. Huge numbers flocked to the call of duty, but by February 1916 there was still a

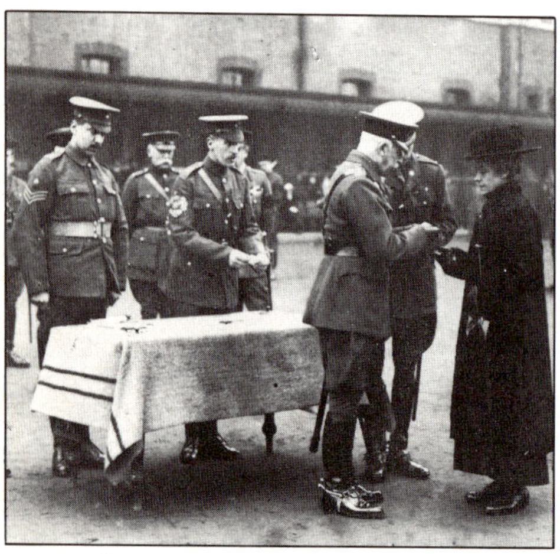

HONOURING A DEAD SOLDIER (**left**). *Men who died in combat were awarded posthumous medals, often received by their widows.*

THE WEAPONS OF WAR

Between 1914 and 1918, fully mechanized warfare was born as the full resources of industry were harnessed to the war effort. The development of the aeroplane, then in its infancy, was spurred on, and planes were used for reconnaissance and increasingly for dropping bombs and aerial fighting. The war on the seas was revolutionized by the German U-boat, and trench warfare stimulated the refinement of the machine gun which in turn led to the invention of the tank. The British Vickers medium machine gun and the German Howitzer (heavy artillery) proved particularly lethal. Poisoned gas was first used (by the Germans) in 1915, giving birth to the modern chemical warfare industry. Nevertheless, in spite of the deployment of new technology, neither side was able to solve the problem of interminable deadlock in trench engagements. Many divisions fought each other for months on end, only to gain or lose a mile or two of ground. Casualties on both sides were out of all proportion to results, until, in August 1918, the Allies launched their final, victorious offensive with American support.

BRITISH MARK V TANK. *Britain was the first to use the new armoured vehicle, the tank, but it was not until late in the war, after a series of modifications, that it proved successful. Its shape was dictated by various factors: for example, it had to cross wide trenches as well as fit the narrow railway wagons on which it was transported. Mark I went into action in September 1916. Out of a potential force of 49 only 18 managed to assemble. But at Cambrai, late in 1917, 350 Mark IV tanks were deployed in a 6-mile front with devastating effect. Eventually the tank was to make trench warfare obsolete.*

shortage of soldiers, and conscription was introduced. Britain was by now fighting not only in western Europe but also in Turkey, the Middle East and Italy. Activity in France had meanwhile intensified, and jingoistic songs gave way to grimmer verses: 'If you want to find the old battalion, I know where they are, They're hanging on the old barbed wire, I've seen 'em.' The names of the longest, bloodiest battles, such as the Marne, the Somme, Ypres and Passchendaele, remain engraved on the nation's hearts and war monuments. In the first day of the assault on the Somme (1 July 1916), some 20,000 British lives were lost.

The home front

The war caused great social and economic changes. For the first time, women worked as the equals of men, many finding a new opportunity to earn a realistic wage in armaments factories, on public transport or on the land. By 1917 the German submarine offensive was so effective that strict rationing was introduced. Nor was the civilian population safe from direct German hostility. The raids of the Zeppelin airships on south-east England, followed by those of the Gotha bombers, were a totally new form of attack, causing over a thousand casualties and occasional symptoms of panic in the capital.

Poets and leaders

Mounting dread, and the unfamiliar experience of wartime frustration, gave rise to two important developments of the British psyche. One was a virulent and unattractive hatred of Germany and all things German, which was fostered by an energetic government propaganda machine. The shooting of Nurse Edith Cavell in 1916 was grist to this mill – there were scores of atrocity stories, and even pictures suggesting German cannibalism. The other was the flowering of war poetry, expressing the horrors of life in the trenches. An agonizing sense of the monstrosities of combat was also reflected in many war diaries, memoirs and novels of the period. Photographs, and paintings by the official war artists, provide a chilling visual record.

WILFRED OWEN (***right***) *in 1917. One of the most eloquent and indignant of the war poets, Owen (1893–1918) told a story that shattered all illusions. He railed against 'the old lie:* Dulce et decorum est pro patria mori' *(It is sweet and fitting to die for one's country), and described scenes of death, mutilation, shell-shock and gas-poisoning in the muddy trenches.*

GERMAN ZEPPELIN AIRSHIP. *The Zeppelin 'rigid dirigible' airship, invented by Count von Zeppelin, was conceived both as a reconnaissance craft and as a bomber. It proved unwieldy, however, and vulnerable to anti-aircraft fire. The German Gotha biplane, modified for extra range, took over the Zeppelin's role in bombing English cities. The British did not develop long-range bombers until after 1918.*

GERMAN U-BOAT (***below***). *The German onslaught under the seas was far more effective than the surface force. With their deadly U-boat, the Germans countered the blockade imposed on them and began, from February 1917, a campaign of unrestricted submarine warfare.*

BRITISH DREADNOUGHT (***below***). *HMS* Dreadnought, *built at great cost and launched in 1906, rendered all earlier battleships obsolete. It combined heavy armour with a dozen 12-inch guns (with all-round fire capability) and engines that could drive it at over 20 knots. The development of the ship prompted an armaments race with Germany which contributed to the outbreak of war. By 1914 the British Fleet, stationed at Scapa Flow in the Orkney Islands, was the stronger; it had a family of 20 Dreadnoughts and superior numbers of battlecruisers, cruisers, destroyers and even submarines. The only major naval engagement of the Great War, the Battle of Jutland (31 May–1 June 1916), was an extraordinary set-piece battle (almost in the tradition of Trafalgar) in which the two fleets pitted all their might against each other. Neither could claim victory, but the great German High Seas Fleet remained in harbour for the rest of the war.*

The attempts of politicians to curtail the nightmare of wasted lives proved ineffective, as much of the real power had passed from them to the Army generals, who were backed by the strident encouragements of the Press. It was the Army which had first (almost secretly) committed Britain to a military alliance with France. Every significant change, from the replacement of Asquith by Lloyd George as Prime Minister in 1916 to the creation of a new Commander-in-Chief in France, was connived at by senior soldiers through the medium of the Press. Only the end of conscription and the swift dismantling of the Army after the Armistice destroyed the generals' excessive power. In the 1920s and 1930s there was a widespread conviction that the great commanders, such as Earl Haig and Field Marshal French, and even the young Winston Churchill (who had, as First Lord of the Admiralty, masterminded the Gallipoli invasion fiasco), had drastically over-committed the nation's forces.

When the war ended in 1918 there were scenes of wild rejoicing, but the victory turned out to be a hollow one. About seven million men had been sent to fight, and a tenth of them never returned. The riches and power of Imperial Britain had wasted away in supporting the struggle, and the swift re-emergence of a German threat underlined the futility of the sacrifice.

CONNECTIONS
The first aeroplanes: 180–81 *The plane-makers*
Homes for heroes: 240–41 *Suburbia*
Military history: 122–3 *The armed forces*
Women at work: 90–91 *Women and the family*

The Second World War

THE BATTLE OF BRITAIN

The German occupation of Poland, Denmark, Norway, Holland, Belgium and France left Britain isolated and vulnerable. Hitler conceived a plan for a seaborne invasion – Operation Sealion, for which orders were given in July 1940 – but it could only be undertaken after the Germans had gained supremacy in the air. Goering, in command of the *Luftwaffe* (air force), claimed to the Führer that all he needed was five days of fine weather. Meanwhile, the British prepared themselves for the possibility of invasion by taking down nameboards from railway stations and removing roadsigns. Parts of the south and east coasts were cordoned off as 'Defence Areas'. And over 1,700 British subjects were interned in case they were informers in the German employ.

The first step towards invasion, taken on 10 July, was an attack by bombers on merchant convoys in the English Channel. After further such attacks, the *Luftwaffe* turned to the task of destroying the RAF and the airfields of southern England. It met with efficient and courageous opposition, underpinned by the technology of coastal radar stations. The fast British fighter planes proved slightly superior to the German Messerschmitts, and huge casualties were inflicted on the enemy despite their greater numbers. A British pilot who was shot down would often escape by parachute and go into action again on the same day. Faced with such resistance, the Germans changed their strategy and began on 7 September to make massive bombing raids on London and other major targets. British morale remained astonishingly high throughout this period of the Blitz. In the biggest daylight onslaught, on 15 September, 56 German planes were brought down. This was the climax of the Battle of Britain. Thereafter, raids were scaled down and Operation Sealion postponed indefinitely. Churchill declared over countless crackling wireless sets: 'Never in the field of human conflict was so much owed by so many to so few.'

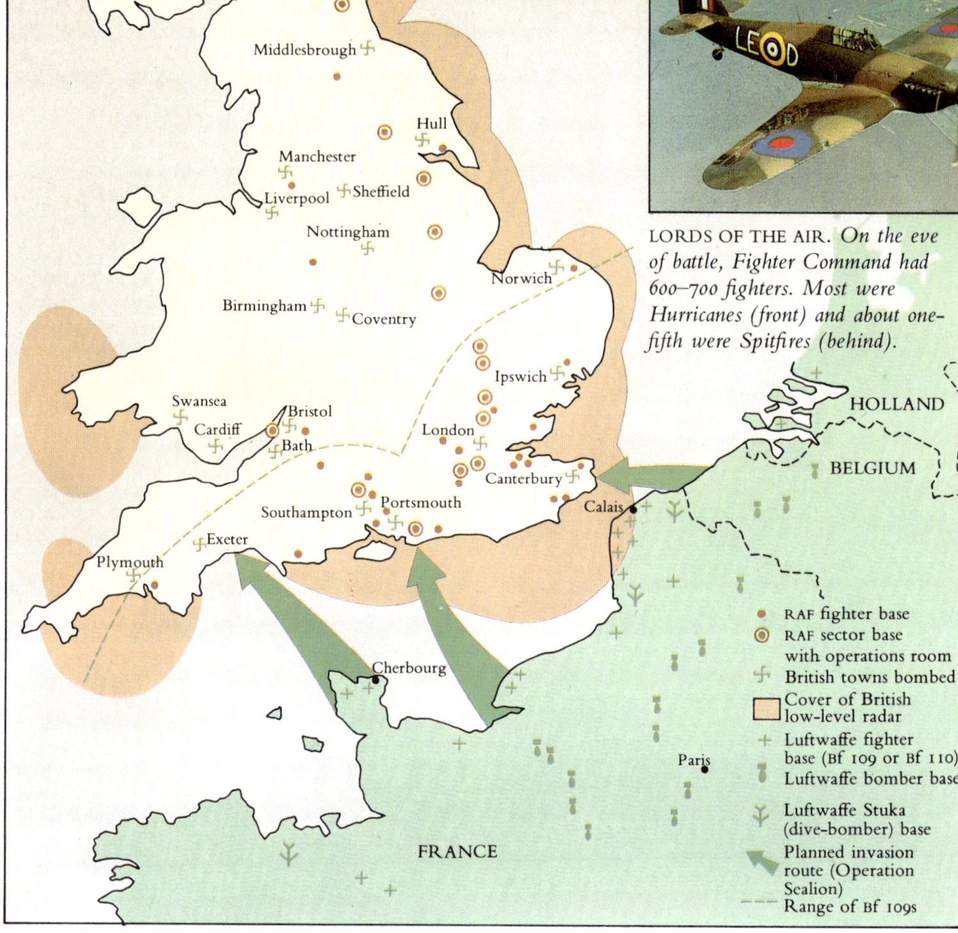

LORDS OF THE AIR. *On the eve of battle, Fighter Command had 600–700 fighters. Most were Hurricanes (front) and about one-fifth were Spitfires (behind).*

Hardly a home in Britain was left unaffected by the Second World War. Not only were lives and buildings lost; also, some of the rigid features of British society were dissolved, to the long-term benefit of the nation. Patriotism, courage and grief were dominant among the reactions of the people. But there was also a sense of being at the mercy of an all-pervasive official control, which requisitioned houses, commandeered spare bedrooms and dispersed families. For a country involved in total war, it was clear that privacy and family ties were not sacrosanct.

The course of the conflict

War was declared on Germany on 3 September 1939 after Hitler invaded Poland. For a while, any dread of heavy casualties to come seemed quite unfounded: the months of 'phoney war' bred a mood of false optimism, although thorough preparations were made. Britain concentrated on clearing the seas of German shipping and setting up an army in France, while at home fear of bombing raids on the cities led to an evacuation programme

BOMB DAMAGE (**left**). *The Blitz on London began between 5 and 6 p.m. on 7 September, when about 320 German bombers, escorted by over 600 fighters, flew up the Thames and dropped their load on key targets such as Westminster, Woolwich Arsenal and the docks.*

in which children from urban areas were moved to the countryside. This was the beginning of a series of internal movements of population on an unprecedented scale. Many slum children were given a glimpse of an utterly different way of life, which was sometimes a happier one. Other precautions included the issue of gas-masks and the imposition of a nocturnal black-out.

The phoney war came to an end in April 1940 when Germany invaded Norway. Prime Minister Neville Chamberlain, accused of bungling preparations for the war, was replaced by a coalition government under Winston Churchill, who took office on the day (10 May) that Hitler launched his successful attack on the western front. When France fell, 320,000 British and French troops were evacuated from Dunkirk and nearby beaches. The heroic saga in which civilians came to the rescue in

THE WAR AT SEA *fared badly at first for Britain. German* U*-boats hunted on the surface in 'wolf-packs'. However, by the end of 1942 the Allies were beginning to regain mastery.*

THE UNDERGROUND *during an air-raid. When the sirens sounded, people in London took refuge in tube stations and cellars as well as in special shelters.*

THE LAND ARMY GIRLS *served as farm labourers, so that more men were available for combat. At a time of severe food shortages, full agricultural productivity was critical.*

small boats was made much of by official propaganda; but in reality most of the soldiers were brought back by the Royal Navy, and a great many of them were in such a disorganized and pitiable condition that those who saw them could not doubt that the country had suffered a catastrophe. It was at this moment that the titanic figure of Churchill stepped to the centre of the international stage. His golden oratory gave expression to a deeply felt, reckless defiance. Many veterans of the First World War were banded together in crudely armed, scarcely uniformed Home Guard units to help the regular Army contest a fight to the finish.

In the summer and autumn of 1940 the people of south-east England watched the RAF defeat the *Luftwaffe* in the Battle of Britain. The British victory sounded what was to be for many years a lonely note of triumph. Even before it had been won, the German bombers had started their Blitz on British cities. Acres of buildings all over the country were gutted and bomb-damaged, and there was a high toll of casualties. Coventry was devastated, and London was ravaged by great fires which threatened to get out of control. By May 1941 there was a real danger that the capital would become uninhabitable. The only relief was the opening of Hitler's Russian campaign, which diverted the pressure from Britain.

The British endured endless discomforts and inconveniences as well as serious physical dangers. Even in daytime, travel could not be undertaken lightly, as petrol was available only for official purposes and train timetables were disrupted by the Blitz. By 1941 the total number of evacuees had risen to about three million, and food rationing, introduced in 1940, became increasingly strict. But perhaps hardest of all to bear were the bitter years of military defeat. Important bastions fell – Crete, Tobruk, Singapore – and the Royal Navy's *Hood*, *Prince of Wales* and *Repulse* were sunk: these were merely some of the greatest setbacks in a long litany of disaster.

The Second World War brought the British only a third of the casualties they had endured in the previous nightmare, yet the death-toll was still formidable – about 264,000 servicemen and 60,000 civilians. The tide began to swing against Germany in late 1942; but there were still further horrors in store. The Germans' V1 flying bomb and V2 rocket campaigns of 1944 brought a new wave of misery and death before victory was finally achieved.

Warfare and welfare

British society underwent profound changes during the war. Legions of people needed special kinds of help – bombed-out families, young widows, children whose mothers were working in vital industries, and many others. To cater for these needs, the government expanded the social services, bringing in supplementary pensions, home-helps for the sick and aged, immunization against diphtheria, and subsidized milk and school meals. These measures were the basis of the Welfare State. At the same time, new attitudes broke down the rigidity of a conformist social tradition. Women were called upon for a far fuller participation in the war effort than in 1914–18, and acquired new freedoms which they never subsequently lost. Changes were also caused by the great numbers of foreign troops in the country. By late 1942, as well as Europeans and Colonials, there were over 170,000 American servicemen in Britain. These foreigners brought new habits into society, and added new words to the vocabulary.

When the ordeal of war was over, a weary, drab and damaged country wished only for a fresh start. Turning against Churchill and the Conservatives in the election of July 1945, the people voted against a return to pre-war policies. Under a new Labour government, it seemed that an age of peace, full employment and comprehensive social welfare would miraculously dawn.

CONNECTIONS
Military history: 122–3 *The armed forces*
Post-war London: 250–51 *London*
Sea and air power: 178–9 *Shipbuilding;* **180–81** *The plane-makers;* **270–71** *Aviation*
War artists: 288–9 *The artist's eye*
Warfare and welfare: 88–9 *The growth of the Welfare State*

WAR GAMES. *In this cartoon Churchill, in partnership with Franklin D. Roosevelt of the United States, plays a double-six at dominoes against Hitler and Mussolini. Emperor Hirohito of Japan looks over Hitler's shoulder, while Stalin (whose ambitions in Europe increasingly aroused Churchill's suspicions) is standing to the right.*

Conserving the past

The historical and cultural achievements of Britain survive in a multitude of monuments, large and small. These range from whole sectors of towns such as York or Edinburgh to small farmhouses or railway stations tucked away in remote folds of countryside. The threat to this great heritage is a monster with many heads – environmental pollution, commercialism, inflation, ignorance. The visible past is gradually being eaten up. Many a fine building has had to concede its place in the urban townscape to a new shopping complex or multistorey office block. The countryside too has shared in this onslaught. Too many historic villages have acquired an ill-suited cladding of commuter estates, and traditional landscapes have had the integrity of their vernacular building styles intruded upon by prefabricated structures and discordant bungalows. Local authorities, no less than private developers, have been instrumental in such acts of barbarism.

Town and country

The most pressing problems for conservationists have attended the massive redevelopment of towns. The architectural heritage of towns such as Worcester, Shrewsbury and Hereford is now apparent only from side streets. In 1965 the Council for British Archaeology compiled a list of 322 historic towns which included 51 whose protection was seen as a matter of 'national concern'. The government response was to conduct a survey of the plight of four historic centres: York, Chichester, Bath and Chester. In York the problem was not so much redevelopment as the lack of a ring-road, leading to heavy traffic flow in the city centre. This has not only detracted from the character of one of the country's finest medieval walled towns, it has even threatened the structural stability of the Minster and other buildings. The Inner Ring Road devised in 1967 would have run outside the town walls, but at the cost of Georgian frontages. The successful opposition of 'York 2000' to this scheme provided a model for other urban protest groups.

Conservation action in the countryside has taken two forms. Items of what might be called the 'portable past' have been gathered together in countryside and open-air museums, which are rapidly proliferating. Among the most developed of them is the Welsh Folk Museum at St Fagans, near Cardiff, with its reconstructed farm buildings and workshops and its fine collection of country artefacts. In England there are a number of splendid regional museums in which the rural life of the area forms a central theme – for example, the North of England Open Air Museum at Beamish Hall (Durham) and the Museum of Lakeland Life at Kendal. A second form of rural conservation has grappled with the task of maintaining whole segments of the landscape. One instance of this is the survival of the open-field system at Laxton

BARN OF THE 16th CENTURY *at the Welsh Folk Museum, St Fagans (S. Glam.). This thatched, timber-framed barn, originally at Pennley (Clwyd), was dismantled, re-erected on the new site and carefully restored.*

Watchdogs of the heritage

The response to such widespread destruction has been more evident in public opinion than in planning practice. However, organized forces of opposition have sprung up, some of which, such as the Council for British Archaeology, have assumed a national role as watchdogs. Smaller bodies, such as the Georgian and Victorian Societies, have focused their efforts on particular periods. But perhaps the most significant and vocal of the conservationist lobbies have been the numerous Conservation or Civic Trusts in towns throughout the country – over 1,200 registered by 1981, each acting as a critical commentator on local planning.

Fresh laws on planning procedure have been introduced as a result of these activities. In addition to the designation of 'listed' buildings by the Department of the Environment (a safeguard against easy demolition), the 1967 Civic Amenities Act has empowered the Department to protect whole areas from radical change. And since the 1974 Town and Country Planning Act, local authorities have been forced to think constructively about the conservation of Britain's threatened urban and rural landscapes.

RESTORATION

Restoration of damaged monuments and works of art demands not only craftsmen trained in ancient crafts – glaziers, plasterers, bricklayers, masons and others – but also the invention of techniques to cope with 20th-century atmospheric pollution. It also calls for a great deal of money.

Since the 1950s some success has been achieved in coating outdoor sculpture with protective silane – for example, at Barfreston Church (Kent) and Wells Cathedral. But sometimes skilled craftsmen have had to be employed to replace damaged work entirely: the famous sculpted heads guarding Oxford's Sheldonian Theatre were completely renewed in 1971–2.

A particularly exciting challenge to restoration is being posed by Henry VIII's warship *Mary Rose*, discovered in the mud of the Solent: her timbers will require a 20-year course of treatment.

CLEANING SOILED MASONRY. *Numerous buildings and outdoor sculptures have been rejuvenated by blasting (**above**), by chemical treatment or by spraying with water. Blasting is now considered by experts to be too abrasive.*

RESTORING STAINED GLASS. *Despite weathering, vandalism and other hazards, a considerable amount of medieval stained glass survives. At Canterbury, in 1973, the Stained Glass Studio began painstakingly to remove (**right**) and restore (**above**) the Cathedral's great 12th- and 13th-century windows. Fragments of early glass are now collected in a special museum at Ely.*

ST ALBANS CATHEDRAL *was altered by Sir Edmund Beckett (later Lord Grimthorpe) in the 19th century in what was probably the most destructive restoration ever performed on an English cathedral. The west front is shown before and after the changes (**above** and **right**). Beckett added novel motifs copied from his favourite 13th-century churches. The* Builder *called him 'an architectural pretender . . . amusing himself . . . with the property of the nation'.*

(Nottinghamshire); another is the attempt to preserve the former crofting township at Auchindrain in Argyll. Generally, this type of conservation is most successful within the national parks, where planning objectives are clearly defined.

Historic buildings

In recent years a broader view of the national architectural heritage has gained purchase. The preservation of the great country houses remains a compelling duty, admirably discharged by the National Trust. But equal interest is now shown in humbler architecture. The Landmark Trust has been set up for the conservation and appreciation of small but precious habitable buildings, including the Martello Tower at Aldeburgh (Suffolk), the Gothick temple at Stowe (Buckinghamshire) and the railway station at Alton (Staffordshire). The restoration of artisan dwellings at Robert Owen's New Lanark or of the cottages built by the Great Western Railway for its workers in Swindon belong to the same category of concern. In the case of large commercial buildings, adaptation has proved both a redemption and a profitable investment, as at St Katherine's Dock in London, which has attracted a cluster of craft shops.

Sometimes the flagrant destruction of a particular type of building has suddenly prompted new appreciation. The cavalier demolition of the Firestone Factory on the Great West Road out of London has encouraged concern for another notable example of inter-war industrial architecture in London, the Hoover Factory in Perivale. Similarly, inner city development in cities such as Liverpool and Glasgow has awakened many people to the merits of some Victorian townscapes.

THE PINEAPPLE, *c. 1760, near Stirling, central Scotland. Part of a range of outbuildings (where pineapples were grown) on a great estate, this folly is run by the Landmark Trust as a holiday home.*

GEORGIAN BATH. *The city's precious centre, including the famous Crescents and the Circus (**above**), was protected by the Bath Corporation Act of 1937. But a development plan in the 1950s ravaged much of the suburbs, producing out-of-scale hotels, flats and shopping arcades.*

CONNECTIONS

The architectural heritage: 192–256

The industrial heritage: 146–7 *Relics of the industrial past;* **266–7** *Enjoying the railways today*

Rural architecture: 220–21 *Cottages and rural homes;* **232–3** *Farms*

Rural traditions: 86–7 *Vanishing skills*

Farming & industry

Many features in the agricultural and industrial landscapes of Britain would be utterly baffling to a time-traveller from even as recent an era as the 1920s. But widely scattered among the modern manifestations of technology – the huge globes of a nuclear power station, the computerized milking machines of an up-to-date dairy farm – are fascinating relics of older methods. This section of the book celebrates the ingenuity, old and new, that has made Britain both a humming workshop and a garden rich with the fruits of the earth.

Medieval agriculture

The rural landscapes of medieval Britain would have seemed very strange to modern eyes: there were few of the dispersed farmsteads, hedgerows or dry-stone walls, or regularly planted shelter belts and coppices that characterize them today. The majority of medieval husbandmen clustered in villages or townships and cultivated the surrounding ground on an open-field system, whereby each person's holding was subdivided into strips, or selions, scattered over all the arable land. These arrangements of the cultivated land gave rise to a splendid range of vernacular descriptive terms such as stitchmeal in south-west England, offaldfal in the Wash area, rudvall in Pembrokeshire and runrig in Scotland.

Some of these farming communities had their strips scattered haphazardly. Sometimes, though, the entire layout of the settlement followed a regular plan: each landholder's strips and parcels of land would be arranged in the same way in each of the different furlongs or arable plots, so that each person always had the same neighbours. These regular layouts of land division were often based on regional traditions. In eastern England and Scotland, for example, villages and townships made use of a division whereby landholders were allocated strips on either the sunny (eastern and southern) or shadow (western and northern) side of each furlong.

The open fields

Open fields posed practical problems for the individual farmers. They largely overcame these by treating their entire lands as a single communal unit of husbandry. Every task, from ploughing and seeding to weeding and harvesting, was performed on a joint basis. The larger communities usually operated a number of common plough-teams, to

MEDIEVAL LAND USE
Medieval field systems, or the way in which farming communities of the period organized their land for the purposes of cropping and grazing, displayed broad regional differences.

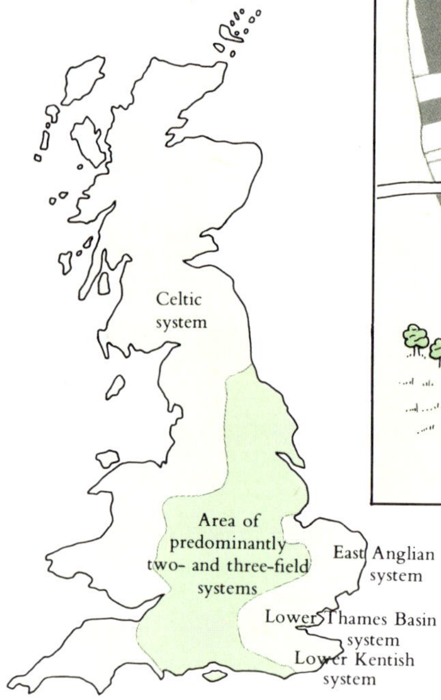

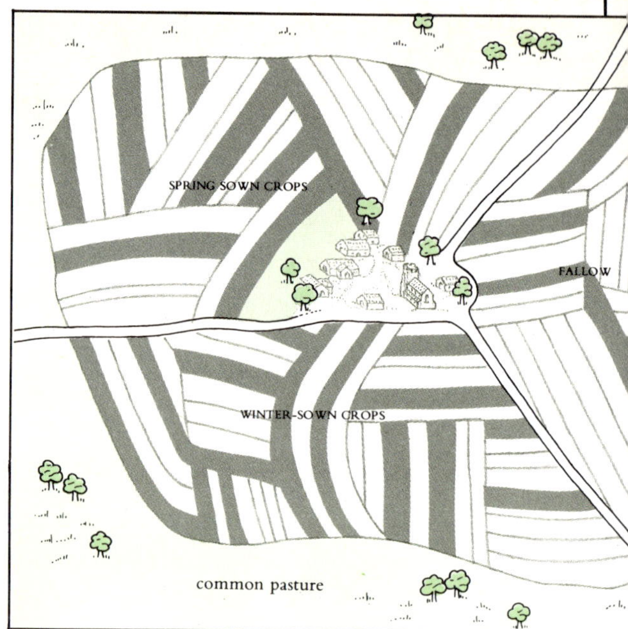

A TYPICAL THREE-FIELD SYSTEM, *with one field under a winter-sown grain, another under a spring-sown grain and the third lying fallow. Here the strips are regular and distributed between the landholders in an orderly way, but in other cases the strips might appear irregularly shaped and a landholder might have his strips concentrated in one area. The larger field systems could involve up to 50 different landholders.*

The main field system was the two- or three-field type. Originally considered to have been confined to the Midlands, its full distribution is now seen as extending north-westwards as far as Lancashire, north-eastwards as far as Northumberland and southwards into counties such as Somerset, Dorset and Hampshire. A similar type of open-field system was to be found in East Anglia, but there historians now prefer to stress the fold-course system, whereby the lords of the manor assumed the right to fold their sheep flocks over the harvest stubble of the village. Fully developed open-field systems were less widely found in the extreme south-east. The county of Kent, for example, experienced some fragmentation and intermixing of property due to piecemeal colonization of virgin land and the operation of a local inheritance custom known as gavelkind, whereby land was divided among inheriting sons. In upland areas of Britain the main type of open-field system was that of infield–outfield, although a diverse range of pastures was also found.

HARVESTING SCENE (***below***) *from the 14th-century Luttrell Psalter. The harvesters are being overlooked by the reeve, who acted as the lord's foreman. The sheaves were kept small to ease drying and handling.*

LAXTON IN NOTTINGHAMSHIRE (*left*) *is the finest surviving example of medieval open-field agriculture. Seen from the air, the corrugated grain imposed on the snow-covered countryside can be seen clearly and we can appreciate how relatively open and naked the medieval farming scene was. The area still operates as an open-field system and each year the boundaries of the common grass and arable strips are inspected and then freshly marked out by members of the Manor Court.*

THE MEDIEVAL PLOUGH *was a notoriously difficult implement to manage. Cumbersome in motion and with a draught of up to 8 oxen, it needed a small army of ploughmen and ploughboys both to goad and direct the plough-team and to keep the plough in the ground. Its clumsiness was most evident when it had to be turned at the end of each furrow, and most villages set aside a separate strip of headland for this task. In upland areas the spade was often preferred to the plough.*

THE RIDGES AND FURROWS *of medieval fields were produced by the action of a swing plough with a fixed mouldboard. The coulter made a vertical cut in the soil and then the share cut horizontally. Immediately after the share came the mouldboard, set at a slight angle to the direction of the plough, which turned over the slice of earth cut by the coulter and share and laid it alongside to the right, parallel to the direction of the plough.*

which the various landholders would contribute plough-irons, plough-timbers or draught beasts.

Pasture and meadowland were also subject to communal controls. Landholders supplied stock to a common herd in proportion to the amount of land they held in the settlement as a whole. Identical arrangements regulated the allocation of valuable stubble grazing left in the fields after harvesting. Indeed, it was this interest in common grazing over the stubble that militated against enclosures and in favour of 'open' or common fields. Only in such areas as the south-west of both England and Wales, where the strength of communal co-operation in agrarian matters was patently weak, did individual landholders opt out of the common grazing of harvest stubble by somewhat perversely enclosing their strips on a piecemeal basis.

The agreements reached by open-field communities over ploughing, herding and other tasks had repercussions on how their fields were organized for cropping. To have landholders harmoniously ploughing, harrowing, planting, harvesting and fallowing together, or moving their stock between the common pasture and harvest stubble in step with each other, meant that the entire system had to be put under the same cropping routine. The most widely adopted scheme was the two- or three-field system that grouped all the different furlongs of the village into two or three large cropping sectors. Under a two-field system, one field was cropped with a winter-sown or spring-sown grain (mainly wheat or barley) and the other left fallow. The three-field system involved cropping one sector with a winter-sown grain (mainly wheat), another with a spring-sown grain (mainly barley or oats), and letting the third lie fallow.

Around the highland areas of Britain more diverse systems of husbandry were to be found, of which the most widespread was the infield-outfield system. The infield occupied the better land close to the farmsteads and was cultivated intensively with crops such as oats and barley. The poorer, more distant arable land was known as outfield. It was cultivated by a cycle of partial and temporary cropping, the land being switched between arable and grass in regular succession.

Feudal relationships on the land

In the medieval period, relationships between lord and peasant were based on feudal ideas. Broadly speaking, feudalism controlled lord–peasant relationships through the manor, an institution that placed lord and peasant at opposite ends of the scale in terms of economic and legal standing. In those parts of lowland Britain where feudalism was strong and where the manor tended to be a single village, the typical husbandman was of unfree (villein) status. He held his land in return for labour services discharged on the demesne – that is, the part of the village that the lord kept in his own hands. This, the classic type of manor, was mainly to be found in the Midlands and southern-central England. Historians today are more appreciative of how the manor could deviate from this classic type. In the prime agricultural area of East Anglia, for example, villages commonly embraced two or more manors and often carried significant numbers of free tenants (locally called 'sokemen') as opposed to unfree villeins. The proportion of land given over to demesne was a further source of variety: this reached a peak during the 13th century, after which the proportion declined.

Away from the main arable districts, the hand of feudalism rested more lightly on the farming community. Towards both the north and south-west of England, and across the Welsh border, large territorial manors covered a number of different settlements. The links between lord and peasant in these areas were weaker, and relationships were often measured in cash rather than service (especially in the uplands).

CONNECTIONS
Barns and dovecotes: 232–3 *Farms*
Feudalism: 74–5 *Class in Britain*
Post-medieval agriculture: 134–5 *The agricultural revolution;* 136–7 *The impact of the new farming*
Wool: 142–3 *The wool trade*

The agricultural revolution

The word revolution suggests dramatic and sometimes violent change over a short period, but the so-called 'agricultural revolution' in Britain is misnamed in these respects. We use the term to describe gradual but fundamental and far-reaching changes in the methods of agricultural production and in the system of landholding from the mid-16th century to the end of the 19th century. These changes are bound up with the shift from a feudal economy to an increasingly commercial or 'capitalist' system.

Basic to this transformation of British agriculture was the reform of landholding. Under the feudal system of management, land had been seen in one sense as a common asset, to be used by people with common rights over it (of cultivation and cattle grazing, for example). In the 16th and 17th centuries, land became, more and more, a valuable commodity in which to invest, and highly sought-after by aristocratic families, merchants, lawyers, courtiers, administrators and other wealthy groups. The precise nature of the new developments was affected by complicated and often localized landholding systems and land inheritance patterns. For example, in areas where much of the land was under the control of a powerful manorial lord, it was easier to introduce a new mode of holding and management.

The momentum of enclosure

A key feature of the agricultural revolution was 'enclosure': the physical bounding of a piece of land by a hedge, fence, wall or ditch to create the fields – very different from the open fields of the medieval system – with which we are familiar in our 20th-century rural landscape. The term enclosure also refers to the equally important legal process, involving the removal of common rights of use and the substitution of exclusive individual rights of use – individual ownership as we know it.

Although enclosure (in both physical and legal senses) had been a continuous process since very early times in Britain, the most intensive waves occurred from the 17th to the 19th century. From 1750 to 1819, 3,828 private Acts of Parliament were passed for enclosure in England alone. The timing and effects varied from place to place, and some areas never experienced the change at all. On the whole, arable and meadow land was enclosed first, upland commons and wastes later.

The earlier parliamentary enclosure Acts were specific to particular parishes. But in the 19th century a number of general Acts were passed by parliament (1801, 1836, 1840 and 1845), which were designed to make enclosure cheaper and which in turn facilitated the fencing off of poorer-quality land. In the 1760s and 1770s the arable fields in the Midlands and in East Yorkshire had been enclosed, but during the period of the Revolutionary and Napoleonic wars (1793–1815) more counties and a greater variety of types of land experienced enclosure, including marginal wastelands brought into cultivation because of wartime food shortages and higher food prices. By the mid-19th century almost all the arable open fields were fenced off and the enclosure of upland wastes and commons continued.

ENCLOSURE SURVEYORS AT WORK (***right***). *The land was carefully surveyed and appropriate legal titles to it were established before it was distributed by the commissioners appointed under each enclosure act.*

THE HOLKHAM MONUMENT

This celebrates the career of Thomas Coke (1752–1842), a famous exponent of agricultural improvement. Erected in commemoration of him by the grateful 'yeomen of Norfolk', it depicts some of the means by which he effected an increase and improvement in cultivation and production. For many years Coke held an annual sheep-shearing festival at Holkham (***below***), originally just for his guests and tenants, but eventually for interested farmers from all over Britain and beyond. Visitors could see an agricultural revolution in action and afterwards return home to try the new methods for themselves.

THE HOLKHAM DEVON OX. *This stately beast represents the herd of red Devon cattle introduced to Norfolk by Coke.*

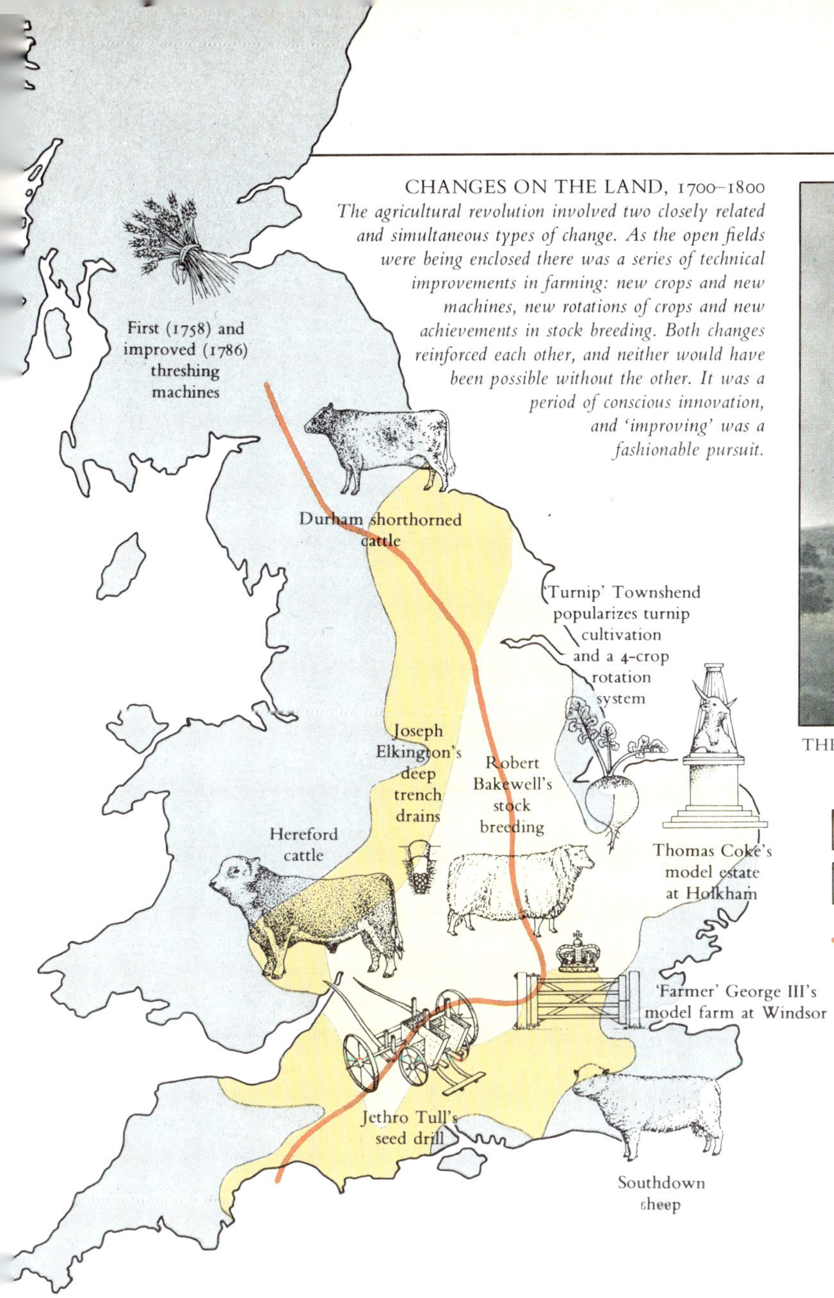

CHANGES ON THE LAND, 1700–1800 *The agricultural revolution involved two closely related and simultaneous types of change. As the open fields were being enclosed there was a series of technical improvements in farming: new crops and new machines, new rotations of crops and new achievements in stock breeding. Both changes reinforced each other, and neither would have been possible without the other. It was a period of conscious innovation, and 'improving' was a fashionable pursuit.*

THE DURHAM OX *was bred by the Colling brothers of Ketton near Darlington.*

In the areas of south Wales where the Norman influence had been strong, arable open fields were rare in the 18th century, because most of them had probably been enclosed before the start of the parliamentary enclosure movement. However, large areas of upland were affected by private and general parliamentary enclosure Acts in the 18th and 19th centuries. The relative pace of change is indicated by the fact that although there were only four enclosure awards for south Wales before 1793, involving 5,784 acres (2,341 ha), in the period 1800–95 there were 104 awards relating to approximately 155,000 acres (63,000 ha).

New crops and techniques

In general, the enclosed fields provided a basic framework for the introduction of new systems of farming which could not have been *extensively* introduced into the former open-field system. A major feature of the agricultural revolution was the widespread adoption of new crops, cropping systems, management techniques and various labour-saving devices including agricultural machinery (the latter quite late in the day). It is quite wrong to assume, as many people still do, that the new crops and rotation systems were not introduced until well into the 18th century: the turnip, for example, had been introduced to England by the Romans, but was reintroduced by Dutch merchants in East Anglia in the 16th century, and it was in East Anglia that it was used in the famous Norfolk four-course rotation.

The essential ingredients of the new cropping systems were root crops and grasses, which fulfilled several functions including those of increasing the number of animals that could be fed on green land, and of improving the soil by the addition of nitrogen (in the case of clover and the new grasses). The technique of using the new sown grasses (as opposed to the natural sward) in rotation with fodder crops was part of a system of 'convertible husbandry': that is, of rotating cultivation of one crop with a crop of sown grass, the grass being a temporary rather than a permanent feature. It is claimed that convertible husbandry spread rapidly in the 17th century, with the introduction of clover and the increasing adoption of the turnip.

The most publicized form of convertible husbandry was the Norfolk four-course rotation involving the rotation of two cereal crops (wheat and barley) with two fodder crops (clover and turnips), usually in the sequence: turnips, barley, clover, wheat. The fact that it was widely vaunted did not, however, mean that it was the only efficient system of land use. Indeed, in time it was considerably modified to suit soil and climatic conditions different from those of the light-soil areas of Norfolk. The publicity, like that of other agricultural innovations of the period, owed much to publicists such as Thomas Coke of Holkham ('Coke of Norfolk'). A still more important advocate of improved farming was Arthur Young, Secretary to the Board of Agriculture (1793).

There are many other examples of successfully introduced innovations in the period of the agricultural revolution. Among them are the swede (swedish turnip), mangold-wurzel, lucerne, sainfoin and Italian rye-grass; the floated watermeadow (a system of irrigation to produce greatest grass growth on chalklands); and the products of experimental animal breeding, such as the new Leicester sheep bred by Robert Bakewell at Dishley. The degree to which the new rotations were adopted (often in combination with the more intensive stocking of land with improved livestock) varied enormously with time and place. Generally, they were first applied in the light-soil regions of East Anglia, but spread in modified form at a later date to the heavy clay-soil areas farther west.

A quieter revolution involved changes in methods of land drainage, which progressed from basic surface drainage furrows to subsurface drainage systems. Major progress was made with the introduction of tile drains in the 1830s and 1840s, and government loans were available to assist with clayland drainage costs.

CONNECTIONS
Enclosure in Leicestershire: 36–7 *Man and the landscape*
Farm buildings: 232–3 *Farms*
Farming and the railways: 264–5 *The railway revolution*
The open fields: 32–3 *Medieval agriculture*
Settlement patterns: 222–3 *Villages and hamlets*

The impact of the new farming

The agricultural revolution was not beneficial to the whole rural populace. For those who lost common rights, enclosure ultimately spelt misery, even though there was much work initially, such as hedging, fencing and initiating new practices. Dissatisfaction led to migration to the factory towns, or emigration abroad, and sometimes to violent protest. By the early 19th century, small farmers had all but disappeared, except in parts of Wales, Scotland and areas in the north such as the Pennine dales. Instead, British farming came to be dominated by the triple division into great landlords, the tenant-farmers of large farms, and landless hired labourers. There was tension in the countryside as social divisions widened: the labourers spoke and dressed in much the same way as before, but their masters were now gentleman farmers who favoured the fashions of the town, and whose wives and daughters took up genteel pursuits such as the piano.

The application of invention and innovation was a slow and uneven process, however, especially where the availability of cheap labour discouraged investment in machinery. Although various improved forms of plough, including the Rotherham plough and the Sussex iron plough, were introduced in the 18th century, much of the improvement in productivity came from minor modifications to very traditional implements. The disc plough, whose main feature was the substitution of revolving convex discs in place of the old share and mouldboard, was only introduced towards the end of the 19th century.

The most dramatic aspect of mechanization was the introduction of steam ploughing, beginning around 1800, and usually involving the traction of the plough by a cable or rope attached to a steam engine. It was only a matter of time before steampower was applied to other processes, including threshing, and among the outstanding developments in 19th-century farming was the invention of machines for reaping, threshing and binding. Although several horse-drawn reaping machines had existed earlier in the century the greatest impact came from the exhibition (at the Crystal Palace in 1851) of two American machines, the Hussey and the McCormick reapers.

The Scottish story

The Scottish experience of the agricultural revolution was different. In considering it, the modernizing Lowlands have to be distinguished from the, broadly speaking, more traditional and 'tribal' Highlands and islands where subsistence peasants were settled in ancestral areas under chieftains, or lairds, of their own kin. In the Lowlands enclosure followed on from a feudal system similar to that of most of the rest of Britain and by the early 19th century progressive agricultural practices had become a hallmark of the region.

But when the Highland lairds began to behave like ordinary landlords, that is doing with their 'property' what they pleased, a painful and, to the crofters, immoral process of disruption ensued. In the days when the laird's status was based on the number of men he could muster to his allegiance in wartime it made sense to allow the number of small proprietors on the clan's land to multiply. But the lairds could only achieve the status and lifestyle of their southern landholding counterparts by 'clearing' the hilly land of crofters to make way for labour-saving sheep.

THE CROFTERS' PLIGHT. *As the Highland lairds cleared their hilly land to make way for flocks of sheep, many of the dispossessed crofters emigrated overseas. Those remaining crowded into already congested areas and suffered a miniature version of the Irish Famine in the middle 1840s, when the potato crop failed.*

AN ENGLISH DAIRYMAID CHURNING BUTTER. *As cereals and new crops conquered 19th-century British agriculture, there was less general dairying. It was traditionally skilled and relatively well-paid women's work, although extremely demanding physically. Under the farmer's wife, dairymaids worked from early morning until late at night in summer.*

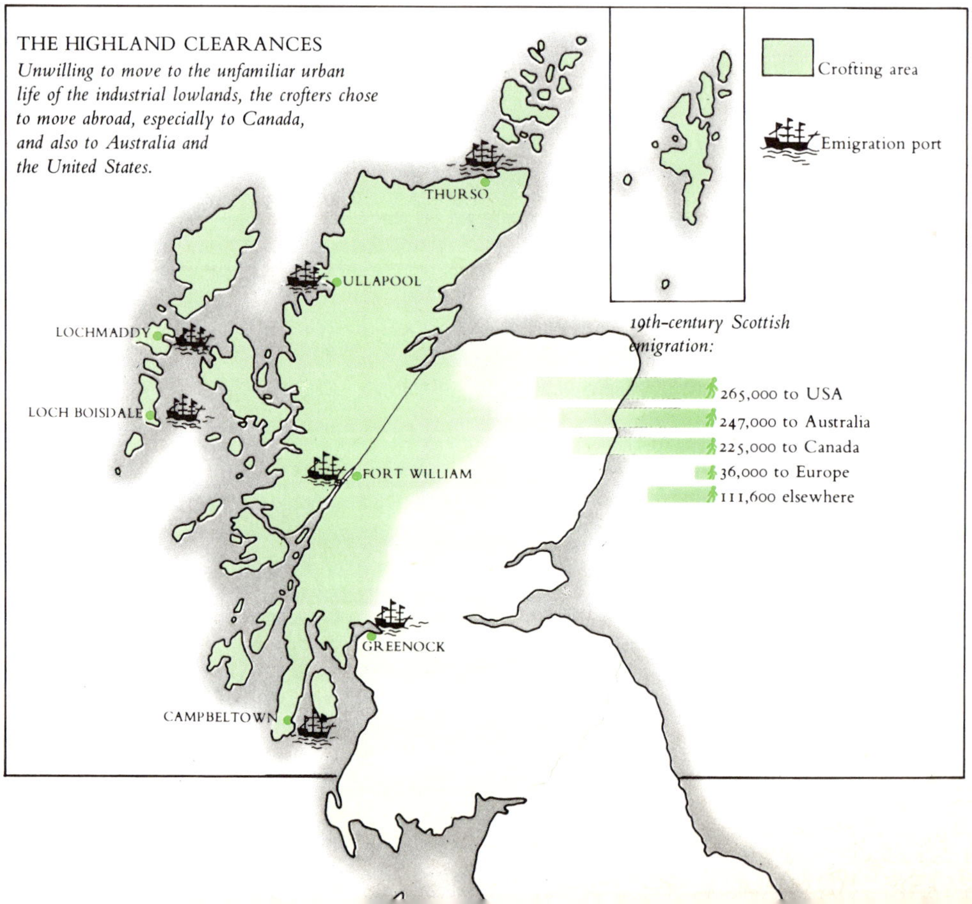

THE GOLDEN YEARS. *This idyllic English harvesting scene belongs to the period after 1850, when migration had reduced the rural surplus, leaving more work for those remaining. Foreign competition was not yet a problem.*

THE STATE OF THE COUNTRY (***below***). *A contemporary cartoon captures some of the elements in the 1830–1 'Swing' uprising in 7 low-wage corn-growing counties of the south and east. Threshing machines made many labourers redundant.*

THE REAPING REVOLUTION

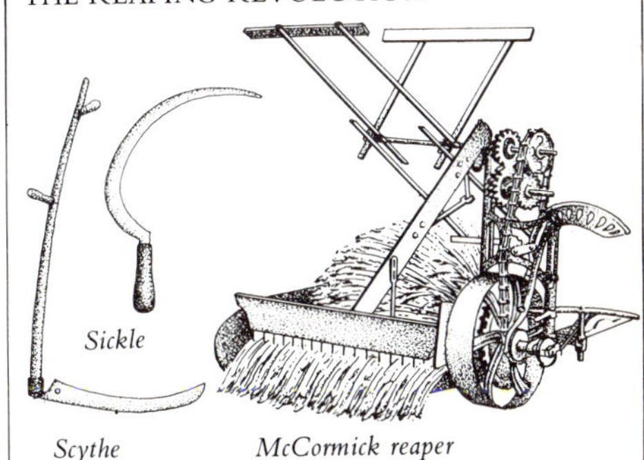

From ancient times the hook-shaped sickle was the reaper's tool, but it was increasingly replaced in the 19th century by the heavier but faster scythe, which in turn, from the 1850s onwards, yielded place to the first mechanical reapers.

CONNECTIONS

Agrarian unrest: 84–5 *Workers' movements;* **108–9** *Riot and revolution*
Enclosure: 134–5 *The agricultural revolution*
Farming in literature: 296–9 *Writers and places*
The Highlands: 62–3 *Scottish clans and tartans*

Modern agriculture

The second half of the 20th century has seen changes on the land as dramatic as those that occurred in the period of the agricultural revolution. Modern farming is increasingly science-based and mechanized. Working horses are now rare and tractors ubiquitous. Haymaking has been transformed by tractor-mounted mowers, while at corn harvest time huge combine harvesters simultaneously cut the corn and thresh the grain. As late as 1939, there were less than 100 combines in Britain, but today great numbers of them announce the coming of autumn over vast tracts of arable land. The straw they leave is either burnt or baled into neat, machine-handled blocks, which now characterize the harvest landscape, superseding the stooks of bound sheaves that used to be left in the sun to dry. Haystacks, and milk churns by the roadside, are also things of the past.

The changing 'farmscape'
In order to operate efficiently, big agricultural machines need wide, open spaces. Today, especially in the eastern counties, hedgeless 'prairies', undoing the parcels of the enclosure movement, are conquering Britain. Thanks to the achievements of plant breeders, farmers are now growing new crops such as a special type of maize better suited to British conditions. An especially conspicuous newcomer, adding patches of lurid yellow to the countryside, is oilseed rape (used to supply vegetable oil for the food industry). Modern agriculture also takes advantage of disease-resistant and high-yielding varieties of traditional crops such as wheat. Crop rotation is no longer such a pressing need now that pesticides and herbicides can be used to cleanse the land, and synthetic fertilizers give life to tired soil that would otherwise have required a spell of lying fallow.

Some farm animals, once a familiar sight in the rural outdoors, are now seldom to be seen. Pigs and poultry are kept in controlled indoor environments. (The prototypes of modern battery units first appeared in the late 1920s.) Many types of dairy cattle have been ousted by the black-and-white Friesian, which is now the dominant breed. Developments in animal genetics have also helped to alter the farmer's work routines. The heyday of the local bull, for example, was brought to an end by the introduction of artificial insemination in the 1940s: this is now the predominant method.

Farming as 'agri-business'
The new look of the agricultural landscape reflects the way in which farming has become increasingly business-like since the Second World War. The

FARMING TYPES *Lowland areas with low rainfall generally favour crops; highland areas with poorer soil and high rainfall favour livestock.*

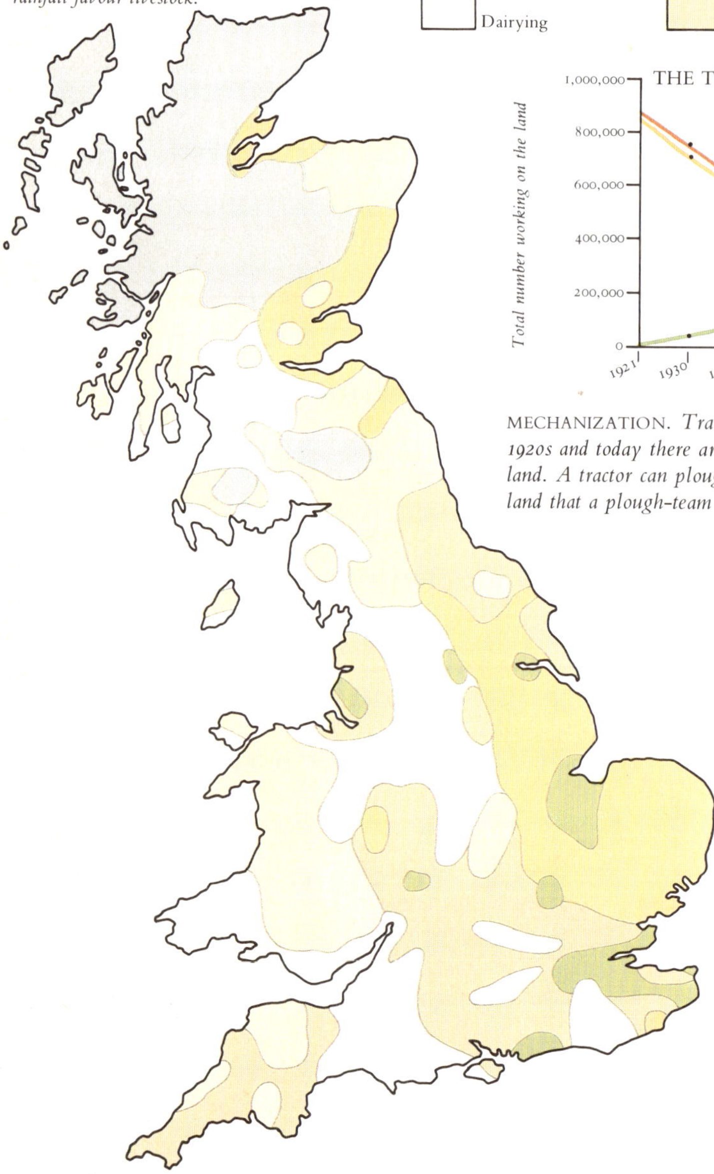

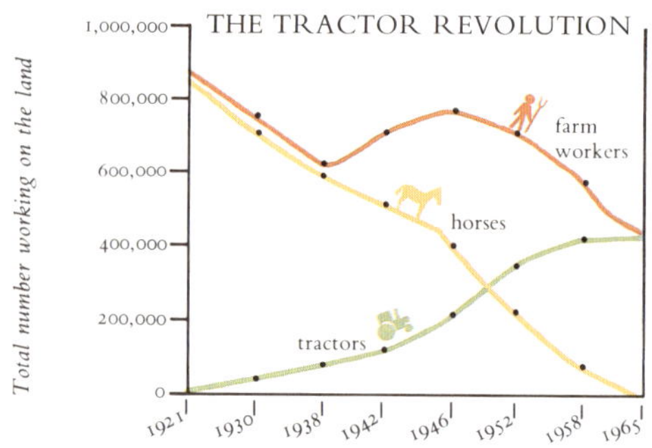

MECHANIZATION. *Tractors first appeared in the 1920s and today there are around 435,000 on the land. A tractor can plough 25 times the amount of land that a plough-team could in a day.*

CHAROLLAIS CATTLE. *The first creamy white Charollais bulls were imported from Burgundy in 1961. When they are crossed with dairy cows, quick-maturing beef calves are produced.*

BEFORE THE TRACTOR, *the Suffolk Punch was East Anglia's plough horse. It is still valued today on light soils, which are unlikely to stick to the horse's legs, but horses no longer operate in great numbers.*

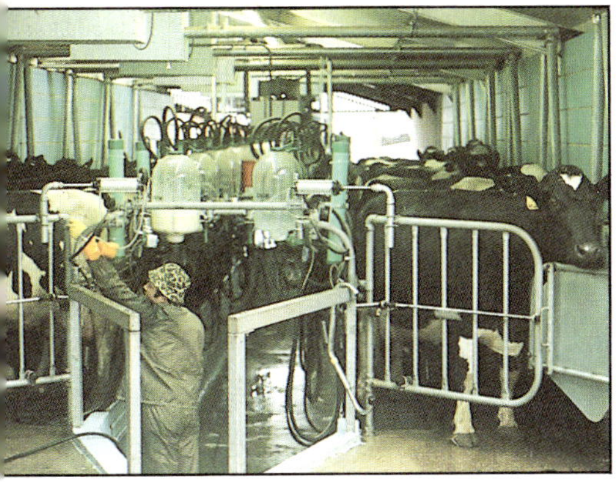

MILKING TIME. *In the old days cows were milked twice a day, but on the most modern farms they are milked by machine in round-the-clock relays.*

BANBURY CATTLE MARKET, OXON. *Markets promote the best use of different kinds of land by facilitating the transfer of animals. Cattle reared in highland areas are fattened by lowland farmers.*

modern farm has a great deal of capital invested in it, much of it tied up in specialized buildings and equipment.

The context in which the farmer-businessman operates is national and international. His activities are influenced by government policy and by the Common Agricultural Policy of the European Economic Community. External aid to farmers has taken the form of price guarantees, charges on imports and direct grants to encourage new emphases in the pattern of farming production. State assistance was given in the First World War to promote a greater output of cereals, and in one form or another has been available continuously since the 1947 Agricultural Act.

British farms have grown in size but declined in numbers since the 19th century. Today more than three-quarters of farms are 100 acres (40 ha) or more, and the average size of holdings is around 250 acres (100 ha). However, mechanization has meant that even large farms such as these generally employ a small workforce on a permanent basis, though use is often made of seasonal labour. In 1851 some 22 per cent of the total work force of the

A COMBINE HARVESTER *cuts the corn, threshes the grain and stores it in a tank until it is unloaded into trailers that transport it to the corn dryer. Although costly, these machines enable the farmer to take maximum advantage of fine weather at harvest time.*

country was engaged in agriculture and fishing. By 1931 this had fallen to 6 per cent; and the present figure is around 3 per cent.

Regional variations

Advances in transport in the 19th and 20th centuries have made it easier and cheaper to move perishables such as milk or eggs. Such progress has made the location of horticulture, originally determined by the demand from towns, more flexible. However, the farming of some bulky products, such as potatoes and sugar beet, is still limited by the necessity of nearby sources of demand, and proximity to processing centres is an important consideration in vegetable production for canning and freezing.

In spite of all the pressures towards uniformity, farming today retains something of its regionalized character. The age-old factors of soil, climate, altitude and topography still come very much into play. Yet the dominant impression, for an observer of the modern farming scene, is one of rapid change. One current trend is towards barley at the expense of livestock, as it is costly to feed animals on cereals, and more efficient ways of feeding them on grass have not yet been thoroughly explored. But agriculture is now so unsettled that such generalizations can quickly become outdated.

BATTERY HENS (**below**). *Eighty per cent of British laying birds live in the controlled environments of battery houses, where they are automatically fed on a uniform diet. Under these conditions a hen can lay about 300 eggs a year, compared with 90 in 1946.*

CONNECTIONS

The changing diet: 184–5 *Food in Britain;* **186–7** *Drink in Britain*

Farm buildings: 232–3 *Farms*

The mechanization of farming: 134–5 *The agricultural revolution*

Fishing

TYPES OF FISHING GEAR

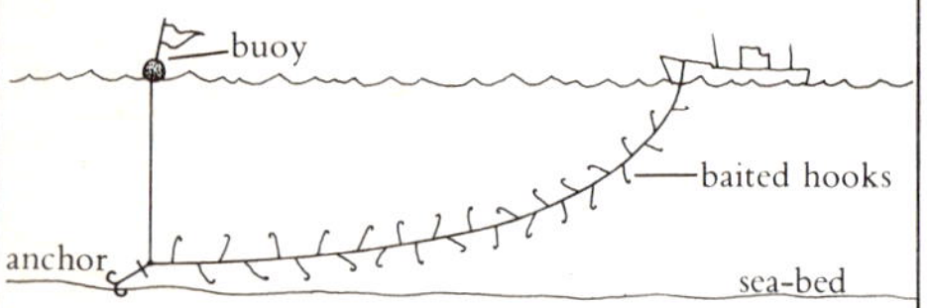

LONG-LINING. *Used for centuries, for example by medieval cod fishermen off Iceland, and today by some inshore fishermen. The hooks are usually baited with mackerel.*

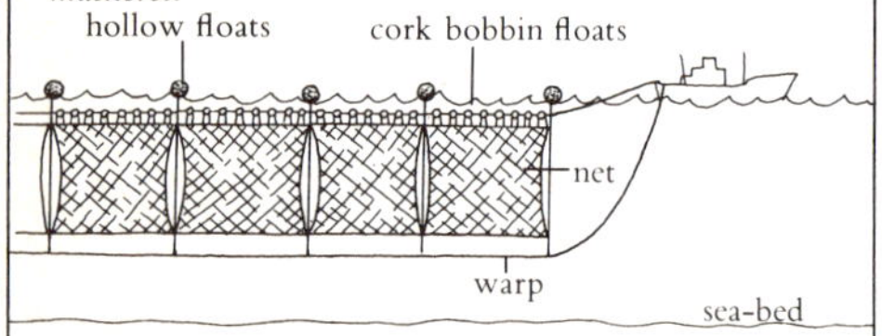

DRIFTING. *Traditional but now uncommon way of catching herring and other pelagic (surface or middle depth) fish. Still used by a few vessels in the south-west.*

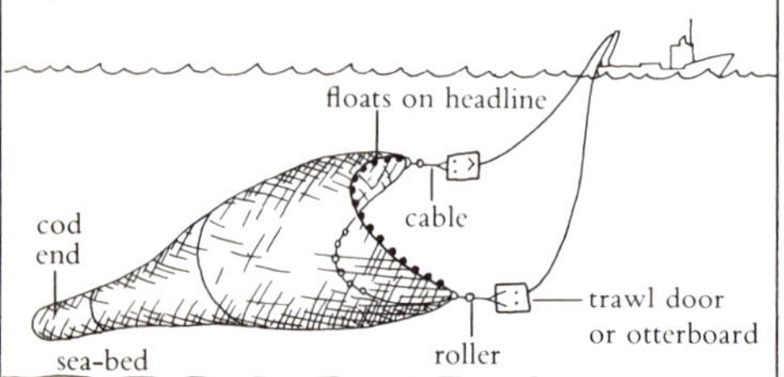

TRAWLING. *Spread during the 19th century as an improved way of catching demersal (sea-bed) fish such as cod. Mackerel trawling is now a major activity.*

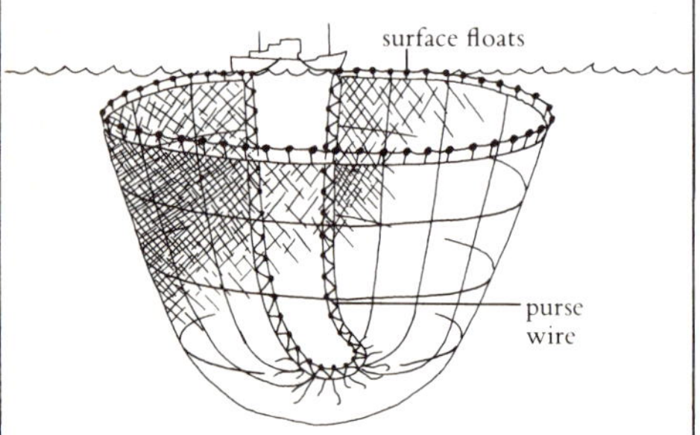

PURSE-SEINING. *Highly effective way of catching pelagic fish. After the shoal has been encircled with the net, the purse-wire is drawn tight. The vast catches are often pumped on board.*

Sea fishing in Britain pre-dates the origins of farming. Primitive techniques, involving spears, lines, hooks, traps and nets, were in use some 5,000–4,000 years ago, in conjunction with crudely constructed boats. Gradually, fish ceased to be merely a local subsistence food and became an important item of trade, caught progressively farther from the coasts and sold ever deeper inland. Records of the 6th century describe the activities of fish traders in the English Channel and North Sea. By the 12th century the long history of British fishing around Iceland had begun. Cod and herring, which remained the mainstay of the fishing industry until the 1970s, were the principal species sought in the Middle Ages. The improvement of curing methods, such as drying, salting and smoking, allowed catches to be preserved for longer periods and sold in greater quantities to Britain's growing medieval towns.

Improved catching techniques gradually evolved, but sparked off controversy before they were widely accepted. In 1376, for example, a group of Thames Estuary fishermen petitioned Edward III about the threat to their livelihood posed by the use of a 'wondyrchoun' (literally, a wondrous device). The reference was to a net that was dragged along the sea-floor: it caught immature fish as well as full-grown ones, and disrupted breeding grounds. The technique was banned as requested and did not become legal again until the 17th century, but persisted illicitly and evolved into the variety of trawl nets used in modern times.

Expansion and contraction

The industrial revolution produced the markets and the technological means for a massive expansion of the fishing industry during the 18th and 19th centuries. Steam-power and the internal combustion engine meant that larger, faster vessels could be built, while the development of the railways improved distribution. Ice from North America and, later, Norway was used for preserving fish during transportation before the development of ice production by mechanical means.

The practice of trawling spread rapidly in the 19th century as an efficient way of catching cod and other demersal (sea-bed) species. The first British steam trawlers were launched at Hull and Grimsby in 1882. Drift-netting, a technique borrowed from the Dutch and developed to exploit

FISHING PORTS AND THEIR LANDINGS

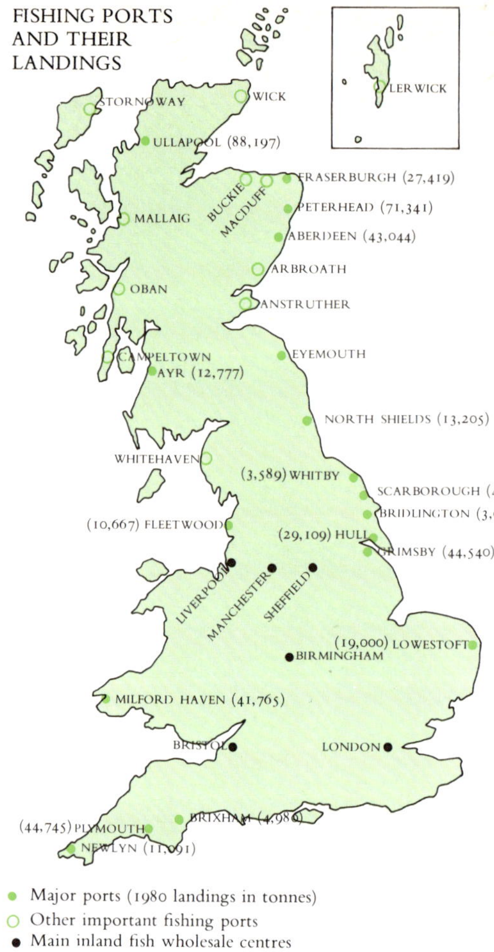

PURSE-SEINER AT PLYMOUTH. *The first British purse-seining vessel was built in 1968. Although fish are a renewable resource, there is no species that can withstand uncontrolled purse-seining.*

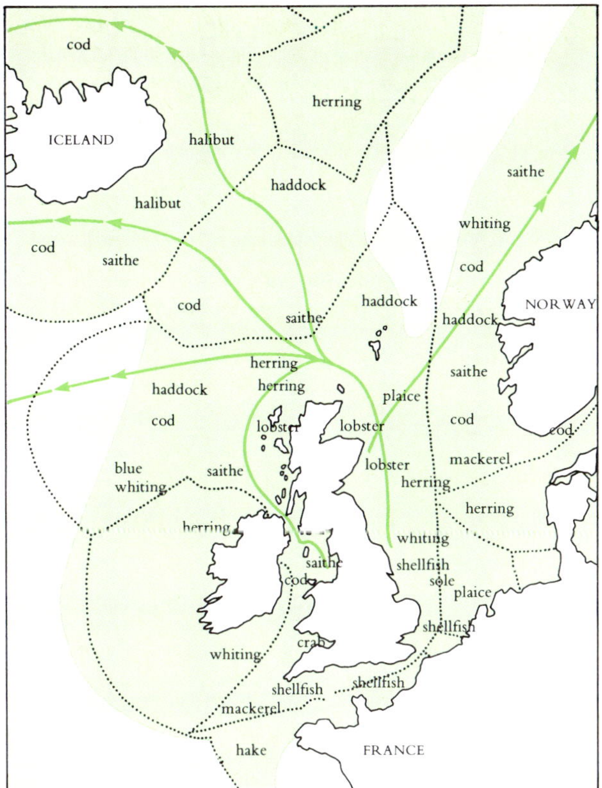

BRITAIN'S NEAR AND MIDDLE FISHING GROUNDS

Main fishing areas

.... 200-mile/median limits

Directions of distant-water fishing effort prior to spread of 200-mile limits

BILLINGSGATE MARKET, *1981. London's historic wholesale fish market was moved from here to the Isle of Dogs in January 1982.*

the rich herring fisheries that stretched from the Shetlands to East Anglia, was also modernized. Steam drifters, introduced about 1900, enabled tide and wind to be conquered, and highly mobile fleets to pursue the shoals virtually all year round.

In recent times overfishing has led to the ejection of fishermen from Icelandic, Norwegian and North American fishing grounds. Consequently, the British fishing effort has contracted back towards home waters, and ports based on distant-water fishing, such as Hull, have sadly declined.

THE FATE OF THE NORTH SEA HERRING

From spawning grounds off northern Britain, young herring larvae drift eastwards to nursery areas near Continental coasts. For centuries, cured herring was an important source of protein throughout Europe; until recently the kipper was a familiar food on British tables. From 1945, however, 'industrial' herring fishing for reduction to meal and oil was increasingly practised by the Danes and Norwegians, aided by new equipment such as the purse-seine net. The British, who still fished with traditional herring drifters, were alarmed to see their livelihood threatened. But inevitably, some were soon investing in purse-seiners of their own and new catching capacities initially led to an increase in landings (1960–65). The classic overfishing cycle was completed when the catch fell to a mere 44,200 tonnes in 1977. The East Anglian fishery had collapsed, and by 1975 the last Shetland herring drifter had ceased operations. After years of prevarication a ban was placed on North Sea herring fishing in 1977 in a desperately belated effort to save a once great fishery.

HERRING LANDINGS
Overfishing has led to a dramatic decline in the North Sea herring catches of British fishermen.

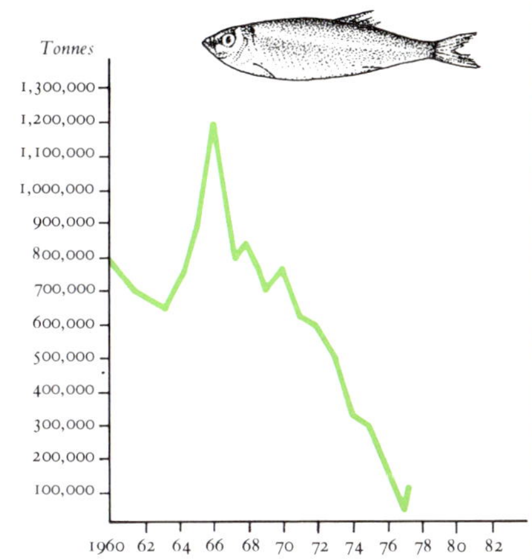

YARMOUTH IN THE 1920s. *The land-bound women of this important herring-fishing community, many of whom were imported from Scotland, were engaged in maintaining and mending the drift-nets (**below**) and in gutting, sorting and curing the herrings.*

COD WAR CONFRONTATION (***left***). *Between 1958 and 1975 Britain clashed with Iceland in a series of 'cod wars' as the Icelanders, alarmed at declining cod yields and concerned to protect a resource vital to their economy, progressively extended their national fishing limit.*

CONNECTIONS
Fish in the British diet: 184–5 *Food in Britain*
Fishing ports and the railways: 264–5 *The railway revolution*

The wool trade

Until the 18th century wool was the staple manufacture of England. Its prominence dated back to the 12th and 13th centuries, when many of the newly founded abbeys took to sheep-farming as a source of income. Using their network of overseas contacts, the abbeys exported most of their wool to Continental Europe, but by the end of the 13th century their interest was waning and the flocks maintained by lay landowners became responsible for an increasing share of the wool produced. At the same time, the export trade in raw wool declined as home demand grew with the expansion of England's own woollen cloth industry in the 14th and 15th centuries.

A MEDIEVAL SHEEP-SHEARER. *Shearing takes place in summer. Using mechanical clipping machines instead of the old hand shears, modern sheep shearers can remove an entire fleece in one piece.*

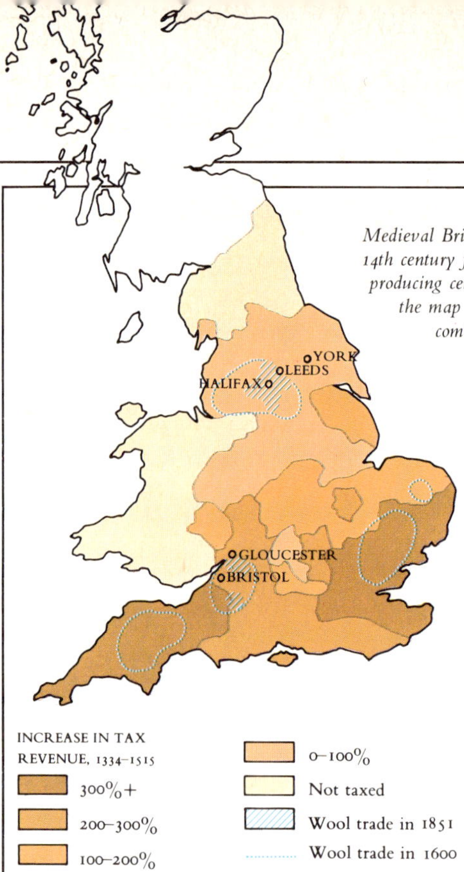

WOOL AND WEALTH
*Medieval Britain's main centre of wealth shifted dramatically after the mid-14th century from the crop-producing Midlands to the sheep runs and cloth-producing centres of the south-east and south-west. This shift is evident on the map (**left**), which shows changes in medieval tax levies. With the coming of industrialization, the wool trade became concentrated on centres in Yorkshire and the West Country.*

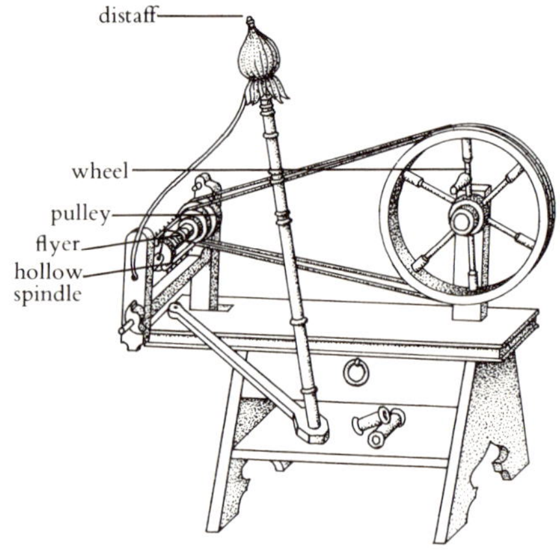

A SPINNING WHEEL, c. *1480. Wool-spinners were ubiquitous in medieval Britain. Nearly every household had a spinning wheel or distaff as part of the furniture.*

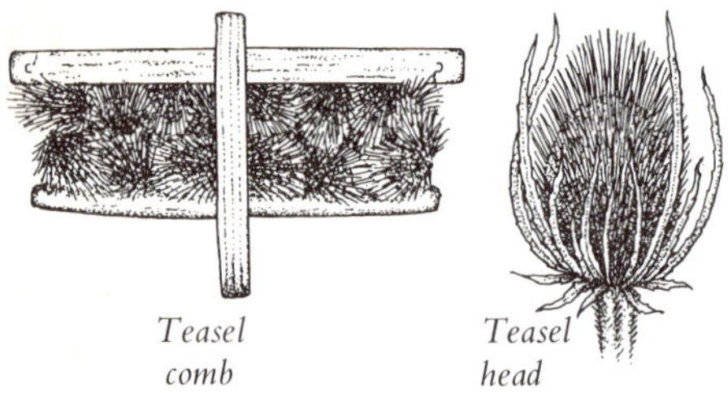

A WELSH TEASEL COMB. *This simple implement, made of teasel-heads, served to open out the wool fibres prior to spinning and weaving in the days when the wool trade was still a cottage industry. Teasels were also used for raising the nap.*

WOOL-DYEING ON THE ISLE OF LEWIS, *1936. The woollen industry of the Hebrides has retained its essentially croft-based character.*

A HERDWICK SHEEP. *Since the industrial revolution farmers have been most interested in sheep for their meat, but the Herdwick, which predominates in the Lake District, is kept primarily for its wool.*

There is probably not an area in the whole of Britain that has not been at one time or another connected with the manufacture of woollen cloth. The geographical range of this activity was especially wide in the Middle Ages, when new rural areas were drawn in not only to supply the wool but also to carry out processes such as carding or combing, spinning, weaving and fulling (cleansing and thickening the woven cloth). The local specialities of a host of minor wool districts imparted great diversity to the industry: products ranged from the cheap white cloth of mid-Wales to the hand-knitted hosiery of the east Midlands. Until the 18th century, however, the wool trade was concentrated in the manufacturing districts of East Anglia, the West Country (especially Somerset, Gloucestershire and Wiltshire) and Yorkshire.

The cloth and worsted trades
The woollen trade was divided into two main branches: cloth (or woollens) and worsteds (or stuffs). Whereas the cloth trade used short-staple wool which was carded before spinning, the worsted trade used long-staple wool which was combed. After spinning and weaving, woollen cloth passed through various fulling and finishing processes, but these were not applied to worsteds.

The West Country was the centre of the cloth trade, while East Anglia was the centre of the worsted trade, having benefited most from the expertise of émigré Flemish weavers. The clothiers of Yorkshire were initially based on towns such as York and Beverley. By the 14th century, however, the northern trade's focus had started to shift westwards into the Pennine valleys, and by the 18th century the districts around Leeds, Halifax and Wakefield were the main centres, producing a cheap, narrow cloth.

Until the late 18th century the wool trade was organized on a domestic basis: all the different stages of manufacture were performed by artisans in their own homes. The links between each process were provided by the local marketplace or, increasingly, by merchants who organized the scattered artisans into a coherent system of production by providing them with materials and credit. Only the processes of fulling and dyeing were divorced from this predominantly domestic context. Fulling had been mechanized as early as the 13th century with the introduction of the water-powered fulling mill, an innovation that did much to orientate the industry towards the fast-flowing streams of the countryside. Dyeing required such an array of exotic dyes that its control was invariably in the hands of enterprising merchants.

From cottages to factories
The industrial revolution led to the mechanization of the basic processes of the wool trade and their transfer from cottages to factories. Spinning was

PIECE HALL, HALIFAX

The wool trade of Halifax dates back to the 15th century, although the town's heyday, to which the impressive Piece Hall bears witness, was the late 18th and the 19th century. The building was started in 1775 when the wool merchants of Halifax joined together to establish a new trading centre – a place where pieces of cloth could be bought and sold. The three-storeyed complex has 315 rooms, ranged around a courtyard (***below***). Over the entrance is a weather-vane in the shape of a fleece. The elaborate coat of arms (***left***) testifies to the self-confident prosperity of Halifax's wool merchants at this time. Today, Piece Hall houses craft shops and textile exhibits.

WEAVING IN HUDDERSFIELD TODAY (***left***). *These modern, fully automatic, high-speed Rapier looms can produce woollen and worsted fabrics in a variety of designs using several different-coloured yarns.*

the first process to be mechanized to any great effect. It was transformed by a sequence of innovations – the spinning jenny, water frame and mule – that had been pioneered in the cotton industry and were adopted by the wool trade from the 1780s onwards. Weaving became mechanized when the use of the power loom became general in the second quarter of the 19th century, and thereafter integrated spinning and weaving factories were possible.

The Yorkshire woollen cloth and worsted trades were the first to respond to these innovations. However, Yorkshire's domination of the woollen trade was achieved over the century *prior to* the industrial revolution: the area's relatively speedy response to mechanization, and the availability of coal for driving the new machines, merely emphasized this dominance. The West Country introduced mechanized spinning during the 1790s, but the mechanization of weaving was a slow affair, involving much labour trouble and high social costs. Least responsive of all was East Anglia, whose output and importance declined over the late 18th and early 19th centuries.

Today, most of the raw wool for Britain's use is imported from Australia, New Zealand and South Africa, and electricity has replaced steam-power. The wool textile industry is still largely concentrated in the towns of West Yorkshire. A number of smaller areas of production have survived, however, specializing in unique products of high quality – Harris tweed from the Outer Hebrides, cashmere, knitwear and tweeds from elsewhere in Scotland, blankets from Whitney.

A distinct and comparatively recent branch of the industry is the manufacture of tweed, which developed from the traditional shepherd checks produced from the late 18th century in the Scottish Southern Uplands. Encouraged by the fashionable success of tartans, clothiers from the region began to devise a wide range of checks for trousers, shawls and other garments, laying the foundations of the modern tweed industry.

CONNECTIONS

Other textiles: 160–63 *Cotton*

Watermills: 148–9 *Wind, water and steam*

Wool and wealth: 204–5 *Parish churches*

Wool towns: 222–3 *Villages and hamlets;* **224–5** *Market towns*

The birth of industry

The two most truly momentous episodes in the history of the world have been the invention of agriculture and the industrial revolution. The latter was at first an exclusively British phenomenon, which took place gradually from the later 18th century. It was activated by a coincidence of favourable circumstances – social stability, prosperity based on agriculture and protected trading power, a variety of natural resources (notably iron and coal), a good water transport system, a growing population to provide labour and a demand for cheap manufactured goods, and colonies to supply raw materials and exclusive markets. When these potentialities were realized by a massive input of technological and entrepreneurial talent, fundamental changes took place in society. By 1800 the various small, scattered cottage industries of Britain, organized by merchant businessmen who distributed the raw materials and collected the finished goods, were on the wane. New manufacturing techniques and new sources of power had resulted in a large-scale re-organization of industry – the emergence of the factory system, which made Britain the workshop of the world.

SIR RICHARD ARKWRIGHT, *the most dynamic and successful of the cotton magnates.*

ARKWRIGHT'S CROMFORD
The power for Arkwright's cotton mills at Cromford, Derbys., came from Bonsall Brook (a tributary of the Derwent) and Cromford Sough (a lead-mining drain).

Arkwright's Old Mill, in its original form

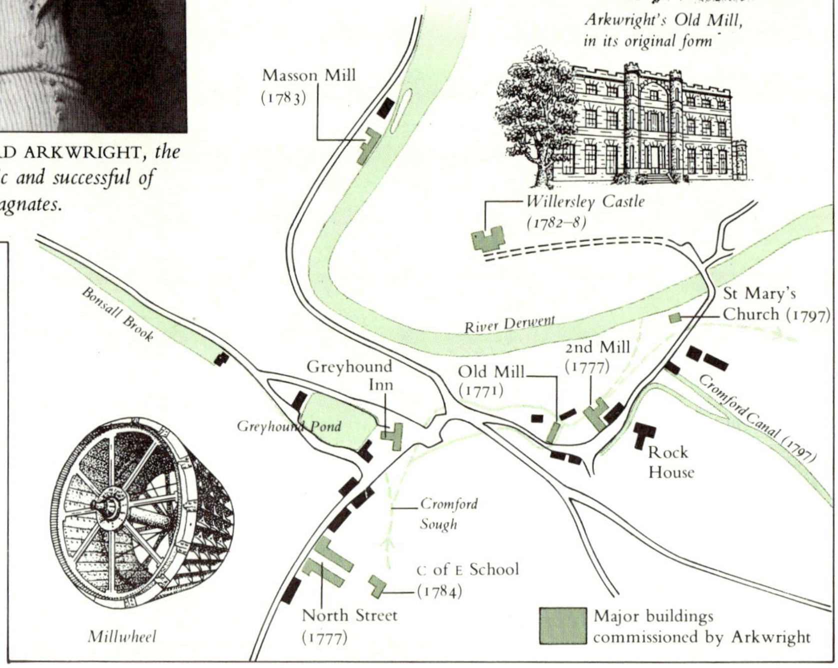

HARGREAVES' SPINNING JENNY (1764). *One operator could now spin a number of threads at once, simply by turning a handle. Some 20,000 of these jennies (the term is a contraction of 'engine') were in use by 1788.*

A BOULTON & WATT ROTATIVE ENGINE, *built in 1788 and now in London's Science Museum. A separate condenser condensed the steam without cooling the cylinder and piston. The beam was fixed to a connecting rod which turned a flywheel. The 'sun and planet' gear, an improvement suggested by W. Murdoch, doubled the speed of the axle.*
a *Cylinder containing steam-driven double-acting piston*
b *Sun and planet gear*
c *Connecting rod*
d *Beam*

Enterprise and invention

The largest British industry in the early 18th century was the cloth trade. The export of woollen goods alone produced nearly half the country's total export earnings. But it was cotton that led the way in industrialization. A series of inventions enabled the raw cotton that was coming into the country (imports of cotton *goods* were banned in 1721) to be used to the fullest. John Kay's flying shuttle (1733) increased the output of weavers and in turn stimulated a demand for improved methods of spinning, which was supplied by James Hargreaves' spinning jenny (1764), Richard Arkwright's water frame (1769) and Samuel Crompton's 'mule' (1779).

The most prosperous and hard-headed of these inventors was Richard Arkwright (1732–92), a Preston-born tailor's son who had worked as a barber and itinerant wig-maker. Hearing that Hargreaves' jenny had been smashed by Lancashire workers who believed that it endangered their jobs, Arkwright moved to Nottingham where he formed a partnership with the hosiery manufacturer Jedediah Strutt. In 1771 they built the world's first water-powered cotton mill at Cromford (Derbyshire), where the River Derwent flows rapidly through a narrow gorge. Arkwright went on to build other mills, not only in Derbyshire but also in Lancashire, Scotland and elsewhere. The factory system had been born.

Weaving lagged behind these changes in spinning and remained for a time a domestic handicraft. However, the handloom weavers felt threatened in the 1780s by Edmund Cartright's power loom, even though it still awaited the availability of a suitable material for construction. Like the spinners of earlier decades, some of them resisted change by factory-burning or machine-smashing. Their instinct was right: by the 1840s the power loom reigned supreme in the cotton world.

THE SEVERN GORGE AT COALBROOKDALE (*above*) *in the late 18th century. Abraham Darby II's coke ovens, on the same site as his father's ironworks, opened the way for a great expansion of iron-smelting in the second half of the century.*

Steam, coal and iron

The power loom was driven by steam. As early as the 1770s steam-power, provided by a type of engine introduced by Thomas Newcomen, had been used for pumping water out of coal mines, for supplying water to towns and for blowing blast furnaces. The Scotsman James Watt greatly improved Newcomen's engine and joined with Matthew Boulton, a Birmingham hardware manufacturer, to produce pumps for the Cornish tin and copper mines. But it was the application of rotary motion, in 1781, that properly inaugurated the age of steam, for it multiplied the kinds of machine to which steam-power could be harnessed. By 1800 Boulton & Watt were supplying engines to sugar refineries, flour mills, waterworks, breweries and other factories. Manufacturers were now liberated from the need to site their works where there were fast-flowing streams, instead concentrating their activities on coalfield towns which rapidly expanded.

Coal-mining itself, and the transport of coal, were made more efficient in response not only to the increasing popularity of the steam engine but also to the demand for iron. Charcoal was the material traditionally used for smelting, but the shortage of timber stimulated the search for new methods. Attempts to use coal for smelting were a failure, but in 1709 Abraham Darby successfully smelted iron ore with coke (which was derived from coal) at Coalbrookdale, Shropshire. The technique was improved by Abraham Darby II, and from the 1760s mining and smelting took place in areas where both ore and coal were available.

THE WORLD'S FIRST IRON BRIDGE (1779), *built over the Severn by Abraham Darby III. The town that grew up nearby, Ironbridge, now has a fine museum of the industrial past.*

NEW LANARK (*left*), *the cotton settlement on the banks of the Clyde (early 19th century). Robert Owen, on becoming partner-manager, replaced workers' slums with decent new housing.*

Developments in transport, as well as in power and manufacturing techniques, were an important premise of the industrial revolution. The building of new canals such as the Trent and Mersey was of immense significance in facilitating the movement of both raw materials and finished products. And when the railways caught the entrepreneurial imagination, from the mid-1830s onwards, a new phase of industrialization had begun that gave added importance to steam as a source of power and iron as a basic material.

The factory settlements

In the days when cotton mills were water-powered and were miles from any town, the owners sometimes put up 'apprentice houses' and peopled them with pauper children from the workhouses. Later, in the steam age, when factories had an urban location, the workers lived in industrial slums. A few employers stand out as comparatively enlightened and humanitarian. At Cromford and Belper (both in Derbyshire), Arkwright and Strutt built comfortable new villages for cotton workers. Since women and children were needed in greater quantities than skilled men, surplus males worked in other industries – lead-mining and frame-knitting at Cromford, nail-making at Belper. The most humanitarian of all factory-owners, however, was Robert Owen, manager of the New Lanark Mills in Scotland from 1800 to 1825. Not only did he provide schools and other facilities for his working community, and shortened working hours, but also, after 1830, he interested himself in trade unionism.

CONNECTIONS

Cotton mills: 160–63 *Cotton*

Industrial archaeology: 146–7 *Relics of the industrial past*

Industrial communities: 234–5 *Coal mining towns;* **236–7** *Factory towns*

Natural resources: 148–9 *Wind, water and steam;* **150–51** *Coal;* **152–5** *The bowels of the earth;* **158–9** *Iron and steel*

Relics of the industrial past

Few parts of mainland Britain are not within striking distance of one or more reminders of 18th- or 19th-century industry – perhaps a forge, a furnace, an engine-house, a horse-gin or a stretch of canal. Such monuments were long undervalued, but the coining of the term 'industrial archaeology' (first used in print in 1955) reflected a new sensitivity. Before long, appreciation of the industrial past had become a popular pursuit, a trend that was encouraged by the growth of industrial museums and by the conservation of relics.

To get the most out of Britain's industrial

FRANCIS DARBY *(1783–1850)* ***(right)****: son of Abraham Darby III, and manager of the Coalbrookdale Ironworks from 1810. Paintings that bring alive the personalities of the industrial past are to be found in many local museums.*

A HORSE-GIN, *reconstructed in the Nottingham Industrial Museum, Wollaton Park, Notts. In some areas, horse-gins such as this were used for raising coal until the early 20th century.*

A PRINTING SHOP *at the Blists Hill Open Air Museum, Ironbridge, Salop. A butcher's shop, cobbler's shop and sawmill have also been re-created at this museum, to form the basis of a 19th-century industrial village.*

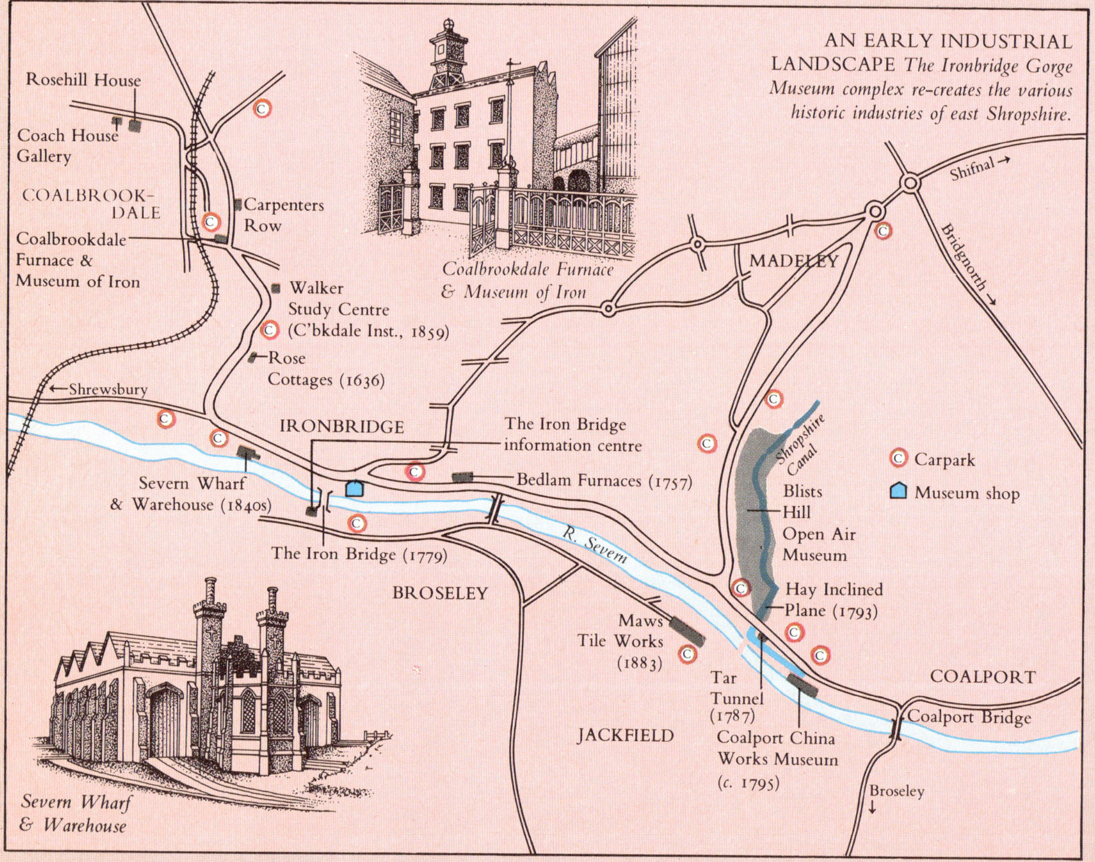

AN EARLY INDUSTRIAL LANDSCAPE *The Ironbridge Gorge Museum complex re-creates the various historic industries of east Shropshire.*

heritage, it is necessary to respond to a sense of place. Every site exists in a complex interrelationship with neighbouring sites, with the topographical and social character of the region and with available sources of power and transport. Recognition of the importance of these geographical factors has led to the creation of open-air museums in which important structures are often left *in situ*. One of the most successful is the North of England Open Air Museum at Beamish, Co. Durham, which portrays the social history of the north-east by reconstructing industrial, agricultural and urban features. Just south of Sheffield is the Abbeydale Industrial Hamlet, where the making of crucible steel and the forging of scythe blades are explained in a series of exhibits. Most ambitious of all, however, is the museum complex in the Ironbridge Gorge, along a three-mile stretch of the Severn valley in Shropshire. Like Cromford in Derbyshire, the gorge was a cradle of the industrial revolution. Abraham Darby's original iron-smelting furnace is preserved at Coalbrookdale, while upstream from here is the Blists Hill Open Air Museum, where a colliery steam winding-engine is in regular operation.

More modest but still highly significant efforts at conservation have been made in many other parts of Britain. The numerous factories that have been adapted to form museums include the Quarry Bank Mill at Styal in Cheshire (built for Samuel Greg in 1784) and the Moorside Mills, near Bradford. Many historic factories have been converted to other uses, but their exteriors are still of great interest to the inquiring amateur. Among them are William Strutt's 'fireproof' North Mill (1804) at Belper, Derbyshire, and the handsome late 18th-century silk mills of Macclesfield.

STRETHAM DRAINAGE ENGINE HOUSE, CAMBS., *still has its original beam engine (1831).*

THE HAY INCLINE (***left***), *in the Blists Hill Open Air Museum. With the help of rails and winding gear, tub-boats could be lowered on a wheeled trolley from the Shropshire Canal to the Coalport Canal at the bottom. Substantial remains of dock and engine-house can still be seen.*

Many people are addicted to steam engines. The sight of a massive beam engine in steam can be an unforgettable experience, and fortunately it is one that can still be savoured, thanks to the activities of numerous preservation societies. Examples range from the 1812 Boulton & Watt engine preserved at Crofton pumping station, Wiltshire, on the Kennet & Avon Canal, to the 1907 horizontal mill engine at the Dee Mill, Shaw (near Oldham).

The history of mining also has its devotees, who spend hours exploring derelict engine-houses or tracing lead-miners' rakes over desolate moorland. For the novice, the best initiation into these pleasures is to visit a museum such as the excellent Mining Museum at Matlock Bath, Derbyshire, or the more elaborate display provided by the Chatterley Whitfield Colliery, Tunstall (Staffordshire), where the visitor can go below ground.

CONNECTIONS
The Gladstone Pottery Museum: 164–5 *Pottery and porcelain*
Mining relics: 152–5 *The bowels of the earth*
Steam engines: 148–9 *Wind, water and steam*
Transport relics: 260–61 *The canals;* **266–7** *Enjoying the railways today*

Wind, water and steam

Before steam engines were first put to commercial uses in the 18th century, water and wind had long been successfully exploited, with relatively unsophisticated machinery, to provide power. Windmills have been used for fulling cloth and sawing timber, as well as for grinding corn and draining the land (in the Fens and the Norfolk Broads), but they have played only a mimimal role in manufacturing. However, stream power, which has a longer history, has also been much more versatile.

PITSTONE POSTMILL, *Bucks., is one of Britain's oldest mills, built in the 17th century.*

Waterwheels were crucial to early industrialization, and nowadays, long after the steam engine has become almost an antiquated curiosity, the potential contribution of hydro-electricity and tidal power to Britain's energy prospects is still optimistically under review.

Windmills and watermills

Windmills made their first appearance in England in the 12th century, and proliferated particularly in the corn-growing regions of the east and south-east. The earliest type was the post mill, which was pivoted so that the whole body could be turned to face the wind. On later post mills the orientation was adjusted automatically by a projecting fantail (patented by Edmund Lee in 1745) – a windvane, which was mounted above a circular track which ran round the mill.

From the 15th century there were also tower mills: on top of the fixed cylindrical tower was mounted a movable cap which carried the sails and fantail. An early variant of this type, taperingly octagonal in shape with a timbered upper part, is known as the smock mill (because it resembled a man in a smock).

The sails of a windmill were originally of canvas mounted on a wood frame, and needed to be reefed and unreefed like the sails of a ship, but this inconvenience was eliminated by the invention by Andrew Meikle (in 1772) of a sail fitted with shutters which could be regulated by the miller from inside.

Waterwheels were built by the Romans and the Saxons, and there were 5,624 in use in England by the time of the Domesday survey (1086). Their main purpose was grinding corn, by means of millstones, but they were applied to cloth-making as early as the 13th century. Greater power was possible after the invention of the 'overshot' wheel, which was turned not by the force of the current but by the weight of water in buckets attached to the wheel's rim. Further design improvements in the later 18th century, by James Smeaton and other experimenters, gradually increased efficiency. By 1820 sophisticated sluice-gates to control the water flow, well-designed buckets and the use of cast iron had transformed the traditional techniques. The three-quarter-mile tunnel and expensive 100-horsepower wheel built by Samuel Greg at his

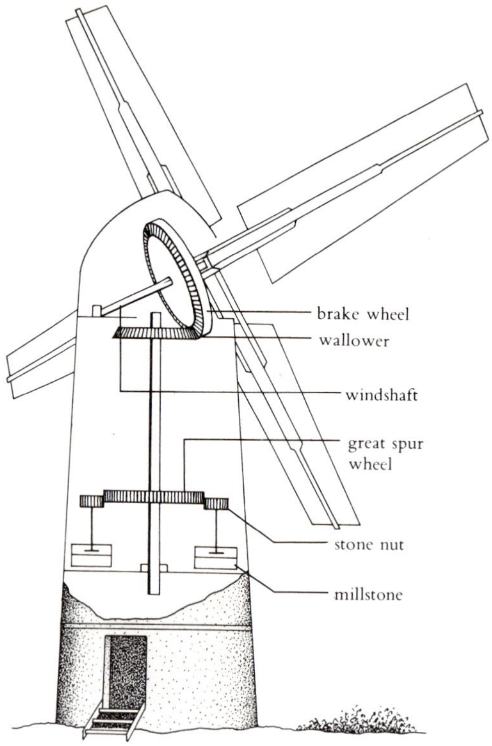

ANATOMY OF A TOWER MILL
The sails turn the windshaft, on which is mounted the brake wheel, geared to a horizontal 'wallower' (see photograph, ***above left****). This turns the main central shaft, which by a further system of gears operates the mill-stones.*

TYPES OF WATERWHEEL

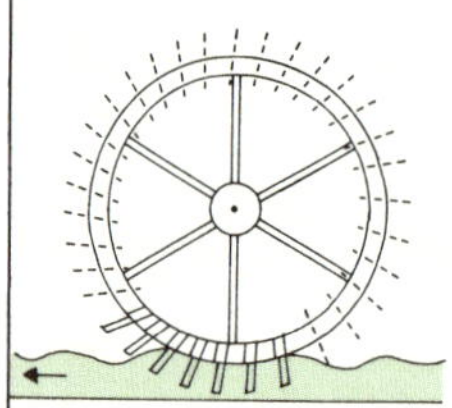

Undershot

The undershot was the oldest and simplest of vertical waterwheels, and it was the only type that could be installed on rivers in low-lying areas. Always fitted with blades or paddles.

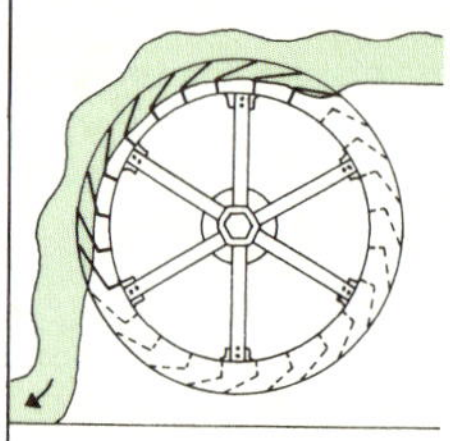

Overshot

The overshot wheel has buckets (or troughs) set into its rim. Water is carried to the top of the wheel from a channel (leat), often fed from a mill-pond. Found where there was a limited but reliable supply of water.

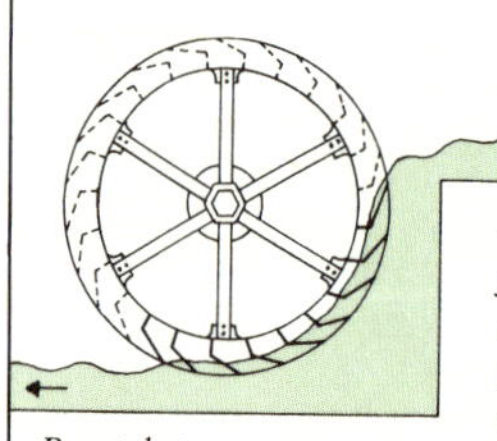

Breastshot

The breastshot wheel was a later type, again with buckets rather than blades. Used where there was not quite enough head of water for an overshot. Another later type of wheel was the pitchback – an overshot designed to turn in the reverse direction, making it easier to operate in times of flood.

CASTLE MILL, DORKING, *in Surrey, showing the undershot wheel. Now a private house.*

It is unusual nowadays to find an intact wheel made entirely of wood, but there are many hybrid types combining timber and cast iron. The largest waterwheel in Britain is the Lady Isabella at Laxey on the Isle of Man, built in 1854 to pump water from a lead mine; its diameter is 22 m ($72\frac{1}{2}$ ft). Many watermills have been preserved in excellent working order.

PAPPLEWICK PUMPS. *The Victorian waterworks at Papplewick, north of Nottingham, features a pumping station equipped with twin beam engines (1884), which drew up water from an outcrop of red bunter sandstone: they are still periodically set in action. The engine house, ornately decorated inside (**below**), stands beside a cooling pond (**right**).*

STEAM IN THE FAIRGROUND (***below***). *Steam-power provided a new thrill for fair-goers – the colourful merry-go-round. This one, dating from the 1920s, is now to be found in the Age of Steam collection, Crowlas, Cornwall.*

A STEAM FIRE ENGINE *of the Victorian era. The London Fire Engine Establishment, equipped with the latest horse-drawn steam pumps, was the most up-to-date force in the world. The horses were specially trained not to be frightened by a raging fire.*

Quarry Bank Mill at Styal, Cheshire (1818), were typical of the elaborate lengths to which some owners went in their quest for maximum efficiency. The applications of water power were manifold, ranging from rock-crushing machines in Cornwall to the operation of the bellows in smelting furnaces.

Steam–power

In 1698 the Cornishman William Savery patented an engine which could pump water out of a mine by a combination of atmospheric and steam pressure. Although nicknamed the 'Miner's Friend', it was never reliable, but in 1708 a more efficient version was invented by Thomas Newcomen, a blacksmith and ironmonger from Dartmouth. Steam generated by a boiler was fed into a cylinder housing a piston which was connected via a pivoted beam to the vertical pump rods. As the piston rose, the pump rods correspondingly descended until a jet of cold water supplied from a cistern condensed the steam in the cylinder. This created a vacuum beneath the piston, which was then forced downwards by atmospheric pressure, pulling the pump rods up again. The repetition of this cycle operated the pump.

Most of the early Newcomen engines were supplied to coal mines, and as they burnt unwanted coal it did not matter that their rate of fuel consumption was high. A more efficient design was provided, however, by James Watt, who discovered in 1765 that heat loss could be reduced by condensing the steam in a separate vessel instead of in the cylinder.

In 1774 Watt moved down from Scotland to Birmingham to enter a partnership with Matthew Boulton, and at the Soho works there they began to produce steam engines commercially, assisted by John Wilkinson, who had hit upon a way of making precision-bored cylinders. Most of the output went to the Cornish tin and copper mines. The economic utilization of steam engines in manufacturing awaited Watt's introduction of the more versatile rotative engine. By 1800 Boulton and Watt had set up more than 300 engines all over Britain, most of them of the rotative type.

The most important advance of the first half of the 19th century was the high-pressure engine, patented by Richard Trevithick in 1802. A series of explosions seemed to justify James Watt's belief that this was too dangerous to develop further, but the idea made progress nevertheless. Although beam engines were built throughout the 19th century, they were gradually outnumbered by the faster, more versatile direct-action engines using high-pressure steam. It was these that made possible the new era of steam – the railway age – which did not end until the last steam locomotive in Britain (appropriately named *Evening Star*) was built in 1960.

CONNECTIONS
Drainage of mines: 150–51 *Coal;* **152–5** *The bowels of the earth*
Drainage windmills: 20–21 *The lowlands*
Hydro-electricity: 166–7 *Electricity*
Steam engines: 144–5 *The birth of industry*

Coal

In just two hundred years the mining of coal – a combustible carbonaceous rock derived from vegetable matter – developed from an ancient but small-scale industry into a pillar of Britain's industrial revolution. The coal industry began to expand in the 16th century when shrinking timber resources provoked serious interest in an alternative, mineral fuel. By the 17th century, coal was not only being increasingly used domestically, for heating, but was also being exploited in glass and brick manufacture and in baking and sugar refining. The concentration of these activities in coal-less London soon accelerated the coastal shipping of coal from Newcastle and gave rise to a colloquial phrase signifying a futile gesture – 'taking coals to Newcastle'.

Coal and the industrial revolution

In 1709 Abraham Darby I (1678–1717) succeeded in using coke derived from coal (instead of charcoal derived from timber) for smelting iron, with the result that iron could henceforth be produced in unprecedented quantities. Not long afterwards Henry Cort (1740–1800) invented a puddling and rolling technique that made coke-blast iron as malleable and capable of supporting stress as charcoal-smelted iron. The result of these advances was that coal's central place in the economy was confirmed.

The importance of coal encouraged the development of easier and less perilous ways of getting at it. Major improvements came with the application of steam-power (itself conditional on plentiful supplies of coal), first to the drainage of deep mines and then to the haulage of coal, and miners, to the surface. But the deadly problems associated with suffocating and explosive gases remained. Traditionally, the caged canary, more sensitive than humans to the toxic effects of gases, acted as the miner's warning device. Then Sir Humphry Davy's safety lamp (1815) gave a more effective remedy, providing light while avoiding the risk of underground explosions.

The fivefold increase in coal output in the 18th century was simultaneously a symptom of, and a stimulus to, the gathering momentum of the industrial revolution. The canals, for example, were often built with a view to transporting coal cheaply; and the first railways also carried the fuel. In 1800 the total output of coal was nearly eleven million tonnes and by 1900 this had increased to about 225 million tonnes. The 1900 figure reflects not only new technology and increased demand, but also important changes in the organization of the industry: the change from small units with relatively shallow pits to large companies employing a large workforce and mining at great depths.

The rapid advent of coal as a major industry had profound social effects and, ultimately, legislative repercussions. The hazardous nature of mining was first impressed upon the community at large after the *First Report* of the Children's Employment Commission in 1842, which told of the suffering of children (and women) working underground for long hours, carrying or pulling extremely heavy loads. The resultant Miners' Act (1842) and a

GETTING AT THE COAL

At first, coal was picked up on beach outcrops. When these were used up, coal-seekers had to follow a seam inland and, if it was not too far underground, quarry the coal in an open-cast mine (**d**). The first real mines were simple bell pits (**a**). They were so shallow that there were no serious flooding or ventilation problems. Sometimes, the coal would be drawn up from a bell pit by a horse-powered windlass. But when the search for coal necessitated deeper mines, the unfortunate result of piercing the water-table was that water accumulated at the shaft bases. Attempts to get at coal-bearing strata via horizontal drift mines (**b**) were of limited value. Successful deep mining (**c**) awaited the application of steam-power, first for pumping out water and later for winding purposes.

Winding gear long remained primitive, but was greatly improved by the introduction of wire rope, and of specially designed 'cages' for moving miners up and down the shafts.

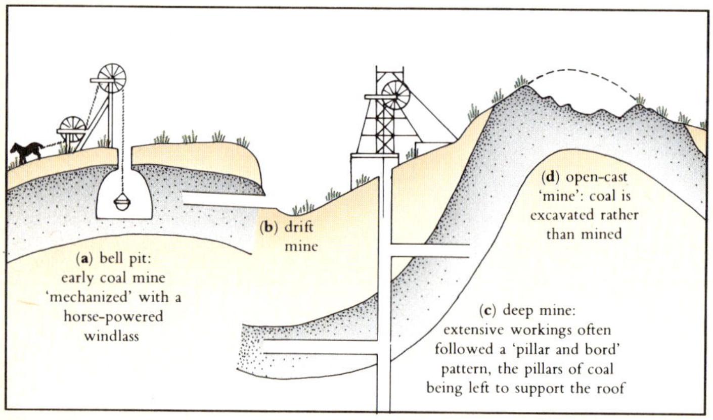

A YORKSHIRE COLLIER OF 1814. *With a basket of his own coal on his arm, this jaunty miner is on his way home from the Middleton Colliery near Leeds, which was unusually well mechanized for this period. Behind him, John Blenkinsop's steam locomotive – Blenkinsop was agent for this colliery – hauls 'corves' (trollies) of coal and steam-driven winding gear brings coal to the surface. In those days mining villages were hardly different from rural villages, for the coal industry was not yet highly capitalized or mechanized, and whole families were involved. Despite the hazardous nature of the work, miners in the early 19th century were healthier than their successors, because they worked underground less intensively.*

In this period, over half the coal output – and possibly as much as two-thirds – was for burning at home. The iron industry absorbed 10–15 per cent.

HEWERS, HOLERS AND PUTTERS (***right***). *This 19th-century hewer is cutting into the face to 'get' or 'win' coal, while the holer, using a different kind of pick, is attacking an underseam in an extremely cramped space. The putters load the coal into a wagon (here drawn by a pit pony) to be taken to the pit bottom, which might be more than two miles away. One of the putters here is a boy. In the early days wagons were often pulled by women or young children, though hewers were always adult men.*

further Act of 1850 'For the Inspection of Coal Mines in Great Britain' improved mine-working conditions, though the impact was neither dramatic nor universal.

Coal this century

Important changes have taken place in this century. The coal industry sank from its 19th-century heights after the First World War, owing to the exhaustion of some of the best seams, the loss of export markets and competition from newer energy sources, especially oil. In 1947 the mines were nationalized, and the National Coal Board was set up to rationalize production.

A number of older mines are nearing exhaustion and many have been closed, but under an NCB plan of 1974 new mines have been sunk, and extensive explorations are now being undertaken for the coalfields of the future. Untapped reserves have been identified to the east of the Yorkshire-Derby-Nottingham field (particularly at Selby in Yorkshire, where a very large drift mine is already under construction), in north-east Leicestershire (the Vale of Belvoir) and in Warwickshire. These are all extensions of coalfields that are already exploited, but it is possible that a new field in Oxfordshire will prove workable. However, it may be that alternative sources of fuel will eliminate the need for further exploitation.

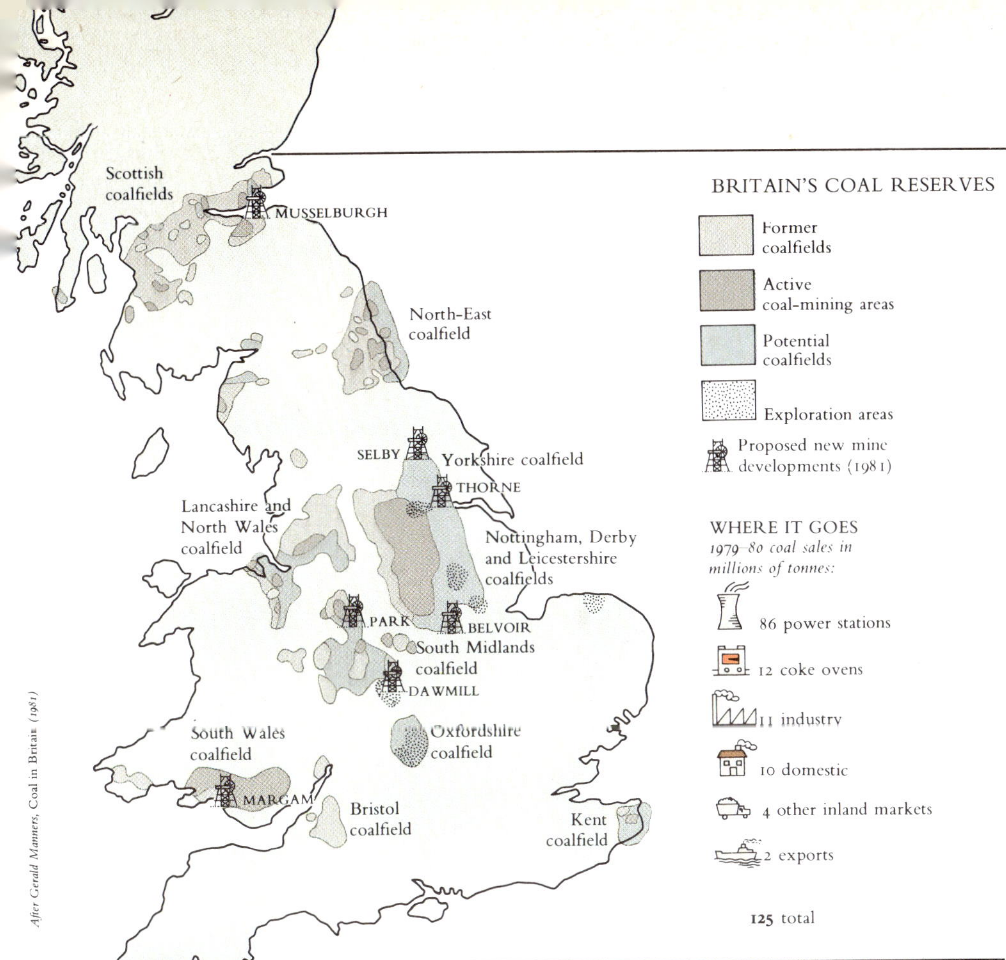

OPEN-CAST MINING TODAY. *The first primitive mines were open-cast, but modern open-cast operations in Britain were started in 1942 as a wartime expedient. Short-term open-cast mining is profitable and need not scar the countryside permanently, as is demonstrated by this pleasant scene – a landscaped former open-cast site at Shipley in Derbyshire.*

MECHANICAL MINING (**left**). *A coal-cutting 'shearer' in action at the Nantgarw/Windsor Colliery in south Wales, near Cardiff.*

CONNECTIONS

Coke: **144–5** *The birth of industry;* **158–9** *Iron and steel*
The miners: **234–5** *Coal mining towns*
Steam power: **148–9** *Wind, water and steam*
Transport of coal: **260–61** *The canals;* **262–3** *The railway age;* **264–5** *The railway revolution*

The bowels of the earth

GOLDMINERS IN WALES, *late 19th century. In more recent times the most productive mines (now closed) have been those of the Mawddach valley north of Dolgellau (Gwynedd).*

MINING FOR METALS
Silver, not shown on the map, has been extracted from lead ore at Ceredigion (Dyfed) and elsewhere.

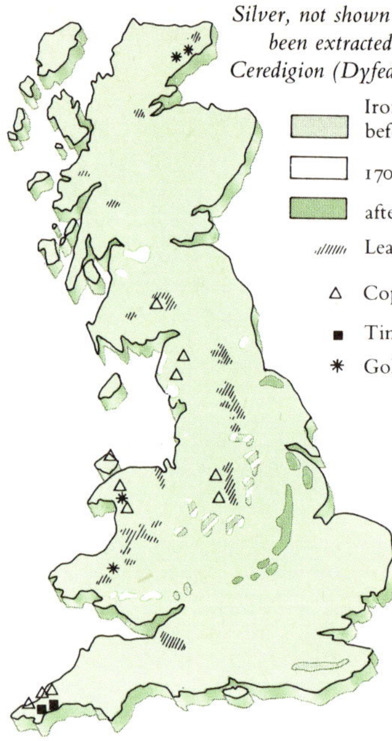

usually obtained as a by-product of lead working, has generally offered a surer prospect of riches.

Galena, or lead ore, has long been the most widely exploited of the commoner metal ores. The antiquity of lead mining has been demonstrated by the discovery of bars ('pigs') of lead stamped with Roman inscriptions. During the medieval period the major centres were the Mendips and the Peak District of Derbyshire. Production in both areas was based on small leasehold mines, and their lease and operation were regulated through local courts, such as the Barmoot Court in Derbyshire.

Lead mining in the Mendips began to be organized on a more capitalist basis during the 16th

THE BRAZEN DISH, *made of bronze in the reign of Henry VIII, is the standard measure of ore in the Low Peak of Derbyshire. It is kept in the Barmoot Hall at Wirksworth, where the miners' court still meets twice annually.*

SLIME TABLES OF THE 1930s, *for dressing the ore (that is, removing the waste) at the Millclose Lead Mine in Derbyshire. The mine closed in 1939–40 owing to flooding and dwindling reserves.*

Many a miner or quarryman must have shared the sentiments of the émigré German miners in Cumbria in the 16th century who gave the name Gotes Gab (God's Gift) to one of their copper workings. However, the extraction of underground wealth has always been highly speculative, and many enterprises have come to grief as lodes or veins have given out unexpectedly, or as markets have suddenly slumped.

Gold, silver and lead

Gold mining has never been practised on a large scale in Britain, but it has a long tradition, dating back to Celtic times. The Romans worked for gold at Dolaucothi (Dyfed), using both open-cast methods and underground galleries (adits). There was particular excitement over gold in the mid-19th century, when the old Roman workings were extended. However, for the British miner, silver,

THE MAGPIE LEAD MINE

Derbyshire's Magpie Mine, near Sheldon, has a remarkably complete and varied collection of remains. Its history, which goes back to the 1740s, is a sad saga of closures and false starts. By the time the drainage problems were eventually solved in the later 19th century, falling lead prices had caused additional difficulties. The mine was finally abandoned in 1958.

THE MAGPIE RELICS (***right***). *The ruined engine house contained a pump which successfully drained the mine dry in 1871.*

PLAN OF THE SITE
Visitors should first contact the Mining Museum at Matlock Bath.

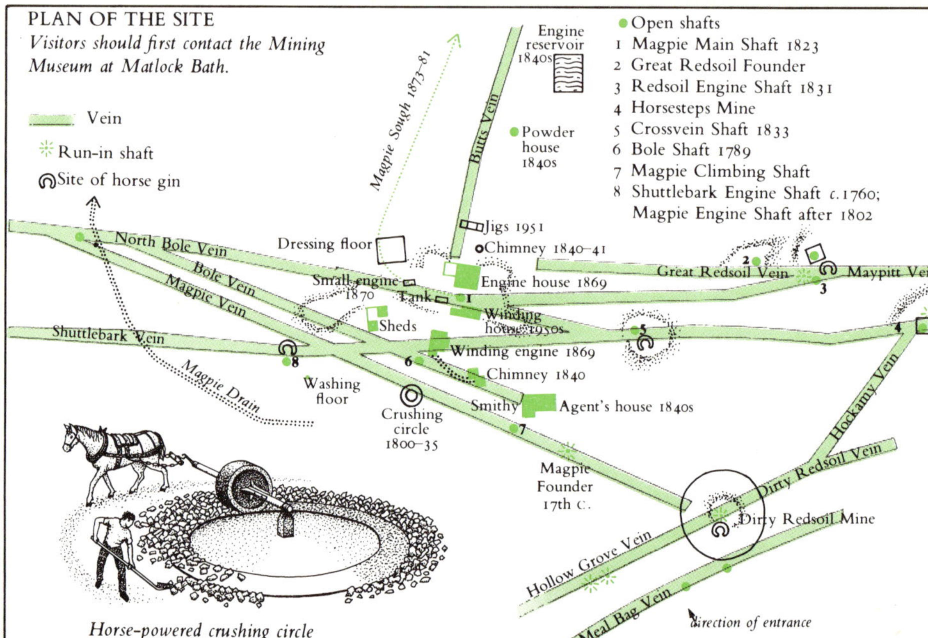

and 17th centuries. Mining had ceased by 1850, although spoil was re-worked in some places until the early years of the present century.

The Derbyshire mines' main phase of expansion culminated in about 1750. Although there was considerable capital investment (for example, by the London Lead Company), the mining capitalists played a less prominent role here than they did in the northern Pennines. There was a rapid shrinkage after 1860, but lead mining was kept alive by the Mill Close Mine, Darley Dale. Today, the mineral fluorspar, formerly discarded by the miners of the Peak, is more valuable than lead, which is now exploited only as a by-product.

Lead mining in Wales enjoyed its heyday during the 19th century, when new discoveries began to augment the old sources, a notable example being the Van mine in Powys, from which ore was first raised in 1866.

Lead extraction has disfigured many a mile of landscape. Early miners confined themselves to surface veins, a practice which left the terrain scarred by shallow trenches (rakes or lanes) from which the ore had been removed. Around such trenches lay spoil tips and abandoned dressing floors, the whole forming a topography which time has usually done little to disguise; in the Mendips it is known as 'gruffy ground'.

During the 17th century, miners in the Peak District and elsewhere began to tap deeper veins and delve below the watertable. The traditional solution to the formidable problem of drainage was to excavate channels (soughs) under the workings; some of these, such as Meerbrook Sough (built in the 1770s), were major feats of surveying and engineering. The cutting of soughs sometimes revealed valuable new veins, from which the mineral was carried by boat.

With the introduction of water-pressure and steam pumping engines it was possible to dig below sough level, and pump the water up to the sough. However, for some mines the bugbear was not excess water but lack of it, for it was needed to dress the ore and to drive machinery. Leats, or channels, sometimes provided water for both these purposes. Dressing and crushing floors can still be seen at many old mines.

Most early mines also smelted the ore on site, using simple 'wind hearths', but in time smelting became detached from mining. With the advent of the reverberatory furnace in the 18th century, smelting operations were located with more regard to coal than to ore supplies. High in the Yorkshire Pennines, however, smelt hearths built close to the mines were still active in the late 19th century, using peat as a fuel.

TIN MINING TODAY, *in the Wheal Jane Mine in Cornwall. The miners are drilling prior to a blasting operation on the main lode.*

A RELIC OF TIN-MINING (***left***), *at East Pool, Cornwall. This engine house contains a winding engine (or whim) installed in 1887.*

Tin and copper

Tin seems to have been extracted in modest quantities in Cornwall by the second millenium BC. Early methods were based on 'streaming' – the panning of river gravels. By the Middle Ages, production had become organized into districts known as stannaries, each equipped with its own court. Before 1600, miners discovered the lodes from which stream tin was derived and began to extract it from shaft workings.

The Cornish landscape has also been etched into by copper mining, which flourished over the 18th and 19th centuries, stimulated by the demand for brass, for shipbuilding and engineering. The areas of most vigorous activity were the Penwith peninsula, and around Redruth and Camborne.

A notable feature of the Cornish mines was their use of massive steam-driven pumping engines, of the kind invented by the Cornishman Richard Trevithick. There were approximately 700 steam engines in use in Cornwall and west Devon between 1850 and 1860, and derelict engine-houses, with their monolithic chimney stacks, still punctuate the skyline in large numbers.

Quarrying for stone

Britain's rich vernacular tradition of architecture owes as much to the variety of building stones employed as to the diversity of styles. The warm brown stone of the Cotswolds, the grey Pennine grits and other local materials, locally employed, have helped to create their own distinctive landscapes. Some building stones, however, achieved a wider appeal. In the Portland peninsula, limestone has been quarried for four centuries, and has been exploited in some of Britain's finest buildings, including St Paul's and the British Museum. The cavernous Rubislaw quarry provided granite for the building of Aberdeen, but other granite quarries marketed their stone on a national basis: Bonawe quarry in Argyll, for example, helped to pave the streets of both Glasgow and London.

A LIMESTONE QUARRY (***right***) *in Derbys. Modern machinery (such as walking grabs and crushing plants) has greatly improved the efficiency of limestone quarries.*

THE COPPER MOUNTAIN (***below***), *in a watercolour of 1758. Towards the end of the 19th century, the Parys Mountain Mine, Anglesey, was the most productive copper mine in Europe.*

AN ANGLESEY PENNY (***left***). *Copper pennies and halfpennies were minted by the Parys Mines Company between 1787 and 1793.*

Slate

Slate had an even wider appeal. Although long used in north-west Wales and Cumbria, where it was quarried, it spread farther afield with the rapid urban growth of the 19th century and its general adoption for roofing.

The north Wales slate industry reached its peak between 1830 and 1880, after which there was a gradual decline. The dominant centres of production were the great quarries around Blaenau Ffestiniog, Bethesda, Llanberis and Nantlle, and in this region the industry has left spectacular marks on the landscape. In some places, whole hillsides were cut in massive step-like galleries. The Penrhyn quarry, for example, possessed twenty-one galleries rising like a giant staircase up the side of Elidir mountain. At other sites, mining rather than quarrying techniques were employed, leaving behind vast underground chambers such as the one at Llechwedd, now the basis of a visitors' centre. Tramways carried slate to the central dressing sheds of each quarry (Penrhyn had over fifty miles of track), and a network of railways took the dressed slate to ports such as Bangor, Porthmadog and Towyn.

During the 19th century slate quarrying penetrated the Highlands and islands of Scotland. The long, tidy rows of workers' cottages at Easdale, Cullipool, Balvicar and Toberonochy bear witness to the scale of former activity no less than the abandoned quarries themselves.

Slate is no longer Britain's principal roofing material, but some of the old Welsh quarries are still in production on a modest scale, and the green slate of the Lake District is now a popular form of ornamental cladding.

Limestone, chalk, sand and gravel

The 20th-century decline in the traditional quarrying of building stone is the result of the increased use of more economical materials. Some types, such as Bath stone from the Cotswolds, are still fairly widely extracted, but mostly for cladding new buildings in conservation areas, or for restoring historic buildings. Chalk and limestone works, however, are busily engaged in the blasting and crushing of stone for use in the production of cement and concrete.

Sand and gravel for concrete are mainstays of the

modern construction industry. Since deposits are widely spread, the location of workings is often determined by the pattern of consumption. London, for example, is served by a large concentration of gravel pits, notably to the west of the city, at Staines. Bristol and south Wales have tapped the sandbanks of the Bristol Channel for their concrete industry.

China clay and potash

One of the most striking landscapes to be found anywhere in Britain is that produced by the extraction of china clay and china stone in Cornwall – deposits formed by the 'kaolinization' of granite. First exploited in the 18th century, they were used not only by the ceramics industry, but also in the manufacture of such diverse products as paper, calico and medicines. The main areas of production lie just north of St Austell on Henbarrow, but there are also minor centres in west Penwith and on Bodmin Moor. As much as 90 per cent of the material removed by the china clay quarriers is waste (largely silica), which has been dumped in ghostly white cone-like tips.

Further exploitation of the materials beneath Britain's skin is continuously demanded by the growth of the younger industries. Among the developments of recent decades has been the mining of potash in North Yorkshire, to supply the manufacturers of fertilizers.

SALT MINING IN CHESHIRE

In Roman Britain salt was produced in coastal salt pans by evaporation of sea water, and during medieval and early modern times this practice was widespread. However the rock salt resources of Cheshire, discovered in the 1670s, also gave birth to a substantial industry. Salt from the Cheshire mines (for example, those at Northwich and Nantwich) was transported to Liverpool by canal (***below***), to supply the chemical plants of the Merseyside region.

Latterly, there has been a shift in the method of working the salt deposits: extraction is now largely based on pumping out natural brine, though some mines have been deliberately flooded to produce 'bastard brine'. Salt mining has brought severe environmental problems for the county. Many areas have experienced subsidence, and flooded depressions (flashes) are a common feature.

OLD LIME KILNS, *Beadnell, Northumb. (inset,* ***left****). Lime, produced by burning limestone or chalk, was once commonly used in agriculture and in bleaching, and to make mortar for the building trade.*

THE SLATE QUARRY AT PENRHYN, *in north Wales (****left****). Some notable Welsh slate quarries, such as those at Dinorwic and Penrhyn, were already showing signs of decline by the 1860s. Most of the larger quarries ceased production in the 1960s, though the vast Penrhyn quarry is still worked to a limited degree. At Llechwedd, Ffestiniog, a reconstructed dressing shed (****above****) commemorates the age of the 'slate rush'.*

EXTRACTION OF SAND AND GRAVEL *at Stanway, near Colchester, Essex. The dug-out material is transferred by crane to the conveyor. It is then taken to the processing plant just visible in the distance.*

CONNECTIONS

Building materials: 170–71 *Building*

China clay: 36–7 *Man and the landscape;* **164–5** *Pottery and porcelain*

Coal mining: 150–51 *Coal*

Iron ore: 158–9 *Iron and steel*

Mineral resources: 14–15 *Beneath the landscape*

Gas and oil

THE GAS REVOLUTION

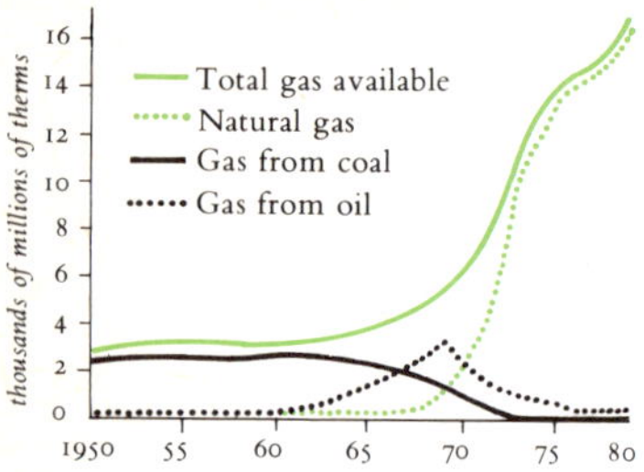

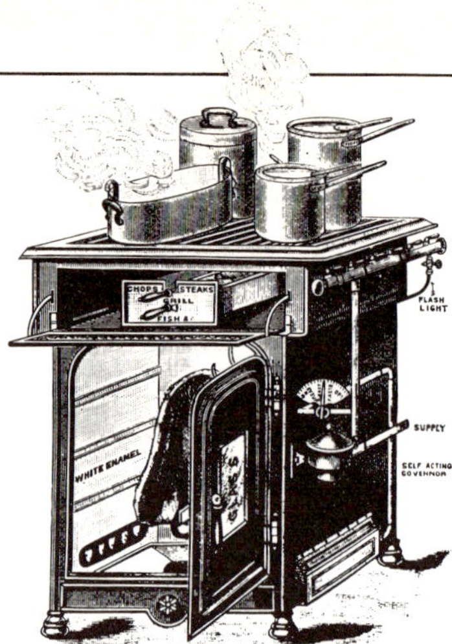

A GAS COOKER *with a grill. This was an innovation of 1886.*

DISCHARGING COKE *from a vertical gas retort, in 1912 (**left**).*

BECKTON GASWORKS, *London, 1950s (**below**). The coal-gas produced was stored in vast round gasholders.*

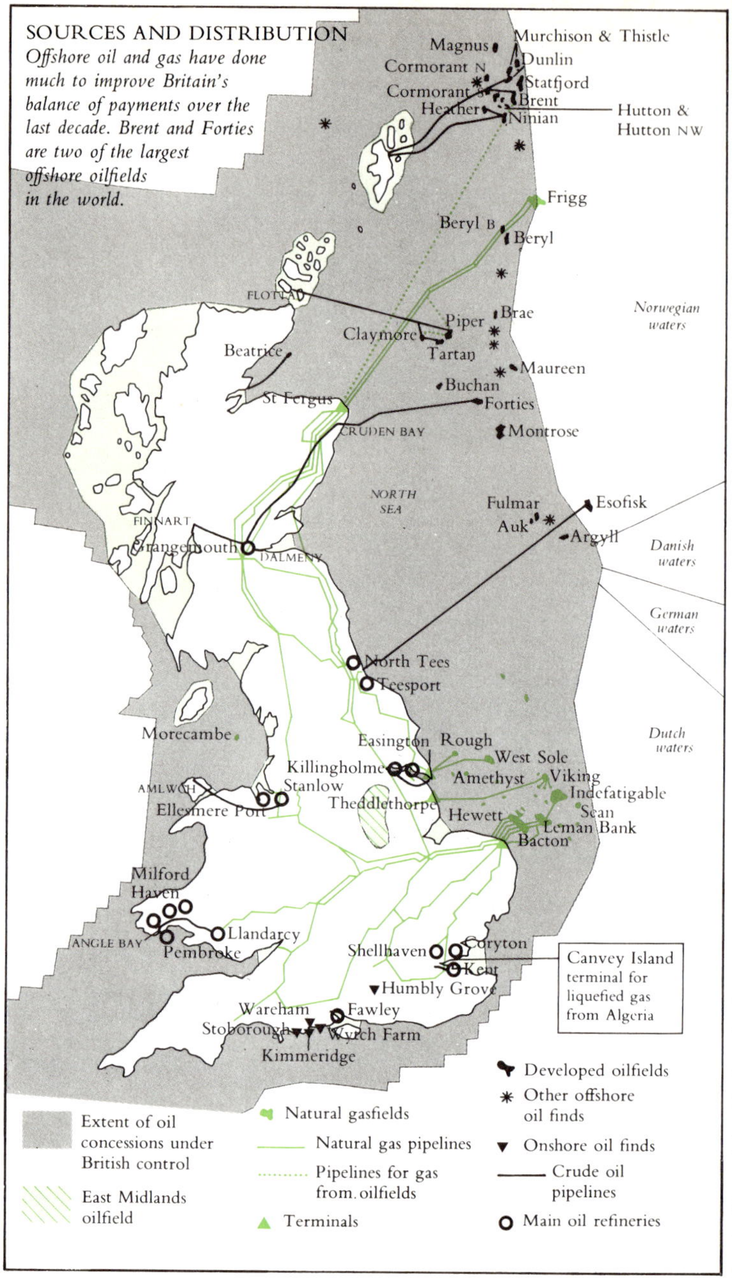

Over the past decade the profile of Britain's energy consumption has been completely overturned. There has been a decline in the use of coal, counterbalanced by the meteoric rise of natural gas. Although there has been a drop in oil consumption, a major development has been a growing degree of self-sufficiency with the exploitation of the North Sea oilfields.

Coal-gas

An 18th-century experimenter, the Earl of Dundonald, used gas obtained as a by-product of a tar-making process to provide lighting at his Fifeshire home. It was the manufacturing partnership of Boulton and Watt, however, that introduced gas lighting to industry: in 1798 William Murdock lit their famous Soho factory in Birmingham by coal-gas produced in iron retorts, and the company went on to instal gasworks for other firms.

Frederick Winsor, a German emigré, saw great possibilities in the idea of underground pipelines. He lit part of Pall Mall with gas piped from his own house, and later obtained a government charter for his Gas Light and Coke Company. By April 1814 there was gas lighting in a parish of Westminster, and gasworks operated in fifteen large towns by 1820. For many years gas was used solely for illumination: a variety of gas cookers had been exhibited by mid-century, but they were regarded merely as prototypes, and the first successful gas fire did not appear until 1882.

Throughout the century, advances were made in the design of retorts, and the process of discharging (that is, emptying the coke by-product) was streamlined. Methods of storage were also improved, and by 1887 a telescopic gasholder had been devised that dispensed with the need for a massive surrounding framework.

By the end of the 19th century, electric lighting was beginning to rival gas, but the invention of the incandescent mantle delayed obsolescence. Electricity caught up by the mid-1930s, but there was gas lighting in Covent Garden as recently as 1975.

Natural gas

Coal-gas needs to be purified before use and the production process is expensive. In any case, by the mid-1960s reserves of suitable coal were dwindling, and efforts now began to be concentrated on oil-based gas, which assumed great importance with the growth of the petroleum industry. However, the new age of gas produced from oil lasted only a decade, as it was cut short by another energy revolution: the rise of natural gas.

In 1959 the first tanker-load of natural gas (from Louisiana) was landed at Canvey Island, Essex. Regular imports from Algeria began in 1963. The natural gas was converted to 'town gas', which was distributed by a grid of pipelines which extended as far north as Leeds.

British Petroleum's *Sea Gem* exploration rig struck natural gas under the North Sea – the West Sole Field – in 1965, and the first supplies were piped to the British mainland two years later. The government adopted a policy of rapid exploitation of the newly found resource. Recent developments have included the increasing exploitation of gas found in association with the offshore oilfields, and experiments in producing a substitute natural gas (SNG) to cope with the foreseen exhaustion of North Sea supplies.

Oil

By 1968 oil was providing nearly 40 per cent of Britain's energy requirements. Although some of it came from onshore fields in Nottinghamshire (worked since the 1930s), by far the greater part was imported, and was processed at refineries close to the ports that received it. The closure of the Suez Canal in 1967 led to a need for larger tankers in order to reduce the cost of the journey round Cape Horn. Since these ships were too large for the oil ports, special terminals were built for them on deep-water inlets on the west coast: from here the oil was piped or shipped to existing refineries.

In the 1970s political crises in the Middle East contributed to rising costs of oil imports. The situation was saved by the discovery of oil under the North Sea in 1969. By 1979, four years after it had first been brought ashore, consumption of North Sea oil (39.1 per cent) had overtaken that of coal (36.3 per cent), but in absolute terms it had dropped owing to competition from natural gas.

In addition to 750 miles of submarine pipeline connecting the offshore oilfields with the east coast, underground pipes are used to distribute crude oil to the refineries, and refined products to major marketing areas.

Unlike the gas industry (which became public in 1949), oil remains in the private sector. The British National Oil Corporation (set up in 1976) plays a major role in trading and exploration.

'GRASSHOPPER' OIL PUMPING UNIT (***below***) *at Kimmeridge, Dorset. There is currently a renewal of interest in exploring onshore oilfields.*

OIL PRODUCTION PLATFORM *in the Forties oilfield. Oil is raised from wells in the sea bed by natural pressure, assisted by injected natural gas and seawater. Excess gas is burned off on a 'flare boom'. Each platform carries equipment for drilling the wells and for cleaning the oil and pumping it to Grangemouth. The structure is anchored by 11 piles driven into the sea-bed.*

STANLOW REFINERY, MERSEYSIDE (***right***). *Some of the crude oil distilled in a refinery is treated further to produce light oils such as gasoline.*

CONNECTIONS
Oil terminals: 230–31 *Ports*
Other sources of power: 166–7 *Electricity;* **168–9** *Nuclear power*
Petrochemicals: 176–7 *The chemical industry*

Iron and steel

The manufacture of iron was such a significant skill for early society that archaeologists characterize a whole period of prehistory by its innovation and spread, referring to the period from about 750 BC as the Iron Age. The ancient method of making iron was the bloomery process, which involved heating iron ore with charcoal on a hearth and drawing off the iron that gathered as a 'bloom' at the base. The output of a bloomery (hearth) was small, but in the 15th century the introduction of blast furnaces which made use of water-powered bellows greatly improved productivity.

Iron ore was abundant, but the smelting process required charcoal (derived from wood) as well as proximity to fast-flowing streams. It is not surprising, therefore, that the earliest blast furnaces were built in the forests of the Weald. When the builders of ships and houses began to compete for the Weald's resources, many ironmasters moved northwards and westwards, above all to the Forest of Dean, which became the premier iron-smelting district in the 17th century.

The coming of coke-blast iron

As the country's timber resources dwindled, the need for a substitute fuel became apparent. At the old ironworks in Coalbrookdale in Shropshire, Abraham Darby (1678–1717) made the first successful attempt to use coke (obtained from coal) for smelting. The idea of using coke had been toyed with before Darby's breakthrough in 1709, but the difficulty was that coke-smelting removed a smaller proportion of the impurities from iron ore than did charcoal. Darby got round this by using a very clean ore and superior coke, but even so, coke-blast iron was far more brittle than charcoal-blast iron.

It was the invention of the puddling and rolling technique by the naval agent Henry Cort (1740–1800) that eventually ensured the triumph of coke. Henceforth, the iron industry was no longer tied to timber, and the harnessing of steam power for blasting freed it of the need to be close to a source of water. By the 1780s south Wales and the west Midlands were key iron-smelting centres.

J.B. Neilson's 'hot blast' method (1828) improved output and led to savings in fuel costs. It was of particular benefit to the Clyde valley industry, enabling the region to exploit local ore and coal to produce iron very cheaply. Before long, this was the foremost iron-making area. Continued refinements in fuel technology later made access to vast amounts of ore, in areas such as Cleveland, the paramount factor in the industry's location.

BLAST FURNACES *of the 1860s. Iron-plate furnaces such as these, lined with refractory bricks, superseded the earlier brick and stone structures.*

A CAST-IRON FIREBACK, *1636. Prior to being worked, molten iron was run into 'pigs' – shapes moulded in sand (resembling a sow feeding her litter). However, some objects were cast in molten iron that was poured straight from the blast furnace into a purpose-made mould.*

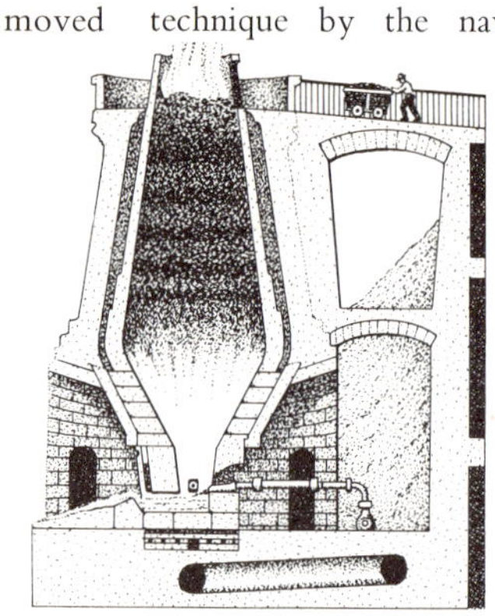

The blast furnace

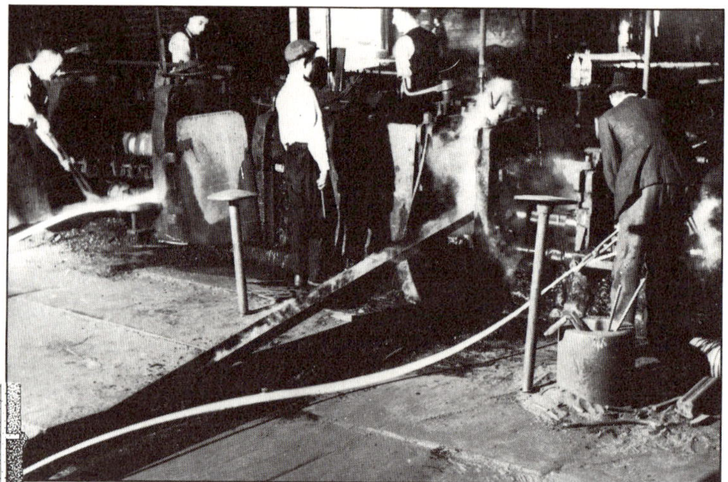

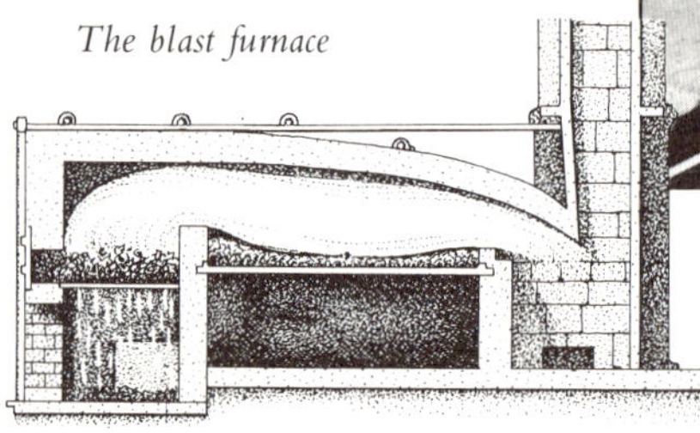

The puddling furnace

MAKING WROUGHT IRON. *In a Cort puddling furnace pig iron was alternately heated and cooled until the wrought iron could be separated out by reason of its higher melting-point. After some preliminary hammering, the rolling mill (**above**) squeezed out the dross, shaping the iron and turning out an unlimited number of standardized crude shapes, such as bars, beams and rails, for the insatiable industries of the new iron age.*

ARTISTRY IN IRON. *The magnificent 18th-century gates of Castle Ashby, a mansion in Northamptonshire, demonstrate how wrought iron (unlike cast iron, which is brittle) lends itself to the forging of delicate ornamental shapes.*

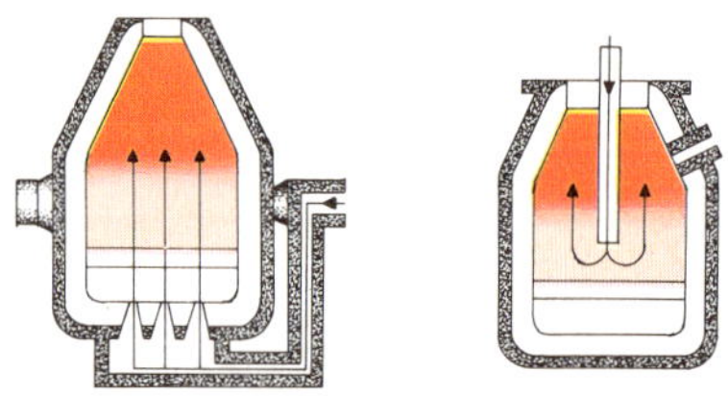

IRON TO STEEL. *Since the 1960s the Bessemer conversion process (left) has been largely replaced by the modern Basic Oxygen method (right) in which oxygen gas is blown onto the metal. The oxygen combines with carbon and other elements, thus eliminating these impurities from the molten pig iron, and producing steel.*

The age of steel

Before the 19th century, steel was made (for swords and cutlery, for example) by the slow, expensive 'cementation' method, which depended on imported high-grade pig iron. Benjamin Huntsman invented a method of refining steel in the 1740s, but it still relied on the cementation process. The picture was radically changed, however, after Henry Bessemer, in 1856, devised a means of mass-producing steel in a 'converter', which blew air through molten iron to burn out the impurities. Once started, the process continued without the addition of extra fuel, and so it became cheaper to produce steel than iron at a time when there was a growing demand for girders, rails,

A STEEL-MAKING INFERNO. *When all the steel has been tapped the converter is turned upside down. Then, the residual slag – oxidized impurities which have been separated from the molten charge – is tipped into a ladle ready for removal to the slag pool.*

tools, wire ropes and other goods for which the hardness of steel was perfectly suited.

An alternative method of making mild steel was William Siemens' open-hearth process (1866), which could convert scrap iron at high temperatures. There was a sizeable investment in open-hearth furnaces in the Swansea district, where the tin-plate industry provided a ready market.

Neither the Bessemer converter nor the open-hearth furnace could use iron with a high phosphorus content, but in the 1870s Sidney Gilchrist Thomas discovered how to remove the phosphorus using limestone. This advance led to a revaluation of phosphoric ore in the east Midlands and steel works at Corby and elsewhere.

Because of the increasing reliance on imported ores, the large integrated iron and steel works which dominate the industry today (for example, that at Port Talbot in south Wales) have shown a preference for coastal sites, especially since the formation of the British Steel Corporation in 1948. The recent contraction of the industry has worked to the same effect, for it is the inland sites, such as Ebbw Vale, that have suffered most from closure.

CONNECTIONS
Charcoal-burning: 86–7 *Vanishing skills*
Abraham Darby: 144–5 *The birth of industry*
Iron ships: 178–9 *Shipbuilding*
Uses of iron and steel: 170–71 *Building;* 174–5 *Engineering;* 262–3 *The railway age*

Cotton

In the 16th century, Lancashire had a varied textile industry, producing woollens, linens and silks on a limited scale. The first use of cotton wool for the manufacture of cloth probably took place during the early 17th century, when the making of fustian spread from East Anglia and took root around towns such as Manchester, Bolton and Blackburn in central Lancashire. Fustian was a mixed cloth, made from a flax warp and a cotton weft. Its manufacture soon became widespread among the families who lived along the western flanks of the Pennines: the women and children were responsible for carding the raw cotton or dressing the flax, and then spinning it into yarn, while the men wove the yarn into cloth.

The increasing activities of the East India Company in the 17th century led not only to improved supplies of cotton wool, mainly from Syria and Cyprus, but also to the import of fine printed cottons from India. The lightness, colour and variety of these textiles made them fashionable among the rich for both dress and furnishings. Bearing in mind that earlier cloths (with the exception of luxurious silk) had been coarse, heavy and dull, we can readily appreciate the appeal of cottons. If the costs could be reduced, the market potential would be limitless.

The triumph of cotton

The manufacture of fustian attracted entrepreneurial interest from the outset. Through the medium of travelling 'broggers' and 'chapmen', merchants supplied the scattered army of spinners and weavers with raw cotton and yarn, and then despatched the finished grey cloth to centres such as London for bleaching and dyeing. The full measure of the merchants' shrewdness became apparent in the 18th century. In response to growing opposition from the woollen and silk industries, legislation enacted in 1700 banned the import of Indian printed cottons or calicoes. The Lancashire merchants then acted quickly to fill the gap. The fustians they commissioned more and more resembled Indian cotton, and eventually they shifted to pure cotton production with the help of raw material supplied by the plantations of the West Indies and North America.

When Daniel Defoe visited Manchester in 1727, he wrote of cotton as 'the grand manufacture which has so much raised this town'. He implied that the expansion had begun at the turn of the century. But despite its vigorous growth, the cotton industry continued to be organized on a domestic or 'putting-out' basis, and the merchants could only expand by scouring the countryside for new pairs of hands. There were also problems in balancing the output of spinners with the rate at which the weavers worked, the latter needing a greater number of spinners to maintain them even in part-time employment. Historians see these twin difficulties as the context in which the great technical innovations occurred within the industry later in the 18th century, as the cotton trade became the pace-setter of industrialization.

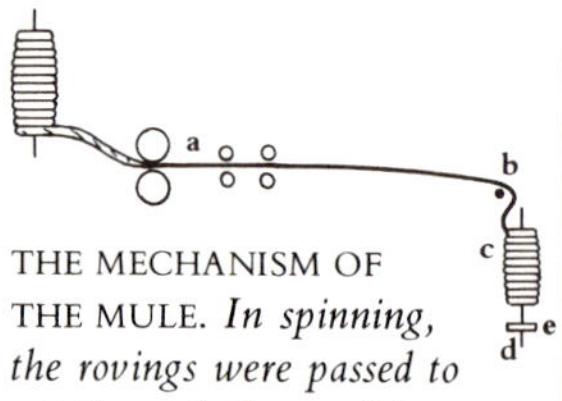

THE MECHANISM OF THE MULE. *In spinning, the rovings were passed to rotating spindles, and from there to this movable wheeled carriage, which drew out the rovings and at the same time twisted them. Three rollers (a) revolved at different speeds. The yarn was guided by wires (b) on to bobbins (c), which were mounted on spindles (d) and pulled by pulleys (e).*

CROMPTON'S MULE *was so called because it was a cross-breed from the jenny and the water frame. It spun such strong, fine yarns that British weavers were now able to compete with the calicoes and muslins of India. In spite of his great invention, Crompton died poor.*

'BATTING' THE COTTON. *After the raw cotton had been cleaned – a particularly unpleasant task – the fibres had to be 'batted' into a thick mat before they could be carded. All this preparatory work was usually executed by women and children, as it did not have to be done in a factory. Nowadays, instead of being batted, the raw cotton is pressed through beater cylinders.*

SEEDHILL MILLS, PAISLEY (***right***), c. 1812. *Scottish spinning mills such as this one produced yarn for independent weavers who worked from domestic workshops in the surrounding area. Many merchants had turned to cotton after a decline in the tobacco trade.*

THE CARDING PROCESS, *1843. Carding machines (the first one was produced in 1748) disentangled the cotton fibres and arranged them lengthwise. The next stage was roving, by which the fibres were drawn out and lightly twisted into a delicate rope. After this came the spinning itself.*

PREPARING THE WARP FOR THE LOOM, c. *1905. In weaving, two yarns are employed: the warp, a set of lengthwise strands held firmly on the loom; and the weft, which is carried laterally through the alternately parted warp strands by a fast shuttle.*

LADIES IN LACE, c. *1850. Machine-made cotton lace was a British invention. The industry still flourishes in the Midlands, particularly in Nottingham.*

Machines and mills

Ironically, the first major invention compounded rather than eased the infant industry's problems. This was John Kay's flying shuttle (1733), which increased the output of the weaver. After the shuttle's widespread adoption in the 1760s, it was now desperately important to improve the means of spinning. The first real breakthrough came with James Hargreaves's spinning jenny, invented in 1765 and patented in 1770. The jenny enabled one person to spin on as many as eight (and eventually as many as 120) spindles simultaneously. Shortly afterwards, Richard Arkwright developed his water frame (patented 1769), a water-powered spinning machine which produced a yarn strong enough to serve as both warp and weft. However, the main impact of the jenny and the water frame was not felt until the appearance of Samuel Crompton's Mule (1779).

With the application of Boulton and Watt's steam engine to drive the mule, the stage was set for a remarkable expansion of the cotton industry. However, the old bottleneck of supply had now been transferred to weaving. A notable attempt to improve on weaving efficiency was made by Edmund Cartright. Cartright's power loom, though, suffered from technical hitches as well as from opposition by the hand-weavers themselves, vigorous as always in the protection of their trade. An effective solution to the crisis of weaving capacity did not come until the 1820s, when the first efficient power looms were introduced.

In major centres such as Manchester and Bolton, as well as in outlying country districts where land was cheap and the water supply plentiful, men of capital began to build mills to house the new machinery. Mills built before 1800 were still small, employing 100–200 people at the most – a fact which helps to explain why there were already as many as 900 of them by 1797. The rapidly emerging cotton towns, such as Oldham, Rochdale and Ashton, were usually composed of a dense cluster of spinning mills encircled by weavers' cottages. Weavers were absorbed into the factories only with the spread of the steam-driven loom from the 1820s onwards. This coincided with the development of Richard Roberts's 'self-acting' mule, and their combined impact caused new factories to be built on a much larger scale from the 1830s onwards.

The siting of the first mills was determined by the availability of water-power, so the Pennine valleys of south Lancashire and Derbyshire were for a while predominant. Steam-power gradually encouraged a movement towards the central Lancashire coalfield. By 1840 only 13 per cent of the industry's energy needs came from water. There was also a tendency for spinning to be more strongly represented in southern areas (such as north-west Derbyshire) and for weaving to be predominant in the north (for example, around Blackburn and Preston).

The growth of factory production after 1780 also saw the creation of an entirely new region of cotton manufacturing in south-west Scotland. By 1834 there were 134 mills, largely devoted to spinning. These were mostly in the Paisley and Glasgow area. However, there were famous cotton mills in other parts of Scotland by the early 19th century, such as those at New Lanark (south-east of Glasgow), Langholm (in Eskdale) and Deanston (near Stirling).

The finishing of the cloth

Once woven, cotton cloth had to be bleached, and in this form it was used for a variety of household items, such as sheets and pillowcases, as well as for clothing. Some uses, though, called for more elaborate treatment. Together, the bleaching, dyeing and printing trades formed a vital adjunct to the cotton industry, their origins dating back to the late 16th century and the earliest attempts to produce fustian in East Anglia. Early methods were crude and laborious. Bleaching took months, as the cloth was given a long soaking in sour milk and then set out on tenterhooks in the 'bleach-fields'. The technical advances which enabled bleaching to catch up with the increased efficiency of manufacture came in the mid-18th century with the introduction of sulphuric acid and, later, of chlorine. Bleaching now took hours to complete instead of months.

Progress in dyeing and printing was retarded at first by legislation which made it illegal to dye or print calicoes. After this restriction was lifted in 1736, new skills were soon developed. A major innovation was cylinder rolling (*c.* 1785), which facilitated large-scale printing of cotton cloth at a rapid rate. Important innovations such as these resulted in a re-orientation of the finishing trades from their traditional areas around London to Lancashire and, before long, to the Clyde valley.

A VICTORIAN SHAWL SHOP (***left***), *reconstructed in the Museum of Costume, Bath. Shawls first became fashionable in the late 18th century.*

A PAISLEY SHAWL (*detail,* ***below***), *c. 1822. Just as English cotton initially copied Indian designs, so Scottish wool manufacturers emulated the shawls imported from Kashmir, using techniques pioneered in the cotton trade.*

CLOTHES FOR EVERY TASTE

Until the rise of cotton in the late 18th century, wool dominated British textiles, although there was also a sizeable linen industry and a small but significant silk industry. Because it was relatively easy to wash and suitable for wearing next to the skin, linen was synonymous with underwear. Cotton undercut the price of linen, but was considered a socially inferior substitute until the end of the 19th century. Linen production prospered, especially in the east-central region of Scotland.

The silk trade was not substantially affected by the expansion of cotton, and Spitalfields in London remained an important centre. In the 18th century, rising demand for this luxurious material also enabled areas such as Surrey to take up production of silk stockings, while Coventry specialized in ribbon. The first silk spinning mill was opened in Derby in 1724. The expansion of the industry came to a halt in the mid-19th century when the import duty on French silk was eventually removed.

A NAVAHO BLANKET (***below***). *The weavers of this American Indian tribe made their own dyes from roots and plants, but the brilliant red colour in so many of their products came to them from far-off Manchester. Acquiring coloured cotton fabrics through trade with white Americans, they unravelled the threads and incorporated them into their own designs.*

Aspects of growth

The extraordinary transformation of the cotton industry between 1770 and 1850 set off ripples of change in many other areas of the British economy. With the introduction of steam-power, a new stimulus was given to coal mining. Such bulky commodities as coal and cotton needed cheap and effective transport – a requirement met by canals such as the Manchester, Bolton and Bury Canal (1791), the Rochdale Canal (1779–1804) and, in a later period, the Manchester Ship Canal (1894), which brought ocean-going vessels to within easy reach of mills and warehouses. Cotton was also a major item of freight on the railways.

Equally significant was the cotton industry's stimulation of mechanical engineering in Lancashire and the Clyde valley. The first machines, such as Arkwright's water frames, were largely of wood, but iron was increasingly used, as it was longer-lasting, fireproof and easier to clean. It was also more economical on space, so that a mill-owner could buy more machines without enlarging his building.

The triumph of cotton relied as much on a marketing revolution as on the much-vaunted revolution in manufacturing. By entrepreneurial resourcefulness, cotton was turned into an item of mass consumption, one that was flexible enough to adapt to all the fickle changes of fashion in clothing and furnishing fabrics. Both the Lancashire and Scottish branches of the industry showed great resourcefulness in design. Patterns of the 18th century which were formerly ascribed to Paris are now believed to have originated in Britain, and to have been closely connected with the marketing of printed cottons. Variety of product also became important, especially in the Scottish industry: a late starter, it thrived through diversity, with a range of products that by 1850 embraced ginghams, muslins, poplins, zephyrs, shirting, fustian and many other types.

The scale of cotton's success, however, depended on more than just the home market, for it was essentially an export industry. By the time of Victoria's accession, it was supplying vast quantities of cloth to Europe, America, Africa and even, by a reversal of the earlier traffic, to India, the most important customer by 1843. The ports of Liverpool and Glasgow profited hugely from this traffic, as well as from the influx of raw cotton, which was by far Britain's most significant import from 1825 until 1873.

The 20th-century decline

The story of the cotton industry after its peak of expansion in 1912 is one of rapid and inevitable decline. Countries which once yielded raw cotton to Britain now had the urge to make more cloth themselves. India, for example, had begun to build her own cotton mills within a decade of Britain's lifting of the ban on the export of textile

THE DINNER HOUR, WIGAN, *1878. The long hours of arduous work demanded in the 19th-century cotton mills, coupled with an unrestrained use of women's and children's labour, precipitated the first legislation on factory employment. This romanticized painting blurs the grimmer realities.*

machinery (1843). By 1958, imports of cotton goods to Britain exceeded exports.

The decline has been accelerated by rivalry from new artificial fibres, many of which were invented or developed in Britain. For example, Terylene, invented in 1941, began to be produced on a commercial scale from the mid-1950s. The modern industry responded to its perilous conditions by increasing capital investment to mitigate labour costs, by developing new machinery and by adapting inventions from other producer countries. The contraction, though, could not be halted. Many closures took place, mills were altered to new uses, and in many parts of Lancashire cotton passed into history.

COTTON IN CONTEXT (***left***): *a fresh white apron, clean underwear and cotton lace curtains, in a reconstructed Victorian kitchen. Cotton was a symbol of respectability: 'Cleanliness is next to godliness.'*

CONNECTIONS
Cotton centres: 236–7 *Factory towns;* **252–3** *Manchester*
Dyeing: 176–7 *The chemical industry*
The importance of the cotton industry: 144–5 *The birth of industry*
Wool: 142–3 *The wool trade*

Pottery and porcelain

The ceramics industry has yielded an enormous variety of products, including tiles, bricks, baths, pipes and electrical insulators. Pottery and porcelain have a special place in this output, on account of their rich possibilities for decorative expression.

The age of experiment

Clays are of almost universal abundance, and are the materials with which ordinary earthenware pottery has been made since Neolithic times. Pots were hand-built at first but a simple potter's wheel was introduced during the Iron Age.

In the Roman period Castor in Northamptonshire produced a wide range of domestic pottery, and the New Forest was also an important centre of manufacture. Technical advances of the Middle Ages included a faster wheel and the use of lead glazes. There was a great interest in tile-making, for the floors of cathedrals and abbeys.

A tradition of hard-fired earthenware decorated with trailed white slip (diluted clay) gave rise to some vigorously decorated pieces during the 17th century. The Toft family of Staffordshire were the most important potters of this period, but fine work was also done at Wrotham (Kent) and in Devon.

In the 18th century there was a strong impulse towards greater refinement, and Continental techniques were widely influential. White salt-glazed stoneware in the German manner was popular, while the production of tin-glazed earthenware in the Low Countries stimulated imitators in Norwich, London (Aldgate, Lambeth and Southwark), Bristol and Liverpool.

Some types of stoneware resembled Chinese porcelain, which Europeans had admired since the 15th century. Attempts to produce more exact imitations began when the taste for drinking tea, coffee and chocolate caught on in Europe, and it was necessary to make vessels that could withstand hot liquids, to supplement imported wares from China. The formula for porcelain (which employed kaolin, or china clay) was discovered in Germany in 1708, but it was another sixty years before William Cookworthy of Plymouth took out the first English patent. The china clay pits of Cornwall soon became the key to a new industry, which began with the opening of a porcelain factory at Chelsea in 1745. Only three factories – Plymouth, Bristol and New Hall (Staffordshire) – succeeded in making Chinese-style 'hard-paste' porcelain, but a convincing 'soft-paste' substitute was used for figures and tableware by numerous manufacturers in England and Wales. The only porcelain works still operating today is that of the Royal Worcester Porcelain Company (whose factory can be visited).

The pottery industry

The most notable figure in the ceramics industry of the 18th century was Josiah Wedgwood (1730–95), who came from a long line of Staffordshire potters. Although Wedgwood is perhaps best known for his jasperware, which was in tune with the neo-classical tastes of the time, his real importance lay in the manufacture of less expensive cream-coloured earthenware for a wide middle-class market, and in the pioneering of mass-production techniques.

A further development in Staffordshire came around 1805 when Josiah Spode of Stoke perfected the manufacture of bone china (using bone ash with kaolin). This was to become one of the distinctive products of the Potteries – an area that soon became synonymous with the growing ceramics industry.

There are many reasons why the Potteries – based on six villages of north Staffordshire, which soon became towns – acquired this importance. Initially, the most potent of these was a long local tradition of the potter's craft. This tradition owed its tenacity to local supplies of clay and to the presence of long-flame coals that were ideal for firing. From the 1770s the canals, notably the Grand Trunk Canal from the Trent to the Mersey, facilitated the import of raw materials that were not available close by: china clay from Cornwall, ball clay from Devon, flint (used for ironstone

A POTBANK IN THE MID-19TH CENTURY

As the ceramics industry of the north Staffordshire villages expanded, hundreds of smoke- and soot-ridden potbanks, with their bottle ovens, became inextricably mixed up with the workers' terraced housing. The typical potbank (***right***) was a square of buildings in which the ware was made, with a handsome façade and a large arched entrance to the yard. At the edge of the yard were the bottle ovens, of different shapes to cater for the different firing temperatures required. An old potbank in Longton now houses the award-winning Gladstone Pottery Museum.

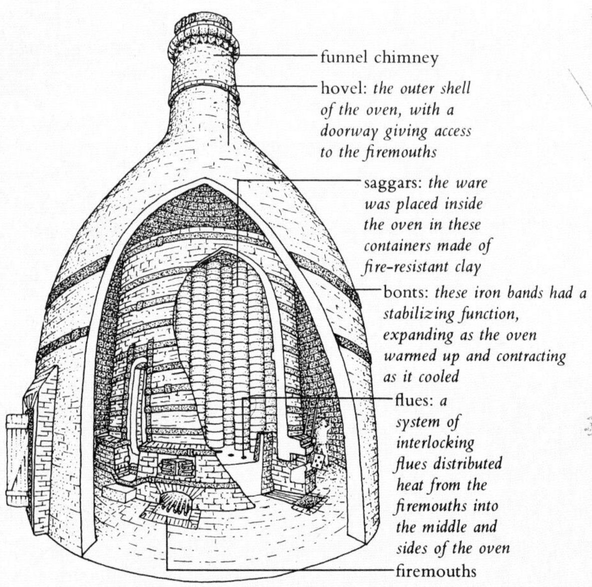

ANATOMY OF A BOTTLE OVEN: *its shape was designed to ensure even firing of the wares.*

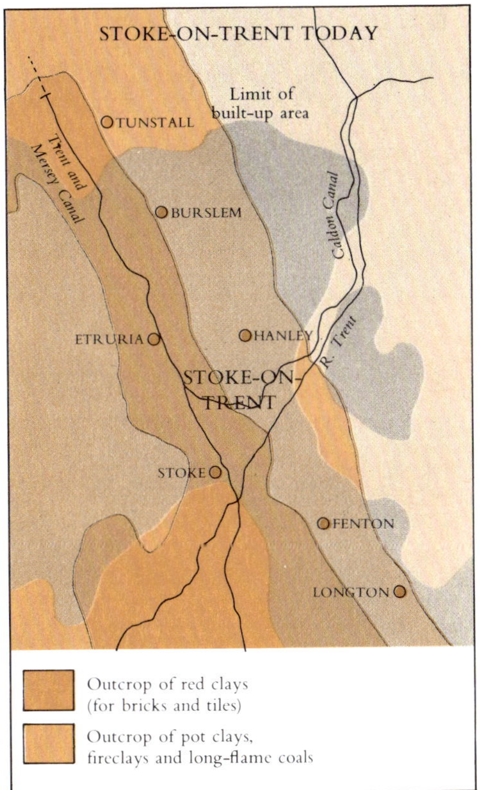

A MARL PIT IN LONGTON, *1905. Red firing clay, or marl (used for common earthenware), was the most easily obtainable of the Potteries' raw materials. It was excavated virtually on the potbank doorstep. The pits were used as dumps for potters' debris.*

POTTERY VERSUS PORCELAIN
As the north Staffordshire potteries rose to dominance in the ceramics industry, the porcelain centres declined (see map ***right****, which gives the dates of the major factories). In 1910 the original towns of the Potteries (****above****) were united to form one city – Stoke-on-Trent.*

COMMEMORATIVE CUP. *Pottery of a high standard was often made in 17th-century Britain. This slipware 'tyg' is vigorously decorated.*

PORCELAIN SAUCEBOAT. *This elegant china sauceboat from Bristol shows the leap forward in ceramic expertise in the 18th century.*

TILE-MAKING IN 1910. *Mass-produced tiles first found a ready market among the hygiene-conscious Victorians. As one worker (extreme left) is showing, the tiles were manufactured by whirling the flying presses. Young assistants stacked the fragile tiles in 'saggars', ready for firing.*

ware and other products) from the south-east.

In the 19th century transfer-printing (a technique particularly associated with Sadler and Green of Liverpool) was used for the decoration of countless 'willow pattern' tablewares. Newer, more expensive methods – for example, a metallic lustrous effect created by gold and platinum – often led to hideous overdecoration. In the second half of the century there was some dissatisfaction with the factory system, and a number of pottery studios sprang up, such as those of William de Morgan and the Minton firm in London.

The continued pre-eminence of the Potteries in the modern industry is underpinned by increasing automation. The proverbial smoke and pollution have disappeared with the exploitation of new energy sources. Before the Second World War, J. Wedgwood and Sons opened a new factory at Barlaston (south of the historic Wedgwood site at Etruria) and began to employ tunnel ovens, in which the wares were fired on a moving trolley. These have now supplanted the old bottle ovens, most of which have been demolished. The canals are also now unused, except by pleasure traffic, and china clay is brought from Cornwall by special 'clayliner' trains.

CONNECTIONS
Ceramics collections: 292–3 *Great art collections*
China clay: 152–5 *The bowels of the earth*
The Grand Trunk Canal: 260–61 *The canals*
Josiah Wedgwood: 284–5 *The artist's eye*

MICHAEL FARADAY *(1791–1867). In 1831 Faraday discovered the principles of the electric motor and dynamo.*

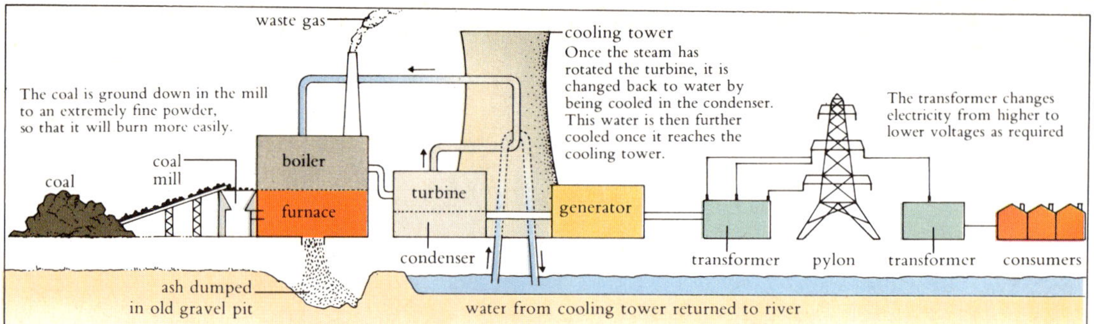

ANATOMY OF A TRENT VALLEY POWER STATION. *In areas with large, fast-flowing rivers, generators can be rotated by water-power, but in England steam-power is generally more practicable. The steam (produced from water heated by burning pulverized coal) revolves the blades of the turbine (just as a stream drives a water-wheel), and this provides the initial power for the electricity generating process.*

THE POWER HOUSE OF ENGLAND

The stations currently operating in the valley of the River Trent below Burton produce more than a quarter of all the electricity used in England and Wales. The area is ideal for the siting of power stations: the Trent and its tributaries supply vast quantities of water for steam generation and cooling, and coal is available near by from the east Midlands coalfields. Most of the power stations were built from 1950 onwards, and with their prominent cooling towers they stand out as conspicuous features of the landscape. The stations are directly linked to the super grid – high-voltage lines that can be seen traversing the countryside, supported on transmission towers. About half of the electricity produced in the Trent Valley stations is 'exported', especially to London, which is incapable of generating all its own electricity with the same degree of economy.

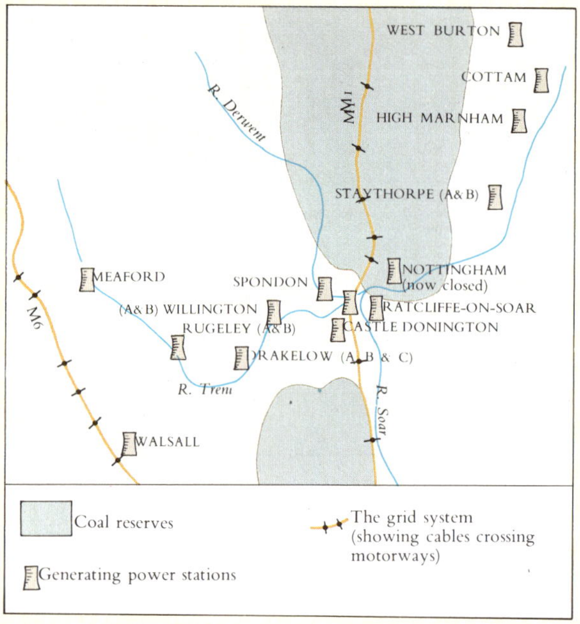

RATCLIFFE-ON-SOAR POWER STATION *is one of the largest and most efficient in the country.*

Electricity is a form of energy that is produced from other forms of energy, such as mechanical rotation or chemical reaction. Experiments carried out by Michael Faraday in 1831 laid the basis for the mechanical production of electricity. However, it was another fifty years before Faraday's discoveries were sufficiently developed to make possible the building of electric generators, or dynamos, that were capable of supplying whole communities with electricity on a commercial basis. Once that was feasible, it was another thirty years before the electrification of Britain got going in earnest.

Godalming in Surrey was the first community to have a public electricity supply. This was in September 1881, when the townspeople experienced the miracle of streets illuminated by the flick of a switch, which operated a generator in a watermill on the River Wey. Before long, other towns followed Godalming's precedent, beginning with Chesterfield and Norwich. In 1882 the first steam-powered stations were opened in London (in Holborn) and in Brighton, and by 1900 there were more than 400 small electricity undertakings in Britain. The Electric Lighting Act of 1909 allowed local authorities and specially formed companies to generate and supply electricity. The first electric cooker was in use in 1891, and the early years of the 20th century saw an increasing electrification of everyday life: the vacuum cleaner (1904), the washing machine (1908), the dishwasher (1910) and the refrigerator (1913).

From national to super grid

Soon there were enough power stations and enough customers to make electricity relatively cheap. In 1926 the stations began to be linked together by cable to form a 'national grid' (fully operational in 1936), whereby shortages of power in one area could be remedied by using power from another. By 1939 almost three-quarters of the houses in Britain had electricity laid on, but there were big differences between the prices charged by the many different electricity companies. In 1948 the electricity supply industry was brought into public ownership with the formation of the British Electricity Authority. This was to become the Central Electricity Authority and then, by the Electricity Act of 1957, the Central Electricity Generating Board (CEGB). This became responsible for generation and primary transmission, while area boards looked after supply and sales. The original grid system has been upgraded in various stages into a 'super grid', which enables electricity to be transmitted more economically for greater distances by means of the high-voltage cables.

Sources of energy

The first electric generators, like the historic one at Godalming, were driven by water power, a source that has the advantage of being virtually inexhaustible. Hydro-electricity is today the best method in highland areas with heavy rainfall: although it provides only a small proportion of the national total of electricity (1.3 per cent), it is very important in Scotland and in parts of Wales. In England most electricity is produced from coal.

In the late 1950s and the 1960s, when the demand for electricity was continuing to rise, the first oil-fired stations were built near oil refineries such as Milford Haven in south Wales. Nuclear power also began to be utilized. Although the cost of building safe nuclear power stations remains high, a half-kilo of uranium will produce 10,000 units of electricity, whereas the same weight of coal produces one unit.

In addition to the use of coal, nuclear power, oil and water, five other ways of generating electricity have recently been investigated: geothermal power, tapping the natural heat of rocks thousands of metres below the Earth's surface; wind power, operating giant windmills; tidal power, in areas with a large tidal range (such as the Bristol Channel); wave power, which is really another form of wind power; and solar power.

One hundred years after the first ventures in public electrification, Britain has the largest electricity supply organization in the world, with 132 generating stations supplying more than 20 million customers. The CEGB continues to be an innovator in methods of both generation and transmission. In hydro-electricity, it has experimented with 'pumped storage': the principle is that during off-peak hours, when consumption falls, the surplus power available is used to pump water back uphill to the main storage area, so that the same water can be used many times to provide power. One of the first ever pumped storage schemes was built at Ffestiniog in north Wales, and Dinorwic, also in north Wales, is the largest pumped storage scheme in Europe.

ELECTRIC EXTRAVAGANZA *along the famous promenade at Blackpool, Lancs.*

THE UPPER RESERVOIR, FFESTINIOG (***left***). *At night, water for recycling is pumped up electrically from the lower reservoir. During the day, this water is released back to the lower reservoir, generating electricity in the process.*

CONNECTIONS
Electrical engineering: 174–5 *Engineering*
Michael Faraday: 116–17 *Science*
Sources of electricity: 148–9 *Wind, water and steam;* **150–51** *Coal;* **156–7** *Gas and oil;* **168–9** *Nuclear power*

Nuclear power

BRITAIN'S REACTORS: THE TWO GENERATIONS

The advanced gas-cooled reactors, intended to supplement the earlier Magnox stations, produce more energy per tonne of fuel used and for a given output are more compact in size. Other types of modern reactor include the demonstration fast breeder at Dounreay.

ERNEST RUTHERFORD (1871–1937) *worked under J.J. Thompson at Cambridge in the experiments that led to the discovery of the electron in 1897. His subsequent research helped to make possible the development of nuclear energy as a source of either electrical power or military destruction.*

SAFETY MEASURES (***right***). *In the vicinity of the Hunterston nuclear power stations on the Clyde coast, a Health Physics Monitor takes seaweed samples, to test for radioactivity.*

INSIDE A REACTOR (***below***): *the last of the Magnox stations, at Wylfa, on Anglesey.*

When the nucleus of a heavy atom is split in two by the process termed 'fission', a tremendous amount of energy is released. In nuclear reactors fission takes place under controlled conditions, and the resultant energy is harnessed to produce steam and, through turbines, to generate electricity. The fissile material on which the nuclear power industry has been built is a type (technically speaking, an isotope) of uranium – U-235. Because uranium ore contains only a small quantity of U-235, methods have been developed to increase the proportion by 'enrichment'. About 14% of the country's energy is now supplied by nuclear reactors and by the year 2000 the proportion may be as high as a third.

Britain's pioneering of nuclear power in the early 1950s depended on earlier experiments in British universities, especially at Cambridge's Cavendish Laboratory. In the Second World War knowledge

of fission was extended by British scientists working in the United States on the military applications of atomic energy, and many of them helped to build up Britain's nuclear power programme after the war ended. In 1946 an atomic energy research station was founded at Harwell, near Oxford, and by 1952 a series of nuclear factories had been built at Springfields, Capenhurst and Windscale to produce and process fuels.

The 1950s was a decade of great excitement for the nuclear physicists. Work was begun on the world's first large nuclear power station in 1953, at Calder Hall on the bleak Cumbrian coast. Its construction was stimulated by the need for the by-product plutonium-239 for use in nuclear defence. By the time the first reactor-generated electricity had surged into the national grid (in October 1956), the government had announced an ambitious scheme for further reactors.

The reactors

The first phase of the nuclear power programme was the building of nine Magnox stations, all completed by 1971. These use natural uranium as a fuel and take their name from the magnesium alloy cladding around the uranium rods.

A second nuclear programme, announced in 1964, was based on the more efficient advanced gas-cooled reactor (AGR). This uses the same coolant as the Magnox (carbon dioxide gas) and the same 'moderator' to slow down the neutrons to

THE FAST BREEDER EXPERIMENT *at Dounreay (Highland), whose sphere became a well-known landmark, ceased operation in 1977. It was superseded by a more powerful Prototype Fast Reactor, completed in 1974.*

facilitate fission (graphite), but differs in using a slightly enriched uranium oxide fuel. The full implementation of the AGR programme has suffered delays, owing to technical hiccups.

When the need became clear for an alternative to Magnox, a counter-proposal to the AGR which attracted the majority of support was the pressurized water reactor (PWR), using water instead of gas as a coolant; this is the main type of reactor in use overseas. The Central Electricity Generating Board has recently proposed a PWR at Sizewell in Suffolk, and this will go ahead if the necessary consents and safety clearances are obtained.

A further category of reactor is represented by the fast breeder at Dounreay in the north of Scotland, based on a prototype opened in 1959. A fast breeder can produce more fuel (in the form of the plutonium by-product) than it consumes, thus reducing dependence on imported uranium.

It was partly the fear of radioactive leakage that caused the earliest reactors to be built in remote regions, but new stations at Hartlepool and Heysham, closer to well-populated areas, reflect an increased confidence within the industry. Nevertheless there is a vociferous lobby that is alarmed by the possibility of a nuclear accident. The biggest bone of contention is the disposal of waste fuel. Highly radioactive wastes are currently being stored on-site while methods of disposal are under development.

ANTI-NUCLEAR DEMONSTRATORS, *1980. Protest became especially vigorous after a reactor fire accident at Windscale in October 1937, which resulted in low-level contamination of some milk supplies.*

CONNECTIONS
The national grid: 166–7 *Electricity*
Other sources of power: 148–9 *Wind, water and steam*
Safety in industry: 176–7 *The chemical industry*

THE NUCLEAR LANDSCAPE (***below***). *As with a conventional electricity generating plant, a nuclear power station inevitably makes an undisguisable impact on the landscape. However, it is considerably quieter and cleaner.*

Building

The modern building industry is still very much concerned with the provision of housing – indeed, the word building is derived from an Old English term meaning dwelling place. The industry is now involved with a wide range of structures, including roads, sewerage systems, harbours and sea defences. But it is designs for domestic living that have aroused the strongest responses, critical and otherwise, from public opinion, especially since the 1950s.

MEDIEVAL BUILDING *depended largely upon brawn, but masons guarded their secrets, and designs were often founded on complex mathematical calculations.*

BUILDING IN THE 18TH CENTURY, *a contemporary engraving. Traditional tasks included mortaring (B), truing (or levelling) courses (C) and marking stone for cutting (D).*

THATCHING (***below centre***) *was the traditional roofing method before slates and tiles became prevalent. It is now expensive, but long-lasting.*

PARGETING (***below***), *The Sun Inn, Saffron Walden (Essex). A form of raised ornamental plasterwork, popular in the 16th and 17th centuries.*

Vernacular styles

The cathedrals, churches, castles and stately homes of Britain have attracted most attention from visitors, but much of the architectural richness of the country lies in humbler domestic structures. The countryside of England and Wales is particularly richly endowed with houses of remarkable age, including some that are claimed to have been continuously occupied since the Norman period. One of the most fascinating aspects of these dwellings is the way in which they display vernacular styles – that is, regional characteristics dependent upon local variations in culture or building materials.

Bricks were first introduced by the Romans, but after their departure brickmaking was not fully re-established until the 14th and 15th centuries. In the intervening period (and up to the 17th century in some areas) timber buildings were widespread, and rural builders also exploited more primitive materials, notably wattle and daub. Stone building developed rapidly after the Norman conquest, but in many places stone was a rare commodity and too expensive to import for all but the grandest

REINFORCED CONCRETE, *which forms the sweeping ramps of the Penguin Pool, London Zoo (1938), was first developed in the 1890s. The reinforcement is provided by a skeleton of steel bars.*

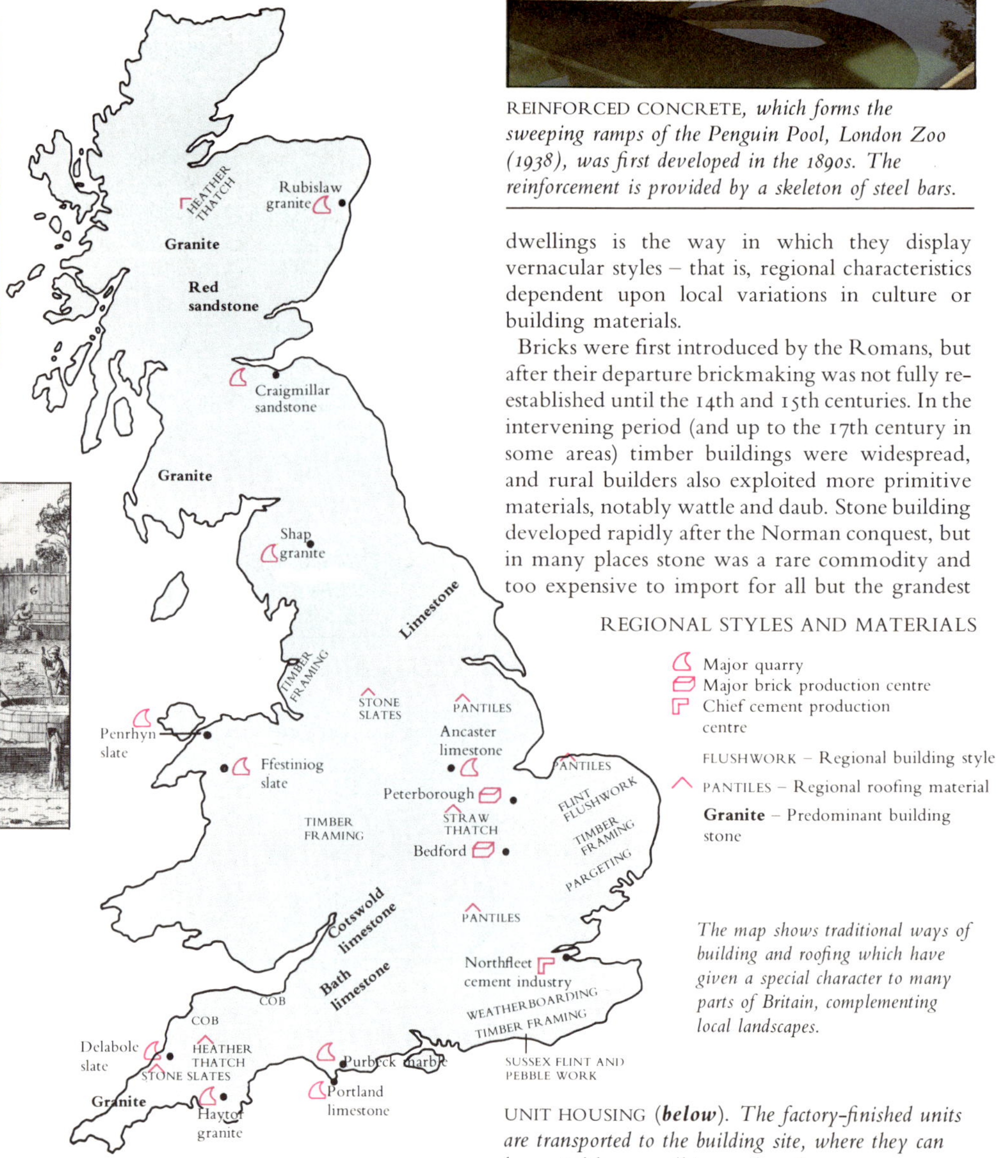

The map shows traditional ways of building and roofing which have given a special character to many parts of Britain, complementing local landscapes.

UNIT HOUSING (***below***). *The factory-finished units are transported to the building site, where they can be erected by a small team of workers.*

constructions. Builders were therefore inventive with local materials.

Typical of much domestic architecture in England and Wales was the use of load-bearing timber frames infilled with wattle and daub and coated with lime for protection. There was a major difference between the timber-frame traditions of the north and west (where the cruck frame employed huge curved timbers that were joined in a gable shape) and those of the south-east (where the more adaptable box frame house was usual). In general, the use of wood-and-plaster and flint-and-pebble is most prevalent in the south-east, but the extraordinary half-timbered houses of Cheshire and Lancashire are outstanding. Surprisingly, since local stone is not lacking, Devon is remarkable for buildings with thick walls of roughly fashioned cob (a mixture of clay and chopped straw).

Bricks and roofing

When the use of brick returned to Britain it was at first confined to the south-east. Dutch and Flemish brickmakers were imported, and eventually various elements of Continental brick building styles were also brought in (such as the curved Dutch gable). Brick came into widespread use for ordinary houses in the 17th century. After the Great Fire of 1666, London was largely rebuilt in this

STATEMENT IN STEEL AND GLASS: *the imposing History Faculty building, Cambridge University (1968), by the prestigious Glasgow-born architect James Stirling.*

CONSTRUCTION TECHNIQUES OF THE 1970s *have produced what is believed to be the world's tallest cantilevered structure, the National Westminster Tower in London, which was opened in 1981. The reinforced concrete cantilevers, which carry units of steel ribs and columns, project from a central concrete core which rests on foundations plunging deep into the London clay.*

material. Except in regions well provided with strong local stone, brickmaking flourished. Red brick was most common, since most clay and sand has a measure of iron, but in London and in the Norwich area of Norfolk local chalk has produced a yellow variety.

Roofing material was also subject to considerable diversification for many centuries. Pantiles (S-shaped tiles first imported from Flanders) were common in the south-east, and eventually came into general use. Thatching, originally a poor man's roofing, was practised in many areas, but it was brought to perfection in Norfolk. By the 17th and 18th centuries slate roofs were becoming frequent, but their heyday was the Victorian age.

Iron, steel and concrete

During the 18th century the idea of a load-bearing frame with non-load-bearing walls was revived, but now using iron, and later steel, for the frames – mainly for large buildings such as factories and market halls. London's Crystal Palace of 1851 demonstrated the significance of iron combined with glass as a building material. In 1904 work was started on the Ritz Hotel, the first of many steel-framed buildings in London. Reinforced concrete also became increasingly important; the first patent for its use in building was taken out in 1854, just thirty years after the invention of Portland cement. The cement industry, and the quarrying of chalk to support it, grew rapidly after concrete came into general use.

The era of bulk freight transport and the adoption of economic building styles have tended to extinguish the traditional use of local styles and materials. Compact structures composed of mass-produced units have been employed for housing, successfully reducing the soaring costs incurred by traditional labour-intensive building methods. And in the building of schools an influential event of 1957 was the banding together of local authorities to develop the CLASP system of prefabrication.

Pre-stressed concrete has given scope for extraordinarily imaginative designs and has proved the strongest, most economic material for large buildings and engineering works. A recent development is that of glass-reinforced cement composites, consisting of ordinary Portland cement and sand combined with glass fibre. Glass-faced, steel-framed structures and traditional red brick have both enjoyed a revival.

CONNECTIONS
Brick: 208–9 *The great country houses*
Building in London: 242–51 *London*
Housing: 226–7 *Town houses;* **228–9** *Town planning*
Sources of stone: 152–5 *The bowels of the earth*
Timber-framed architecture: 220–21 *Cottages and rural homes*

Manufacturing

HENRY WICKHAM (1846–1928), *a pioneer rubber planter, proved to be one of the greatest benefactors of the European rubber industry. The rubber tree seeds which he collected in Brazil were nurtured in Kew Gardens, London, and transplanted to south-east Asia. By the end of the 19th century British rubber firms producing tyres, hoses, belting, cables and clothing competed fiercely for supplies.*

THE IMPORTANCE OF DUNLOP

The Dunlop group, one of the largest tyre manufacturing concerns in Europe, owes its existence to a simple but revolutionary invention – the first practicable pneumatic tyre, which was created in 1888 by John Boyd Dunlop (1840–1921) (***right***). The initial step in his introduction of tyres to bicycle manufacture was an experiment in which he attached a rubber hose to a child's tricycle. By 1900 his company had captured the lion's share of a vast market and was established as a supplier to the up-and-coming motor car industry. The Fort Dunlop works at Birmingham (***below***) was built in the 1930s, by which time the firm's activities had extended to footwear, clothing, foam rubber (with the invention of 'Dunlopillo' in 1929) and sports equipment.

The prodigious variety of goods produced by Britain's manufacturing industries is matched by vastly varying patterns of ownership and organization. The giants – such as Dunlop and Unilever – are almost imperial in their size and complexity, but a feature of recent industrial development has been the application of the principle that 'small is beautiful'. Firms with fewer than twenty employees now account for one fifth of the output.

In recent decades, manufacturing has undergone great changes, many of them inevitably painful. Some of these have been caused by profound technological advances, particularly where new synthetic materials have come into use. Others have been stimulated by adjustments in the international equation of supply and demand. For example, electrical engineering and the aviation and petrochemical industries have enormously expanded, while textiles and shipbuilding have suffered a sharp decline.

Since the 1960s the proportion of the labour force involved in manufacturing has diminished, partly because of the biting winds of the economic climate, and partly because of the widespread adoption of automation.

Metal products and furniture

In addition to iron and steel production and the machine tool industry, Britain boasts a wide spectrum of metal products. Typical of the continuous changes that have affected manufacturing since the industrial revolution was the introduction of electro-plating (in 1840), which effectively put an end to the profitable manufacture of Sheffield plate. Metal goods became concentrated around Birmingham and the west Midlands, and Sheffield; and despite the advances of mechanization a number of small workshops have continued to thrive here, producing cutlery, nails and similar items. One remarkably profitable branch of metal manufacturing is the production of hand tools, and there is still a large domestic and export market for jewellery in gold and silver and other metals.

Furniture-making emerged as a fully fledged industry at the end of the 17th century, although it was not until the mid-20th century that it penetrated significant markets overseas. London de-

MAJOR MANUFACTURING ZONES

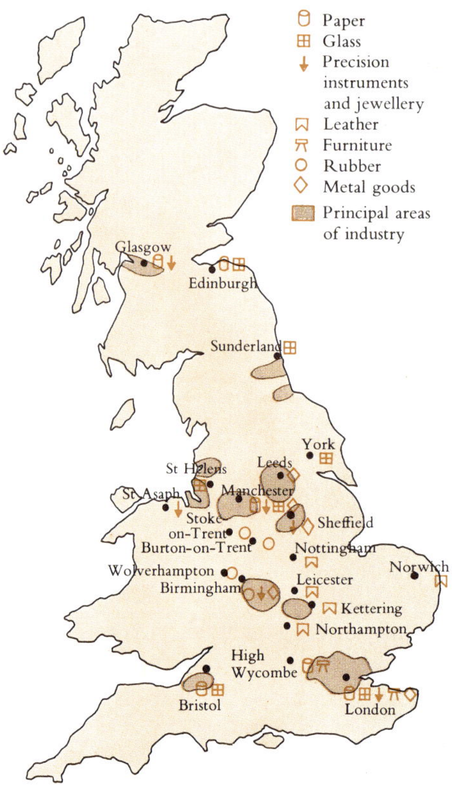

A predominant pattern in the distribution of manufacturing industries was evident by the 19th century – a broad manufacturing belt from London to Lancashire and another across lowland Scotland.

SHOE-MAKING *today still makes use of traditional methods of stitching and gluing uppers to soles, but in some factories computer stitching and injection moulding have been introduced.*

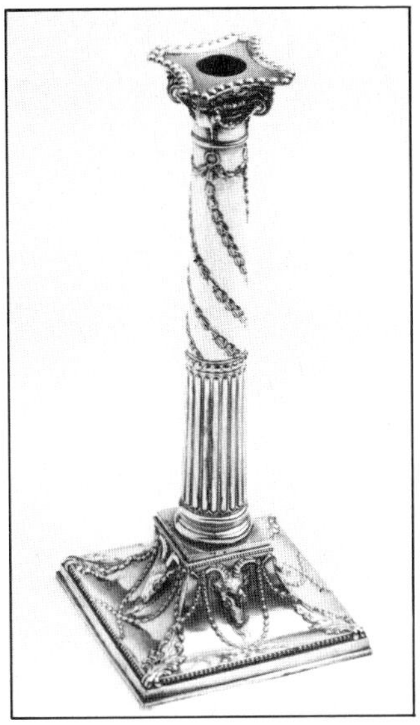

SHEFFIELD PLATING *(the process of fusing copper with an outer layer of silver) flourished from the late 18th century until the 1830s.*

GLASSMAKING IN THE 18TH CENTURY. *Many of the techniques used in the 18th century, such as gathering, blowing and 'marvering' (rolling the hot glass on a slab of stone or iron), are still current in the modern handmade glass industry.*

veloped as the major centre for the manufacture of quality pieces, and by the 1880s there was a clearly defined furniture district in the East End. Outside the capital the other principal furniture-making town was (and still is) High Wycombe in Buckinghamshire, where local supplies of beechwood benefited the growth of the industry. Small specialist craft firms are now enjoying renewed demand, but cheap, functional 'unit' furniture is making serious inroads into the market.

Leather and footwear

By the 17th century, good supplies of raw material had firmly established the leather and footwear industries in the Midlands, for this was a major cattle-fattening area with good supplies of oak-bark (an essential ingredient of the tanning process). By 1900 mineral salts had replaced oak-bark in tanning, and a large quantity of hides was being imported. Ports then became important centres of the heavy leather industry, but boots and shoes continued to be produced mainly in the Midlands. The first bulk order (for 10,000 pairs of military footwear) went to Northampton as early as 1642. Stafford and Norwich were also important footwear centres, later to be joined by Leicester. An efficient method of riveting soles to uppers was patented by Thomas Crick of Leicester in 1853. After 1890 a large export trade developed, but after 1918 the leather shoe trade faced mounting problems owing to rivalry from synthetic materials and cheaper imported products.

Glass and paper

Britain's glass industry is one of the largest in the world, with containers, flat glass and safety glass accounting for most of the more highly mechanized aspects of production. However, until the end of the 19th century, most glass was handmade. The basic raw materials were sand, alkali (soda or potash) and various fluxes.

Glass-making in Britain dates from pre-Roman times, but experienced its first great period of expansion in the 16th and 17th centuries. Areas such as the Sussex Weald and the Forest of Dean, with their plentiful supplies of timber for fuel, were particularly important, but as the forests were progressively denuded, and coal was introduced, new centres emerged. St Helens in Lancashire was especially favoured by suitable deposits of sands and nearby coalfields.

In the 20th century glass technology has been undergoing continuous change, but a number of small craft firms specializing in lead crystal have been notably successful.

Like the glass industry, papermaking in Britain is of international significance. By the end of the 18th century there were about 500 rag-paper mills scattered throughout the country. The main raw materials by the mid-19th century, however, were straw and wood pulp, together with certain chemicals. Paper mills have become larger and fewer, but specialized types of paper are still produced by small companies. Recently, there has been an increase in the use of recycled waste paper.

Rubber

There was a factory in London processing natural rubber by 1820, and in 1823 the Scotsman Charles Macintosh produced the first rubberized raincoat, but the greatest boost to rubber manufacture in the 19th century was Dunlop's invention of the pneumatic tyre. It stimulated the bicycle industry, which in turn contributed to the development of the first motor cars – and today, car tyres and tubes account for half of Britain's rubber production. Since the Second World War synthetic rubber has risen to importance, and the industry has become closely linked with petrochemicals.

FLOAT GLASSMAKING, *invented in the 1950s, was a radically new process for flat glass manufacture. Glass is poured from the furnace onto the surface of a bath of molten tin. The result is glass of uniform thickness with a brilliant polish.*

CONNECTIONS
Ceramics: 164–5 *Pottery and porcelain*
Exports: 100–101 *Britain in the world marketplace*
Metals: 158–9 *Iron and steel*
Petrochemicals: 176–7 *The chemical industry*
Ships, aeroplanes and cars: 178–83
Textiles: 160–63 *Cotton*

Engineering

The many-headed engineering industry began with, and once begun further stimulated, the industrial revolution. In Britain today the word 'engineer' stands both for the skilled metalworker and for the specialized technologist – an ambiguity reflecting engineering's early flowering in a country whose precocious industrialization produced a demand for metal, not only for machines, engines and tools, but also for bridges, pipes, building materials and domestic utensils.

The first engineers were associated with the development of the steam engine. In their famous Soho workshop in Birmingham the partnership of Matthew Boulton, the industrialist, and James Watt, the inventor, pioneered the mass production of efficient machinery and by 1800 had produced some 500 engines.

BRIDGE-BUILDING, 1797. *The construction of a cast-iron bridge over the Wear. It was another 50 years before iron ships made a convincing appearance.*

Civil and mechanical engineering

Heavy constructional engineering – called 'civil' to distinguish it from engineering in its original military sense – grew up in the 18th century with the development of canals, roads, bridges and, much later, the railways. The engineered environment of Britain called for a new precision and new skills to which, initially, many traditionally trained craftsmen applied themselves. Thus, the canal-builder James Brindley (1716–72) started his career as a millwright, while the Scot Thomas Telford (1757–1834) began as a stonemason but eventually became one of the greatest early civil engineers. In 1818 the Institution of Civil Engineers was founded to mark the establishment of a new profession.

One of the greatest challenges in civil engineering has been the provision of bridges. The most monumental 19th-century solutions have included two bridges over the Menai Strait – the suspension bridge by Telford and the tubular Britannia Bridge by Robert Stephenson – and the formidable Forth Bridge.

By the mid-19th century, mechanical engineering industries were well established in the lowlands of Scotland, north-east England, Lancashire, Yorkshire, the west Midlands and south Wales. By 1900 few large towns were without a factory making use of iron and steel. The type of engineering found in such towns either met local needs for specific products, such as agricultural machinery in Ipswich, or was associated with a metalworking tradition based on local supplies of coal and iron.

However, not all engineering has been dependent on iron and steel: non-ferrous metals, especially copper and brass in the 19th century and zinc, nickel chromium and aluminium in the 20th, have also been employed. The 19th-century non-ferrous smelting industry was predominantly

A TREADLE-OPERATED LATHE (***below***), *in a 19th-century workshop.*

MAKING CAPSTON LATHES, c.*1960. The mass production of machine tools was pioneered by Victorian engineers such as Henry Maudslay and his pupils James Nasmyth and Joseph Whitworth.*

A VICTORIAN ENGINEER FOR ALL SEASONS

Isambard Kingdom Brunel (1806–59) combined in his brilliant career the skills of civil, marine and mechanical engineering. He was the son of Sir Marc Brunel, a French-born engineer who masterminded the first tunnel under the Thames. In 1829 Brunel designed the Clifton Suspension Bridge (completed in 1864), and in 1833 he became engineer to the Great Western Railway, for whom he designed the magnificent Royal Albert, or Saltash, Bridge – finished in the year of his death – which spans the River Tamar to link Devon and Cornwall (***below***).

Brunel was also famous for his innovative iron steamships: the *Great Britain* (1843), powered by screw propeller, and the *Great Eastern* (1858), in which the screw propeller was combined with paddles. The latter remained the world's largest ship for over 40 years, and laid the first telegraphic cable between Britain and North America.

based on the Swansea region, but Birmingham was the major centre of non-ferrous manufacturing; its brass-engineering enterprises were particularly associated with steam engines. Today, nearly half of the non-ferrous metal industry is still located in the Midlands.

All the engineering industries rely on machine tools – tools which are themselves machines, designed to cut, shape or join metal and other substances – and this branch of engineering is one of the strongest in Britain.

The most important machine tool, known since antiquity, is the lathe, which works by facilitating the rotation of a piece of metal or wood while a cutting edge is applied to it, to produce an even smooth cut. Henry Maudslay (1771–1831) extended the first primitive attempts to mechanize this essential tool with his slide-rest lathe, in which the cutting tool was held rigid and operated mechanically, instead of by hand. He also developed a screw-cutting lathe, and was responsible for the invention of the micrometer – and for the beer pump which soon graced every public house. He was a pupil of another great engineer, Joseph Bramah (1748–1814).

The most important kinds of machine tools today continue to be milling, grinding and turning machines. There has recently been a rapid development in automatic control systems.

HOW THE BARRIER WORKS. *The 9 piers, each built on a giant concrete plug sunk into the river-bed, support curved gates which can be swung from their horizontal resting places (some just above and some just below the water) into a vertical position. So that shipping is not disrupted, the 61-metre gaps between 5 of the piers are wide enough to allow even the biggest vessels to pass through.*

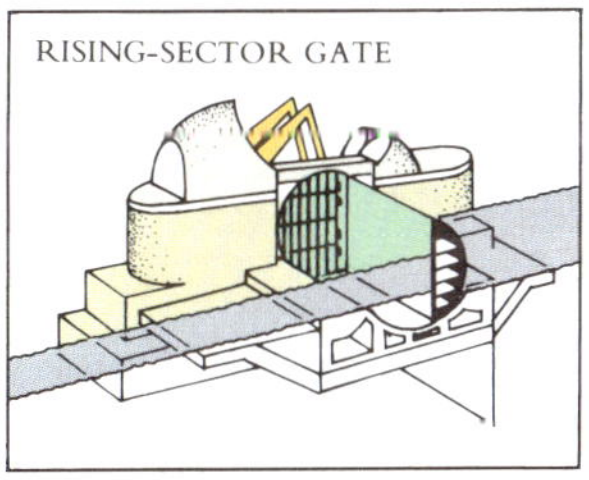

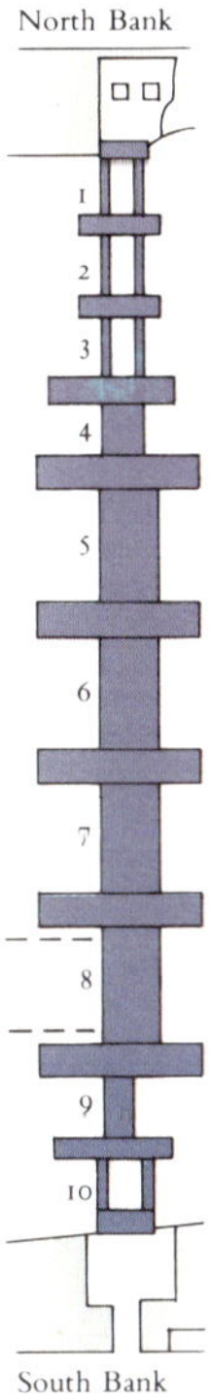

Falling radial gates 1, 2, 3, 10
Rising-sector gates 4, 5, 6, 7, 9
Channel for ship navigation 8

THE THAMES FLOOD BARRIER, *here shown under construction (1981), is designed to protect London from flooding by halting the advance of tidal surges from the North Sea. The hoods on the piers house sophisticated machinery for closing the flood gates, which can be done within minutes of a warning.*

A ROBOT WELDER. *Modern machine tools such as this, eliminating the possibilities of human error, are stages on the way towards the realization of the futuristic concept of the unmanned factory.*

The younger engineering industries

Electrical engineering dates from the end of the 19th century, when the electrification of Britain was begun, with its concomitant demand for electricity-generating machinery, domestic appliances and equipment for motor vehicles and aircraft. Today, the applications of the rapidly expanding electronics industry include radio and television, sound recording, computers and aerospace and navigation equipment. Some of this industry is located in areas formerly noted for 'heavier' kinds of engineering, such as Tyneside and the west Midlands, but a large sector is concentrated in areas such as south-east England, hitherto not associated with metalworking.

CONNECTIONS
Civil engineering: 260–61 *The canals;* **262–3** *The railway age;* **266–7** *Enjoying the railways today*
The materials: 158–9 *Iron and steel*
Transport engineering: 178–9 *Shipbuilding;* **180–81** *The plane-makers;* **182–3** *The motor industry;* **264–5** *The railway revolution*

The chemical industry

The chemical industry is a vast and rapidly expanding sector of manufacturing – the third most important in the country – and affects almost every aspect of our lives.

Pharmaceuticals and toilet preparations, strongly orientated towards the consumer, account for a substantial share of the total output. These are categorized as 'light' chemicals, and are produced by labour-intensive methods, mainly in the south-east. However, a much greater part of the industry, chiefly located in the north, is concerned with the bulk manufacture of 'heavy' chemicals in large, capital-intensive plants. These substances are primarily for industrial use, and cover a bewilderingly vast spectrum of both organic and inorganic materials (organic chemicals are those which are compounds of carbon). Among the most familiar products are oils, acids, chlorine, dyestuffs, soaps, starch, fertilizers, pesticides, explosives and paints. Plastics and synthetic fibres have shown spectacular growth over the past thirty years, with the shift from coal to petroleum as the basic raw material of the industry.

SOAP-MAKING (***left***) *in the late 18th century, using alkali made from plant ash and limestone.*

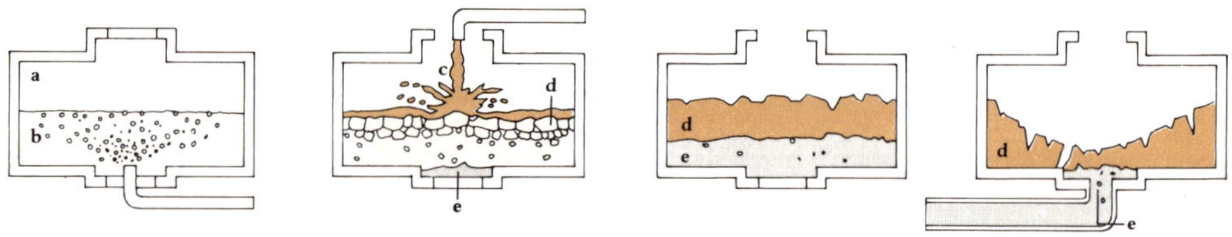

MODERN SOAP-MAKING (***below***) *relies upon an ancient chemical process: the saponification of fat and alkali into soap and glycerol. Fats and oils (b) are reacted with water at high temperature and pressure (a). Alkali (c) is added to the resulting mixture to produce soap (d) and glycerol (e). The glycerol is washed out with brine and separated from the soap in a centrifuge.*

Early developments

The chemical industry is often thought of as quintessentially modern, but in fact its origins can be traced to the late 18th century, when the growth of the textiles industry in Lancashire created the need for increased supplies of various kinds of soaps, dyes and bleach.

The manufacture of soap requires a cheap and plentiful supply of soda (alkali), which initially was obtained from the ashes of burnt vegetable matter. The French chemist Nicholas Leblanc discovered in 1787 what was to be one of the most important chemical processes of the 19th century: namely, the conversion of common salt into soda by treating it with sulphuric acid.

The organic chemical side of the industry (embracing dyes, plastics and drugs) owes much to the early dye trade, and in particular to the work of Sir William Perkin. His discovery of the first truly synthetic dye (aniline purple) revolutionized an activity which had previously relied upon animal and vegetable extracts. In 1869 Perkin went on to discover how to process the useful chemical known as alizarin, but unfortunately the patent was obtained by a German company one day before he put in his own application. Subsequently much of the initiative in synthetic dyestuffs was lost to the Germans.

The later 19th century saw much activity in other fields: the large-scale production of fertilizers, the use of phosphorus in matchmaking, the manufacture of nitro-explosives and the synthesis of chemical drugs were just a few of the important advances being made. By the early 1900s the chemical industry – essentially the alkali industry – was controlled by about fifty companies clustered on

HAZARDS OF THE INDUSTRY

On 1 June 1974 a major explosion occurred at the Nypro chemical plant at Flixborough (Humberside), where cyclohexane was oxidized to produce intermediates for the production of nylon (***above***). As a result, an Advisory Committee on Major Hazards was set up to investigate the attendant risks of industrial processes, and stringent safety measures were subsequently enforced.

Atmospheric and river pollution has always been a problem in the chemical industry, particularly in the regions of Widnes and St Helens in the 19th century. However, rivers foaming with effluents and dotted with dead fish are now an evil of the past, as modern legislation requires factories to install machines for the disposal of chemical waste. It is also compulsory to control smoke, dirt and fumes, and drivers of vehicles containing dangerous chemicals are specially trained.

SYNTHETIC FIBRES (***below***) *such as nylon, terylene and acrylic are made entirely from chemicals and have a wide range of applications. Nylon is much stronger than natural fibre and was used for parachutes during the Second World War.*

THE ICI COMPLEX AT WILTON, TEESSIDE, *where petrochemicals and plastics are produced. This site, first developed in 1946, now covers an area of over 1,400 acres (556 ha). It is the largest complex of its kind in Europe, and employs about 10,000 people.*

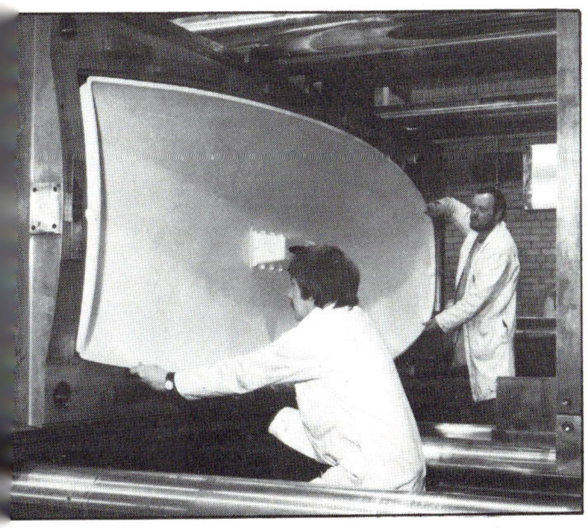

INJECTION MOULDING *is an extremely versatile process, used for moulding thermoplastics (plastics which soften on heating). Britain has recently developed the biggest injection-moulding project in the world, allowing the production of a sailing dinghy hull in just 7 minutes.*

THE BRITISH CHEMICAL INDUSTRY

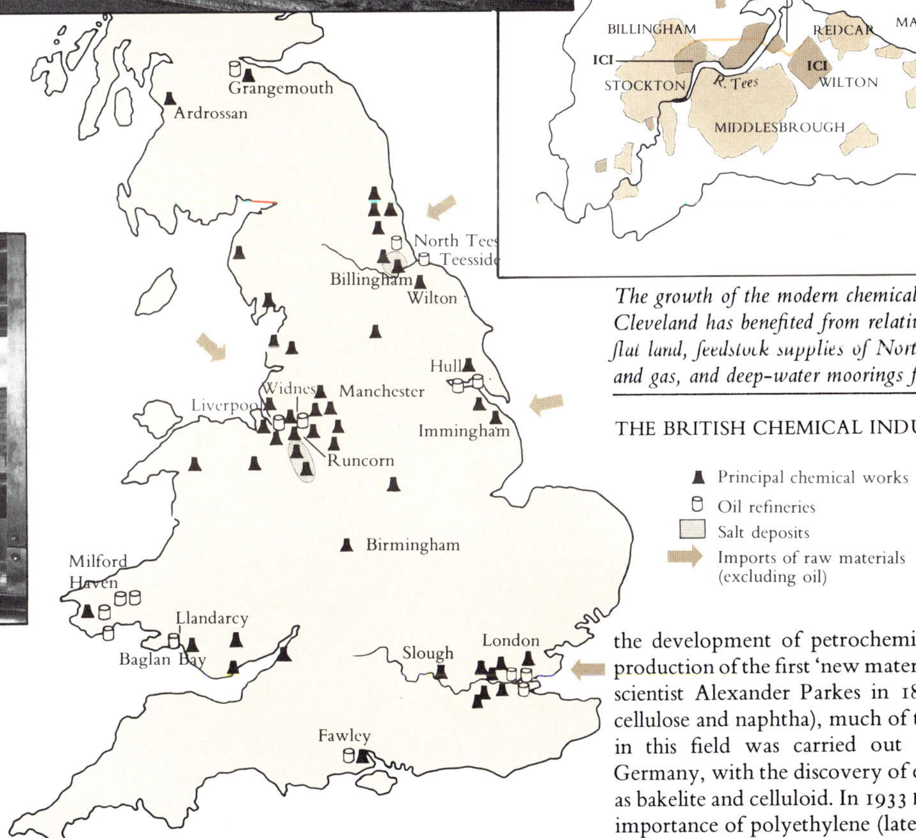

Merseyside and Tyneside. The location of these firms was no accident: abundant supplies of three of the basic raw materials (salt, lime and coal) could be obtained from local deposits and the fourth (sulphur) could be cheaply imported via the docks. Proximity to customers (such as the glassmaking concerns at St Helens, which needed vast quantities of alkali) was also a crucial factor.

Fierce competition within the rapidly expanding industry led to mergers of small companies for more efficient and economic production. The most significant structural change in the trade occurred in 1926 when four leading firms – British Dyestuffs Corporation, United Alkali Company, Nobel Industries and Brunner, Mond and Company – combined to form Imperial Chemical Industries (ICI). This organization is now a giant. It employs some 92,000 workers in the United Kingdom and over 58,000 overseas, and is in the forefront of chemical research.

Petrochemicals

Since the 1950s perhaps the most spectacular development has been in petrochemicals: that is, chemicals derived from crude petroleum by way of the feedstock naphtha. After the Second World War several large petroleum companies established oil refineries in Britain, and the chemical industry found new sources of raw materials from their by-products. Unlike coal, petroleum products can be transported by pipeline, such as the one that links the Shell refinery at Stanlow with the Carrington works on the Mersey. Perhaps the most famous pipeline, however, is the Trans-Pennine, which connects the chemical industries of Lancashire and Merseyside with those of Teesside.

The growth of the plastics industry owes much to the development of petrochemicals. Despite the production of the first 'new material' by the British scientist Alexander Parkes in 1862 (using nitrocellulose and naphtha), much of the early research in this field was carried out in America and Germany, with the discovery of early plastics such as bakelite and celluloid. In 1933 ICI discovered the importance of polyethylene (later polythene), but it was not until the 1950s that the plastics industry became firmly established in Britain.

CHEMICALS ON TEESSIDE

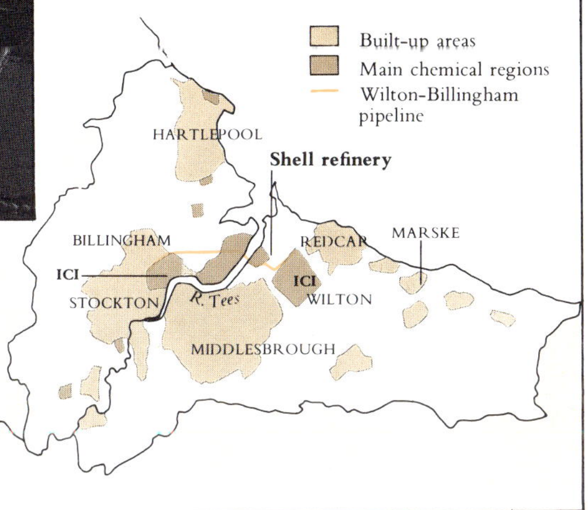

The growth of the modern chemical industry in Cleveland has benefited from relatively cheap, flat land, feedstock supplies of North Sea oil and gas, and deep-water moorings for tankers.

CONNECTIONS
Early chemists: 116–17 *Science*
Glass: 172–3 *Manufacturing*
Petrochemicals: 156–7 *Gas and oil*
Textiles: 160–63 *Cotton*

Shipbuilding

THE GOLDEN HIND: *a modern replica of Francis Drake's famous 16th-century galleon, setting sail for California. The relatively low forecastle of a galleon made it more manoeuvrable than earlier ships.*

It was the naval policies of the Tudors, combined with developing trade and the urge to explore unchartered seas, that laid the foundations of British shipbuilding. The warship emerged as a specialized vessel in the reign of Henry VIII, who greatly extended the royal dockyards and encouraged the construction of bigger, more elaborately rigged ships. But it was the magnificent galleons of Elizabeth's reign that most elegantly symbolized the urge to rule the waves.

As the volume of mercantile shipping increased during the 17th century, other countries in Europe made great progress in the design of ocean-going vessels. By 1680, probably as much as a quarter of English merchant shipping was foreign-built, mainly by the Dutch. Britain experienced sixty-five years of war between 1689 and 1815, so there was also an urgent need for warships. Many of these were built in the royal dockyards at Chatham, Deptford, Woolwich or Portsmouth, but as the demand outstripped the supply, contracts were often awarded to the civilian yards of the Thames estuary. Among the technological advances of the 18th century were the introduction of wheel steering and the use of copper sheathing to protect hulls from shipworm.

To meet the challenge of the Napoleonic wars (as well as to supply the East India Company with merchantmen), the shipyards buzzed with activity. One of the most important was Buckler's Hard on the River Hamble in Hampshire. The more permanent sites had sail-lofts and mast-houses as well as launchways, sawpits, timber stacks and a mould loft (where loftsmen marked out the plans with scriving knives). Only a few yards had rope-walks, as rope-making was a specialized job requiring a great deal of money and space.

About 700 large oak trees were required to build Nelson's *Victory* (at Chatham) in 1759. The problem of timber shortage was solved by the use of iron, which also enabled ships to be larger. An iron barge was built on the Severn in 1787 and a number of iron craft for river and estuary work were launched in the early 19th century. On larger vessels wooden planking was combined with iron frames to create a curious breed of composite ship.

THE FIGHTING TÉMÉRAIRE: *Turner's painting (1838) shows the warship en route along the Thames to be broken up at Rotherhithe. It had been launched in 1798, at Chatham.*

Steamships

The potential of iron was not fully exploited in shipbuilding until the adoption of steam-power. To begin with, steam was merely an auxiliary of sail, although there were some notable exceptions to this, such as I.K. Brunel's transatlantic steamship the *Great Western*, driven by paddle wheels. Because the early steamships were inefficient, sail power (and especially the great clippers such as the *Cutty Sark*) remained a competitive alternative.

The technological revolution which brought iron, and later steel, to the forefront of shipbuilding was accompanied by a major relocation of the industry, caused by the demand for cheap labour and for massive supplies of raw materials. The Thames yards closed one by one throughout the century, and four main areas became predominant: the Clyde estuary, north-east England (the Tyne, Wear and Tees), Merseyside, and Barrow-in-

THE GREAT BRITAIN *being launched (1843) at Bristol (where it is preserved today). This iron-hulled vessel, by Brunel, was driven by screw propeller, a method of propulsion that became increasingly popular.*

SHIPBUILDING CENTRES TODAY

British Shipbuilders' yards produce 85 per cent of merchant shipbuilding tonnage and 99 per cent of naval building in the UK.

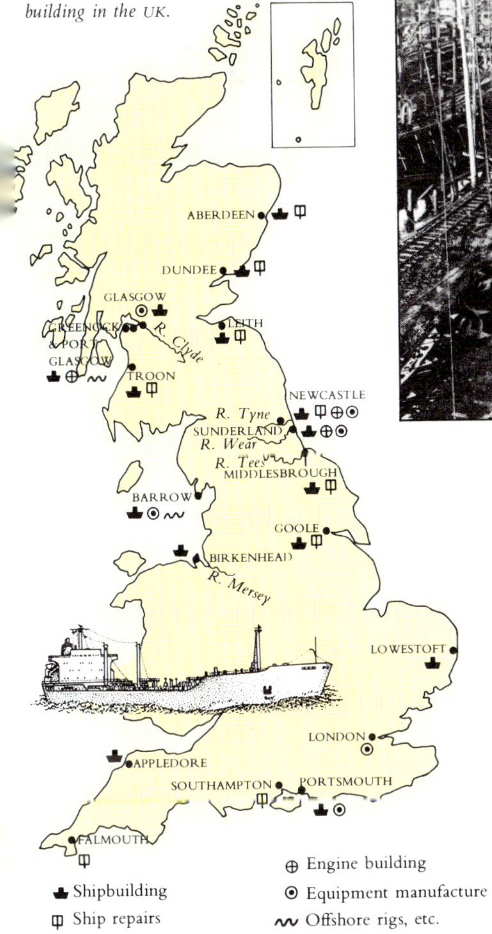

JOHN BROWN'S SHIPYARD (***left***) *at Clydebank, c.1910. The ship is the Cunard liner* Aquitania, *which crossed the Atlantic about 600 times.*

Furness in Cumbria. (In Northern Ireland, Belfast was also of major importance.)

Clydeside has produced the greatest variety of ships, but it is best-known for its liners. Among them was the ill-fated *Lusitania* (built by John Brown's for the Cunard line in 1907), which helped to promote the steam turbine as a means of propulsion. John Brown's other great Cunarders were the *Queen Mary* (1934), the *Queen Elizabeth* (1936) and the *QE II* (1965).

The change from coal to oil for firing ships' boilers, first put into effect around 1910, not only benefited the transatlantic liners but also, by allowing greater space for cargo and by simplifying refuelling, it prepared the way for the bulk carriers of later years.

A NAVAL SHIPYARD *at the docks at Southampton, belonging to the firm of Vosper Thorneycroft Ltd.*

A SUBMARINE IN DRY DOCK AT PORTSMOUTH. *Submarine construction in Britain dates from the early years of this century, when Barrow-in-Furness was an important centre.*

A COVERED BUILDING BERTH: *Sunderland Shipbuilders Ltd's Pallion Yard. The ship under construction is a freighter intended for India.*

The post-war scene

After 1945 British shipbuilding came up against increasing competition from other countries, although the demand for oil tankers gave a boost to the industry in the 1950s. The stagnation of seaborne trade in the 1970s led to the closure of some yards on Tyneside and Clydebank but the modernization and reorganization of others. In 1977 the main shipbuilding companies, combined with a number of firms producing engines, were nationalized to form British Shipbuilders.

One of the major technical developments of the post-war period has been the change from rivetting to mechanized welding, which has facilitated prefabrication. Large ships are now built not on sloping slipways but in shallow docks spanned by travelling cranes. An interesting trend of recent years is for smaller ships to be built in covered building berths (such as that at Appledore in Devon).

CONNECTIONS

I.K. Brunel: 174–5 *Engineering*

The Royal Navy: 122–3 *The armed forces;* 124–5 *The First World War;* 126–7 *The Second World War*

Sources of timber: 30–31 *Woodlands and forests*

The plane-makers

The formation of the Royal Aeronautical Society (1866) and the Aero Club (1901) reflected an early fascination with flying which was translated into a positive drive towards a British aircraft industry after the first decade of the 20th century.

The first flying machines

When the Wright brothers made the first ever flight in an engine-powered machine in North Carolina in 1903, British engineers showed an immediate interest in the event. In 1909 the first flight over British territory in a native-made aeroplane was achieved by Alliot Verdon-Roe, a Manchester man whose 'Avroplane' (a triplane) swooped over the Lea Marshes in London. The same year the Short brothers built their famous biplane in Kent.

Although early flying machines were highly accident-prone, there was no want of courageous pilots, and a number of private aircraft companies were founded within a short space of time. Verdon-Roe's company, set up in 1910, was swiftly followed by the Bristol Aircraft Company, which produced no fewer than sixteen biplanes by the end of the year. Among the other leading flyers who had their own companies were Geoffrey de Havilland (undaunted by a spectacular crash in his first machine), Robert Blackburn and Thomas Sopwith. Claude Graham-White set up a renowned flying school at Hendon, in north London. At the Hendon Aerodrome and at Brooklands, an establishment run by Vickers Ltd near Weybridge in Surrey, regular air meetings between French and British flyers provided a stimulating competitive arena for early designers.

The fuselages of early planes were usually timber-framed (spruce or cane), with a fabric covered in 'dope'. The frame was assembled by traditional carpentry techniques and was made rigid by piano wire under tension.

Military and commercial uses

The growth of the industry was immensely stimulated by the onset of the First World War. By 1916 the Royal Aircraft Factory at Farnborough near London (chartered in 1909) had 4,500 workers, but the great majority of military aircraft were built by firms that had had no connection with the industry prior to 1914 (for example, the Siddeley Deasy Motor Car Company). Much of the construction was carried out by sub-contractors, as plane-making was always an assembly industry.

Many designing and manufacturing programmes were cancelled after the war and some manu-

THE SOPWITH CAMEL (***left***), *1916, a famous fighting machine. Some 18,000 Sopwith aeroplanes of various types were built during the First World War.*

THE ROLLS-ROYCE ENGINES

In 1914 the Rolls-Royce Company, which had been formed in 1906 to produce cars, was asked by the government to manufacture French Renault aero engines. Frederick Henry Royce (***right***) declined, and instead designed his own 200 horse-power engine, the Eagle, which was produced in the Derby factory. From these beginnings, the company eventually became one of the world's three leading aero engine manufacturers. A half-sized version of the Eagle, the Falcon, was fitted to an aeroplane made by the Bristol Aircraft Company, and this proved to be one of the most successful machines of the First World War. The celebrated Hawk engine was developed for naval airships. Between 1916 and 1919 6,500 engines were produced at Derby.

It was in long-distance flights in the early 1920s that Rolls-Royce engines gained widespread recognition. In 1927 the Kestrel was selected for use by the RAF. But it was the Merlin that was to become the most famous of all the piston engines, powering the great fighters of the Second World War – the Hurricane and the Spitfire – as well as bombers such as the Lancaster, the Halifax and the Mosquito. The development of the Whittle jet engine was taken over by the firm in 1943, and the

consequent switch from piston to jet engines placed Rolls-Royce in the forefront of aero engine development. The RB211 engine (***right***) was introduced in 1972 and has become one of the most widely used engines in the world, not only for aircraft but also in pumps and power turbines.

A more recent invention is the Olympus Turbojet, developed and manufactured jointly with the French Company SNECMA; the Olympus 593 powers the Anglo-French airliner Concorde.

There are also several engines designed for vertical take-off aircraft. Among these is the Pegasus, notable for its swivelling mechanism, which provides both vertical and horizontal thrust.

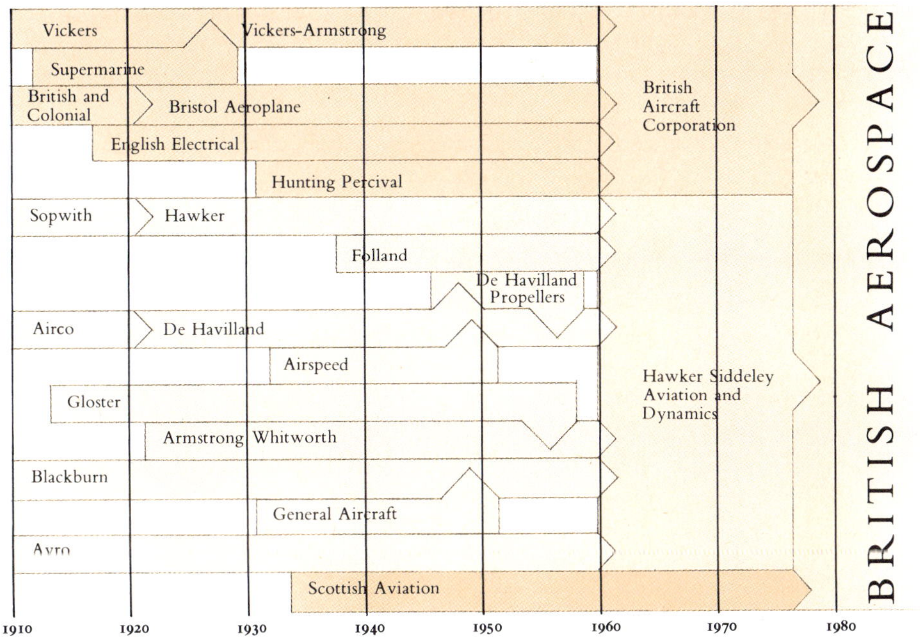

THE ANCESTRY OF BRITISH AEROSPACE. *Numerous companies, many of them pioneers in British aviation history, were combined into the nationalized company of British Aerospace in 1977 (denationalized in 1980). The industry achieved record sales in 1980 – a 50% increase on figures for the previous year.*

THE HAWKER HARRIER JUMP JET, *1968. The Harrier was the West's first fixed-wing 'vertical/short take-off and landing' fighting aircraft.*

facturers failed to survive. However, civil aviation now emerged as a new field for commercial expansion, and the spirit of adventurous flying remained decidedly alive. In 1919 John Alcock and Arthur Whitten Brown made the first non-stop transatlantic flight, in a Vickers Vimy bomber.

The first civil airlines made extensive use of ex-service machines, but before long planes were being purpose-built for passengers. A significant step in the early 1920s was the introduction of all-metal aircraft, but in Britain fabric-covered planes remained in use – and even in production – until 1940 and beyond. Even the large airliners built for Imperial Airways in the early 1930s were backward-looking in technology. On the principle that a flying boat was the safest type of sea-crossing plane, some large ones were built for British Airways by the Short Company.

During the Second World War, under the auspices of the RAF, British designers and manufacturers produced some magnificent aeroplanes, among them the fabric-covered Hawker Hurricane, the all-metal Supermarine Spitfire and the four-engined Avro Lancaster bomber. Helicopters, successfully developed in America, were found to be invaluable for military purposes, and in Britain after the war the Westland Aircraft Company (later well-known for its Hovercraft) built the best American designs under licence for the domestic and Commonwealth markets. With the coming of peace, major technological developments sped forwards. Britain took a lead in developing the gas turbine principle, which dated back to the work of Frank Whittle in the late 1920s.

CONCORDE UNDER CONSTRUCTION. *Developed jointly by the British Aircraft Corporation and France's Aérospatiale, Concorde made its début flight in 1976. It was the world's first supersonic jet airliner, and is instantly recognizable by its 'ogival delta' wings and hinged nose cone.*

The modern industry

The jet age began for airline traffic in 1952 when the de Havilland Comet made the first British commercial jet flight from London to Johannesburg. The British initiative was soon lost to the major American builders, but the 1950s also saw the construction in Britain of the first turbo-propeller airliner (the Vickers Viscount) as well as the de Havilland Heron and the Bristol Freighter.

As the scale of the British aero industry has grown, its structure has demanded radical reorganization. In 1977 the British Aircraft Corporation and Hawker Siddeley Aviation, together with Hawker Siddeley Dynamics and Scottish Aviation, joined together to form British Aerospace. In that year the aerospace industry employed about 200,000 people, with a further workforce of 40,000 engaged in the manufacture of electronic components.

Since the development of the North Sea oil rigs, helicopter manufacture has become a more significant branch of the industry. In the field of light aircraft one of the most exciting of current developments is the fan-driven Edgeley Optica, with its all-round-vision cockpit.

CONNECTIONS
Air services: 270–71 *Aviation*
Rolls-Royce: 182–3 *The motor industry*
The Royal Air Force: 122–3 *The armed forces;* **124–5** *The First World War;* **126–7** *The Second World War*

The motor industry

One of the industries that most typically reflects the increased affluence of 20th-century Western society is the motor trade. Unlike the industries that developed in the 19th century, it relies not on a few sources of bulky raw materials but on an input of small manufactured components, often requiring thousands of parts for the making of one vehicle. Output is based on mass production in assembly lines. It is often described as one of the 'footloose' industries, which means that the location of factories is not determined by proximity to sources of materials. More important are good accessibility by road and availability of labour.

Early motor cars

The technological breakthroughs that stimulated the early motor trade were made not in Britain but in France and Germany: British engineers were preoccupied instead with the exploitation of steam and electricity as methods of propulsion. Both had their serious drawbacks, and it soon became clear that these lines of development were blind alleys: steam cars were slow starters and difficult to operate, while electric cars required frequent battery charges and were suitable only for towns.

Two Germans – Gottlieb Daimler and Carl Benz

THE ROLLS-ROYCE SILVER GHOST, *1907, probably the most famous car in the world. This luxurious, silent-running limousine was within the reach only of a wealthy élite.*

– independently produced the first petrol-driven cars in 1885–6, in a design indebted to the horse-drawn vehicles of the period. A notable British experiment was the three-wheeler made by J.H. Knight in 1895, perhaps the first British petrol-driven vehicle to run on a public road.

In 1896 two significant events in Britain preluded the era of serious motoring. One was the repeal of the Road Acts of 1861 and 1865, which had stipulated that all motor vehicles be preceded by a person carrying a red warning flag; the other was the establishment of the Daimler Motor Company in Coventry, as a result of Frederick Simms' acquisition, in 1893, of the British rights to manufacture Daimler cars.

The early years of the 20th century saw much activity within the industry. Not only were new firms mushrooming all over the country, but considerable advances were being made in speed, comfort and reliability. Pneumatic tyres revolutionized the motor car, as did electric ignition, which encouraged women to take the wheel by making it physically easier to start a car.

Of the many new firms, a few are worthy of special mention: Rover and Standard, both at Coventry (1903); Austin at Longbridge, Birmingham (1905); Rolls-Royce at Manchester (1906); Ford (a branch of the American company), also at Manchester (1911); and Morris at Oxford (1913). By 1913 there were 149 firms scattered throughout Britain, although eleven of these were responsible for about three-quarters of the output. The remarkable proliferation of factories had important consequences for the many small companies whose owners were far-sighted enough to adapt themselves to the needs of the new industry. One such man of vision was Joseph Lucas. In 1860 he was merely a dealer in buckets; in 1867 he added illuminating oil to his trade, and before long was making acetylene lamps; and by 1910 the Lucas firm was providing a complete range of electrical equipment for cars.

A BEDFORD VAN *of 1936. The* BYC *12/15 cwt model, powered by a 2.4 litre 6-cylinder engine. The 4-speed synchromesh gearbox was advertised as being capable of facilitating 'fast getaways in traffic'.*

Towards mass production

The introduction of mass-production techniques, which were already practised in America, owed much to Henry Ford and his Model T. This internationally successful vehicle was easy to drive, solidly and compactly built and capable of carrying five passengers, and in 1914 the car sold for £135. The Manchester Ford factory, at Trafford Park, was an assembly plant only, using imported components. However, the larger Ford factory at Dagenham (Essex), opened in 1931, was equipped with its own blast furnace, foundry, jetty and power station. In its first full year of production it produced 25,571 cars and trucks.

The invasion of the British market by cheap, mass-produced American cars evoked a patriotic response, notably from William Morris and Herbert Austin. Models such as the 1924 Morris Cowley (popularly known as the 'Bullnose') and the 1923 Austin Seven cornered an important part of the market. By emulating transatlantic assembly methods, British factories were now able to produce reliable cars for middle-class families.

By 1929 the number of firms had shrunk to 31, and on the eve of the Second World War 90 per

THE POST-WAR BOOM (***below***)*: final assembly of the Morris Eight series* E *saloon at Cowley, in 1946. This family car had a 918 cc engine. About 120,000 models were made (from 1938 to 1948).*

PROFILE OF A MODERN FACTORY

The Longbridge factory in Birmingham belongs to British Leyland Ltd, the largest motor manufacturer in Britain and one of the biggest earners of foreign currency. The plant covers a total area of 375 acres (152 ha) and employs a workforce of approximately 17,000 (with up to five times as many employed in supporting industries).

Recent investment in the manufacture of the Austin Mini Metro, which has required the building of a new body works (begun in 1977), has made Longbridge one of the most up-to-date, fully integrated, car-making plants in Europe, employing high-level welding technology and extensive computerized control. A special railway siding allows body pressings to be brought directly into the factory.

THE BUILDING OF THE METRO

A The West Works has the capacity to manufacture 6,500 Metro bodies a week. A single Metro is made up of 179 separate steel pressings welded together into 21 sub-assemblies. The largest parts are the body sides and the underframe, which eventually come together to form a recognizable car body. Before the bodies are despatched to the South Works, electronic sensors measure 24 critical dimensions of the structure for quality control.

B The unpainted body store has a computer-controlled storage system which allows for optimum batching to the paint shops.

C In the paint shops the bodies are cleaned, then primed, undersealed and coated with paint by automatic spraying machines. A final injection of wax is applied before the bodies are moved to the painted body store.

D The car assembly building contains three trim tracks, three assembly tracks and a quality audit area. Along the trim tracks the painted bodies are fitted with windows, carpets, door handles, seats, and other accessories. Meanwhile, on the assembly tracks, the suspension, engine, gearbox, brakes and exhaust system are assembled. The trimmed body is then lowered on to the mechanical components, the wheels are fitted, and – for the first time – the Metro stands unaided. It is then subjected to a rigorous series of tests and checks, culminating in a final inspection line in the customer validation building (**E**) before despatch to the public.

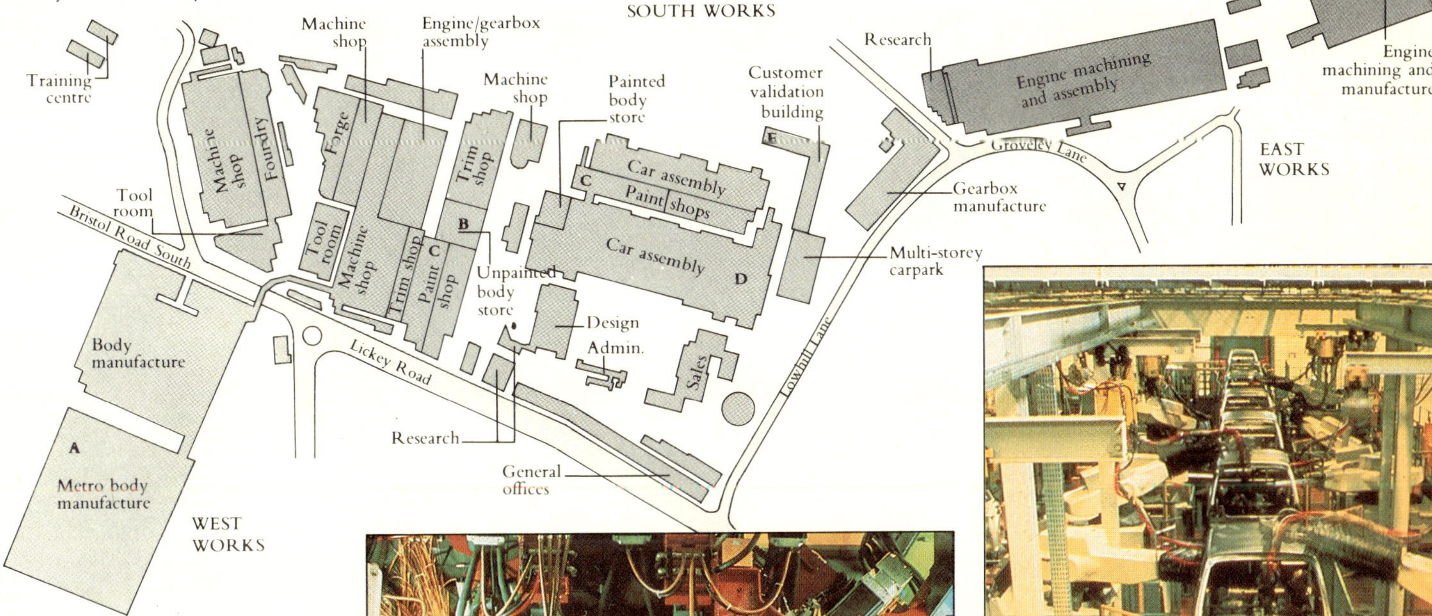

A SCIAKY MULTI-WELDER (***right***) *jigs and spot-welds a Metro roof panel on to the body shell (see A in the key, above right). A multi-welder applies several welds simultaneously.*

ROBOT WELDING (***far right***). *Bodies travel down the robot line for finish welding. Each robot performs several welds in a programmed sequence.*

cent of the total output was divided between only six organizations – Morris, Ford, Austin, Vauxhall, Rootes and Standard.

The modern industry

The post-war years were a period of great expansion, with a major emphasis on exports. Manufacturers strove towards greater comfort and ease of use, installing such refinements as heaters, synchromesh gearboxes and power-assisted brakes and steering. In 1949 Alec Issigoni's wide-tracked Morris Minor appeared, to be followed ten years later by his masterpiece, the Morris Mini Minor, which inaugurated the era of the small four-seater.

Meanwhile, concentration of the industry continued: Austin and Morris combined to form the British Motor Corporation (BMC); Rootes became part of the American Chrysler organization; and Leyland bought out Standard-Triumph and Rover. In 1968 Leyland merged with BMC to create the group that became British Leyland Ltd (BL).

The last decade had witnessed such severe competition from foreign firms that imports now exceed exports. By 1980 the combined annual output of the four leading producers – Ford, BL, Vauxhall and Talbot (formerly Chrysler) – had fallen to 919,000. Although a few small firms still survive (notably, Rolls-Royce), the recent history of the industry has been one of contraction.

CONNECTIONS
Car ownership: 240–41 *Suburbia*
Motor car tyres: 172–3 *Manufacturing*
Roads: 268–9 *The road network*
Rolls-Royce: 180–81 *The plane-makers*

Food in Britain

In 300 BC, Pytheas of Marseilles travelled to Britain and reported it to be a damp, foggy country where the people grew corn. Even at that time, corn-based bread was the staple British foodstuff. In later centuries, its importance in the national diet was reflected by its use as a social symbol: a servant, in Anglo-Saxon times, was known as a *hlaf-oeten* (loaf-eater), while the wife of a chieftain was a *hlaf-dige* (distributor of bread).

The British diet

Bread-making became Britain's earliest commercial food industry. The inhabitants of the expanding towns of the 10th and 11th centuries were not always able to bake their loaves in a communal, municipal oven, and began to buy them ready-baked from specialist tradesmen. The bread was frequently made from a mixture of cereals, expensive wheat often being combined with cheaper, coarser rye, barley, oatmeal bran or bean flour. By the 13th century, the first of many laws had been passed in the attempt to guarantee the quality of commercially made loaves.

Like bread, dairy produce was a staple of the early British diet, and cheese was especially important. It was first known in Britain about 2,000

THE BAKERS OF YORK, *1595. The strict regulations governing the weight of a loaf, and various other conditions of sale to the public, were introduced by the Assize of Bread (1266).*

BRITISH LOAVES

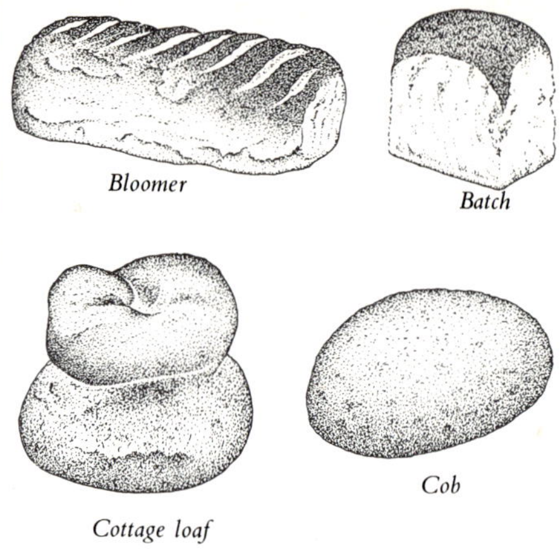

The bloomer, or seedy twist, is popular in London and the south-east, while the soft-sided batch is particularly associated with Scotland. The cob is the easiest shape for home-baking. Cottage loaves are said to date back to Roman times, when their shape facilitated maximum use of the oven.

THE GREAT CHEESES

British cheese-making suffered greatly from the cattle epidemic of 1860, when thousands of cows had to be killed. The result was a massive inflow of American factory-made Cheddar, which stimulated the industrialization of cheese production in Britain. Further damage was done by the Second World War. In modern times, however, there has been a revival of many of the traditional local cheeses that were once in danger of extinction.

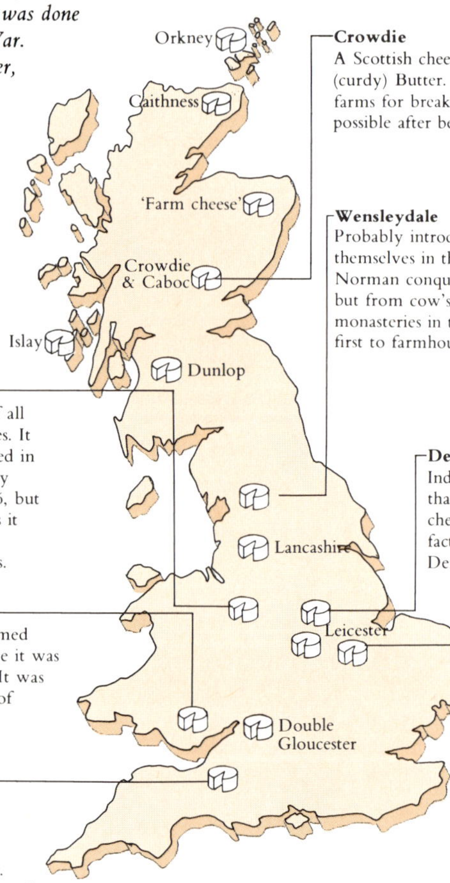

Crowdie
A Scottish cheese, once called Cruddy (curdy) Butter. Traditionally eaten on farms for breakfast (as soon as possible after being made).

Wensleydale
Probably introduced by monks who established themselves in the Yorkshire Dales after the Norman conquest. Originally made from ewe's milk, but from cow's milk after the dissolution of the monasteries in the 16th c. Production moved first to farmhouses, later to small dairies.

Cheshire
The oldest of all British cheeses. It was mentioned in the Domesday Book of 1086, but folklore dates it back to pre-Roman times.

Derby
Industrialized earlier than any other English cheese: the first factory opened in Derby in 1870.

Caerphilly
A quick-ripening cheese, named after the Welsh village where it was made from the early 1800s. It was also made throughout Vale of Glamorgan. Now produced exclusively in England.

Blue Stilton
The 'King of English cheeses'. Esteemed since the early 18th c., when it was sold to travellers on the Great North Road. Daniel Defoe, in 1727, mentioned 'Stilton, a town famous for cheese'. However, its precise origins are obscure. It is now made by about a dozen dairies scattered over Leics., Derbys. and Notts.

Cheddar
The most widely produced cheese in the world. First made near the Somerset village of Cheddar. Today, only about 25 farms in the West Country make it by traditional methods.

A HARVEST FESTIVAL (***below***). *The custom of offering the first fruits of the earth in thanksgiving is as old as harvesting itself, but the church-based harvest festival is a Victorian invention, introduced by the Cornish vicar, Robert Stephen Hawkes.*

A MEAL OF PASTIES *in a Cornish mine, 1897. The meat and vegetable-stuffed pastry was a traditional portable meal for the miners, fishermen and labourers of Cornwall. It was over twice the size of the pasties that are commercially available today.*

years ago. Many regional varieties developed, but they were not widely distributed until the 17th century, and even then they were available only to those with sufficient wealth and enthusiasm to arrange for the slow and costly transport of a favourite variety.

Cheese-making was an excellent method of preserving milk, but for meat and fish to be preserved it was necessary for them to undergo heavy curing (by salting, smoking or pickling). These techniques, in a modified form, have produced some of Britain's most famous and enjoyable foods, including Yorkshire ham, Wiltshire bacon and Arbroath smoked herrings. However, until the 18th century, cured foodstuffs were a monotonously regular item of everyday diet for all but the rich, and were often somewhat unpalatable. Bacon was the meat most people consumed, and bacon and pease pudding (dried split peas that have been soaked and boiled) is one of England's oldest dishes.

Apart from dried beans and peas, vegetables were scarce in British diets until the 17th century, when the art of vegetable growing was developed and market gardens began to spring up around most major towns. At the same time trade with Asia and the Americas introduced many new foodstuffs into Britain. One of these was the potato. It was another two centuries before it was accepted, but eventually it proved to be of enormous importance to the rural poor and contributed to some of Britain's best-known national dishes.

The increase in vegetable growing preceded more radical changes in farming in the 18th century. As more land was put over to wheat the price of wheat flour plummeted, and even the poor could now afford to reject coarser substitutes. Also, the use of new fodder crops (such as turnips) for stall-feeding of livestock during the winter meant that fresh meat could be available all year round, at least to the upper and middle classes.

Supplying food to the growing urban populations of an increasingly industrial Britain presented great obstacles. Large quantities of produce reached its destination in an advanced state of decay, and the adulteration of foodstuffs assumed an unprecedented scale as unscrupulous producers and vendors 'improved' the appearance of poor-quality products.

The industrialization of food

By the mid-19th century, technological and economic developments had begun to change the whole structure of food production and processing in Britain. Trade was more fluid than it had been for centuries, and wheat in particular was being imported in enormous quantities from the newly opened prairies of North America. Fast, reliable railway transport solved the problems of carrying perishables to the towns, and the ready availability of bulk quantities of raw materials made possible the mass production of food to supply the growing urban population. One of the first 'convenience foods' to appear was 'Mr Bird's' instant custard powder, introduced from the United States in the 1840s.

The technology of food production, by this time, was changing rapidly. New methods of grinding and milling wheat made bread manufacture cheaper and the end-product whiter (and less nutritious). Chemical raising agents for flour for the first time enabled cakes to be mass-produced cheaply and quickly. With the introduction of machinery for grinding cocoa beans, chocolate ceased to be a luxury item. Cheap jams appeared, and the first substitute butter (butterine, or oleomargarine) was patented in 1869. The development of meat canning (attempted as early as the late 18th century) enabled meat to be imported from the Americas and Australia, and around 1880 the first successful refrigerated ships were launched. It was now possible to produce dried vegetables (mainly for use at sea), and the same principle could be applied to milk.

In the 20th century, food technology has continued to develop at a phenomenal pace. Increased automation has led to a shift from farmhouse to factory and the disappearance of many small-scale traditional food industries. Some compensation for this loss is to be found in the continual appearance of new products, including those introduced by the 20th-century immigrant communities from Asia and the Caribbean. At the same time, a revival of interest in traditional foods is reflected in the increasing variety of regional products now available on supermarket shelves throughout Britain – from Eccles cakes and Bath buns to Wiltshire sausages and Double Gloucester cheese.

STRAWBERRY CANNING. *Modern canning techniques were foreshadowed by the experiments of the Royal Navy during the Napoleonic Wars. Today, red fruit is packed into lacquered cans, which maintain its true colour.*

CONNECTIONS
Distribution of food: **102–3** *Reaching the consumer;* **264–5** *The railway revolution*
Farming and fishing: **132–41**
Kitchens and dining rooms: **210–11** *Rooms in country houses*

Drink in Britain

GLENDULLAN STILLHOUSE, GRAMPIAN. *After distillation in a stillhouse and the long process of maturation, most whiskies go to the blender, where as many as 40 different single whiskies may be combined to produce the great blends of Scotch.*

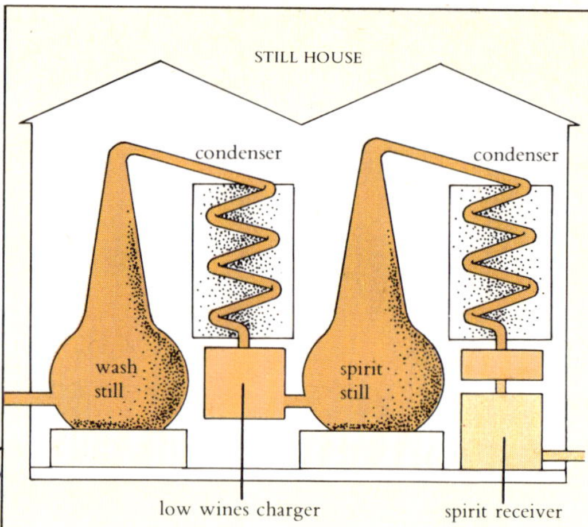

SINGLE MALT WHISKY

Malt whisky (as distinct from grain whisky) is made by distilling a fermented wash of water and malted barley in heated pot stills – huge copper kettles whose shape can affect flavour. The evaporation from the stills is condensed to form 'low wines', which are then re-distilled in spirit stills. Only the middle part of this distillation is acceptable in the whisky-making process. After it has been checked to ensure the right alcohol content, it is then casked in oak barrels. It must remain here at least three years before it can be termed whisky.

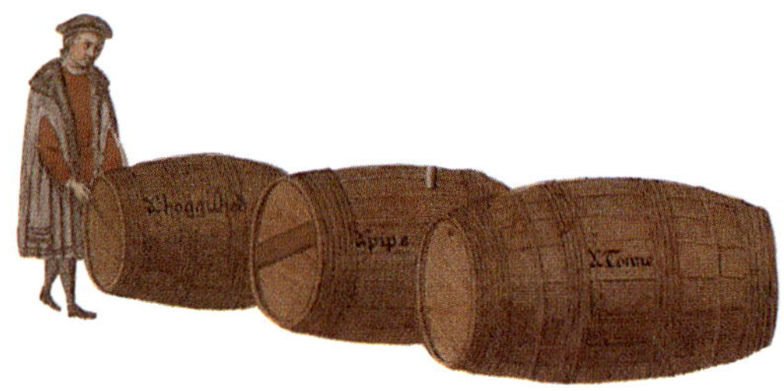

ENGLISH WINE MEASURES *of the 15th century included the hogshead, pipe (two hogsheads) and tonne (two pipes). The size of sailing ships was measured according to their tonne-carrying capacity.*

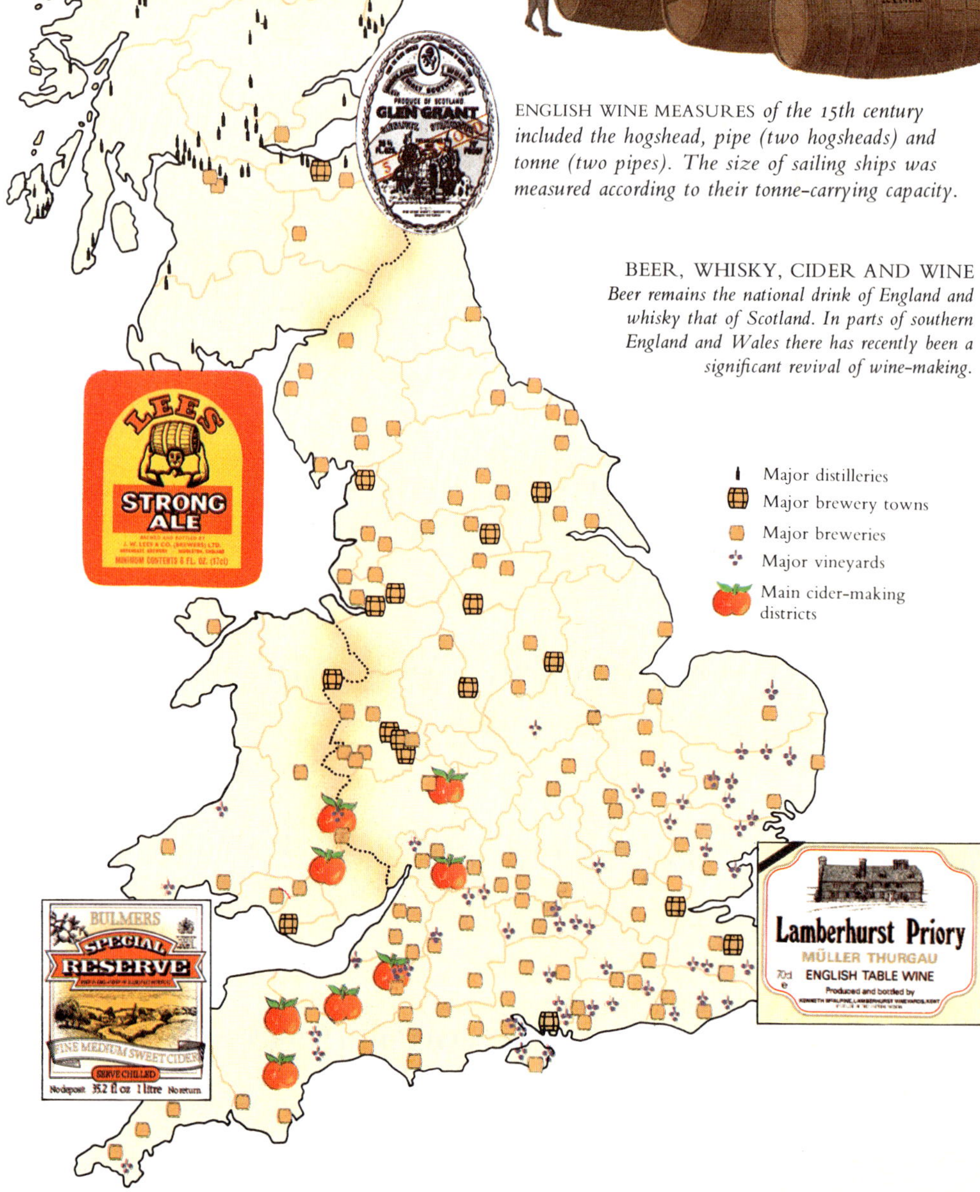

BEER, WHISKY, CIDER AND WINE *Beer remains the national drink of England and whisky that of Scotland. In parts of southern England and Wales there has recently been a significant revival of wine-making.*

Unimpressed by the native ales, the Romans in Britain imported vines so that they could make their own wine. The climate was not conducive to particularly good vintages but efforts at wine-making continued after the Romans' withdrawal, and the monasteries became important centres of viticulture (vine culture) in the Middle Ages. The art died with Henry VIII's attack on monasticism, but in the 12th century the first shiploads of French wine had arrived in Britain, after Henry II's acquisition of Bordeaux in 1152. Although this trade continued, wine was not widely popular, for it was viewed by many people as an undesirable foreign drink.

The list of traditional British drinks includes mead, cider and perry. Made from fermented honey, mead has been drunk since Anglo-Saxon times. The great manor houses of medieval times made vast quantities of it, and it was a favourite drink of Elizabeth I. Metheglin, a kind of mead fermented with yeast and flavoured with herbs, was especially popular with the Welsh.

Cider and perry were introduced into Britain by the Normans. Hedgerows of scrubby crab apple bushes for cider-making were originally planted in Kent and Sussex, but after the 17th century, when the first modern cider apple was produced and cider orchards were established, cultivation moved westwards. Perry, made from the juice of pears, has for long been a traditional speciality of Worcestershire and Herefordshire.

Brewing

In spite of the introduction of cider and perry, ale remained for a long time the staple drink for most of the population. A cheap and simple brew, made from fermented barley with perhaps a few herbs for flavouring, it bore little resemblance to today's ales. The forerunner of the modern 'pub pint' was not known in Britain until the 15th century, when

HARVESTING CIDER APPLES *near Hereford. The word cider comes from the Latin* sicera, *meaning 'strong drink'. Special apples for cider were first grown in the 17th century. The old orchards are today being replaced by heavy-cropping bushes.*

OAST HOUSES, *with their distinctive ventilation cowls, dominate the hopfields of Kent and Sussex. They house the kilns in which hops are dried and pressed before being sent to the brewers.*

THE ENGLISH PUB. *The pub as we know it today is largely a Victorian creation, although ale houses date back to before the Roman occupation.*

Flemish immigrants introduced their type of ale, known as 'biere'. More bitter than British ale, biere obtained its characteristic flavour from the hops that were added before fermentation.

At first hopped ale met with intense suspicion from conservative British brewers. Hops were felt to be highly injurious to health and character, and in 1424 the City of London authorities petitioned the King to outlaw the use of the plant. However, despite such opposition, beer grew steadily more popular, and Flemish settlers in south-east England soon began to grow hops for brewing.

Waters of life

At about the same time, another new drink was coming into vogue. Distilled spirits, or *aqua vitae* (water of life), as they were then collectively called, were made indiscriminately from beer, wine, cider or any other available raw material. They were at first extremely expensive and were used purely medicinally, although such applications ranged from slight indigestion to old age. Gradually spirits became cheaper and more widely available as increasing quantities were imported (particularly of Holland gin) and as whisky and gin distilleries in Britain multiplied. In 1621 there were more than 300 distilleries in Westminster and the City of London alone.

By the 18th century, the cheapness and ready availability of spirits had created a major social problem. Mass-produced 'bath tub' gin offered an inexpensive escape for thousands of urban poor trapped in Britain's slums.

By 1760 the public had turned to weaker and less hazardous beverages – to tea (now cheap enough to be bought by most households) and to new types of cheap, weak, mass-produced beer, encouraged by the government as a preferable alternative to gin.

In the 19th century, manufacturing improvements (particularly in temperature control) went hand in hand with the emergence of larger, more efficient breweries. These were especially concentrated in London (which specialized in porter) and in Burton upon Trent (famous for its pale ales and bitters). With the invention of the hydrometer, it was possible to introduce (in 1880) a beer tax related to alcoholic strength.

In recent years there has been a reaction against commercial keg beers in favour of traditional beers. The dying skills of the local brewer have been revived, and 'real ales' are available in most parts of the country. A similar process is taking place in other branches of the drinks industry: traditional strong, still ciders are now widely on sale; mead is available again; and the aristocrat of all British drinks – best-quality, single malt Scotch whisky – is reaching a wider market.

CONNECTIONS
'Gin Lane': 246–7 *London*
Temperance: 54–5 *Christian minorities;* **236–7** *Factory towns*

THOMAS COOK *(1808–92). Cook, a Baptist lay preacher and a temperance activist, was also a significant figure in the development of tourism. He opened his own firm in 1845.*

A POSTCARD FROM SCOTLAND (***below***), *sent in the late Victorian period (postcards were first introduced in 1870). The enthusiasm of Queen Victoria and the writings of Sir Walter Scott did much to promote the emergence of Scotland as a holiday centre in the 19th century. Today, winter sports have joined the repertoire of leisure pursuits available there.*

It is common to hear tourists spoken of in a derogatory tone. This attitude is undeserved, as tourism is a major contributor to the economic well-being of the country, and one which has shown remarkable resilience during periods of economic uncertainty. It is also an important generator of jobs.

It is now more than fifty years since the British government made its first tentative steps to encourage overseas holiday-makers, with its 'Come to Britain' campaign. Gradually, the tourist industry acquired a formal administrative structure, with the British Tourist Authority at the apex of the pyramid and regional boards at its base.

The response to the industry's blandishments has always justified the cost involved. Throughout the inter-war and early post-war years, overseas visitors came in significant numbers. During the 1950s and 1960s, numbers increased fivefold or sixfold, but the decade of greatest growth was the 1970s: in 1980 there were twelve million visitors, compared with half that number ten years earlier.

A WALKING TOUR (***below***), c. *1900, in north Wales.*

Holidays at home

Overseas tourism on a significant scale is a relatively recent development, but domestic tourism boasts a more ancient lineage, dating back to the later 18th century. Before 1750, journeys were so uncomfortable that it took an exceptionally curious mind not to be deterred. When the going got easier, travel became a fashionable activity for the wealthy, although it seems to have served as much to harden the prejudices as to broaden the mind. One indication of this is the number of condescending accounts of local customs. Another is the reaction to the landscape itself: appreciation of the Sublime and the Picturesque imposed severe constraints upon the areas that were visited, the Lake District and Wye valley being among the favourite regions. Not everyone, however, was convinced that crags must be 'beetling' or chasms 'bottomless', and the satirists had a field day.

The popularity of the Picturesque tour in Britain owed much to the closure of the Continent to Grand Tourists during the Napoleonic blockade.

SOUVENIRS AT WINDSOR CASTLE. *The distant ancestors of such keepsakes are the badges and phials of holy water brought by medieval pilgrims from the shrines they had visited.*

A GROUP OUTING TO BATH (***right***), *1980. In that year, foreign exchange earnings brought by overseas visitors approached £3,800 million.*

When the Continent ceased to be out of bounds, the rich returned to their former haunts, and found others elsewhere. At the same time, tourism became less exclusive. The expansion of the railways in the 1840s brought new leisure possibilities to the middle classes, and later in the century the growth of resorts such as Blackpool and Great Yarmouth was stimulated by the increasing acceptance of the worker's right to an annual holiday. This right was finally enshrined in the Holidays with Pay Act of 1938, and the stage was now set for the 'Butlinism' of the post-war period. When William Butlin proposed a new holiday camp in Pwllheli (opened in 1945), the authorities had difficulty in deciding whether he should be prevented, for fear of causing environmental damage to the Welsh mountains, or praised, for a scheme that would introduce many people to an area of great beauty. This dilemma still underlies tourist policy today.

CONNECTIONS

The impact of the railways: 264–5 *The railway revolution*

Pleasure-towns: 238–9 *Spas and seaside resorts*

The romantization of Scotland: 294–5 *Artists and places;* **296–7** *Writers and places*

A PLEASURE TRIP *at Longleat House, Wilts. Britain's stately homes offer fresh air and family amusements as well as culture.*

A CARAVAN VILLAGE *near Marlow, Bucks. The caravan symbolizes the ambivalences and paradoxes of tourism: adventure without risk, nature without inconvenience. Although caravans can be used for inexpensive touring holidays of coast or countryside, they can also be an expression of the herd instinct.*

Buildings & places

Buildings and settlements are living organisms. They may expand or contract, and may change their uses – a parish church may become a cathedral, a seaport may become an inland town as the sea recedes. The following pages examine historically the vast range of building and community types in Britain. Five towns, of different kinds of importance, are singled out at the end of the section for detailed treatment.

SKARA BRAE, ORKNEY: A NEOLITHIC VILLAGE

This cluster of 10 drystone huts (see plan, ***right***), revealed by excavations in the 1920s, is substantially intact. The settlement was inhabited in the 2nd millenium BC by a small, self-sufficient community which relied on fishing and on the keeping of a few livestock.

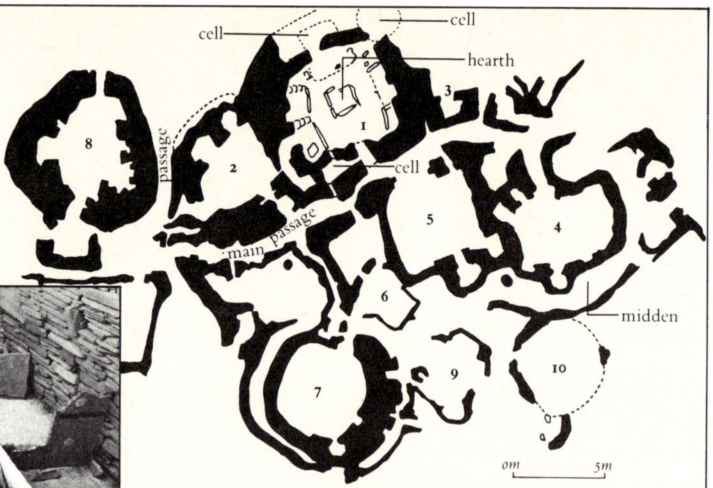

THE REMAINS AT SKARA BRAE *present an extraordinarily complete picture of an ancient lifestyle. Each hut has stone beds, wall cupboards, a two-shelved 'sideboard' and a central stone-rimmed hearth (**left**) where peat was burned. The stone floors have sunken storeholes where liquids or shellfish could be kept. There are underground drains and a communal dumping ground (midden). Tools of stone and bone have been discovered, as well as ropes (of heather), mortars, pestles, decorated pottery and beads. The motifs on the pottery include lozenges, triangles and, in one case, a spiral.*

A FERTILITY GODDESS, *fashioned in chalk. This was found in the Neolithic flint mines at Grime's Graves in Norfolk, where over 350 mine shafts were plotted.*

PENTRE IFAN CROMLECH, DYFED (***below***): *the nucleus of a Bronze Age burial chamber mound. The massive capstone perches on the pointed ends of three megaliths.*

SILBURY HILL, WILTS. *Silbury, the largest prehistoric monument in Europe – 36 m (130 ft) high – is still a mystery. Modern dating methods suggest a date of around 2500 BC. There is no trace of a burial.*

Signs of the activities of Britain's prehistoric peoples are scattered over the landscape, in remains that vary from the debris of primitive cave sites to huge henge monuments and massive hillforts.

Evidence of early man

Communities of the Palaeolithic period (which lasted until *c.* 8300 BC) were small and isolated. The few surviving relics include products of their stone-based technology (such as roughly fashioned hand-axes, spear-points and arrow-heads) and the bones of hunted animals, which have been found in cave shelters (notably Creswell Crags in Derbyshire) and near upland cooking hearths.

In the Mesolithic period (*c.* 8300–4000 BC) a slightly more sophisticated way of life is apparent. A settlement site such as Star Carr (N. Yorkshire) was elaborate by earlier standards: used only during the winter months, it consisted of a timber occupation platform raised above marshy ground.

It was during the Neolithic age (*c.* 4000–1800 BC) that early man began to farm and to make pottery. The first farmers may well have been pastoralists, and when cultivation was introduced it was initially in areas that were only temporarily cleared of woodland: after a few years of cropping, the forest cover was allowed to regenerate.

The greatest impact of the Neolithic people on the present landscape was made not by farming (pollen samples provide the most substantial evidence of this), nor by settlements, but by funerary monuments. From this period come the great long burial mounds (barrows) of southern England and the smaller chambered tombs of western and northern Britain (known as cromlechs in Wales). In terms of effort and function, the barrows, constructed from tons of earth and rubble, are the Neolithic equivalent of the Egyptian pyramids. But the chambered tombs are in one way still more impressive, for they involved the placing of huge

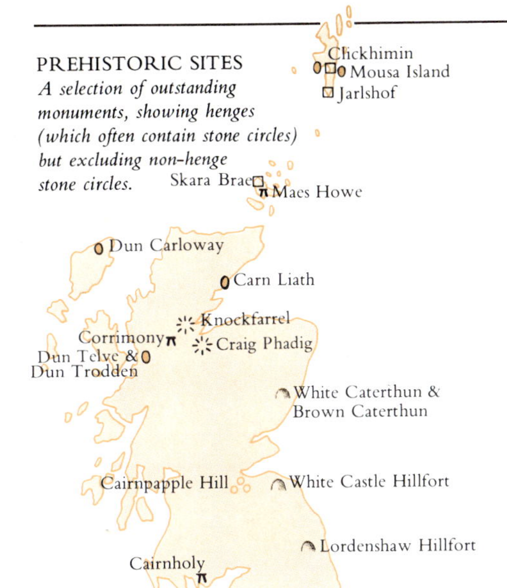

PREHISTORIC SITES *A selection of outstanding monuments, showing henges (which often contain stone circles) but excluding non-henge stone circles.*

GOLD CUP (*left*) *from Rillation, Cornwall: a Bronze Age treasure from a round barrow.*

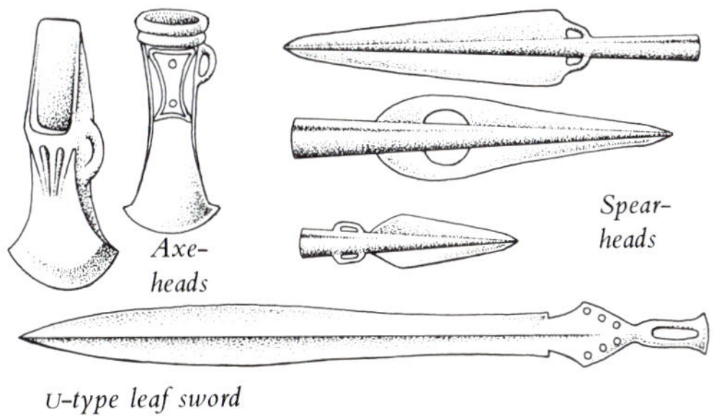

WEAPONRY ITEMS (*below*) *from the Bronze Age, from various sites.*

stones (megaliths) to create portals and chambers, the lifting of a heavy capping stone, and the covering of the entire structure with turf or stone.

The first causewayed camps, such as Maiden Castle in Dorset, are also of the Neolithic period and reflect the strongly tribal organization that developed in comparatively populous areas of Britain such as Wessex. Such camps, characterized by enclosures of ditches and banks (later augmented with further defences and with gates protected by outworks), were built primarily as meeting places, for tribal gatherings and feastings.

A bank-and-ditch enclosure was also the basic structure of a type of ritual monument known as a henge. The most famous examples are Stonehenge and Avebury Henge (both in Wiltshire), but their standing stones were added later and probably reflect a somewhat different religious development. Also known from the Neolithic period are a number of sites where the raw materials for axes were mined, such as Grime's Graves in Norfolk and Great Langdale in Cumbria.

Bronze Age monuments

The greater number of stone circles in Britain belong to the Bronze Age (*c.* 1800–750 BC). The most celebrated of all, Stonehenge, was built in various stages from *c.* 2750 BC to *c.* 1300 BC, using stones from as far away as south-west Wales, as well as massive local monoliths. Like other stone circles, it seems to be laid out according to sophisticated geometrical principles, and in a way that was probably linked to important calendrical events, such as the summer solstice and the start of ploughing. The sky-oriented religion which Stonehenge reflects may have given way by the mid-Bronze Age to worship of water gods.

The Bronze Age was the first of the metal-using cultures, and the first in which permanent arable fields were laid out. Many such fields, which were square or rectangular, have survived in a fossilized state on the chalkland of southern England (for example, at Fyfield Down, Sussex), but it seems that in the north and west the practice of temporary cultivation continued.

Iron Age forts

The Iron Age (*c.* 750–54 BC) saw a further increase in the range and quantity of metal tools and weaponry, and society correspondingly seems to have become more quarrelsome, with inter-tribal feuding. The violence of the times is attested in numerous hillforts, with multiple bank-and-ditch ramparts, timber palisades, and even some use of stone (as at South Cadbury in Somerset). Some of the largest, extending to well over 20 acres (about 8 ha), occur in southern England – notably Hod Hill in Dorset and Danebury in Hampshire.

Scotland had its own type of defensive homestead – a tapered, round, stone tower known as a broch – and a distinctive type of 'vitrified' fort, constructed by combining timber with stones and firing the whole to produce a rock-like structure.

Iron Age villages

In addition to the forts, there are various remains of Iron Age domestic settlements, all on a small scale. In the south these are typified by Little Woodbury in Wiltshire, where there are traces of round, timber-framed huts and food stores set within an encircling stockade. To the north and west, timber gave way to stone, and the survivals (such as Chysauster in Cornwall) are generally more impressive.

AVEBURY HENGE, WILTS. *The bank and ditch, through which the village high street runs, enclose a vast area. The stones, which are unhewn, date from the 2nd millenium BC.*

The lake dwellings (crannogs) that have been recently discovered in the west Highlands of Scotland (for example, along the edges of Lochs Awe and Tay) also date from the later Iron Age. They were strange artificial islands made of timber and stone on which small timber-framed dwellings were built, secure from the possibility of a surprise attack. They have an English counterpart in lake dwellings such as those at Glastonbury and Meare in Somerset.

CONNECTIONS
Ancient field systems: 36–7 *Man and the landscape*
Ancient roads: 268–9 *The road network*
The archaeology of glaciation: 18–19 *The legacy of the ice ages*

Roman Britain

ALBION AND HIBERNIA (**right**) c. AD 150. *The last great classical astronomer and mathematician, Clausius Ptolemy of Alexandria, drew this map on the basis of the latest information available to the Romans about the topography of Britain and Ireland.*

COLONIAL BRITAIN. *This map (**below right**) shows towns, forts and frontiers, as well as the mineral resources that interested the Romans. Throughout their rule they put a great emphasis on urbanization and the creation of good communications. By the mid-2nd century Britain was a civilized province wholly accepting Roman authority. London was the administrative and financial capital of the colony.*

THE REMAINS AT WROXETER (**below**). *The tribal centre of the Cornovii, Wroxeter was the fourth largest town in Britannia. This masonry, once part of an exercise hall for bathers, has survived centuries of pillaging and weathering.*

ROMAN COUNTRY HOUSES. *Villas ranged from luxurious mansions, such as Lullingstone (reconstructed **below**) and Fishbourne (the latter more accurately described as a palace), to small farmhouses. The estates were often worked by slaves. The map (**bottom**) shows the villas which have most to offer the visitor.*

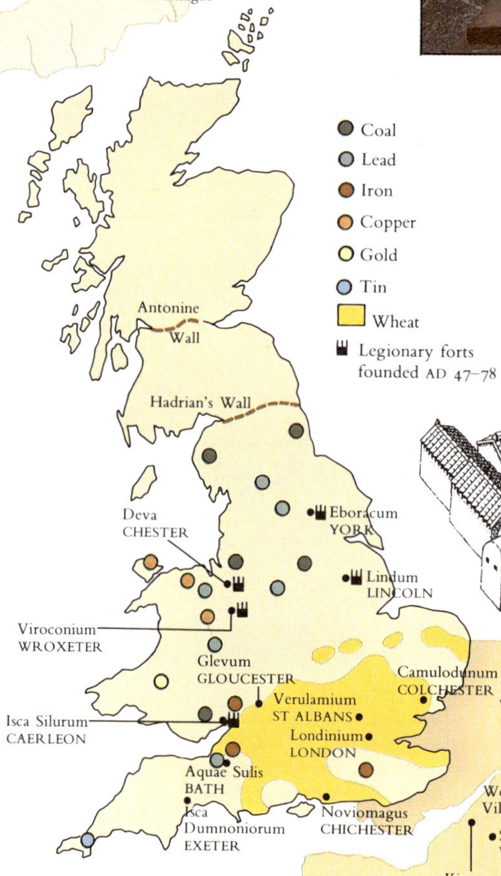

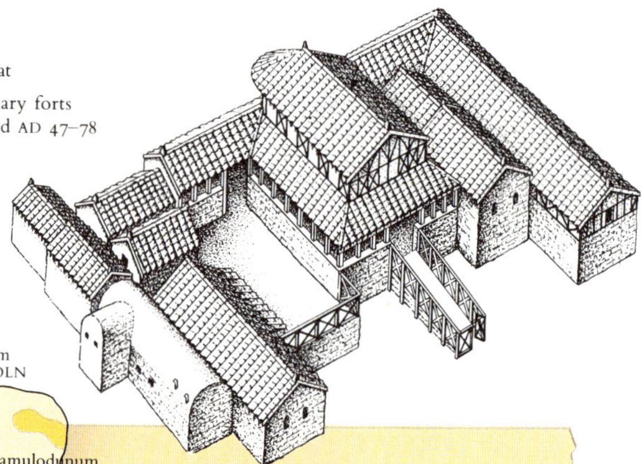

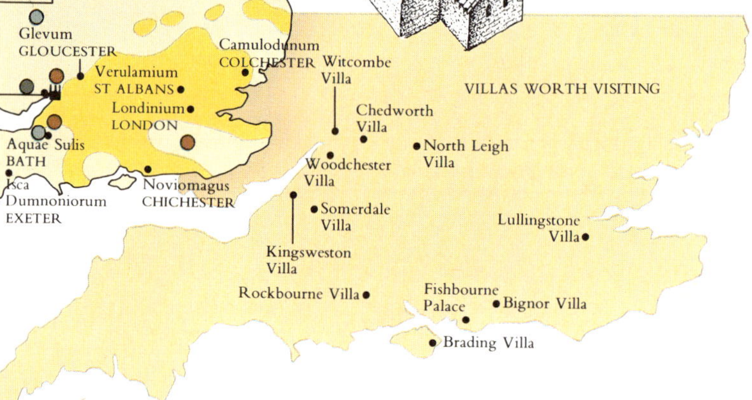

To the Romans Britain was a mysterious Druidic island known to be rich in minerals, and it attracted them in much the same way as the New World drew the Elizabethans. Moreover, it made strategic sense to seek control of a potential source of aid to the unruly Gauls on the Continent. This motive induced Julius Caesar to probe Britain in 55 and 54 BC, but it was nearly a hundred years later, in AD 43, when the Roman conquest began in earnest.

By AD 61 the Romans controlled England as far north as the Humber. Wales was subdued by AD 80 and eventually the legions penetrated the lowlands of Scotland. However, the area that most interested the conquerors was southern England, their activities in the far north being designed merely to secure a stable frontier. Although there was an excursion into central Scotland in the reign of the Emperor Antonius Pius, resulting in the building of the Antonine Wall between the Firths of Clyde and Forth (AD 142), the real northern frontier was Hadrian's Wall. Garrisoned by troops from all over the Roman empire, it was not finally abandoned until AD 383.

THE AMPHITHEATRE, CAERLEON, *near Newport, Gwent. This structure, serving the legionary fortress, was used for military training as well as for entertainment.*

The impact of the Romans

The nature of the Roman presence varied greatly from one part of the country to another. In the far north and in Wales it never lost its military character, expressed in a series of heavily defended garrison bases and smaller forts. Further south, legionary fortresses such as Chester or Colchester were often elaborate and well appointed.

In the south and east of England the consequences of the invasion were more far-reaching, but it would be a mistake to think of Britons straining under the Roman yoke. The upper classes were proud to be citizens of a great empire, but life for ordinary people was not greatly changed. Tribal loyalties remained more important than national ones. In AD 60 the revolt of the Iceni of East Anglia, under their warrior queen Boudicca, was mercilessly crushed, but after this the Romans took care not to tread on tribal toes.

Town and country

The Romans encouraged the growth of the capitals of tribal cantons (*civitates*), and among the towns that fell into this category were Cirencester and Canterbury. Some towns, such as Colchester and Lincoln, started as settlements for retired soldiers (*coloniae*), while others, such as St Albans, earned the status of *municipa* through their trading activities. Sometimes a settlement would develop in response to more specialized conditions: Bath, for example, grew from what was probably a small cult centre into a prosperous spa.

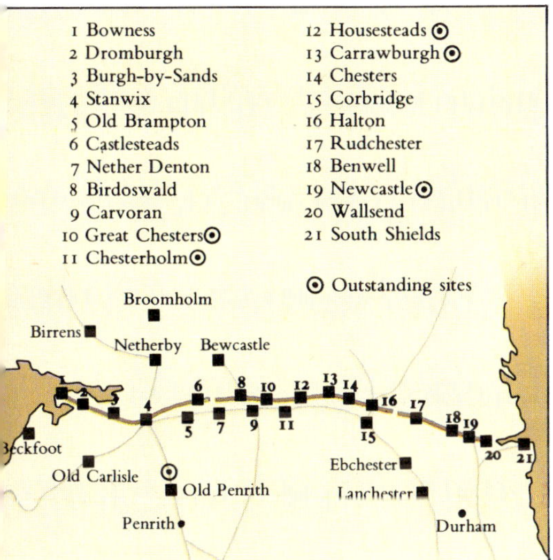

HADRIAN'S WALL *showing the forts and associated towns of Britain's largest Roman site.*

HADRIAN'S WALL. *The central section of this 73-mile fortification (begun in AD 120) passes through rugged landscapes. Along its length were fortlets (milecastles), larger forts and a ditch.*

Roman town planning was highly logical, and was based on a rectilinear grid plan. Each major settlement had its forum, basilica (hall of justice), temples, public baths, shops, private houses (sometimes of brick) and a water supply. The streets were paved, and some had main drains beneath them. Communities were allowed considerable control over their own affairs, and the specially privileged *coloniae* were virtually self-governing.

The settlement of the countryside by Roman or Romanized landowners ebbed and flowed according to political pressures. Some landowners confiscated property from British tribes and families, but others may have bought land. The characteristic architectural feature of areas settled by big landowners was the villa, whose main period of expansion has been identified as the late 3rd and early 4th centuries.

Villas were found largely in the southern half of England, with extensions north into the Vale of York and west into south Wales. There were none in Devon and Cornwall, and they were also conspicuously absent from parts of Wessex (such as Salisbury Plain) and the Fens, which had a dense network of farms.

The classic villa was the headquarters of an estate. The complex of narrow, elongated buildings, arranged on a regular plan around a central courtyard, conformed to a style found elsewhere in the Roman empire. In addition to premises devoted to the function of a large farm, such as craft workshops and grain stores, some villas accommodated more luxurious facilities. Mosaic floors, frescoes, baths and underfloor heating testify to a lifestyle that was far from rude. The walls of the country mansion at Fishbourne in Sussex were decorated with marble from Italy and Greece, and the garden was landscaped with paths, hedges and fountains.

Recently, the idea that villas were abandoned when the Romans withdrew from Britain at the end of the 5th century has been questioned by several historians. Certainly, many of the estates were taken over by the Saxons, even if the villas themselves fell into disuse.

A MOSAIC, *found at Cirencester (Glos.). The wealth that accrued from corn- and wool-producing villa estates is shown by rich mosaics, such as this figure representing autumn. They were commissioned by affluent Romans, or Romano-Britons, who could afford to sustain a Mediterranean lifestyle in the province of Britannia.*

CONNECTIONS
Roman Christianity: 46–7 *The coming of Christianity*
Roman London: 242–3 *London*
Roman mining: 152–5 *The bowels of the earth*
The Romans' withdrawal: 42–3 *The movement of peoples*

Castles

The earliest type of residential castle in Britain, excluding Roman forts and primitive earthworks, was the 'motte and bailey', of which there are several thousand examples. It is a characteristically Norman phenomenon, although some were built before 1066. The motte, so called after the Norman word for turf, was an artificial mound on which a tower encircled by a palisade could be built. There is a splendid motte at York, on which Clifford's Tower was built in the mid-13th century, but the largest in England, on the site of an Iron Age fort, is at Thetford in Norfolk; it now lacks fortifications.

The bailey was an adjacent enclosure, defended by a ditch and stockaded rampart and containing numerous outbuildings (such as stables, kennels and granaries) ranged along the inner sides of the walls. Just as the motte could be dispensed with if a natural slope or crag could serve the same purpose, the bailey, similarly, made the best use of the lie of the land. A convenient river or precipice saved much labour. No two motte and bailey castles are identical in design, and their fascination lies in discovering how the basic pattern has been adapted to match the circumstances. Often, the motte became the core of a much more elaborate castle built round it in later centuries, for example at Caernarfon (Gwynedd), Warwick and Kenilworth (Warwickshire).

Building castles in stone instead of wood began soon after the Conquest. A stone tower (keep or donjon) housed the lord and his family as well as his servants and garrison. It varied in ground plan, but the space inside was always limited, as comfort came a poor second to security. Because artificial mounds were relatively unstable, the keep would usually be built on the natural level. There was often no ground-floor entrance. The lower masonry was impenetrably massive, sometimes with slit-like openings but never windows, and the steep outside staircase made it impossible to use a battering ram against the door. The keeps of Castle Hedingham (Essex), Rochester (Kent) and Castle Rising (Norfolk) are especially mighty-looking. To protect the vulnerable corners of a keep from assault by caterpult or ram, it was realized, in the 12th century, that round corner towers were a useful addition.

ROCHESTER CASTLE, KENT. *The 12th-century keep, built of rough rubble, was undermined by the forces of King John in 1215 after a five-month siege. The square tower that was damaged was later replaced by a round one, and the keep was given a coat of whitewash.*

Before the 12th century was over, it became common practice to replace the palisade surmounting the motte by a curtain wall of stone, to form a 'shell keep'. Excellent ones survive at Restormel in Cornwall and Carisbrooke on the Isle of Wight.

Strongholds of a later age

The 13th century was a period of great experiment and elaboration in castle building, due largely to experience gained in the Crusades by Westerners who studied the impressive fortifications of the Saracens. A vogue came in for keeps that were round in plan instead of square.

A disadvantage of the single tower design was that defenders who abandoned the bailey and retired to the keep surrendered to the enemy their horses and livestock and, very often, their water supply. Moreover, the defending archers were limited in their angle of fire. The latter problem

WARKWORTH CASTLE, NORTHUM. (***below***). *A motte and bailey castle was built here before 1158, then strengthened in the 13th and 14th centuries. The old keep was replaced by a magnificent tower-house sometime before the siege of 1405, when Henvy IV captured the castle from the rebellious Earl of Northumberland.*

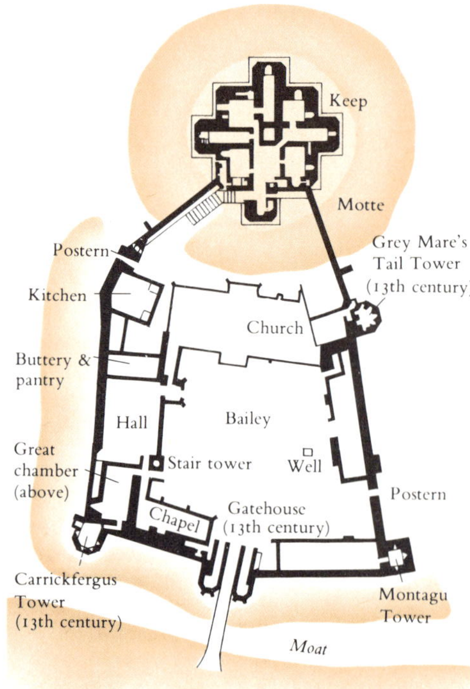

Plan of Warkworth Castle

CASTLES AND GUNFORTS

The strongholds that have most to offer the visitor, by way of either aesthetic or architectural interest, are labelled in capital letters.

- ■ Castle with substantial Norman remains
- ♛ Welsh castle built or improved by Edward I
- ✣ Gunforts of Henry VIII
- ▲ Dramatically sited castles
- ! Notable haunted castles

was solved by the *enceinte* design of castle: a courtyard enclosed by high walls which had a projecting round tower at each angle. The archers could then aim *along* the walls, bringing crossfire to bear on the besiegers. The walls themselves carried, on top, a parapet walk screened by battlements. The embrasures (that is, the gaps between the solid parts, or merlons) were sometimes provided with hinged shutters, which gave extra protection to the archers. More elaborately, wooden galleries known as brattices or hoardings were often suspended from the battlements: they had a trapdoor in the floor through which rocks or quicklime could be dropped on to besiegers. Towards the end of the 13th century, hoardings began to be superseded by projecting masonry parapets held up by corbels with drop-holes (machicolations) in between. Magnificent machicolated towers survive today at Warwick, Raglan (Gwent) and Caerlaverock (Dumfries and Galloway).

As the 13th century progressed, the keep gradually diminished in importance, until it became simply a place of final refuge, as at Pembroke. Its residential function was taken over by an immensely strong keep-gatehouse. The problem now was to fit a drawbridge, porticullis and other defensive devices into a structure that also accommodated the main staterooms. One solution was to relegate the staterooms to the second floor, above the lifting gear.

There are two keep-gatehouses at Beaumaris (Anglesey), which is also remarkable for the symmetry of its plan. Its double line of encircling walls, providing two tiers of defence, qualify it as one of a group of 'concentric' castles, of which the supreme example is the Tower of London as enlarged by Henry III and Edward I. Begun in 1295 and defensible (though not complete) by 1298, Beaumaris absorbed the attentions of about thirty smiths and carpenters, 400 masons and 2,000

DUNNOTTAR CASTLE, GRAMPIAN (***below***). *The typically Scottish 14th-century tower-house which dominates the rock is on the site of an old Pictish stronghold. On the far side is a ruined palace of the 16th and 17th centuries.*

DEFENDING THE ENTRANCE

Castle moats were sometimes crossed by a bridge which stopped short of the gatehouse. The gap was spanned by a drawbridge. Additional defence was provided by a portcullis – a heavy grille which ran up and down slots in the wall of the entrance passage. A gatehouse often had openings in the passage roof through which intruders could be speared.

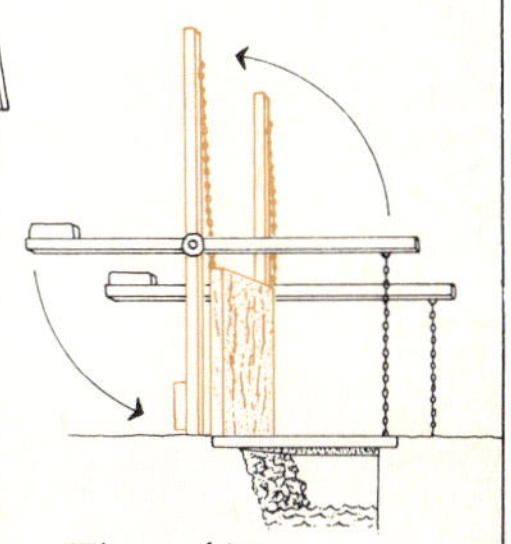

The working of a drawbridge

*A fortified entrance, from inside (**left**)*
1 Windlass
2 Portcullis
3 Gate hall

labourers. It was one of the great castles put up for Edward to consolidate his establishment of English rule in Wales. The borderlands – the Welsh Marches – already had a string of castles such as Ludlow and Chepstow, used by the Anglo-Norman barons to keep Welsh raiders in check. Now were added to these, on or near the coast, the superbly designed castles of Caernarfon, Conway, Harlech and Ruddlan, as well as Beaumaris.

Edward I tried long but in vain to bring Scotland under the same degree of subjection. The region north of the Tees remained disorderly, and a fortified home was a prime requirement of any lord or squire. A northern type of castle known as the 'tower-house' emerged in the 14th century, perfectly exemplified in its starkest, simplest form by Threave (Dumfries and Galloway). Typically, castle entrances in Scotland were protected by 'yetts' – gates of intersecting iron bars.

Castles against cannons

Cannons came into use about 1325, and were common by the end of the 14th century, introducing fresh considerations into castle design. For example, at Bodiam in Sussex the lower part of the gatehouse has keyhole gunports; the nose of the cannon sat in the round hole at the bottom and the gunner peered through the slit above. The first English castle to fall to gunpowder, in 1464, was Bamburgh in Northumberland. For defence against invasion, Henry VIII sited some gunforts along the south-east coast – low and squat with symmetrically arranged bastions like clover leaves.

By this time the mainstream of castle architecture had changed course. Many castles, even before the Wars of the Roses, were built for show instead of defence. Tattershall in Lincolnshire, a machicolated brick tower-house planned along French lines, has large windows that would have been extremely vulnerable in an attack. The last phase of *practical* military architecture in England is rep-

CAERNARFON CASTLE

Caernarfon, whose lofty curtain walls and polygonal towers rise above the Menai Strait, is the most splendid of Edward I's Welsh castles. Intended as the royal headquarters in the conquered principality, it was begun in 1283, after the King's victory over Llywelyn.

The defences were so skilfully designed that they could be held by a garrison of merely a hundred men. Galleries below the parapet were provided with numerous arrow slits, some of which were arranged in threes, converging on one point, so that they could be used by three archers firing in rapid succession. The immensely strong Eagle Tower, triple-turreted, retains the character of a Norman keep.

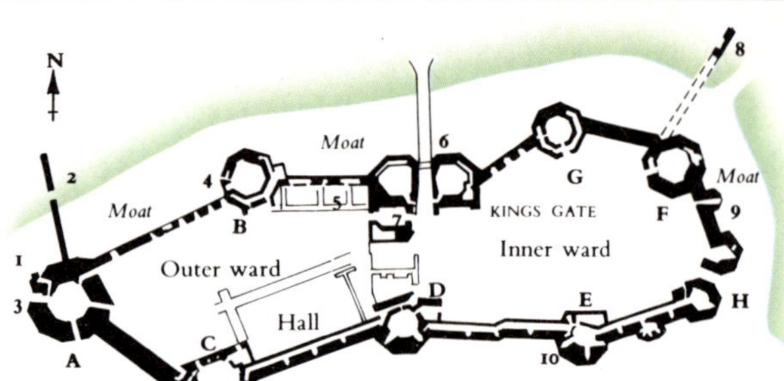

1 Water gate (unfinished)
2 Town wall
3 Postern
4 Postern
5 Kitchen wing
6 Intended drawbridge
7 Prison tower
8 Town wall
9 Watch tower
10 Cistern tower
A Eagle Tower
B Well Tower
C Queen's Tower
D Chamberlain Tower
E Black Tower
F North-east Tower
G Granary Tower
H Queen's Gate

SIEGE WARFARE

Before the advent of gunpowder, war machines such as catapults and mangonels were used. Afterwards, picks and shovels would be deployed under a movable shelter (penthouse). The most effective means of attack was 'mining': a tunnel dug under part of the stronghold was supported by timber props, which were set alight so that the tunnel collapsed and the masonry above cracked.

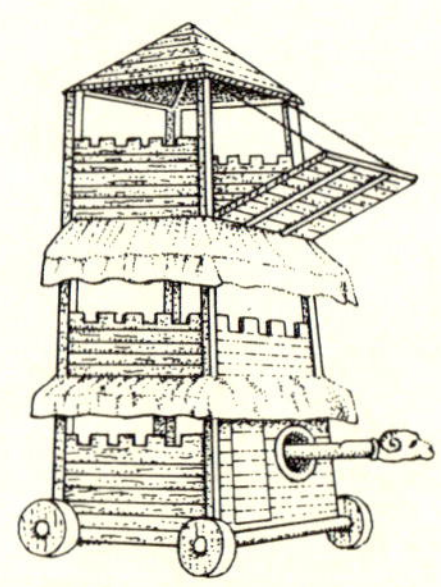

Siege tower with bridge and battering ram

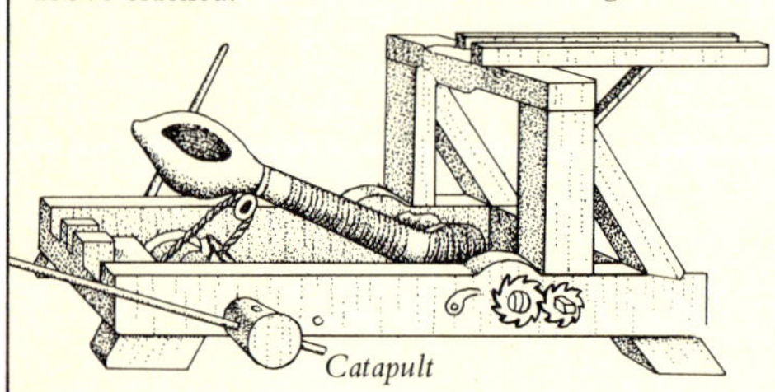

THE SIEGE OF RAGLAN. *The existing ruins of Raglan Castle, Gwent, date largely from the 15th century. The five-storey 'Yellow Tower of Gwent', on the left of the photograph, has its own moat and elaborate drawbridge arrangements. It is thought to embody the core of a Norman motte in its basement, and the rest of the castle may be on the site of the original bailey. This self-contained fortress of last resort was mutilated in 1646 by Cromwell's men after the castle (which was the centre of Royalist organization in the West Country) had survived the longest siege of the war—a fierce onslaught of cannon.*

THE RETAINERS' HALL AT DOUNE. *This castle, one of the finest in Scotland, was begun in the 1380s. The entrance was defended by a tower which served as both gatehouse and keep and contained the lord's hall, and by the adjacent retainers' hall.*

resented by work at Kirby Muxloe (Leicestershire), at Raglan (Gwent) and, as late as 1511, at Thornbury (Avon).

When the Civil War broke out, the old castles could hardly have been expected to withstand 17th-century artillery, but many of them, such as Corfe, Kenilworth, Scarborough and Raglan, survived remarkably well. The worst damage, in some cases, was done after Cromwell had triumphed; many castles, including Corfe, were now demolished, or 'slighted', to render them useless should the Royalist cause be revived.

After the last siege in Britain had been forgotten, castles retained a romantic hold on the imagination. In the late 18th and 19th centuries the ideal still erupted into reality, in the shape of new castles like Robert Adam's Culzean (Strathclyde), and of re-creations such as Arundel (Sussex).

CONNECTIONS
Civil War sieges: 72–3 *The Civil War*
Edinburgh Castle: 256–7 *Edinburgh*
Fortified homes: 208–9 *The great country houses*
Palaces: 214–15 *Royal retreats*
Prehistoric forts: 192–3 *Marks on the landscape*

BODIAM CASTLE, SUSSEX. *A text-book 14th-century castle, built under royal licence by Sir Edward Dalynrigge against the threat of a French invasion. The gatehouse is equipped, at the lowest level, with keyhole-shaped gunports.*

HENRY VIII'S GUNFORT AT WALMER. *Such coastal defences continued on a smaller scale the concentric principle of design that had been initiated at Caerphilly in the 13th century. Early in the 18th century Walmer was adapted to become the residence of the Warden of the Cinque Ports.*

CORFE CASTLE, DORSET. *This was the favourite residence of King John, who added to the original stone keep, built c.1100. By 1285 all that survives today had been built. Corfe lasted through a six-week Parliamentarian siege in 1643, but was later captured by a strategem and partly dismantled.*

The springtime of church architecture

ANGLO-SAXON CHURCH EXTERIOR. *All Saints, Brixworth (Northants), was built mainly in the 7th century. Roman bricks were reused in the masonry. The spire and battlements are much later.*

NORMAN NAVE (***below***). *Durham Cathedral was begun in 1093. The chequered 'diaper' and chevron motifs are splendidly uninhibited.*

THE STRUCTURE OF A CATHEDRAL. *Section through nave, with view of a single bay*

Wall passages at the triforium and clerestory levels were a constant feature of the great medieval churches

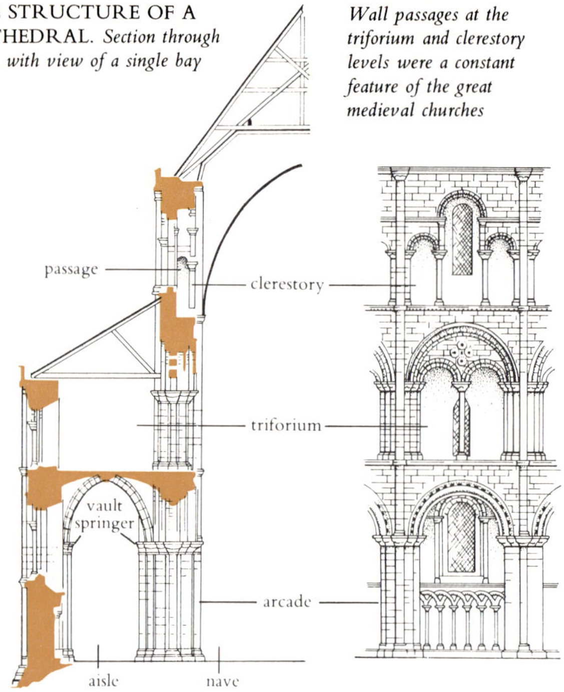

MEDIEVAL VAULTING

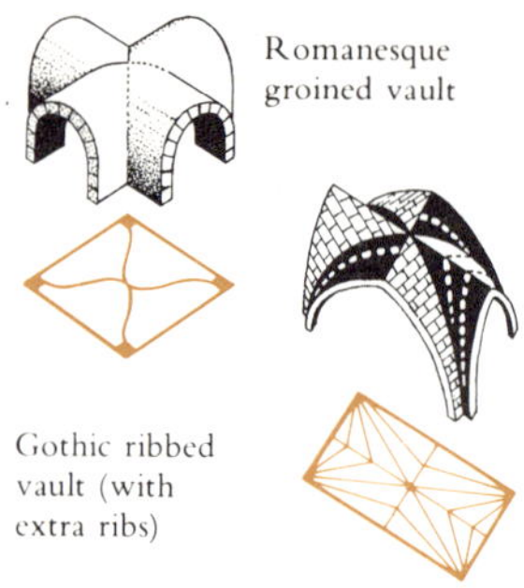

The groined vault, built of intersecting tunnel (or barrel) vaults, was properly suitable only for covering a square space. By contrast, the pointed arches of the Gothic rib vault, which made for greater flexibility, allowed rectangular bays to be spanned. Sometimes the crisscrossing pattern was complicated with extra ribs (liernes or tiercerons).

THE EVOLUTION OF MEDIEVAL WINDOW DESIGN

Plate tracery appeared in Early English buildings. Bar tracery, from the Decorated period on, allowed greater fantasies of ornament

At the time of the Norman Conquest in 1066, England had been Christian for a little more than four hundred years, and the land was dotted with Anglo-Saxon churches, most of which were of wood. Very few even of the stone ones are complete today, but those that are, together with numerous fragments, show a naive approach to design. The dimensions of a Saxon church were small, and the chancel – that is, the eastern limb where the altar stood – was a tiny annexe to the nave. Sometimes, a crude pattern of long, thin stones was let into the exterior of the rubble wall. This can be seen on the Saxon tower at Earl's Barton in Northamptonshire, which also exemplifies the favourite technique of 'long and short' work on the corners – upright squared stones alternating with flat slabs.

The arrival of the Romanesque style

The Normans revolutionized ecclesiastical architecture. Rebuilding of all the major churches was undertaken within a generation in an imported style – Romanesque – characterized by round arches, huge piers or cylindrical columns and thick walls. One feature that was to be of major importance in subsequent architectural developments was the division of the interior wall of a large church into an arcade (flanking the aisle), a row of windows (clerestory) above the level of the aisle roof (sometimes with a passage in the thickness of the wall), and between these tiers a small decorative arcade with a more spacious passageway behind – the triforium or gallery.

The second generation of Norman architecture abandoned the plainness of the first. Exterior walls were embellished with a screen of round arches, sometimes interlaced and ornamented. The semicircular space over a doorway – the tympanum – was treated with special elaboration. Inside, piers

PERPENDICULAR TOWER. *Parapets, pinnacles, traceried windows and echoing stone panels adorn the tower of St Andrew, Mells (Somerset).*

DECORATED WEST FRONT (**left**). *Exeter Cathedral's façade, with tiers of sculpture and a huge traceried window, is a curious composition in three distinct layers.*

and arcades were articulated with ornamented mouldings. Durham Cathedral, in particular, is a masterpiece of Norman pattern, with its bold yet not too riotous display of chevron, trellis and dogtooth designs.

The aspirations of Gothic

Durham Cathedral was the first European building with crisscrossing ribs supporting the vaults, and one of the earliest to have pointed transverse arches in the nave. These elements look forward to the Gothic style, of which the pointed arch is the basic premise. Its early appearance at Durham may be related to a group of monastic houses, belonging to the French-based Cistercian Order, which were founded in the north of England in the 12th century, notably the abbeys of Fountains and Rievaulx in Yorkshire.

Pointed arches had a structural advantage in that they allowed a ribbed vault to be put up over a rectangular space of any dimensions. Once this method had come into general use, following achievements in the cathedrals of Canterbury and Wells in the late 12th century, the pattern of ribbing was gradually elaborated. The Early English style of Gothic, which developed from about 1180 to 1250, was characterized by simplicity and airiness of design, triumphantly exemplified at Salisbury Cathedral. Another feature of this early phase was the use of contrasting stones, such as dark Purbeck against light limestone, a fashion introduced at Canterbury.

The Decorated style which followed carried architectural ornament through to the window openings, previously relatively plain, now richly articulated with tracery. A great sinuosity of line is evident in tracery designs (and in sculpture) in this period, from about 1250 to 1340. Striking examples of decorative invention appear in the parish church of St Botolph's, Boston (Lincolnshire), and in the cathedrals of Bristol, Ely, Exeter and Wells. Lincoln Cathedral's Angel Choir, completed around 1280, illustrates the beginning of the predilection for complexly patterned vaults.

Late medieval flourishes

The final development of medieval English Gothic, the Perpendicular style, flowered from about 1330 to 1540. The style penetrated Wales, whose churches had been influenced by England since Norman times, but not Scotland, which developed its own rather archaic 'late Gothic' style. Perpendicular is characterized by the use of rectangular tracery panels with inscribed arches. Interiors could be aesthetically unified by panelling which was applied both to windows and to wall surfaces. The choir of Gloucester Cathedral is the first surviving example of this innovation. With the invention of fan-vaulting, in the cloister at Gloucester, the standard Perpendicular panels of decoration were carried through to the vaults, which took the form of a double series of inverted half-cones with concave sides.

The integrated decoration of the mature Perpendicular style could produce a delicately bejewelled box-like effect, though sometimes on a grandiose scale, for instance at King's College Chapel, Cambridge, and St George's Chapel, Windsor. A last flourish of decorative and structural virtuosity crowns a few late medieval buildings. In Henry VII's Chapel, Westminster Abbey, for example, fan vaults departing from the walls meet a central group of 'pendent bosses'—ornamental knobs suspended from inverted cones.

If one views English medieval church architecture as a development towards a system of unified overall decoration, this had been fully accomplished by the early 16th century.

PERPENDICULAR VAULT. *The fan vault of Henry VII's Chapel, Westminster Abbey, London, is the most elaborate decorative roof in Britain.*

CONNECTIONS
Abbey churches: 206–7 *Monasteries*
The Gothic style: 202–3 *The great cathedrals;* **204–5** *Parish churches*
King's College Chapel, Cambridge: 254–5 *Oxford and Cambridge*
Medieval art: 280–81 *The artist's eye*

The great cathedrals

A characteristic feature of Britain's medieval cathedrals is their comparative seclusion, set aside from town centres in spacious precincts, and the sometimes vast extent of their dependent buildings. In fact, several cathedrals combined their functions with those of a major monastic church, a practice which was partly the legacy of the early Christian Celtic Church, whose abbots played a role comparable to that of a bishop. In England the bishops of the Dark Ages were harboured in monastic communities, and most of these were situated in rural areas. It was only in the 11th century (in the 12th century in Scotland) that a thorough reorganization of the dioceses took place and several cathedrals were refounded in towns.

Spiritual fortresses and precincts
Bishops, through their religious authority and as major landowners, were important members of the king's court and powerful political figures. Their palaces or, in some cases, their episcopal castles, built near the cathedral church, reflected their temporal importance. Theoretically the right of their election lay with the monks or canons who served the cathedral, but the king always sought to promote his own candidate. In some cases open conflict resulted, as at Durham in 1197 when the monks fought the bishop's soldiers in the great church itself.

Monastic foundations required a great number of buildings – a cloister and a chapter house where community business could be discussed, besides the living accommodation, refectory, wash house and so forth. Secular foundations, which were served by canons, were organized and planned rather like the monastic communities, with chapter houses and cloisters. The canons took monastic vows but did not seclude themselves and often lived in individual houses situated around the cathedral close. The whole complex of monastic buildings is well preserved at Durham, and those of a secular foundation at Wells.

Interior arrangements
The internal arrangement of most medieval cathedrals reflects the influence of monastic practice. Having vowed not to mix with the outside world, the monks were separated from the congregation by two screens: the stone pulpitum, shutting off the choir from the nave, and the wooden rood screen, usually one bay to the west. The rood screen carried the rood, a large crucifix, the only surviving example (dating from the 15th century) being at St Albans. Secular cathedrals usually had a pulpitum only. The only Scottish example is at St Mungo's, Glasgow, but a number of fine English examples survive, as at Canterbury and Exeter. In the choir, monks and canons were provided with wooden choir stalls: many survive with their misericords (brackets beneath hinged seats) showing a sometimes riotous variety of carved scenes.

Chapels and chantries
The number of monks who were ordained priests increased considerably during the Middle Ages, and therefore so did the number of altars in the monastic cathedrals. There was also a growing tendency for individuals to endow masses, and for wealthy men to endow chantry chapels where masses could be said for their souls during their life and after death. Chantry chapels were often freestanding structures, built in cathedrals and in a few parish churches. The finest chapels of all, however, were the Lady Chapels, inspired by the cult of the Virgin Mary, which originated in England in the 12th century. The cult had its own liturgy requiring a special place of celebration. The chapel might achieve the proportion of a small church attached to the east end of the cathedral, as at Ely.

STAINED GLASS WINDOW. *Canterbury Cathedral boasts one of the finest displays of medieval glass in the country (c. late 12th and 13th C.).*

SALISBURY CATHEDRAL FROM THE SOUTH-WEST. *Salisbury is unusually integrated in style, mainly early English but with a Decorated spire. Most medieval cathedrals are architectural patchworks, built and rebuilt in sections in different periods.*

Post-Reformation cathedrals
At the time of the dissolution of the monasteries, in the 16th century, there were seventeen cathedrals in England. Henry VIII refounded five former monastic churches as cathedrals: Bristol, Chester, Gloucester, Oxford and Peterborough. With these new foundations and the relatively slow growth of population, no new cathedrals were needed for some three centuries. The only new construction was St Paul's in London, which replaced the Gothic cathedral destroyed in the Great Fire of 1666. Its plan, based on Italian models, was unique in England, and reflected the Protestant determination to give the congregation a greater involvement in services.

In the 19th century many diocesan boundaries were redrawn and new dioceses created. Some

LINCOLN CATHEDRAL'S NAVE. *Though parts of the Norman church survived an earthquake in 1185, much was rebuilt, including the nave (c. 1220–50). A pulpitum or screen of stone seals off the choir.*

THE CATHEDRALS OF BRITAIN
The styles, or building periods, of the major parts of each cathedral are denoted. Ruined buildings are shown only where the remains are substantial, and former cathedrals now acting as parish churches are not included. No distinction is made between the Presbyterian and Episcopalian cathedrals in Scotland.

CHRIST THE KING, LIVERPOOL. *Completed in 1967, this Roman Catholic cathedral with its central altar embodies the concept of full lay involvement.*

COVENTRY CATHEDRAL. *The Gothic ruin was once a parish church, elevated to cathedral status but destroyed in the Second World War and replaced by the famous modern cathedral, which boasts fine sculpture, tapestry and stained glass.*

large medieval parish churches were made cathedrals. After the emancipation of the Catholics in 1829 several new Catholic cathedrals were built, notably the Byzantine-style brick masterpiece at Westminster.

England is blessed by the number of her ancient cathedrals that have withstood the ravages of time, the supreme creations of the Middle Ages. Even the ruins of some, such as St Andrews and Elgin in Scotland, still reflect former glory. The miracle is that despite the decline of the faith, the tradition of glorifying the great houses of God survives still.

CONNECTIONS
Abbey churches: 206–7 *Monasteries*
The Gothic style: 200–201 *The springtime of church architecture*
Medieval art: 280–81 *The artist's eye*
St Paul's Cathedral: 212–13 *The Italian influence in architecture;* **244–5** *London*

Parish churches

Although not achieving the grandiloquence of cathedrals, parish churches not only provide a richer view of changing religious practices over the centuries, but also, in many cases, offer aesthetic delights that are all the more welcome for being comparatively untrumpeted. The great churches, such as Beverley Minster, or St Martin-in-the-Fields, London, have a steady stream of visitors. But elsewhere, a beautiful tower, stained-glass window, brass memorial or stone tomb, rood screen or timber ceiling can often be savoured with extra intensity because it is off the main tourist circuit. The achievement is seldom of the first order, in a European perspective. Yet parish churches, paradoxically, are Britain's most individual contribution to the story of Romanesque and Gothic architecture.

The Middle Ages

Churches were built from the earliest period of the Roman and Celtic missions, but the oldest surviving are late 7th century – notably Brixworth (Northamptonshire) and Bradwell-on-Sea (Essex). The finance and organization of these early buildings is obscure, but it is likely that many were established and owned by local landowners. In medieval times the practice of advowson, whereby a landowner had the right to bestow the 'living' of a church on a priest of his own choice, who became rector, was widespread. The rector paid for part of the upkeep of the church out of the 'tithes', the offerings of a tenth part of the produce of the parish lands. Advowsons could also be held by a monastery or a university college.

The close connection between the church and local magnate is witnessed in the fact that many churches are veritable mausolea of the local squirearchy. St Mary's, Warwick, for example, is famous for its vigorous 15th-century monument to Richard Beauchamp, Earl of Warwick.

During the later Middle Ages, with the rise of a wealthy mercantile class, new churches were often funded by merchants (individually or in syndicates) or religious guilds. The major contribution was in commercial centres such as London, York, Bristol and Norwich, and in the wool-producing areas of the Cotswolds and East Anglia. Today the splendid 'wool churches' (for example, Chipping Camden in Gloucestershire or Long Melford in Suffolk) sometimes seem disproportionate to their modest settings.

Greater wealth inspired sumptuous invention. It was apparent in the pinnacled Perpendicular towers of Somerset churches and in the decorative exterior stonework of 15th-century East Anglian examples. This was also the period of the great hammerbeam timber roofs.

A VISITORS' GUIDE

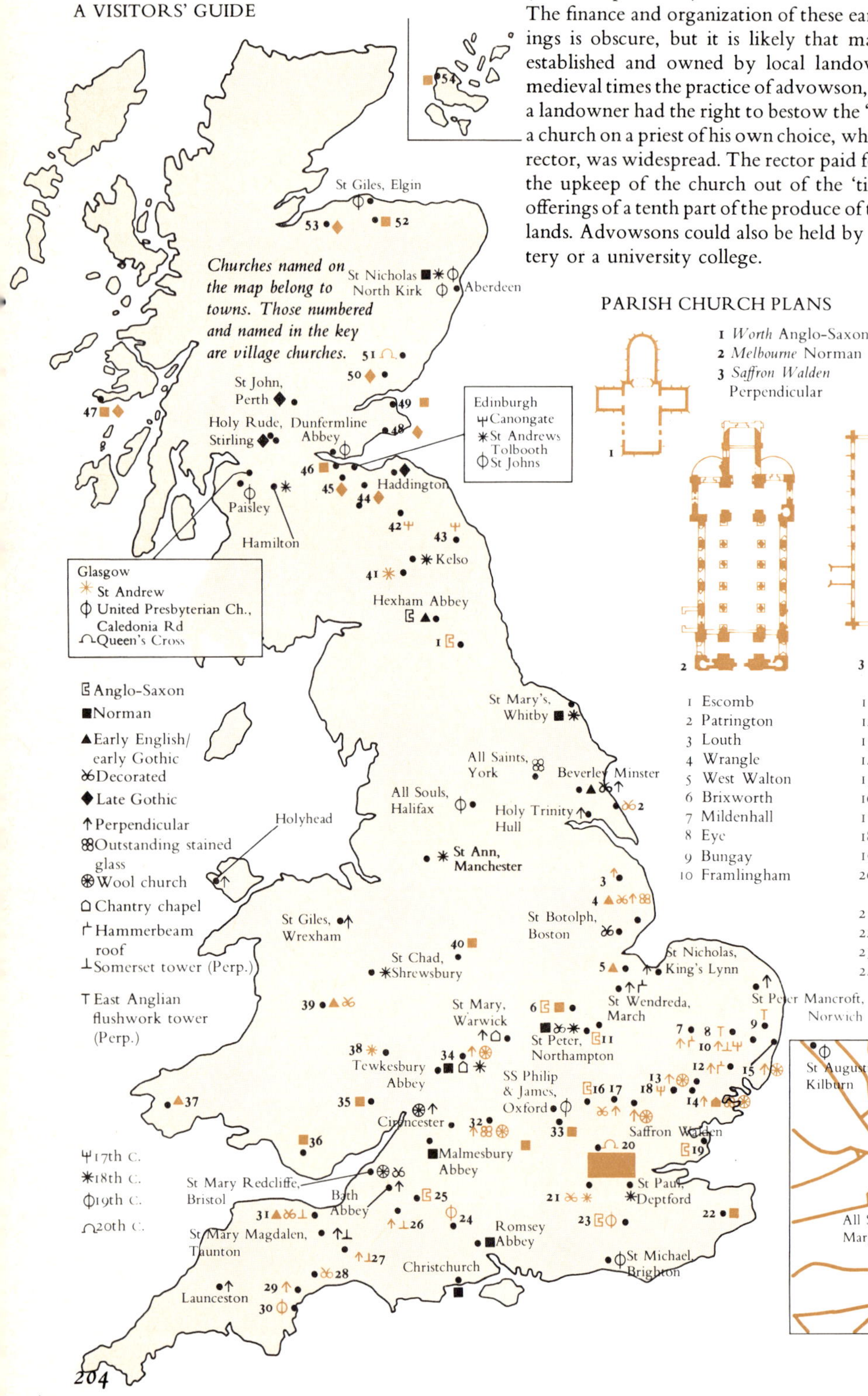

PARISH CHURCH PLANS

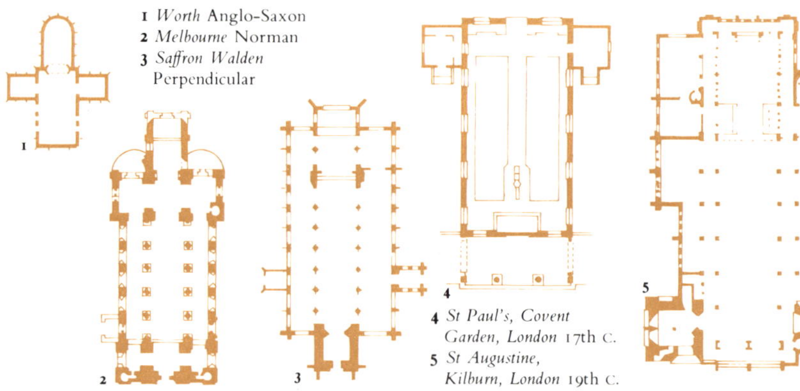

1 *Worth* Anglo-Saxon
2 *Melbourne* Norman
3 *Saffron Walden* Perpendicular
4 *St Paul's, Covent Garden, London* 17th c.
5 *St Augustine, Kilburn, London* 19th c.

1 Escomb	11 Earls Barton	25 Bradford-on-Avon	40 Melbourne
2 Patrington	12 Needham Market	26 Mells	41 Roxburgh
3 Louth	13 Lavenham	27 Ilminster	42 Lauder
4 Wrangle	14 Long Melford	28 Ottery St Mary	43 Lyne
5 West Walton	15 Blythburgh	29 Ashton	44 Roslin
6 Brixworth	16 Wing	30 Babbacombe	45 Corstorphine
7 Mildenhall	17 Ashwell	31 Kingston St Mary	46 Dalmeny
8 Eye	18 Kedington	32 Fairford	47 Iona
9 Bungay	19 Bradwell-on-Sea	33 Iffley	48 St Monance
10 Framlingham	20 St Jude, Hampstead Garden Suburb	34 Chipping Campden	49 Leuchars
	21 St Peter, Petersham	35 Kilpeck	50 Fowlis Easter
	22 Barfreston	36 Ewenni Priory	51 Kirriemuir
	23 Worth	37 Haverfordwest	52 Birnie
	24 St Mary's, Wilton	38 Shobdon	53 Barevan
		39 Llanidloes	54 Orphir

LONDON. *Wren churches are mapped on pp 244–5.*

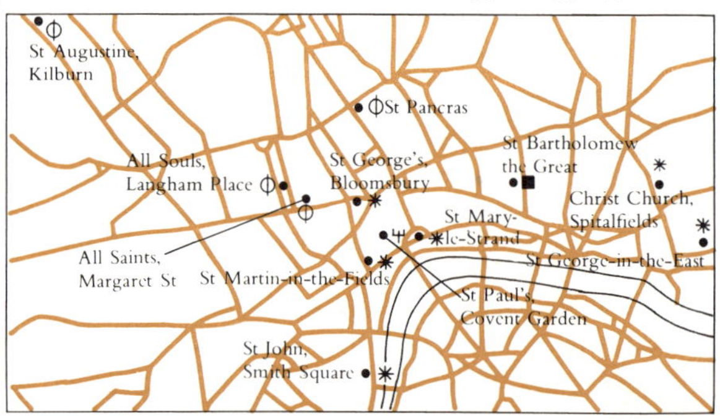

LAVENHAM, SUFFOLK. *A testament to the wealth of the wool trade, Lavenham has East Anglian 'flushwork' – dressed flint with stone panels.*

ST STEPHEN WALBROOK, LONDON (***above right***). *Wren's parish church (1670) anticipated St Paul's in its dome and open plan. The pulpit is a glorious three-decker. The church was carefully restored after its partial destruction in 1941.*

SHOBDON, HEREFORDSHIRE. *Shobdon's tiny Norman church was converted, elegantly, for an 18th-century squire. His private pew was unusually comfortably furnished.*

The reformed Church

With the Reformation, the sovereign became the head of the Church, a fact sometimes boldly proclaimed to worshippers in a large royal coat-of-arms. To make the service more accessible, the rood screen, which had separated the chancel from the nave in medieval churches, was removed. Often the altar was placed in the nave, and took the form of a simple table around which the congregation sat. Meanwhile, all the more colourful paraphernalia of the medieval faith were swept away as idolatrous. Among the victims of the purge were countless items of stained glass, woodwork, painting and statuary. The extreme changes at the height of the Puritan influence in the mid-17th century were later somewhat reversed, but the stress on preaching was maintained.

Architecturally, the new tendencies are illustrated in St Paul's, Covent Garden (1631–8), in London – 'the handsomest barn in England'. Italian Renaissance and baroque idioms were afterwards exploited in London with great individuality and ingenuity by Sir Christopher Wren and, later, James Gibbs and Nicholas Hawksmoor. One of the finest provincial churches of the late Georgian period is the circular St Chad's, Shrewsbury (1790–92).

The 19th-century revival

In the early 19th century the rapid spread of Nonconformist sects led to the building of chapels all over the country, in a stark architectural manner that reflected the severity of the new beliefs. At the same time, the burgeoning of the urban population created a demand for new parish churches. Inspired by the Tractarian (Oxford) Movement and the Camden Society, theologians identified 13th-century Christianity as the most perfect form of worship, and, by analogy, Early English architecture was greatly admired. A great number of neo-Gothic churches were built, with the traditional arrangement of nave, screened-off chancel and sanctuary. Many medieval churches were vulgarly restored. As the century progressed, influences became acceptable from a wider range of older styles, including Italian Romanesque.

One of the few remarkable parish churches of the 20th century is St Jude in Hampstead Garden Suburb, London: a masterpiece by Sir Edwin Lutyens, part medieval in style but modified by an almost classical restraint of detail.

BABBACOMBE, DEVON. *The multi-coloured bricks, screens, tiles and sculpture in William Butterfield's Victorian confection recall the love of colour and ornament that distinguished many medieval churches.*

CONNECTIONS
The Gothic style: 200–201 *The springtime of church architecture*
Jones, Wren, Gibbs and Hawksmoor: 212–13 *The Italian influence in architecture*
Post-Reformation styles: 282–7 *The artist's eye*
The Reformation: 48–9 *Church and State*

Monasteries

The monastic Orders made a vital contribution to the social, cultural, economic and even physical landscapes of medieval Britain. By the 14th century the number of houses in England and Wales alone had risen above 2,000. However, this assessment embraces hospitals, cathedral monasteries and other establishments in towns, as well as the more secluded rural foundations. Although some of the Orders were wholly dedicated to an ideal of godly isolation from all aspects of secular life, others felt that an important part of their religious duty involved the assumption of a charitable role within the lay community.

The Orders

Britain first experienced monasticism in one of its most austere forms. In the 6th century, Celtic monasticism was brought over from Ireland. Settlements were established in remote western parts, such as Iona off the coast of Scotland, and Tintagel in Cornwall. Monasteries in the Celtic tradition consisted simply of groups of cramped individual cells clustered round a modest church – usually the only communal building.

A more formal kind of monastic life was the Benedictine rule, brought to south-east England by St Augustine in AD 597. This version gradually became pre-eminent. The Benedictines' orderly routine of prayer and work, their rigorous self-discipline (the day often starting at 2 or 3 a.m.) and their vows of poverty, chastity and obedience, came to be seen as the archetype of the devotional life. Gradually, however, more and more emphasis was placed on liturgy at the expense of manual labour. This trend reached a climax in the elaborate ceremonies of the Benedictine-based Cluniac Order, whose headquarters were at Cluny in France.

The number of foundations soared after the Norman conquest. It was the beginning of an age of great monastic wealth, based on land ownership. Benefactors would sometimes enlarge a monastic estate by a gift of land, not necessarily near the abbey itself (which could even be in Normandy): in such cases, a small dependent priory (or cell) would be established, whose monks supervised the running of the abbey's property. Some priories eventually became independent.

THE TITHE BARN, GREAT COXWELL, OXON. *Villages within monastic lands paid tithes – a portion of their produce – to their landlords, in this case Beaulieu Abbey.*

1 Abbey church
2 Cloister
3 Gatehouse
4 Bakery and brewhouses
5 Mills and kiln
6 Guest houses
7 Barns
8 Stables
9 Cellar
10 Frater
11 Dorter
12 Garden

TYNEMOUTH PRIORY, TYNE AND WEAR: *the plan. Most of the buildings of this Benedictine priory are reduced to low walls, although parts of the church remain.*

THE CELLARIUM, FOUNTAINS ABBEY, N. YORKS., *was used to store wool, which by the end of the 13th century had made this the richest monastery in England, with revenues from 15,000 sheep.*

During the 12th century, there was an active reform movement, dominated by the Cistercians who advocated a strict interpretation of the Benedictine rule, with a renewed accent on physical labour. The first Cistercian house in England was founded in Surrey, in 1128, but the main Cistercian centres were in remote sites in Wales and northern England, the best known abbeys being Fountains and Rievaulx in Yorkshire and Tintern in Gwent. Other reforming Orders included the Gilbertines, the Premonstratensians and the Carthusians, the latter following a discipline of hermetic austerity.

Monastic buildings

After the Norman conquest the disposition of monastic buildings had developed a basic plan, followed with minor variations by most monastic Orders. The abbey church was bordered by the quadrangular cloister, a place for seclusion and contemplation. Adjacent to one side of the cloister

MOUNT ST BERNARD ABBEY, LEICS. *A Trappist Cistercian community has flourished here since 1835. The domestic buildings were, in the main, designed by the Victorian architect A.W.N. Pugin.*

(usually the east) was the dorter (or dormitory), and behind it the reredorter (or lavatory block). On the side opposite the church was the frater (or refectory), while to the west was the monastic cellar, which often had an extra accommodation block above it. The farmery (or infirmary) was most often located well outside the main court. By the gate house there might be guest houses and an almonry, from which alms were distributed to the poor. Whole complexes of this kind survive in a good state of preservation in some of the cathedral monasteries; while elsewhere there are some splendid isolated survivals – for example, the cellar at Fountains, the great gatehouse at Bury St Edmunds and the Abbot's Kitchen at Glastonbury.

Dissolution and revival

After the dissolution, although many abbeys fell into ruin, great numbers of them were converted into secular residences. This was the fate, for example, of Lacock Abbey in Wiltshire, and at Buckland near Plymouth the church itself was remodelled as a house by Sir Richard Grenville.

The emancipation of the Catholics, beginning with the Catholic Relief Act of 1791, made possible a revival of the monastic Orders of medieval times – notably the Benedictines and the Cistercians. In pace with the momentum of the Anglo-Catholic movement the first Anglican communities ('sisterhoods' and 'brotherhoods') were also established, overcoming centuries of prejudice by their outstanding performance in charity work.

The monastic revival has continued into the 20th century. Many Catholic and Anglo-Catholic monasteries run excellent schools and hospitals. At the same time, secluded communities in remote areas have continued the tradition of the contemplative life.

MONKS AT WORSHIP: *Benedictines in their church at St Michael's, Farnborough.*

MONKS AT WORK, *St Michael's, Farnborough (Hants.). Bookbinding and calligraphy are time-honoured monastic pursuits.*

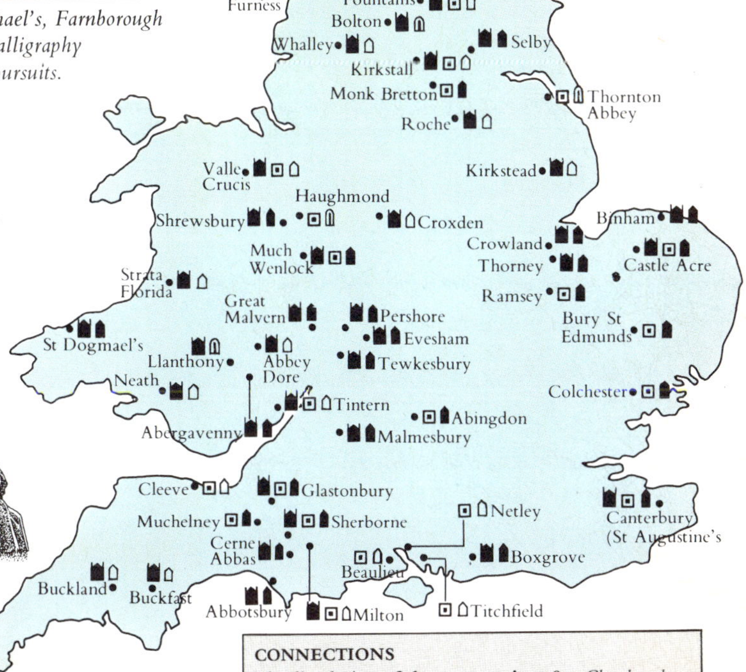

THE GREAT MONASTERIES OF ENGLAND AND WALES

The monasteries represented here are mostly ruins, but many of these are substantial. Some surviving abbey churches, such as that at Tewkesbury, are in use as parish churches. (Monasteries attached to cathedrals are not shown.)

BENEDICTINE MONKS: *sculpture from a 14th-century tomb in Winchester Cathedral (Hants.)*

CONNECTIONS
The dissolution of the monasteries: 48–9 *Church and State*
Early monasticism: 46–7 *The coming of Christianity*
Monastic art: 280–81 *The artist's eye*

The great country houses

STOKESAY CASTLE, SALOP (*left*): *a 13th-century moated manor house, with a show of castle-like crenellation added for its merchant owner.*

Britain's historic country houses are for many visitors a summary of all that is meant by the term 'heritage'. Yet this word fossilizes them, implying that they are merely jewel-boxes and denying the fluidity of their evolution – the various ways in which landowners have used them to express power and prestige and to enjoy their leisure.

Manorial homes

In the later Middle Ages the main residential building type for the wealthy was no longer the great castle stronghold. Although warfare was far from being reduced to a distant memory, spacious manor houses had appeared that were designed for convenience and display rather than for safety. The battlements and towers of a house such as Compton Wynyates in Warwickshire (15th century) were principally ornamental, though they were also symbols of a chivalric ideal.

The prodigy houses

By the Elizabethan and Jacobean periods, many families, such as the Cecils, the Knollys and the Leicesters, had acquired new wealth by service to the Crown or to powerful individuals, or by success in commerce. The emblems of their achievement were the so-called 'prodigy houses', of which the first was Longleat in Wiltshire, designed in 1568 for a steward to the Duke of Somerset. Still more impressive, certainly in proportions, were the mansions built by two Lord Treasurers: William Cecil, who became Lord Burghley, doubled the size of Burghley House in Cambridgeshire (begun 1552) from the proceeds of his office, while Lord Suffolk's home at Audley End in Essex (1603–16) was declared by James I to be 'too big for a king'. The size of such houses reflected not only the pretensions of their owners, but also their expectations of a royal visit. The provision of what amounted to an extra house in the form of state apartments could be ruinously expensive. Audley End, by the 18th century, had become a great white elephant, and parts of it were demolished.

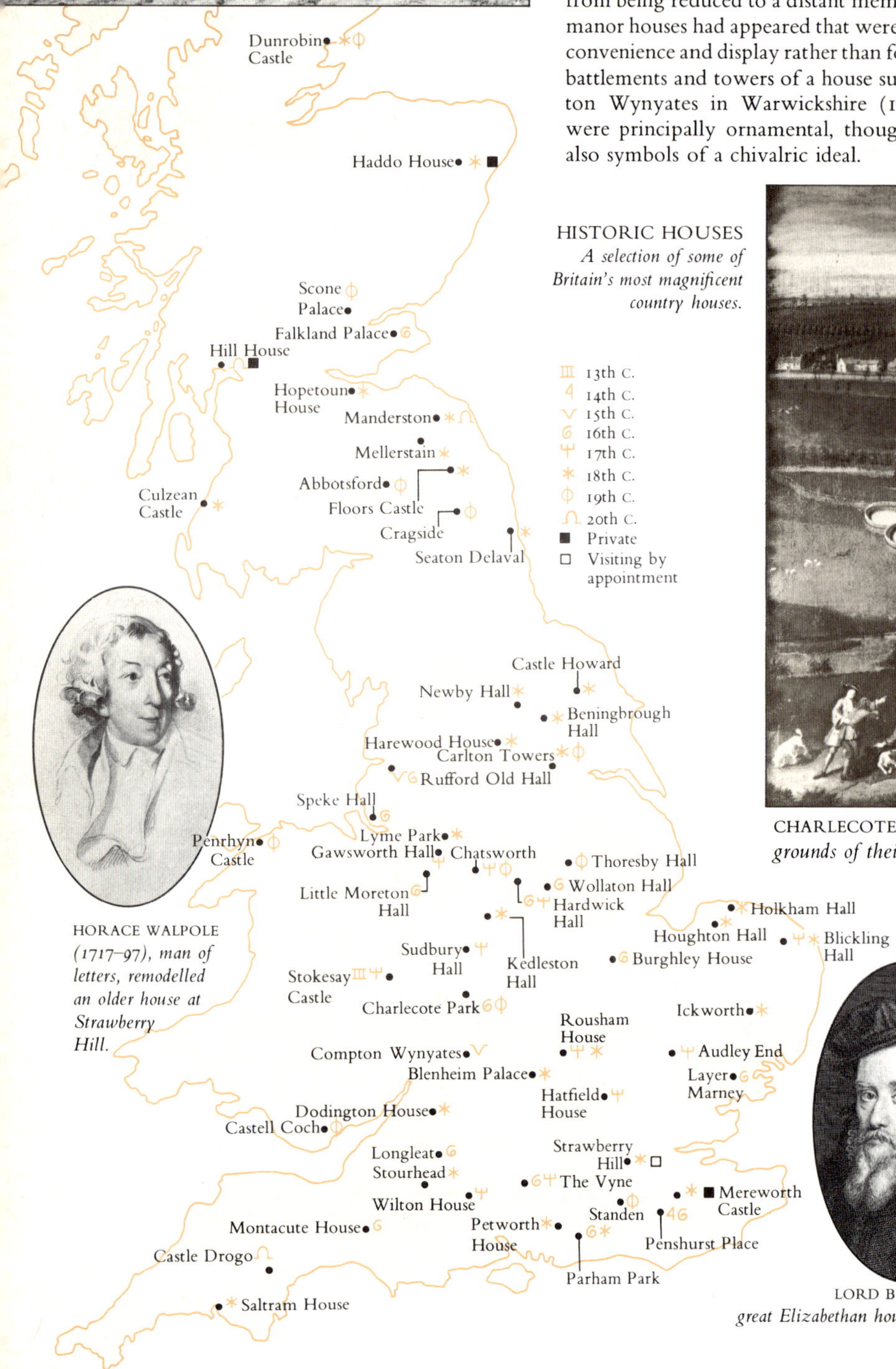

HISTORIC HOUSES
A selection of some of Britain's most magnificent country houses.

HORACE WALPOLE *(1717–97), man of letters, remodelled an older house at Strawberry Hill.*

CHARLECOTE PARK, WARKS.: *a view of c.1690, showing the Lucy family in the grounds of their Elizabethan mansion (now altered).*

LORD BURGHLEY, *great Elizabethan house builder.*

Monumental grandeur

During and after the Civil War there was, for a time, a decline in the building of grand country houses. Before long a restrained and dignified building style was evolved, reaching perfection at the beginning of the 18th century in the Queen Anne house. In contrast to this architectural modesty (influenced by the Dutch style) are the great baroque houses, particularly the twin masterpieces of Vanbrugh – Blenheim Palace in Oxfordshire, with its spread-eagled kitchen and stable blocks, and the aggressive-looking Castle Howard in North Yorkshire, built for the third Earl of Carlisle. Blenheim seemed monstrously impractical to its critics – 'Tis very grand and very fine, But where d'ye eat and where d'ye dine?' – but houses such as this were built for a clientele who at

WOLLATON HALL, NOTTS. *Imposingly turreted and covered with carved ornament, Wollaton is one of the greatest Elizabethan 'prodigy houses', built for Sir Francis Willoughby between 1580 and 1588.*

CULZEAN CASTLE, STRATHCLYDE, *1777–92, by Robert Adam, combines a neoclassical interior with a typically Scottish fortress-style exterior.*

times seemed to place a greater premium on grandeur than on comfort.

The architecture of an 18th-century country house tended to be a close reflection of the personal taste of its owner. Aristocrats such as Lord Burlington and new men such as the banker Henry Hoare (owner of Stourhead in Wiltshire) shared a connoisseurish attitude towards the arts, and expected every aspect of their homes to afford aesthetic pleasure. Sometimes, their personal preferences shouted loudly from every corner of a room, as in Horace Walpole's neo-Gothic fantasy at Strawberry Hill, near Twickenham, Greater London. Unlike the old lords of the manor, many such owners played little part in local life (although some became agricultural improvers), and duty or pleasure often kept them away from the country for long stretches at a time. The Prime Minister Sir Robert Walpole, for example, only managed to spend one month per year at his palatial Norfolk home, Houghton Hall.

CASTLE HOWARD, N. YORKS.: *detail of the central block. The house was Sir John Vanbrugh's first work as an architect (1699). Horace Walpole described it as 'a palace, a town, a fortified city'.*

The new castles

Victorian country houses turned to the grand scale and to extrovert splendour. The neo-Gothic extravaganza of Scarisbrick Hall, near Ormskirk in Lancashire, the neo-Elizabethan Thoresby Hall in Nottinghamshire, and the neo-Romanesque Penrhyn Castle in north Wales all have resoundingly baronial connotations, reflecting a profoundly romantic nostalgia. An increasing proportion of manufacturers and bankers now bought or built country houses, which symbolized their new wealth and expressed their social aspirations. If they could master the complexities of an elaborate code of etiquette, the *nouveaux riches* usually had little difficulty in getting themselves accepted by the older families, especially if the latter had benefited from the industrial revolution by the mineral wealth of their estates.

In the late Victorian houses of Norman Shaw (such as Cragside in Northumberland) there were signs of a return to a homelier traditionalism, which was picturesque rather than overwhelmingly ostentatious. This theme was to become more significant in the Edwardian era. C.F.A. Voysey's houses blended comfortable rusticity with a forward-looking plainness, while the early

HARLAXTON MANOR, LINCS., *by Anthony Salvin. Every detail of this neo-Gothic house of the 1830s was designed to convey baronial splendour.*

creations of Sir Edwin Lutyens were brilliant distillations of the vernacular tradition, warm and reassuring. It was Lutyens who built the last of the grand country houses, in 1910–30 – Castle Drogo in Devon, a granite stronghold commissioned by the founder of the Home and Colonial Stores, Julian Drewe, who made his fortune early and retired at the age of thirty-three.

CONNECTIONS
Architectural styles: 282–7 *The artist's eye;* **212–13** *The Italian influence in architecture*
Blenheim Palace: 92–3 *Landownership*
Interiors: 210–11 *Rooms in country houses;* **290–93** *Great art collections*
Settings: 216–19 *Gardens*

Rooms in country houses

THE CHAPEL, CHATSWORTH HOUSE, DERBYS. *Every great country house had a chapel, but none surpassed this 17th-century baroque masterpiece at Chatsworth. Family prayers were particularly important to the Victorians.*

THE GREAT HALL, HATFIELD HOUSE, HERTS. (***left***), *is the Jacobean successor to the medieval Great Hall. The lord's table was raised on a dais beneath the minstrel's gallery at the opposite end of the hall from the kitchen.*

Perhaps more than any other building type, country houses have been highly susceptible to the patchwork effect of successive refurbishings, additions and demolitions, as owners have met the claims of comfort or fashion or have adapted their homes to suit changes in lifestyle. The outcome for the visitor can be a bewildering heterogeneity, but in many houses there are individual rooms which perfectly recapture the essence of a period.

The decline of the hall

Complete preserved interiors of the Middle Ages are extremely rare, but several late medieval manors preserve a distinctive arrangement – small private rooms and service rooms arranged on either side of a great hall. The hall was the focal point of household life, where the whole community ate and where retainers and servants slept. One of the finest surviving examples is that of Penshurst Place in Kent, where the original central hearth is preserved.

By the end of the 16th century, although the arrangement of the hall was not radically different, there were now one or more sumptuous rooms on the first floor. Of these, the grandest was the solar, or great chamber, where the lord slept, received guests and sometimes had meals. At Hardwick Hall, Derbyshire, there was also a second-floor state room, which survives with its original Elizabethan decoration.

By the late 17th century, as life had become increasingly concentrated on the first floor, the significance of the hall had dwindled, its function usurped by dining rooms and saloons. However, in the great 18th-century houses it came into its own

COUNTRY HOUSE PLANS

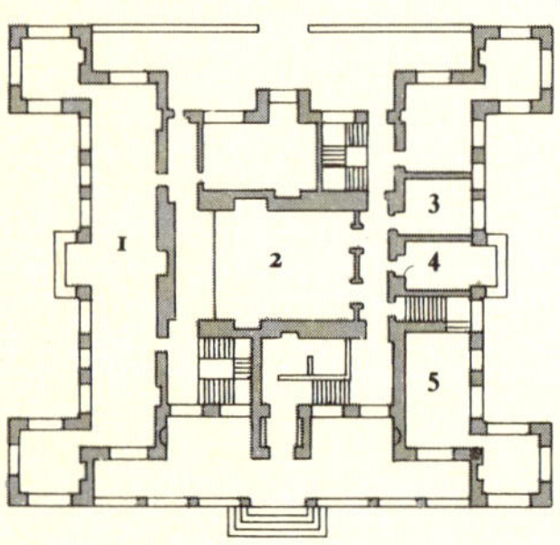

1 Gallery (over)
2 Hall
3 Pantry
4 Buttery
5 Kitchen
←

1 Nursery
2 Bathroom
3 Bedroom
4 Governess's rooms
5 Schoolroom
↓

6 Dressing room
7 Boudoir
8 Garden hall
9 Billiard room
10 Drawing room
11 Library
12 Breakfast room
13 Dining room
14 Hall
15 Serving room
16 Glass pantry

17 Butler's pantry
18 Menservants' rooms
19 Kitchen maids
20 Kitchen

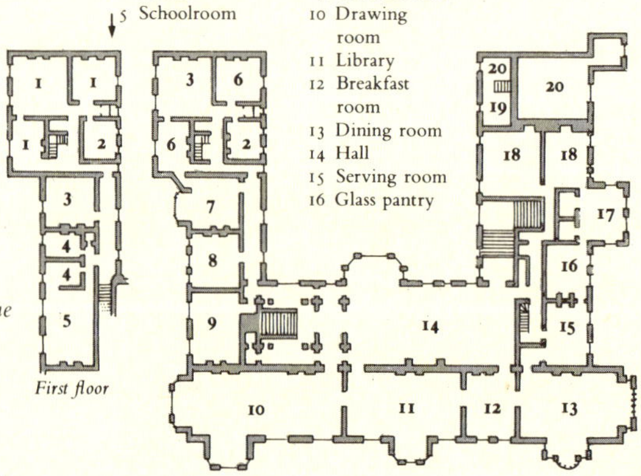

*Strictly symmetrical plans (some E-shaped, some with a central courtyard) emerged in the Elizabethan age, for example at Wollaton Hall, Notts. (**above**), and enjoyed a vogue until the return of asymmetry in the late 18th century. Victorian houses, such as Thoresby (also in Notts.) (**right**), run riot by comparison.*

as an imposing vestibule, and the Victorians revived the medieval-style hall for use as a huge living room and for occasional festivities.

The cultural life

The multiplication of specialized rooms was a natural result of the increasing sophistication of country house life from the Renaissance onwards. One of the great contributions of the 16th and 17th centuries was the long gallery, a room for gentle exercise and for the hanging of paintings. There is an early example at The Vyne, Hampshire.

In the 17th century, an age of retirement and scholarship, two rooms of special importance were the library and closet, the latter a refuge for reading and writing. Ham House (Richmond, Greater London) has unaltered examples of each, dating from the 1670s. The notion that 'books do furnish a room' dates from the 18th century, when libraries began to develop into book-lined living rooms.

Family rooms

As the dinner hour gradually grew later in the 18th century, the drawing room gained prominence as a feminine after-dinner retreat. (Its forebear was the

THE GREAT PARLOUR, ROUSHAM PARK, OXON., *remodelled in 1764, was originally the library. Parlours, used as informal sitting rooms, date back to Elizabethan times: Longleat had three.*

THE KITCHEN, CASTLE DROGO, DEVON (***right***). *The service block of Lutyens' grand Edwardian castle still has its original fitments.*

'withdrawing room' of the Elizabethan and Jacobean house, between the solar and the bedchamber.) In the 19th century the drawing room became the centre of the tea ceremony for all the family. The Victorian male preserve was the smoking room (there is a sumptuous one at Castell Coch in south Wales), sometimes combined with the billiards room.

Children also had their special domain, for the nursery was ruled by the head nursery maid (or nanny), and parents were often unwelcome intruders. The complement of the nursery was the schoolroom, ruled by the governess.

THE DRAWING ROOM, PENRHYN CASTLE, GWYNEDD (***left***): *a typically Victorian blend of baronialism and bourgeois comfort. The wealth of the family was based on the local slate mines.*

Servants and services

Service rooms in country homes have survived more rarely than the rooms used by the family. The idea that servants should maintain a low visibility was fully defined in the late 18th century with the development of separate servants' wings. Under the Victorians the division became emphatic, and one architect was led to remark that 'it was the affectation of the time that work was done by magic; it was vulgar to recognize its existence or even to see anybody doing it.'

In the interests of morality, the bedrooms of the female servants were as far as possible from those of the men. The numerous duties of the servants, and the complexity of their hierarchy, inspired labyrinthine passages and specialized rooms – still room, store room, knife room, shoe room, lamp room, scullery, wash house, and many more. One of the best places to recapture the flavour of such multiplicity is the service block of Lanhydrock House, near Bodmin in Cornwall, where the kitchen includes its original, somewhat cumbersome equipment.

THE HOLBEIN BEDROOM, STRAWBERRY HILL, GREATER LONDON, *illustrates Horace Walpole's predilection for a lightweight neo-Gothic style.*

The luxury of the family apartments offered a striking contrast to the servants' quarters. However, even the owners sometimes suffered relatively primitive conditions of hygiene, and the outside privy was all too common. Not until the late 19th century did the modern water closet and plumbed bathroom become widespread.

CONNECTIONS
Décor: 212–13 *The Italian influence in architecture;* **282–6** *The artist's eye;* **292–3** *Great art collections*
Exteriors: 208–9 *The great country houses*

The Italian influence in architecture

LAYER MARNEY TOWER, ESSEX, *begun in 1520, is an impressive showpiece of creamy Italian terracotta decoration (the work of imported craftsmen) set in panels between layers of rich Tudor red brick.*

Few towns in Britain are without traces of the profound impact of Italy's historic architecture upon British architects. The debt is not only to Roman antiquity, with its connotations of imperial power and patrician dignity, but also to Italian Late Gothic and to the innovations of the Renaissance and the baroque. Rival styles from other European countries made their impression – for example, the robust charm of the Netherlands, or the heavy solemnity of ancient Greece – but Italian styles were a potent influence in Britain for nearly 300 years.

The first steps towards classicism

By the mid-16th century, architects of the Italian Renaissance, who imitated the serene harmony, as well as the structural and decorative details, of ancient Roman architecture, had invested their cities with buildings of supreme architectural excitement. Tudor England, in its anti-papal isolation, was ill-placed to be fertilized by these ideas, but by the early 16th century a few aristocratic houses had already acquired superficial Italianate flourishes. Rather more significant developments were stimulated by the appearance in 1563 of the first English architectural treatise, John Shute's *The First and Chief Groundes of Architecture*, the fruit of an architectural study tour of Italy. Shute described the Classical Orders (of columns, capitals and surmounting entablatures) which Renaissance designers had adapted from the ancients – the solid-looking Doric, the fluted Ionic, and the delicate Corinthian or Composite column with its acanthus-leaved capital. Before long, the Orders were being used decoratively, as badges of high fashion, on the façades of English country houses such as Longleat in Wiltshire (1572–80) and Burghley House, Cambridgeshire.

Jones and Palladio

The first decades of the 17th century saw the emergence of a more thorough-going classicism. This was the achievement of one man, Inigo Jones (1573–1652), who had spent several years in Italy, where he acquired the architectural treatise upon which he was to base his style, Palladio's *I Quattro Libri*. Palladio, the greatest Italian architect of the late 16th century, had brilliantly adapted the ancient Roman style in his villas around Vicenza and his Venetian churches.

Jones's work, as Surveyor General of the King's Works from 1615, must have seemed totally alien to the English public. The Banqueting House in Whitehall, the Queen's House at Greenwich, and the Single- and Double-cube Rooms at Wilton House (Wiltshire) all reflect the Palladian emphasis on harmonic proportions and the sensitive use of the Orders. The effect was close to Jones's stated ideal of architecture – that its outward ornament should be 'solid, proportionable according to the rules, masculine and unaffected'.

THE QUEEN'S HOUSE, GREENWICH, *by Inigo Jones. Begun in 1616 and designed as a weekend retreat for James I's queen, this house was England's introduction to the pure, classical ideal of architecture.*

ST MARY-LE-STRAND, LONDON (***below***) *1714–17, by James Gibbs. Gibbs's church reflects the impact of Wren and his own training in Rome with a leading baroque architect.*

THE VYNE, HAMPSHIRE, (***below right***), *has a temple-like portico, designed by John Webb in 1650. It was the prototype of the standard centrepiece of the 18th-century English Palladian country house.*

The English baroque

In Italy, meanwhile, the early 17th century had seen the dawn of baroque, with its dramatic sweeping forms and rich illusionism. If the high priest of Italian baroque, Gianlorenzo Bernini, had an English counterpart, it was undoubtedly Sir Christopher Wren (1632–1723), who rejected the most fantastic baroque decorative flourishes but was deeply impressed by Bernini's bold and massive groupings. The main source of Wren's great new domed St Paul's, an astonishing departure from the English tradition, was St Peter's in Rome, but there was also a debt to the baroque vitality of Francesco Borromini, for example in the curves and countercurves of the west towers. Convincing echoes of Bernini and Borromini are also to be found in the London churches of Wren's younger contemporary Thomas Archer: St John's, Smith Square, and St Paul's, Deptford.

The Palladians and neoclassicists

After the death of Queen Anne, the new land-owning Whig aristocracy associated the English baroque with a hated despotism: the overwhelming grandeur of Wren, Vanbrugh and Hawksmoor was highly autocratic. What was sought was something quieter, less emotive, less Roman. The answer to this need was a return to the simplicity and precision of Palladio and Inigo Jones in a reaction led by Colen Campbell (1676–1729) and his patron Lord Burlington (1694–1753). In the 1720s they both created direct imitations (at Mereworth Castle, Kent, and Chiswick House, London, respectively) of Palladio's famous Villa Rotonda outside Vicenza.

The critics of the Palladians accused them of impractical academicism, and indeed it would be hard to defend Burlington's Assembly Rooms in York (1731–2) from this criticism: the internal colonnades are so narrowly spaced that a lady in a hooped petticoat would not have been able to pass through them. However, there were also many marvellous triumphs, such as William Kent's Holkham Hall (Norfolk) with its fine colonnaded screens (inspired by Palladio's Venetian churches), James Paine's exquisite little chapel at Gibside near

THE ENTRANCE HALL AT HOLKHAM, NORFOLK, *by William Kent. Begun in 1734, Holkham magnificently demonstrates the features of Palladianism, including screens of columns (painted in imitation of Italian marble), apse-ended rooms with coffered ceilings, and sculpted friezes.*

Newcastle, and the splendid Georgian townscapes of Edinburgh, Bath and Buxton.

In the mid-18th century archaeological discoveries in Italy and in the provinces of the Roman Empire encouraged a new architectural style, neoclassicism, based on imitation of the antique. A key event was the appearance in 1764 of a study of the Roman ruins at Spalato by Robert Adam (1728–92). In the interiors of his own buildings, such as Syon House near London, Adam added gaiety to Palladianism. He translated his knowledge of Roman, Pompeiian, 'Etruscan' and Renaissance styles into a versatile repertoire of ornament, which he combined with ingenious room plans inspired by the Roman public baths.

The 19th century

Adam's eclecticism presaged the magpie spirit of the later 18th and early 19th centuries. John Nash, leader of the Picturesque movement, built a villa in an Italianate vernacular style at Cronkhill, Shropshire, and a corner of Sir John Soane's Bank of England is a facsimile of the ancient Temple of

THE TEMPLETON FACTORY, GLASGOW, *1889, is one of the most bizarre Victorian imitations of the Gothic Doge's Palace in Venice.*

Vesta at Tivoli. But such echoes of Italy were part of a polyphony in which Gothick was now one of the loudest strains. Many classically inclined architects soon began to favour Greek rather than Roman models, but there were two major Italian themes in the Victorians' recycling of historic styles. One was the revival of Italian Gothic (or Romanesque); the other was the neo-Renaissance style which decked many a British bank in the dress of a Renaissance palazzo.

CONNECTIONS
Classical styles: 208–9 *The great country houses;* **210–11** *Rooms in country houses;* **282–5** *The artist's eye*
Neo-Gothic: 204–5 *Parish churches;* **286–7** *The artist's eye*
St Paul's Cathedral: 244–5 *London*

Royal retreats

HAMPTON COURT PALACE, GREATER LONDON. *The Tudor buildings, near the river, are easily distinguishable from the apartments added by Sir Christopher Wren (from 1689), surrounding the Fountain Court. The small central courtyard – Clock Court – contains an astronomical clock made for Henry VIII in 1540.*

THE ROYAL PAVILION, BRIGHTON (***below***). *The pleasure domes added a touch of fantasy to Regency Britain's leading seaside resort. The Prince Regent's extravagance, particularly his spending on the Chinese-style interior decoration, was severely censured in Parliament.*

Castles were seldom particularly comfortable, and unless there was some crisis when considerations of security overrode questions of comfort, even medieval monarchs preferred the space and luxury of a palace or the privacy of a hunting lodge. The sombre Tower of London complex, which was begun by William the Conqueror, was simultaneously a palace, a fortress and a prison but it was never popular as a home. By contrast, Windsor Castle outside the capital, started by William as a wooden fortress, was extended by subsequent rulers into a comfortable retreat. Edward III made it the headquarters of his new Order of the Garter. The present appearance of the buildings owes much to extensive restoration in the 1820s, in the reign of George IV; this was carried out by Sir Jeffry Wyatville, who heightened the round tower and created a whole new range of state apartments. The brightest jewel at Windsor, though, is the sumptuous St George's Chapel (begun *c.* 1478), where Charles I is buried.

The gorgeous palaces

Even before the Normans arrived there had been a palace at Westminster. But when it was burnt down in 1512, Henry VIII built St James's Palace instead, and he also transformed Cardinal Wolsey's magnificent York Place into the Palace of Whitehall. Near Epsom in Surrey this good-living monarch raised the fantasy palace of Nonsuch, which Charles II eventually gave to his mistress, Lady Castlemaine, and which she sold advantageously for demolition and redevelopment. Gone too is that favourite family palace of the Tudors, Greenwich, where Henry VIII was born, as were his daughters, Mary and Elizabeth.

Most of the outlying royal residences were within easy reach of the capital by boat or on horse-back. There was a palace at Sheen in Surrey as far back as 1125, later much loved by Richard II, who demolished it in his grief at the death of his first queen, Anne of Bohemia. Rebuilt, and again accidentally destroyed by fire, it was restored by Henry VII and renamed Richmond after the Yorkshire town of which he had been Earl. It was at the Thames-side palace of Richmond, of which nothing except for its great park now remains, that Elizabeth I died, and Charles II, as a child, had his own household there as Prince of Wales.

Many royal homes, stately and less stately, are partly open to visitors, while others, such as Balmoral, can only be gazed at from a respectful distance. Supreme showplace is Hampton Court, which the worldly Cardinal Wolsey began in 1514 only to have it filched by Henry VIII. Five of Henry's wives lived in this, his favourite home, and two of them, Jane Seymour and Catherine Howard, are said to haunt it still. There the bluebeard monarch enjoyed jousting and playing tennis – the closed court can still be seen. The asthmatic William III also succumbed to Hampton Court's charms, which he preferred to smoky London, and many of the additions, as well as the laying out of the gardens, are due to William and Mary's affection for this pleasant riverside retreat.

William also bought Kensington Palace, then set in the unspoilt countryside, but handier for West-

AWAY FROM IT ALL

Queen Victoria took advantage of the railways to move around her realm to those favourite retreats – Windsor, Balmoral and Osborne – where she could enjoy being a devoted wife to her beloved Albert and the mother of many children (at Windsor, ***right***). The high-minded Albert reformed the chaotic administration of the royal households and took great interest in every detail of their management and design. He insisted, for example, that the ancient custom of discarding candles once they had been lit, even if they were incompletely used, be discontinued. After his death (1861) no new pictures were hung on the walls at Windsor, for, as Victoria decreed, those already there had been put in their places by Albert and his decisions were eternal.

Balmoral was the best loved royal retreat and twice yearly, in spring and autumn, Victoria went northwards on the long pilgrimage to the Highlands and her 'dear paradise'. There she was blissfully happy and when away would remember with affection Albert's stalkings, the building of a cairn, the evening walk when she lost her way, torchlit dances and expeditions to other parts of Scotland under an assumed name. Victoria bought Balmoral House, a small residence in the wilds of Grampian, in 1852 and under Albert's inspiration it was replaced by a great granite castle in the Scottish baronial style, skilfully arranged so as to command the finest views of the surrounding mountains and the River Dee. By contrast Osborne House on the Isle of Wight, purchased in 1845, was rebuilt as an Italian palazzo. The photograph (***below right***) shows a party in the grounds: Victoria was in her 79th year.

As the widow of Windsor, arrayed in deepest mourning, Victoria passed dolefully from Windsor to Osborne and from there to Balmoral. On the 26th of August each year – Albert's birthday – the bereaved Queen, her family, her court, her servants and her tenantry met together at the foot of the bronze statue of Albert (in highland dress) that stood in the hall at Balmoral, and in silence drank to his beloved memory. When Victoria emerged from this secluded phase in the 1870s it was to the blandishments of the artful Disraeli. As a token of her esteem she sent him bunches of spring flowers, among them his favourite primroses, picked by herself and her ladies in the woods at Osborne. 'They show,' he told her, 'that your Majesty's sceptre has touched the enchanted isle.'

minster. One can walk today through the state apartments planned by Christopher Wren and adorned with wainscotting crafted by Grinling Gibbons. Kensington was used by sovereigns until the death of George II in 1760. George III preferred Kew – first Kew House and, after its demolition, the Dutch House (or Kew Palace), which still stands.

Retreating by rail

Buckingham Palace was built in 1703 for the Duke of Buckingham and remodelled for George IV by John Nash. It became the favourite London home of royalty with the accession of Queen Victoria in 1837, but the development of the railways meant that she could seek country quiet far beyond the Thames Valley. Her happiest days were spent at Balmoral in the Scottish Highlands, a baronial mansion that was largely the personal creation of her adored husband, Albert, who supervised its planning, its decor (a wealth of tartan and stags' heads) and the layout of its grounds.

It was the energetic Prince Albert, also, who planned Victoria's seaside home, Osborne House on the Isle of Wight. But this edifice pales in comparison with that earlier seaside retreat, the flamboyantly oriental Brighton Pavilion, designed by John Nash for the Prince Regent in 1817. The future Edward VII broke new ground by acquiring Sandringham House in Norfolk, but today the royal family has gone west. The Prince and Princess of Wales at Highgrove House in Gloucestershire are near-neighbours to Princess Anne at Gatcombe. Curiously, there has never been a royal household (as opposed to strategic castles such as those of Edward I) established in Wales. Farthest north of all, the Queen Mother uses the Castle of Mey, formerly Barrogill Castle, overlooking the Pentland Firth, as her summer retreat.

QUEEN ELIZABETH II AT BALMORAL (***left***). *As a place of refuge, Balmoral has special attractions for a royal family beleaguered by the Press.*

CONNECTIONS
Aristocratic retreats: 208–9 *The great country houses*
The Palace of Holyroodhouse: 256–7 *Edinburgh*
Royal strongholds: 196–9 *Castles*
Royal wealth: 58–9. *Monarchy and display*

Gardens

A VISITOR'S GUIDE
Only a small selection of Britain's most rewarding gardens is shown here. Except for Hestercombe (which can be seen by arrangement), all these examples are open to the public, either daily or on a regular basis. The National Trust alone has over 100 gardens that can be visited. Many private gardens open occasionally to raise funds for charity.

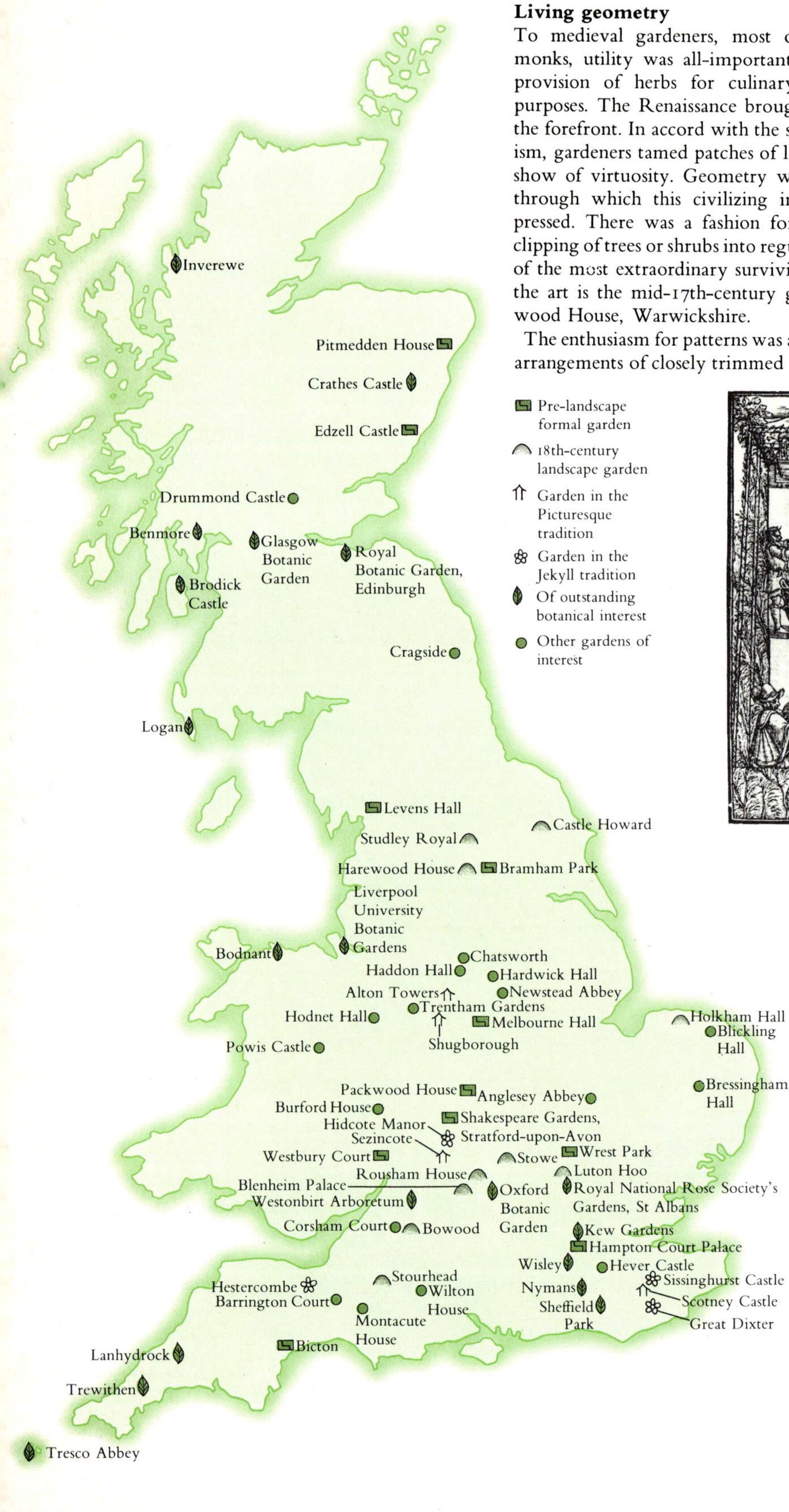

Francis Bacon, in an essay of 1623, wrote that gardens offer 'the greatest refreshment to the spirits of man'. The gardener's art has been treated with such high seriousness since Tudor times, inspiring learned treatises, passionate debates in print and some marvellous poetry.

Living geometry

To medieval gardeners, most of whom were monks, utility was all-important, especially the provision of herbs for culinary or medicinal purposes. The Renaissance brought aesthetics to the forefront. In accord with the spirit of humanism, gardeners tamed patches of landscape with a show of virtuosity. Geometry was the medium through which this civilizing instinct was expressed. There was a fashion for topiary – the clipping of trees or shrubs into regular shapes. One of the most extraordinary surviving examples of the art is the mid-17th-century garden at Packwood House, Warwickshire.

The enthusiasm for patterns was also expressed in arrangements of closely trimmed shrubs or herbs, known as knot gardens. Their ultimate inspiration was probably the penitential mazes of the early Christian Church. No knot gardens survive in their original form, but there are some interesting reconstructions, notably at Hampton Court Palace and Stratford-upon-Avon.

Early gardens were usually enclosed by a wall, but this did not imply total hermeticism. A common feature was a grassy or brick-and-timber mound, or mount, from which the outside world could be observed. Mounts would sometimes be placed in the corners of a garden, and were often topped by viewing pavilions (gazebos) reached by steps. The walls and corner pavilions at Montacute House in Somerset are the most beautiful of all survivals from the Elizabethan period of garden architecture.

Exotic plants increasingly captured the imagination of British gardeners. There was some aristocratic correspondence about the purchase of orange trees as early as 1561, and hundreds of orangeries were built in the 17th century to give winter protection to trees that in summer were

A RENAISSANCE GARDEN, *with a watering machine, from the 1586 edition of Thomas Hill's* The Gardener's Labyrinth. *Hill's book was the first comprehensive guide to English gardening.*

TOPIARY AT LEVENS HALL, CUMBRIA. *Among the ancient topiary, cut in yew and box, are some 19th-century additions, but parts of the original late 17th-century garden still survive.*

trundled out in tubs for an ornamental airing. The foundation of the first botanical garden in England – the Oxford Physic Garden in 1621 – bore witness to a new scientific approach to plants. In the same period the Tradescant family built up a superb plant collection at Lambeth.

The appeal of exotics was paralleled by an admiration for the gardening styles that were flourishing in Italy, France and Holland. The French influence gave birth to a fashion for parterres – level areas laid out with symmetrical designs of flowerbeds, plants and ornaments. From the Continent too came rectangular 'canals', sometimes with a pavilion mirrored at one end.

WESTBURY COURT, GLOS. (***left***): *a fine Dutch-style canal garden of the late 17th century. There are two canals – a straight one centred on a pavilion, and a T-shaped one with a Neptune statue.*

THE QUEEN'S GARDEN (***below***), *part of the Royal Botanic Gardens at Kew, Greater London, is in the 17th-century style. There is a formal parterre and a mount topped by a wrought-iron pavilion overlooking the Thames.*

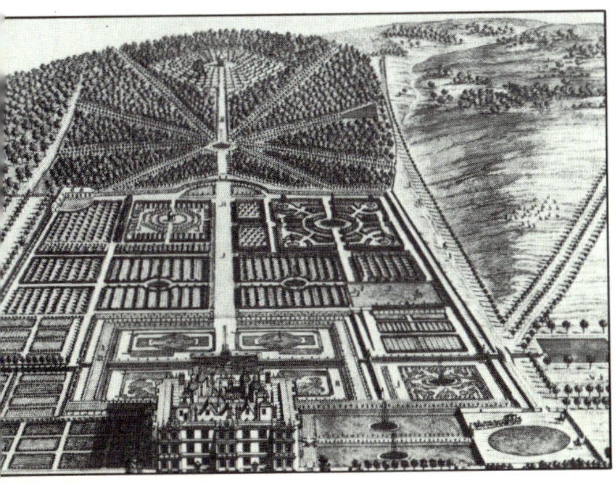

THE CLASSIC FRENCH-STYLE GARDEN (***left***) *in the grand manner, with a* patte d'oie. *Like most other examples, this one at Longleat House (by George London) was destroyed in the 18th century.*

England has nothing to match the great radiating formal gardens of André Le Nôtre in France, but in the late 17th and early 18th centuries Gallicism was rampant. The hallmarks of the French style were the *allée* (a straight walk bordered by closely shaven shrubs or trees) and the *patte d'oie* (literally, 'goose's foot': a splayed arrangement of *allées*). Like most gardens before the mid-18th century, the manifestations of Gallic formalism have been largely obliterated by the landscape movement. But an impressive reminder has escaped its clutches at Bramham Park in West Yorkshire, and the work of the most distinguished gardeners of the time, George London and Henry Wise, can still be appreciated at Melbourne Hall, Derbyshire.

The softer touch

The tyranny of ruler and protractor caused inevitable ripples of unrest. The first hesitant steps away from the formal were taken by William Kent at Chiswick House, and by the poet Alexander Pope in his own small plot at Twickenham. More boldly original, though, was John Aislabie's garden at Studley Royal (1720–42) in North Yorkshire, still geometric in the layout of its canals and pools but novel in its choice of a wooded valley setting to create a mood of introspection.

It was Kent who emerged, around 1730, as the first true master of the landscape. At Stowe in Buckinghamshire (now a boys' school) he 'leapt the fence and saw all Nature was a garden', giving mature expression for the first time to the idea of the man-made landscape as an idyllic composition in the manner of the painters Claude Lorraine or Salvator Rosa. The disposition of trees, glades and architectural 'eyecatchers' was artfully planned as a series of pleasurable surprises. In contrast to the softened contours of the garden, the house itself stood to attention in the Palladian style. This was echoed in the classical garden buildings, which evoked ancient Rome.

CHISWICK HOUSE, GREATER LONDON. *Much of this garden is highly formal, but when William Kent modified it for Lord Burlington in the 1720s, he subtly softened the geometry.*

The style was often repeated, and by none so tirelessly as Lancelot ('Capability') Brown (1716–83). After setting up in business in 1751, Brown created some two hundred landscapes, including magnificent examples at Blenheim

(Oxfordshire) and Bowood (Wiltshire). Most adhered to a simple recipe: lawns rolling right up to the house, a serpentine lake, clumps and belts of trees and a scattering of eyecatchers.

After Brown's death, colour was added to the landscape garden by Humphry Repton (1752–1818), who re-introduced flowers and terraces, as well as favouring a greater variety of trees and shrubs. But despite Repton's modifications, the Brown formula was felt by the end of the century to be wearisomely repetitive – 'one uniform, eternal green'.

The quest for greater incident was taken up by the Picturesque school of garden design. A classical

STOWE, BUCKS. (***below***): *the Palladian bridge was one of a number of classical garden buildings in this 18th-century landscape by William Kent. Similar bridges were built at Wilton House (Wilts.) and Prior Park (near Bath).*

STOURHEAD, WILTS., *made by its owner Henry Hoare from c. 1744, is the most beautiful of all gardens of the landscape movement. Hoare dammed a stream to create a series of lakes, and planted trees (mainly beech and spruce) on the valley sides. In the background of this photograph is the Pantheon; other eyecatchers include the Temple of Apollo and the Gothic Cottage. A great deal of new planting was added from the late 18th century onwards.*

A SCHEME BY HUMPHRY REPTON (***left***). *Repton re-introduced the terrace to make a more gradual transition between house and landscape. This is a page from one of his* Red Books, *which he used to present designs to clients.*

Roman temple could now be found in the company of a ruined Gothic tower or ivy-mantled cottage. The riotous medley of styles at Alton Towers, Staffordshire (1814–35), shows the extremes to which this route could lead.

Victorian gardens

When, in the early 19th century, gardening more and more became a passion of the middle classes, it was to the writings of J.C. Loudon that the new amateurs turned for instruction. Loudon encouraged the widespread adoption of what he called the 'gardenesque' approach, based on commonsense eclecticism. He was influential too in his promotion of municipal parks and botanic gardens (with labelled exhibits for the public).

The Victorians went in for botany on an unprecedented scale. Plant-collectors such as J.D. Hooker brought species from as far afield as the Himalayas and China. Hybridization further fattened the catalogue. Protection for the exotics was often afforded by greenhouses heated by boilers and cast-iron water pipes. One of the most famous of all was the Great Stove (now vanished) at Chatsworth in Derbyshire, where in 1849 its designer Joseph Paxton became the first to achieve the flowering of the giant South American water-lily (*Victoria amazonica*).

Greenhouses were crucial to the popular method of plant rotation known as bedding-out, whereby showy-flowered half-hardy annuals were kept heated under glass until they were ready for transference to outdoor beds in tightly packed masses of colour. An alternative solution to the difficulties of growing tender exotics was to exploit the warm currents of the Gulf Stream. This led to some delectable gardens in the extreme west, such as Tresco Abbey in the Scillies and Inverewe in north-west Scotland. Inverewe is a fine illus-

SIR JOSEPH DALTON HOOKER (*1817–1911*), *in 1850, returned from the Himalayas with 43 new rhododendron species.*

THE RHODODENDRON ARBOREUM (***left***) *was introduced from the Himalayas in the 1820s. Being vulnerable to frosts, the Himalayan species were crossed with hardier sorts.*

THE PALM HOUSE AT KEW GARDENS, *designed and built by Sir Joseph Paxton from 1836 to 1840. Paxton was probably the greatest gardener of his century. For 32 years he served the 6th Duke of Devonshire at Chatsworth.*

THE GLORY OF SISSINGHURST. *This highly influential garden in Kent, begun in 1930, was made by Vita Sackville-West and her husband Sir Harold Nicolson. It was ingeniously planned to provide beauty at all times of year.*

THE ROYAL BOTANIC GARDEN, EDINBURGH: *the interior of the modern plant house (1967), suspended on exterior steel cables which leave the interior uncluttered. There are 6 sections, each with different temperatures and humidities.*

tration of the Victorian predilection for woodland gardens, many of which were started as havens for rhododendrons and azaleas.

The most potent influence in the 20th century was Gertrude Jekyll, who was inspired by her friend William Robinson's promotion of the 'wild garden', and by the cottage gardens of her native Surrey. Her best achievements were her collaborations with the architect Edwin Lutyens: he supplied a formal yet vernacular architectural framework, she the planting that breathed life into it. Variety was attained by treating a garden as a series of outdoor rooms, each with its own character. The best-preserved of the Jekyll-Lutyens creations is at Hestercombe in Surrey.

The Jekyll style inspired some of the most glorious gardens of the 20th century, such as Hidcote Manor in the Cotswolds and Crathes Castle near Aberdeen. Some designers, however, preferred a return to formality. One was Harold Peto, whose Italianate manner can be seen at Buscot Park, Oxfordshire.

The post-war years have been relatively lean for British gardens. One of the more imaginative innovations has been the idea of 'island beds', publicized in the 1950s by Alan Bloom in his own garden at Bressingham Hall in Norfolk. Outstanding gardens have also been created by Russell Page (author of the influential book *The Education of a Gardener*), whose work can be seen at Longleat.

CONNECTIONS
Garden cities: 228–9 *Town planning*
Palladian architecture: 208–9 *The great country houses;* **212–13** *The Italian influence in architecture*
The Picturesque: 188–9 *Tourism;* **284–5** *The artist's eye;* **294–5** *Artists and places;* **296–9** *Writers and places*

Cottages and rural homes

THE CRUCK HOUSE

The cruck house differs from other types of timber-frame construction in that the roof is an integral part of its structure. Pairs of curved or elbowed timbers ('blades'), joined to create arches and tied with horizontal beams, form the basis. Like most timber-frame structures, the cruck frame was cut in a carpenter's workshop, or 'framynplace', where separate pieces were marked with numerals before being assembled and infilled on the site. The commonest filling was wattle and daub.

Cruck houses are unknown in the east and south-east English lowlands, but are fairly widely distributed elsewhere in England and Wales.

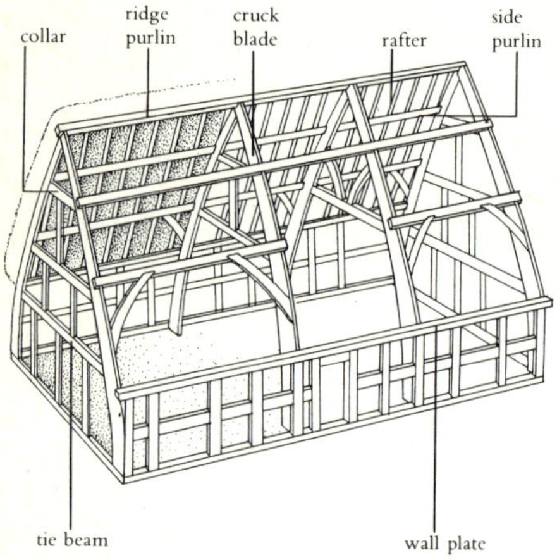

THE CRUCK-FRAME PRINCIPLE: *a 16th-century example. The hall extended to the roof, but part of the house was two-storeyed.*

A WEALDEN HOUSE. *The 'Old Shop', Bignor, Sussex, is a celebrated 15th-century example showing the characteristic form: a 2-storey central hall flanked by jettied upper chambers, all under a single hipped roof. The original façade has been concealed by the addition of brickwork, some of it in a herringbone pattern.*

A CRUCK COTTAGE, *with a typical thatched roof, at Sandhurst, Glos. One of many cruck houses with exposed frames in this region.*

There was a time when cottages planted deep in the countryside were held in low esteem. Underlying this attitude were the harsh realities of rural life. In some areas, hardly any advance was made upon the rude accommodation of the Anglo-Saxon cottar's home. Windowless dwellings of sod or turf persisted in the Scottish Highlands, as well as in the Isle of Man, until the end of the 19th century, and for the poor the general standard of rural housing remained low until well into the 20th.

With the Picturesque movement of the late 18th century, however, rusticity became a fashionable ideal. Today, the magnetism of the cottage is stronger that ever: it has become an idyllic retreat cherished by thousands of urban escapees.

Early traditions

One of the most persistent kinds of rural dwelling, built in turf in the north of England as long ago as the 9th century and in the south from the 12th century onwards, is the longhouse. This was initially a simple single-storey hut, divided into two areas, one for cattle and one for humans, with a passage running from front to back between. After the 17th century, a standard northern type developed, with an inner room leading off from the main living space and with a fireplace backing on to the passage. Many examples in stone still survive in an altered form.

Before the Middle Ages, the commonest material used for yeomen's cottages was cob, or unbaked clay, usually strengthened by straw or heather. In the West Country, where the tradition was especially long-lived, villages such as Dunsford, Iddesleigh and Whimple have typical cob buildings of the 18th and early 19th centuries; while in East Anglia the local practice of building in clay blocks (known as bats or lumps) can still be seen in 19th-century cottages in a belt of villages stretching from Thetford to Diss.

In the post-conquest period, substantial timber-framed cottages were erected by well-to-do yeomen and farmers in southern England. The oldest surviving timber buildings are in the cruck form, widely used until the end of the 18th century: there is a famous 14th-century example at Didbrook in Gloucestershire, but most surviving cruck houses are of later date. Of the more elaborate types, one of the grandest was the generously sized Wealden house of the south-east, prevalent from the late 14th until the early 16th century. In Kent and Essex, timber-framed houses were often clad in weather-boarding, using imported Scandinavian timber.

As timber supplies diminished, there was a tendency for the frames of half-timbered houses to become thinner, and the walls to be covered with plaster to disguise the poor-quality wood. Amateur restorers have often tended to expose the original timbers regardless of whether this is the appropriate treatment. It is doubtful, moreover, whether many of the so-called 'black and white' buildings had their present appearance in pre-Victorian times: a permanent black was unobtainable on the timbers, and bright colours seem often to have been preferred for the infill panels.

Brick and stone

During the rebuilding of rural England in the late 16th and early 17th centuries, the timber-framed tradition continued in some areas (such as the Welsh Borders), but elsewhere local stone was widely employed for the first time. The most attractive of all stone cottages are perhaps the limestone dwellings of the Cotswolds, with their mullioned windows, and dormers set into steeply pitched roofs of stone 'slates'. In Northamptonshire, many ironstone cottages carry datestones of the 17th century.

Brick was originally a prestige material, and yeomen's cottages were not commonly built in it until the 18th century, although it was used for chimney-stacks before this, and for replacing the original wattle and daub on many timber-frame

COTSWOLD STONE COTTAGES *at Bibury, Glos. These early 17th-century cottages display the characteristic roofs and gables of the region.*

A COTTAGE ORNÉ (***left***) *at Blaise Hamlet, Avon. It is one of 10 Picturesque houses built by John Nash for a Quaker banker's retired tenants (1811).*

COTTAGES OF FLINT AND BRICK *at Brancaster, Norfolk. Flint walls with brick dressings round the openings and at the corners are a typical Norfolk feature. Sometimes, flint is combined with sea pebbles or chunks of chalk.*

houses. In the south-east, where brick eventually became the most widespread material, brickwork exhibited many local variations, such as patterning with flint, and numerous kinds of bonding.

The cottage orné

Some cottages were built in neat terraces at a surprisingly early date, but these did not suit the Picturesque taste of the late 18th century. To those who admired the Picturesque, the terrace was a denial of rusticity. Although many wealthy landowners of the time provided their workers with rows of identical cottages, the irregular *cottage orné*, built with a conscious effect of charm, was closer to the fashionable ideal. Great Tew in Oxfordshire acquired early 19th-century versions of 17th-century Cotswold cottages. The most famous *cottages ornés* of all, however, are those at Blaise Hamlet, near Bristol. Cottage life, by the Regency period, had risen sharply in social status, and a cottage home was considered no disgrace for a retiring middle-class family such as Jane Austen's Wentworths (in *Sense and Sensibility*).

Today, the modernization of old cottages is widely criticized by purists who are concerned about the loss of 'character'. However, adaptation to new uses or circumstances has always been an important aspect of the built environment of the countryside, and many historic cottages owe their present form to a process of transformation over the centuries.

A TILED BRICK TERRACE *at Buckler's Hard, Hants., built in the late 18th century. By the Georgian period, the use of bricks had percolated to the yeoman class, and many of the cottages still lining most village streets can be dated to this time.*

CONNECTIONS
Building techniques: 170–71 *Building*
Villages: 222–3 *Villages and hamlets*

Villages and hamlets

It was until recently assumed that the large village grouped around its focal green or pond – that comfortable form that dominates so much writing on English rural life – was an immediate by-product of the Anglo-Saxon conquest. This is now disputed because initially the Anglo-Saxons adapted themselves to the hamlets and dispersed farmsteads that the Romano-Britons had already established on the uplands and in low-lying valley areas. The classic village type began to develop only later, during the 9th and 10th centuries. Its emergence was bound up with social and economic changes within society, which led to the abandonment of existing hamlets and dispersed farms and the gathering together of landholders into larger, more concentrated settlements.

SETTLEMENT PATTERNS *There are, broadly speaking, two types of village: those with a regular plan and a clear nucleus, which generally originated as a result of planning in the 12th and 14th centuries; and those that are relatively formless and perhaps evolved from the accretion of dwellings to one original farmstead. Hamlets and dispersed farms are more usual in areas where the terrain is difficult and the population sparse.*

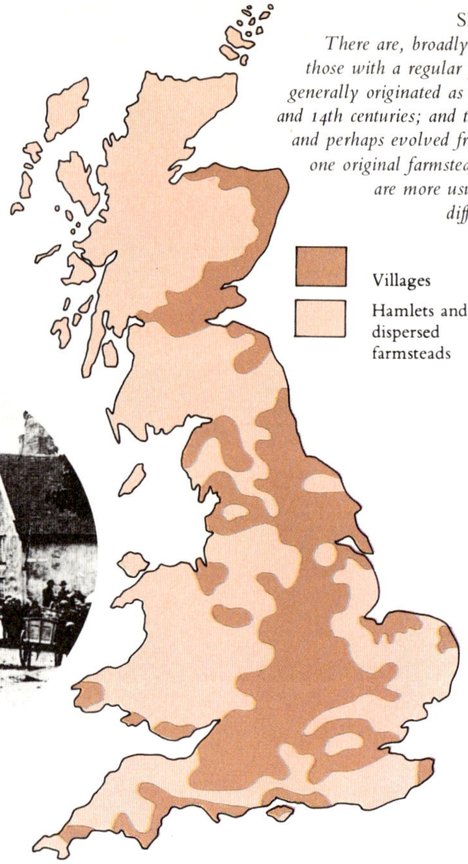

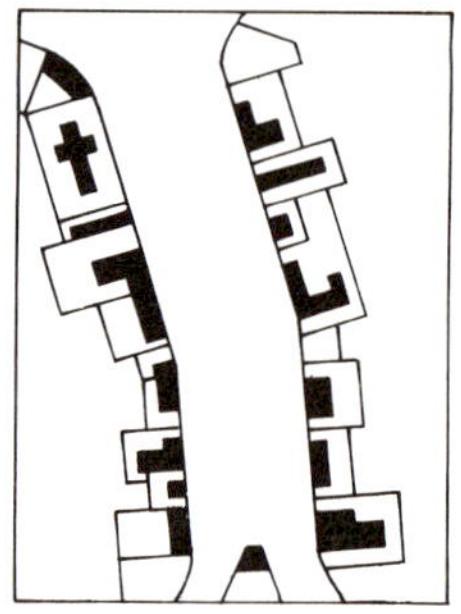

'regular' planned village

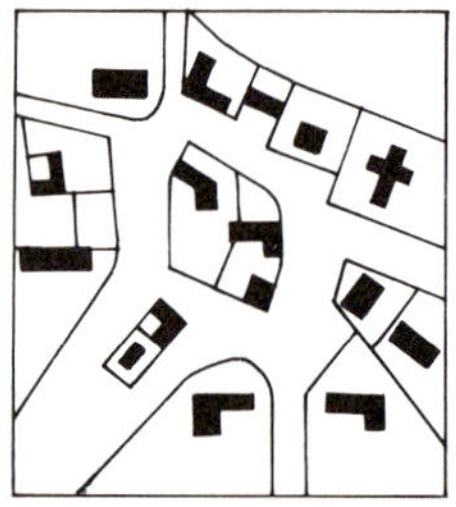

'agglomerated'

LAVENHAM, SUFFOLK, c. *1860s. The close network of Tudor streets in this former 'wool town' gives it an urban feel, but by modern standards of size and population it is considered a village.*

A PLANNED 'TOWNSHIP' ON THE ISLE OF LEWIS, *Scotland. Its origin is in the clearances of the 19th century, when crofters were re-settled to make way for sheep and deer.*

MILTON ABBAS, DORSET. *A model estate village built by Joseph Damer, Earl of Dorchester, in the late 17th century. The original settlement was razed because it spoilt the view from his house.*

Shifting and splitting villages

Villages, once they had been founded, did not always remain entirely static in form. After the devastations of the Conqueror's army in 1069–70, many villages in the north of England took on a new shape. In the same way, Anglo-Scottish warring during the 14th and, later, the 16th century helped to re-draw the layout of many a Border village. Historical studies of Norfolk villages have highlighted another type of change: the shifting of some settlements to a new site near by. One example of this is Grantchester, near Cambridge, where Rupert Brooke imagined that he could lie in the grass 'until the centuries blend and blur': the village is now known to have shifted its site before the 12th century.

The splitting of villages into two or more separate settlements was a further source of change up to the mid-14th century. It can be detected in groups of villages that bear a common 'surname' but are distinguished from each other by place-name prefixes such as East or West, Nether or Upper. Such division often sprang from the inheritance of an estate-cum-village by co-heirs, or its break-up between different landowners. Some settlement groups have a parent-daughter relationship, one village having been spawned as an offshoot of the other. The Danish place-name element *thorp(e)*, as in Ashwell and Ashwell Thorpe in Norfolk, denotes that this sort of fission has occurred. In more recent centuries, the enclosure of open fields precipitated a further change of settlement layout, as farmers moved away from the old village centre to new farmsteads within their separate holdings.

After a change of site in medieval times, some settlements were rebuilt according to a definite plan. Especially distinctive are those known as 'regular' villages. These occur widely in the north-east of England, in Yorkshire and in scattered parts of the Midlands. They can be recognized by the fact that their tofts (the large rectangular enclosures on which every house was sited) are laid out in a grid-like fashion along either side of a main street. Some examples were based around three or four rows of tofts, and some left space in between for a village green.

Modern estate villages display regularity of a different sort. Built from the 18th century onwards, they are distinguished by stone-built cottages, which usually conform to a distinct style of estate architecture, and by their modest gardens (instead of tofts). Nuneham Courtney near

UPPER SLAUGHTER, GLOS., *is only a mile away from its twin, Lower Slaughter. The name is nothing to do with massacres: it derives from the Anglo Saxon word slohtre, meaning 'muddy place'.*

FINCHINGFIELD, ESSEX (***left***). *A classic agglomerated village dating from the Norman period. Despite many additions over the ages, notably the 15th-century guildhall, it retains its focal green and pond.*

Oxford was an estate village created in this manner, after the old site was cleared to make way for Nuneham Park.

Hamlets and dispersed farmsteads

Towards the north and west of Britain, settlement has traditionally been dominated more by hamlets and dispersed farmsteads than by villages. In Scotland settlement prior to the 18th century was generally based on small, irregularly shaped clusters, known as clachans in the Highlands and as fermtouns in the Lowlands. Over the 18th century the Lowland fermtouns were abandoned in favour of the modern distribution of scattered farmsteads. From the late 18th century onwards, many of the Highland clachans, under the impact of the 'clearances' (the creation of new sheep runs), were deserted, and some were re-established on poorer coastal sites. Many crofting townships on islands such as Lewis have their origins in this period.

Settlement in upland Wales has also been widely subject to change. During the early medieval period, the most widespread type was the small hamlet occupied by bondmen or serfs. As more and more bondmen acquired free status, their settlement adjusted to a more open, dispersed pattern – the sort that characterizes these areas today. By contrast, on the marginal ground skirting upland massifs such as Snowdonia, there is an extensive scattering of smallholdings that originated as squatters' settlements, created literally overnight on former common lands during the 17th, 18th and 19th centuries.

DESERTED VILLAGES

Scattered all over Britain, but especially in the Midlands, East Anglia and north-east England, more than 2,000 deserted villages are to be found. Raised house platforms, sunken trackways, dried-out ponds and other vestiges of lost communities have sometimes been preserved beneath old pasture. The oldest of such ghost villages are often found in areas such as Dartmoor, where poor soil or harsh climates deterred further settlement after a tentative beginning. Others were deserted after the Black Death of the mid-14th century. The majority, though, were cleared in the 15th and 16th centuries when landlords converted open-field villages into large sheep farms. Deserted villages provide archaeologists with an excellent opportunity for excavating a settlement *in toto*. Investigations have shown, for example, that traces of earlier Romano-British settlement lie beneath many an apparently Saxon village. Lost villages are sometimes visible from the air as an uneven crop pattern.

CHYSAUSTER, CORNWALL, *is one of the earliest and best-preserved deserted villages in Britain. The 2,000-year-old layout of this tin-miners' village can be seen clearly from the air (**above right**). The houses (**above left**) fronted on to a street, and their orderly arrangement possibly reflects a Roman influence.*

CONNECTIONS
Anglo-Saxon settlements: 42–3 *The movement of peoples*
Cottages: 170–71 *Building;* **220–21** *Cottages and rural homes*
Prehistoric settlements: 192–3 *Marks on the landscape*

Market towns

Most country towns have medieval origins. Their growth was an aspect of Britain's awakening from the Dark Ages, and was accompanied by the strengthening of trade and currency and encouraged by the diminished threat of disruptive invasions. Weekly markets were responsible for the growth of many small towns, and often contributed to their names, as in Market Harborough and Chipping Campden ('Chipping' always denotes a market).

Market charters and fairs

A market town could be fairly well assured of prosperity if it could obtain a royal charter, guaranteeing its right to hold a market. (In some cases, such charters were part and parcel of borough status.) Barnstaple in Devon has one of the oldest charters, dating to AD 930. From the 12th century, the sale of charters increased considerably. They were a valuable source of income to the Crown, while the benefits they conferred upon the townspeople had many ramifications. The security they brought fostered the development of market guilds, which controlled the minutiae of market activity and sometimes provided a structure of local government. Charters could also be granted

THE MARKET HALL AT LEDBURY, HEREF. AND WORCS., *1665. The upper storeys were used for guild meetings.*

A NORWICH FLOWER STALL (***right***). *The lively open-air market is held every day except Sunday.*

THE MARKET CROSS AT MALMESBURY, WILTS., *dating from c. 1500: a photograph of the 1930s. Malmesbury was a Saxon foundation which developed into a major medieval town.*

THE MARKET HALL, CHIPPING CAMPDEN (***right***), *1627: the focus of the wool market. This is one of many towns built on a single-street axis that was wide enough to accomodate the market. The High Street has numerous wool merchants' houses.*

MARKET SCENES (***below***): *a pair of sketches published as etchings in 1802.*

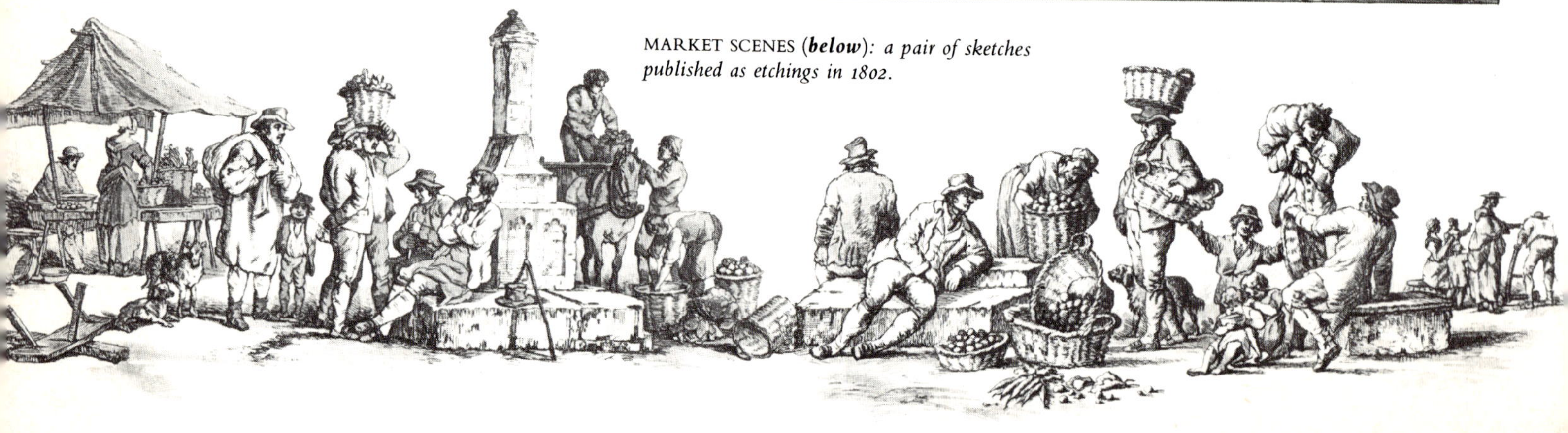

RICHMOND, N. YORKS. *On Saturdays, the 18th-century obelisk rises from a sea of stalls. The market square is one of the largest in Britain.*

to individual lords, who founded local markets for their tenants. The tenacity of market customs is well demonstrated by Market Drayton, Shropshire, which has held a Wednesday market for over 700 years.

The gatherings that became most widely famous were the specialist and seasonal fairs, which attracted merchants from distant parts. Winchester had its St Giles Fair, Nottingham its Goose Fair, and there was also a celebrated fair at Stourbridge on the River Cam. Most impressive of all were the wool fairs in 'staple towns' such as Cirencester.

Many market towns reached new heights of prosperity during the later Middle Ages. The symbols of this success are the market crosses, which were sometimes grandiose: most magnificent of all is the 16th-century one at Chichester, West Sussex. There are also some distinguished late

GUILDFORD HIGH STREET, SURREY (***left***). *The clock projects from the magnificent Guildhall, which has a 17th-century façade on a Tudor core.*

medieval market halls. In the late 17th and the 18th centuries, many old irregular marketplaces were rebuilt as handsome squares, with new town halls.

Today, all too many marketplaces are mere fractions of their former selves. However, in a number of towns where the market was held in a broad thoroughfare instead of on a rectangular or triangular plot, the space has not been violated. Among such precious survivals are Marlborough and Thame.

CONNECTIONS
Farming: 132–9
Marketplaces: 102–3 *Reaching the consumer*
Wool: 142–3 *The wool trade*

Town houses

Of the earliest town houses, little remains but the ground plans. The most common Roman type seems to have been a long, narrow, timber or half-timbered building arranged at right angles to the street, with the living quarters on an upper floor. Wealthier houses were sometimes planned round a courtyard. Anglo-Saxon town dwellings were timber-frame structures infilled with a variety of possible materials, including wattle and daub.

In the post-conquest period, the urban merchants' need for increased storage space led to the more frequent construction of storeyed buildings, although the central hall extending up to the roof was still a common feature. The use of stone was exceptional, and denoted prosperity. A notable survival is the Jew's House in the Strait at Lincoln.

In the 'Great Rebuilding' of the 16th and 17th centuries, most town houses continued to be built of wood. The addition of a jettied (that is, overhanging) storey often provided extra space above ground level, giving rise to closely packed alleys such as those which survive at York (in the Shambles). Lavenham in Suffolk, once a busy wool town, has some marvellous 15th- and 16th-century houses with carved decoration on their exposed ground-floor timbers.

A GEORGIAN DRAWING ROOM *in Bristol's 'Georgian House' (on Great George Street), the well-preserved fashionable home of a wealthy Bristol sugar merchant.*

A GEORGIAN DOORWAY *in Bedford Square, London, with typical decorative fanlight (and ornate cast-iron bootscrapers).*

SLUMS IN GLASGOW, *1868. The tenements of the Gorbals district were notorious slums. In Scotland, better-quality tenements were also a feature of middle- and upper-class urban life.*

Terraces, tenements and flats

From the 17th century onwards, there were rapid changes in urban building styles. Timber was replaced by brick, and in some crowded cities (such as Edinburgh, notable for its high-rise tenements) houses became taller. In London the period after the Great Fire of 1666 was marked by the standardization of design. The Commissioners for Rebuilding dictated standard heights and other dimensions, forbade the hazardous jetties and outlawed the use of materials other than brick or stone.

Elegant detached town houses of the late 17th century were built in the 'Queen Anne' style, with hipped roofs (that is, sloping from eaves to ridge on all four sides), tall sash windows, quoins (corner stones) on the angles, and canopies over the doorways. By this period, however, a new building form had already made an appearance: the terrace.

The first terraces were built in London by speculators such as the Earl of Southampton and Nicholas Barbon. English middle- and upper-class families soon accepted the idea of living in a house identical with that of the next-door neighbours, and in the Georgian period the terraced house became synonymous with a stylish urban lifestyle. Built in brick, it typically had two main rooms on each floor, with the reception rooms on the first floor. In London the street level was raised, so that the front basement looked out into a deep 'area' between the house frontage and the railings. One of the most sumptuous of all London houses is Robert Adam's Home House (1773–7) in Portman Square. Although London, Bath and Edinburgh are richest of all in Georgian domestic architecture, impressive examples can also be seen in many other towns, such as Winchester, Wisbech and Ludlow.

Georgian elegance was carried through into the Regency period (1810–20) and the reign of George IV. The typical Regency house was tall and had stuccoed outer walls, often with elaborate wrought-iron balconies. Such houses appeared not only in London but also, in great numbers, in the newly fashionable south coast resorts.

Until the 19th century the houses of different classes were mostly based on similar designs, differing principally in size and décor. In Victoria's reign, however, the disparity between dwellings for the monied and for the poor became very sharp indeed. Slum-like tenements grew up in some cities, and mean back-to-back terraces in industrial towns such as Leeds and Bradford. Model workers' homes, such as those provided by the Edinburgh distillers, were all too rare. Newcastle upon Tyne had its own type of working-class flats, in-

SWAN HOUSE, CHELSEA EMBANKMENT, LONDON *(1875), by Norman Shaw. The Queen Anne Revival style is ingeniously combined with earlier idioms: note, for example, the first-floor oriel windows.*

distinguishable from ordinary terraced housing except for the paired doors, one of which led to the upstairs flat. Minimum requirements of size and construction were laid down in the Artisans' Dwellings Act of 1868. Among the successful lower-class blocks built by the London County Council from the 1890s onwards was the Millbank Estate at Westminster (1898).

More prosperous citizens adopted the Continental apartment idea (which was also traditional in Scotland) in the later 19th century. The pioneer of this format in England was Richard Norman Shaw, who in the 1870s built Kensington's Albert Hall Mansions in the Queen Anne Revival style.

In the 20th century, private detached houses have become a rarity in big cities (except in the suburbs). The most adventurous urban architects of the modern age have concentrated (by necessity) on flats, attempting to avoid the pitfalls of high-rise blocks in a variety of ways.

A VICTORIAN TERRACE *in Leeds. This housing was originally relatively grand, but Leeds was also notorious for its cramped back-to-back terraces.*

THE BYKER WALL, NEWCASTLE (***below***), *begun in 1970: a long, curving housing block designed to shut out traffic noise. The architect Ralph Erskine encouraged the future inhabitants to become involved in the planning of the project.*

CONNECTIONS
The capital: 242–51 *London*
Fashionable towns: 238–9 *Spas and seaside resorts*
Planning: 228–9 *Town planning*
Suburban houses: 240–41 *Suburbia*
Working-class houses: 234–5 *Coal mining towns;* **236–7** *Factory towns;* **252–3** *Manchester*

Town planning

The Romans were the first in Britain to think purposefully about how urban living spaces should be arranged. Silchester, Colchester and Cirencester are among the Roman towns with impressively regular grid plans. However, archaeologists' reconstructions are unclear about whether they followed precisely the classic city model, based on a cross of principal axes.

The Anglo-Saxons took over some Roman towns, which then began to grow organically, but also added new towns to the urban system. Among the most interesting are the fortified *burhs* of Wessex (such as Wantage), laid out on a grid plan.

Boroughs and burgages

By the 11th century, the Anglo-Saxon *burh* had evolved into the medieval borough, with its 'burgage' tenements – standardized plots occupied by commercially privileged citizens known as burgesses. Between 1066 and 1400, over 500 boroughs were created by the Crown and by the greater barons. New Winchelsea (East Sussex) shows all the characteristics. Its strictly rectilinear plan, laid out by the Crown in 1288, is clearly visible today, in contrast to that of more successful new towns of the Middle Ages such as Newcastle-upon-Tyne (1080–1130) or Liverpool (1207), where later accretions have obliterated the grid.

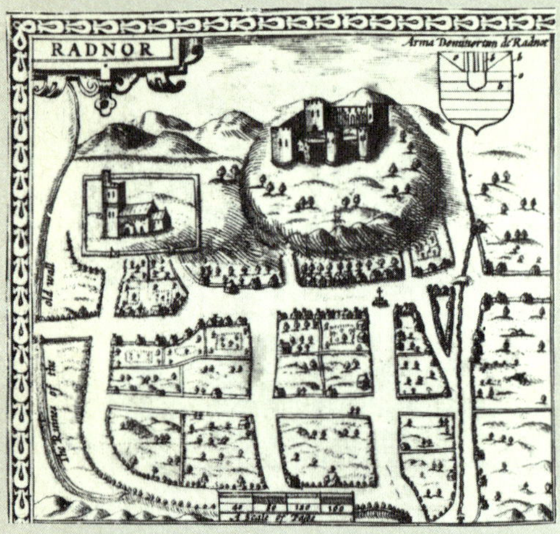

A PLAN OF NEW RADNOR, POWYS, *1611. This 13th-century new town has a grid plan with a main street leading to its key feature, the castle.*

Urban expansion

In subsequent centuries until the 19th, town planning was preoccupied with expansion rather than renewal. Until they were rebuilt in stone, many large towns in the south and east (such as Exeter, Norwich and London) were affected by devastating fires, but such opportunities for radical rethinking were allowed to pass. Even in the expansion of urban areas, design was usually somewhat random. There were exceptions, however. Inigo Jones's design for the Bedford estate in the 1630s, with quality housing arranged round a square (Covent Garden), followed a Parisian model. Such formal planning became more widespread in the Georgian period. The showpiece is unquestionably John Nash's Regent's Park estate (1811–31), with its counterpoint of 'natural' park and grand, unified terraces.

By this time, Georgian townscapes had begun to appear outside London, the finest of them at Edinburgh and the spa towns. The two John Woods, at Bath, had anticipated Nash by making each individual residence subordinate to a grand design. John Wood the Elder's Circus (1754) and the Younger's Royal Crescent (1767–75) were copied at Buxton, Derbyshire, by John Carr, and later by Robert Adam in Edinburgh. Squares, crescents and terraces were eventually acquired by the larger commercial and industrial towns: Clifton (Bristol) had its Brunswick Square, Liverpool its Falkner and Abercrombie Squares.

PORT SUNLIGHT, MERSEYSIDE (***right***)*: the acme of philanthropic planning, founded by Lord Lever for his soap-workers in 1888.*

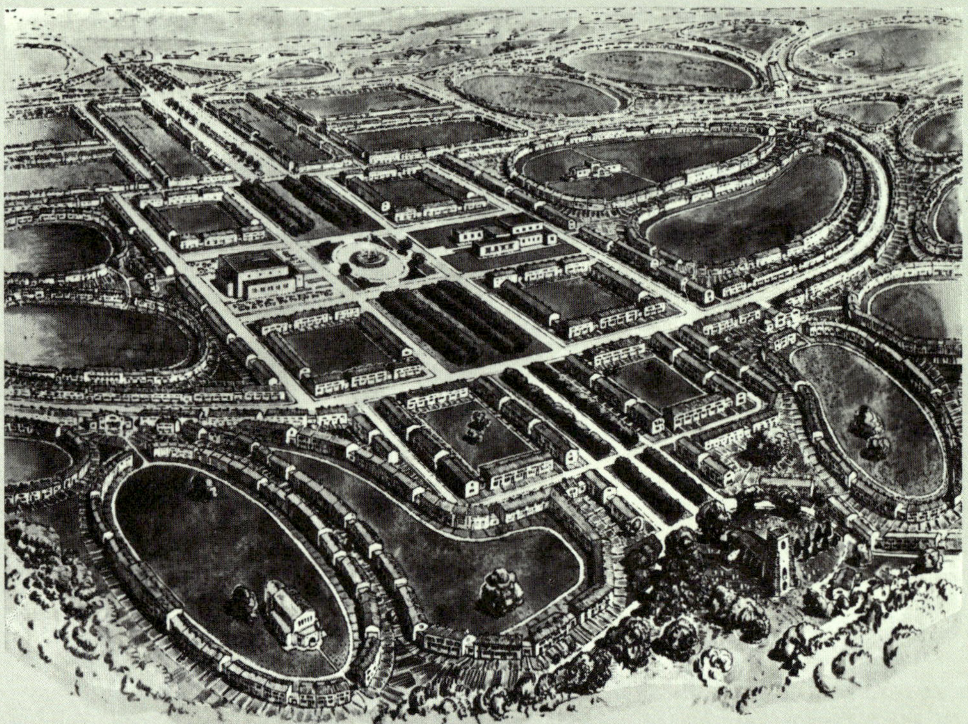

THE BIRKENHEAD PLAN (***below***), *1947. Charles Reilly's utopian plans for this war-ravaged Merseyside town were too ambitious to be realized.*

GREY STREET, NEWCASTLE (***below***), *1835–9: the masterpiece of John Dobson. With Grainger Street, it cleared the old centre of congestion.*

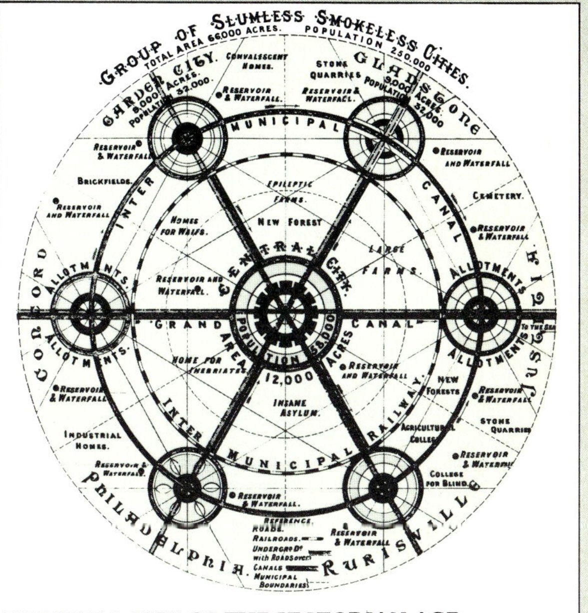

THE IDEAL CITY OF THE VICTORIAN AGE

Ebenezer Howard's scheme for a ring of slumless, smokeless, self-sufficient cities was published in 1898 in his book *Tomorrow*, which had a huge influence on contemporary planning. Howard placed a major emphasis on low-density housing, integrated into a patchwork of large gardens and woods.

In the 18th and 19th centuries, a handful of new, modestly sized planned settlements were founded by landowners. Several of them survive, relatively unchanged, in Scotland. The Duke of Argyll's burgh of Inveraray (Strathclyde), started in the 1740s, has a basically T-shaped plan, while in the north-east towns such as New Cullen and Fochabers have rather spartan grid plans, relieved only by market squares. One of the most attractive foundations of the period is Helensburgh (Strathclyde), named after the wife of its founder Sir James Colquhoun. Begun in 1776, it employs a regular grid, but with liberal use of green spaces.

Garden cities and new towns

In the rapid urban growth of the 19th century there was little thought for a better environment, but not all towns lacked design or amenities. The Improvement Commissioners who laid out Birkenhead in the mid-19th century provided spacious open squares, as well as parks created by Joseph Paxton, the foremost park designer of his day. The concept of the park as lungs for the working class soon spread to other new industrial towns, such as Middlesbrough. By the end of the century, an appreciation of the need for a less congested environment had flowered into the planning of spacious towns, full of greenery, such as Port Sunlight (1888). The fully worked out garden city concept was the brainchild of Ebenezer Howard, who put his theories into practice at Letchworth (begun in 1903) and, later, at Welwyn Garden City (1920).

The new towns of the modern era, less idealistic than Howard's schemes, emerged out of housing problems exacerbated by the Second World War. The first generation included eight new towns for the Home Counties area, with others designed to revive depressed areas, such as the coalfields of north-east England. Each was built upon principles that were to become standard, including low-density housing and the separation of pedestrians and traffic. The latest phase of new towns, dating from the 1960s and including regional centres such as Milton Keynes and Telford, has similarly provided an abundance of opportunity for experiments with urban design.

CONNECTIONS
Cities: 242–51 *London;* 252–3 *Manchester;* 256–7 *Edinburgh*
Conservation: 128–9 *Conserving the past*
Georgian planning: 238–9 *Spas and seaside resorts*
Industrial communities: 144–5 *The birth of industry;* 236–7 *Factory towns*
The suburbs: 240–41 *Suburbia*

CUMBERNAULD, STRATHCLYDE (**below**), *1956, has the characteristic amenities of a new town, including pedestrian precincts*

Ports

BRISTOL DOCKS *in the 18th century. Bristol's great tidal range meant that a ship in port would be grounded twice daily. Ships pursuing regular trade with the city had to have their hulls strengthened.*

In the Middle Ages, when Britain's overseas trade was concentrated on Europe and the Mediterranean, the busiest ports were those facing the English Channel and the North Sea. This bias was reflected in the trading success of the Cinque Ports (Dover, Sandwich, Romney, Hythe and Hastings), which from Anglo-Saxon times until the 16th century were awarded special privileges in return for supplying ships and crews for royal service. However, with the rise of the Atlantic economy in the 16th and 17th centuries, many merchants began to turn their attention to the west-facing ports. An indication of this trend was the rise of Bristol. London, though, continued to handle the greatest volume of traffic: as Daniel Defoe was later to remark, it 'sucked the vitals of trade in this island to itself'.

Modernization

At the end of the 18th century, all ports were still at the mercy of the tides. At London, ships either tied up at the wharves and at low tide lay on the bottom, or moored mid-stream and were serviced by small craft known as lighters. Around 1700, however, the first wet dock was opened at Rotherhithe: a basin with a constant level of water, which ships could enter by means of locks. Many wet docks were added to major British ports between the 1790s and the 1820s.

Liverpool overtook Bristol in importance in the later 18th century. A gradual programme of modernization resulted by 1890 in a dock system stretching over 6 miles along the Mersey. Glasgow enjoyed a marked expansion of shipping with the canalization of the Clyde after the 1770s, but relied entirely on marginal quays until 1867.

London, meanwhile, had acquired a highly elaborate complex. The first phase of expansion

A CUTTER-SUCTION DREDGER (***below***) *removing chalk for the construction of new berths at Ramsgate, Kent. The principle is that of a vacuum-cleaner.*

THE PORT OF LIVERPOOL

The image of the Liverpool merchant in the 18th century is distorted by his links with the slave trade, but the port was also a major import centre for tobacco and sugar. In the 19th century a vast range of cargoes was handled, including cotton, grain, timber and rubber for import, and coal and metal and cotton goods for export. Facilities developed rapidly after the completion of the first wet dock in 1720.

In the 19th-century expansion of the dock estate, the central figure was Jesse Hartley. During his period as dock engineer from 1824 until his death in 1860, he more than doubled the total area of berths. It was he who gave the dockland the heavily fortified appearance it still bears today: he protected his docks behind a high stone wall.

In modern times the greatest development has been the Royal Seaforth Dock, built on a stretch of reclaimed foreshore and opened in 1973. It has specialized facilities for grain, meat, timber and containers, as well as highly efficient general cargo berths.

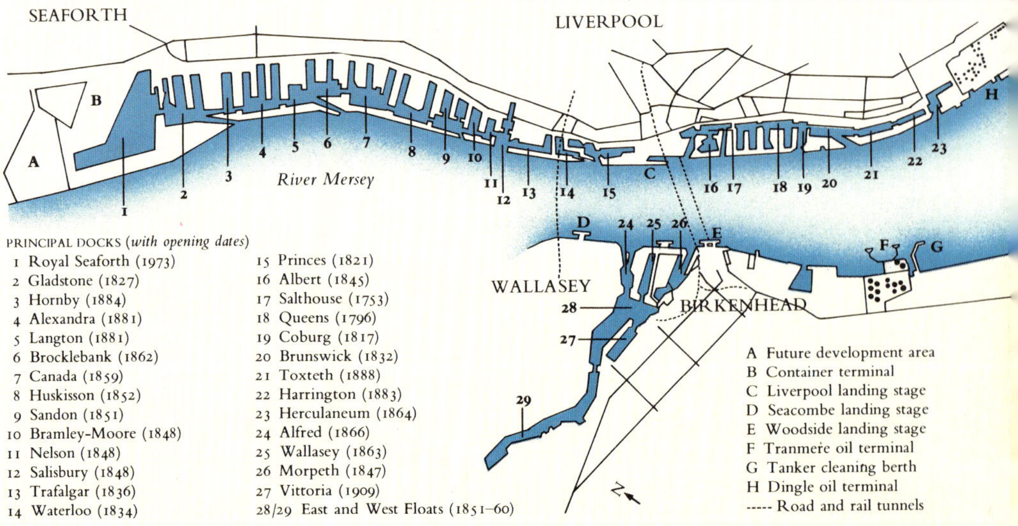

PRINCIPAL DOCKS (*with opening dates*)

1 Royal Seaforth (1973)
2 Gladstone (1827)
3 Hornby (1884)
4 Alexandra (1881)
5 Langton (1881)
6 Brocklebank (1862)
7 Canada (1859)
8 Huskisson (1852)
9 Sandon (1851)
10 Bramley-Moore (1848)
11 Nelson (1848)
12 Salisbury (1848)
13 Trafalgar (1836)
14 Waterloo (1834)
15 Princes (1821)
16 Albert (1845)
17 Salthouse (1753)
18 Queens (1796)
19 Coburg (1817)
20 Brunswick (1832)
21 Toxteth (1888)
22 Harrington (1883)
23 Herculaneum (1864)
24 Alfred (1866)
25 Wallasey (1863)
26 Morpeth (1847)
27 Vittoria (1909)
28/29 East and West Floats (1851–60)

A Future development area
B Container terminal
C Liverpool landing stage
D Seacombe landing stage
E Woodside landing stage
F Tranmere oil terminal
G Tanker cleaning berth
H Dingle oil terminal
----- Road and rail tunnels

THE TILBURY COMPLEX (*left*). *The original Tilbury docks were opened in 1886. From the mid-1960s the site was massively redeveloped for the handling of container and bulk grain traffic and packaged forest products. Tilbury continues to handle more conventional cargoes, however.*

ALBERT DOCK, *opened in 1845, is Jesse Hartley's masterpiece. It incorporated the latest hydraulic machinery.*

created the West India Docks (1802), the Surrey Commercial Docks (1807) and St Katharine Dock (1828), the latter taking the unprecedented step of bringing its warehouses right up to the water's edge. In 1855 the Victoria Dock was opened down-river, the first of three great Royal Docks, and the first in the country to have direct rail links to its quays. All over Britain the railways were having a profound effect on the ports. Southampton's rapid development as a passenger port followed the acquisition of its docking facilities by a railway company in the 1890s.

By the end of the 19th century, the increase in the size of ships was putting pressure on many of the ports, and this could only be eased by the construction of more generously sized berths. At the same time ports were beginning to acquire more specialized dock systems. Silos were provided for grain, stacking yards for timber. The south Wales coal-exporting ports of Swansea, Barry and Newport were the first to become totally specialized.

The 20th century

The continuing trend towards specialization in modern times is represented by great oil terminals like Milford Haven and by the terminals developed to cater for bulk ore carriers, such as those at Port Talbot and Immingham.

The history of the ports in the 20th century has become closely bound up with the need for deep-water facilities. This has stimulated a migration towards the estuary mouths, sometimes leaving derelict areas of dockland up-river. The classic case is London. In the 1950s the Royal Docks acquired new equipment for the mechanical handling of chilled meat and special sheds for fruit and vegetables, but in the early years of the following decade the Port of London Authority (PLA) recognized that its future lay instead at Tilbury, near the mouth of the Thames.

A HOVERCRAFT UNLOADING *at Pegwell Bay, Ramsgate. A regular service to Calais is operated, carrying cars and passengers. The first commercial hovercraft made its maiden voyage in 1959.*

Tilbury is now the largest non-fuel seaport in Britain. It has led the way in the growth of container traffic – the use of standardized containers which are either loaded on and off ship by crane (the LO-LO system) or, at ports with roll-on/roll-off (RO-RO) facilities, are driven on and off in container lorries which travel in the ship's hold.

Ports such as Dover, Felixstowe, Harwich and Hull have shared handsomely in the expansion of container traffic. Felixstowe, for example, has grown from a small grain and timber dock, in the 1950s, to become a major RO-RO port.

CONNECTIONS
The Port of London: 248–9 *London*
The Royal Navy: 122–3 *The armed forces*
Trade with the world: 100–101 *Britain in the world marketplace*

Farms

Farm buildings, of whatever period, take us close to the everyday realities of living in the countryside. As with factories, the form is usually the perfect expression of the function. Present-day farm architecture conveys the complex dynamics of the modern farming scene, while historic buildings can serve as illuminating guide-posts to the economic past, identifying periods and regions of relative prosperity. Many old farming structures have undergone changes of use: for example, stables (originally used for oxen as well as horses) were sometimes turned into milking parlours.

Farm buildings and farmsteads

Surviving medieval farm buildings do not represent the whole range of farming practice, since most types were rudely built in ephemeral materials. However, the barns and dovecotes of wealthy estates were often made of stone, and those that endure today are telling indicators of the strict hierarchy of medieval society. The tithes owed to ecclesiastical landowners by their tenants demanded vast, secure barns for storage, such as those at Bradford-on-Avon (Wiltshire) and at Great Coxwell (Oxfordshire).

The dovecote symbolizes secular rather than ecclesiastical authority. The keeping of pigeons or doves for fresh meat at times of the year when little else was available was for long a seigneurial privilege, although nesting-boxes became a regular feature of many farms in the 17th century.

In the post-medieval period, styles of agricultural architecture were slow to change. It was not until the end of the 18th century, for example, that the old style of barn was transformed. The traditional barn generally had two pairs of large doors on opposite walls. Between them was a central passageway (through which the cart passed during unloading), with storage bays to either side. The passage was also used as a threshing floor, and winnowing was assisted by having both sets of doors open to create a through-draught. Mechanized threshing equipment, which could be taken into the fields, had begun to make the threshing barn redundant by the mid-19th century. There was a transitional period, however, when horse-powered and steam-powered machinery was used in barns, some of which acquired wheel-houses or incongruous chimneys.

An interesting variant of the barn was the field barn, used on hilly terrain for corn storage and threshing, to avoid having to cart corn to the farmstead itself. It was usually attached to a shed and foldyard for a few cattle, which converted the straw to manure, again avoiding difficult journeys. Field barns ceased to be built around 1850, and

A MEDIEVAL DOVECOTE (***below***), *at Richmond Castle, Heref. and Worcs. The circular design was typical.*

A MODEL DAIRY (***left***) *at Easton Farm Park, Suffolk, 1870. An unusually ornate example, with tiled floor, cooling fountain, marble shelves and stained-glass windows. This dairy was a separate building, but most were part of the farmhouse.*

A VICTORIAN MODEL FARM

This large farm – an extraordinarily self-reliant complex – was devised by Sir Thomas Tancred in the later 19th century. Although the plan was never carried out, it is not totally fantastic, as many farms of the period followed the same principle of rationalization, with an ordered layout of multiple yards, and steam-powered mechanization. Note in particular the tramways in the stackyard and the chimney-topped engine-house.

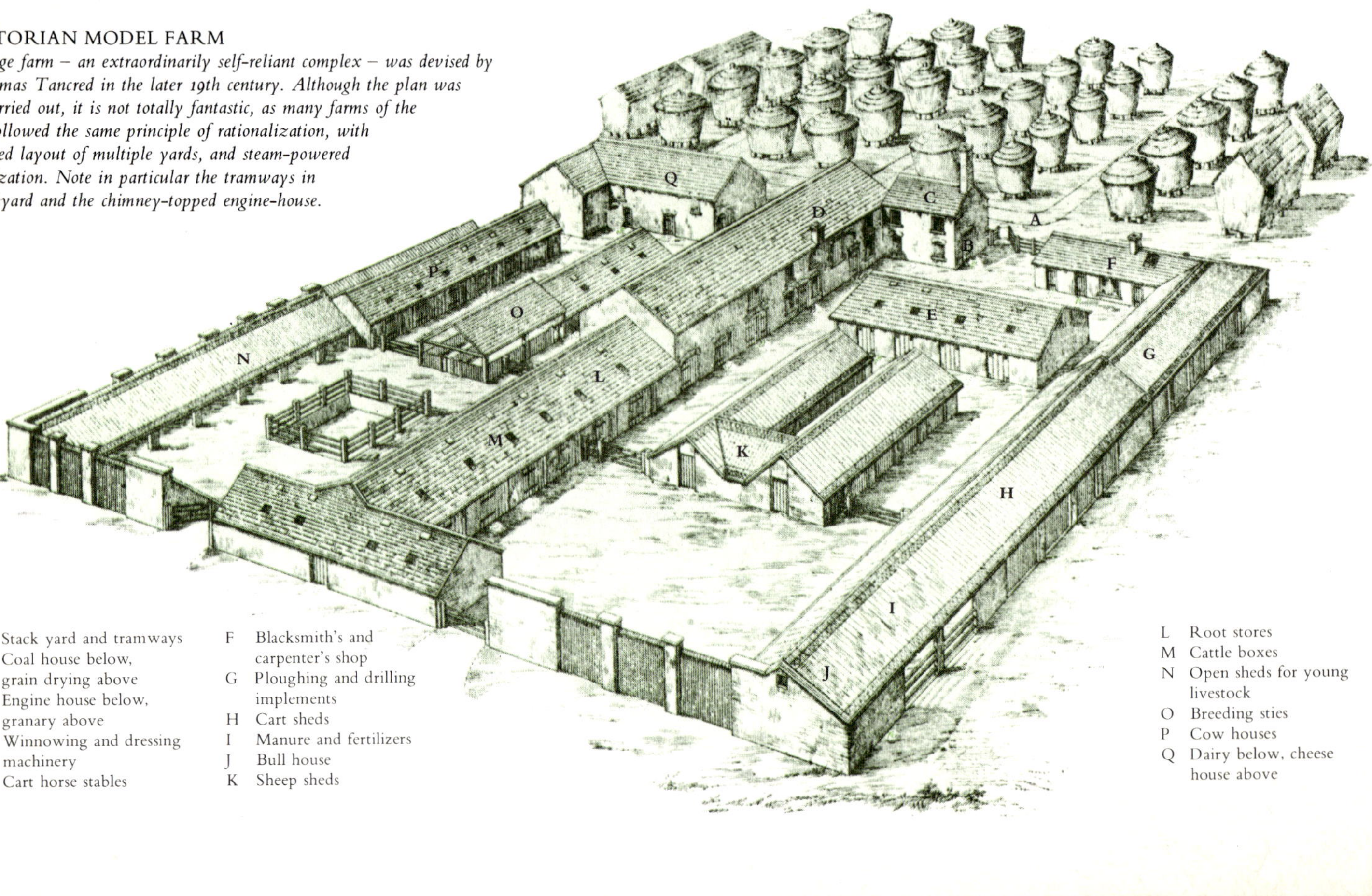

- A Stack yard and tramways
- B Coal house below, grain drying above
- C Engine house below, granary above
- D Winnowing and dressing machinery
- E Cart horse stables
- F Blacksmith's and carpenter's shop
- G Ploughing and drilling implements
- H Cart sheds
- I Manure and fertilizers
- J Bull house
- K Sheep sheds
- L Root stores
- M Cattle boxes
- N Open sheds for young livestock
- O Breeding sties
- P Cow houses
- Q Dairy below, cheese house above

those that have not disappeared are now mostly derelict. A cousin of the conventional threshing barn was the wall-less Dutch barn, used for storage of hay or straw but seldom for grain. This type was built in considerable numbers after about 1880. The later examples were iron-framed with a corrugated roof.

Livestock has been accommodated in a great variety of regional building types. In the Pennines and the Welsh uplands, the longhouse, which sheltered cattle and household under the same roof, remained standard until well into the 19th century. Other styles included the open-fronted Worcestershire cowhouse and the Devonshire linhay – again open-fronted, but with an open loft above.

The piggery, surprisingly, is a building of relatively recent origin. Pigs were originally kept in woodlands under the care of the village swineherd, and it was not until the 17th and 18th centuries that they were brought into the farmyard. Usually they were housed in a sty – a warm shelter adjacent to a walled run. On dairy farms, where the pigs were fattened on by-products of butter-making and cheese-making, sties were often built in long rows.

Most of the farmsteads of the present day have a layout dating from the period 1750–1880, when many old farms were modernized and many new ones built (often on a regular plan round one or two yards with one open side, although in the 19th century some of the richer farms were based on multiple yards).

The modern farm

Few new farm buildings were constructed in the first three decades of the present century, but since the Second World War the rate of transformation has been rapid. Modern practices have required new structures. As long ago as 1968 it was estimated that one third of all existing farm buildings were erected after 1957 (when government grants became available). Since then, the pace of change has become even faster. The traditional granary, for example – a small storehouse, usually raised on mushroom-shaped 'staddle stones' to protect the grain from vermin – has been superseded by far more sophisticated grain stores. Other new building types include specialist units for pigs and poultry.

The most up-to-date farms are unromantic complexes of steel, concrete and asbestos, built to a national rather than a regional pattern, and essentially industrial in spirit. Luckily, however, among the prefabricated units, an old stable, cowshed, piggery or cartshed may often be found intact, although adapted to modern needs.

A FARMSTEAD (***below***) *at Howgill, near Sedburgh, N. Yorks., as it was in the 1940s. The external staircases were a common feature of traditional farm architecture: they usually gave access to a granary, built over a cartshed open at one side.*

IN THE COMPOST YARD. *Manure manufacture is now a specialized industry, which is highly mechanized.*

A MODERN BEEF FEED LOT *at Severn Springs, Glos. Many agricultural landscapes have been transformed by tower silos, in which grass is stored in a vacuum to conserve its moisture. Grass is a more nutritious cattle feed than hay, and wet weather does not interfere with its making.*

CONNECTIONS

The feudal system: 132–3 *Medieval agriculture*
Technology on the farm: 134–5 *The agricultural revolution;* **136–7** *The impact of the new farming;* **138–9** *Modern agriculture*
Tithe barns: 206–7 *Monasteries*

Coal mining towns

The popular image of a coal mining community is of an isolated colony of grim houses hastily put up around a pit-head in the 19th century, a settlement wholly dependent on coal (and hence the colliery owner) for its survival. This view is simplistic. Not all mining settlements, for example, were totally isolated. Many miners lived in sizeable towns such as Leeds or in the sort of urban sprawl that grew up in the Rhondda valley and elsewhere. Neither were miners always at the mercy of a single employer. Pit-owners exerted tremendous social power, but most miners had access to more than one pit and would sometimes move from one colliery to another to better their lot.

Bricks and mortar

In the early phase of the industry, coal mining was a part-time occupation for workers who also kept animals and grew vegetables. Modernization in the 19th century, and the need for a large labour force, lead to the growth of special housing. Colliery-owners augmented existing villages by the addition of colliers' 'rows', or built new planned settlements, which usually comprised ranks of terraces on a linear or square plan. Dwellings on a monotonous grid layout were especially characteristic of Northumberland and Durham.

In Scotland and north-east England, single-storey houses were common, while two-storey dwellings were the rule in other regions. In the north-east a miner's house was usually of rubble stone with a slate roof and a floor of beaten earth (later replaced by tiles or wooden planking). One (or sometimes two) rooms were provided on the ground floor, with an upstairs room (reached by a ladder) where the children slept. The kitchen-cum-living room was dominated by a large metal range with an oven, boiler and fire-grate.

Towards the end of the 19th century, houses tended to become somewhat larger, with two upper rooms, and the quality of sanitation and water supply was also belatedly improved. Shops, churches and other public buildings (apart from pubs) were generally slow in coming, and when they did it was usually through the communities' own efforts: the mine-owner might provide land for a chapel but the major cost of building was shouldered by the miners and their families. The same spirit of self-improvement is evidenced by the growth of the Co-operative stores, and by the successful efforts of some miners to purchase their own homes out of their savings.

THE DURHAM MINE DISASTER *of 1908, in which 14 miners lost their lives owing to a firedamp (or methane) explosion. In spite of the Davy lamp, naked lights were still frequently used. A postcard such as this would have been sold to raise money for the bereaved.*

A PIT PONY (***below***) *in 1938. Ponies were often kept in underground stables, but were generally well looked after. This horse had been specially groomed to take part in the Royal Horse Show at Cardiff.*

TAYLORSTOWN, THE RHONDDA VALLEY (***below***). *This was a region in which individual house-ownership was not uncommon, even in the 19th century. By 1900 almost one fifth of all houses in the south Wales coalfield were owned by colliery workers.*

A MINER'S LIVING ROOM (***right***)*: a reconstructed interior of the 1890s. The bed was folded up during the day into a sideboard.*

THE MINESCAPE OF SOUTH WALES. *The wheels of the pit-head machinery loom over miners' terraces in the village of Abercynon.*

The mining community

The history of the coal industry is grimly overshadowed by appalling working conditions and, on the whole, cramped, unhealthy housing. The first of a long sequence of tragic mine explosions was at Gateshead Colliery, Tyneside, in 1705. The Davy lamp, over a century later, made an important contribution to safety, but explosions still happened. One of the most serious was in 1913, when a coal-dust explosion in the Senghenydd Colliery in the Aber valley caused 439 deaths.

The shared dangers of the mining community engendered a strong community spirit. There was a powerful will to improve conditions, which led to the formation of the first unions in the north-east in the 1840s. However, not until the first decade of the 20th century was a united fighting front achieved. Among the crises that lay ahead were the general misery of the 1926 strike and the Depression, and the closure of 229 pits between 1965 and 1971 in the context of reduced oil prices.

Home and leisure

The nature of a miner's work caused great disruption to domestic life, and his wife's lot was correspondingly arduous. Families tended to be large. Extra housework was caused by the multiple-shift system: in a family with working sons there was always someone who needed feeding and bathing. The latter took place in a tin tub – by the early 20th century pit baths were still a rarity, and miners had to pay to use them.

The custom of paying wages in pubs strengthened the miners' reputation for drunkenness, and some employers opened libraries and reading rooms, as well as non-licensed clubs, as rival attractions. However, there were already more sober pursuits to occupy the precious time above ground. Horticulture was very popular, and allotment-grown leeks and flowers carried off prizes at exhibitions. Pigeon-racing also had its enthusiasts, and many colliery bands and choirs made more than a local name for themselves.

CONNECTIONS
The coal industry: 150–51 *Coal*
The Co-operative movement: 102–3 *Reaching the consumer*
Unionization: 84–5 *Workers' movements*

Factory towns

SALTAIRE: PATERNALISM IN PRACTICE

The working community of Saltaire, W. Yorks., was begun in 1851 in a pleasant valley on the River Aire. Its founder Sir Titus Salt (1803–76) (***right***), a Bradford wool-manufacturer, saw it as his Christian duty to put the welfare of his workers before personal profit. In addition to well-planned and relatively comfortable houses, the workers at his new textile mill had access to various specially provided amenities such as gardens, allotments, shops, a hospital, and almshouses for the old. Significantly, though, no provision was made in Saltaire for public houses, as Sir Titus felt that intemperance had contributed to the squalor of Bradford, where he had made his fortune.

By the mid-19th century more British people lived in towns and cities than in country areas, as the concentration of large labour forces had made the factories a focus of early urban growth. The early industrial period was the age of the 'walking city': workers lived close to their factories so that they could walk to work. Accordingly, workers' housing tended towards dense, multi-storeyed dwellings, crowding in as many people as possible.

The court dwellings of the first factory towns had an especially bad reputation. Jerry-built, they offered cramped, inadequately lit living quarters and only the most rudimentary sanitation, with open drains, ash pits (not water closets) and communal water supplies. Change came partly through statutory reforms, which began to produce a visible improvement in the quality of working-class housing from the mid-19th century onwards. The court layout was increasingly superseded by streets of terraced back-to-back houses.

Perhaps the most interesting new towns of the Victorian age were those that mushroomed from small beginnings. Middlesbrough (Cleveland) was one such place. In 1801 it comprised a hamlet with four houses and twenty-five people; by 1851 it had 7,000 inhabitants; but by 1900 the population had reached 90,000. Behind this increase lay Middlesbrough's success, first as a coal-exporting town and, after the mid-century, as a centre of iron-smelting and, later, of steelmaking. In 1830 the embryo of the new town was laid out along geometric lines on a marshy site beside the River Tees. Before long, housing development was rapidly inundating the open land lying south of the railway. This new growth had a bare, functional appearance – a townscape described by a contemporary as 'hastily located, instantly occupied', formed of 'rows of little brown streets'.

Industrial feudalism

Not all industrial settlements were built as cheaply and quickly as possible by the factory masters. Some employers provided decent housing and

A KNOCKER-UP (***left***) *in 1929. The knocker-up's job, originating in the days when few working-class households had a clock, was to give early-morning calls to factory hands, using his wire-pronged pole.*

OLDHAM, LANCS. (***right***), *in 1936. Typified by long rows of terraced housing and tall factory chimneys, 'coketowns' such as this sprang up with the expansion of the cotton trade and engineering.*

FACTORY LIFE IN THE 1950s. *The exodus from Austin's Motor Works at Birmingham at the end of the working day* (***above***)*; and a mill-workers' lunch-break in a factory canteen in the Lancashire town of Shaw* (***right***).

improved working conditions for their employees. Notable among such enlightened industrialists was Robert Owen of New Lanark (Strathclyde). Like Josiah Wedgwood, who built his mansion at Etruria in the Potteries within sight of his kilns, Owen placed his own house right among his workers' dwellings. Until the late 19th century many of the 'masters' in smaller industrial towns, such as Wakefield or Huddersfield, shared this preference for living among the sights, sounds and smells of their enterprises. The relative integration of these industrialists into the communities which they had helped to create earned them an almost feudal loyalty from the lowlier inhabitants. Factory workers participated in jamborees for the coming of age of millowners' eldest sons, and often followed their masters' voting behaviour. By contrast, after the middle of the century, the employing classes of large cities were moving to 'villas' in the greener suburbs, which they alone could afford to penetrate.

The modern age

Factories of the 20th century have been more 'footloose' than their Victorian forebears. Liberated by the transport revolution from the need to be close to coalfields, the modern light industries have concentrated on the Midlands–Greater London axis, often in areas where there is no working-class tradition. Industrial estates, made up of factories, have grown up all over the country, beginning with Trafford Park, Manchester.

In the north, the working-class tradition persists, but it has been weakened by socio-economic changes. Home-ownership and the television have damaged even such well-established communal foci as the pub and the football match.

CONNECTIONS
Housing: 226–7 *Town houses;* **228–9** *Town planning*
L.S. Lowry's Salford: 294–5 *Artists and places*
New Lanark: 144–5 *The birth of industry*
Recreation: 118–19 *Sporting Britain*
Textiles: 160–63 *Cotton*
Town expansion: 240–41 *Suburbia*

Spas and seaside resorts

BRITAIN'S FINEST SPAS
The growth of the early resorts was influenced by travellers' experiences of the Continental spas after the Civil War. British spas reached the zenith of their popularity in the 18th century, when they acquired distinctive and impressive townscapes.
Today, the architecture and atmosphere of many of these pleasure-towns is extremely well preserved, and some, such as Bath and Buxton, are important cultural centres.

BATHING AT LOWESTOFT, *Suffolk,* c. *1900. Bathers changed close to the sea in bathing machines, and the sexes were segregated.*

TAKING THE WATERS *at Bath, by Thomas Rowlandson, 1798. The Pump Room was the spa's social centre.*

BATHING BELLES AT BUTLIN'S. *The commercial holiday camps begun by William Butlin at Skegness (Lincs.) in 1937 created a new style of holiday, with regimented fun and games.*

Water's healing and therapeutic properties have been recognized from an early date. The mineral waters of Buxton in Derbyshire were appreciated by the Romans, and the pleasurable therapy of bathing in hot springs also made Bath a popular Roman resort. In the Middle Ages, curative springs and wells were thought to have religious potency, and were much frequented. However the rise of the modern spa (and, later, of the seaside resort) was stimulated by the recommendations of fashionable physicians, and by the urge to cut a dash among high society in the pursuit of health.

Fashionable watering-places

The first town to match the popularity of any of the Continental spas was Tunbridge Wells in Kent. A nobleman suffering from overindulgence in the capital was cured by drinking Tunbridge waters in the early 17th century. Then, in 1630, Queen Henrietta Maria was sent there by her physician to recuperate from childbirth. London society and a range of new entertainments followed in her wake. The Puritans referred to the town's springs as the 'waters of scandal', but the growth of the new pleasure-centres was unstoppable. In the Restoration period, spa therapy, rationalized by doctors and encouraged by property developers, was undoubtedly a boom industry.

The 18th-century renaissance of Bath was in large part the work of Queen Anne (a visitor in 1702) and of the socially talented Richard ('Beau') Nash, who gave a heightened elegance to the water-taking ceremony. Bath's rapid rise in prosperity was soon reflected in the building of a splendid set of Assembly Rooms (1769–71) and a new Pump Room (1789–99), where three glasses of water were taken before lunch and another three afterwards, to an accompaniment of music, conversation and the arrangement of marriages. Other spas, such as Buxton and Cheltenham, followed Bath in acquiring spacious layouts with promenades and gardens.

In the Victorian age, the jewel of all the spas was Harrogate, where at the height of its popularity there were a thousand treatments daily. Matlock Bath in Derbyshire, dominated by John Smedley's Hydro building (1852), was also a flourishing resort until the eve of the First World War.

The bracing sea air

In the 1730s an enthusiasm for the benefits of cold bathing inspired the growth of a small spa at Scarborough on the Yorkshire coast. This was the first of a new species of resort. In 1752 a Dr Russell of Lewes published a medical treatise on the healthful properties of sea-water – for drinking as

ST IVES, CORNWALL. *It was not until the early 20th century that the Cornish fishing villages were turned into popular resorts.*

A SEASIDE SWEET SHOP, *Llandudno (Gwynedd). Sticky treats (especially rock and candy floss) are the stock-in-trade of the seaside salesman.*

TENBY, DYFED. *The town was rescued from decline in the 19th century by Sir William Paxton and other developers.*

THE PALACE PIER, BRIGHTON, E. SUSSEX: *the most famous of all pleasure piers, begun in 1891 as a replacement for the old Chain Pier, which was reaching the end of its life. Just to the west is the famous pier (1863–6) by Eugenius Birch.*

well as for self-immersion. Two years earlier he had settled at Brighthelmstone, soon to be known as Brighton. Dr Johnson was among the early visitors to this increasingly popular resort, but a greater cachet was the presence of the Prince of Wales, who came to live here in 1784.

At first the flavour of resorts such as Brighton, Lyme Regis or Bournemouth did not much differ from that of the spas, but in the 19th century there was a movement down the social scale, brought about by the advent of cheap, efficient transport. Even before the first railways, working-class day-trippers travelled from London to Margate, Ramsgate and Southend by steamboat. Trains enlarged the flow, as well as promoting the growth of new resorts, particularly in the north. Blackpool, especially, became a mecca for mill-workers, its first pier opening in 1863. As wages rose and holidays lengthened, entertainments in the seaside resorts multiplied, and new regions such as the south-west were unlocked to holiday-makers.

Today, the most popular of the resorts have an atmosphere that is often brash, always very English and usually somewhat old-fashioned.

CONNECTIONS

Coastal scenery: 26–7 *The changing shoreline*

Festivals in spas: 300–301 *Music and song*

Fishing villages: 140–41 *Fishing*

The impact of the railways: 264–5 *The railway revolution*

Royalty at Brighton: 214–15 *Royal retreats*

Suburbia

Suburbia as we think of it today is largely a creation of the 1920s and 1930s. It has been subjected to savage criticism as a residential environment. The International Congress of Modern Architecture (1933) declared that 'the suburb is a symbol of waste . . . a kind of scum churning against the wall of the city'. It was attacked on many fronts – for upholding the values of selfish individualism at a time when collectivism was a more respectable doctrine, for tarnishing town and country alike with a formless sprawl of ill-designed houses, for clogging with traffic the approach roads to town centres. The planner Thomas Sharp, who claimed that suburban development was a distraction from the pressing need for urban renewal, put his finger on the suburban paradox in 1940: 'anyone who goes to the suburbs seeking the edge of the countryside pushes the countryside away from someone else.'

BEDFORD PARK, CHISWICK, *west London. The first planned garden suburb, laid out by Norman Shaw in 1875. There was a high proportion of artists and writers among the original inhabitants.*

A HORSE TRAM IN PORTSMOUTH (***below***), *1901. Portsmouth was quick to take advantage of the 1870 Tramway Act, which empowered local authorities to buy up certain private tramways.*

CLEANING THE MORRIS EIGHT (***left***) *outside a suburban 'semi' of the 1930s. The number of car-owners rose from 109,000 in 1919 to 2 million by 1939.*

THE LURE OF THE COUNTRYSIDE (***below***): *a London Underground poster of 1908. In those days the tube train surfaced right in the midst of the rural landscape, reinforcing the sharp contrast of town and country.*

These dismissals ignored the fact that the inter-war semi-detached suburban house was the exact fulfilment of an ideal. It provided the freedom and status of house-ownership, the luxury of a large rear garden and countless other comforts and conveniences to millions of families. Unlike many of the dreams cherished by architects, it was an ideal that has never become obsolete.

Centrifugal forces

The first wave of fashionable suburbanization dates from the 17th century. In London the plague of 1665 and the Great Fire accelerated the aristocratic drift to the developing West End. In the following century the appeal of the Picturesque took Londoners to outlying villages such as Hampstead or Greenwich. One of the most elegant planned suburbs of the period was St John's Wood (1794–1830), with its layout of detached and semi-detached houses. Parallel tendencies were also evident in provincial towns: Edgbaston, for example, was created by Sir Henry Gough as an exclusive satellite of Birmingham.

Generally, the Victorian middle classes were repelled by the towns which made them wealthy. The unhealthy conditions, and the proximity of workers whose discontent might at any moment break out into violence, made it preferable to live in the outskirts. In the suburban belt created by this centrifugal movement, the unified, Georgian style of planning continued at first to be fashionable. Before long, however, individualism became the norm. The chronology of suburban planning is well illustrated at Oxford: Park Town (1853–5), the earliest residential extension, was a haven of terraced crescents and public gardens, but further growth northwards in the 1860s was based on the detached villa with a large garden.

By the last quarter of the 19th century, the suburban arcadia was no longer the exclusive domain of the wealthy. Cheaper public transport extended its social range. In London, where the spreading net of the railways determined the pattern of expansion, the outward drift was encouraged by the introduction of the first workman's fare (1864). Trams, which first appeared in 1860, at Birkenhead, had the same effect. By the end of Victoria's reign, there were eighty-nine private tram systems, as well as sixty-one in the control of local authorities. To accommodate the lower income groups now being admitted to the suburbs, smaller, cheaper houses were built. The Dutch-influenced 'Queen Anne' manner popularized by R. Norman Shaw was still influential, but by the 1880s and 1890s simple terraced houses, for rent, were also making an appearance.

The inter-war boom

Denigrators of suburbia forgot the practical achievement: Lloyd George's catchphrase 'Homes for heroes' was the starting-signal for a tremendous building boom. In the two decades after 1919, over 4 million new dwellings were built, nearly 3 million of them by private enterprise. Rented housing was provided for the working classes on council estates, but for many of the middle classes the lowering of building society interest rates realized for the first time the dream of ownership. In 1937 a suburban 'semi' with a garage and a large garden could cost as little as £480.

The continued extension of public transport took the suburbs right into the heart of the country. The fastest rate of growth was achieved by London's Metropolitan line, whose posters tempted families into 'Metro-land' with a powerful tug of rural imagery. The houses themselves were agglomerations of symbols. False timbers on the 'Tudor-

THE GRANADA CINEMA, TOOTING, *south London. Inter-war suburbanites had a great appetite for Hollywood-style fantasy. Their cathedrals were the ornate super-cinemas of the 1930s.*

bethan' gables conjured up a golden age of English achievement, while the ubiquitous sunrise motif (especially on garden gates) was appropriate to the view of suburbia as a land of promise. Garden gnomes, initially imported from Germany, had a cluster of symbolic meanings, including fertility, industriousness, guardianship. Many houses had exterior walls of 'pebbledash' – a status-asserting simulacrum of stone.

Such a wealth of associations was inimical to the Modernist spirit of architecture, which regarded a house as a machine for living in. Modernism made two significant contributions to suburbia: the functional London tube stations designed by Charles Holden (for example Arnos Grove) and the 'Sun-trap' house, with its plain lines and curved windows. The first of a number of 'Sun-trap' estates was built at Edgware in 1932. The more avant-garde flat-roofed 'Sunspan' house, however, was never popular. The obstacle to its acceptance was that Modernism was the fashionable language of factories and office blocks. Suburbanites wanted their houses to be homely: as in the 19th century, home and work had to be poles apart.

CONNECTIONS
Garden cities: 228–9 *Town planning*
The growth of London: 244–51 *London*
The growth of Manchester: 252–3 *Manchester*
Housing: 226–7 *Town houses*
The railways: 262–3 *The railway age;* **264–5** *The railway revolution*

PRUNING THE ANIMALS. *Individualism in the suburbs is often expressed in the garden. These topiary dogs, at Wolverhampton, W. Midlands, deny the myth that suburbia is always bland.*

THE NINE MUSES IN SUBURBIA. *In the living room of a 'semi' in Leyton, east London, the painter Gerald Binns has covered the entire walls and ceiling with an elaborate* trompe l'œil *allegory.*

'EXECUTIVE' HOUSING (***below***) *at Shenfield, Essex. Shuttered windows, pedimented doorways and bow windows are the totems of the 'executive' style.*

London/*The beginnings of a capital*

It was the Romans who, shortly after their invasion of Britain in AD 43, first recognized the gravel beds by the Thames as the ideal site for a bridge and a tidal port. The original settlement did not last long. In AD 61 it was burnt to the ground by Queen Boudicca's warriors, who massacred the inhabitants, tossed severed heads into the River Walbrook (the skulls have been dug up near the Mansion House) and razed every fragile building. But by now the Romans knew Londinium to be the key to their British province. It was quickly built again over 325 acres (130 ha) and later enclosed by a three-mile wall, of which parts are still visible.

A few so-called Roman remains, like the ancient bath near the Strand, may be dubious, and the whole of Roman London is now some six metres (19 ft) below the present street level. However, it is certainly true that, until the Empire fell apart in the 5th century, London was one of Rome's important provincial centres. Foreign ships crowded the wharves; good roads radiated from the gates; and the forum and basilica – a vast complex of public buildings – formed one of the largest such centres in Roman Europe.

The legions left as the Roman Empire crumbled. But London remained, decayed though never deserted, even in the darkest of the Dark Ages. In the Anglo-Saxon era Ethelbert, King of Kent, probably had a palace where the Roman fort had been. He appointed the earliest bishop in 604 and began building the first St Paul's. Other Saxon churches sprang up, such as All Hallows by the Tower, where a good Saxon arch can still be seen. Invading Danes sacked and burnt the city, but King Alfred (871–99) made it strong again. When the Vikings sailed up in a hundred galleys to attack London Bridge, they were driven off. However, when the Dane Canute became King of England in 1016 he proved a great stimulus to London's prosperity. The church of St Clement Danes stands on the grave of his son, Harold Harefoot. Few traces of that stormy time remain, apart from drawings in Anglo-Saxon manuscripts and small objects, such as the Viking combs and gambling counters now in the London Museum. True, Edward the Confessor (1042–66) founded Westminster Abbey, but of course it is not his church that we see today.

The Middle Ages

With the Norman Conquest of 1066 London began to acquire some of its still familiar landmarks. William himself commissioned the building of the White Tower, the core of the Tower of London. At the Palace of Westminster his son Rufus built the great hall, though its roof dates from Richard II's reign. The crumbling city walls were built up again and remained the boundary of the city proper, though never in fact assailed in war. Slowly the population crept back to its level in Roman times (about 45,000), but it was still only 50,000 in 1509.

Many people preferred to live outside the city walls. Names like Smithfield and St-Martin-in-the-Fields recall the open country where the townsfolk enjoyed their archery and other sports. But by degrees the houses spread in many directions.

From 1176 to 1209 the foundations of London Bridge were rebuilt in stone – they lasted until 1831. On the far bank the suburb of Southwark, the starting-point for Chaucer's Canterbury pilgrims, grew larger. Westwards, what with the royal palace, the Abbey and the Law Courts, Westminster became another little city in itself, linked with the original London by a ribbon-development of houses along the bank, or 'strand', of the Thames. Lawyers began to live together in big hostels or 'inns': the Old Hall at Lincoln's Inn can still be seen. The rich merchants, like Dick Whittington, who died in 1423, built great mansions in the old quarter. Part of one such, Crosby Hall, built by a grocer in Bishopsgate in 1466,

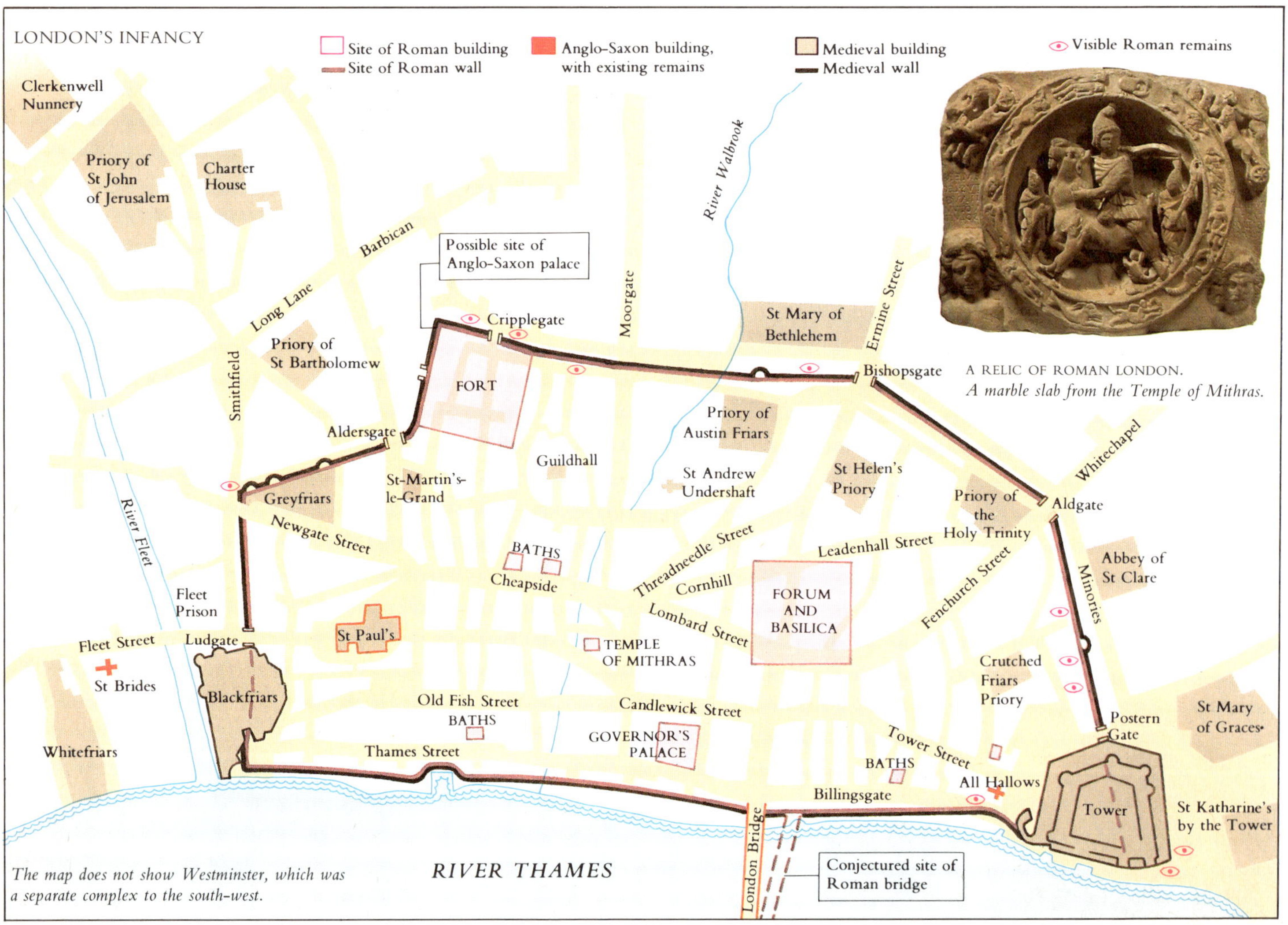

The map does not show Westminster, which was a separate complex to the south-west.

A RELIC OF ROMAN LONDON.
A marble slab from the Temple of Mithras.

THE GREAT HALL, WESTMINSTER *This, the hub of the administration, is the only important survival of the original royal seat. Henry Yevele designed the superb hammerbeam roof.*

THE WHITE TOWER (***right***). *A miniature of c.1500 purporting to show the time when the Duke of Orleans was a prisoner in the Tower following his capture at Agincourt.*

STAPLE INN, 338 HIGH HOLBORN. *The building is unique in London as an example of an Elizabethan domestic exterior.*

ELIZABETHAN LONDON *The City and Westminster are now united. The theatres tended to be sited outside the City's jurisdiction.*

stands today in Chelsea, whither it was transferred stone by stone. At Guildhall, where these merchant princes met as aldermen to run the affairs of their city, the 15th-century crypt is an impressive survival of medieval London.

The Tudor town

Henry VII's superb late Gothic chapel in Westminster Abbey gives us a visible reminder of the transition from medieval to Tudor London. In the 16th century the population grew fourfold: at Elizabeth's death in 1603 it was about two million. When Henry VIII dissolved the monasteries, the precincts of those in London were grabbed for development. New houses mushroomed where cloisters and herb gardens had been. Blackfriars, Whitefriars, Crutched Friars and Charterhouse became names on a street plan. Other buildings seeped out into the 'green belt', despite every royal attempt to check such growth. The new playhouses of Shakespeare's time were established in Finsbury Fields across the Thames on Bankside.

Time and the Great Fire, and later development, have left all too few traces of that 16th-century city. The restored frontage of Staple Inn in High Holborn is a rare Elizabethan survival. We have parts of St James's Palace, built by Henry VIII, and the governor's lodging in the Tower. We also have the church of St Andrew Undershaft (1520–32), worth visiting to see the alabaster bust of John Stow, the tailor whose heart was really in local history and whose *Survey of London*, published in 1598, is an invaluable record of the city he knew. It is in his pages and the other rich literature of his time – everything from ballads and nursery rhymes to the plays of Ben Jonson – that we can really feel closest to the citizens of that age.

CONNECTIONS
Elizabethan theatres: 302–3 *Britain and the theatre*
The Romans: 194–5 *Roman Britain*
The route to Canterbury: 52–3 *Medieval saints and shrines*
Saxons, Vikings and Normans: 42–3 *The movement of peoples*

London/*The age of Pepys*

Many aspects of London in the 17th century – a period of almost hectic transformation – are captured in the *Diary* (1660–69) of Samuel Pepys, an Admiralty official who reveals himself as an engaging, bustling, flirtatious character. He lived through some of the most dramatic events of the city's history. Born near Fleet Street in 1633, Pepys used to trudge as a boy up Ludgate Hill to St Paul's School, which was then in the shadow of the dilapidated medieval cathedral. He was not yet sixteen when he stood in the crowd at Whitehall to see Charles I beheaded in front of the superb Italianate Banqueting House (1625) designed by Inigo Jones. That building serves today as a visible landmark for the beginning of this period; to mark its end we have the great domed St Paul's, which was slowly nearing completion when Pepys died in 1703.

In his seventy years Pepys lived in various parts of the city. He began his married life in Westminster, then moved to Seething Lane, near Tower Hill, adjoining the Navy Office. Later he took a fine house in Buckingham Street, being by then so important in the Admiralty that he simply moved

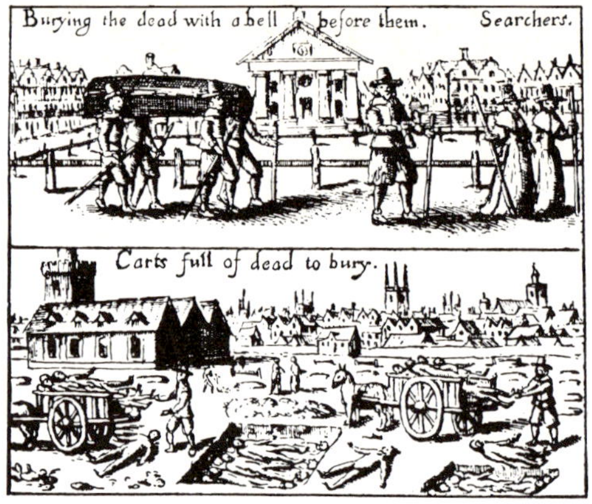

SCENES OF THE PLAGUE. *This contemporary broadsheet shows grim tableaux from the last and most serious outbreak in 1665, when over 70,000 people were recorded to have died.*

A COFFEE-HOUSE (***below right***). *Such meeting-places were introduced after the Civil War and quickly became enormously popular.*

The beginnings of the West End

Up to the outbreak of the Civil War in 1642, the main pressure to build was on the largely open fields to the west. The chief growth areas of London in Pepys's day were in Pall Mall, Piccadilly and St Giles's Fields. In 1611 Piccadilly Hall was built by a tradesman who had made his money from lace collars, or piccadills. By 1627, as other houses sprang up, the road westward became known as Piccadilly. The Lammas Fields owned by the Earl of Leicester were built over, and only one small open space remained, as Leicester Square. The Earl of Salisbury laid out St Martin's Lane where cattle had previously pastured, and the Earl of Bedford commissioned Inigo Jones to lay out an Italian-style piazza over the former monastic grounds still known as Covent Garden. Lincoln's Inn Fields – despite angry protests from the lawyers – were developed by a speculative builder named William Newton. But one grandiose scheme was never realized – a new Whitehall Palace, of which the Banqueting House was only the beginning.

THE RIVER THAMES AT WHITEHALL. *An engraving of the landing stairs by Wenceslaus Hollar.*

THE MARCH OF THE FIRE

1 Leicester House
2 Piccadilly Hall
3 Burlington House
4 Clarendon House
5 St James's Fields
6 St James's Palace
7 Westminster Abbey
8 Westminster Hall
9 Westminster Stairs
10 Whitehall Palace
11 Banqueting House
12 Buckingham Street
13 St Clement Danes
14 Temple Stairs
15 Blackfriars Stairs
16 St Paul's Cathedral
17 Guildhall
18 Royal Exchange
19 The Monument
20 St Olave's
21 Seething Lane

This map shows the extent of the Great Fire of 1666 in the City, and the new 17th-century developments in the West End.

his department with him. He died at the then rural village of Clapham, but was buried beside his wife at St Olave's church, where the couple had worshipped in their Seething Lane days. They lie there still, and we can see the memorial that Pepys erected to his frivolous, trying and much-tried young Elizabeth, for St Olave's survived the Blitz of the Second World War just as it had previously escaped the Great Fire.

That disaster in 1666, following fast on the heels of the Plague, transformed much of the face of the old London. The Great Fire started in a baker's shop in Pudding Lane and swept eastwards through the City for three days. The conflagration reduced to ashes 13,000 houses, the old St Paul's, 87 parish churches and many public buildings. It never reached outlying districts such as the rapidly developing West End, however, and there were few deaths, although more than half of London's population was rendered homeless.

Restoration racketeers

With the Restoration of Charles II in 1660 the interrupted development was resumed at hectic speed, not least because the King, ever short of cash, rewarded his supporters with slices of land. Pepys's first departmental chief, the notorious political fixer George Downing, appropriately secured the site which he profitably developed as the street that still bears his name. Jermyn Street recalls the equally unscrupulous Henry Jermyn, who was leased St James's Field, including the present square and the surrounding streets which he named after Charles II, the Duke of York and others he wished to flatter. The King restored the long-neglected St James's Park and threw it open to the public. The game of *paille maille* (an odd mixture of golf and croquet) was transferred from Pall Mall to the Mall. The former ground was then built on; Nell Gwynne had a house there, and Pepys once saw her there, chatting over the garden wall with the King.

Pepys's day

The King, Nell Gwynne and Pepys himself, and many others who figure in his diary, are vividly represented in the National Portrait Gallery. Surviving objects from that era are, of course, numer-

THE SURVIVING 'WREN' CHURCHES IN THE CITY

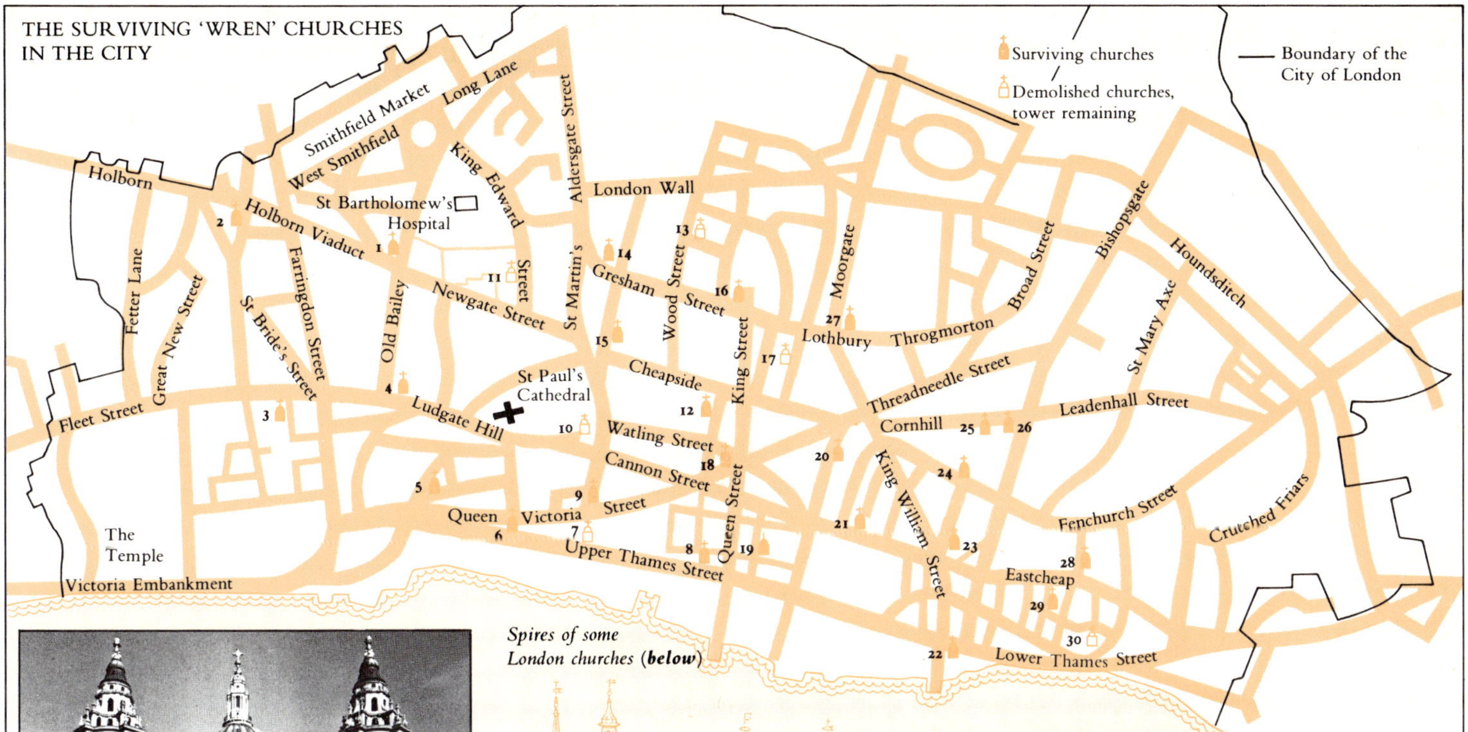

Spires of some London churches (***below***)

ST PAUL'S CATHEDRAL (***left***). *The façade.*

1 St Sepulchre
2 St Andrew, Holborn
3 St Bride
4 St Martin, Ludgate
5 St Andrew-by-the-Wardrobe
6 St Benet, Paul's Wharf
7 St Mary Somerset
8 St James Garlickhithe
9 St Nicholas Cole Abbey
10 St Augustine
11 Christ Church, Newgate Street
12 St Mary-le-Bow
13 St Alban
14 SS Anne and Agnes
15 St Vedast
16 St Lawrence Jewry
17 St Olave, Old Jewry
18 St Mary Aldermary
19 St Michael Paternoster Royal
20 St Stephen Walbrook
21 St Mary Abchurch
22 St Magnus
23 St Clement Eastcheap
24 St Edmund the King
25 St Michael Cornhill
26 St Peter Cornhill
27 St Margaret, Lothbury
28 St Margaret Pattens
29 St Mary-at-Hill
30 St Dunstan-in-the-East

ous, though perhaps none so eloquent as the handbell (in the London Museum) signalling the approach of the death-carts during the Plague. But to re-create the atmosphere of London there is nothing to match the *Diary*. We see the indefatigable Pepys rising at four in the morning to start his office-work – and still roistering with friends at supper till midnight. We see him at the playhouse, book-browsing in St Paul's churchyard, gossiping in taverns, proudly parading his new coach amid the fashionable throng in Hyde Park, or taking a boat upriver to wait on King or Parliament. His London had our own problems: overcrowding, smoke pollution – and traffic jams. Often the Thames provided the quickest highway, with its stairs or landing-stages along both banks, and boatmen plying like today's taxi drivers.

The genius of Wren

Though Wren's imaginative reconstruction plan after the Great Fire was not adopted, his genius set its mark on the rebuilt city. The Monument, a fluted Doric column soaring to sixty-two metres (202 ft), was his commemoration of the catastrophe, but his own memorial, as he declared, was the new St Paul's. Over fifty other 'Wren' churches were built under his supervision, though only a few were designed by him in detail. Many were destroyed in the Blitz, but his handiwork remains in a number, such as St Bride's, St Mary-le-Bow and St James's, Piccadilly. In this last the spirit of the period lingers evocatively. Grinling Gibbons carved the magnificent limewood altarpiece and the case for the organ. Another brilliant architectural achievement is St Stephen, Walbrook, in which Wren tried out some of the ideas later used in St Paul's. It is not only in the churches that Wren's achievements can be admired. His surviving secular work includes the south and east wings of Hampton Court, the Royal Hospital at Chelsea and the grand Baroque composition of Greenwich Hospital (1705).

THE BANQUETING HOUSE. *The Palladian-style building designed by Inigo Jones was intended to be part of a splendid royal palace at Whitehall, but the rest was never realized. Charles I knighted Rubens for the fine painted ceiling.*

CONNECTIONS
Grinling Gibbons: 282–3 *The artist's eye*
Hampton Court Palace: 214–15 *Royal retreats*
Jones and Wren: 212–13 *The Italian influence on architecture*
The Plague: 40–41 *The growth of population*

London/*The age of elegance*

CUMBERLAND TERRACE, REGENT'S PARK. *Built by John Nash, 1821–30.*

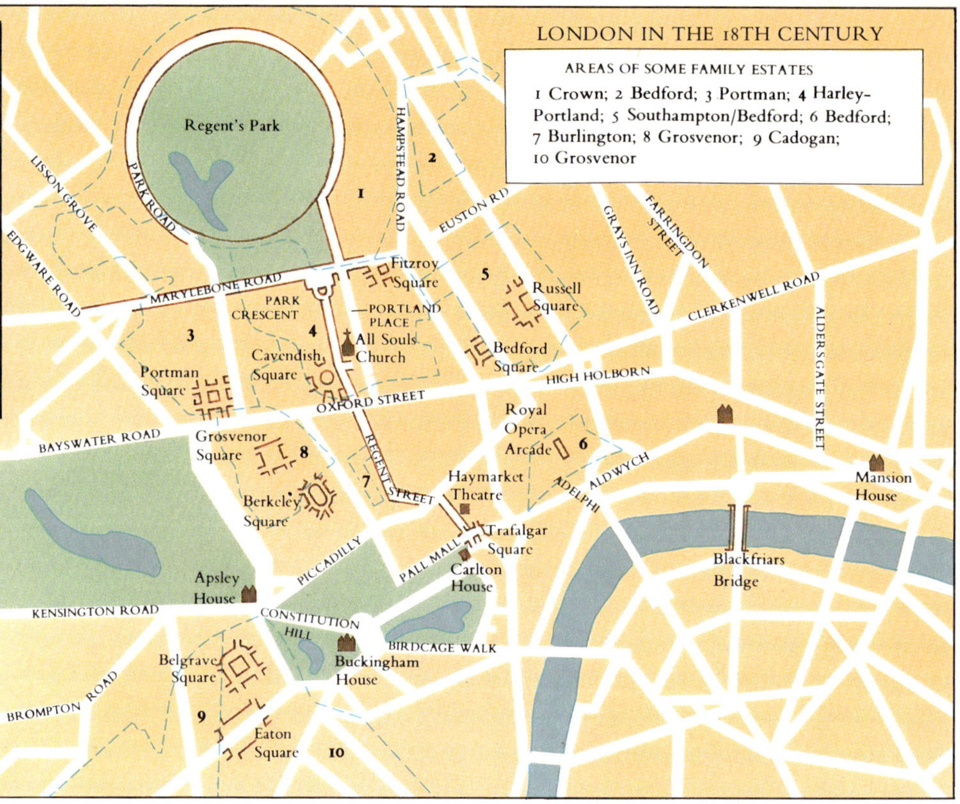

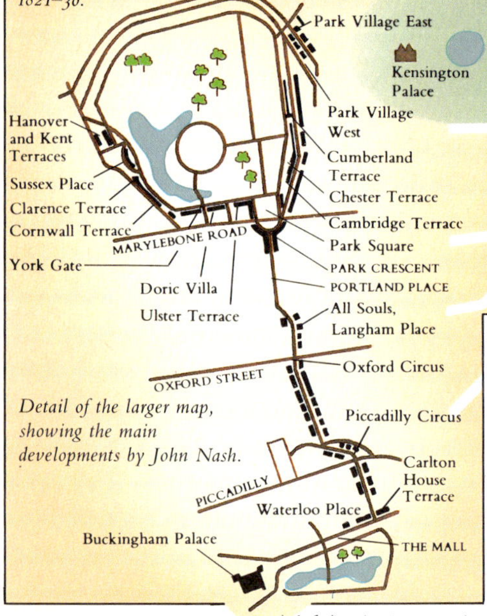

Detail of the larger map, showing the main developments by John Nash.

GROSVENOR SQUARE, 1754 (***right***). *A view north to the villages of Hampstead and Highgate.*

DR JOHNSON'S HOUSE (***below***). *Johnson worked on his dictionary in the attic at 17 Gough Square.*

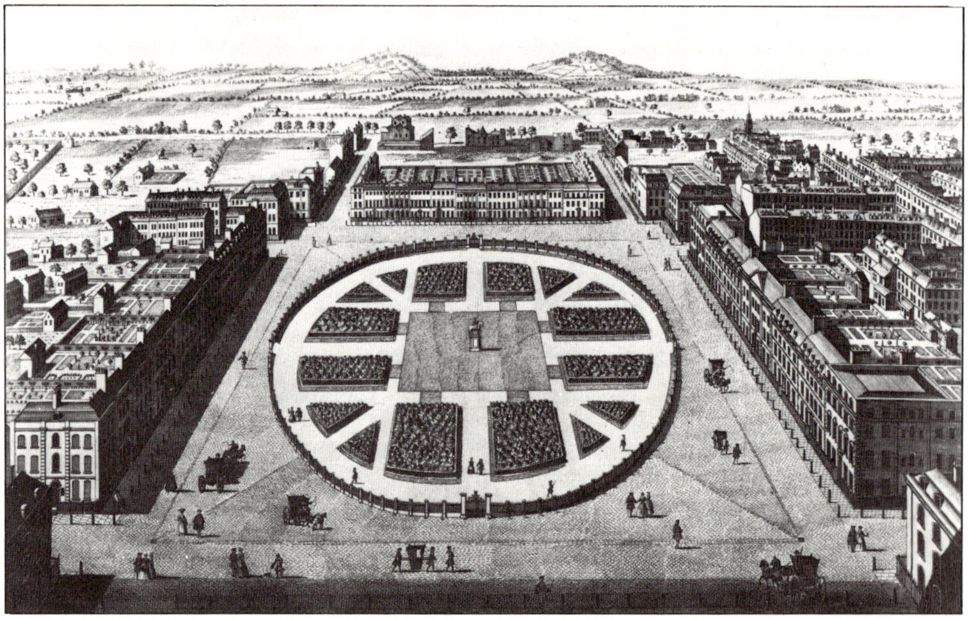

Sir Christopher Wren influenced a line of highly gifted successors, who gave London some of its greatest buildings. His assistant, Nicholas Hawksmoor, continued his work at Kensington Palace, where he collaborated with another exponent of the English Baroque, Sir John Vanbrugh, on the Orangery (1704–05); the magnificent carvings inside are by Grinling Gibbons. A fine example of Hawksmoor's ecclesiastical architecture is St George's, Bloomsbury, with its Corinthian portico and statue of George I surmounting the steeple; the latter was 'a masterstroke of absurdity', according to Horace Walpole. St George's is one of six London churches Hawksmoor designed as a consequence of the Act of Building Fifty New Churches, passed in 1711.

More building at Kensington, which had become the favoured home of the sovereign, was carried out by the architect and designer William Kent. It was George I himself who planned the Broad Walk and the Round Pond, while George II's queen, Caroline, had the little Westbourne river dammed to form a lake – the Serpentine. Kent's best-known building is probably the Horse Guards in Whitehall (1749–59). Too many of his other achievements, such as Devonshire House – outstanding among the aristocratic town houses that multiplied in this period – have disappeared.

At this period no great family, whatever stately homes it possessed elsewhere, could be without a mansion in the fashionable West End. For the growing upper middle class there were new streets and squares of tall, four-storey terraced houses, with sash windows, semicircular fanlights over the doors, and staircases with wrought-iron balustrades – the quintessential Georgian style. Each house had its staff of servants, and separate accommodation at the rear – the mews – for coachman, horses and carriage. Vast tracts of this kind of housing were frequently developed and let by a single landowner, who was also sometimes the contractor or architect. This system facilitated coherent town planning on a large scale.

A major figure on the London property market, and a brilliant architect, was Robert Adam, who built Apsley House (later home of the Duke of Wellington) and many other West End houses including the south and east sides of Fitzroy Square. With his three brothers he developed, from 1768, the Adelphi complex (now demolished) from the Strand down to the river, inspired by the grand ruins of the Roman Emperor Diocletian's palace at Split in modern Yugoslavia. Adam's contemporary and fellow Scot, William Chambers, is best remembered for Somerset House and Kew Gardens, with its pagoda.

VAUXHALL GARDENS. *A watercolour by Thomas Rowlandson showing the fashionable pleasure garden.*

HOGARTH'S 'GIN LANE'. *The church in the background is St George's, Bloomsbury.*

Squalor and prosperity

This was the age of Dr Johnson and his circle, who gathered in the taverns and coffee-houses of Fleet Street and the Strand, arguing furiously, scribbling frenziedly, about politics and literature and other topics of the moment. It was also the age of the theatre, of David Garrick and Sarah Siddons, and of the public pleasure gardens at Vauxhall, Ranelagh and Sadler's Wells. In contrast to this raffish glamour, the slums of London were places of appalling squalor, especially when, for a time, the consumption of cheap gin struck the working population like a second plague. In one Holborn parish, out of 2,000 houses, 506 were selling the spirit. 'Drunk for a penny, dead drunk for twopence,' ran the saying, 'clean straw for nothing.'

However, the 18th century was also a time of hard work and extraordinary commercial progress. As the British Empire expanded, and with it Britain's supremacy in world trade, the City of London rose to fresh heights of importance. Some institutions, such as the Bank of England and Lloyd's, date from the end of the 17th century, but it was the 18th that saw them develop. Most of their buildings have been replaced, or masked, by even vaster modern structures, but the Mansion House (completed in 1753) still stands.

Before long, the City had acquired a second bridge, Blackfriars. Westminster had had its own river crossing since 1750. The first years of the next century produced a succession of new docks below London Bridge. Meanwhile the shops of the West End became ever more alluring. 'Lovely Oxford Street,' enthused a foreign lady in 1786; she described in covetous detail the wide, well-lit thoroughfare with its 'great glass windows' where everything you could think of was 'neatly, attractively displayed'.

The Regency dream

The period closes with the Prince Regent, later George IV, whose favourite architect, John Nash, left as distinctive a signature on the London scene as Wren. He was an inspired scenic artist, excelling in vistas and façades. It was his dream, never fully realized, to develop Regent's Park (planned 1811–13) and connect its gracious terraces by a long processional route with the Prince's residence, the now-vanished Carlton House (which Nash designed Carlton House Terrace to replace). His versatility may be judged from other works that survive, ranging from the massive Haymarket Theatre to the charming Royal Opera Arcade close by; and from All Souls Church, Langham Place, to the garden frontage of Buckingham Palace, which his patron planned to occupy on his accession but, in the event, never did.

CONNECTIONS
Alcohol and society: 186–7 *Drink in Britain*
Architecture: 226–7 *Town houses*
The arts in the 18th century: 284–5 *The artist's eye*
David Garrick: 302–3 *Britain and the theatre*
Musicians in London: 300–301 *Music and song*

THE THAMES AND THE CITY OF LONDON FROM RICHMOND HOUSE *(detail). Canaletto lent a distinct Venetian air to his elegant townscape.*

The population of London soared in Victorian times. It was approaching half a million when Pepys started his diary and it had not gone far beyond that mark by 1700. When the first census was taken in 1801 it had reached 864,845; by 1831 it was one and a half million, and at the time of Victoria's Diamond Jubilee in 1897 it was over five million. London shared in the general population explosion of the time, but the capital's population was also continually swollen by new arrivals from the provinces and from overseas. To the largest city in the world came the provincial cabinetmaker in search of metropolitan experience, the rural labourer for casual employment, or the down-and-out interested in the ministrations of the capital's rich charities. Late Victorian London held more Scots that Aberdeen, more Irish than Dublin and more Jews than Palestine.

OVER LONDON BY RAIL (***below***). *Gustave Doré's image shows how the railways blighted London with shabby dark houses in their interstices.*

EDWARDIAN PICCADILLY (***right***). *The statue that has become popularly known as 'Eros' is in fact meant to symbolize the angel of Christian charity. A memorial to the philanthropic Lord Shaftesbury, it was unveiled in 1893 and is the focus of some half-dozen West End thoroughfares.*

The veins of London

The Victorian revolution in transport reinforced London's magnetism, because the railway network was centred upon the metropolis. The first railway station (London Bridge) was opened in 1836, the year before Victoria became Queen. For the next thirty-two years new termini followed each other in rapid succession as different companies cut their way into the city from every direction. This was Victorian private enterprise at its most dynamic. Armies of navvies, with nothing but shovel, barrow and brawn, dug cuttings and threw up embankments. New bridges crossed the river. Long viaducts curved majestically above the roof-tops. Tunnels bored inexorably through the higher ground. It all added up to a prodigious engineering achievement, employment for many – and misery for the many more displaced by the demolition of thousands of homes. Its most lasting result, though, was the creation of the more distant suburbs, the birth of the Greater London we see today. The boundaries of the capital city became confusingly blurred – the age of the commuter had begun.

Those who did not move so far out still needed transport for shorter journeys across the ever-spreading city. Not all could afford to hire cabs, the sedate four-wheel 'growlers' or the shiny two-wheel hansoms, and private carriages were for an even smaller minority. The solution for middle-class passengers was the omnibus. The first, in 1829, had three horses and carried twenty-two passengers, all inside, and soon there were bigger vehicles with open seats on top. Rival companies, each in its own bright, distinctive colours, competed briskly. When the streets became intolerably congested there came the fantastic new proposal that railway tunnels should be made below the streets. In 1863 the Underground was born, with steam locomotives drawing smut-speckled passengers in open trucks. Horse-drawn trams began in the 1860s, but the electrical type, 'the gondolas of the people', which many more travellers could afford to use, were not introduced until 1903.

The building of an imperial city

There had been much destruction of the old London. But it was nothing compared with the construction that year by year produced so many of today's architectural landmarks. On her accession, the young Victoria moved into Buckingham Palace, making it at last the sovereign's London home. She made further changes to the buildings, though the east frontage familiar to the public was altered again in 1913. The Admiralty Arch at the far end of the Mall and the Queen Victoria Memorial in front of the Palace were both tributes to her, erected soon after her death. Oddly enough, one of the most conspicuous features designed in her lifetime – a ponderous and ornate gateway for the Palace – proved too narrow for the carriages and now stands, a useless white elephant, as Marble Arch.

The Houses of Parliament were built by Barry after the fire of 1834 – in the neo-Gothic style that seemed to many Victorians to have an ethical appropriateness derived from its ecclesiastical associations. Later, the various government departments of Whitehall began to raise their massive blocks in the debased classical idiom that was the favoured alternative. Only the Law Courts quitted Westminster for their present buildings in the Strand. Trafalgar Square was completed and Nelson's Column added. Among the other notable additions was the Albert Memorial, designed by Sir G. Gilbert Scott in 1872.

The cleansing of the underworld

Environmental improvement in London was tackled with great energy, although the horrors of the Dickensian slums were not easily eradicated. Sometimes the incentive to provide better conditions for the lower orders was moral; it was believed that a bad physical environment was responsible for undesirable habits such as drinking, gambling and atheism. This moral concern was also tinged with a social anxiety, for as the respectable classes moved to suburbs or grand estates, London became more segregated socially and the lower orders were left without any 'good example' in uncivilized inner areas. It was known too that cholera and typhoid had no respect for class, and it was in the interests of all to make London a healthier place.

DENS OF INIQUITY. *The wide streets of 19th-century London were often cut through the 'rookeries' – the foci of crime, cholera and Chartism, all abhorrent to 'respectable' Londoners. The building of New Oxford Street (1850–56) necessitated the demolition of St Giles rookery, rendering 5,000 persons homeless.*

THE RAILWAYS. *All lines led to the metropolis. London's thirteen termini, notably the neo-Gothic St Pancras reflected in grandiose designs an age of unprecedented traffic and trade.*

St Pancras Hotel (1869)

Houses of Parliament (1840–50)

VICTORIAN LONDON
As the capital grew, it spread beyond its original nucleus like a 'swelling pudding splashed beyond its envelope'.

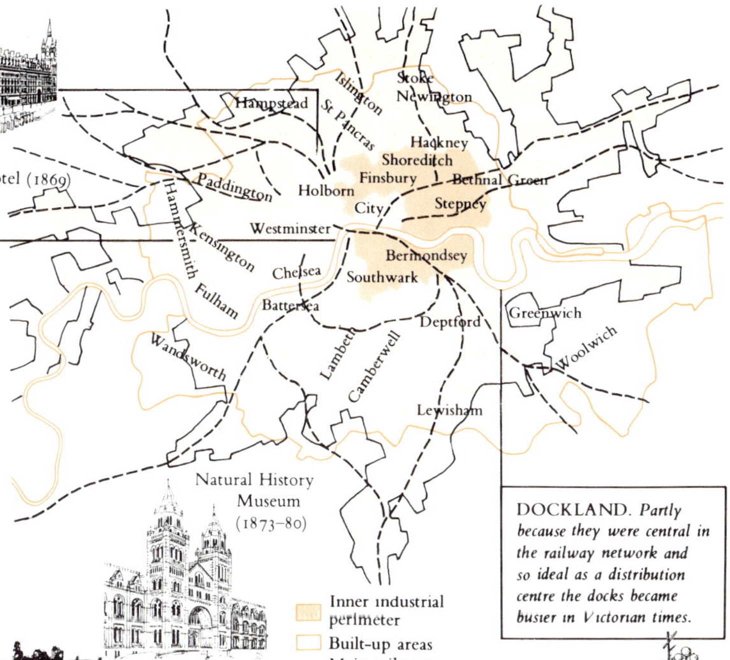

Natural History Museum (1873–80)

DOCKLAND. *Partly because they were central in the railway network and so ideal as a distribution centre the docks became busier in Victorian times.*

THE THAMES EMBANKMENT *(1864–70). This helped to solve London's sanitation problems, for beneath the handsome promenade a great sewer collected all the capital's waste and carried it safely downriver before discharging it.*

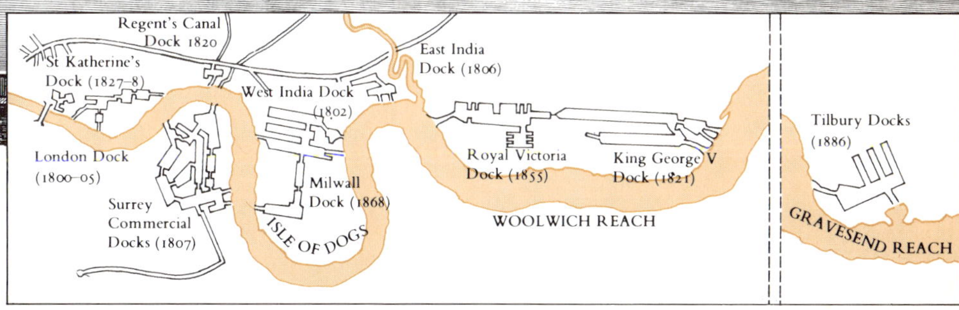

THE PORT OF LONDON. *Old docks were enlarged in the 19th century and new ones built. Extra space had to be cleared for warehouses.*

The Metropolitan Board of Works, set up in 1855, had established the main sewage system by the mid-1860s. By the 1880s the water supply, though still insufficient, was taken from better sources, stored in reservoirs and properly filtered. Other contributions to public health were the first proper public conveniences – their building often motivated by the belief of temperance reformers that a man might not be tempted to enter a public house if he could relieve himself without doing so – and large cemeteries such as Highgate.

The lights of London

Just as fine new street-lighting made London brighter, so entertainments multiplied, with Irving at the Lyceum, pantomime at Drury Lane, opera at Covent Garden and Gilbert and Sullivan at the Savoy – a theatre built along with one of the big new hotels that were a Victorian innovation. It was the heyday of the music-hall, at the Empire, the Oxford, the London Pavilion, and many more. Sedater pleasures included the Zoo, the permanent art galleries, the much enlarged British Museum, the new Natural History and the Victoria and Albert museums, and more temporary attractions like the Great Exhibition of 1851.

CONNECTIONS
The East End: 44–5 *Foreign settlers*
Galleries and museums: 290–93 *Great art collections*
The London of Dickens: 296–9 *Writers and places*
The London suburbs: 240–41 *Suburbia*
Theatreland: 302–3 *Britain and the theatre*
Transport: 262–3 *The railway age*

Edwardian London demonstrated all the contrasts and contradictions of Britain when she was simultaneously the world's greatest imperial power, the first progenitor of industrial squalor and the home of disinterested liberal social reform. It is a mistake to lament the years before the First World War as a lost golden age. Sweat-shops in London's East End, trade union and suffragette violence in 1911 and after, and sober Fabian tracts are as central to the scene as the cockaded coachmen still driving carriages among the growing throng of motorcars, omnibuses, taxis and lorries. The keynote of continuing confidence in imperial destiny was sounded by the luxurious Ritz Hotel (1904), an early steel-framed building rising in Piccadilly on a massive arcade of Portland stone. The slums of 'outcast London' were the other side of the coin.

The twenties and thirties

After the war there was a natural tendency to carry on as before. The vista of Kingsway, that dull, broad Edwardian thoroughfare, was closed at its Aldwych end by Bush House (1920) and India House (1930). But great architectural changes were in the air. The Art Deco style, which mingled modernity with a backward glance at ancient Egypt, left its brash mark, particularly on cinemas and factories; while modernism banished fussy decoration and concentrated on form and function. Each year brought at least one lasting landmark to the London scene – in 1931 Broadcasting House; then in 1932 Shell-Mex House looming over the Thames; and in the same year the completed County Hall on the opposite bank. Berthold Lubetkin's Penguin Pool was added to the Zoo in 1933–35. Experiments in housing ranged from the Highpoint I flats at Highgate (1935) to the Kensal House scheme in Ladbroke Grove (1936). Outstanding new shops included the Peter Jones Store in Sloane Square (1935–36), with its undulating façade. For most Londoners, however, new local authority housing in such boroughs as Bermondsey, and the Hyde Park Lido – inspirations of George Lansbury, the East End's representative in the Labour governments of 1923 and 1929–31 – were probably more welcome.

ENTRANCE TO THE HOOVER BUILDING, PERIVALE. *An Art Deco masterpiece (1932–3) on the Great West Road out of London.*

THE HAYWARD GALLERY (***right***). *The uncompromisingly stark Hayward Gallery (1968), which houses the Arts Council's exhibitions, is part of the South Bank arts complex. This includes the National Theatre (designed by Denys Lasdun; opened 1976), the National Film Theatre, the Royal Festival Hall and its smaller counterpart, the Queen Elizabeth Hall (1967). Rough concrete textures are the unifying design motif.*

VIEW OF LONDON FROM THE TOP OF THE SHELL CENTRE, BY DAVID THOMAS, 1968 (*detail*).

1 Charing Cross Station	9 St Mary-le-Strand	17 Savoy
2 Post Office Tower	10 Bush House	18 Royal Festival Hall
3 Centre Point	11 Australia House	19 Queen Elizabeth Hall
4 Shell-Mex House	12 Law Courts	20 Hayward Gallery
5 St George's, Bloomsbury	13 St Dunstan-in-the-West	21 Waterloo Bridge
6 Freemasons' Hall	14 Inns of Court (Temple)	22 Old Bailey
7 St Pancras Station	15 St Bride's	23 Britannic House
8 Somerset House	16 City of London School	24 St Paul's Cathedral

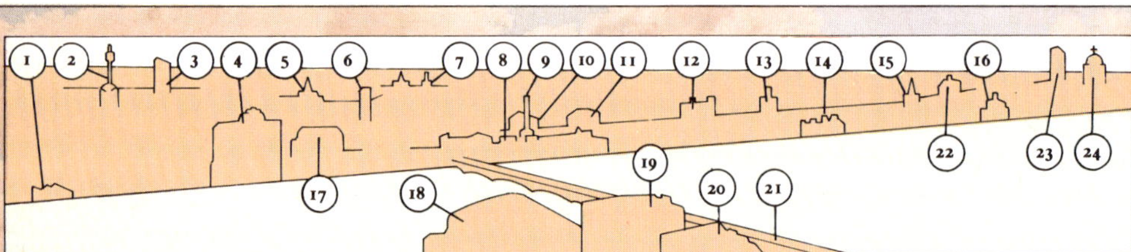

SOHO. *The centre of London's nightlife, studded with sex shops, strip clubs, food shops and markets.*

MODERN LONDON

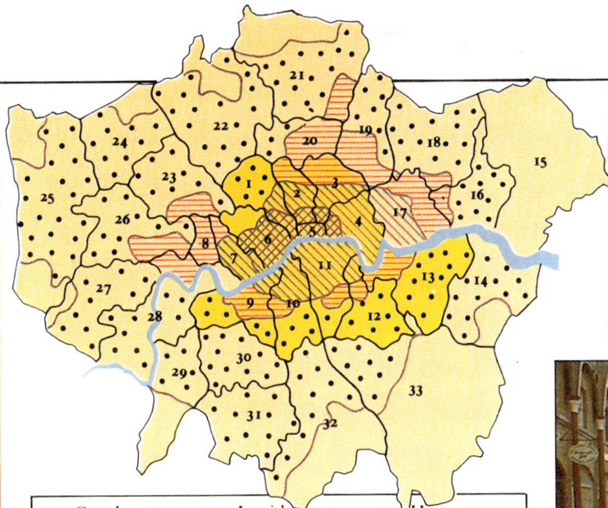

COVENT GARDEN. *London's famous fruit and vegetable market has partly been converted (1981) into a shopping arcade.*

HYDE PARK (***left***). *The pleasures of the park include a surprising number of rare trees, unappreciated by most visitors.*

THE NOTTING HILL CARNIVAL (***above***). *An annual event staged by the West Indian community. The modern housing makes an incongruous setting.*

After the Second World War

The air raids, in particular the incendiary bombs of the 1940 Blitz, devastated whole areas, and many historic buildings. The damage gave an opportunity to build afresh, and many worthy, if dull, public housing estates were built. A symbol of Britain's recovery from the war and of the spirit of reconstruction was the Festival of Britain of 1951, housed on the devastated south bank of the Thames. The surviving monument to the festival, not completed until 1965, is the Royal Festival Hall, a concert hall with a superb interior.

In the end, the speculators did more damage to historical London than all of Hitler's bombs. Between the wars, vast council housing estates and similar private developments spread over the urban landscape. In 1956 the thirty metres (100 ft) limit on the height of buildings was removed, and 'high-rise' flats now seemed the answer to overcrowding. The Roehampton estate (1952–59) was one of the earliest and best, but dramatically taller buildings soon sprang up – hardly skyscrapers by American standards, but high enough to transform the skyline. Tall *public* buildings could have this effect less criminally, as no one had to live in them. The latest and highest, Richard Seifert's National Westminster Bank tower at Bishopsgate (begun 1977), soars to some thirty storeys and 200 metres (638 ft), its graceful vertical lines like a cluster of organ pipes. The new Stock Exchange (1973) and the Barbican (begun 1962), with its three triangular towers of flats at 125 metres (400 ft), are other City landmarks. Elsewhere in London, there are office blocks like Centre Point (1960–64, also by Seifert), massive multistorey hotels in Mayfair and the column-like Post Office Tower (1964).

London is still one of the few truly great cities of the world. Yet it is under threat on all flanks. Some areas, such as Southall and Brixton, have a recent history of unrest linked with unemployment and racial tensions. In the centre, the main danger is that the architectural conservationists will lose their battle against commercialism.

CONNECTIONS
The Alexandra Palace: 276–7 *Radio and television*
The London suburbs: 240–41 *Suburbia*
Modern architecture: 170–71 *Building;* **288–9** *The artist's eye*
Wartime London: 126–7 *The Second World War*

Manchester

FRIEDRICH ENGELS *(1820–95). Manchester in the 19th century was the home of many contentious ideas, including* laissez-faire *capitalism, Liberalism and left-wing radicalism. The latter was promoted by Engels, sent to Manchester in 1842 to manage a branch of his father's cotton firm. Much of his studying was done in Chetham's, the first public library in the country (founded 1653).*

THE CITY CENTRE

Buildings of interest:

1 Co-operative Insurance Society Building (tower, 1962)
2 Chetham's Hospital, School and Library (17th c.)
3 Cathedral (Victorian ext., 15th-c. int.)
4 Old Wellington Inn (Tudor)
5 Royal Exchange (1874)
6 Barton Arcade (1871)
7 St Ann's Church (1709)
8 Sawyers Arms (Victorian pub frontage)
9 Rylands Library (1890–99)
10 Magistrates' Court (1971)
11 Free Trade Hall (1856)
12 Theatre Royal (1845)
13 Midland Hotel (1898–1903)
14 Central Reference Library (1934)
15 Town Hall (1868–77)
16 Old Bank of England (1845)
17 Lombardy Chambers (1868)
18 National Westminster Bank (1969)
19 Reform Club (1871)
20 City Art Gallery (1825)
21 Athenaeum (1837)
22 Cook & Watts Warehouse (1851)
23 Pickles Building (1870)
24 Refuge Assurance Building (1891–1910)

Approximate extent of built-up area in 1750

Designated Conservation Areas, containing Listed Buildings

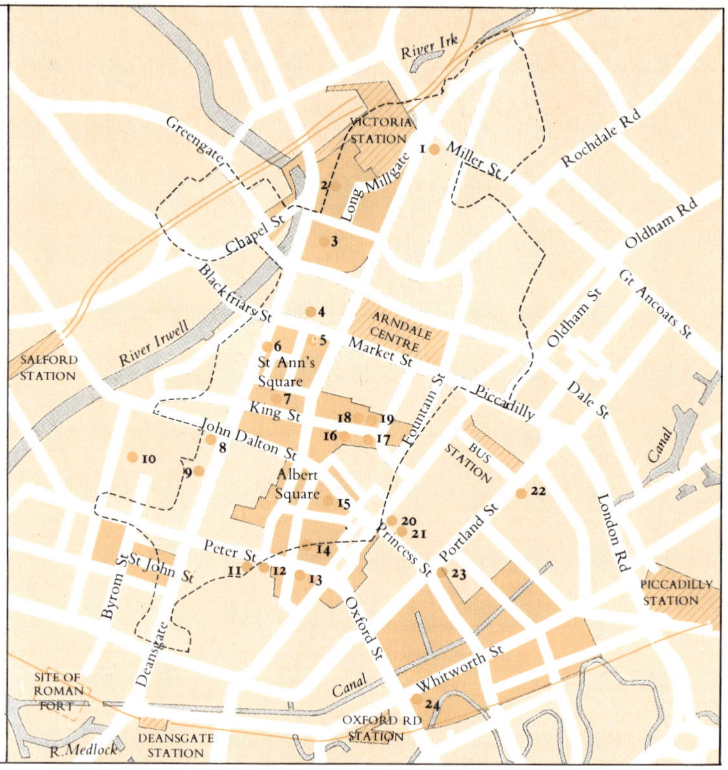

The shape of Manchester, like its status, has been changing constantly since the origins of the settlement. Yet its commercial centre, like that of its close neighbour Salford, has never strayed far from the banks of the Irk, Irwell and Medlock – rivers that today seem insignificant amid the jumbled townscape of bulky Victorian grandiloquence and modern commercial anonymity. The city has made a major contribution to British culture. Among its most famous products have been the principle of Free Trade, the *Guardian* newspaper and the Hallé orchestra.

The beginnings

First to settle were the Celts, who established an encampment called Mancenion, or 'place of tents'. The Romans built a fort on a defensible spur overlooking the Medlock; quite substantial traces of their occupation have been found. Saxon Mamecaster, founded two centuries after the Romans' departure, was a little farther north, by the junction of the Irk and Irwell. There was a thriving village there by 1086, when the Domesday Book recorded St Mary's church. This probably stood on the site now occupied by the 15th-century collegiate church, which was raised to cathedral status in 1847 and partly rebuilt in 1867.

During the Middle Ages Manchester became a modestly sized but regionally important centre for the production and distribution of woollens and textiles. The soft local water was well suited for finishing processes. By 1282 the town had a market and two mills, one for fulling, the other for corn-grinding. The arrival of a group of Flemish weavers in the late 14th century further augmented its importance. By 1650 there were three main streets radiating from the centre. Building was largely limited to the road frontages. Of the houses that stood then, the Old Wellington Inn, a Tudor half-timbered structure, survives today. The pattern of roads had filled in by 1750, although the extent of the town was still only about half a mile in each direction.

Some fine Georgian houses were put up by wealthy manufacturers, but most have long since disappeared. The best-preserved part of Georgian Manchester is St John Street, but there are other reminders of vanished elegance in Kennedy Street, King Street and Portland Street.

MANCUNIAN CHIMNEYS, *surrounding Victoria Bridge, 1859. The profusion of chimneys in Victorian times made Manchester a synonym for grime and smog. Campaigners in the 1840s wanted to impose restrictions on smoke from chimneys, but John Bright and other factory owners had the pertinent clause removed from the 1848 Public Health Act. Not until 1866 was a legal restraint applied. Thereafter, the smoke abatement movement gathered strength. But the final breakthrough did not come until 1952, when part of the central business area was declared a smokeless zone. Fogs are now less frequent.*

MANCHESTER COMES OF AGE

Modern Manchester is an amorphous Metropolitan District, housing one-sixth of the 2.6 million people who live in Greater Manchester County. The map shows the rapid growth of the built-up area since 1845.

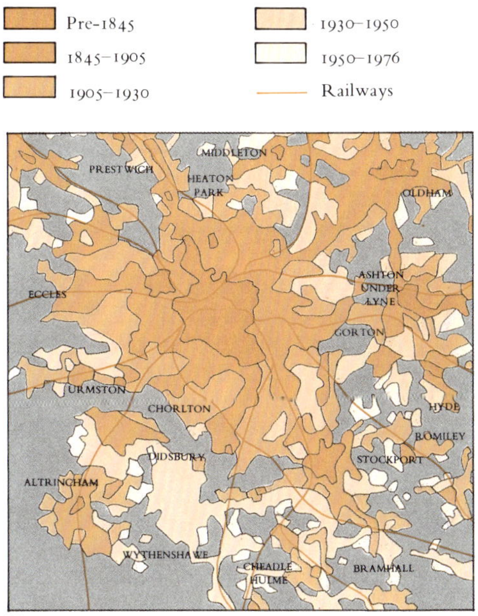

A SYMBOL OF CIVIC PRIDE

Between 1860 and 1880 the area now called Albert Square was redeveloped. The architectural masterpiece of the scheme was Alfred Waterhouse's Town Hall (1868–77), in the 13th-century Gothic style. Appropriately, the interior decoration included cotton motifs and the bees of industry.

MURAL FOR THE TOWN HALL: *one of a series of 12 by the Pre-Raphaelite painter Ford Madox Brown, illustrating scenes from Manchester's history (with more regard for composition and colour than for historical accuracy). The artist wanted to include a view of the 'Peterloo Massacre' – the famous cavalry attack on a group of radical reformers at St Peter's Fields in 1819 – but the council committee felt that the subject was politically much too sensitive.*

THE TOWN HALL *and Albert Square (**left**). Waterhouse's design, a neo-Gothic* tour de force, *was chosen from a plethora of rival submissions; it was admired for 'the supply of light, the facility of ventilation, the ease of access and the general excellence of the plan'. There is a fine hammerbeam roof in the Great Hall. The tower has a beautiful peal of 21 bells, each of which bears a line from Tennyson's* In Memoriam.

Cottonopolis

Manchester was the hub of the expanding cotton trade, which was the pace-setter of the industrial revolution. The town's experience of rapid industrial advances transformed it beyond recognition, a metamorphosis greatly accelerated by the proximity of coal. The population rose at an extraordinary rate – 18,000 in 1752, 70,000 by 1801 and 182,000 by 1831. It was the world's first truly industrial city, a role symbolized by the first commercial use of a steam engine in 1783, at Richard Arkwright's cotton-spinning factory.

Before long the town had come to illustrate a paradox of the early industrial age: social degradation as a by-product of wealth. This was observed by European visitors such as Alexis de Tocqueville, who thought it a 'foul drain' from which 'the greatest stream of industry flows out to fertilize the whole world'. The most vivid (but exaggerated) account of the slums appeared in Friedrich Engels' *The Condition of the Working Class in England* (1845). Some employers, such as Robert Greg, provided valuable social services, but the quality of life among the poor remained appalling. Part of the problem was the cramped, unhealthy workers' housing built near factories between 1800 and 1840. The banning of back-to-back houses in 1844 was one step in a gradual process of social cleansing that by this time was well under way.

Meanwhile, Manchester's communications network had become formidably impressive. The Duke of Bridgewater had brought Britain's first cross-country canal into the city in 1764, and others soon pierced the townscape. In 1830 Manchester was linked to Liverpool by the first passenger railway. Other lines followed, dispersing people and factories to peripheral towns and villages. No longer now a factory town, Manchester became a great European centre for the collection and export of textiles. Warehouses sprang up by the score, many in the Italianate *palazzo* style. By 1861 the editor of *Building News* found Manchester 'a more interesting city to walk over than London'.

The completion of the Manchester Ship Canal in 1894 turned the city into a major inland port and opened the way for the mushrooming of new industries. After the decline of cotton, the canal turned out to be Manchester's lifeblood, keeping the engineering and distributive trades healthy throughout the region.

Manchester now

Manchester's most recent great buildings are the Central Library (1934) and the Town Hall extension (1938), both by Vincent Harris. In the post-war era the town has been architecturally unlucky. One of the worst eyesores is the massively characterless Arndale shopping centre. Other modern buildings, such as those south of the city centre on what is now Europe's largest educational precinct, remind us of Manchester's importance as a centre for scientific and medical research – a tradition that stretches back to John Dalton's conception of the atomic theory in the early 19th century.

THE ROYAL EXCHANGE THEATRE. *Parked like a space capsule in the 19th-century cotton exchange, the theatre (built in 1976) daringly solves the problem of adapting an old building to a new use.*

CONNECTIONS
The cotton industry: 160–63 *Cotton*
Free Trade: 100–101 *Britain in the world marketplace*
The *Guardian*: 120–21 *The Press*
The Hallé Orchestra: 300–301 *Music and song*
The Peterloo Massacre: 108–9 *Riot and revolution*
Transport: 260–61 *The canals*

Oxford and Cambridge/*The universities*

In the two most ancient universities of Britain time-locked quadrangles create an impression of a mysterious, almost hallowed life of learning. Each university is closely enmeshed with the provincial town which has evolved in step with it (although there are various appendages, such as Oxford's Cowley, where its motor industry is based). The colleges – over thirty in each town – are scattered through a picturesque tangle of narrow, crowded streets, forming an incredible conglomeration of architectural gems.

The colleges

Both universities developed haphazardly from centres where young scholars flocked to hear famous teachers. Oxford, as a town, was already renowned for learning when a group of masters and their pupils migrated there from Paris in 1167, reinforcing its reputation. By the early 13th century its schools had coalesced into a *universitas* authorized by papal charter. A conflict between town and gown in 1209 forced a group of scholars into exile. They moved to Cambridge, which over the next two centuries rose to national importance as a centre of learning, and acquired European prestige with the coming of Erasmus in 1510.

The earliest colleges provided accommodation for masters only, and the pupils—many of them as young as fourteen—had to fend for themselves in halls of residence. (One such was St Edmund Hall in Oxford, which did not achieve collegiate status until 1957.) By the late 13th century, several

OXFORD FROM ABOVE
Colleges are listed with their dates of foundation

1 New College 1379
2 Hertford College *c.*1283
3 Queen's College 1340
4 St Edmund Hall *c.* 1220
5 Magdalen College 1458
6 Examination Schools
7 University College 1249
8 Oriel College 1326
9 Merton College 1264
10 Corpus Christi College 1517
11 St Frideswide's Church
12 Christ Church College 1525
13 Pembroke College 1624
14 Lincoln College 1429
15 Brasenose College 1509
16 St Mary's Church
17 Jesus College 1571
18 Exeter College 1314
19 Radcliffe Camera
20 Sheldonian Theatre
21 Bodleian Library
22 Trinity College 1555
23 Balliol College 1265
24 St John's College 1555
25 Wadham College 1610

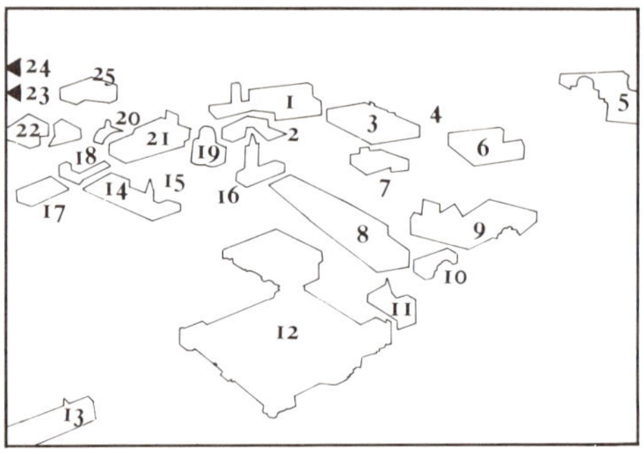

THE BODLEIAN LIBRARY, OXFORD

The Bodleian, one of the world's greatest libraries, was founded in 1598 by the retired diplomat and scholar Sir Thomas Bodley (1545–1613). He replenished Duke Humfrey's Library (founded 1480) and extended it with an annexe in the new Schools Quadrangle (begun 1613), which was later given over entirely to the Bodleian. Bodley laid down some rigorous statutes: even Charles I was unable to plunder a book from the massive hoard. Today there are over 4 million volumes on over 70 miles of shelving, which extend to labyrinthine underground stacks and a large modern building on Broad Street (built in 1935 by Sir Giles Scott).

SIR THOMAS BODLEY. *Bodley's portrait, by an anonymous artist, is one of the 15 surviving panels from a 17th-century ceiling in the library.*

KING'S COLLEGE, CAMBRIDGE (*left*): *a view across the River Cam. Henry VI established King's, the first royal foundation in Cambridge. The chapel, completed in 1515, is a Perpendicular masterpiece. To the right is the elegantly classical Fellows' Building (1723) by James Gibbs.*

THE CHANCELLOR'S PROCESSION, OXFORD. *Stately processions are part of the pageantry of academic life in both universities. The Chancellor's office is now largely honorific, but in bygone days the head of the university had considerable power. His election was often contentious.*

'A VARSITY TRICK—SMUGGLING IN'. *Rowlandson's watercolour caricature of student antics was painted sometime before 1810. In later times, the risky business of secreting a woman into a college against regulations has been amusingly described in numerous novels and memoirs.*

colleges had been founded in Oxford, including University College (1249), Merton (1264) and Balliol (*c.* 1265), and Peterhouse (1284) in Cambridge. Balliol came into being as an act of penance by John de Balliol, father of the Scottish king. Its fabric today is largely Victorian, whereas Merton still has some of its original buildings. Further foundations were made by merchants, statesmen and royalty, and their endowments sometimes laid the basis for great wealth.

The spate of foundations ceased after the 16th century, but began again in the 19th. At Cambridge no new colleges emerged between Sidney Sussex (1596) and Downing (1800). However, existing colleges were enlarged or rebuilt during this period. Of the Victorian foundations, Oxford's Keble College (opened 1870), its first for 120 years, is the most outstanding architecturally: William Butterfield's neo-Gothic structure of two-coloured brick strikes a note of adventurous dissonance.

Keble broke with the 'Oxbridge' pattern in having rooms arranged along corridors instead of on staircases. The traditional arrangement derives from Oxford's New College, massively endowed by William of Wykeham in 1379. Gatehouses, in which the porter has his lodge, lead into monastic-style quadrangles ('courts' at Cambridge) from which open doorways and stairs lead up to the students' rooms. Other important parts of the college, often open to the public, are the dining hall (which is especially magnificent at Christ Church, Oxford), the chapel (of which the supreme example is King's College, Cambridge), the library and the garden.

The collegiate system still operates, but the colleges have gradually come to work more closely together, sharing lectures, examinations and buildings. At Oxford, Sir Christopher Wren's Sheldonian Theatre (1669), an eccentric version of an ancient Roman model, is used for full-dress ceremonial occasions. Another famous shared facility is the Bodleian Library, with its superb domed rotunda, the Radcliffe Camera (1749) by James Gibbs. It was Gibbs too who designed Senate House (1730), Cambridge's equivalent, in function, of the Sheldonian.

Tradition and change

In the 20th century many of the conventional restraints of university life at Oxford and Cambridge have been relaxed. The social mix is wider, gowns are no longer everyday wear, and women are playing an increasing part in establishments that were formerly male enclaves. The first women's college – Lady Margaret Hall, Oxford – was founded in 1878, and the rule of single-sex colleges was breached in 1972 at Cambridge (Clare and King's). Yet many old traditions, some very strange, have survived. Because Christ Church, Oxford, had 101 members in its original foundation, its massive bell strikes 101 times at five past nine each evening; this was formerly the signal for all the colleges to close their gates. At Cambridge, quaintly, the magnificent gilded clock on Trinity Chapel tower strikes each hour twice over. Perhaps the most enjoyable of the college customs are the Christmas carol services at King's, Cambridge, and the May Morning choral singing on top of Magdalen Tower, Oxford.

PUNTING AT CAMBRIDGE, *under the Bridge of Sighs. This is also a popular pursuit on the River Cherwell at Oxford.*

CONNECTIONS

The Fitzwilliam and Ashmolean Museums: 290–93 *Great art collections*

The Oxford Movement: 50–51 *Catholics and Protestants*

Oxford's suburbs: 240–41 *Suburbia*

Universities: 112–13 *Higher education*

Edinburgh

Edinburgh, the 'Athens of the North', is a town that is dominated by the physical realities of its setting. Its backbone is a volcanic plug which, during the Ice Ages, acquired a long tail of glacial debris: together these features form Castle Rock and the foundations of the Old Town. To the north-east and south-east are two further volcanic outcrops, Calton Hill and the more grandly scaled craggy heights of Arthur's Seat. The north-eastern prospect from Castle Rock is a magnificent panorama over the gorge-like valley below to the Firth of Forth in the far distance; and looking south from Calton Hill, the steep cliffs sweeping up to the Castle give an impression of the incomparable defensive qualities of the site.

The rise of the Old Town

The name 'Edinburgh' is sometimes said to mean Edwin's burh – a fortified settlement built by Edwin of Northumbria in the late 7th century. It was in the 11th century that the Scottish king David I established a new burh to the east of Castle Rock, along the sloping line of what is now the Royal Mile. The city expanded to the south and south-east in the 14th and 15th centuries, and the Flodden Wall, begun in 1514, was built to embrace these areas of recent growth. The Lawnmarket, the Grassmarket and the Cowgate were within this girdle.

The special character of the Old Town is partly the result of the constraints imposed by the walls. As the population grew, the long narrow plots between the High Street and Cowgate were slowly infilled with more houses and 'lands' – tall tenement-like buildings, arranged in blocks and separated by narrow alleyways known as wynds or closes. The lands were built higher and higher, reaching five or six storeys by the end of the 17th century. By now the town was a veritable rabbit warren, a confined and densely settled community. Among the many outstanding survivals of the Old Town are a ramshackle 15th-century building said to have housed the theologian John Knox and the towering 17th-century block called 'Gladstone's Land'.

The enlightened capital

Edinburgh had emerged as Scotland's capital city by the mid-15th century. It acquired a great kirk (St Giles) and a grandiose royal palace at Holyrood (begun in 1500 by James IV). The Castle, with its piecemeal accretions of the Middle Ages, was further extended in the early 17th century. Following the Act of Union (1707), the city's political significance dwindled, but it was soon to emerge as one of Europe's leading cultural centres, with an immense social vitality.

The city's golden age extended from about 1760 to 1830. Among its literati were James Boswell, Sir Walter Scott and James Hogg, and other Edinburgh luminaries included the philosopher David Hume, the economist Adam Smith and a number of scientists, all contributing to an ambience of creativity. Yet Edinburgh also earned a reputation for villainy: it nurtured the thieving town councillor Deacon Brodie and the notorious body-snatchers Burke and Hare.

The New Town

Edinburgh's Enlightenment was accompanied by the fulfilment of an ambitious scheme for expanding the town northwards. The ravine left by the drainage of Nor' Loch was spanned by the North Bridge (completed 1772), and on the far side a bold start was made with the building of Robert Adam's Register House (1772–88). The Town Council approved a scheme produced by James Craig in 1767: a broad main street (George Street) with a square at either end. This early portion of the New Town is a highpoint of Regency town development.

After 1800 attention began to focus on other areas. The Greek Revival architecture of William Playfair and Thomas Hamilton – the Assembly Hall, the National Gallery, the Royal High School – added an Athenian touch appropriate to the rocky terrain.

'Auld Reekie'

Rich and poor became sharply segregated as the rich evacuated the Old Town for the New. However, modern Edinburgh comprises a great deal more than these two sectors. Since the early 19th century, its population has grown from just over 10,000 to over half a million, an increase sustained by a far more diverse range of employment than the city's traditional 'three Bs' – books, beer and biscuits. To house the 19th-century worker, rows of tenements sprang up, such as those in Pilrig, Dalry and Gorgie, while in marked

THE GRASSMARKET *was once a place of execution, where Covenanters died for their dissenting religious beliefs in the 17th century. Today, antique and fashion shops line the square.*

THE LAWNMARKET *lies on the Royal Mile, to the east of the Castle. The surviving 'lands' of the 17th century are squeezed between 19th-century tenements.*

THE EDINBURGH FESTIVAL (***below***), *founded in 1946, has become one of the world's major festivals of music and drama. As well as grand occasions such as the opera or the military Tattoo, numerous fringe activities take place.*

MARY, QUEEN OF SCOTS *(1542–87) spent six stormy years of her tragic reign at the Palace of Holyroodhouse.*

contrast were the genteel middle-class suburbs of Morningside and Newington. Shops and hotels invaded Princes Street. The Old Town suffered increasingly from overcrowding, smog and bad sanitation (earning the city its nickname, 'Auld Reekie') although some attempts were made to clear the slums before the close of the century.

In more recent years, the character of the New Town has been affected by its emergence as a commercial quarter. George Square was considerably spoilt by the intrusion of modern office development in the 1960s. However, the conservation movement has guarded much of the New Town with success, and some parts of the Old Town have been imaginatively restored.

CONNECTIONS
Robert Adam: 212–13 *The Italian influence in architecture;* 284–5 *The artist's eye*
Anglo-Scottish relations: 60–61 *Scotland and England*
The Edinburgh Festival: 300–301 *Music and song*
Tenement housing: 226–7 *Town houses*

CHARLOTTE SQUARE (***below***), *the jewel of the early New Town (1791), was one of the most elegant creations of the Scottish architect Robert Adam (1728–92), who trained in his father's Edinburgh office and attended Edinburgh University.*

THE CITY TODAY (***bottom***). *The railway runs right under the National Galleries (left and centre of the photograph) past the foot of Castle Rock. On the right is the Scott Monument (1840s), towering over Princes Street.*

Transport & communications

The limits of what can humanly be done in a day, an hour, a minute or a second have been continually expanded. In the pages that follow, the story of this expansion is told, from Roman roads to the most up-to-date developments in British telecommunications.

The canals

THE CANAL SYSTEM TODAY

At the height of their importance in the 1830s, Britain's waterways covered more than 4,000 miles and linked most of the big industrial towns. After 1840, however, there was a decline as many canals fell into disuse and some were lost forever. About 2,000 miles of navigable waterway remain in existence today, and one can still travel along many of those that made engineering and economic history a century and a half ago, while many of the neglected ones are important refuges for wildlife.

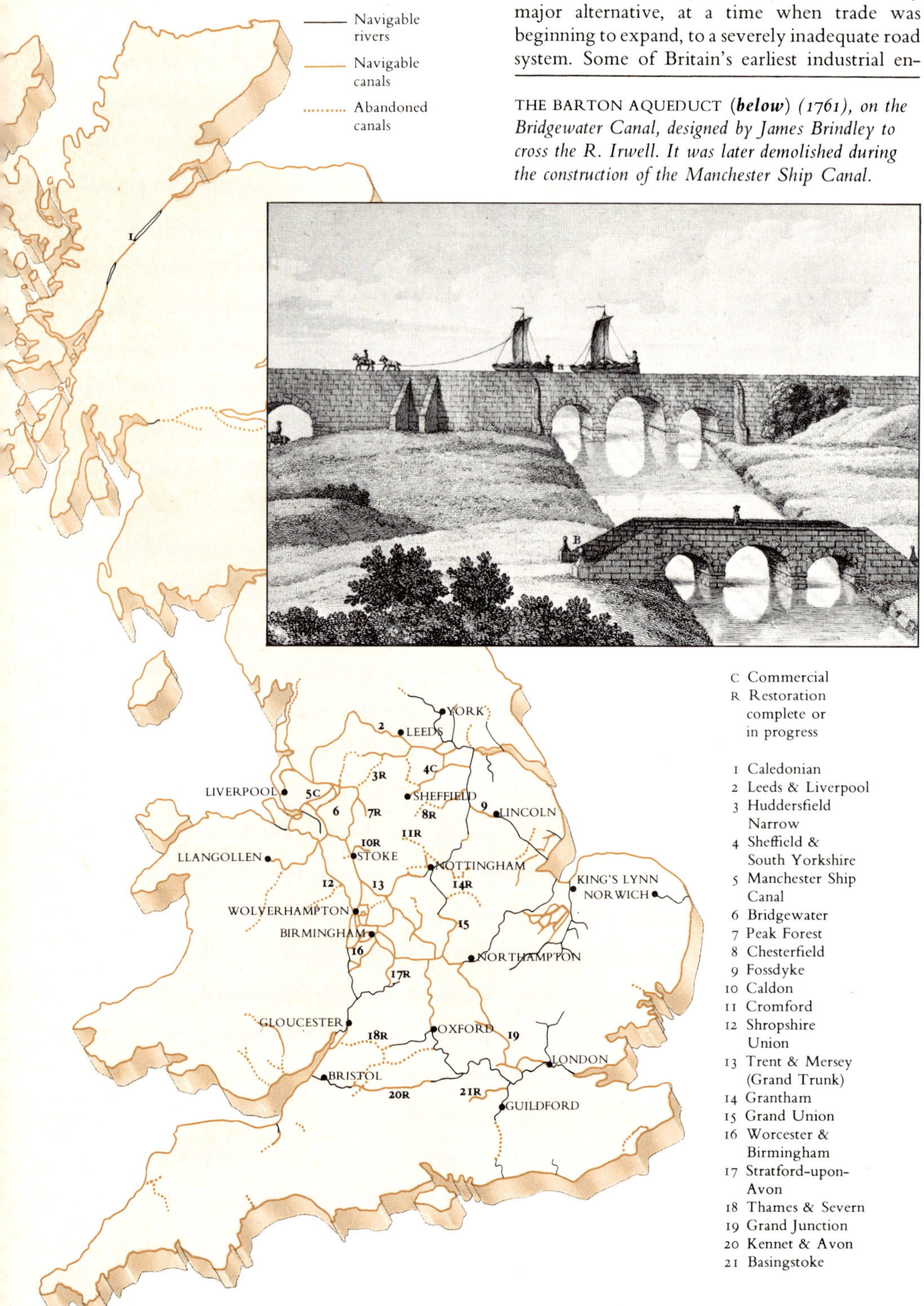

Britain's first canal, the Fossdyke, was built around AD200 by the Romans to form a link between Lincoln and the River Trent. Other small stretches of waterway were dug in the Roman period, but after the departure of the legions canal construction was abandoned and the rivers remained virtually the only form of water transport for more than a thousand years.

Navigable rivers assumed particular importance during the Middle Ages, as they offered the only major alternative, at a time when trade was beginning to expand, to a severely inadequate road system. Some of Britain's earliest industrial enterprises – for example, the extraction and refining of Cheshire salt – depended entirely on rivers for moving bulky raw materials and goods. In time these routeways inevitably had to be improved: artificial channels were built to shorten meandering rivers and primitive locks were constructed to overcome changes in level. The engineering techniques developed at this time proved invaluable when canal building resumed in the 18th century.

THE BARTON AQUEDUCT (***below***) *(1761), on the Bridgewater Canal, designed by James Brindley to cross the R. Irwell. It was later demolished during the construction of the Manchester Ship Canal.*

The great canals

The first of the 18th-century canals, completed in 1757, was the Sankey Brook Canal in south Lancashire. Until this date, the development of the Lancashire coal industry had been severely handicapped by lack of access to markets – there were no navigable rivers, and land carriage of coal, even over three or four miles, was cripplingly expensive. This pioneering waterway, which marked the beginning of the great age of canals in Britain, overcame the problem by connecting the St Helens collieries with the Mersey, thereby opening up the markets of Manchester and Liverpool. As a result, the price of coal in Manchester was halved, and became the lowest in Britain.

The Sankey Brook Canal was followed in 1761 by the Bridgewater Canal, built by the former millwright James Brindley to carry coal from the Duke of Bridgewater's mines at Worsley to Manchester, seven miles away. The waterway encouraged many similar ventures, for it was a great commercial success, reducing the freight charges for bulky goods to about one third of the wagoners' rates. But the most ambitious project of Brindley's canal-building career was the Grand Trunk (or Trent and Mersey), which was partly financed by Josiah Wedgwood and was completed in 1776, four years after Brindley's death from overwork. The canal provided a navigable link between the east and west coasts of England. Its benefit to Wedgwood was that it reduced the price of transporting a ton of goods from Liverpool to the Potteries from 50 to 13 shillings.

By 1830 engineering techniques had become increasingly sophisticated in the effort to minimize the number of locks without producing unduly circuitous routes. Cuttings and tunnels were essential in hilly areas, and most of the trunk canals involved civil engineering on a scale hitherto unknown. Three major canals burrowed through the Pennines, and the Grand Junction Canal from London to Birmingham negotiated the awkward topography of the Chilterns and Cotswolds with complex flights of locks and several tunnels. The last important canal to be completed, the Shropshire Union, cuts across country in long, direct, level stretches, achieved by a combination of cuttings and embankments which foreshadowed the techniques of the railway engineer.

The canals in decline

Travel by horse-drawn barge was slow and subject to frequent and often acrimonious delays at locks, tunnels and congested basins. The introduction of steam and, later, diesel power to the canals could do nothing to arrest the decline in trade caused by competition from the railways. Although many navigations continued to carry commercial traffic

LIFE ON THE BARGES (***left***). *The distinctive lifestyle of bargees and their families began to evolve in the 1840s. Until then canal boats were worked by all-male crews, but when competition from the railways resulted in drastically reduced wages, bargees could no longer afford shore accommodation, and captains dispersed their crews and took their wives and children on board. The barges then became homes, as well as places of work, for whole families.*

THE ROCHDALE CANAL, *abandoned by commerce in 1952, now provides water for industry.*

into the 1950s, the network is now largely disused as a means of industrial transport. The only canal of any commercial significance today is the South Yorkshire Navigation, which carries coal.

Canals are unlikely to return to their former industrial importance, although there is a vigorous movement in favour of reviving them. In theory, barges could transport bulky goods far more cheaply than the road and rail systems, but several factors militate against their revival. Enormous investment would be required to restore sufficient stretches of waterway to the required standards for commercial traffic, and most of the original canals are in any case too narrow to transport economic quantities of goods. Moreover, the industrial geography of the country has shifted, and many canals no longer link manufacturers with suitable markets and sources of raw materials.

However, canals have today acquired a new role as pleasure-cruising routes, and some formerly derelict cuts, such as the Stratford-on-Avon Navigation, have been restored for recreational traffic.

CONNECTIONS
James Brindley: 174–5 *Engineering*
Cheshire salt: 152–5 *The bowels of the earth*
Thomas Telford: 268–9 *The road network*
Josiah Wedgwood: 164–5 *Pottery and porcelain*

CANAL ENGINEERING

The canals built in the late 18th century by Brindley and others were very narrow: the 7-foot gauge was particularly popular. Later engineers continued to build narrow waterways, but larger budgets and greater technological resources allowed them to be more ambitious in their schemes. The ten-lock Foxton Flight (1808) in Leicestershire (***right***) is one of the great canal monuments. A different kind of engineering is represented by Thomas Telford's beautiful Pont Cysyllte Aqueduct carrying the Ellesmere Canal over the Dee valley. Inclined planes, with rails and winding gear, were sometimes used to transfer loads from one canal to another at a different level.

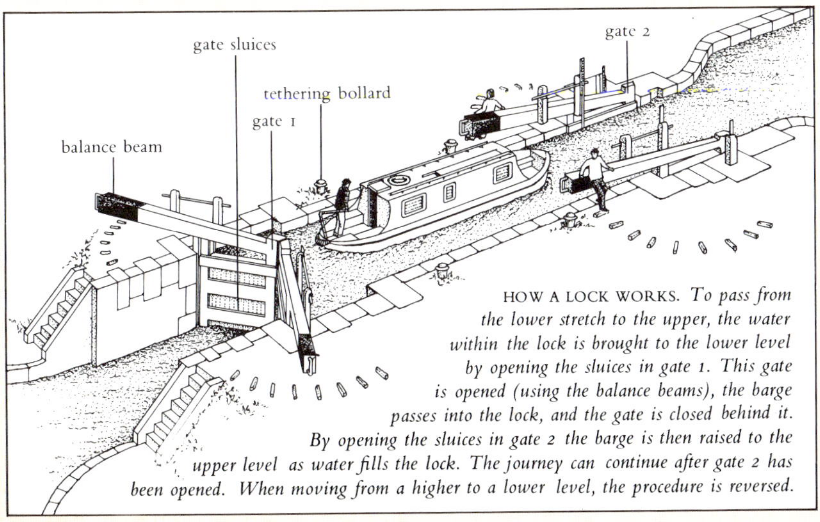

HOW A LOCK WORKS. *To pass from the lower stretch to the upper, the water within the lock is brought to the lower level by opening the sluices in gate 1. This gate is opened (using the balance beams), the barge passes into the lock, and the gate is closed behind it. By opening the sluices in gate 2 the barge is then raised to the upper level as water fills the lock. The journey can continue after gate 2 has been opened. When moving from a higher to a lower level, the procedure is reversed.*

The railway age

PUFFING BILLY, *built by William Hedley in 1813, carried coal at the Wylam Colliery, Northumb., for 49 years. It could pull 9 laden wagons at 5 m.p.h. Now in London's Science Museum, it is the oldest surviving steam locomotive.*

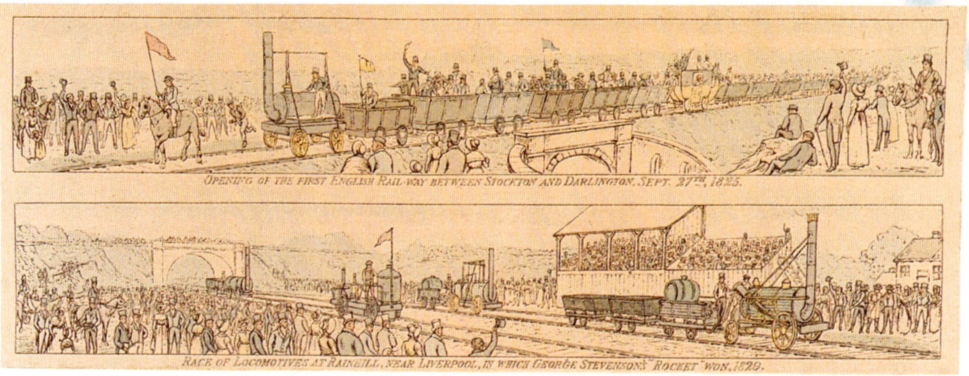

THE PUBLIC RESPONSE (***above***). *The opening of the Stockton–Darlington line (1825) was loudly cheered (top), and a special stand was built for spectators when the Stephensons'* Rocket *raced against other steam locomotives in the Rainhill Trials of 1829 (bottom).*

A RURAL BRANCH LINE (***below***). *Drawing away from Banyards station in Sussex, an Ivatt 2-6-2 locomotive heads along the branch line towards Horsham. That was in 1963. Since then, the service has been withdrawn, the line has closed and the station is now a private house.*

'Canals will last my lifetime, but what I fear is those damned tramways.' These words of the Duke of Bridgewater, uttered in the early 19th century, referred to the horse-drawn 'railways' which had been used for about two centuries to carry coal from mines to the nearest navigable waterway. Although the Duke's anxiety proved prophetic, he did not foresee the circumstances that made it so. The crucial development was not iron rails in themselves but their combination with steam-powered locomotives.

James Watt, in the 1780s, had experimented briefly with steam-powered transport, and in 1804 a locomotive built by the Cornishman Richard Trevithick pulled five wagons and a passenger coach along a ten-mile stretch of tramway in south Wales. Further such experiments caught the imagination of the engine-wright George Stephenson (1781–1848), whose famous Stockton–Darlington railway (1825) linked the coal mines of south Durham with the river port of Stockton. The venture was a great success, and inspired the construction of a railway between Liverpool and Manchester, with Stephenson as Chief Engineer. This line, opened in 1830, was the first exclusively to employ steam locomotives and to provide regular freight and passenger services; it was the true starting-point of the railway age.

Widespread enthusiasm for the Liverpool–Manchester line was soon reflected in the formation, by private Acts of Parliament, of a series of railway companies all over the country. Railway mania gripped the nation, and by 1840 there were already 1,860 miles of track (rising to 8,000 by 1855, and over 15,000 by 1870). From the 1870s onwards, mass-produced steel rails were employed.

Many of the early railways were designed to meet purely local requirements, but once it was realized that larger companies could offer long-distance services, mergers became common. In the mining and manufacturing districts commercial clashes took place between rival railway titans, such as the London and North Western (formed in 1846) and the slightly older Midland Railway. The west of England gradually came under the influence of the Great Western Railway (GWR), which gradually expanded to become Britain's largest system in terms of miles of track.

The GWR's Chief Engineer was Isambard Kingdom Brunel, whose remarkable projects included the masterly two-mile tunnel at Box Hill. Although the majority of Britain's railways followed Stephenson in conforming to a gauge of 4 feet 8½ inches, Brunel and the GWR favoured the 7-foot gauge. However, they failed to persuade other companies to imitate them in this practice, and by 1982 the GWR had converted all its broad tracks to the standard width.

Further extension of the rail network in the late

THE SPREADING NETWORK *By 1840 more than 1,500 miles of track were in operation. The network was at its most extensive in 1920, but the seeds of decline were already sown. Within three years the first line closures were being made.*

STEAM LOCOMOTION: THE INSIDE STORY

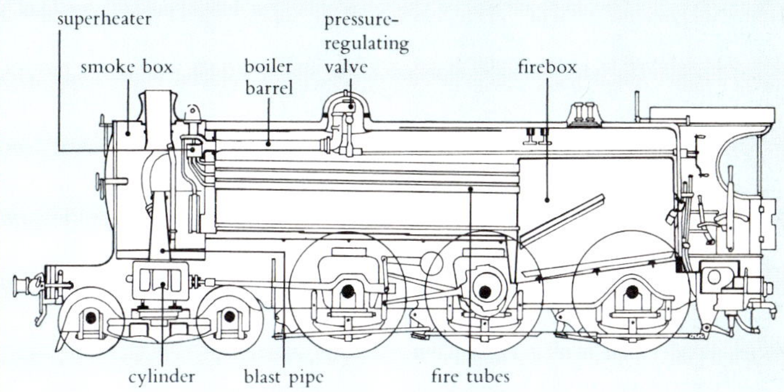

The heating process is aided by channelling hot gases from the firebox through firetubes immersed in the water of the boiler. The steam pressure, increased by a superheater, is released into the cylinder, from which the power is supplied to the wheels. The exhaust through the blast pipe sharpens the draught and increases the rate of steam raising.

HIGH-SPEED TRAVEL. *Designed to travel at speeds of up to 155 miles per hour, British Rail's Advanced Passenger Train (APT) can do the London–Glasgow run in just over 4 hours.*

19th century was accompanied by improved efficiency and standards of comfort. Restaurant and sleeping cars were introduced in the 1870s and corridor carriages in the 90s. The 1890s also saw the opening of the first deep underground lines in London (the earliest ones had been only a few metres below the surface). In the following decades the first railway electrification schemes were put into practice: the electrification of suburban services south of London began in 1898.

The problem years

In 1921 Britain's 123 independent railway companies were re-grouped into four major systems: the London, Midland & Scottish (LMS), London & North Eastern Railway (LNER), Southern Railway (SR) and Great Western. This re-organization improved management efficiency, but was insufficient to meet the increasing challenge from freight and passenger road transport. Long-distance passenger runs continued to be well patronized, but many rural branch lines with stations remote from village centres lost traffic to the more flexible and economic bus services, which dropped passengers closer to their destinations.

Between 1923 and 1939 local passenger services were closed on more than 1,000 miles of track, and there was also a withdrawal of trains in many industrial regions which had been hit by the depression. Further difficulties were caused by the Second World War, which added the problem of dilapidated locomotives and rolling stock to the railways' catalogue of complaints. Lack of maintenance and German bombing left many bridges, stations and sections of track in a pitiable state.

British Railways, which was formed as a nationalized concern in 1948, recorded its first overall financial deficit in the early 1950s, and shortly afterwards an ambitious modernization plan was introduced in an effort to win back lost markets. Steam locomotives were to be replaced by diesel and electric, freight handling was to be re-organized using high-speed expresses, and unprofitable passenger services were again to be reduced. However, the decline continued in spite of these measures. British Rail lost £87 million in 1962. In 1963 an inquiry headed by Dr Reginald Beeching came to the painful conclusion that a further 5,000 miles of line and 2,000 stations had to be closed, and future investment had to be concentrated on a limited system of fast inter-city services. This drastic plan for survival was substantially modified in the late 1960s when the government subsidized uneconomic passenger services in country regions, where the railways afforded the principal contact with the outside world.

Today, the future for freight-carrying railways looks bleak, but the development of new high-speed trains and the introduction of fare-saving schemes have helped to bring about a minor renaissance in passenger rail travel.

CONNECTIONS
I.K. Brunel: 174–5 *Engineering*
The impact of the railways: 264–5 *The railway revolution*
Relics of the steam age: 266–7 *Enjoying the railways today*
Suburban railways: 240–41 *Suburbia*

The railway revolution

FRESH MILK FOR TOWNS, c. *1915. The railway companies' comprehensive 'milk train' services transported freshly filled churns from remote rural districts into the hearts of cities.*

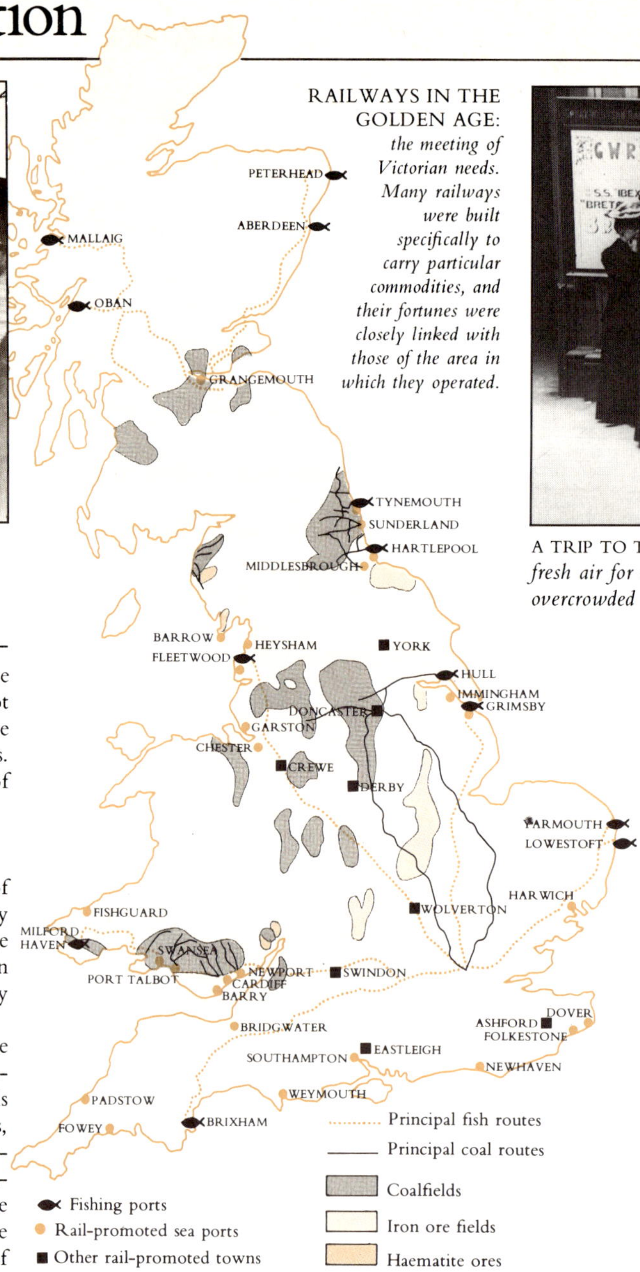

RAILWAYS IN THE GOLDEN AGE: *the meeting of Victorian needs. Many railways were built specifically to carry particular commodities, and their fortunes were closely linked with those of the area in which they operated.*

A TRIP TO THE SEASIDE *by rail meant a breath of fresh air for the inhabitants of Britain's grimy and overcrowded industrial areas.*

ORGANIZED OUTINGS *advertised by the railway companies encouraged the growing enthusiasm for travel.*

Canals and turnpike roads played a large part in the early success of industrialization but they could not match the speed or range of services offered by the railways, which steadily captured their markets. In the process, the economic and social life of Britain was altered beyond recognition.

Industry and farming

Industry was quick to recognize the advantages of the new mode of transport, and the railside factory became a familiar feature of the landscape. Large companies owned their own rail wagons, on which their names and products were proudly emblazoned.

The iron, coal and engineering industries were massively stimulated by the railways, which provided them with rapid transport of bulky materials and goods, and a new market, hungry for engines, rolling stock, miles of iron track, ancillary equipment and large quantities of fuel. Building materials also accounted for a significant share of the freight: Midland brick and Welsh slate were carried nationwide, leading to the obsolescence of traditional building styles in local materials.

Away from the heavy manufacturing areas, the railways relied largely on fishing and agriculture. Easy delivery of fertilizers, cattle feed and agricultural machinery, combined with the expansion of markets, made it possible in the 1850s to practise 'high farming' – high output based on heavy investment. Droving became a thing of the past. The new opportunities for long-distance transport of perishables encouraged a boom in market gardening and fruit growing, and the expansion of fishing ports. Special trains were laid on to bring turkeys from Norfolk, broccoli from Cornwall, fruit from the south-east, wheat from East Anglia.

The railways may have destroyed some of the individuality of Britain's rural areas, but it also brought them new prosperity by offering, for the first time, the chance of trading on a large scale with the towns.

Trains and the people

The main objective of most of the pioneering railways was the carriage of freight, but it was soon realized that the traffic in passengers could be equally lucrative. It was substantially cheaper to go by train than by coach. Particularly on routes where rival companies operated services, intense competition reduced fares sufficiently to attract even the relatively badly off, who had never travelled before. Because railway journeys were much quicker than road journeys, they also attracted the wealthy, who were provided with comfortable first-class carriages.

PASSENGERS AND FREIGHT *on the Liverpool and Manchester line (**below** and **opposite**). Passenger traffic was the more profitable until about 1850.*

SPEED AND TIME

In the glorious early days of steam, timed races between locomotives were common, and the companies whose services covered similar routes were soon vying with each other to shave minutes off journey times. By the end of the 19th century a few long-distance expresses had achieved average speeds of more than 60 m.p.h. After the coming of the bus and the motor car, the need to survive in a competitive market was met by faster services such as the LNER Silver Jubilee Express.

The fact that railways ran to a published timetable (the first one was published in 1839) led to greater exactitude in the nation's awareness of time. Travellers set their pocket watches by the station clocks, which were nationally synchronized. The result was a uniformity of timekeeping unknown, and unnecessary, in the era of more leisurely modes of travel.

THE FLYING SCOTSMAN, *one of the most famous of all British expresses, raced between Edinburgh and London. Its first non-stop run was in 1928. The photograph shows a more recent journey for steam enthusiasts.*

QUEEN VICTORIA'S SALOON. *The sumptuous fittings of royal saloons contrasted with the bare boards and benches of 3rd-class compartments.*

THE SHRINKING JOURNEY

Times of travel from London

	1750 *(by road)* Days	1850 *(by rail)* Hours · mins	1982 *(by rail)* Hours · mins
PERTH	10–	18 · 30	7 · 24
EDINBURGH	10–12	17 · 30	4 · 37
GLASGOW		16 · 30	5 · 8
CARLISLE		13 · 45	3 · 43
NEWCASTLE	6	9 · 45	2 · 58
HOLYHEAD		8 · 30	4 · 27
PLYMOUTH		7 · 15	3 · 13
LIVERPOOL	3	7 · 15	2 · 30
MANCHESTER	$3\frac{1}{6}$	6 · 30	2 · 28
BIRMINGHAM	2	3 · 15	1 · 31
BATH	2	3 · 45	1 · 10
DOVER	1	4	1 · 30
IPSWICH	1	3 · 30	1 · 10
BRIGHTON	1	3 · 30	58

A RAILWAY CLOCK, *Birkdale Station, Lancs. A common 19th-century design.*

NAVVIES AT WORK *on the London Underground. The term 'navvies', meaning casual labourers, comes from 'navigators', the men who had built the canals.*

Third-class conditions, in the early days, were exceedingly spartan, the railway companies showing their disregard for the poor by making them ride in open trucks. However, a great improvement was made by Gladstone's Railways Act (1844), which laid down rules for third-class travel. At least one train a day, in each direction, had to halt at every station and give third-class passengers a seated, covered ride at a maximum charge of a penny per mile.

Shorter journey times and low-cost excursions provided many of the poorer classes with the innovation of a day at the seaside. The Duke of Wellington's complaint that the railways enabled 'the lower orders to go uselessly wandering around the country' was an arrogant exaggeration, but daytrips and annual holidays to the seaside indeed became ever more popular, and the railway companies built their own hotels to cater for the expanding clientele. Typical of the railway-promoted seaside resorts are towns such as Blackpool, Skegness and Margate.

The railway altered habits of work as well as of leisure. By providing a quick and reliable method of travelling into city centres, the spread of suburban rail services played an important part in producing a new breed of city worker – the daily commuter – and great rings of satellite housing were built to answer his needs. Another new category of worker was the railway engineer, and he too had his own type of community. One of the new towns that grew around the railway workshops was Crewe, whose population (after the purchase of land by the Grand Junction company) multiplied from 203 in 1841 to 18,000 in 1871.

CONNECTIONS
Delivery of mail: 272–3 *The Post Office*
The railways and leisure: 188–9 *Tourism*
The railways in London: 248–9 *London*
Seaside towns: 238–9 *Spas and seaside resorts*
Suburban lines: 240–41 *Suburbia*
Transport of food: 186–7 *Food in Britain*

Enjoying the railways today

In the context of post-war shrinkage, the rise of tourism made the preservation of some railways a viable and indeed dynamic commercial proposition. Some of the earliest rescue bids concentrated on narrow-gauge mineral lines, beginning with the Talyllyn Railway (Dyfed), saved in 1951. In the 1960s abandoned branch lines were bought or leased by preservationists and re-opened as private ventures. For steam devotees there are also museums and steam centres throughout the country, where locomotives are sometimes operated along short stretches of track.

Between 1830 and 1860 alone about a quarter of a million railway bridges were built in Britain. Many 19th-century bridges and viaducts survive in relatively unaltered condition, and most are still in use. They include the grand viaducts of the Pennines, of which the most memorable is the double red-brick monster at Stockport. In the realm of railway architecture, the Midland Hotel, St Pancras, towers high but not alone. More modest but no less satisfying delights are to be found in the stations of spa towns such as Malvern, in the suburbs of Liverpool and Newcastle, and in countless other unexpected places.

THE SQUIRREL SEAT. *Fine workmanship and delicate detail were applied to the fittings of the humblest Victorian station. This example is in the National Railway Museum, York, but many others, with more sober paintwork, can still be seen* in situ.

SAVED FROM THE SCRAPYARD. *The National Railway Museum at York, opened in 1928, houses a magnificent display of some 30 steam locomotives (including the record-breaking* Mallard*).*

THE TRAIN SHED AT BRIGHTON STATION *(1881–3)* (***below***), *with its slender colonnades, is one of the most satisfying of all monuments of railway architecture.*

THE BLUEBELL RAILWAY

Running 5 miles through the Sussex countryside, the Bluebell Railway sustains the atmosphere and leisurely pace of a typical branch line of southern England. It was closed by British Railways in 1958, but within a year a preservation society had acquired the track, two steam locomotives and several coaches, and by August 1960 the line had been re-opened. Today, there are many more locomotives, which chug back and forth between Horsted Keynes and Sheffield Park, carrying 400,000 passengers each year past the flower-strewn banks which have given the line its name.

Among the 30 historic coaches is the London, Brighton and South Coast Railway directors' saloon, built in 1914. Sheffield Park Station, which opened in 1882, is a well-preserved example of a Victorian rural halt. Its oil-lit platform lamps are still intact. On platform 2 there is a museum of railway relics.

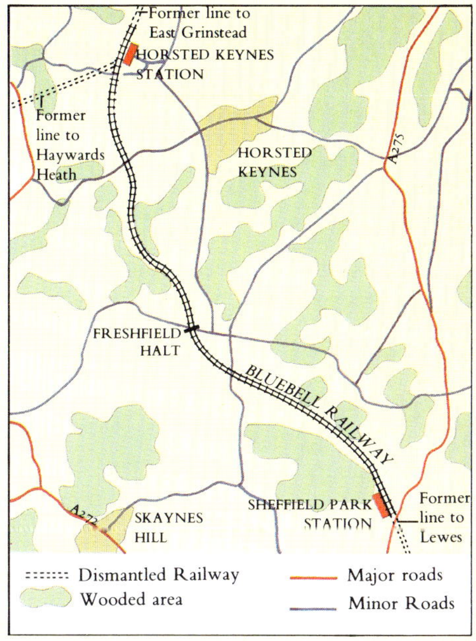

THE NEW RAILWAY MANIA

Inter-city lines, many of them passing through superb countryside, provide high-speed services between most British cities. For the steam enthusiast, however, there are other joys. Many old lines have been revived by preservation societies, and steam trains also run periodically on selected routes of the main line system.

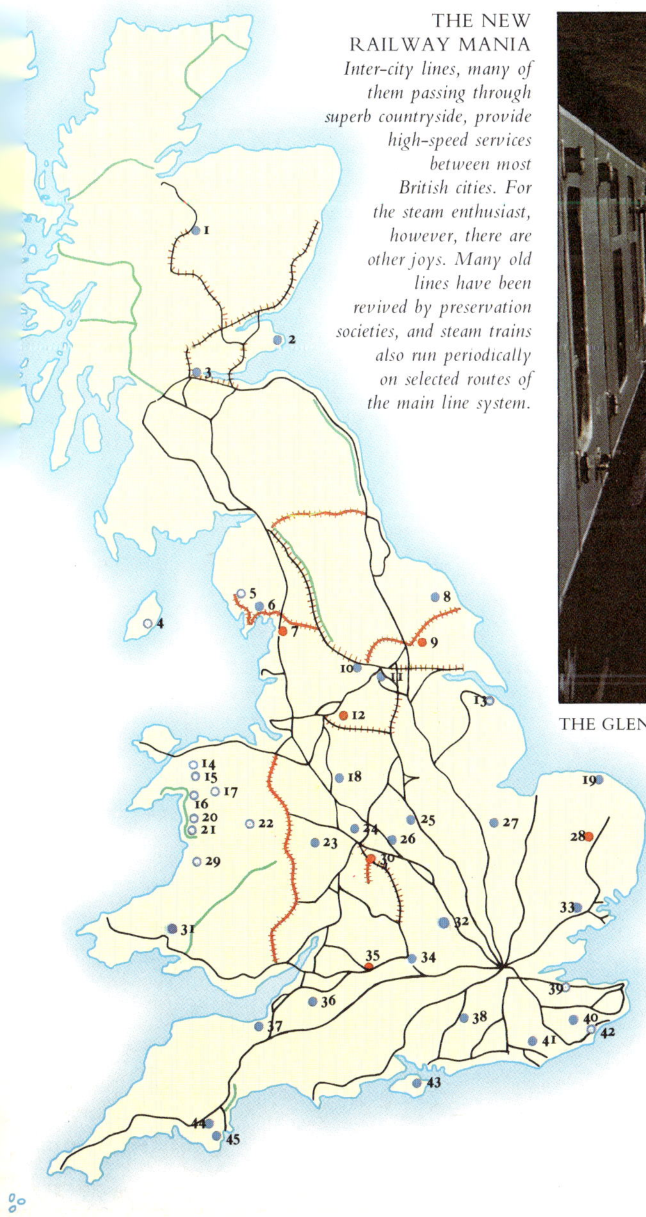

Inter-city services

Routes with regular steam workings

PRESERVED RAILWAYS:
- standard gauge
- narrow gauge
- Steam centre or railway museum

Scenic routes on the BR system

THE GLENFINNAN VIADUCT, HIGHLAND: *the first concrete viaduct (1897–1901), an early McAlpines' contract.*

1 Strathspey Rlwy **2** Lochty Private Rlwy **3** Scottish Rlwy Preservation Society, Falkirk **4** Isle of Man Rlwy **5** Ravenglass & Eskdale Rlwy **6** Lakeside & Haverthwaite Rlwy **7** Steamtown, Carnforth **8** North Yorks. Moors Rlwy, Pickering **9** National Rlwy Museum, York **10** Worth Valley Rlwy, Haworth **11** Middleton Rlwy, Leeds **12** Dinting Rlwy Centre, Glossop **13** Lincs. Coast Light Rlwy, Humberstone **14** Snowdon Mountain Rlwy **15** Llanberis Lake Rlwy **16** Ffestiniog Rlwy, Porthmadog **17** Bala Lake Rlwy **18** Foxfield Light Rlwy, Dilhorne **19** North Norfolk Rlwy, Sheringham **20** Fairbourne Rlwy **21** Talyllyn Rlwy **22** Welshpool & Llanfair Light Rlwy **23** Severn Valley Rlwy, Bewdley **24** Chasewater Light Rlwy **25** Main Line Steam Trust, Loughborough **26** Shackerstone Rlwy Society **27** Nene Valley Rlwy, Wansford **28** Bressingham Steam Museum, Diss **29** Vale of Rheidol Rlwy, Aberystwyth **30** Birmingham Rlwy Museum **31** Gwili Rlwy **32** Quainton Rlwy Centre, Aylesbury **33** Stour Valley Rlwy **34** Great Western Rlwy Centre, Didcot **35** Great Western Rlwy Museum, Swindon **36** East Somerset Rlwy, Cranmore **37** West Somerset Rlwy, Minehead **38** Mid-Hants. Rlwy **39** Sittingbourne & Kemsley Light Rlwy **40** Kent & East Sussex Rlwy, Tenterden **41** Bluebell Rlwy **42** Romney, Hythe & Dymchurch Rlwy **43** Isle of Wight Steam Rlwy Centre **44** Dart Valley Rlwy, Buckfastleigh **45** Torbay & Dartmouth Rlwy

The road network

Prehistoric Britons had little need to travel beyond their immediate communities, and the few long-distance tracks that existed were probably created as routeways to important religious sites. Many of these early roads, such as the Ridgeway (or Icknield Way), followed the crestlines of chalk downland in southern England, and several routes converged at religious centres such as Avebury in Wiltshire. When the Romans invaded Britain, however, they were anxious to consolidate their conquest with a road network designed largely for rapid military movements, a strategy reflected in the long, straight routes (such as Ermine Street and Watling Street) radiating out from centres of military or civil power.

Medieval trade

After the collapse of Roman rule, large sections of this first national road system decayed. Most of those that survived are now only minor roads or bridle-ways. However, some of the more important, such as Watling Street, acquired a new function as medieval trade routes, and a number have been incorporated as major arteries in the modern trunk road network. These Roman survivals, together with other routes that grew to cater for the limited commercial and industrial trade of the medieval period, were of variable quality and frequently became impassable in bad weather. By the late 17th century, the failings of the road system had become a serious hindrance to the growing need for more reliable transport between major towns.

Medieval legislation stipulated that the upkeep of major routes was the responsibility of each parish through which they passed. But this ruling was

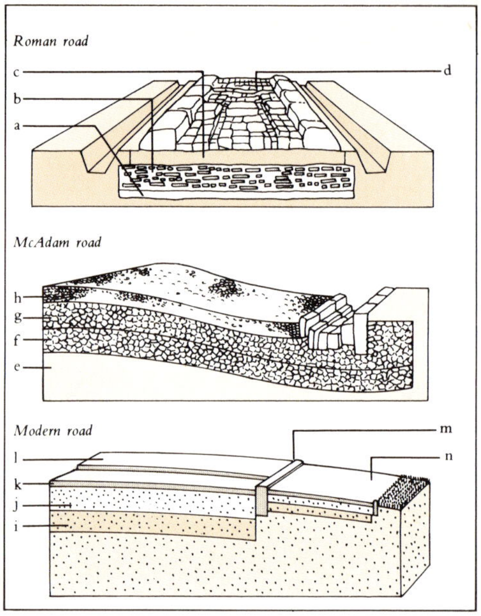

FROM STONES TO ASPHALT (***right***). *The Roman road had earth footing (a), then a layer of small stones in mortar (b), a hard filling (c) and a stone slab surface (d). The McAdam road had a cambered earth footing (e), a base course of stones (f), a middle course of stones (g) and a wearing surface of small stones (h). A typical modern road has a granular sub-base (i), a base layer of concrete (j), a layer of tar or rolled asphalt (k), a wearing course of rolled asphalt (l), a concrete haunch (m) and a hard shoulder of asphalt on a concrete base (n).*

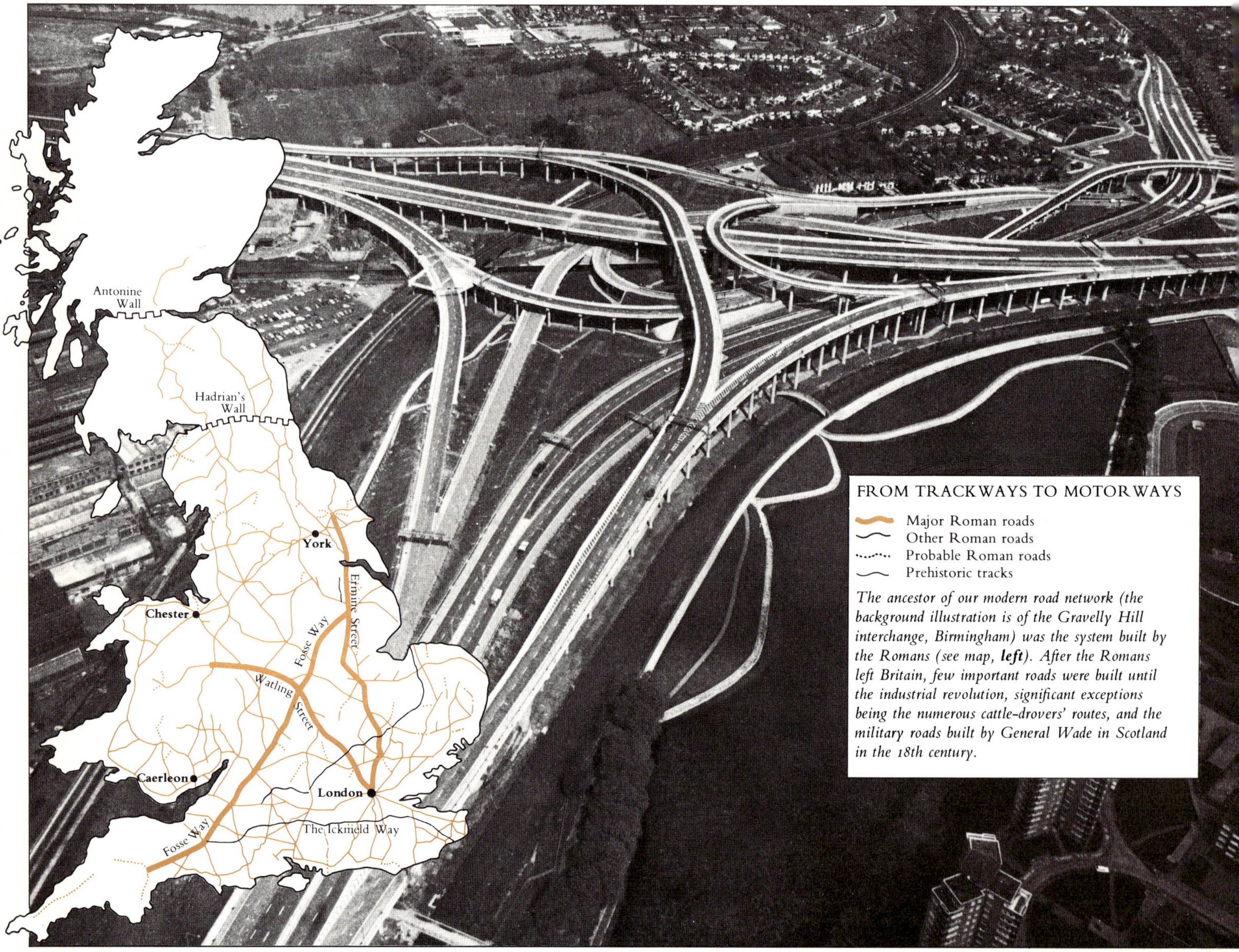

The ancestor of our modern road network (the background illustration is of the Gravelly Hill interchange, Birmingham) was the system built by the Romans (see map, ***left****). After the Romans left Britain, few important roads were built until the industrial revolution, significant exceptions being the numerous cattle-drovers' routes, and the military roads built by General Wade in Scotland in the 18th century.*

A TOLLGATE, *1794. For about 250 years after 1663, key routes in Britain were maintained with the money exacted from road-users at tollgates. The last turnpike was abolished in 1895.*

TRAVELLING BY COACH, c. *1810* ***(left)****. The stage-coaches, which began to carry mail and passengers from about 1640 onwards, resembled large private coaches. Coach speeds improved in the 18th century when night stops were discontinued and relay horses began to be used.*

rarely heeded, and after 1663 the first experiments were made in turnpiking, a practice whereby specific lengths of road were maintained in good order using money from tolls levied on traffic passing over them. The Great North Road was one of the first major routes to be improved in this way. Tolls ranged from a penny to two shillings.

The building of toll roads was stimulated in the 18th century by the increased movement of coal, ironstone, clay and other bulky raw materials of the industrial revolution, and turnpike trusts to administer these roads were established throughout Britain. Although progress was piecemeal and uncoordinated, by the late 1830s more than 22,000 miles of toll road were in use, and thanks to the achievements of men such as Thomas Telford (1757–1834) and John McAdam (1756–1836), road-building had been established as a respected branch of civil engineering. Telford's Menai Suspension Bridge (1826), which carried his London–Holyhead road over the Menai Straits, was one of the wonders of the age.

Mail coach to motorcar

The turnpike road network, in addition to lowering the costs of freight carriage, also made possible the introduction of regular stage-coach and mail-coach services which linked all the principal cities and towns. And these in turn were supplemented by village carriers, whose wagons connected each market town with its rural hinterland. The turnpike system, together with the canals and navigable rivers, carried the bulk of industrial traffic in Britain during the country's greatest period of economic expansion. Although steam-powered road vehicles were operated with some measure of success in the early 19th century, the greater attractions of the railway resulted in the rapid decline of the horse-drawn stage-coach.

By the time of the First World War, the reliability of the motor vehicle had been convincingly established. The steady increase in both private and commercial traffic in the 1920s soon exposed the inadequacies of the road system, which had stagnated in the heyday of the railways. The success achieved by the pioneer Italian motorways stimulated calls from motoring interests for similar innovations in Britain. By-passes were provided for the more seriously congested towns, such as Kingston upon Thames and Winchester, and a few arterial roads were designed for fast motor traffic, including the Western and Eastern Avenues out of London and the East Lancashire Road between Liverpool and Manchester. Such improvements were few, however, and the new trunk routes were subject to traffic jams.

CARS OF THE PEOPLE, 1922. *Motor charabancs (or motor coaches) taking members of the Ancient Order of Foresters on their annual outing. The introduction of the motor vehicle led to the establishment of the Ministry of Transport in 1920.*

The arrival of the motorway

Recommendations for a national motoring network were made to the government in the 1930s, but war interrupted positive planning, and official proposals did not appear until 1946. In 1958 Britain's first motorway, the Preston by-pass, was opened. This was followed a year later by the completion of the southern section of the M1 from St Albans to Rugby. In 1963, a more ambitious plan for building 1,000 miles of motorway was announced. These entirely new routes were also to be supplemented by widespread improvement schemes for the conventional road system. For example, circuitous coastal routes were shortened by building bridges over the Severn, Humber, Forth and Tay estuaries. Economic problems in the late 1970s led to a slower rate of road-building than was first anticipated, but by 1981 most major projects had been completed and Britain's 1,660 miles of motorway now carry about 10 per cent of all traffic.

Traffic problems still exist, however. The concentration of population into large conurbations, and the increasing numbers of private, public and commercial vehicles using urban roads, are creating serious congestion in most of Britain's towns and cities. Urban roads now carry about half of all traffic, and there is an urgent need for their further improvement. The demands of the motorist for better roads in Britain as a whole must, however, be balanced not only against the need to conserve the historical and architectural heritage that many British towns and cities possess, but also against the ecological consequences of too much traffic, and the needs of pedestrians.

CONNECTIONS
Consequences of urban traffic: 128–9 *Conserving the past*
Road vehicles: 182–3 *The motor industry*
Upkeep of medieval roads: 80–81 *Local government and the Civil Service*

VINCENZO LUNARDI *was the first in Britain to make an ascent by hydrogen balloon, in 1798. The idea of commercial aviation by airship was not abandoned until 1930.*

IMPERIAL AIRWAYS *was based initially on Croydon (**below**), shown here in 1929. The London–Paris service (**below right**) was used mainly by businessmen.*

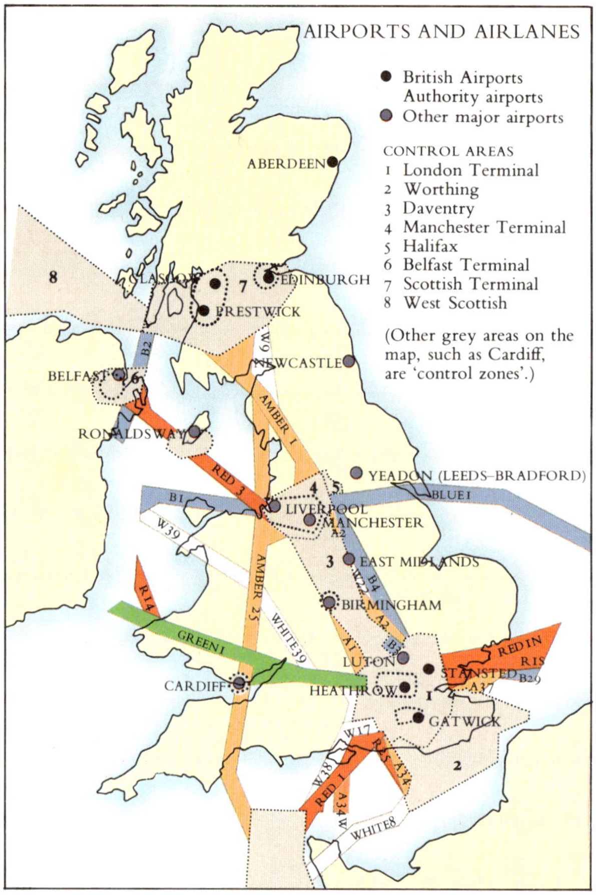

The UK *Airways System consists of air corridors with a minimum width of 10 miles, extending upwards to 25,000 ft (7,620 m).*

DEPARTURE GATE *at Edinburgh (**below**). The continuous re-assessment and improvement of passenger flow and baggage handling facilities is a major aspect of airport development.*

The emergence of the first commercial airlines in Britain was a phenomenon of the 1920s and depended enormously upon flying experience gained by pilots in the First World War. Initially, the emphasis was on the development of overseas services. The first daily international flight, on 25 August 1919, was to Paris from Hounslow Heath, an aerodrome which Aircraft Transport and Travel Ltd had borrowed from the RAF.

Croydon became the chief international airport in 1920, and throughout the inter-war years was virtually the only one handling international traffic. Several companies attempted to provide services to Europe but foundered on the rock of French competition. The British government therefore created Imperial Airways (1924) as a subsidized monopoly. It concentrated on developing long-distance overseas routes, but complaints that Europe was being neglected led in the 1930s to an attempt to redress the balance, culminating in the establishment of British European Airways (BEA) in 1946. By 1949 all British routes were controlled by BEA and the British Overseas Airways Corporation (BOAC), later to be merged as British Airways (1972).

Consolidation

Air travel within Britain seemed to offer fewer opportunities. Not only was there an absence of suitable airfields: in addition, low cruising speeds resulted in flight times that had only a slight edge over existing rail timings.

In 1929 municipal airports opened in Nottingham, Blackpool and Hull, with a temporary one at Manchester. By the 1930s average speeds had increased to 200 m.p.h., improved navigational aids were available and over ninety regular air services were operating within and around the UK. Of the advantages of air travel between mainland Britain, Ireland and the Scottish islands, no-one needed much convincing. However, between major cities on the mainland the railways could still offer shorter journey times, and the volume of air passengers was therefore small and the profits marginal. Adequate terminal facilities were slow in coming: by 1939 there were still no paved runways on civil airfields.

After 1945 there was a growth of public confidence in aviation, partly because of advances made during the war. When flight times were substantially cut by jetliners such as the Comet, air travel

EDINBURGH AIRPORT: *refuelling. New BP and Esso fuel terminals were opened here in 1980 and 1981. Passenger levels at Edinburgh dropped slightly over this period.*

became even more of an attractive proposition. The volume of passengers on international flights in 1939 was a mere 170,000, but by 1970 it had risen to 21 million, and by 1979 to 41 million. The sharp increase of the last two decades owes much to the growth of all-inclusive package tours in the 1960s and to the price-cutting war which followed the introduction of Laker Airways' walk-on trans-atlantic service in 1977.

Internal traffic has also increased, despite competition from high-speed trains. Relaxation of the state monopoly in 1960 allowed private companies to re-enter the domestic market. Today, British Airways, together with about fifty independent airlines (of which the largest is British Caledonian), provides a comprehensive network of services throughout the country. The Scottish services linking mainland airports with the islands yield little or no profit, but these links are recognized by the government as lifelines to the island communities, and some of them are subsidized.

London's airports

Around London, the pre-war airfields at Croydon, Heston and Hendon proved totally unsuited to major expansion, so international flights became centred on Heathrow, only fifteen miles from the centre of the capital. As Heathrow was progressively modernized, Gatwick became the secondary terminal, and was rebuilt in the 1950s, while Luton came into the limelight as the focus of package holidays. Overcrowding at Heathrow became especially troublesome in the late 1960s, and the controversial search for a third London airport site was begun. The selection of an existing airport at Stanstead, Essex, was eventually abandoned by the Roskill Commission in favour of a virgin site at Foulness (on the Thames estuary), but the British Airports Authority has lately put forward a renewed proposal to develop Stanstead.

THE BUSIEST AIRPORT

Heathrow is Britain's major airport for cargo as well as passengers. The layout of runways was designed to avoid interference from cross-winds—a requirement that is now outmoded.

Heathrow's shortage of capacity at busy periods has led to a policy of re-routing some traffic to Gatwick, which will ultimately have a capacity of 25 million passengers per year.

R1 R2 R3 Main runways
T1 T2 Terminals 1 and 2
T3d Terminal 3 Departures
T3a Terminal 3 Arrivals
T4 Terminal 4 (under construction: to be opened 1985. The terminal will be linked to a new Underground railway loop)
⊖ Heathrow Underground station
C Control tower
Ca Cargo terminal
Cp Carparks
F Fire station
G General aviation building ('General aviation' is the term for all aircraft movements other than commercial and military)
H Helicopter strip
M Maintenance area
P Perimeter road
Q Queen's Building
S Snow base

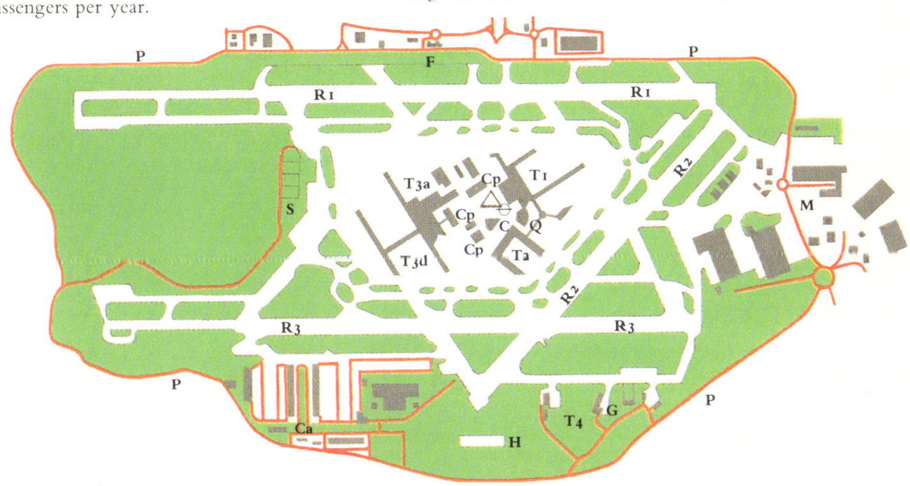

HEATHROW: *a view from the east. The photograph was taken in the autumn of 1980.*

CONNECTIONS
The aero industry: 180–81 *The plane-makers*
Wartime flying: 124–5 *The First World War;* **126–7** *The Second World War*

The Post Office

The British postal service is one of the oldest in the world, with a history going back more than 300 years. It was Charles I who founded the public post, in 1635, but its genesis can be traced back further than this. In Henry VIII's reign, mail was conveyed regularly along the main routes to and from London. However, this was strictly the King's mail: unofficial use of the service was discouraged, though it could not be entirely prevented.

The birth of the public postal service in the 17th century satisfied a growing demand, and at the same time provided the government of the day with a useful source of revenue. Postage was paid by the recipient of a letter, who was charged by mileage and the number of sheets the letter contained. In 1660, an Act of Parliament established the General Post Office as a state monopoly and banned private competition.

By the middle of the 18th century, the expansion of commerce and the growth of the letter-writing habit had greatly increased the demands upon the postal service. In response, an extensive programme of road building was launched in 1765, preparing the way for the stage-coach. By 1830 a stage-coach could collect and deliver over a distance of 120 miles within a 24-hour time-span.

A RURAL POSTMAN (***right***), c. *1900. With the introduction of the parcel post in 1883, letter-carriers became known as postmen. In due course their 'penny farthing' cycles were replaced by safety bicycles and, eventually, by motor vans.*

A PENNY BLACK (***right***). *In May 1840, when a uniform penny letter rate was adopted, the world's first postage stamps were issued – the Penny Blacks, of which 66 million were produced before the colour was changed to red (1841).*

WANGFORD POST OFFICE, SUFFOLK (***right***), c. *1912. By this time the local post office had become a central institution in everyday life*

This was also the year when post was carried by rail for the first time, on George Stephenson's new Manchester–Liverpool line.

Modernization

The real revolution was to come ten years later, with the reforms of Rowland Hill (1795–1879). By introducing a uniform cheap rate of postage to be paid by the sender rather than by the recipient, Hill made the post accessible to the populace, in a way it had never been before. Under the new system, postage was no longer charged by distance but by weight: a letter of half an ounce or less could be sent anywhere inland for a flat rate of one penny. Proof of payment was furnished by a postage stamp affixed to the letter before sending.

The sale of stamps marked the beginning of the Post Office counter service. Within fifteen years, post boxes were set up throughout the country (replacing the more expensive letter-receiving offices), and letter boxes – at first just slits in front

THE DISAPPEARING MAIL POUCH: *a photograph of 1960. This track-side apparatus, first demonstrated in 1839, enables mailbags to be snatched on to fast-moving trains.*

doors – came into being to facilitate delivery.

The mid-19th century was the beginning of the great age of railways and steamships, permitting a faster, more reliable postal service at home and abroad. Travelling post offices – railway carriages for sorting mail in transit – made an important contribution; they were in use on the Birmingham–Liverpool and London–Preston lines as early as 1838. By the end of the century the extension of the railway network, and technical improvements such as mail-snatching apparatus on trains, had so speeded up the service that deliveries were possible the day after posting at distances of more than 400 miles.

The 20th century

With the dawning of the 20th century, a new and valuable addition was made to the Post Office transport armoury – the aeroplane. Just eight years after the Wright brothers' historic flight, the world's first airmail service was launched between Hendon and Windsor, as part of King George V's coronation celebrations in 1911. In 1919, there followed the first regular international airmail link, between London and Paris. The development of the jet engine, permitting much faster travel, and the widespread adoption of the lightweight air-letter after the Second World War, greatly accelerated the growth of airmail traffic. Now, every working day of the week, a vast armada of aeroplanes, boats, trains, motor vehicles and foot-slogging postmen is deployed in moving a vast volume of mail, comprising some 35 million letters and 600,000 parcels.

LONDON'S SECRET UNDERGROUND, *in the 1960s: driverless electric trains linking sorting offices with main railway termini. The system opened in 1927.*

A LETTER AT THE SORTING OFFICE

Modern letter-sorting operations are based on the postcode (first introduced in 1959) and sophisticated technologies. At the sorting office, parcels and letters are first separated in the drum of a segregator, which is revolved so that letters slip out through the hinged flaps on its sides. Special scanners then locate the stamps, twist round the letters to ensure they are all the same way up, divide them into first and second class, and pass them on for franking. At a coding desk, an operator then reads the postcode on each letter and copies it on his keyboard. This feeds impulses to a computor-like translator which impresses a series of phosphorescent dots in two lines on the envelope. When the letter passes to the sorting scanner, these dots are 'read', and enable the machine to allocate the letter correctly. The machine can be used to sort letters for onward transmission (using the bottom row of phosphorescent dots) or, alternatively, for local delivery (using the top and bottom rows of dots in combination). If the postcode is absent, delivery may be delayed.

LETTERS *passing through the segregator's flaps are immediately divided into streams, depending on their size and shape.*

SCANNING *the stamp.*

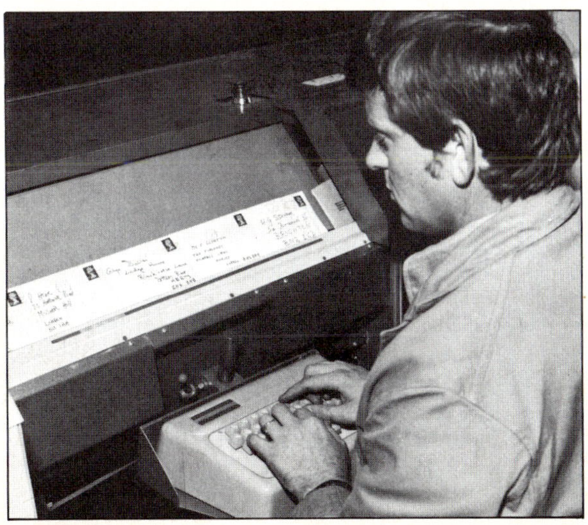

A CODING DESK OPERATOR *at work. Postcodes are essential for mechanical sorting operations, which hold down costs.*

CONNECTIONS

The growth of commerce: 100–101 *Britain in the world marketplace;* **102–3** *Reaching the consumer*

Literacy: 112–13 *Learning and the people*

Postcards: 188–9 *Tourism*

Telecommunications: 274–5 *Telegraph and telephones*

Telegraph and telephones

AN EARLY TELEPHONE EXCHANGE (*1910*). *On the roof* (**below**) *was a cumbersome distribution frame, with heavy overhead wires. The plug-and-socket style of switchboard* (**right**) *was gradually superseded by an automatic system designed by Almon B. Strowger, an undertaker from Kansas City.*

A WALL TELEPHONE, *of c. 1890, incorporating a carbon microphone (invented 1877).*

In 1981 British Telecom, the fourth largest telecommunications organization in the world, was officially separated from the Post Office, so closing a chapter in the history of communications technology in which the Post Office had played a major role.

The telegraph

Telecommunications is a relatively new development, originating in the 19th century with the invention of telegraphy. Basically, this is a method of sending messages, codified into electrical impulses, along wires. Pioneering work was carried out both in Britain and in the United States, where a successful telegraphic device was developed by Samuel Morse, who gave his name to the famous code. At about the same time William Cooke and Charles Wheatstone produced a British model, which they patented in 1837. This was the basis of the world's first commercial telegraph. Thirteen years later the first submarine telegraphic cable was laid, between England and France, and in 1866 a similar link was established with the United States. For nearly four decades, telegraphy provided the quickest means of long-distance communication.

The age of the telephone

In 1876 Alexander Graham Bell, a Scotsman living in the USA, astonished the world with his new invention, the telephone. Britain was quick to seize upon its advantages. The first British telephone company was the Telephone Company Ltd, which opened an exchange in August 1879 with eight subscribers.

In 1891 the first international telephone link was formed, between London and Paris. At that time the Post Office held a state monopoly over telegraph offices, conferred twenty years before. This did not extend, however, to telephones. There were now about 45,000 in the country, run by a combination of seven private companies, the Post Office and several municipal corporations.

Early in the following century, negotiations began with a view to unifying the system under the aegis of the Post Office. As most of the licences granted to private companies in the 1880s ran out by 1912, this was the date chosen for the takeover. When the time came, the bulk of the companies had already been absorbed into the Post Office or its most serious rival, the National Telephone Company. An Act of Parliament now gave the Post Office a telephone monopoly, thus creating a single, co-ordinated network.

An important milestone in British telecommunication history was the installation, in 1912, of an automatic telephone exchange at Epsom in Surrey. For the first time subscribers could make a local call without having to go through the operator. As the web of cables and telephones spread throughout the country, the technology moved forwards in leaps and bounds. In 1930 the Post Office introduced an 'on demand' service for long-distance calls, and in 1936 the world's first high-capacity coaxial cable was laid, between London and Birmingham. This made it possible for several hundred conversations to be transmitted simultaneously over one pair of wires.

It was not until 1956 that the first transatlantic telephone cable (TAT 1) was in operation, connecting Scotland and Newfoundland. This long-awaited development depended on a breakthrough made by Post Office engineers five years earlier: the evolution of a new type of deep-sea cable with a central steel core. Previously, calls to North America had been transmitted by radio, and the quality of reception had been variable; now they could be handled semi-automatically by a single operator. The new type of oceanic cable was a foundation stone of a fully automated worldwide telephone network. In 1958 the introduction

BRITISH TELECOM'S NAVY (**below**). *The* Iris, *seen here laying experimental optical fibre cable in Loch Fyne (western Scotland), is one of the ships that maintains Britain's underwater cables.*

LINKING THE WORLD BY SATELLITE

Satellites and their Earth stations carry an increasing share of global telecommunications. A typical satellite telephone call goes first to a local exchange, then to an international exchange, and from there to one of Britain's two Earth stations – Goonhilly near the tip of Cornwall or Madley near Hereford. From the Earth station the call is beamed up to a satellite by microwave radio and re-transmitted to Earth in another country. Satellites (among the most up-to-date is the Intelsat V, **below**) are placed in an almost perfect geostationary orbit. However, they are not quite stationary as seen from an Earth station, so the aerial (the one shown, **right**, is Aerial 4 at Goonhilly) has to be directed so that the satellite is brought within its beam. When this has been achieved, the Earth station picks up a beacon signal transmitted by the satellite, and this is used to provide automatic tracking.

Both the Goonhilly and Madley stations contain a repeater station which links the satellite system with the inland transmission network. Future systems are likely to employ low-cost Earth terminals located in cities.

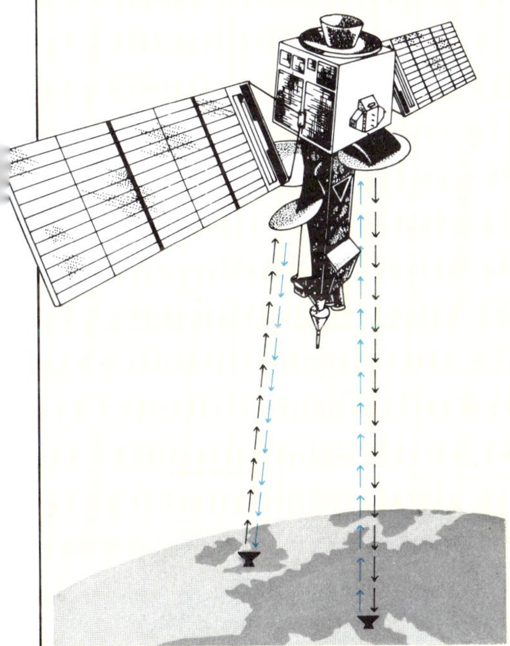

of Subscriber Trunk Dialling (STD) in Britain (initially in Bristol) enabled long-distance calls to be made direct. It was followed in 1963 by the opening of the first automatic international exchange link between London and Paris. London and New York were similarly connected in 1970, and links with other major European cities were created not long afterwards.

The shrinking world

The space age added a new dimension to telecommunications. *Telstar*, the first satellite, was launched in 1962. Linked with the 'Earth station' at Goonhilly Down in Cornwall (not far from where Marconi first transmitted his radio messages across the Atlantic), it could receive and beam down signals, providing telephone and television links with the United States.

Telstar was a pioneer satellite, whose rapid movement in low orbit called for very accurate tracking. In 1965, however, the first commercial communications satellite, *Early Bird* (INTELSAT I), was launched into geostationary orbit – in other words, it circled the globe at the same speed as the Earth spins on its axis, and could thus be kept in constant position over the Atlantic. Other satellites followed, and in 1969 the last step towards full global coverage was taken. Today, Britain has the second largest stake in the international satellite network, which handles television broadcasts, telex, data and facsimile calls, telegrams, messages to ships at sea and two-thirds of all intercontinental telephone calls.

In recent years, terrestrial transmission has also undergone something of a revolution. In 1978, just two years after the closure of the last manual exchange (at Portree on the Isle of Skye), the first telephone call in Europe was made using optical fibre transmission. This is a method of sending information, in the form of pulses of light, through hair-thin strands of glass. A single pair of fibres can transmit up to 2,000 telephone conversations simultaneously. Optical fibre cables, each consisting of between four and twelve fibrous strands, will gradually replace the old, coaxial cables which have been in use since the 1930s.

Coupled with this development, an extended electronic switching system (launched in 1979) will enable tomorrow's subscriber to use simplified dialling codes, receive automatic alarm calls, divert calls or block unwanted calls, and hold three-way long-distance conversations.

CONNECTIONS

Communications in the pre-electronic age: 272–3 *The Post Office*

The Post Office Tower: 250–51 *London*

Radio and television

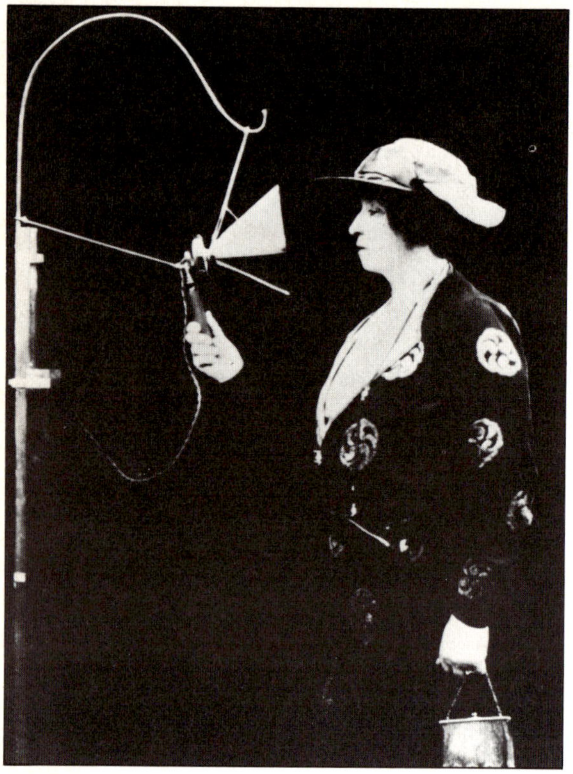

THE FIRST RADIO ENTERTAINMENT PROGRAMME (***left***), *on 15 June 1920, was a song recital by Dame Nellie Melba, broadcast from the Marconi Studio at Chelmsford, Essex.*

THE FIRST RADIO NEWS BROADCAST (***below***), *on 23 February 1920. The announcer was W.T. Ditcham. Today, the General News Service at Broadcasting House, London, distributes news by teleprinter to various London and regional centres.*

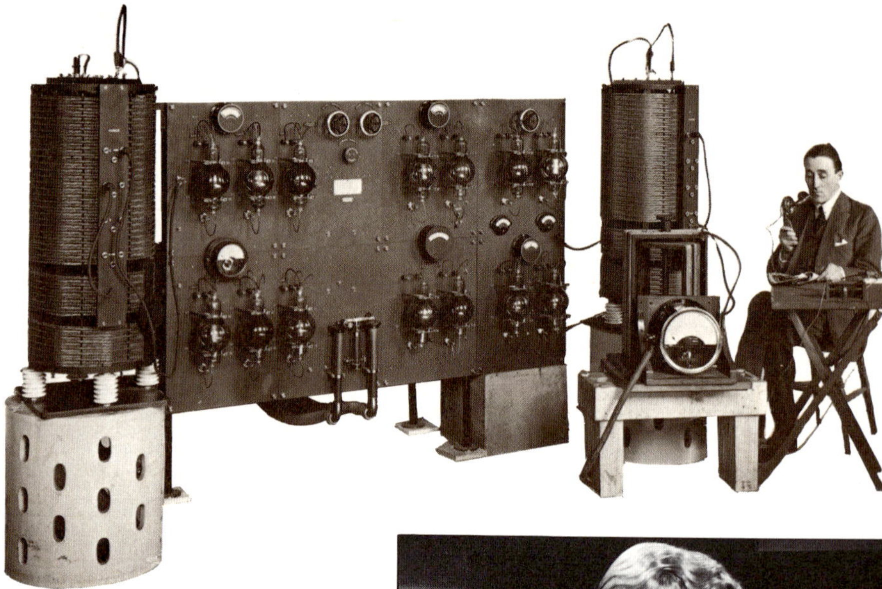

Radio and television have done more than provide a way of killing time. They have also been a powerful educative force and have played a major role as patrons of drama and music, as well as in the promotion of democracy, public accountability in politics, community awareness and the erosion of class barriers. Radio has also had the effect of standardizing educated speech, although the current tendency is towards a rather self-conscious revival of regional differences. On the debit side, many self-made forms of entertainment have suffered from the growth of popular broadcasting.

The radio years

A major event in the pre-history of broadcasting took place in 1901, when Gugliemo Marconi (1874–1937) transmitted radio signals from Cornwall to Newfoundland. The success of this attempt, and the first transmission of speech and music in Massachusetts in 1906, encouraged hundreds of amateur experimenters. Public broadcasting was banned by the Post Office in 1920, on the grounds that it interfered with important communications. However, in January 1922, in response to a petition of 63 wireless societies, the Marconi Company was allowed to go ahead with a daily 15-minute programme of speech and music. The authorities still feared that undisciplined broadcasting would lead to impossible cacophony on the airwaves, and the British Broadcasting Company was set up in October 1922 in order to regularize the situation. Daily broadcasting began the following month, from the old Marconi 2LO station in the Strand, London. The first programmes consisted mostly of election results. By 1924, the number of ten-shilling licence holders had passed the million mark, and the figure had doubled by 1927. By this time, a long-wave transmitter at Daventry in Northamptonshire, in conjunction with regional transmitters, provided a truly national network from the studios at Savoy Hill. In 1927 the Crawford Committee advised that future broadcasting be conducted by a public corporation 'acting as trustee for the national interest'. Accordingly, the British Broadcasting Corporation was established by royal charter. It functioned under the dynamic director-generalship of Sir John Reith, whose Empire Service (1932) was the antecedent of the famous World Service.

The arrival of television

Meanwhile, television was still in its infancy. John Logie Baird (1888–1946) had made his first public demonstrations in 1925, but it was not until 1936 that the BBC transmitted the world's first regular service, from the Alexandra Palace in north London. There were just 400 television sets in the country. By 1939 this number had risen to 20,000. But just before the outbreak of war, the service was shut down for fear that enemy bombers would home in on the transmitters.

Radio, however, grew immensely in importance during the Second World War. Popular programmes such as Tommy Handley's comedy show *ITMA* (*It's That Man Again*) and *The Brains Trust* quiz, and the rallying speeches of Winston Churchill, made the 'wireless' a vital morale-booster. The BBC emerged from the war with its prestige enhanced and its monopoly intact.

The era of competition

Television started up again in June 1946, with an hour of programmes in the afternoon and 90 minutes in the evening. The Coronation (1953) was seen by over 20 million viewers, and was a great stimulus to the sale of sets. Aerials crowded the urban rooflines. At this period, there was intense concern about the BBC monopoly. The verdict of the Beveridge Committee (1949) was that if broadcasting were to have a social purpose it had to be protected from the degrading effects of competition. However, a skilful pressure-group crusade succeeded in establishing commercial TV by an Act of 1954: an Independent Television Authority (ITA) was set up to control a federal, regionalized structure of companies whose revenue would come from advertising. Most channels prospered, and the sale of sets was boosted. By 1957 TV licences outnumbered radio licences for the first time.

RADIO GLAMOUR: *a new set on display at Radiolympia in 1934. Receivers such as this introduced millions of people to serious music: the BBC Symphony Orchestra was established in 1930.*

THE ALEXANDRA PALACE. *When the first regular* TV *broadcast was made from here in 1936, the range of the transmitter was only 30 miles.*

THE DAWN OF THE TV ERA: *a Press demonstration in 1933. The major problem was poor definition.*

Under Hugh Greene, the BBC staged a fight-back in the 1960s. In 1962 the Pilkington Committee castigated commercial television for the low quality of its programming, and recommended that a third channel be allocated to its rival. The first BBC 2 transmission was on 20 April 1964. Four years later all three channels were able to offer colour television.

Radio broadcasting was also transformed. The transistor and the establishment of BBC Radio One (in 1967) combined to give a new dimension to popular music. Eight local radio stations were also opened between the autumn of 1967 and the summer of 1968. The growth of commercial local radio after 1970 called for a widening of the ITA's umbrella: the organization was consequently re-designated as the Independent Broadcasting Authority in 1972. In the world of television, meanwhile, the controversy over the allocation of a fourth channel had already begun: it was eventually granted to commercial TV in November 1980.

The new technologies

Broadcasting is currently going through a change as profound as anything since the 1920s. The main catalyst in this process is the video cassette recorder (VCR), which has begun to free television from the strait-jacketing dimension of time, as well as providing a valuable new teaching medium. Most homes in Britain are likely to have a VCR in the near future. Other foreseeable developments are the expansion of cable TV, the growth of new satellite channels, and an increasing emphasis on payment by subscription. No longer merely a receiver for conventional programmed broadcasting, the television set can already offer a multi-purpose service which is almost as flexible as electricity itself.

CONNECTIONS
Churchill's broadcasts: 126–7 *The Second World War*
News services: 120–21 *The Press*

QUESTION TIME (***below***): *public figures answer questions from a* TV *studio audience, under the chairmanship of Sir Robin Day. The principle of audience participation has inspired some excellent programmes, both on commercial and* BBC *television, and in the form of radio 'phone-ins', which can perform a valuable advisory service.*

The arts

British painters, sculptors, architects, writers and musicians have often shown great responsiveness to the spirit of place. This theme and others are explored in the following pages, which include an historical survey of the visual arts in Britain ('The artist's eye').

When the Roman legions left Britain in the early 5th century, the so-called 'Dark Ages' began. The popular image of this period is one of predominant barbarism, with Anglo-Saxons penetrating Britain and, later, bloodthirsty Vikings plundering and destroying settlements. Yet the evidence from these centuries, gleaned from isolated remnants and some spectacular archaeological finds, suggests a surprisingly high level of artistic sophistication.

The Celtic tradition

The classical tradition, with its realistic portrayal of people and objects, had indeed disappeared. The Romans had favoured formal patterns such as the guilloche (interwoven wavy bands), but they had used them to surround mythological scenes. Now, Britain reverted to an art that was abstract and symbolic, using stylized animal forms which are presumed to have come from the art of the Celtic tribes. Buckles and clasps showing workmanship of unmatched dexterity, in gold, glass and enamel, were recovered from the sensationally rich 7th-century ship burial of Sutton Hoo in Suffolk.

The coming of Christianity did not immediately change this pagan style, for the Celtic Irish missionaries who brought their religion to Scotland (in the 6th century) and then to the north of England reinforced this heritage. A number of magnificently decorated sacred manuscripts, above all the Lindisfarne Gospels (created in an isolated Northumberland monastery in the late 7th century, and now in the British Museum), have pages devoted to Celtic patterns. The portraits of evangelists in these books, and the figures carved on the great stone crosses of this period, are strangely awkward and stiff by comparison.

GOLD BUCKLE (***below***), *7th century* AD. *The Sutton Hoo hoard demonstrates the survival of a style established by the Celts in Britain by the 3rd century* BC.
British Museum, London

NORMAN CARVED PORTALS

France may have created the most magnificent sculpted portals of the early Middle Ages, but England's finest examples have a vigour and eccentricity of their own. An enormous repertoire of decorative motifs included interlaced foliage and beak-heads (which glower down from the inner arch of the Kilpeck portal, ***above***) and chevron and diaper patterns. The traditional Viking ornament of intertwined dragon-like beasts was also absorbed into Norman art. Fine examples of the small, highly carved portal are also found at Barfreston (Kent), and at Ely Cathedral in the prior's doorway, with its magnificent Christ in Majesty tympanum (arched panel). Church sculpture did not exclude secular subjects, such as grotesque figures.

Anglo-Saxon culture

The 'renaissance' of the arts in the north of England in the 7th century was disrupted by the pressure of the invading Vikings, but a strong new cultural identity had emerged by the 11th century. In the small stone church of Bradford-on-Avon in Wiltshire, carvings of angels show that a strongly representational style had been established. Furthermore, a distinctive school of manuscript illumination had developed in the south in the 10th and 11th centuries, influenced by the art of the Frankish Empire of Charlemagne (800–814). The Bayeux tapestry, completed in 1077, is a superb example of Anglo-Saxon embroidery; ironically, it was employed in recording the victory of the Normans.

The conquest of art

The Norman conquest of 1066 shattered the Anglo-Saxon world and brought England into the orbit of France. The Normans brought with them the Romanesque style, with its masterly development of round-arched architecture and church sculpture. Occasionally, on capitals and portals, the entwining organic forms of the pre-Conquest age appeared, as on the portal of the church of Kilpeck, near Hereford. The grander Norman achievements include the awesome carved Apostles in the south porch of Malmesbury Abbey (Wiltshire) and superb 12th-century reliefs in Chichester Cathedral.

The arts were now thriving on a greater scale than ever before, and the focus of this flowering was the

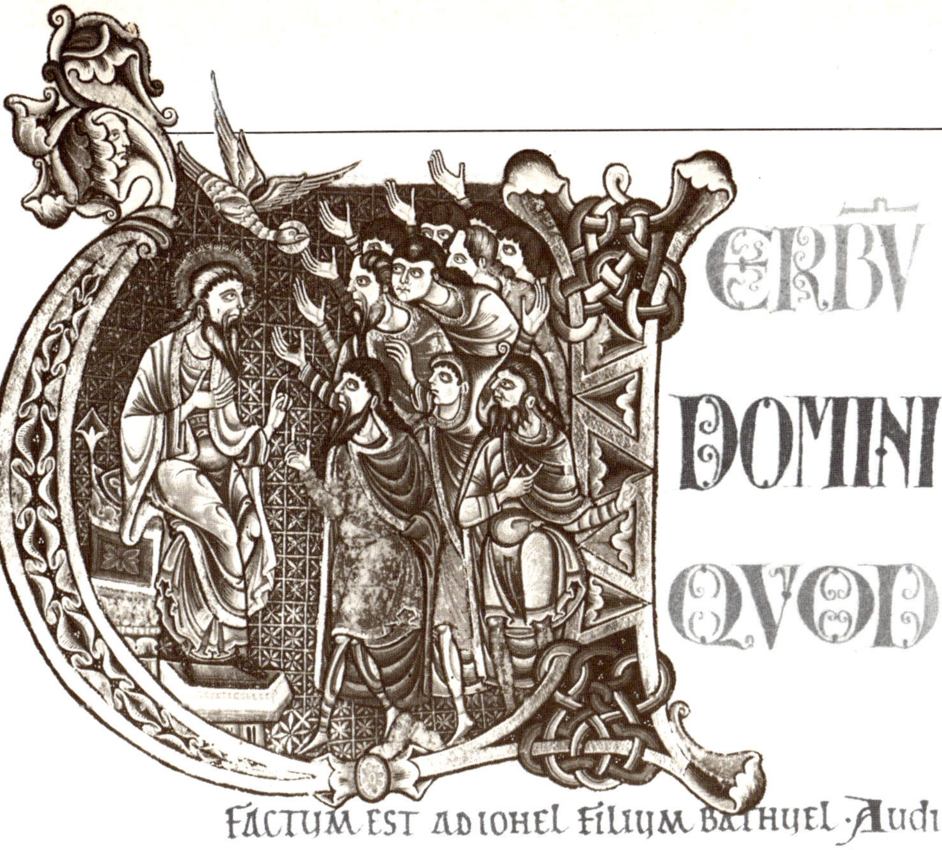

CHRIST AND THE APOSTLES, *an initial from the Winchester Bible,* c.*1160–70. Richly coloured figures, drawn in a dramatic, animated style, illustrate the Bishop of Winchester's giant Bible.* Winchester Cathedral Library

TOMB OF EDWARD II *(*d.*1327), Gloucester Cathedral. The idealization of the effigy – the King had been horribly murdered – and the softly flowing sculptural style are quintessentially 14th-century.*

THE WILTON DIPTYCH (***left***), c. *1380. Richard II, portrayed here praying to the Virgin, was a patron of the International Gothic style, whose hallmarks were linear richness and subtle vitality.*
National Gallery, London

Church – its buildings, its sacred manuscripts and liturgical objects. A rare surviving example of early 12th-century precious metalwork is the Gloucester Candlestick, in the Victoria and Albert Museum. It is as intricate as the decorative pages of the Lindisfarne Gospels, but it is three-dimensional, formed of a mass of bronze-gilt foliage, animals and human figures. England in the 12th century also cultivated some of the greatest schools of illumination in Europe, producing magnificent psalters and bibles, at Winchester, Canterbury, St Albans and Bury St Edmunds. Mural paintings from the period have survived more rarely.

Gothic masterpieces

Late in the 12th century, just as Romanesque was at its height, a new style was imported from France. Gothic art abandoned the massive solemnity of the Norman manner and a heightened elegance now emerged. The great new churches of the 13th century, such as Wells Cathedral and Westminster Abbey, were embellished with graceful reliefs and free-standing statues. Intricate displays of stained glass were made possible by elaborate patterns of stone tracery in church windows. England became famous for religious vestments, decorated with gold- and silver-figured embroidery known as *Opus Anglicanum*; this work was coveted as far afield as Rome.

In the later Middle Ages the secular powers – royalty and nobles – began to have a greater impact on culture. Luxurious clothes, devotional ivories and small altarpieces were in demand. By the 14th century, secular themes were increasingly appearing in the manuscripts produced for the great courts of Europe, and the prevailing delicate, linear style was enlivened by naturalistic detail. Embellishment became increasingly sumptuous, sometimes with backgrounds of tooled gold.

Throughout the Middle Ages, there was no distinction between the artist and the craftsman, and creative work was almost always anonymous, and dedicated to the glory of God. The age of a predominantly private art and of secular patronage, and the concept of individual artistic genius, did not emerge until the 16th century.

CONNECTIONS
Celtic traditions: 46–7 *The coming of Christianity*
College architecture: 254–5 *Oxford and Cambridge*
Medieval churches: 200–207
Roman art: 194–5 *Roman Britain*
Saxons, Vikings and Normans: 42–3 *The movement of peoples*

THE AMBASSADORS (*left*), *1533, by Hans Holbein the Younger, the first truly great Renaissance painter to visit England. This canvas is outstanding for its meticulous still-life background and the virtuoso foreshortening of the symbolic skull.*
National Gallery, London

THE ARMADA JEWEL, *interior* (*below*), c.*1600, attributed to Nicholas Hilliard. Queen Elizabeth I's portrait, and a Tudor rose, are enclosed by a locket of enamelled gold with rubies and diamonds. The jewel was given to the Queen by her Treasurer.*
Victoria and Albert Museum, London

The Renaissance – the great European artistic flowering that began in 14th-century Italy – did not make its first impressions on Britain until the 16th century. The Tudor dynasty, launched by Henry VII in 1485, revelled in thoroughly secular visual splendour and admired artistic styles from the Continent, but at first the response was fitful and cautious.

The transition

The fruits of Tudor patronage were evident early in the 16th century in Henry VII's Chapel in Westminster Abbey, London. It was built in the exquisite late Gothic style, and was given a focal-point in Henry's magnificent marble tomb, sculpted between 1512 and 1518 by an Italian, Pietro Torrigiano, fellow-pupil of Michelangelo. The King's recumbent effigy, startlingly realistic, is accompanied by thoroughly Renaissance motifs, notably the graceful cherubs or *putti*, which hark back to ancient Rome.

Henry VIII's break with the Roman Catholic Church in 1534 was the final death-blow for Church patronage. The new centres of artistic creativity were private houses and palaces. A very English adaptation of Renaissance motifs is apparent in the terracotta decorations of the most extravagant Tudor palace, Hampton Court in Surrey, begun in 1514. The small study lined with paintings was clearly an attempt to rival the private studies (*studioli*) of the Italian Renaissance princes.

Since the Reformation had practically destroyed the finer traditions of English painting, Henry VIII turned to a Swiss-German artist, Hans Holbein the Younger, for flattering records of his own resplendent figure. Holbein spent two spells in England, in the 1520s and again from 1532 to 1543. His characteristic style was extraordinarily realistic and often sumptuous. Holbein was the brightest star in 16th-century English painting, but, like his immediate successors, he was still a court servant rather than an honoured genius. He was followed at court by Guillim Scrots (from the Netherlands), who had a slight but elegant mannerist style, and pandered to the Elizabethan taste for allegory and complex symbolism.

Elizabethan aristocrats

Court patronage languished in the reign of Elizabeth I, but the luxury-loving nobles of England were eager patrons of the arts. In portraits of the period, their somewhat stiffly posed figures are gaudily decked with jewellery, lace and rich textiles. One of the finest painters was in fact a miniaturist, Nicholas Hilliard, whose tiny, intimate portraits were given as keepsakes (and perhaps exchanged by lovers). Elizabethan sculpture was in general less sophisticated, though the best tomb sculptures also showed a strong preoccupation with rich costumery.

The great art studios of this period were the grand houses of the aristocracy. Hardwick Hall in Derbyshire and Longleat House in Wiltshire exemplify a new mode of architecture – 'all window and no wall', with a concern for symmetry and a delight in various decorative motifs, both Renaissance and Netherlandish. Classical pilasters (thin, flat columns) were applied to exteriors, while the interior decoration often had an almost rustic vigour. The plaster friezes of Montacute House in Somerset and the oak screens of Parham Hall in Surrey are characteristically, almost monstrously, Elizabethan. Such houses were liberally hung with tapestries (mostly imported) and provided with rich tableware and ostentatiously carved furniture. Scotland in the 16th century achieved its own Renaissance splendour at Linlithgow Castle (Lothian), Falkland Palace (Fife) and elsewhere.

ELIZABETHAN EMBROIDERY. *The Bradford table carpet* (*below*), *dated to the late 16th century, is stitched in* petit point *in silks. Needlework was a popular aristocratic pastime, and the great houses of the period were gloriously decorated with embroidered hangings, table covers and curtains. Some panels by Mary Queen of Scots, depicting plants, animals and various emblematic devices, still survive at Oxburgh Hall in Norfolk.*
Victoria and Albert Museum, London

Stuart grandeur

It was the Stuart monarchy that presided over the full flowering of the Renaissance in Britain, when it rivalled that of Italy and France. Charles I brought over the Flemish artist Van Dyck, and commissioned paintings from Rubens; both were knighted at his sparkling court. He encouraged the outstanding royal tapestry weavers at Mortlake in London and commissioned the first thoroughly Italianate buildings in England – notably the Banqueting House in Whitehall, London, designed by Inigo Jones. This new style, imitating the Italian architecture of Palladio, was radically to affect the whole course of English architecture.

Van Dyckian portraiture established a standard of elegant grandeur and psychological insight, which was successfully followed by two English painters, William Dobson and Robert Walker. Their subjects – doomed Cavaliers and stalwart Parliamentarians – were usually endowed with a grand monumentality vastly different from the etiolated, bejewelled aristocrats of Elizabethan portraiture.

The Stuart court and nobility looked to France for guidance in taste, and were influenced by the Gallic fashion for vast mythological paintings. After the disruption of the Civil War, the Frenchman Louis Laguerre (who had worked at Versailles) and the Neapolitan Antonio Verrio were both invited over to undertake huge decorative schemes.

The leading portraitist of the Restoration was Sir Peter Lely, whose flattering and fluent style was enormously popular, though it was quite superficial. The outstanding artistic development was in architecture: the phenomenon of the English baroque, dominated by the undisputed genius of Sir Christopher Wren (1632–1723), whose massive, dynamic compositions sounded a new note of high drama.

CONNECTIONS
Architecture and décor: 208–9 *The great country houses;* 210–11 *Rooms in country houses;* 212–13 *The Italian influence in architecture*
Painting and the decorative arts: 290–93 *Great art collections*
Royal patronage: 58–9 *Monarchy and display*

THOMAS KILLIGREW AND LORD CROFTS, *1638, by Sir Anthony Van Dyck. Van Dyck's exquisitely elegant baroque portraits, such as this study of two royalist gentlemen, had a profound and lasting influence on English portraiture. He also painted religious and mythological subjects.*
Windsor Castle, Royal Collection

GRINLING GIBBONS: MASTER CARVER OF RESTORATION ENGLAND

GIBBONS AT CAMBRIDGE (***above*** *and* ***right***). *From 1691 Gibbons carved portrait busts and delicate limewood panels of fruit, flowers and coats of arms for the bookcases and alcoves of Wren's handsome new library for Trinity College (1676–84).*

GIBBONS AT PETWORTH (***right***). *In 1692 Gibbons began work for the Duke of Somerset at Petworth House in Sussex. The east wall of the Carved Room includes astounding three-dimensional song birds in cages and putti with trumpets.*

Grinling Gibbons was the finest decorative wood-carver in Europe in the late 17th century. He carried out numerous schemes for churches and palaces. Fine examples can still be seen at London's St Paul's Cathedral, Blenheim Palace (Oxfordshire) and elsewhere. Gibbons delighted in flourishes of *trompe-l'oeil* virtuosity: he made a fine cravat carved in limewood (now in the Victoria and Albert Museum), which was reputedly worn by Horace Walpole.

MARRIAGE A LA MODE: *'Shortly after the marriage', 1743, by William Hogarth. Hogarth's* tableaux *of a collapsed marriage were an unprecedented success.*
National Gallery, London

THE ARTIST'S DAUGHTERS (***below***), c.*1765, by Thomas Gainsborough. The artist's daughters have as much elegance as his aristocratic sitters.*
National Gallery, London

The fertility of invention and the variety of styles in 18th-century British art were born of a new prosperity and peace. Britain was emerging as a leading world power, its great wealth based on trade and on pioneering triumphs in industrial manufacture. The gentry and the rising middle classes formed a new category of patrons, who demanded excellence in all branches of the arts, and encouraged it in British artists. Continental art was still collected avidly but the traffic was now two-way: for the first time, British art was influential abroad.

The late baroque style

In the first years of the 18th century the grand style that had been promoted by the Stuart aristocracy continued the note of luxurious display. The gargantuan palaces built by Sir John Vanbrugh (with the collaboration of Nicholas Hawksmoor) – Blenheim (1705–24) in Oxfordshire and Castle Howard (1699–1712) in North Yorkshire – are masterpieces at the summit of English baroque. Hawksmoor's London churches and the buildings of James Gibbs show brilliance and flamboyance in smaller dimensions.

The next phase in architecture was a return to the Palladianism of Inigo Jones, in the restrained, sober classicism developed by Lord Burlington, Colen Campbell and William Kent. Interiors remained rich and exuberant. Sir James Thornhill surpassed his foreign mentors in vast allegorical murals and ceiling paintings. His Painted Hall in Wren's Greenwich Hospital, London, is perhaps the finest illusionistic painting of the baroque period in England – a grand composition on a grand scale.

The English school of painting

From about 1725 painting in England entered its golden age. William Hogarth (1697–1764), often claimed as the greatest of all English painters, was the first to depict the rich variety of English life and culture. His 'modern moral subjects' – satirical scenes painted for sets of engravings that reached a wide public – are brilliantly deft and vivid, and cruelly witty. Hogarth wished to establish an English school in another field – history painting – and was given scope for his large canvases in the Grand Manner by the enlightened patronage of Thomas Coram. But his work in this vein is hugely ponderous, and he was far more successful in his portraits, which realized a grand but unforced profundity of vision. By 1740 Hogarth had broken decisively with the Van Dyckian tradition, which had limped on into the early 18th century, in a debased form, in the portraits of Sir Godfrey Kneller.

The Royal Academy

In 1768 the Royal Academy was founded, with the aim of raising the status of artists. Its early years were dominated by rivalry between Hogarth and the first President, Sir Joshua Reynolds. Reynolds practised, and preached, a scholastic Grand Manner. In portraits, he enveloped his fashionable sitters in classical dress, such as the Montgomery sisters wear in *Three Ladies adorning a Term of Hymen*, 1733 (Tate Gallery).

HANDEL'S TOMB, *1761, by Louis François Roubiliac. Tomb sculptors abandoned the old 'effigy in death' for lively portraits. Here, Handel conducts a celestial orchestra in Westminster Abbey.*

The new elegance

The shift in taste from the formal Grand Manner to the lighter, more graceful mode of the mid-18th century is illustrated by the popularity of Thomas Gainsborough (1727–88), also a founder member

A CHEETAH WITH TWO INDIANS (***right***), c.*1765, by George Stubbs. George III commissioned England's finest animal painter to portray this cheetah, given to him by the Governor of Madras.*
Manchester City Art Gallery

THE LIBRARY, KENWOOD HOUSE, *London, 1767–9, by Robert Adam. Adam studied Roman art and applied his knowledge to nearly every aspect of design, from ceilings to carpets and furniture. The library at Kenwood is, typically, unified by its classical themes and by its delicate colour scheme, and is distinguished by a thoroughly neoclassical restraint. Adam's style was widely imitated.*

of the Academy. He trained in the French rococo style, and evolved a free, fluid technique, full of sensuous delight in delicate textures. Perhaps even more intimate were George Romney's portraits, notably those of the infamous Lady Hamilton. The lighter manner was simultaneously developed by watercolour artists, and was also embodied in figurines made by the Bow and Chelsea porcelain factories. Pastoral simplicity was a dominant theme.

The taste for the informal came into play in the decorative arts, where French rococo vied with pseudo-Chinese effects (chinoiserie) as well as quaint versions of English 'Gothick'. The furniture designer Thomas Chippendale exploited both, but also achieved a classical elegance, notably in a fine set of pieces for Harewood House, West Yorkshire, in the 1760s. Delicate straight-lined furniture, associated with Hepplewhite and Sheraton, later superseded the swirling contours of the rococo style.

Neoclassicism

Classicism had been the dominant architectural style throughout the 18th century, but now it gave way to *neo*classicism, in part a reaction against the decadent frivolity of the rococo. It entailed a stricter emulation of the arts of ancient Greece and Rome, which were closely studied. Archaeological expeditions were sent to the Mediterranean (for example, by the Society of Dilettanti), and several outstanding collections of antiquities were formed. The Scottish architect and designer Robert Adam (1728–92) was particularly influential in developing neoclassical interior decoration. In ceramics the leader was Josiah Wedgwood, whose decorated pieces characteristically featured white classical figures applied to a blue or other coloured ground.

By the end of the century British painting had freed itself from the tyranny of portraiture. Landscape painting had been established (notably by Richard Wilson, Alexander Cozens, Joseph Wright of Derby and Gainsborough) and history painting gained a new lease of life in the works of Benjamin West. Meanwhile, in the medium of watercolour, Thomas Rowlandson's satire and William Blake's mysticism were startlingly original. Sporting art was transformed in the meticulously executed canvases of George Stubbs. Painting in England now had a variety and vigour that by earlier standards were quite extraordinary.

NEOCLASSICAL POTTERY

It was Josiah Wedgwood's ambition to produce wares fashioned after the classical treasures that were being excavated by archaeologists at Herculaneum and Pompeii. This was fulfilled in 1769 with the foundation of his new factory, Etruria, near Stoke-on-Trent in Staffordshire. The factory soon became famous for its black Basaltes ware with painted Grecian designs and its Jasper ware (from 1774), which had relief decorations in white on grounds of pale blue, dark blue, sage green, lilac, yellow, or black. Jasper ware was used as a medium for fine portrait plaques, among other things, and was much imitated, for example by Sèvres.

Wedgwood employed several notable artists to design the reliefs, among them George Stubbs and John Flaxman. The latter made the model for the vase showing *Apollo and the Nine Muses* (***left***). The factory exploited authentic Greek shapes – urns and drinking cups – but antique relief ornament was also applied to everyday 18th-century teapots. Wedgwood's most popular products were in an elegant, classically restrained, cream-coloured earthenware known from *c.*1765 as Queen's Ware, after Queen Charlotte. His greatest contribution to ceramics was the development of attractive pottery that was also durable and inexpensive.

CONNECTIONS
Baroque and neoclassical styles: 208–9 *The great country houses;* **210–11** *Rooms in country houses;* **212–13** *The Italian influence in architecture*
Georg Friedrich Handel: 300–301 *Music and song*
Landscape painting: 294–5 *Artists and places*
Josiah Wedgwood: 164–5 *Pottery and porcelain*

THE BARD *(**left**), 1817, by John Martin. The last Welsh bard curses Edward I from a towering crag. Martin's impact depended on impossible magnification of scale and drama. A master of populist art, he was a forerunner of the modern disaster-movie maker.*
Laing Art Gallery, Newcastle-upon-Tyne

The 19th century was the period of Britain's greatest power in the world arena – a peak of national self-confidence. It was also a time of artistic efflorescence, and of public display on an unprecedented scale – at huge international exhibitions and in vast public buildings. At no time previously had British artists been so much lauded or so well paid. Sculpture was generally bland but British painting, although it could be emptily grandiose, was often very inventive.

Romanticism

From about 1790 until 1840 British art was dominated by a huge European phenomenon: the Romantic movement. In an increasingly mechanized world, exploited by capitalists and explained by scientists, the Romantics were haunted by a sense of doom and catastrophe, and their art often expressed their own highly subjective responses to the world. British Romanticism embraced the extraordinarily diverse talents of William Blake, and those twin champions of the landscape, John Constable and J.M.W. Turner. Sir Thomas Lawrence and Sir Henry Raeburn dominated portraiture in London and Edinburgh respectively.

Blake (1757–1827), the painter, poet and unworldly eccentric, evolved a muscular yet delicate watercolour style, drawing on the arts of Raphael and Michelangelo. He created his own mythological world. Both he and his disciple Samuel Palmer had visionary experiences, and the imaginative power of their work inspired a small group of young followers, 'The Ancients'. Greater popular success, however, was won by the series of apocalyptic extravaganzas painted and engraved by John Martin.

In the mainstream of British Romanticism, artists were more impressed by Turner. He was the leading Academician from the early 1800s, and painted huge canvases in which nature was coupled with drama or with tender melancholy. In hundreds of private studies, as well as mature works such as *Rain, Steam and Speed* (1843, Tate Gallery), he explored atmospheric space and colour, anticipating (and even inspiring) the French Impressionists. Constable's work, directly concerned with the simple beauty of the countryside, had less impact on his contemporaries in England, but was much admired in France.

Victorianization

After the accession of Queen Victoria in 1837 an official style of art emerged. Landscapes and nudes were demoted in favour of the genre paintings – versions of everyday themes treated in a busy, narrative fashion. William Frith's *Derby Day* of 1858 (Tate Gallery), a feast of detailed contemporary observation, is a climax of this trend. Piety, patriotism and melodrama were dominant moods, and there was a strong strain of the sentimental, for example in the ragged urchins and pretty country girls of Sir David Wilkie.

From the early years of the 19th century, the decorative arts had been dominated by free-flowing eclecticism. The masterpiece of the Regency was Sir John Nash's Brighton Pavilion (1815–22), with its mixture of Indian, Moorish and Chinese ornament. Neo-Gothic, which had its roots in the 18th-century Picturesque movement, was also popular at this time. In the Victorian age the magpie-like attitude towards older styles was even more pronounced, and the result was a plethora of revivals.

In architecture a battle raged from the 1840s to the 1870s between neoclassical (both Greek and Roman) and neo-Gothic. The Houses of Parliament (by Sir Charles Barry) were a triumph for Gothic, whose principal champion was A.W.N. Pugin. But many classical monuments of civic pride also appeared, such as Leeds Town Hall.

The most rebellious advance in painting in the mid-19th century was the formation of the Pre-

OPHELIA, *1852, by J.E. Millais. Pre-Raphaelite artists took painting from the life to astonishing extremes. Lizzie Siddal, the model for this beautiful drowning virgin, had to lie in a cold bath for many hours.*
Tate Gallery, London

THE ALBERT MEMORIAL AND THE ALBERT HALL, *London* ***(below left)****, 1863–72 and 1867–71. The architecture of Kensington's cultural centre, inspired by Prince Albert, displays the revival of Gothic, Renaissance and Classical styles. The Memorial was designed by George Gilbert Scott.*

STAFFORDSHIRE PLATE ***(below right)****, late 19th century. The pottery towns responded to the demand for bright, ornamental ware by developing new techniques for mass production.*

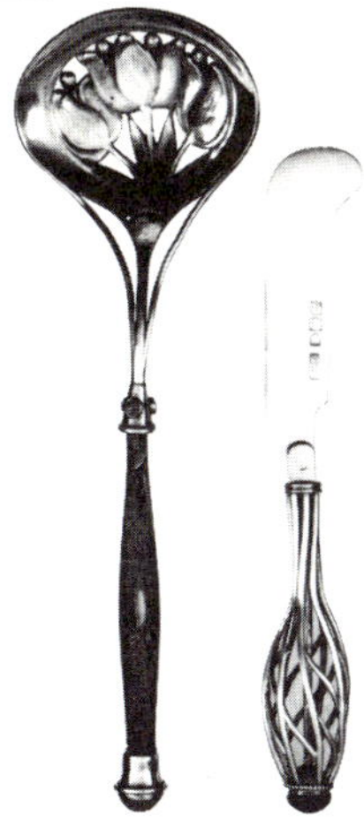

LATE VICTORIAN DECORATIVE ARTS

Mass production was repellent to William Morris and to the Arts and Crafts Movement, which was inspired by his theories. Morris espoused a richly coloured ornamental style and, with his company of craftsmen, he produced tapestries, stained glass, wallpapers and furniture (***below***). His style was superseded in the 1890s by the more austere, linear grace of Walter Crane's book illustrations and C.R. Ashbee's silverwork (***left***). Both Crane and Ashbee discarded the heavier, medieval overtones of Morris's work. Ashbee's designs are closely related to the Art Nouveau manner, which was characterized by sensuous, swirling shapes and owed much of its popularity to its promotion by Liberty's new department store in Regent Street, London.

Raphaelite Brotherhood in 1848. A small group of painters (principally D.G. Rossetti, W. Holman Hunt and J.E. Millais) was determined to reject the current notion of beauty and return to a sharp, almost primitive clarity of colour and draughtsmanship, which they associated with the style of the early Renaissance. Their first exhibition of 1850 outraged the Establishment: John Millais' *Christ in the House of His Parents* (1851, Tate Gallery) was described in *The Times* as plainly revolting. But the heavily moral and romantically medieval subjects of the PRB are now seen as quintessentially Victorian.

The Pre-Raphaelite painters soon split up and their styles diverged. Rossetti's became softer and more luxuriant. He influenced Edward Burne-Jones, who designed tapestries and stained glass as well as painted. Burne-Jones's languid ladies with erotic undertones belong to the broad current of Symbolism in Europe. Eroticism appeared also as a new strain in the official style. The leading Academy painters in the 1880s, notably Frederick Lord Leighton and Sir Lawrence Alma-Tadema, produced extraordinarily decadent scenes of women in Roman baths and Turkish harems.

The most controversial painter of the period was the American-born aesthete James McNeill Whistler (1834–1903), who declared that painting could be pure art, like music, without literary or narrative content. He shared the concerns of the French Post-Impressionists, and reduced his scenes of the Thames in London to patterns of muted colours. He was, however, an isolated phenomenon, and most of the British avant garde (such as Philip Wilson Steer) hung on to the coat-tails of the less revolutionary Impressionists.

Technology and craftsmanship

The manufacture of artefacts, meanwhile, became increasingly industrialized. In 1851 the power of industry was absolute and the Great Exhibition, held in the revolutionary iron-and-glass structure of the Crystal Palace in London, proclaimed it to the world – in mass-produced furniture, ceramics, glassware, metalwork and textiles.

The mania for mechanization led to a sharp reaction, a nostalgic return to an age of honest

craftsmanship. The great protagonists were John Ruskin (who was appalled to hear a stone-sculptor swearing while he was at work on the Pitt-Rivers Museum at Oxford) and William Morris, for whom craftsmanship had profound moral and religious associations. For Morris the Middle Ages, when craftsmanship was dedicated to God, were a paradise lost. He was an inspiration to the Arts and Crafts Movement, but never fully achieved his aims. For he was heroically trying to stem an irresistible tide: the advance towards an effective marriage of design and machinery, which came about in the 20th century.

CONNECTIONS
Church restoration: 204–5 *Parish churches*
Landscape painting: 294–5 *Artists and places*
John Nash: 214–15 *Royal retreats;* **246–7** *London*
Victorian architecture: 248–9 *London*
Victorian country houses: 208–9 *The great country houses;* **210–11** *Rooms in country houses*

THE ROCK DRILL (**below**), *1913, by Sir Jacob Epstein. When originally exhibited, this sculpture was set on a real rock drill.*
Tate Gallery, London

THE LIBRARY, GLASGOW SCHOOL OF ART (**left**), *1907–9, by C.R. Mackintosh. Mackintosh's version of Art Nouveau has none of the hot-house sensuality of the Continental style. The subtle linear composition was a triumph for abstract design, and the furniture was carefully integrated.*

In the 20th century the visual arts in Britain, as elsewhere in the world, have been characterized by extreme and, to many, disturbing upheavals. Artists and designers have pioneered new forms and styles in a heroic endeavour to meet the challenge of machine production and to express new ideas that have questioned the comfortable assumptions underlying the arts of the past. Yet alongside the most radical developments there have been many signs of nostalgia.

The turn of the century

The Arts and Crafts Movement was still a potent force in the first decade of the 20th century, but a change of heart was now apparent. C.R. Ashbee, for one, began to lose his faith in handicrafts, and stated in 1910 that 'modern civilization rests on machinery'. The greatest British exponent of the Art Nouveau style, C.R. Mackintosh (1868–1928), was little interested in details of individual craftsmanship, and in his furniture preferred painted wood to the appearance of the natural grain. Mackintosh's achievement as an architect, a field in which he freed himself from academic convention and created dynamic spatial compositions, was rivalled only by the austere country houses of Charles Voysey and the inventive traditionalism of Sir Edwin Lutyens.

The new abstraction

In painting the treacherous path between the popular anecdotalism of the Victorian age and the refined aestheticism of Whistler was taken by Walter Sickert (1860–1942), who brought something of the immediacy of Impressionism to dour and sombre scenes of everyday life. The younger painters, including Harold Gilman and Spencer Gore (who were to form the Camden Town Group in 1911), admired Sickert's subject matter but rejected his bleak colouring in favour of a brilliance inspired by the French Post-Impressionists.

The Vorticists responded to a new, bracing breeze from the Continent – Cubism. Their periodical *BLAST* (1914–15) was an outcry against all that was most stultifying in bourgeois society. It was the brainchild of Percy Wyndham Lewis (1882–1957), whose harsh, semi-abstract, mechanistic paintings were an important influence on many younger

POWER (**below**), *1930, by E. McKnight-Kauffer. The artist developed a 'Cubo-Vorticist' style in posters made in the 1920s and 1930s for London Transport, patron of the avant garde.*
London Transport Museum

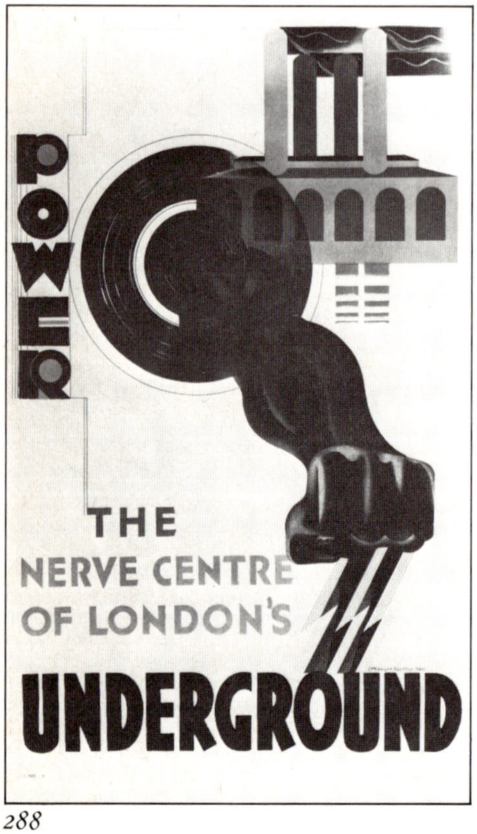

TOTES MEER (**below**), *1940–1, by Paul Nash. The title refers to the 'dead sea' of German aircraft shot down in 1940 – a subject to which Nash gives a surrealist treatment. He was an official war artist.*
Tate Gallery, London

BRITISH SCULPTURE SINCE THE SECOND WORLD WAR

Britain has made her most outstanding contribution to modern art in the field of sculpture. In the 1940s and 1950s first Henry Moore and then Barbara Hepworth established international reputations – Moore above all with his monumental figures, Hepworth with graceful bronzes and abstract carvings. Her wooden *Biolith* (***right***), 1948–9, is a consummate example of the ideal of 'truth to material'. In the 1960s British sculpture was once more transformed, principally by Philip King and Anthony Caro (both pupils of Henry Moore). They rejected organic forms for completely abstract, large-scale sculptures, using iron and steel plates, beams and girders, sometimes brightly coloured with enamel paints. Caro's *Fathom* (***below***) of 1976 exploits the colour and texture of rusted steel, and, typically, lies without a base upon the ground. These sculptors have preferred the industrial techniques of welding and riveting to the more traditional methods of modelling and carving.

artists. The dynamic energy of Lewis was matched by that of Sir Jacob Epstein (1880–1959), who took up the current Continental fascination with primitive sculpture and began, before the First World War, to experiment with non-traditional materials.

By contrast with this ferment, the 1920s presented a calmer picture: the decade was distinguished by the lively (if superficial) portraiture of Augustus John, by Epstein's public portrait busts and monumental work, and by the phenomenon of Art Deco. A more personal vision was achieved in the mystical paintings of Sir Stanley Spencer.

Art in the 1930s

Evidence of burgeoning new energies in British art are found, in the 1930s, in the work of the younger sculptors, who rediscovered the fascination of carving. This return to an old technique was pioneered by Eric Gill as part of a larger campaign for the revival of handicraft. Henry Moore (born 1898) and Barbara Hepworth (1903–75) belong to the same line of development: both rejected the academic traditions of modelling to explore the natural qualities of their materials.

The growing interest in abstract art on the Continent was paralleled by the efforts of architects (such as Berthold Lubetkin) who imported to Britain the austere functionalism of the International Style. Increasing politicization of the arts in the 1930s was reflected in the formation of numerous groups who expressed their aims in dogmatic manifestos. The French Surrealists had their English counterparts – painters such as Paul Nash who provided an alternative style to the geometrical abstraction favoured by Ben Nicholson and others. Opposed to both tendencies was the politically committed realism of the Euston Road School, founded in 1938 by Sir William Coldstream.

Post-war developments

The need to boost morale in the Second World War gave rise to government sponsorship of the arts, and the tendency continued afterwards, notably in the Festival of Britain (1951), where artists of all kinds combined to present an optimistic view of the nation's role in the post-war world. An altogether bleaker vision of man's destiny emerged from the sinister paintings of Francis Bacon (born 1909). Predictably, abstraction has been a powerful ingredient in post-war art, the most distinguished exponent in sculpture being Anthony Caro. By contrast, 'Pop' artists such as Richard Hamilton have turned to mass media as a source of imagery. A more traditional kind of figurative painting is represented by David Hockney and R.B. Kitaj.

Post-war architects have particularly turned their attention to urban development and mass housing. Their solutions to the housing problem – large uniform estates and tower blocks – have seldom met with unanimous approval. However, some examples, such as Alton West Estate (1952–9) at Roehampton in west London, have successfully combined large-scale units with spacious grounds.

CONNECTIONS
Art Nouveau and Art Deco: 292–3 *Great art collections*
David Hockney: 300–301 *Music and song*
Modern architecture: 170–71 *Building;* **240–41** *Suburbia;* **250–51** *London*
Reactions to the landscape: 294–5 *Artists and places*

THREE FIGURES (***right***), *1976, by Francis Bacon. One of the world's leading figurative painters, Bacon horrifically distorts reality to express his view of man as 'an accident, a completely futile being'.*
Tate Gallery, London

Great art collections/*Painting and sculpture*

THE NATIONAL GALLERY, *in the mid-19th century. The idea of a national collection was immediately popular, and at auctions sales to the gallery were cheered. Sir Charles Eastlake bought 139 paintings in the decade before his death in 1865.*

DIONE AND APHRODITE, *in the British Museum. Lord Elgin, between 1801 and 1805, acquired many of the classical sculptures from the Parthenon temple at Athens. He originally planned only to draw the marbles, but eventually obtained permission to ship them to England. He sold them to the British Museum for £35,000.*

SEVEN GREAT COLLECTORS

1 Charles I (1600–49). Of his treasures, still in the royal collection are Mantegna's *Triumphs* (Hampton Court) and the Sistine Chapel tapestry cartoons by Raphael (on loan to the Victoria and Albert Museum).

2 2nd Earl of Arundel (1586–1646). A passionate patron and collector, the Earl imported paintings and antiquities, many now in the Ashmolean, Oxford.

3 Sir Hans Sloane (1660–1753). This King's physician's library and cabinet of curiosities (including Egyptian, Etruscan and classical art) formed the nucleus of the British Museum.

4 Thomas Coke, 1st Earl of Leicester (1697–1759). Coke embarked on his Grand Tour of Italy in 1712, aged 15. He housed his collection at Holkham, his Palladian villa in Norfolk.

5 George IV (1762–1830). A compulsive, extravagant collector, George IV built and rebuilt four great palaces, and filled them with tapestries, bronzes, carpets and porcelain. Most of his collection of 17th-century Dutch masters are now in Buckingham Palace.

6 4th Marquess of Hertford (1800–70). Hertford inherited a fine collection of Dutch and French art (the latter from Versailles) and himself rapaciously amassed 18th-century French paintings.

7 Lord Leverhulme (1821–1925). The soap baron worshipped contemporary giants of the Royal Academy – Leighton, Alma-Tadema and others – and built a gallery for employees at Port Sunlight, near Liverpool.

THE LONG GALLERY, HARDWICK HALL. *The collection includes likenesses of luxuriously dressed and bejewelled Elizabethans.*

The first British art collections were set up in the 16th century in the houses of extravagant aristocrats. The Renaissance passion for collecting antique works of art had as yet made no impact on Britain. Instead, in their grand new mansions, dukes and earls amassed portraits. By the late 16th century, a gallery (for promenades as well as paintings) had become a fashionable feature; a splendid and spacious one at Hardwick Hall, Derbyshire, has over a hundred Tudor and Elizabethan portraits.

The early connoisseurs

With the Renaissance, collecting became an obsession, first in Italy and then in the royal and aristocratic palaces of France, Germany and Spain. Serious connoisseurship did not affect Britain, however, until Charles I, even before he came to the throne, set an extraordinary example in the 17th century. His lavish patronage of the arts and appetite for importing great works of Old Masters (such as Raphael) were probably stimulated by visits to royal courts on the Continent. He inspired a small but glittering group of aristocratic cognoscenti (for example, the Earl of Arundel and the Dukes of Buckingham and Somerset) to compete with him as collectors and patrons. Both Rubens and Van Dyck were treated to great hospitality at court. Perhaps the King's most impressive acquisition was most of the Renaissance collection of the dukes of Mantua. The Civil War disrupted such activities. Arundel emigrated with his treasures in 1642, and Charles's pictures were largely sold off by Parliament in the early 1650s. The cream of the collection was dispersed over Europe, into the hands of Philip IV of Spain and other wealthy buyers. The best of the residue can be seen at Hampton Court, Windsor Castle and the Victoria and Albert Museum.

After the Restoration

Royalist sympathizers who toured the Continent to escape the Commonwealth came back well versed in European trends in art. Visits continued after the Restoration, laying the foundations of the Grand Tour, which became *de rigueur* for cultured gentlemen of the 18th century. Some Grand

Tourists, as well as dealers and agents, returned with paintings and sculpture to glorify Britain's great houses. Several collections of this period were so vast that one home was not enough for them. By the 1770s the Duke of Devonshire had great works of art in each of four country houses including Chatsworth in Derbyshire. Another notable 18th-century collector was Lord Burlington, who designed the ground-floor rooms of his villa, Chiswick House in London, especially to show the fruits of his connoisseurship.

Taste in the early part of the 18th century favoured Italian painting, and in the context of this predilection it is not surprising that Canaletto made his livelihood from English patrons. Claude Lorraine's mellow landscapes of the 17th century were eagerly sought. The neoclassical taste led to importation of classical antiquities. Some fine Roman sculpture found its way into Lord Leicester's collection at Holkham Hall, Norfolk. After the mid-18th century collectors became attracted to the landscape paintings of 17th-century Dutch art. The third Marquess of Hertford's collection, now part of the Wallace Collection, London, includes the sunny, peaceful scenes of Aelbert Cuyp, who is still better represented in English galleries than in his native Holland.

BACCHUS AND ARIADNE, *by Titian, in the National Gallery. The gallery acquired this brilliant mythology, painted in the 1520s, in the early 19th century. Titian was one of the favourite painters of Charles I. Prince Albert's collection of Italian paintings joined the gallery in 1861.*

Art for the public

In the 19th century a different type of collection appeared. After Napoleon's massive development of the Louvre as a public museum, similar institutions began to emerge all over Europe. Britain resisted the trend at first but gradually gave in. The National Gallery was founded in 1824 (based on the collection of a successful banker, J. J. Angerstein) amid cries that the public would not be interested. A popular success, it moved to its present site in Trafalgar Square in 1838 and became particularly strong in early Italian Renaissance art under the vigorous directorship of Sir Charles Eastlake. Botticelli's *The Adoration of the Magi* is one of the legacies of his shrewd buying policy. Today the National Gallery is one of the best places in the world to study the evolution of European art from Giotto to Cézanne. A tour of its most important pictures would inevitably include Van Eyck's *Arnolfini Marriage*, the Early Netherlandish study of a contemplative bride and her groom.

London's Tate Gallery was founded in the last decade of the 19th century under pressure from a group who believed that British art was inadequately displayed to the public. Its core was sixty or so paintings acquired by the sugar magnate Henry Tate. A vastly extended British collection (*c.* 1545–*c.* 1900) is now complemented by the National collection of modern art (1870 onwards), with Bonnards, Matisses, Braques and Picassos among its highlights, and by modern sculpture.

THE SAINSBURY CENTRE FOR VISUAL ARTS, *University of East Anglia. The collection reflects today's fascination with tribal art.*

Public galleries were regarded as a way of expressing not only national but also civic and individual prestige. There are some excellent provincial collections, in Liverpool, Brighton, Oxford (the Ashmolean), Cambridge (the Fitzwilliam) and elsewhere. The Lady Lever Art Gallery at Port Sunlight exemplifies the benefits of patronage by a local industrialist. Other galleries, for example the Castle Museum at Norwich, which has paintings by the 19th-century Norwich School of landscapists, are a focus for more local interests.

Wealthy connoisseurs have always played an important educative role: one was Samuel Courtauld, whose percipient acquisition of French Impressionist and Post-Impressionist art in the 1920s and 1930s, when contemporary taste was unsympathetic, remains an unforgettable blessing for visitors to the Tate Gallery and Courtauld Institute Galleries. Also in London, the Wallace Collection, famous for its rococo canvases by Watteau and Boucher, and for Fragonard's salacious *The Swing*, is an outstanding testament to 'avant-garde' tastes of the 18th and 19th centuries. It is the largest 19th-century collection intact.

In Scotland, the National Gallery, Edinburgh, has some remarkable treasures, such as Poussin's severe but affecting series of the *Seven Sacraments*; while Glasgow's municipal gallery, one of the best endowed in Britain, is notable for twenty-two works by Degas, and for magnificent pieces by Giorgione, Rembrandt, Whistler, Salvator Rosa and others. Cardiff's Welsh National Museum, founded to celebrate the Welsh cultural heritage, has paintings by Richard Wilson, Augustus John and, more surprisingly, Rubens and Poussin.

CONNECTIONS
Art in country houses: 210–11 *Rooms in country houses*
British landscape art: 294–5 *Artists and places*
British painting and sculpture: 280–89 *The artist's eye*
The decorative arts: 292–3 *Great art collections*
Royal patronage and display: 58–9 *Monarchy and display*; **214–15** *Royal retreats*

THE CANNING JEWEL, *late 16th century, in the Victoria and Albert Museum, London: a pearl transformed by an Italian or Netherlandish jeweller.*

Many of Britain's great collections of the decorative arts – furnishings, silverware, ceramics, glass and other items – were formed at the same time as the first private galleries of painting and sculpture in the country. Horace Walpole, for example, collected both fine art and precious objects, including fine pieces of porcelain, for which he is said to have had a special passion. Yet perhaps because the decorative arts lacked the prestige of fine art, they did not begin to inspire specialized museums until relatively late in the 19th century.

THE STATE BEDROOM, POWIS CASTLE *(Powys), has a rare ensemble of 17th-century carved woodwork and textiles.*

The Victoria and Albert Museum in London is one of the few public museums that was specifically founded for the decorative arts. It began as a design centre, with the aim of stimulating British craftsmen and manufacturers by showing superlative examples of arts and crafts of every style from almost every part of the world. This aim was promoted by the Government School of Design, and the nucleus of the collection, opened by Queen Victoria in 1857, consisted of objects from the Great Exhibition (1851) at the Crystal Palace.

It was the small prelude to an avalanche of acquisitions. The contents of the old Museum of Ornamental Art arrived in the same year, and some outstanding private collections followed – such as the superb maiolica pottery collected by M. Soulages of Toulouse, which the V & A's first director, Sir Henry Cole, waged a determined campaign to acquire. The huge Salting bequest of Chinese ceramics was obtained in 1910, a year after the present vast building in South Kensington was opened. The India Museum – the world's richest single collection of art from India and south-east Asia – merged with the V & A in 1957. The museum's range is enormous and the masterpieces are legion – Shah Jehan's jade drinking-cup from India, the medieval Eltenberg Reliquary from Germany, and the English ivory *Adoration of the Magi* are just a few highlights in a vast repository.

The V & A has reaped a rich harvest of oriental antiquities, and much of its collection reflects the strength of Britain's long tradition of trading and imperial ties with the East. A similar imperial acquisitiveness is responsible for the hoards of antiquities (from the Middle East, Egypt and other parts of Africa) in the British Museum. Diplomats and politicians, such as Sir Stamford Raffles, who accumulated vast amounts of Javan ornamental metalwork and woodwork in the 18th century, were often avid collectors. In the 19th and early 20th centuries, pioneer archaeologists were able to bring back marvellous antiquities to Britain: at that time, few of their countries of origin had laws preventing their export. Two new 20th-century museums, the Percival David Foundation in London (given to London University in 1961) and the Gulbenkian Museum of Oriental Art and Archaeology, Durham University (opened in 1960), have added to the extraordinary wealth of ancient decorative arts on public display.

Provincial museums

The smaller-scale departments of decorative arts in museums and galleries throughout Britain may appear less dazzling than the riches on display in the labyrinthine V & A and the British Museum, but several are unrivalled in particular fields. The Ashmolean Museum in Oxford has an unmatched hoard of silverware wrought by refugee Huguenot craftsmen in the 17th century. The best collection of Tiffany glass in Europe is housed in the Haworth Art Gallery in Accrington (Lancashire), thanks to the generosity of one of the firm's Chicago managers. Some collections are associated with local manufacturing strengths, such as the fine displays of porcelain at Derby and Stoke and the brilliant glass collection at Bristol.

Country house treasures

Country house collections are sometimes made up of functional paraphernalia, not necessarily chosen with a connoisseur's eye. Even so they are often of compelling interest. The late Stuart furniture of Ham House in Richmond is now a rare collection, as are the 17th-century hangings and furnishing at Knole in Kent and at Powis Castle in north Wales. Houses in which the architectural style is complemented by contemporary interior decoration have a particular charm – notably the Regency ensemble of Brighton Pavilion and the Victoriana

THE TAPESTRY ROOM, OSTERLEY PARK *(Greater London),* c. *1774* ***(below)****. The* Loves of the Gods *tapestries, made in the French Gobelins factory after designs by François Boucher, are displayed in a specially designed room.*

SÈVRES JARDINIÈRE, c. *1750, Harewood House (W. Yorks)* ***(below bottom)****. Sèvres and Chinese porcelain were collected at Harewood with a connoisseur's pride by Edwin Lascelles, first Earl of Harewood, in the 18th century.*

RECONSTRUCTED PERIOD ROOMS

One of the most exciting developments in museum presentation in the 20th century is the re-creation of completely furnished rooms in period style. Some of the rooms at Waddesdon Manor, Buckinghamshire, are precursors of this trend – 19th-century ensembles of 18th-century French panelling and furniture. The American Museum in Bath, founded in 1962, has 18 complete rooms imported from the United States, and the Geffrye Museum in east London has a series of furnished chambers dating from about 1600 to recent times, giving a fascinating insight into the way of life of ordinary people of past generations.

THE DAVID VASE, *1351, in the Percival David Foundation, London (**left**): a Yüan vase from a major collection of early, dated Chinese ware.*

HEAD OF A QUEEN MOTHER, *15th–16th century, in the British Museum (**below**): a Benin bronze from the Benin kingdom of south Nigeria, a former French colony.*

of Leighton House in London.

More specialized collections have depended upon the tastes and fortunes of various aristocrats or members of the gentry. Bess of Hardwick, in the Elizabethan age, was a keen collector of tapestries and needlework, and also ordered furniture from the Continent. John Chute, a friend of Horace Walpole, amassed an exceptional English furniture collection at The Vyne in Hampshire. The oriental ceramics collection at Saltram in Devon owes much to the 18th-century passion for chinoiserie, but also to rapaciousness – its basis is the cargo of porcelain captured in 1762 by Captain Parker from a Spanish vessel bound for the Spanish court. Shugborough (Staffordshire) has a mass of Chinese porcelain given to Admiral Anson in 1744 in gratitude for his extinguishing a dangerous fire in Canton. The 18th century was also the period when collectors often prided themselves on their 'cabinet of curiosities', which could contain treasuries of *virtù* (precious objects) as well as curiosities of natural history such as crocodile eggs or fossils.

In the 19th and 20th centuries the increasing numbers of auction rooms have helped to form several great collections. Alice Rothschild acquired a fine display of Sèvres and Meissen china at Waddesdon Manor in Buckinghamshire. One of the richest stores of *objets d'art* in the country was amassed by the Wernher family, in the late 19th and 20th century, at Luton Hoo in Bedfordshire.

CONNECTIONS
British decorative arts: 280–89 *The artist's eye*
Country house collections: 210–11 *Rooms in country houses*
Painting and sculpture: 290–91 *Great art collections*
Royal patronage and display: 58–9 *Monarchy and display;* **214–15** *Royal retreats*

ART NOUVEAU AND ART DECO COLLECTIONS

Both Art Nouveau (a predominantly curvilinear style which swept through Europe between 1890 and 1910) and Art Deco (a more geometrical mode fashionable in the 1920s and 1930s) were great movements of the decorative arts. Years after their demise, the glass, metalwork, jewellery and furniture they inspired have become collectors' pieces. The Hunterian Gallery in Glasgow has an exceptional legacy of Art Nouveau. The Art Deco fan (***above***) and brilliant examples of Lalique glass are to be found in the Brighton City Museum, which has a lively and fast-growing collection of 20th-century decorative arts.

Artists and places

The tradition of landscape painting in Britain has strong roots. Numerous artists have won fame and fortune by successfully capturing the spirit of a place. Sometimes the impact of their achievement has been such that it has coloured our view of a region, so that we have come to see it through a particular artist's eyes. Constable's lush Suffolk meadows and gentle vales are the supreme example, for they have become an ideal against which a much-changed countryside is measured.

The natural landscape was not always a rewarding subject for artists in Britain. To begin with, only limited aspects of the theme were explored. In the 17th century, patrons began to employ topographical painters, for precise records of the land they owned. One such topographer was the Czech Wenceslaus Hollar, who was invited to England in the 1630s, and produced panoramic engravings of the Earl of Arundel's estates at Albury in Surrey. His work, and the honest country-house views of the Fleming Jan Siberechts, represented the small beginnings of scene painting in England.

Canaletto's first visit to England in the 1740s gave a great boost to landscapes. He invested his scenes of London, Warwick Castle and Alnwick (Northumberland) with the watery sunshine of his native Venice, and inspired a number of imitators, most notably Samuel Scott.

KING AND QUEEN *(Shawhead, Dumfries), 1952–3, by Henry Moore. These rugged bronze figures have a potent aura of grim judgement.*

THE LAKE *(the Black Country), 1937, by L. S. Lowry. Such unsentimental scenes of the grim townscape around Salford, Manchester (where Lowry worked as a rent collector), are immensely popular.*
Salford Museum and Art Gallery

SNOWDON (***below***) *c.1770, by Richard Wilson. The 18th-century classical theory of ideal natural beauty informed Wilson's views of Wales.*
Castle Museum, Nottingham

Sublime visions

It was not until the late 18th century that the grandiose, idealized, classical landscape style of Gaspard Poussin and Claude Lorraine made a serious impression on British art. The Welshman Richard Wilson was the first to interpret the natural scenery of England and Wales in terms of classical composition. Gainsborough, in the same period, imitated the Dutch 17th-century realist style, as well as the pastoral mood of French rococo. He also painted one of the most perfect English landscapes – the rolling Suffolk farmland in the portrait *Mr and Mrs Andrews* (*c.*1750, now in the National Gallery).

A taste for the picturesque became ingrained in the second half of the 18th century, promoted by such volumes as the Reverend William Gilpin's *Picturesque Tours*, illustrated with plates of his drawings. Gilpin foreshadowed the Romantics' love of natural beauty, which was shortly to amount to a cult, coinciding with trends in literature. Several painters now asserted the value of the British landscape for itself alone. Thomas Girtin, for example, travelled to parts of Scotland and the north of England to capture the countryside in small, brilliant watercolours that were enviously admired by the greatest artistic prodigy of the day, J. M. W. Turner (1775–1851).

Turner enjoyed considerable success with landscapes in a conventional classical manner, but in other paintings he was a great innovator. A distinctive quality of sultry, tinted light marks his superb views of Norham Castle, Petworth Park and Salisbury Cathedral, while in private sketches, such as those of the Thames at Walton (between 1800 and 1810), he found a fresh spontaneity of vision quite unanticipated in the work of his predecessors. A vast part of his *oeuvre* can be seen in London's Tate Gallery.

The natural landscape

Unlike Turner, John Constable (1776–1837) set out to create a realistic landscape art untouched by high drama or visionary effects. His first and last love was his native Suffolk, where he painted his best-known canvases, *The Hay Wain* (1820, in the National Gallery) and the views of Dedham Vale and the River Stour. His studies of passing clouds and other transient aspects of nature led him to a deep understanding of the particular quality of English light. It was his approach, in contrast to the romantic vision of Turner, the mystical rural scenes of Samuel Palmer at Shoreham (Kent), or the carefully structured views of the Norwich School, that established pure nature as a preeminent subject for artists.

By the 1850s and 1860s, Pre-Raphaelite landscape views, such as those of William Dyce, achieved an almost photographic exactness. The spirit of the romantic sublime lived on in translations of Scottish scenery by Horatio McCulloch and Edwin Landseer. But towards the end of the 19th century, subtleties of form and expression came to the fore, for example in James McNeill Whistler's *Nocturnes*

ARTISTS' BRITAIN

John Constable

DEDHAM VALE *(Suffolk)*, *1828, by John Constable. In canvases such as this, Constable offered an interpretation of scenery based on exact observation.*
National Gallery of Scotland, Edinburgh

THE LAKE, PETWORTH *(Sussex)*, *c.1829–30, by J. M. W. Turner. Turner's Sussex has a golden paradisal glow.* Petworth House

GRETA BRIDGE *(Yorkshire)*, *1805, by John Sell Cotman. With John Crome, Cotman was the leading painter of the Norwich School. While staying with friends in Yorkshire, he made open-air sketches and used them for some of his best-known watercolours.*
British Museum, London

and in the canvases of the visiting French Impressionists – Monet, Pissarro and Sisley – who were fascinated by London and its environs.

The influence of Post-Impressionism and abstraction in the 20th century has not lessened the power of landscape over some British artists. Paul Nash, for example, through suggestive manipulation of images, has managed to capture the essence of the southern English woods and hills. Graham Sutherland's imaginative paraphrases of south Wales also reveal a profound relationship with the countryside. Two exceptional painters – L. S. Lowry, living on the edge of Manchester, and Stanley Spencer at Cookham in Berkshire – enmeshed their art with one place throughout their lives, exploring an intensely personal vision. And a special development in recent decades has been the landscape sculpture of Barbara Hepworth and Henry Moore, both of whom have several works planted almost like prehistoric megaliths in the countryside where they have lived.

CONNECTIONS
British painting and sculpture: 282–9 *The artist's eye*
The Picturesque: 188–9 *Tourism;* **296–7** *Writers and places*
Turner and the Thames: 178–9 *Shipbuilding*

Writers and places

English literature is deeply suffused with a love of place. In the early 19th century, enthusiasm for natural scenery seemed at times to overshadow human concerns. However, a landscape can often command a writer's emotions as a manifestation of the past, and particularly of a golden childhood.

Such reactions would have been unintelligible in the Dark and Middle Ages, when nature in its untamed state was threatening. Chaucer's famous description of April in the opening lines of *The Canterbury Tales* (1387) hints at a new attitude: nature, by this time, could be a profound source of pleasure. Primitive fear of the wilderness gradually passed into literary convention. In Elizabethan literature it was common practice to describe a wood as a place of foreboding. At the opposite pole was the garden, a place for dalliance. Shakespeare's *As You Like It* (1599) represents a different outlook, for here it is the court that holds the dangers, while the wood – the Forest of Arden – is peopled with lovers. This play was one of the greatest expressions of the pastoral tradition, which had its origins in the writings of Theocritus and Virgil. In England the general trend, which Shakespeare's vision transcended, was to see nature as a rural playground inhabited by lovesick, pipe-playing swains and coy maidens. Such figures were actually courtiers in fancy dress.

PASTORAL ENGLAND: *a woodcut illustration from Edmund Spenser's poem* The Shepheards Calender *(1579), a series of dialogues between shepherds.*

SHAKESPEARE IN SILHOUETTE: *the Gower Monument at Stratford-upon-Avon. According to tradition, Shakespeare was born in Henley St, in a house which today contains Shakespearian memorabilia, including the desk he is said to have used at the local grammar school.*

IZAAK WALTON *(1593–1683) wrote biographies of John Donne and George Herbert, but he is best known for* The Compleat Angler *(1653), a discourse on fishing (**right**, in an 18th-century edition). Towards the end of his life, Walton moved to Winchester. He died here and was buried in the south transept of the cathedral, where a memorial window was erected over his tomb in 1914 (**below**).*

The pastoral tradition was extraordinarily long-lived. The finest 17th-century manifestations included Milton's masque *Comus* (first performed in Ludlow Castle in 1634) and Andrew Marvell's poems about mowers.

Poetry and farming

The first poet to concern himself wholeheartedly with scenery was James Thomson in his blank verse sequence *The Seasons* (1726–30). Thomson's landscapes are alive with toiling farm labourers, all of them highly idealized. Prominent among the poets who came closer to the realities of rural life was Robert Burns (1759–96), an Ayrshire cottar's son, born at Alloway. Burns was himself a farm-worker, and his best poems combine earthy optimism with a deeply lyrical strain.

Another poet-peasant, eagerly taken up by fashionable literary society, was John Clare (1793–1864), son of a Cambridgeshire labourer. Clare was one of the workforce involved in agricultural enclosure, which he found deeply inimical: 'inclosure, like a buonaparte', runs his memorable simile.

Agricultural change remained a significant literary theme for another forty years or more. One of the most appealing of the writers who recorded what was happening to the landscape was William Cobbett, well known for his *Rural Rides* through England (collected in 1830).

Two great novelists of the 19th century presented a detailed picture of the agricultural scene as part of their wider vision. One was George Eliot, whose masterpiece was *Middlemarch* (1871–2), a study of a Midland rural community in the pre-Reform era. The other was Thomas Hardy (1840–1928), whose recurrent themes include the impact of the new farming. Most of Hardy's novels are set in 'South Wessex', or Dorset. The landscapes range from the rich dairy valley of the Froom (Frome) as described in *Tess of the D'Urbevilles* (1891) to the inhospitable Egdon Heath, used in *The Return of the Native* (1878) as a symbol of nature's indifference. Egdon Heath exists in real topography as the region around Hardy's birthplace, Higher Bockhampton.

The Picturesque and Romanticism

Hardy's *œuvre* was a late development of Romanticism, a mode of feeling which had grown out of the Picturesque movement of the later 18th century. The exponents of the Picturesque found new pleasures in wild scenery, autumnal melancholy, ruins, transience. Thomas Gray's country churchyard (actually Stoke Poges, Bucks.) in his famous *Elegy* (1750) was one expression of the mood. The Picturesque was more than a merely literary attitude: it coloured every educated person's view of the landscape.

cont'd.

WORDSWORTH AND COLERIDGE

The term 'Lake School' (first used in 1817) applies to three Romantic poets who, in the 19th century, were all Cumbrian residents: Wordsworth, Coleridge and Robert Southey.

Wordsworth saw the Cumbrian mountains as a manifestation of the Sublime, yet under the influence of his sister Dorothy he also appreciated the gentler aspects of nature – the humble celandine, the 'little unpretending rill'.

Coleridge's best descriptive pieces were written in the 1790s, at Nether Stowey (Somerset), at a period when the Wordsworths were also living in the West Country. Because of their suspicious habit of taking nocturnal walks with notebooks, the three of them were investigated as suspected French spies.

Samuel Taylor Coleridge

*William Wordsworth (**below**)*

DOVE COTTAGE, GRASMERE, CUMBRIA. *Wordsworth and his sister lived here from the winter of 1799 onwards. Details of their daily life are recorded in Dorothy's* Journals.

LITERARY BRITAIN

A selection of the many sites which are of interest to the archaeologist of the literary imagination.

B Place of birth
L Place of residence
D Place of death
G Grave or tomb
P Place that has inspired a writer
M Museum, or house on view to public

EDINBURGH
James Hogg 18th–19th C. **LP**
Walter Scott 18th–19th C. **BL**
R.L. Stevenson 19th C. **BLPM**

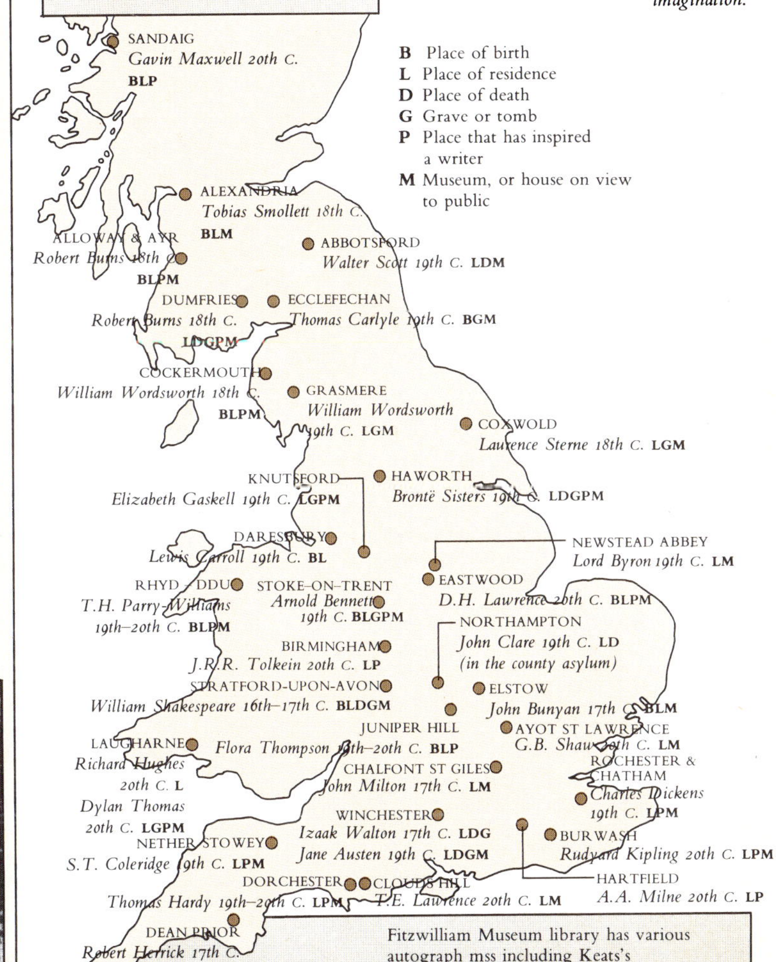

OXFORD
Students commemorated include:
Joseph Addison (Magdalen) *17th–18th C.*
Samuel Johnson (Pembroke) *18th C.*
Percy B. Shelley (University) *19th C.*
Bodleian Library has many mss and 1st editions.

CAMBRIDGE
Students commemorated include:
John Milton 17th C. (Christ's Coll.)
Samuel Pepys 17th C. (Magdalene)
Lord Byron 19th C. (Trinity)
Fitzwilliam Museum library has various autograph mss including Keats's 'Ode to a Nightingale'.

LONDON
Samuel Johnson 18th C. (Gough Sq., City) **LM**
John Keats 19th C. (Hampstead) **LM**
Thomas Carlyle 19th C. (Chelsea) **LDM**
William Morris 19th C. (Bexleyheath and Walthamstow) **LM**
British Museum has various letters and mss including *Beowulf.* Westminster Abbey's 'Poet's Corner' has tomb of Chaucer, grave of Ben Jonson, and monuments to Thomas Gray, Shelley, the Brontës and others.

LORD BYRON *(1788–1824)* ***(left)*** *was repelled by English hypocrisy, and left the country for good in 1816. England is seldom the setting of his poetry. However, the last scenes of his marvellous mock-epic poem* Don Juan *are set in 'Norman Abbey', which corresponds with Newstead Abbey (Notts.), his family home. Canto XIII describes the 'mighty window' of the old abbey church. The photograph* ***(below)*** *shows this window, with the tomb of Byron's dog Boatswain in front.*

ABBOTSFORD, BORDERS: *Sir Walter Scott's home, from 1812 until his death. He built the mansion on the site of a small farm. It was here that he wrote the Waverley novels. After becoming involved in a bankruptcy in 1826, he spent the last six years of his life working feverishly to pay off his creditors.*

Romanticism was the Picturesque taken to extremes. One of its cornerstones was the Sublime, associated by Edmund Burke with a pleasing sensation of horror and belittlement. William Wordsworth found such sensations in abundance, and not only in the mountains of his beloved Lake District. Wordsworth at his most meditative is to be found in his 'Lines composed above Tintern Abbey', where he perceived 'a motion and a spirit' which 'rolls through all things'.

Sir Walter Scott (1771–1832), a contemporary of Wordsworth, was far more popular in their own time. His narrative poem *The Lady of the Lake* (1810) was received with an enthusiasm that rapidly turned Loch Katrine and the Trossachs into a tourist region. Scott brought Scottish history out of the closet. The ghosts of his novels haunt the length and breadth of Scotland, as well as places south of the border such as Kenilworth and Warwick.

By contrast, the Brontës are closely associated with a particular patch of West Yorkshire around Haworth, their parsonage home (now a Brontë museum). Nearby houses appear with fictitious names in Charlotte Brontë's *Jane Eyre* (1847), the classic 'governess novel', while her later novel *Shirley* describes Yorkshire at the time of the Luddite risings. However, it is Emily's *Wuthering Heights* (1847) that has the firmest hold on the popular imagination. In its exploration of the claims of passion (of which the desolate moors are a perfect symbol), it is one of the pinnacles of Romanticism in fiction.

A WATERCOLOUR BY CHARLOTTE BRONTË, *showing Anne's dog Flossie. This watercolour, together with many other relics of the Brontë family, can be seen today in the Old Parsonage at Haworth, W. Yorks.*

CHARLOTTE BRONTË *(1816–55). She died 9 months after her marriage to the curate of Haworth.*

The city and the industrial landscape

Urban themes became significant in literature with the rise of the novel. One of the many 18th-century novelists to concern himself with London was Tobias Smollett, whose scope in *Humphry Clinker* (1771) ranges from the pleasure gardens of Vauxhall to the prison community of the King's Bench. In the following century, a similar fascination with prisons is to be found in the works of Charles Dickens (1812–70).

Dickens's view of London became distinctly bleaker as the years went by. The city described in *Sketches by Boz* and *The Pickwick Papers* (both 1836–7) is pleasingly bustling – a place for which it is still possible to feel uncomplicated affection. With the march of industrialization, London became more threatening. In *Dombey and Son* (1847–8) a passage on the excavation of a railway cutting through Camden Town has powerful overtones of horror. Yet for Dickens the slums, dirt and destruction had a strangely mesmerizing quality. In the same way he was both appalled and fascinated by the costly longwindedness of the legal process (a major theme of *Bleak House*).

Later novelists, such as Virginia Woolf in *Mrs Dalloway* (1925), could portray a London which had been largely purged of such evils. Mrs Dalloway's city is clean and colourful, like a toy town. For the soul, however, there was still no shortage of horrors. Some of them are evoked by T.S. Eliot in his resonant, allusive poem *The Waste Land* (1922). Of the more recent evocations of London life, one of the most successful is Iris Murdoch's brilliant novel *Under the Net* (1954).

The novel of the industrial north belongs to a commodious category of its own. Chronologically it ranges from Elizabeth Gaskell's *Mary Barton* (1848) to the sub-genre of the realistic working-class novel of the 1950s. Between these extremes lie Arnold Bennett's tales of the Potteries and, more significant as works of art, D.H. Lawrence's powerful novels set in the Nottinghamshire coalfield, around Eastwood.

In an industrial society, the country idyll assumes a special intensity that at times becomes almost religious. The popularity in modern times of prose works by H.E. Bates, Flora Thompson and Laurie Lee owes much to their evocation of a rural paradise whose loss is still poignantly recent.

WELSH POETRY

At the head of the Welsh poetic tradition stand the names of Taliesin and Aneirin (both 6th century). The bardic craft enjoyed a golden age in the 12th and 13th centuries and began to decline from the 16th onwards. It was at this period that Welshmen began to write literature in English.

The finest Anglo-Welsh writer is undoubtedly the Swansea-born poet and story-teller Dylan Thomas (1914–53). He moved to London in 1936 and soon acquired a reputation not only for his writings and broadcasts but also for a dissolute lifestyle.

Other important Welsh poets of the 20th century include R.S. Thomas (b. 1913), whose verse draws its imagery from the rural hill-farming communities.

THE BOATHOUSE, LAUGHARNE, DYFED (***above***). *Dylan Thomas wrote* Under Milk Wood *(1952) in the garden shed (**left**). 'Llareggub', the town in which this play for voices is set, is traditionally associated with Laugharne: the characters may have been based on local people. After the poet's death in America, his body was brought back to be buried in the graveyard of St Martin's church.*

CONNECTIONS
Enclosure of the fields: 134–5 *The agricultural revolution;* **136–7** *The impact of the new farming*
Dr Johnson's London: 246–7 *London*
Pepys's London: 244–5 *London*
The Picturesque: 188–9 *Tourism;* **294–5** *Artists and places*
Writers on gardens: 216–19 *Gardens*

Music and song

KING'S COLLEGE CHOIR, CAMBRIDGE. *The singing of England's boy choristers is unrivalled. The tradition dates back to medieval times, when outstanding boy singers were sometimes press-ganged into service at the Chapel Royal.*

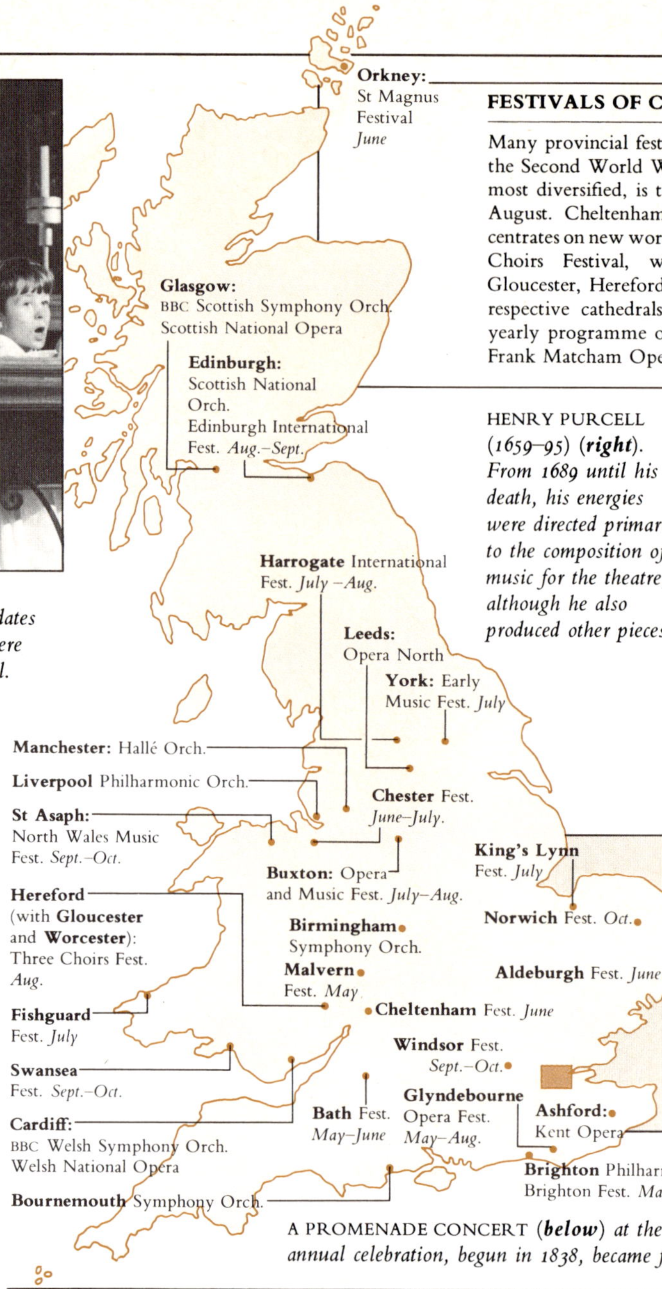

FESTIVALS OF CLASSICAL MUSIC

Many provincial festivals of music have flowered since the Second World War. The grandest, and perhaps the most diversified, is the Edinburgh Festival, held every August. Cheltenham, on a more modest scale, concentrates on new works by British composers. The Three Choirs Festival, which rotates annually between Gloucester, Hereford and Worcester, is focused on the respective cathedrals. Buxton, Derbyshire, mounts a yearly programme of opera and music in the restored Frank Matcham Opera House.

HENRY PURCELL (*1659–95*) (***right***). *From 1689 until his death, his energies were directed primarily to the composition of music for the theatre, although he also produced other pieces.*

'Das Land ohne Musik': the land without music. This was once the popular German misconception of Britain's musical achievement. It is true that the works of, say, the German Romantics have often been of more interest to British music-lovers than native compositions. Even so, there are superlative pieces by native composers in the repertoire.

Songs of praise

The great focus of musical development in the Middle Ages was the Church, whose cathedrals and abbey churches were regularly filled with soaring choral praises. The art of choral music developed from the elaborate polyphonic compositions of the 16th and 17th centuries. Most famous among the composers of Tudor and Stuart England were John Taverner, Thomas Tallis and William Byrd, all of whom served as Organist and Choirmaster of the Chapel Royal in London, and created masses, and songs for divine service, as well as secular entertainments such as madrigals.

The Chapel Royal was also the musical nursery of England's greatest 17th-century composer. Henry Purcell (1659–95) was a tenor in the Chapel and later the organist at Westminster Abbey. His ecclesiastical music, notably a series of magnificent choral odes and anthems, and his one-act *Dido and Aeneas* (one of the earliest English operas), seemed to promise a new era of excellence. With his premature death, the course of English music suffered a grievous blow.

Visiting musicians

By the 18th century, concert-going was gaining ground as one of the chief delights of London life. Few native talents appeared, but Continental music (especially Italian) was much admired. London became a profitable port of call for some eminent foreign musicians. The first important composer to arrive from Europe was Georg Friedrich Handel (1685–1759), who took the capital by storm in 1711 with his opera *Rinaldo*. Handel spent the rest of his life in England, at first composing Italianate operas, then perfecting the

A PROMENADE CONCERT (***below***) *at the Albert Hall, London. This annual celebration, begun in 1838, became famous under Sir Henry Wood.*

GUSTAV HOLST AND RALPH VAUGHAN WILLIAMS (***below***), *photographed on a walking tour in 1913 by the folksong collector W.G. Whittaker. Both Holst and Vaughan Williams brought folksong influences into their music, as did the Bradford-born composer Frederick Delius (1862–1934).*

THE RAKE'S PROGRESS: *the brothel scene from Stravinsky's opera, performed in 1975 at the Glyndebourne Festival (E. Sussex), which takes place in an opera house in the grounds of a Tudor Mansion. The brilliant design in this production was by David Hockney.*

English oratorio. He is particularly cherished for his oratorio *Messiah* (1742).

No other European composer put himself at the mercy of the London public for so long a period, but many made the occasional visit. In 1764 Leopold Mozart brought his prodigiously talented eight-year-old son, Wolfgang Amadeus. Josef Haydn came twice, and his 'London' symphonies were all premièred in the city. Foreign singers, such as Mozart's castrato Rauzzini (who is buried

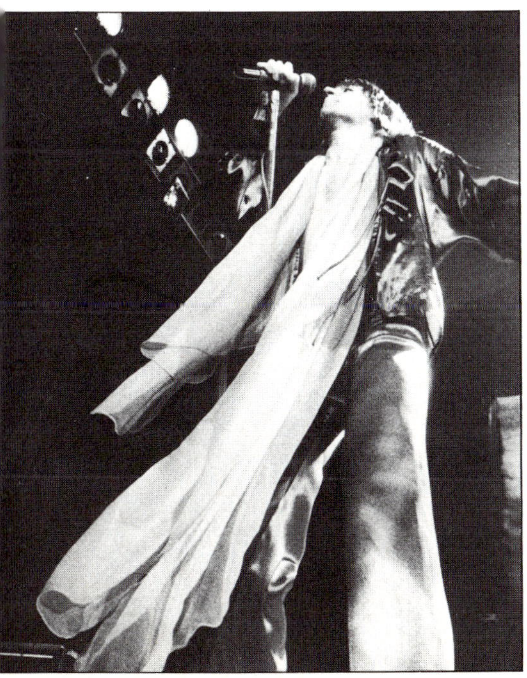

ROD STEWART *is one of many British pop stars who have won cult followings among young people since the Beatlemania of the 1960s.*

in Bath Abbey), also had their successes. In the following century Chopin visited Scotland, and Mendelssohn captured its romantic spirit in his *Scottish Symphony* and *Hebridean Overture*.

A musical rebirth

In the 19th century, the increased prosperity of the provincial cities engendered new cultural amenities for the middle classes. The newly formed regional orchestras included many that flourish today, such as the one founded by Charles Hallé in Manchester (1858). Classical concerts were often given in the grand town halls of the Victorian age; Mendelssohn's *Elijah* had its première at Birmingham Town Hall in 1846. At another level of musical appreciation, the music halls catered for the taste for popular songs and revues, while gatherings round the piano were an important part of middle-class home life.

Increasing opportunities for performance undoubtedly encouraged British composers from the latter part of the 19th century. Edward Elgar (1857–1934) inaugurated a recognizably English style, deeply rooted in the choral tradition but often strongly evocative of the gently rolling Malvern hills, which he loved. Pastoral strains pervade the *Enigma Variations* (1899), but in some pieces it is the self-assertiveness of Edwardian London that is conveyed.

The music of Ralph Vaughan Williams (1872–1958) also drew inspiration from the countryside, but there are influences too from his study of English folksong. At a somewhat later period, the bleak Suffolk coast fired the imagination of Benjamin Britten (1913–76). Two of his operas, *Peter Grimes* (1945) and *Albert Herring* (1947), are set in the small fishing town of Aldeburgh, where he spent most of his adult life and founded the famous festival in 1948. Other important contributions to British music in the post-war period have been made by Sir William Walton (b. 1902) and Sir Michael Tippett (b. 1905).

Folk and pop music

The folk music tradition in Britain is one of immense variety, with roots in many parts of the country and in many different ways of life, from soldiery to farming. Some folksongs have become nationally famous, but many have been preserved only by the efforts of collectors (most notably Cecil Sharp) and of the societies which have grown up since the early 20th century.

The industrial revolution spawned its own folk music – the male choirs of south Wales and the brass bands of northern English towns. These still flourish. Music of more ancient origin – that of Celtic Wales and Gaelic Scotland – is performed at Welsh eisteddfodau and Scottish ceilidhs.

The phenomenal flowering of commercial 'pop' music since the 1950s has owed much to transatlantic trends, but in 1965 the Beatles were awarded the MBE for breaking the American dominance. Two members of the group, John Lennon and Paul McCartney, wrote songs that can stand comparison with any written this century.

Pop music has often transcended its associations with youth politics and fashion. Sophisticated orchestral rock, for example, has produced many excellent compositions, such as Mike Oldfield's *Tubular Bells* (1973).

CONNECTIONS
Handel's tomb: 284–5 *The artist's eye*
Music in Edinburgh: 256–7 *Edinburgh*
Music in Manchester: 252–3 *Manchester*
Music on the radio: 276–7 *Radio and television*
The Royal Festival Hall: 250–51 *London*

Britain and the theatre

In Britain, as on the Continent, the first dramatic performances were under the aegis of the Church. They began with re-enactments of the Easter story, but before long other biblical scenes such as the story of Noah were also included. Whole cycles of these plays (the 'mystery' cycles) were given outdoors, and by the early 14th century their organization had been taken over by the craft guilds. Each scene was presented (on a cart which moved from audience to audience) by a guild that had a special link with the subject-matter: Jonah and the Whale, for example, would be performed by the Fishmongers.

In the later Middle Ages, the range of drama was extended. Itinerant actors, who performed wherever they could, presented the highly popular 'morality' plays such as *Everyman* (*c.* 1495) and John Skelton's *Magnificence* (*c.* 1515). Gradually, a body of secular drama was accumulated.

The first permanent playhouse, known simply as the Theatre, was established in Shoreditch, London, by James Burbage in 1576. Using timber from this building, his sons set up the Globe on Bankside, Southwark, in 1599. Here, Richard Burbage became the leading actor of the Chamberlain's Men, for whom Shakespeare wrote most of his greatest plays. Other permanent theatres – all required by law to be outside the limits of the City – included the Rose (1587), the Swan (1594) and the Fortune (1600). Most playhouses consisted of a raised playing area, an inner stage, a balcony and a dressing room, with audiences sitting in covered galleries or standing in the rowdy pit. Costumes were mostly contemporary, and all the players were male.

DRURY LANE THEATRE, *London, has a far longer theatrical tradition than any other in the country. The first of its succession of four buildings appeared in 1663. Charles II awarded Letters Patent to Drury Lane and Lincoln's Inn Fields (the latter's passing to Covent Garden), conferring on them a monopoly for the presentation of legitimate drama in London. These monopolies lasted until 1843. The third Drury Lane, shown here in 1808, seated over 3,000.*

A MEDIEVAL MYSTERY PLAY *from the York cycle, revived by modern actors. Other versions that have survived include the Chester and Wakefield (or Towneley) cycles.*

VICTORIAN SHAKESPEARE. *In 1897 Mrs Patrick Campbell played Ophelia to Johnston Forbes-Robertson's Hamlet, which was the most subtle portrayal of the period.*

DAVID GARRICK *(1717–79)* ***(left)****, the greatest actor of his day, portrayed here with Mrs Pritchard in a performance of* Macbeth. *Garrick set new standards in naturalistic acting and production at Drury Lane.*

The age of the indoor theatre

The post-Restoration theatre presented a somewhat different picture. All performances had been banned during the Interregnum, but Charles II had become accustomed during his exile to sophisticated court masques. When drama was allowed again, the influence of the masque was far-reaching. Indoor theatres, with painted backcloths, side wings and proscenium arches, became the order of the day. In a relaxed moral atmosphere there was nothing to prevent playwrights such as Sir George Etherege, William Wycherley and William Congreve from producing plays that reflected the bawdy spirit of the age. The use of actresses was essential to the success of a Restoration play.

The 18th century saw the appearance throughout the provinces of innumerable Theatres Royal, licensed for 'legitimate' drama by local magistrates. Such theatres were visited by travelling companies, one of which was Henry Gifford's, in which David Garrick made his first appearances.

The early years of the 19th century were dominated, in London, by the rival histrionics of Edmund Kean and William Charles Macready. Their performances were restricted by the Patent Laws to Covent Garden and Drury Lane, and their repertoire comprised mutilated versions of Shakespeare and other, inferior playwrights, with the emphasis on spectacle on a grand scale.

After the repeal of the Patent Laws in 1843, smaller theatres (which had evaded the ban on straight plays by inserting songs and calling them 'burlesques') grew in popularity but offered only melodrama. There was, at this period, a social stigma attached to actors and actresses. Only with

LONDON'S THEATRELAND *Currently active theatres (1–50) are listed with their opening dates. Defunct theatres (51–76) also have their dates of closure or demolition.*

1 Royal Court (1888)
2 Apollo Victoria (1930)
3 Victoria Palace (1911)
4 Westminster (1931)
5 Whitehall (1930)
6 Mayfair (1963)
7 Her Majesty's (1890)
8 Haymarket (1880)
9 Comedy (1881)
10 Prince of Wales (1884)
11 Criterion (1874)
12 Piccadilly (1928)
13 Windmill (1931)
14 Lyric (1888)
15 Apollo (1901)
16 Globe (1906)
17 Queen's (1907)
18 Prince Edward's (1930)
19 Palace (1890)
20 Phoenix (1930)
21 Palladium (1910)
22 Ambassador's (1913)
23 St Martin's (1916)
24 Cambridge (1930)
25 Arts (1927)
26 Albery (1903)
28 Duke of York's (1892)
29 Garrick (1889)
30 Coliseum (1904)
31 Adelphi (1901)
32 Vaudeville (1891)
33 Savoy (1881)
34 Covent Garden (1847)
35 Fortune (1924)
36 Drury Lane (1812)
37 Duchess (1929)
38 Strand (1905)
39 Aldwych (1905)
40 Mermaid (1959)
41 National Theatre (1976)
42 Young Vic (1970)
43 New London (1973)
44 Shaftesbury (1911)
45 Sadler's Wells (1931)
46 Open Air (1933)
47 Round House (1964)
48 Lyric (1888)
49 Theatre Royal, Stratford East (1884)
50 Barbican (1982)

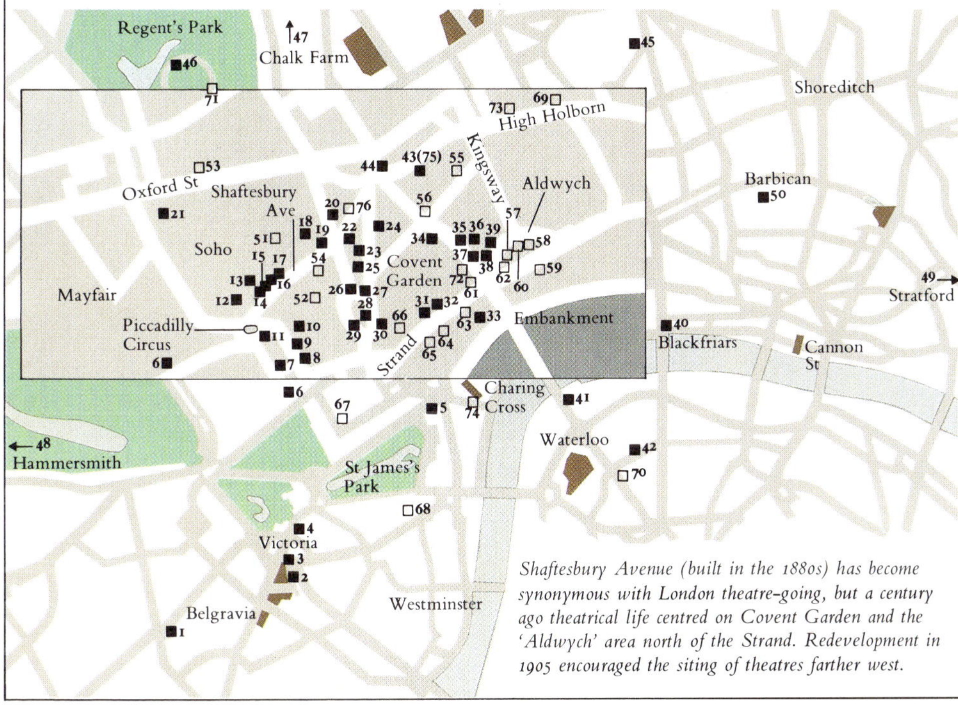

■ Active theatres, presenting plays or musicals
□ Theatres now closed or demolished

51 Royalty, Dean St (1840, *closed 1938*)
52 Daly's, Leicester Sq (1893, *closed 1937*)
53 Princess's, Oxford St (1840, *closed 1902*)
54 Shaftesbury, Shaftesbury Ave (1888, *bombed 1941*)
55 Kingsway, Great Queen St (1882, *closed 1941*)
56 Queen's, Long Acre (1867, *closed 1878*)
57 Olympic, 'Aldwych' (1849, *closed 1905*)
58 Opera Comique, 'Aldwych' (1870, *closed 1899*)
59 Strand, Strand (1831, *closed 1905*)
60 Globe, 'Aldwych' (1868, *closed 1899*)
61 Gaiety (1), 'Aldwych' (1868, *closed 1903*)
62 Gaiety (2), 'Aldwych' (1903, *closed 1939*)
63 Terry's, Strand (1887, *closed 1910*)
64 Tivoli, Strand (1890, *closed 1914*)
65 Toole's, William IV St (1869, *closed 1895*)
66 Little, John Adam St (1910, *bombed 1941*)
67 St James's, King St (1835, *demolished 1957*)
68 Imperial, Tothill St (1876, *closed 1902*)
69 Theatre Royal, High Holborn (1866, *burned down 1880*)
70 Old Vic, Waterloo Rd (1818, *closed 1981*)
71 Scala, Charlotte St (1831, *closed and demolished 1969*)
72 Lyceum, Wellington St (1834, *closed 1939*)
73 Alcazar, High Holborn (1873, *closed 1886*)
74 Playhouse, Northumberland Ave (1882, *closed 1949*)
75 Winter Gardens, Drury Lane (1872, *closed 1960*)
76 Saville, Shaftesbury Ave (1931, *closed 1970*)

Shaftesbury Avenue (built in the 1880s) has become synonymous with London theatre-going, but a century ago theatrical life centred on Covent Garden and the 'Aldwych' area north of the Strand. Redevelopment in 1905 encouraged the siting of theatres farther west.

THE ROYAL SHAKESPEARE COMPANY, *seen here in Peter Brook's revolutionary staging of* A Midsummer Night's Dream *in 1970, has been in the forefront of theatrical 'modernism', showing a constant willingness to experiment. Brook's direction in this production allowed long periods of improvisation in which the cast acquired circus skills such as juggling, plate-spinning and trapeze work. Other 'alienation' effects included a plain white set and very basic costumes. The result was that both players and audience could concentrate more on the text, and the production offered insights into the play which traditional treatments might have overlooked.*

the arrival of 'serious' dramatists such as Henry Arthur Jones and Sir Arthur Wing Pinero in the last fifteen years of the century, and the knighting of Henry Irving in 1895, did the theatre regain any respectability. At the same period it was becoming increasingly popular: between 1880 and 1914 thirty-eight London theatres were built or reconstructed. Improved transport made theatre-going readily available even to suburbanites.

Theatre in the 20th century

The early years of the present century saw the acceptance of the more naturalistic plays of Henrik Ibsen and George Bernard Shaw, and the rapid rise of the repertory movement, which provided most provincial towns with a new production each week. After the Second World War this important source of theatre became the victim of the television age. Nevertheless, new provincial theatres, usually with an open, adaptable stage instead of the more restrictive proscenium arch, continued to be built. The National Theatre opened the first of its new London playhouses in 1976, and in 1982 it was joined by the Barbican Theatre in the City.

CONNECTIONS
Cinemas: 240–41 *Suburbia*
The Royal Exchange, Manchester: 252–3 *Manchester*
Shakespeare's London: 280–81 *London*

Themes & places/*A thematic gazetteer*

The following section is a traveller's guide to Britain, organized according to the themes listed on this page. Within each theme, the arrangement of sites is regional. A list of regions, in the order in which they are covered, is given below. The regions are keyed into the map by numbers.

THE REGIONS

1 The West Country
2 South-east England
3 Greater London
4 The Thames, Chilterns & East Anglia
5 Central England
6 Yorkshire, Humberside & the North-west
7 The North of England
8 Wales
9 Southern Scotland
10 Central Scotland & Strathclyde
11 Northern Scotland & the Islands

THE THEMES

Page numbers are given in italics:

Note *Readers are advised to check on opening times (if applicable) before making a visit.*

Abbreviations

appt.	appointment
c.	century
coll.	collection
incl.	includes/including
m	metre(s)
m.	mile(s)
nr	near
rlwy	railway

AVIATION

Most major airports have visitors' observation areas. See also: 'Military history' (p 315).

THE WEST COUNTRY
Bristol, Avon.
Industrial Museum has coll. of Bristol-built aero-engines.
Helston, Cornwall.
Cornwall Aero Park has Battle of Britain War Gallery, helicopters, hovercraft, Concorde flight deck.
Torbay, Devon.
Aircraft Museum, with 18 historic aircraft.
Yeovilton, Somerset.
Fleet Air Arm Museum has over 40 historic planes.
GREATER LONDON
Hendon.
RAF Museum has over 40 aircraft.
Kensington.
Science Museum (National Aeronautical Coll.) incl. war fighters, Amy Johnson's Gypsy Moth & first jet plane.
THE THAMES, CHILTERNS & EAST ANGLIA
Duxford Airfield, Cambs.
Coll. of both military & civil aeroplanes.
Old Warden, Beds.
Shuttleworth Collection, with 40 types of aircraft.
CENTRAL ENGLAND
Castle Donington, Leics.
East Midlands Airport has aircraft museum.
Derby, Derbys.
Industrial Museum. Rolls-Royce aero-engines & display on aviation history.
Newark, Notts.
Air Museum. Famous aircraft, incl. Meteor & Vampire jets.
Stoke-on-Trent, Staffs.
Spitfire Museum.
Tattershall, Lincs.
Aviation Museum.
Wolverhampton, W. Midlands.
RAF Aerospace Museum, Cosford. 50 aircraft, British & foreign; British Airways civil aircraft coll.
YORKSHIRE, HUMBERSIDE & THE NORTH-WEST
Wakefield, W. Yorks.
Nostell Priory Aviation Museum.
CENTRAL SCOTLAND & STRATHCLYDE
North Berwick, Lothian.
Museum of Flight. 18 aircraft; aero-engines & rockets.

BATTLEFIELDS

THE WEST COUNTRY
Bridgwater, Somerset.
Admiral Blake Museum has model of Battle of Sedgemoor (1685).
SOUTH-EAST ENGLAND
Battle, nr Hastings, E. Sussex.
Site of *Battle of Hastings* (1066). Exhibition with relics from battle & half-size reproduction of Bayeux Tapestry. High altar of *Battle Abbey* (founded by William I) over spot where Harold was killed.
THE THAMES, CHILTERNS & EAST ANGLIA
Newbury, Berks.
Models of both battles (1643, 1644) in local *museum*.
CENTRAL ENGLAND
Bosworth Field, Leics.
Battlefield Centre, with exhibition, battle footpath & model of battle (1485).
Evesham, Heref. & Worcs.
Obelisk in garden of Abbey Manor overlooks site of battle (1265). See also De Montfort room in *Evesham local museum*.
Naseby, Northants.
Battle & Farm Museum. Plans & relics illustrating Civil War battle.
Shrewsbury, Salop.
Battlefield Church, 3 m. to north, founded in memory of fallen in battle of 1403.
Tewkesbury, Glos.
Abbey contains tomb of Prince Edward, slain in battle (1471).
YORKSHIRE, HUMBERSIDE & THE NORTH-WEST
York, N. Yorks.
Castle Museum has model of Battle of Marston Moor (1644) & 17th-C. arms.
CENTRAL SCOTLAND & STRATHCLYDE
Bannockburn, nr Stirling, Central.
Audio-visual display of events leading to Scottish victory (1314).
NORTHERN SCOTLAND & THE ISLANDS
Culloden, Highland.
National Trust Centre, with *audio-visual display* of battle (1746); cairns & scattered commemorative stones.

BRIDGES & VIADUCTS

THE WEST COUNTRY
Bath, Avon.
Pulteney Bridge by Robert Adam, 1770; inspired by Ponte Vecchio, Florence.
Bristol, Avon.
Clifton Suspension Bridge. Earliest engineering feat of I.K. Brunel, designed 1829.

Saltash, Cornwall.
Royal Albert Rlwy Bridge over R. Tamar. Last major work by Brunel, completed 1859.
SOUTH-EAST ENGLAND
Balcombe Viaduct, W. Sussex.
Carried London–Brighton line across R. Ouse, 1839.
Brighton, E. Sussex.
London Road Viaduct, 37 arches, built 1841.
GREATER LONDON
Central London.
Outstanding bridges incl.: *Tower Bridge*, built 1886–94 in Gothic style; *Hammersmith Bridge*, iron suspension bridge, 1887; *Richmond Bridge*, by James Paine, 1774–7.
THE THAMES, CHILTERNS & EAST ANGLIA
Bletchley, Bucks.
Skew Bridge (i.e., at an angle) on Robert Stephenson's London & Birmingham Rlwy, 1838.
CENTRAL ENGLAND
Bakewell, Derbys.
14th-C. *packhorse bridge* over R. Wye.
Brackley, Northants.
Railway *viaduct*, 1899.
Coalbrookdale, Salop.
World's first *iron bridge* (1779), by Abraham Darby III. Exhibition in tollhouse nearby.
Crowland, Lincs.
Unique *triangular bridge*, originally spanning 3 rivers but now on dry land. Late 14th C.
Harringworth, Northants.
82-arch *Welland Viaduct*, 1878–80.
Ilkeston, Notts.
Bennerley Viaduct, wrought-iron, 1879.
Irthlingborough, Northants.
14th-C. bridge with 19 arches.
Lincoln, Lincs.
High Bridge: 12th-C. bridge with timber-framed 16th-C. house on west side.
Monsal Dale, Derbys.
Rlwy *viaduct*, 1860.
Swarkestone, Derbys.
Superb medieval bridge.
YORKSHIRE, HUMBERSIDE & THE NORTH-WEST
Hebden Bridge, W. Yorks.
Packhorse bridge dates from *c.* 1510. Scene of Civil War battle, 1643.
Humber Bridge, Humber.
World's longest single-span *suspension bridge*, 1981.
Ribbleshead Viaduct, N. Yorks.
On Settle–Carlisle rlwy.
Sankey Brook Viaduct, nr Warrington, Cheshire.
First major rlwy *viaduct*, 1830.
THE NORTH OF ENGLAND
Berwick-upon-Tweed, Northumb.
Old Bridge 1610–34; *Royal Border Rlwy Bridge*, 1849.
Middlesbrough, Cleveland.
Transporter bridge of 1911. Suspended carriage carries passengers & cars across river.
Newcastle upon Tyne, Tyne & Wear.
High Level Bridge by Robert Stephenson (1845–9) with rlwy on upper deck, road below. *Swing Bridge* (1876). *Tyne Bridge* (1925–8), a suspension road bridge.
WALES
Aberdare, Mid Glam.
Oldest surviving *tramway bridge*, 1811.
Chepstow, Gwent.
Bridge by I.K. Brunel, partly replaced 1862.
Conwy, Gwynedd.
Estuary spanned by Thomas Telford's mock-medieval *suspension road bridge* (1826), Robert Stephenson's *tubular rlwy bridge* (1848) & modern *road bridge* (1958).
Dolgellau, Gwynedd.
7-arched bridge over R. Wnion, 1638.
Menai Strait, Gwynedd.
Strait crossed by Thomas Telford's *Menai Suspension Bridge* (1826) & Robert Stephenson's *Britannia Tubular Bridge* (1849).
Monmouth, Gwent.
Fortified bridge (13th C.) over R. Monnow.
Newport, Gwent.
Transporter bridge (1906) carries cars & passengers across R. Usk.
Pont Scethin, Gwynedd.
Medieval stone bridge.
SOUTHERN SCOTLAND
Kelso, Borders.
5-arched bridge by John Rennie, 1803.
CENTRAL SCOTLAND & STRATHCLYDE
Queensferry, Lothian.
Forth Rlwy Bridge (1890) earned knighthood for designer Benjamin Baker.
NORTHERN SCOTLAND & THE ISLANDS
Dundee, Tayside.
2-m.-long *Tay Bridge* opened 1888, 9 years after collapse of 1st rlwy bridge.
Glenfinnan Viaduct, Highland.
First concrete *viaduct*, 1897–1901.
Nairn Viaduct, nr Inverness, Highland.
28-arch *viaduct* carrying Highland Rlwy, 1898.

CANALS

See also: map on p 260.

THE WEST COUNTRY
Devizes, Wilts.
Caen Hill Locks: 29 locks on Kennet & Avon.
Dundas Aqueduct, Avon.
Carries Kennet & Avon Canal over R. Avon.
GREATER LONDON
Little Venice.
Regent's Canal & Paddington Arm meet to form *Browning's Pool*.
CENTRAL ENGLAND
Bearly Aqueduct, Warks.
Longest iron aqueduct in England, built in 1813 to carry Stratford-upon-Avon Canal.
Birmingham Canal Navigations, W. Midlands.
Complex canal network on 3 levels, 105 m. long with 139 locks.
Blisworth Tunnel, nr Stoke Bruerne, Northants.
$1\frac{1}{4}$ m. long, completed 1805.
Bratch Locks, Staffs.
3 locks & an octagonal toll-house.
Braunston, Northants.
Meeting-place of Grand Union Canal & Oxford Canal. *Braunston Tunnel* & flight of 6 locks.
Buxworth Canal Basin, Derbys.
Terminal basin for Peak Forest Canal.
Cromford Canal, Derbys.
Late 18th C. Single-span aqueduct carries canal over R. Derwent.
Dudley, W. Midlands.
Canal trips into *Dudley Tunnel* reveal spectacular limestone workings.
Foxton Locks, Leics.
Staircase of 10 locks, built 1810 & still used. Tracks of inclined plane visible.
Fradley Junction, Staffs.
5 locks on Trent & Mersey Canal.
Grand Union Canal.
Stretches $137\frac{3}{4}$ m. from Birmingham to R. Thames. Finest waterway in Britain.
Grantham Canal, Lincs.
Connected R. Trent with Nottingham. Opened 1797. Canal company workshops extant.
Harecastle Tunnel, Staffs.
On Trent & Mersey Canal. By James Brindley, begun 1766. 2nd tunnel by Thomas Telford, begun 1824.
Hatton Locks, Warks.
Grand Union Canal raised by 21 locks. Modernized 1930s.
Longdon Aqueduct, Salop.
By Thomas Telford, 1795: world's first iron aqueduct, on Shrewsbury Canal.
Nottingham, Notts.
Canal Museum in old warehouse (Canal St), with wharfage, sheds, cranes.
River Avon Navigation, Warks.
Lower section (from Tewkesbury to

Evesham) part of Avon Ring. Highly popular for cruising.
Shardlow, nr Derby, Derbys.
Clock Warehouse (1780) has exhibition on canal life.
Shropshire Union Canal.
One of the most popular cruising waterways. Runs 66½ m., 46 locks. Middlewich Branch is 10 m. long.
Stoke Bruerne, Northants.
On Grand Union Canal. *Waterways Museum* shows 200 years of canal history & barge life.
Stourport-on-Severn, Heref. & Worcs.
Canal basin. Stourport is only British town built specifically to serve a canal.
Telford, Salop.
Blists Hill Open Air Museum has Hay Inclined Plane.
Tewkesbury, Glos.
Avon Lock: entrance to Lower Avon from R. Severn.
Trent & Mersey Canal.
93½ m. long, 75 locks. A masterpiece by James Brindley, formerly known as Grand Trunk Canal.
Whaley Bridge, Derbys.
On Peak Forest Canal. *Waterway museum.*
Wormleighton, Warks.
Oxford Canal (by James Brindley) follows contour of hills.

YORKSHIRE, HUMBERSIDE & THE NORTH-WEST
Aire & Calder Navigation, W. & N. Yorks.
From Goole to Leeds, a busy commercial waterway.
Anderton, Cheshire.
Boat lift from R. Weaver to Trent & Mersey Canal, opened 1875.
Ashton Canal, Gr Manchester.
Ashton-under-Lyne to Manchester. Victorian industrial architecture along banks.
Barton-upon-Irwell, Gr Manchester.
Barton Swing Aqueduct (1894) carries Bridgewater Canal over Manchester Ship Canal.
Bingley Five Rise, W. Yorks.
Spectacular *lock staircase* (1774) on Leeds & Liverpool Canal.
Castleford Junction, W. Yorks.
Commercial craft, & barge repair yard (Aire & Calder Navigation).
Dewsbury, W. Yorks.
Canal Museum. By appt.
Ellesmere Port, Cheshire.
Boat Museum, with 30 craft & exhibition of painted boat ware.
Huddersfield, W. Yorks.
Unique *lifting bridge* on Huddersfield Broad Canal.
Leeds & Liverpool Canal.
126½ m. long, 91 locks. Passes through fine moorland.
Lune Aqueduct, Lancs.
Completed 1797. Carries Lancaster Canal over R. Lune.
Manchester Ship Canal, Gr Manchester.
Built to link textile industry with sea, opened 1894.
Marple, Gr Manchester.
'Snake bridge', enabling horse pulling barge to cross river where towpath changes sides. Fine *aqueduct* over R. Goyt (1800).
Sowerby Bridge, W. Yorks.
Largest surviving group of 18th-C. canal *warehouses*.
Stanley Ferry Aqueduct, W. Yorks.
On Wakefield section of Aire & Calder Navigation, opened 1839.
Worsley, Gr Manchester.
Bridgewater Canal by James Brindley, completed 1761. Still in use.

WALES
Chirk Aqueduct & Tunnel, Clwyd.
Aqueduct built 1801 by William Jessop to carry Shropshire Union Canal across Ceiriog valley. Brick-lined tunnel with towpath (1802).
High Cross, nr Rogerstone, Gwent.
Restored section of *Monmouthshire Canal*, with footpath to spectacular flight of 14 locks. *Interpretive Centre.*
Llangollen, Clwyd.
Canal Museum on old wharf.
Pontcysyllte Aqueduct, Clwyd.
Britain's finest aqueduct, carrying Llangollen Canal over R. Dee. By Thomas Telford, 1805.
Pontypridd, Mid Glam.
Glamorganshire Canal (1794), built to carry iron.

CENTRAL SCOTLAND & STRATHCLYDE
Linlithgow, Lothian.
Canal Museum.

NORTHERN SCOTLAND & THE ISLANDS
Banavie, Highland.
Neptune's Staircase (1803–22), 8 locks by Thomas Telford on Caledonian Canal.

CASTLES & FORTS

See also: map on p 197.

THE WEST COUNTRY
Berry Pomeroy Castle, Devon.
12th-C. ruins. Unusual gatehouse with 2 towers.
Corfe Castle, Dorset.
Splendid ruins of 10th–14th C.
Dunster, Somerset.
13th-C. castle. Original gatehouse remains, rest remodelled 19th C.
Launceston, Cornwall.
Norman motte-and-bailey castle, with round tower & shell keep.
Pendennis Castle, nr Falmouth, Cornwall.
Built by *Henry VIII* for coastal defence.
Portland Castle, Dorset.
Moated castle, 16th C.
Restormel Castle, Cornwall.
Fine circular shell keep (13th C.), owned by *Black Prince.*
St Mawes, Cornwall.
Henry VIII coastal fort.
St Michael's Mount, Cornwall.
14th-C. castle & Benedictine chapel.
Tintagel, Cornwall.
Remains of 12th-C. castle, split in two parts by sea. Supposed birthplace of King Arthur.

SOUTH-EAST ENGLAND
Arundel, W. Sussex.
Norman castle, rebuilt 18th & 19th C. Superb paintings & decorative arts.
Bodiam Castle, E. Sussex.
Dramatically sited moated castle, built 1386. Well preserved.
Carisbrooke, Isle of Wight.
Large Norman motte-and-bailey castle, with keep & curtain walls added later.
Deal, Kent.
Largest & best-preserved of *Henry VIII*'s coastal forts.
Dover, Kent.
Massive Norman castle incorporating Roman lighthouse & Saxon church.
Farnham, Surrey.
Impressive ruin of 12th-C. castle with motte, shell keep & well still surviving.
Hever Castle, Kent.
Moated castle (13th C.) where *Henry VIII* courted *Anne Boleyn.* Fine coll. of decorative arts.
Leeds Castle, nr Maidstone, Kent.
Mostly 13th C. Passed into royal ownership 1278. Fine furnishings & gardens.
Lewes, E. Sussex.
Ruins of Norman castle, with shell keep. Gatehouse of 14th C.
Pevensey, E. Sussex.
Ruins of Roman fort incorporated in medieval coastal castle.
Portchester, Hants.
Remains of Roman fort enclose medieval castle, with Norman keep & priory church.
Rochester, Kent.
Castle built in 1086, incorporating Roman city walls. Square keep of 1130.
Upnor Castle, Kent.
Tudor fortress, restored 17th C.
Walmer Castle, Kent.
Henry VIII gunfort, built 1538–80. Official residence of Lord Warden of the Cinque Ports since 18th C.

GREATER LONDON
Tower of London.
Began as Norman earthwork; massive *White Tower c.* 1080. Castle enclosed with walls & towers by Henry III & Edward I. Norman *Chapel of St John.*

THE THAMES, CHILTERNS & EAST ANGLIA
Berkeley, Berks.
Norman motte-and-bailey castle, 1067. Shell keep & inner-bailey walls added in 12th C. *Edward II* murdered here.
Berkhamsted, Herts.
Well-preserved early motte-and-bailey, built soon after 1066. Shell keep of 12th C.
Broughton Castle, Oxon.
Romantic moated castle, 1300–1550. Fine interior, good furniture.
Caister Castle, Norfolk.
Ruins of brick castle built by *Sir John Fastolf*, 15th C.
Castle Hedingham, Essex.
12th-C. stronghold, with thick honeycombed walls. 2 out of 4 corner turrets remain.
Castle Rising, nr King's Lynn, Norfolk.
Norman keep surrounded by earthworks. Bridge & gatehouse.
Colchester, Essex.
Norman castle, with massive great tower. Became a prison until 19th C.
Donnington, Berks.
Remains of 14th-C. castle, surrounded by 17th-C. star-shaped earthworks. Besieged 1642–7.
Framlingham, Suffolk.
Extensive Norman remains (1177–1215).
Norwich, Norfolk.
Restored Norman keep. Now a museum.
Orford, Suffolk.
Castle built by *Henry II*, 1165–73. Unique 3-turreted tower.
Windsor, Berks.
Castle originally built by William I. Henry II added vast stone shell keep to Edward III's great tower. George IV, in 1820s, added a hollow crown, making it tallest castle building in Britain. *St George's Chapel*, begun 1477. Superb coll. of paintings & decorative arts.

CENTRAL ENGLAND
Ashby-de-la-Zouche, Leics.
Norman manor house fortified by Lord Hastings, 1464.
Goodrich Castle, nr Ross-on-Wye, Heref. & Worcs.
Romantic ruins of medieval border castle.
Kenilworth, Warks.
Medieval castle with Norman keep, *John of Gaunt's* private apartments and 16th-C. gatehouse.
Lincoln, Lincs.
Castle built by *William I* (1068). One of 2 mottes has a shell keep. Cobb Hall (13th-C. tower) was site of gallows.
Ludlow, Salop.
Massive ruins of medieval red-stone castle. Circular Norman chapel.
Newark, Notts.
Castle built by bishops of Lincoln in 12th C. West wall survived Civil War. Only grounds are open.
Nottingham, Notts.
Castle was *Prince John's* headquarters, 1192–3. Rebuilt after Civil War, & again after a fire in 1831. Houses museum & art gallery.
Peveril Castle, Castleton, Derbys.
Ruined. Norman keep & 13th-C. round tower.
Rockingham, nr Corby, Northants.
Norman stronghold, incorporating Elizabethan house. Good coll. of furniture & pictures.
Tamworth, Staffs.
Norman castle, built on site of Saxon stronghold. Jacobean interior.
Warwick, Warks.
Fine medieval castle, 14th-C. towers & fortifications. Good coll. of arms, armour, paintings & decorative arts.

YORKSHIRE, HUMBERSIDE & THE NORTH-WEST
Bolton Castle, N. Yorks.
Built by Lord Scrope, from 1378. 'Queen Mary's Bedroom', chapel, dungeon, 19th-C. kitchen.
Conisbrough, S. Yorks.
Imposing fortress. Great tower begun 1180s.
Helmsley, N. Yorks.
Ruins of Norman castle, including keep & curtain walls.
Knaresborough, N. Yorks.
12th-C. castle, rebuilt in 14th C. by *Edward II.* Demolished after Civil War.
Richmond, N. Yorks.
Gatehouse, walls & hall 11th C., keep 12th C. One of earliest stone fortresses in country.
Scarborough, N. Yorks.
Remains of Norman castle on site of Viking stronghold.
Skipton, N. Yorks.
Norman and Tudor castle. Shell of 13th-C. chapel, impressive 13th-C. main gate.
York, N. Yorks.
Clifford's Tower (13th C.), on Norman mound.

THE NORTH OF ENGLAND
Alnwick, Northumb.
14th-C. castle overlooking town. Became stronghold of *Percy family*, 1309. Restored in 1850s.
Bamburgh Castle, Northumb.
Dramatically sited Norman castle with keep & curtain walls. Renovated late 19th C.
Barnard Castle, Durham.
Ruins of 11th/12th C.
Brough, Cumbria.
Castle built *c.* 1170. Restored in 17th C., tower converted to residence.

Brougham Castle, Cumbria.
Built 1170s. Restored in 17th c. by Lady Anne Clifford.
Carlisle, Cumbria.
Castle founded 1092, fine keep.
Dunstanburgh Castle, Northumb.
Ruins of 14th-c. cliff-top castle.
Durham, Durham.
Magnificent stonework of 12th c. on Norman motte-and-bailey.
Norham Castle, Northumb.
Border stronghold owned by bishops of Durham. Norman keep.
Raby Castle, Staindrop, Durham.
Late 14th-c. fortified manor house.
Warkworth, nr Alnwick, Northumb.
Largely 13th-c. castle, with fine 15th-c. keep. Owned by powerful *Percy family* from 1332.

WALES

Beaumaris Castle, Anglesey.
Last of *Edward I*'s castles, almost perfectly concentric. Well preserved.
Caernarfon, Gwynedd.
Castle is jewel of military architecture, begun 1283. Welsh headquarters of *Edward I.*
Caerphilly Castle, Mid Glam.
Pioneering concentric design (13th c.). Largest castle in England & Wales after Windsor.
Cardiff, S. Glam.
Norman & Roman remains in grounds of Victorian castle built by the Marquess of Bute.
Carew Castle, Dyfed.
Norman, strengthened in 13th c. Later became Tudor residence.
Chepstow, Gwent.
Castle mostly 14th c., with Norman keep. Picturesque setting.
Chirk Castle, Clwyd.
Founded by *Edward I.* 18th-c. interior, with work by Robert Adam.
Conwy, Gwynedd.
Castle built by *Edward I*, 1283–7. One of outstanding achievements of military architecture.
Denbigh, Clwyd.
Castle built in reign of *Edward I.* Royalist stronghold in Civil War, besieged 1646.
Dolbadarn Castle, Llanberis, Gwynedd.
Fine tower among 12th-13th-c. ruins.
Dolwyddelan, Gwynedd.
Castle remains incl. 12th-c. keep. Supposed birthplace of *Llywelyn the Great*
Flint, Clwyd.
One of the first Welsh castles of *Edward I* (1277).
Grosmont Castle, Gwent.
Moated border castle of 13th c.
Harlech, Gwynedd.
Dramatically sited castle built by *Edward I*, 1283–90. High inner wall with huge round towers, surrounded by low outer wall. Massive gatehouse.
Kidwelly, Dyfed.
Major concentric castle, inner quadrangle built 1270s. Fine gatehouse.
Manorbier, Dyfed.
Castle mostly 13th-14th-c. Birthplace of Gerald of Wales, the historian.
Oystermouth Castle, nr Swansea, W. Glam.
Norman, rebuilt in present form after being sacked by Welsh, 1287.
Pembroke, Dyfed.
Impressive Norman castle, with circular, roofed keep (*c.* 1200). *Henry Tudor* born here.
Powis Castle, Powys.
Medieval castle transformed into stately house by *Herbert family*.
Raglan Castle, Gwent.
Built mainly 15th-16th c. Hexagonal Great Tower outside castle walls on original motte.
Rhuddlan, Clwyd.
Remains of concentric castle built 1277–83 for *Edward I.*
Skenfrith, Gwent.
13th-c. round tower & curtain walls.

SOUTHERN SCOTLAND

Hermitage Castle, Borders.
Tower-house of 14th c., altered in 15th.

CENTRAL SCOTLAND & STRATHCLYDE

Bothwell Castle, Uddingston, Strathclyde.
Begun 1270s. Great Tower partly demolished in 14th c.
Cadzow Castle, Strathclyde.
Ruins of 16th-c. tower-house.
Crichton Castle, nr Dalkeith, Lothian.
Originally a 14th-c. tower-house, later much altered.
Culzean Castle, nr Ayr, Strathclyde.
Mock castle by *Robert Adam*, 18th c., on site of 16th-c. tower-house.
Doune, nr Stirling, Central.
Castle built by *Robert Stewart* (Regent of Scotland 1406–20). Walled garden.
Duart Castle, Mull, Strathclyde.
One of Scotland's earliest tower-houses (13th c.). Restored 1911.
Edinburgh, Lothian.
Edinburgh Castle has perfect rock-top setting. Fortress since 11th c. Oldest part includes Queen Margaret's Chapel (11th c.). Great Hall built by James IV has fine timbered roof. Also in city: *Craigmillar Castle.* Ruins of 14th-c. keep, with curtain wall.

Newark Castle, nr Selkirk, Strathclyde.
Ruins of 5-storey tower-house, dating from 1423.
Rothesay, Isle of Bute, Strathclyde.
Important medieval castle, with unique circular courtyard.
St Andrews, Fife.
Ruined 12th-c. castle, medieval residence of Archbishops of Scotland.
Stirling, Central.
Castle was favourite royal residence of 15th- & 16th-c. Scottish kings. Incorporates Renaissance palace of James V, Parliament Hall & Chapel Royal of 1594.
Tantallon Castle, nr N. Berwick, Lothian.
Ruins of 14th-c. *Douglas* stronghold, situated on promontory.

NORTHERN SCOTLAND & THE ISLANDS

Braemar, Grampian.
Castle built 1628, partly as hunting seat. Rebuilt *c.* 1748, garrisoned by Hanoverian troops.
Castle Fraser, Grampian.
Spectacular turreted castle, late 16th & early 17th c., built around courtyard.
Cawdor Castle, nr Nairn, Highland.
Central tower built 1372, fortified 1454. Enclosed by 16th-c. buildings.
Crathes Castle, Grampian.
Splendid example of fortified baronial tower-house, 16th c. Unusual painted ceiling, 1602. Walled gardens.
Drum Castle, nr Aberdeen, Grampian.
Massive 13th-c. tower adjoins mansion of 1619.
Dunnottar Castle, nr Stonehaven, Grampian.
Spectacular ruins on rocky cliff. Tower & chapel of 14th c., 15th-c. gateway.
Dunrobin Castle, nr Dornoch, Highland.
Square keep built 1275, much altered in 19th c.
Edzell, Tayside.
Ruin of 16th-c. castle. Outstanding 17th-c. garden.
Glamis Castle, Tayside.
Owes present aspect to 17th c. Oldest part is Duncan's Hall. *Malcolm II* said to have died here.
Kildrummy Castle, nr Alford, Grampian.
13th-c. castle, dismantled 1715.
Loch Leven Castle, nr Kinross, Tayside.
Late 14th-c. tower on tiny island. *Mary Queen of Scots* imprisoned here.
Urquhart Castle, nr Drumnadrochit, Highland.
On west shore of Loch Ness. Built 14th c. Blown up 1692 to prevent Jacobite occupation.

CHURCH ARCHITECTURE

For early monuments, stained glass, sculpture etc., see 'The Dark & Middle Ages' (p 309). See also: maps showing cathedrals (p 203), parish churches (p 204) & monasteries (p 207).

THE WEST COUNTRY

Bath, Avon.
Benedictine *abbey* founded 1499. Restored in 16th c.
Bradford-on-Avon, Wilts.
St Lawrence: Saxon church, restored 19th c.
Bristol, Avon.
Cathedral, originally an abbey church, built on unusual plan with high aisles. Abbey gatehouse & chapter house survive. *St Mary Redcliffe.* Great Gothic church (1280–1380), lavish sculpture.
Christchurch, Dorset.
Christ Church, 11th c. Norman nave, Perpendicular choir.
Exeter, Devon.
Cathedral has Norman towers but is mostly Decorated. Superb ribbed vault. West front has large ensemble of 14th-c. sculpted figures.
Glastonbury, Somerset.
Substantial *ruins* of Benedictine abbey church, 12th-13th c.
Launceston, Cornwall.
St Mary Magdalene (1511–24), famous for granite carvings.
Malmesbury, Wilts.
Benedictine *abbey* with Norman nave still in use. Outstanding 12th-c. tympanum.
Ottery St Mary, Devon.
Church, rebuilt 1338–42. Victorian restoration work by Butterfield.
Salisbury, Wilts.
Cathedral consecrated 1258, built to replace Norman cathedral at Old Sarum. Style is unified Early English. Has large green close, early Decorated cloisters, octagonal chapter house & loftiest spire in Britain.
Taunton, Somerset.
Large church, tall Perpendicular tower; main body rebuilt 15th–16th c.
Wells, Somerset.
Cathedral has most magnificent west front in country, with sculpted figures. Interior marred only by 14th-c. 'scissor' arches. Bishop's Palace (13th–14th c.).

SOUTH-EAST ENGLAND

Barfreston, Kent.
Small Norman church, exquisite sculpted portal.
Bournemouth, Dorset.
St Stephen: 19th-c. church by J.L. Pearson.
Beaulieu, Hants.
Ruins of Cistercian abbey; refectory used as parish church.
Brighton, E. Sussex.
St Michael: 19th-c. church with Pre-Raphaelite glass.
Canterbury, Kent.
Cathedral has outstanding Norman crypt with sculpted capitals, early Gothic choir, Perpendicular nave. Superb stained glass. *St Augustine's Abbey*: remains of Benedictine abbey.
Chichester, W. Sussex.
Cathedral is Norman with Gothic alterations and Perpendicular bell tower. Chagall window (20th c.).
Rochester, Kent.
Cathedral has sculpted portals on west front.
Romsey, Hants.
Surviving Norman church of monastery. Saxon carvings.
Winchester, Hants.
Cathedral: Norman transept, Perpendicular nave. Many chapels & tombs.

GREATER LONDON

City.
St Bartholomew the Great, Smithfield. Oldest London church (Norman), with fine monuments. *St Bride's*, Fleet St, a well-restored Christopher Wren church. *St Mary-le-Bow*, Cheapside, has one of Wren's finest steeples (1683). *St Mary Woolnoth*, by Hawksmoor, 1716–26. *St Paul's Cathedral*, Great Gothic church replaced by Wren's baroque masterpiece (1675–1710). Carvings by Grinling Gibbons, ironwork by Jean Tijou. *St Stephen Walbrook*, rebuilt by Wren, 1672–7. Fine dome.
East London.
Christ Church, Spitalfields, by Hawksmoor, 1714–29. *St George-in-the-East.* Fine church by Hawksmoor, 1714–29, restored in 1960s after bombing in Blitz.
North London.
St Augustine, Kilburn, by J.L. Pearson, begun 1871. *St Pancras*, with Athenian-style caryatid columns in porch (1819–22).
West End.
All Saints, Margaret St, Gothic Revival, mid-19th c. *St George, Bloomsbury*, by Hawksmoor, 1716–31. Unusual steeple. *St Martin-in-the-Fields*, by James Gibbs, 1722–6. Tower & spire above Corinthian portico. Fine plasterwork ceiling. *St Mary-le-Strand*, by Gibbs, 1714–17. Baroque gem. *St Paul's, Covent Garden*, by Inigo Jones, begun in 1631, rebuilt after fire in 1795. Stark semi-classical style: 'the handsomest barn in England'.
Westminster.
St John, Smith Square, 1713, by baroque architect Thomas Archer. *Westminster Abbey*, 13th–16th c. Used for coronations. Henry VII's Chapel has magnificent tomb by Torrigiani & superb fan vaulting. *Westminster Cathedral*, metropolitan Roman Catholic church in colourful late 19th-c. neo-Byzantine style. Stations of the Cross carved by Eric Gill, 1914–18.

THE THAMES, CHILTERNS & EAST ANGLIA

Bury St Edmunds, Suffolk.
Ruins of abbey incl. 2 gatehouses.
Cambridge, Cambs.
Norman *Church of Holy Sepulchre*, on circular plan. Restored 19th c.

See also 'Schools, universities, colleges & libraries' (p 320).
Castle Acre, Norfolk.
Impressive *ruins* of priory, *c.* 1190.
Ely, Cambs.
Cathedral has arcaded west front, majestic interior, unique late Gothic octagon lantern. Prior's Doorway (12th C.) has Christ in Majesty tympanum.
Framlingham, nr Woodbridge, Suffolk.
15th-C. church with superb wooden roof & famous early Renaissance monuments.
Iffley, Oxon.
One of the best small Norman churches in the country.
King's Lynn, Norfolk.
St Nicholas (mainly 1419) has Early English tower. Angel roof.
Lavenham, Suffolk.
Splendid *wool church*, 1480–1530.
Long Melford, Suffolk.
Fine Perpendicular *wool church*, magnificent Lady Chapel.
March, nr Peterborough, Cambs.
St Wendreda has superb hammerbeam angel roof.
Norwich, Norfolk.
Cathedral combines Norman & late Gothic. Fine sculpted portal in cloister (*c.* 1310), elegant Perpendicular vaults. *St Peter Mancroft*, superb 15th-C. church with tomb of Sir Thomas Browne.
Oxford, Oxon.
St Mary's has unusual baroque porch. *See also* 'Schools, universities, colleges & libraries' (p 320).
Peterborough, Cambs.
Cathedral almost entirely Norman, with painted wooden ceiling in nave.
Saffron Walden, Essex.
St Mary the Virgin has superb Perpendicular nave.
St Albans, Herts.
Abbey church acquired *cathedral* status in 1877. Imposing Norman exterior.
Walsingham, Norfolk.
Ruins of priory (12th C.): a pilgrimage centre associated with vision of Virgin.
CENTRAL ENGLAND
Boston, Lincs.
St Botolph, grand church in late Decorated style. Magnificent Perpendicular tower ('Boston Stump').
Brixworth, nr Northampton, Northants.
Largest surviving Anglo-Saxon church. Belfry & spire are 14th C.
Cirencester, Glos.
Splendid *wool church*, fine Lady Chapel.
Clumber, Notts.
Neo-Gothic *chapel* of St Mary, 1889.
Coventry, Warks.
Cathedral, 1962, by Sir Basil Spence (next to Gothic ruins). Stained glass by John Piper, Graham Sutherland tapestry, bronze St Michael by Epstein.
Gloucester, Glos.
Cathedral has Norman nave & Perpendicular choir with superb stained glass. Fan-vaulted cloister.
Hereford, Heref. & Worcs.
Cathedral, with noble central tower. Shrines. Ancient library, medieval maps.
Kilpeck, Heref. & Worcs.
Church has richly carved Norman stonework.
Lichfield, Staffs.
Only English *cathedral* with 3 spires. Much restored. Chapter house, 1249.
Lincoln, Lincs.
Cathedral is arguably finest in country, mostly 13th C. with 14th-C. additions. Beautiful central tower. Norman sculpted frieze on west front. Angel Choir, 1256–80.
Louth, Lincs.
Late Gothic church, lofty spire.

Melbourne, Derbys.
Fine Norman church, *c.* 1130.
Shobdon, nr Leominster, Heref. & Worcs.
St John the Evangelist, 1752–6, in rococo-Gothic fantasy style.
Shrewsbury, Salop.
St Chad, Georgian classical, with round nave.
Southwell, Notts.
Minster, with fine Norman & Early English work. Decorated chapter house has magnificent carved foliage on capitals (13th C.).

Tewkesbury, Glos.
Norman *abbey church*, with original mid-12th-C. tower.
Warwick, Warks.
St Mary: Norman crypt & outstanding 15th-C. Beauchamp Chapel.
Worcester, Heref. & Worcs.
Cathedral. Massive crypt (12th C.). Early English retrochoir. Tomb effigy of King John.
YORKSHIRE, HUMBERSIDE & THE NORTH-WEST
Beverley, Humber.
Minster is largest parish church in England. Percy tomb. *St Mary's* has 16th-C. nave & tower. Restored by Pugin, 19th C.
Bolton, N. Yorks.
Augustinian *priory* founded 1150, nave still in use as parish church.
Fountains Abbey, N. Yorks.
Most extensive Cistercian *ruins* in Britain. Beautiful setting. Abbey founded 1132.
Halifax, W. Yorks.
All Souls, church by Sir George Gilbert Scott, 1859.
Liverpool, Merseyside.
Christ the King, Catholic cathedral (1962–7). Effective interior owes much to stained glass. *Church of Christ*, Anglican cathedral (1902–78), by Giles Gilbert Scott. Largest in Britain.
Manchester, Gr Manchester.
Perpendicular collegiate church given *cathedral* status in 1847. *St Ann*, 18th-C. church in Wren style. Contains Carracci's Descent from the Cross.
Patrington, nr Withernsea, Humber.
St Patrick, built on scale of small cathedral, has glorious Gothic spire.
Rievaulx Abbey, N. Yorks.
Ruins of Cistercian foundation (1131).
Ripon, N. Yorks.
Cathedral has unique Saxon crypt.
Selby, N. Yorks.
Abbey church. Exquisite choir, original 14th-C. glass.
Studley Royal, N. Yorks.
19th-C. church, elaborate spire.
Whitby, N. Yorks.
Cliff-top *ruins* of Benedictine abbey.
York, N. Yorks.
Minster renowned for quantity of medieval stained glass. Fine chapter house. Other York churches incl. *All Saints*, North St, also with fine windows.
THE NORTH OF ENGLAND
Durham, Durham.
Great Norman *cathedral*, with massive carved columns, earliest rib vaults, Early English Galilee Chapel.

Gibside, nr Gateshead, Tyne & Wear.
Private *chapel* in Palladian style by James Paine, late 18th C.
Hexham, nr Newcastle, Northumb.
Abbey church, 12th–13th C. Anglo-Saxon crypt almost intact.
WALES
Bangor, Gwynedd.
Cathedral rebuilt in 19th C. to design by George Gilbert Scott.
Brecon, Powys.
Early English *cathedral*.
Llandaff, nr Cardiff, S. Glam.
12th-C. *cathedral*, greatly restored. Christ in Majesty sculpture by Epstein.
St Asaph, Clwyd.
Norman and Gothic *cathedral church*, much restored.
St David's, Dyfed.
Founded early 6th C., cradle of Christian faith in Wales. Norman arches, Celtic remains.
Strata Florida Abbey, Dyfed.
Cistercian *ruins*.
Tintern Abbey, Gwent.
Picturesque *ruins* of Cistercian foundation (1131), riverside setting.
Valle Crucis Abbey, Clwyd.
Cistercian *ruins*. Monastic buildings became farm house.
Wrexham, Clwyd.
St Giles, late Gothic parish church.
SOUTHERN SCOTLAND
Dryburgh Abbey, Borders.
Ruins of Premonstratensian abbey.
Jedburgh, Borders.
Ruins of Augustinian abbey, Romanesque.
Sweetheart Abbey, Dumf. & Gall.
Splendid *ruins* of Cistercian abbey.
CENTRAL SCOTLAND & STRATHCLYDE
Arbroath Abbey, Tayside.
Ruins of Cluniac abbey (founded 1178), incl. gatehouse tower.
Dunblane, Tayside.
Severe 13th-C. *cathedral* with Romanesque tower. Untouched by Reformation, restored 19th C.
Dunkeld, Tayside.
St Columba, originally a Celtic monastery. Gothic choir restored as parish church.
Edinburgh, Lothian.
Canongate: built 1688 as church of Holyroodhouse & Edinburgh Castle. *St Giles Cathedral*, mainly 15th C. Window by William Morris & Burne-Jones. *Tolbooth*: 16th-C. church with outside stair.
Glasgow, Strathclyde.
St Mungo has 13th-C. choir & splendid crypt. *United Presbyterian Church*, Caledonia Rd, by Alexander Thomson (1856), in Greek style.
Hamilton, Strathclyde.
Octagonal church by William Adam (1732).
Haddington, Lothian.
Late Gothic church, well restored.
Iona, Strathclyde.
13th-C. Benedictine *abbey* on Celtic foundation of St Columba (AD 563).
Leuchars, nr St Andrews, Fife.
Fine Norman church.
Roslin, Lothian.
Collegiate church, founded 1446. Celebrated Apprentice's Pillar (exquisite sculpture).
St Andrews, Fife.
Largest cathedral in Scotland, consecrated 1318. In *ruins*.
NORTHERN SCOTLAND & THE ISLANDS
Aberdeen, Grampian.
Cathedral, mostly 15th C. Wooden nave ceiling dated 1520. *St Nicholas's Kirk*, famous for bells.

Elgin, Grampian.
Ruins of 13th-C. cathedral.
Kirkwall, Orkney.
Romanesque *cathedral* (St Magnus), Gothic additions. Earl's Palace (founded 1137) & Bishop's Palace nearby.

COUNTRY HOUSES

See also: map of country houses on p 208, & 'Gardens' (p 313).

THE WEST COUNTRY
Badminton House, nr Chipping Sodbury, Avon.
Palladian mansion altered mid-18th C. by *William Kent*. Carvings by *Grinling Gibbons*. Coll. of decorative arts.
Castle Drogo, nr Moretonhampstead, Devon.
Granite castle by *Lutyens*, early 20th C.
Dodington House, nr Chipping Sodbury, Avon.
Great 18th-C. house by *James Wyatt*.
Dyrham Park, Avon.
Built 17th & early 18th C. Fine coll. of furniture & Dutch paintings.
Longleat House, nr Warminster, Wilts.
Magnificent Elizabethan house. Sumptuous Regency & Victorian interior. Coll. of decorative arts.
Montacute House, Somerset.
Beautiful E-shaped 16th-C. house, with later additions. Huge long gallery.
Prior Park, nr Bath, Avon.
Palladian villa, by *John Wood the Elder*, 1735–48. Now a school, visitable in holidays.
Saltram House, nr Plymouth, Devon.
Georgian, built around Tudor mansion. Coll. of decorative arts, paintings.
Stourhead, Wilts.
Palladian house completed 1722 for Henry Hoare. Coll. of paintings, & furniture by the younger Chippendale. Landscaped garden.
Wilton House, nr Salisbury, Wilts.
Rebuilding by *Inigo Jones* (completed 1653) incl. famous Double-cube Room. Later additions (from 1801) by *James Wyatt*. Paintings & sculpture.
SOUTH-EAST ENGLAND
Clandon Park, nr Guildford, Surrey.
Palladian house, fine interior. Furniture & porcelain.
Ightham Mote, Sevenoaks, Kent.
Moated manor house, from *c.* 1340. Great hall has original ceiling.
Knole, Kent.
Palatial house of 16th & 17th C. Important coll. of portraits, furniture, textiles, silver.
Osborne House, Isle of Wight.
Queen Victoria's retreat, designed by *Prince Albert* & Thomas Cubitt in Italianate style (1846). Ornate state apartments & Victoria's private rooms.
Parham Park, W. Sussex.
Elizabethan house, original hall & gallery.
Penshurst Place, Kent.
House with Tudor enlargements. Great

Hall 1340. Birthplace of Sir Philip Sidney.
Petworth House, W. Sussex.
Medieval house rebuilt at end of 17th c., Victorian additions. Splendid carvings by *Grinling Gibbons*. Fine coll. of paintings.
Polesden Lacey, Surrey.
Regency house, Edwardian alterations. Furniture, china, paintings.
Standen, East Grinstead, W. Sussex.
Designed by *Philip Webb*, 1894.
Uppark, nr Petersfield, W. Sussex.
Late 17th-c. home, well-preserved flock wallpaper. Furniture & paintings.
The Vyne, nr Basingstoke, Hants.
Tudor house with 17th-c. classical portico.

GREATER LONDON

Chiswick House, Chiswick.
Palladian villa, 1725, by *Lord Burlington*, based on Palladio's Villa Rotonda. Interior decoration by *William Kent*.
Ham House, Richmond.
17th-c. house, Stuart furniture.
Hampton Court Palace, Richmond.
Cardinal Wolsey's red-brick palace begun 1514, much enlarged by *Henry VIII*. Classical additions by *Wren*. Ironwork by *Tijou*. Tapestry & picture colls., incl. Mantegna's 'Triumphs of Caesar'.
Kenwood House, Hampstead.
Remodelled by *Robert Adam*. Splendid library. Rembrandts, Vermeers, English Masters.
Osterley Park House, Isleworth.
Rebuilt by *Robert Adam*, 1761–80. Gobelins tapestry, fine furniture.
Strawberry Hill, Twickenham.
Rebuilt by *Horace Walpole*, mid-18th c., in whimsical neo-Gothic style. Visiting by appt.
Syon House, Isleworth.
15th-c. convent, renovated by *Robert Adam*. Spectacular entrance hall with antique sculpture. Fine paintings.

THE THAMES, CHILTERNS & EAST ANGLIA

Anglesey Abbey, Cambs.
Fairhaven Collection of paintings & furniture.
Audley End, Saffron Walden, Essex.
Vast Jacobean house, partly demolished by Vanbrugh. Fine work by *Robert Adam*.
Blenheim Palace, Woodstock, Oxon.
Vanbrugh's masterpiece, built 1704–16 for Duke of Marlborough. Grounds by 'Capability' Brown. Furniture, paintings.
Blickling Hall, nr Aylsham, Norfolk.
Outstanding Jacobean house, late 18th-c. interior. Long gallery.
Burghley House, nr Stamford, Cambs.
Largest Elizabethan mansion in England, virtually unaltered. Carvings by *Grinling Gibbons*. Paintings, decorative arts.
Buscot Park, Faringdon, Oxon.
18th-c. house, with *Burne-Jones* Room.
Hatfield House, Herts.
Jacobean house by *Robert Cecil*, 1st Earl of Salisbury, completed 1611. Fine portraits. Part of 15th-c. Royal Palace survives nearby.
Holkham Hall, Norfolk.
Palladian mansion by *Thomas Coke*, 1734–59. Superb marble entrance hall.
Houghton Hall, Norfolk.
18th-c. mansion built for Sir Robert Walpole. Interior by *William Kent*.
Ickworth, Suffolk.
Begun 1795 for 4th Earl of Bristol. Central domed rotunda.
Kelmscott Manor, Oxon.
Cotswold stone Tudor house owned by William Morris from 1871 until his death in 1896. Visiting by appt.
Knebworth House, nr Stevenage, Herts.
Victorian Gothic exterior. Tudor hall.
Layer Marney Tower, nr Colchester, Essex.
Massive Tudor gatehouse, Italianate decoration.
Luton Hoo, nr Luton, Beds.
Superb art treasures, incl. Fabergé jewellery.
Somerleyton Hall, Suffolk.
Built for railway magnate in Anglo-Italian style, 1846.
Waddesdon Manor, Bucks.
19th-c. Renaissance-style château with superb French decorative arts of 17th & 18th c.
Wimpole Hall, Accrington, nr Royston, Cambs.
18th c. Contains *Sir John Soane*'s Yellow Drawing Room.
Woburn Abbey, Beds.
East front & Chinese dairy by *Henry Holland*, 18th c. Animal park.

CENTRAL ENGLAND

Althorp, nr Northampton, Northants.
Superb coll. of Old Masters, porcelain, furniture.
Aston Hall, nr Birmingham, W. Midlands.
Jacobean house (1635) with fine staircase, gallery & kitchen.
Charlecote Park, Warks.
Elizabethan, altered 19th c.
Chatsworth, Derbys.
The 'Palace of the Peak', by *William Talman*, 1687–1707, additions by *Wyatville* (1820s). Baroque chapel with paintings by *Verrio* & *Laguerre*. Incomparable setting.
Compton Wynyates, Warks.
Tudor house, very picturesque.
Donington-le-Heath, Leics.
Medieval manor house.
Haddon Hall, Derbys.
Fine medieval house, carefully restored in 1920s. Long gallery. Kitchens still have Tudor fittings.
Hardwick Hall, Derbys.
Elizabethan, built for Bess of Hardwick, Countess of Shrewsbury. Plaster friezes in High Great Chamber. Furniture, needlework, tapestries.
Kedleston Hall, Derbys.
Work by *James Paine* & *Robert Adam*, 18th c. Adam built superb Great Hall. Decorative arts, imperial trophies.

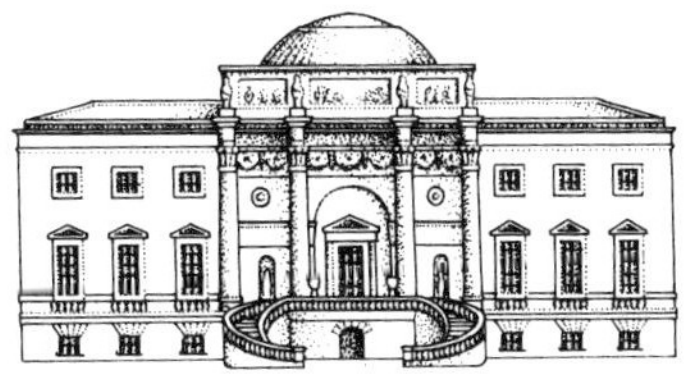

Shugborough, Staffs.
18th-c. home of the Earls of Lichfield. Contains County Museum.
Stokesay Castle, Salop.
Fortified manor house, the Great Hall built *c.* 1270 & almost unchanged. Elizabethan gatehouse.
Sudbury Hall, nr Uttoxeter, Derbys.
Brick mansion of 17th c., richly decorated Charles II rooms. *Grinling Gibbons* carvings.
Thoresby Hall, Notts.
Victorian, heavily furnished. Outstanding 3-storeyed great hall.
Wollaton Hall, Nottingham, Notts.
Elizabethan 'prodigy house', *c.* 1585. Interior altered early 19th c. by *Wyatville*. Now a museum.

YORKSHIRE, HUMBERSIDE & THE NORTH-WEST

Beningbrough Hall, nr Shipton, N. Yorks.
Built 1716, extensively restored. Coll. of portraits. Victorian laundry.
Carlton Towers, N. Yorks.
Victorian, neo-Gothic exterior by *A.W.N. Pugin*. State rooms. Coll. of paintings.
Castle Howard, N. Yorks.
Colossal masterpiece (1700–26) by *Vanbrugh*. Painted & gilded dome, long gallery, chapel. Fine paintings, decorative arts. Mausoleum in landscaped grounds.
Gawsworth Hall, nr Macclesfield, Cheshire.
Late 15th-c. half-timbered manor house, home of Fitton family.
Harewood House, nr Leeds, W. Yorks.
Exterior by *John Carr* (begun 1759), interior by *Robert Adam*, later altered by *Sir Charles Barry*. Superb coll. of Chippendale furniture & oriental porcelain.
Little Moreton Hall, Congleton, Cheshire.
Moated 16th-c. half-timbered house, 16th-c. wall paintings (restored).
Lyme Park, Disley, Cheshire.
Fine Elizabethan rooms, exterior by Leoni, *c.* 1720. Carvings by *Grinling Gibbons*.
Newby Hall, Ripon, N. Yorks.
Small country house (*c.* 1705), with later additions by *Robert Adam*.
Normanby Hall, Scunthorpe, Humber.
By *Sir Robert Smirke*, 1825–9.
Nostell Priory, nr Wakefield, W. Yorks.
Built early 18th c., added to by *Robert Adam*. Chippendale furniture. British paintings (Van Dyck & Hogarth).
Rufford Old Hall, Lancs.
Fine medieval half-timbered hall with hammerbeam roof & unique screen. Coll. of decorative arts.
Speke Hall, Liverpool, Merseyside.
Elizabethan half-timbered courtyard house, rich plasterwork inside.
Tatton Park, Knutsford, Cheshire.
18th-c. neoclassical house.
Temple Newsam, nr Leeds, W. Yorks.
Jacobean house, Georgian décor. English furniture & silver.
Weston Park, Staffs.
Restoration house.

THE NORTH OF ENGLAND

Cragside, nr Rothbury, Northumb.
By *R. Norman Shaw*, completed 1895. Pre-Raphaelite paintings.
Seaton Delaval, nr Whitley Bay, Northumb.
By *Vanbrugh*, begun 1718. Restored after fire. Paintings, furniture, ceramics.
Wallington Hall, nr Morpeth, Northumb.
17th-c. home. Porcelain, furniture, paintings.

WALES

Castell Coch, nr Cardiff, S. Glam.
Castle, remodelled in 19th c. by *William Burges*. Mock-medieval décor.
Erddig, nr Wrexham, Clwyd.
17th c. with 18th-c. additions. Original furniture.
Penrhyn Castle, Bangor, Gwynedd.
19th-c. Norman-style castle built for slate baron.
Powis Castle, Welshpool, Powys.
Castle of 13th–14th c. remodelled in 17th c. Fine plasterwork. Furniture, paintings, tapestry.

SOUTHERN SCOTLAND

Abbotsford, nr Melrose, Borders.
Bought by Sir Walter Scott in 1811. Rebuilt in grand baronial style. Scott memorabilia.
Bowhill, nr Selkirk, Borders.
Home of Duke of Buccleugh & Queensberry. Outstanding paintings, porcelain, furniture.
Drumlanrig Castle, Dumf. & Gall.
Late 17th-c. castle. Paintings, Louis XIV furniture.
Floors Castle, Kelso, Borders.
Built 1721 by *William Adam*, added to by *Playfair*. Paintings, French furniture, porcelain.
Manderston, Borders.
Unaltered Edwardian interior & exterior.
Mellerstain, Gordon, Borders.
Begun by *William Adam* (1725) & finished by his sons. Exquisite decorations & plasterwork, fine library.

CENTRAL SCOTLAND & STRATHCLYDE

Culross Palace, Fife.
Built 1597–1611.
Culzean Castle, Strathclyde.
Fine *Robert Adam* house, built 1777 around ancient core. Superb oval staircase.
Falkland Palace, Fife.
Royal palace, built 1501–41 by James IV on site of 12th-c. palace. Chapel Royal, King's bedchamber, royal tennis court.
Hill House, Helensburgh, Strathclyde.
Art Nouveau version of Scottish baronial home, by *C.R. Mackintosh*, 1902.
Hopetoun House, S. Queensferry, Lothian.
Begun 1696, rebuilt & enlarged in early 18th c. by *the Adams*. Fine paintings.

NORTHERN SCOTLAND & THE ISLANDS

Balmoral Castle, Grampian.
Victorian turreted retreat on estate bought by Prince Albert (1848). Grounds open when Royal Family is absent.
Haddo House, Grampian.
By *William Adam*, 1731. Interior redesigned in 'Adam Revival' style, late 19th c.
Scone Palace, Tayside.
Rebuilt 1803 on site of Scone Abbey. Decorative arts coll.

THE DARK & MIDDLE AGES

This section covers sculpture, stained glass, brasses & precious objects. See also; 'Church architecture' (p 307).

THE WEST COUNTRY

Ashton, Devon.
Church has lavishly carved *bench-ends* & 15th-c. painted *rood screen*.
Exeter, Devon.
Cathedral choir stalls have outstanding 13th-c. *misericords*.
Salisbury, Wilts.
Cathedral has superb recumbent *stone effigy* of armed knight (1226). Large 14th-c. *brass* of Bishop Wyville.

SOUTH-EAST ENGLAND

Canterbury, Kent.
In Cathedral: rare 12th-c. *wall painting* in St Anselm's Chapel. Glorious late 12th-/early 13th-c. *stained glass*, finest in England (especially windows in west transepts, Trinity Chapel & 'corona'). *Tomb effigy* of Black Prince (1376) in choir. Also: shrine of Thomas à Becket.

Chaldon, Surrey.
West wall of church has *mural* (*c.* 1200) showing Ladder of Salvation.
Chichester, W. Sussex.
Exceptional 12th-C. *sculpted stone panels* in south aisle of Cathedral.
Romsey, Hants.
Carved *Saxon crucifixion*, inset in Abbey wall.
Shipley, E. Sussex.
St Mary's church has fine enamelled reliquary casket (13th C.)
Winchester, Hants.
Cathedral has fine 12th-C. sculpted *marble font*, unusual *murals* (*c.* 1225) & 14th-C. *misericords*. Cathedral Library has medieval mss, incl. magnificent *Winchester Bible* (late 12th C).
GREATER LONDON
Bloomsbury.
British Museum has famous 7th-C. Sutton Hoo treasures, Norman metalwork, ivories, enamels. Illuminated mss incl. Lindisfarne Gospels (*c.* 698).
City.
Museum of London (Barbican) has various relics, incl. early 11th-C. carved tombstone showing Viking influence.
Kensington.
Victoria & Albert Museum has early Christian art, fine metalwork (incl. Gloucester Candlestick, *c.* 1110), medieval embroidery & stained glass.
Westminster.
Westminster Abbey: royal tombs incl. bronze effigy of Queen Eleanor (*c.* 1291) & gilt copper effigies of Edward III & Richard II (14th C.).
THE THAMES, CHILTERNS & EAST ANGLIA
Copford Green, Essex.
Celebrated medieval *murals*, mainly 12th C., in parish church.
Dorchester, Oxon.
Abbey has best-preserved Norman figured *lead font* in England.
Ely, Cambs.
Cathedral has stately carved *effigy* of Bishop Kilkenny (d. 1256) & coll. of medieval *stained glass* from many churches.
Eton College, nr Windsor, Berks.
Outstanding late 15th-C. *murals*.
Hitchin, Herts.
Impressive 15th-C. *screens*, *font* & 5 *brasses* in parish church.
Lavenham, Suffolk.
14th-C. carved *choir stalls & rood screen*.
Little Dunmow, Essex.
15th-C. *alabaster effigies* in parish church.
Norwich, Norfolk.
Well-preserved medieval *altarpiece* (1380) in Cathedral. St Peter Hungate Church Museum: 15th-C. *stained glass* & *many illuminated mss*. Church of St Peter Mancroft has good *brasses* & *stained glass* (15th C.).
Oxford, Oxon.
Ashmolean Museum: precious *Anglo-Saxon jewellery*. 9th-C. Alfred Jewel.
Reading, Berks.
Museum has *carved capitals* (12th C.) from cloister of destroyed Reading Abbey.
St Albans, Herts.
Nave piers of cathedral have *wall paintings* of 13th/14th C. Choir contains exceptional *stone rood screen*, *c.* 1380.
Waltham Cross, Herts.
Eleanor Cross, erected by Edward I, 1290.
West Stow, Suffolk.
Reconstructed Anglo-Saxon village has relics on display.
CENTRAL ENGLAND
Chipping Campden, Glos.
Impressive medieval *brasses*, memorials to local wool staplers.

Coventry, W. Midlands.
Guildhall has sturdy 15th-C. wooden *equestrian statue* of St George.
Eardisley, Heref. & Worcs.
Church has superb carved stone font, *c.* 1150.

Fairford, Glos.
Parish church has finest ensemble of 15th- & 16th-C. *stained glass* in England.
Geddington, Northants.
Eleanor Cross, erected by Edward I, 1290.
Gloucester, Glos.
Cathedral has 14th-C. *stained glass*, & alabaster *tomb effigy* of Edward II (d. 1327) beneath ornate stone canopy.
Great Malvern, Heref. & Worcs.
Priory Church has exceptionally complete array of *stained glass*, 15th & 16th C.
Hardingstone, Northants.
Eleanor Cross (1290), perfectly intact.
Hawton, Notts.
Richly decorated stone *Easter Sepulchre* (14th C.) in church.
Hereford, Heref. & Worcs.
Fine 14th-C. carved *misericords* in cathedral. Also: shrine of St Thomas Cantilupe (d. 1282) & chained library.
Lincoln, Lincs.
City & County Museum has major *Saxon coll.*
Oakham, Leics.
Fine *carved capitals* in intact Norman hall.
Warwick, Warks.
In Chantry Chapel of St Mary's Church: 15th-C. life-size copper effigy of Richard Beauchamp, Earl of Warwick, & other *late medieval tombs*.
Worcester, Worcs.
Cathedral has serene recumbent *effigy of King John* (*c.* 1218) in Purbeck marble.
Wrangle, Lincs.
Church has magnificent 14th-C. *stained glass*.
YORKSHIRE, HUMBERSIDE & THE NORTH-WEST
Beverley, Humber.
Minster church contains outstanding early 14th-C. *Percy tomb*, with elaborate canopy.
Chester, Cheshire.
Exquisitely carved *misericords* in Cathedral, amongst finest in England.
Douglas, Isle of Man.
Manx Museum: relics of 9th-C. Norse settlement, incl. *Viking ornaments*.
Manchester, Gr Manchester.
Cathedral (former parish church) has splendid 15th-C. *carvings*, *canopies*, *misericords & screens*.
Nantwich, Cheshire.
Magnificent canopied *choir stalls* with carved misericords, late 14th C.
Pickering, N. Yorks.
Extensive 15th-C. *murals* in nave of church.
Selby, N. Yorks.
Abbey church has impressive 14th-C. *Jesse window*.

York, N. Yorks.
Cathedral has much original late medieval *stained glass*. In All Saints church, North St: *'Prykke of Conscience' window* (mid 15th C.). Yorks. Museum has major coll. of *Viking artefacts* & fine 13th-C. sculpture.
THE NORTH OF ENGLAND
Bewcastle, Cumbria.
St Cuthbert's churchyard has celebrated *Anglo-Saxon cross* (7th C.) sculpted with biblical figures.
Brougham, Cumbria.
St Wilfred's Church has gilt oak reredos with magnificent 15th-C. *altarpiece*.
Durham, Durham.
Cathedral monastic buildings contain *sculpted crosses* of 7th–11th C. & *St Cuthbert's coffin* & grave goods. Illuminated *Bible* in Cathedral Library.
Gosforth, nr Egremont, Cumbria.
Tall Anglo-Saxon *carved cross* with Scandinavian mythical figures.
Patrington, Humber.
Restored medieval *reredos* & fine carved *Easter Sepulchre* in parish church.
WALES
Cardiff, S. Glam.
National Museum of Wales has impressive engraved *church plate* (mid-13th C.).
Gresford, Clwyd.
All Saints has fine 15th-C. *stained glass*.
Llanegryn, Dyfed.
Small church famed for grandiose *rood screen*.
Margam, W. Glam.
Stones Museum: inscribed & sculpted stones incl. 12 early *crosses*, 5th-12th C.
Nevern, nr Cardigan, Dyfed.
Carved stone Celtic *cross*, of 10th C.
Penmon, Anglesey.
5 Celtic *crosses* in St Seiriol's Church.
St David's, Dyfed.
Cathedral has entertaining carved oak *misericords*, 15th C.
SOUTHERN SCOTLAND
Ruthwell, Dumf. & Gall.
Fine 7th-C. carved *cross* with biblical figures.
CENTRAL SCOTLAND & STRATHCLYDE
Edinburgh, Lothian.
National Museum of Antiquities has outstanding *Pictish sculpture & silverwork*.
Fowlis Wester, Fife.
Pictish stone (8th C.) with symbolic carvings.
Iona, Strathclyde.
Celebrated site of early Celtic monastery. Tall carved *crosses* of 9th, 10th & 15th C.
Kilmory Knap, Strathclyde.
MacMillan's Cross outside Chapel of St Maelrubha (14th C.) has some 30 late medieval *sculpted stones*.
St Andrews, Fife.
Cathedral Museum has outstanding sculpted 8th-C. *tombstone* with Celtic ornament & figures.
NORTHERN SCOTLAND & THE ISLANDS
Aberlemno, nr Forfar, Tayside.
Pictish *carved stones*, 6th-8th C., incl. early Christian cross.
Arbroath, Tayside.
St Vigean's Museum has carved *Pictish gravestones*, early Christian period.
Eassie, Tayside.
Pictish stone in grounds of ruined church.
Knocknagael, Grampian.
Boar Stone: carved slab with Pictish symbols.
Meigle, nr Perth, Tayside.
Small museum with 25 sculpted *Celtic stones*, showing beasts & biblical figures.

ENJOYING THE COUNTRYSIDE

There is a map showing National Parks, scenic areas, long-distance footpaths & major nature reserves on p 33. See also: 'Rocks & caves' (p 318).

THE WEST COUNTRY
Avon Gorge, Avon.
Woodland reserve, with rare Bristol whitebeam.
Bodmin Moor, Cornwall.
Open moorland. Granite tors (*Brown Willy, Rough Tor*) give splendid views.
Dartmoor, Devon.
Moorland & upland bog, with granite tors (National Park). Grazed by wild ponies. At *Wistman's Wood*, ancient oaks grow in fantastic shapes.
Exmoor, Devon & Somerset.
High heathery moorland (National Park). Dramatic scenery at *Heddon's Mouth valley*.
Icknield Way, Wilts.
See The Thames, Chilterns & East Anglia.
Land's End, Cornwall.
Treeless outcrop of granite marks England's most westerly point.
Lizard Point, Cornwall.
Southernmost tip of England, culminating in coves below steep cliffs.
Lulworth Cove, Dorset.
Beautiful enclosed bay, much visited.
Marlborough Downs, Wilts.
Chalk uplands, with many ancient monuments.
Savernake Forest, Wilts.
Ancient royal forest, much oak & beech.
Sedgemoor, Somerset.
Formerly a marshy plain with sedges, reeds & rushes. Now farmland, with pollarded willows.
South West Peninsula Path, Somerset, Devon & Cornwall.
515 m. along coast from Minehead, Somerset, round to Lyme Regis, Dorset. In 4 parts (some sections of coast are private). Spectacular scenery.
SOUTH-EAST ENGLAND
Ashdown Forest, nr East Grinstead, E. Sussex.
Ancient forest & sandy heathland, with forest trail (from Gravetye Manor).
Gravel Hill, Horndean, nr Portsmouth, Hants.
Queen Elizabeth Country Park combines downland with beech & conifer forest.
Hampshire Downs, Hants.
Rolling farmland, clumps of beech.
New Forest, Hants.
Open heath & woodland with ancient oaks, beeches. Wild ponies, red deer.
North Downs Way, Kent & Sussex.
140-m. path across steep chalk ridges, thickly wooded.
Epping Forest, Essex.
Remains of old royal forest. Mixed woodland, fine pollarded hornbeams.
Kingley Vale, Chichester, W. Sussex.
Chalk downs, with fine yew wood.
South Downs Way, Sussex.
Bridlepath (80 m.) across Sussex Downs from Beachy Head to W. Sussex/Hants. border.
THE THAMES, CHILTERNS & EAST ANGLIA
Blakeney Point, Norfolk.
Salt-marsh, with interesting bird life.
Burnham Beeches, Bucks.
Large beech wood.
Chilterns, Bucks.
Chalk hills, fine beech woods.
Cotswolds, Oxon.
See Central England.

The Fens, Norfolk, Cambs. & Lincs.
Flat, treeless region around the Wash, crossed by 4 rivers (Witham, Welland, Nene & Ouse). Fields crisscrossed by drainage systems. Nature reserve at Wicken Fen (Cambs.).
Forest of Dean, Glos.
Mixed forest on high plateau.
Hatfield Forest, nr Bishop's Stortford, Essex.
Ancient forest, rich in flora & fauna.
Icknield Way, Norfolk, Cambs., Herts., Bucks., Wilts.
Ancient trade route from Thetford, Norfolk, to source of R. Kennet, Wilts. Beautiful walking countryside.
Norfolk Broads, Norfolk.
Lakes formed by peat-cutting. 5 major broads are Barton, Filby, Hickling, Ormesby & Wroxham. Popular sailing region.
Ridgeway Path, Wilts., Berks., Oxon., Bucks., Herts.
Ancient 85-m. path from Avebury, Wilts., across Berkshire Downs to Ivinghoe Beacon, Bucks. Chalk uplands, ancient hillforts, splendid views.
Thetford Chase, Norfolk.
Lowland pine forest on sandy heath.

CENTRAL ENGLAND

Cotswolds, Glos. & Oxon.
Limestone hills with steep slopes, beautiful valleys. Many lovely villages.
Derbyshire Dales, Derbys.
Series of ridges broken by picturesque river valleys. Most beautiful parts incl. *Dovedale, Wolfscote Dale, Lathkill Dale.*
The Fens, Lincs.
See The Thames, Chilterns & East Anglia.
Long Mynd, Salop.
Moorland, with wooded valleys below.
Malvern Hills, Heref. & Worcs.
Good footpaths over grassy hills, splendid views.
Peak District, Derbys.
National Park, comprising *White Peak* (rolling limestone hills, wooded slopes) & *Dark Peak* (bleaker gritstone region, to north).
Pennine Way, Derbys.
See Yorkshire, Humberside & the North-west.
Vale of Evesham, Heref. & Worcs.
Fertile vale, beautiful blossoms in spring.
Wye valley, Heref. & Worcs.
Well-farmed wooded valley. At *Symonds Yat*, river winds through a dramatic narrow gorge. *See also* Wales.

YORKSHIRE, HUMBERSIDE & THE NORTH-WEST

Cleveland Way, N. Yorks.
Ancient footpath (about 95 m.) along Hambleton & Cleveland hills.
North York Moors, N. Yorks.
National Park. Heathery moorland, rugged coastline.
Pennine Way, mainly N. Yorks. & Northumb.
Spectacular path 248 m. along Pennines, from Edale (Derbys.) through Yorks. Dales & Northumb. National Parks. Ends Scottish Borders.
Wolds Way, N. Yorks.
Begins at Filey Brigg, through Vale of Pickering to Thixendale. Rolling chalk hills, attractive arable land.
Yorkshire Dales, N. Yorks.
National Park: mountain, moorland, dales. Fine limestone scenery, esp. around *Malham Tarn.*

THE NORTH OF ENGLAND

Border Forest Park, Northumb.
Large state forest, mainly spruce.
Cheviots, Northumb.
Sheep-farming uplands; moorlands & bogs on heights. Pennine Way runs along crest.
Hadrian's Wall, Northumb. & Cumbria.
Upland footpath along Roman wall (73 m). *See* 'Roman Britain' (p 319).
Lake District, Cumbria.
National Park featuring England's highest mountains & most of her largest lakes. Scafell Pike, 989 m (3,206 ft), is for serious hill walkers. Helvellyn, 950 m (3,118 ft), has spectacular Striding Edge. Extensive forests (notably Thornthwaite & Grizedale).
Pennine Way, Northumb.
See Yorkshire, Humberside & the North-west.

WALES

Black Mountains, Dyfed & Powys.
2 large ranges in west Wales; deep valleys, oaks, sprucewoods.
Brecon Beacons, Powys.
National Park. Hills, wooded gorges, high reservoirs.
Cadair Idris, Gwynedd.
Spectacular mountain: the 'throne of Idris'. 892 m (2,927 ft).
Cambrian Mountains, mainly Dyfed & Powys.
Windy uplands, ideal walking country.
Gwydyr Forest, Gwynedd.
On Snowdonian foothills, mainly conifers & oak.
Offa's Dyke, Gwent, Heref. & Worcs., Powys, Clwyd.
167-m. footpath from R. Wye to R. Dee, partly along ancient boundary.
Pembrokeshire Coast Path, Dyfed.
Runs 168 m. from St Dogmael's to Amroth. Varied scenery.
Snowdonia, Gwynedd.
National Park covers large area of Gwynedd. Mountainous scenery of forests & lakes. *Dyfi valley* very attractive. Snowdon is highest mountain in England & Wales, 1,085 m (3,650 ft); footpath or rlwy to summit.
Wye valley, Gwent.
Superb limestone gorge from Tintern to Chepstow. Setting of ruined Tintern Abbey inspired famous poem by Wordsworth.

SOUTHERN SCOTLAND

Galloway Forest Park, Dumf. & Gall.
Huge state forest; pine, old oakwoods. Also lovely moors & high hills.

CENTRAL SCOTLAND & STRATHCLYDE

Almondell Country Park, Central.
Valley of *R. Almond* has lovely walks & nature trails. Old drovers' roads over *Pentland Hills.*
Argyll Forest Park, Strathclyde.
Extensive coniferous woodland, mountains & lochs, ideal for walking.
Isle of Arran, Strathclyde.
Splendid mountainous landscape with scenic ridge walks. Magnificent walk through Glen Iorsa.
Mull of Kintyre, Strathclyde.
Remote & craggy peninsula; lochs, streams, caves.
Queen Elizabeth Forest Park, Central.
Large expanse of mountainous land with woods & lochs, incl. *Loch Lomond.*
Trossachs, Central & Strathclyde.
Mountains, glens, lochs, moorland, streams. Splendid views.

NORTHERN SCOTLAND & THE ISLANDS

Ben Lawers, Tayside.
Highest mountain in highly scenic region. Visitor centre at Killin on *Loch Tay.*
Ben Nevis, Highland.
Granite mass towering above Fort William. Britain's highest mountain, 1,344 m (4,418 ft), popular with determined hill walkers.
Cairngorms, Highland & Grampian.
Magnificent mountain range, part of which is a National Nature Reserve. Ski-ing centre at Aviemore; chairlift.
Corrieshralloch Gorge, Highland.
Spectacular gorge near Ullapool with dramatic *Falls of Measach.*
Culbin Forest, nr Nairn, Grampian.
State forest, conifers; also sand dunes.
Falls of Glomach, Highland.
Dramatic waterfall above splendidly wild *Glen Elchaig.* 7-m. walkers' path through hills from Croe Bridge on Loch Duich.
Glen Affric, Highland.
Scenic area of ancient Scots pines.
Glen Torridon, Highland.
Vast estate with several awesome mountains & much-indented coastline.
Glencoe & Dalness, Highland.
Fine mountainous countryside. Dramatic *Pass of Glencoe*, scene of historic massacre. Moorland trails, visitor centre.
Loch Morar, Highland.
Deepest loch in Scotland in mountainous countryside.
Orkney Islands.
65 islands, 30 of which are inhabited. Much unspoilt moorland, practically treeless.
Rannoch Forest, nr Pitlochry, Tayside.
Remains of Caledonian pine forest. *Moor of Rannoch* is largest moor in Scotland.
Isle of Rhum, Highland.
Extraordinary unspoilt island of moors, woods & lochs. Boat from Mallaig.

Shetland Islands.
Britain's most northerly isles. Spectacular cliffs, good nature reserves.
Skye, Highland.
Huge & unspoilt area of moors & hills. *The Cuillins* rise to 1,009 m (3,309 ft).

FAMOUS PEOPLE

See also: maps on 'Artists & places' (p 295) & 'Writers & places' (p 297).

THE WEST COUNTRY

Bovington, nr Wareham, Dorset.
Clouds Hill cottage: home of *T.E. Lawrence* (of Arabia). Furniture, books.
Buckland Abbey, Devon.
Relics of *Sir Francis Drake*, incl. his famous drum.
Dorchester, Dorset.
Dorset County Museum: *Thomas Hardy* memorial room.
Higher Bockhampton, Dorset.
Thomas Hardy's cottage (birthplace).
Nether Stowey, nr Bridgwater, Somerset.
Poet *S.T. Coleridge*'s cottage, 1797–1800. Now a museum.

SOUTH-EAST ENGLAND

Broadstairs, Kent.
Dickens' House Museum: letters & personal belongings of great Victorian novelist.
Burwash, E. Sussex.
Bateman's: home of writer & poet *Rudyard Kipling*. Various exhibits.
Chartwell, nr Westerham, Kent.
Home of *Sir Winston Churchill.* Memorabilia & paintings.
Chawton, Hants.
Chawton House: *Jane Austen*'s home, 1809–17. Personal belongings, charming portrait.
Guildford, Surrey.
Museum has letters & other belongings of *Lewis Carroll*, author of 'Alice in Wonderland'.
Hever Castle, Kent.
Birthplace of *Anne Boleyn.*
Rodmell, nr Lewes, E. Sussex.
Monks House, where writer *Virginia Woolf* lived, 1919–41. Original furnishings, personal possessions.
Polesden Lacey, Surrey.
Home of dramatist *R.B. Sheridan.*
Portsmouth, Hants.
Charles Dickens' birthplace (393 Commercial Rd, Mile End).
Romsey, Hants.
Lord Louis Mountbatten exhibition at Broadlands.
Rye, E. Sussex.
Lamb House: home of novelist *Henry James*, 1898–1916.
Selbourne, Hants.
Gilbert White Museum (The Wakes): relics & books of famous 18th-C. naturalist.
Tenterden, Kent.
Ellen Terry Museum: home of great fin-de-siècle actress. Also contains relics of other actors & actresses (e.g. Irving, Mrs Siddons, David Garrick).
Westerham, Kent.
Quebec House: museum with mementoes of 18th-C. military hero *James Wolfe.*

GREATER LONDON

Bromley.
Down House, Downe: home of 19th-C. naturalist *Charles Darwin.* Personal relics.
Chelsea.
Thomas Carlyle's House (124 Cheyne Row): portraits, letters, furniture & small library belonging to 19th-C. essayist & historian.
Chiswick.
William Hogarth's House (Hogarth Lane): home of English artist, 1749–64.
City.
Dickens' House (48 Doughty St). Various relics. *Dr Johnson's House* (17 Gough Sq.): contains portraits of great critic & lexicographer & of his biographer James Boswell. *St Paul's Cathedral*: crypt has many monuments of famous figures. 'Painters' Corner' has tombs of Reynolds & Turner. Also: tombs of admirals & notable soldiers. *Wesley's House* (14 City Rd). Personal relics of founder of Methodism.
Hampstead.
Keats's House, Keats Grove: personal items, mss. Keats lived here, 1818–20.
Highgate.
Karl Marx's tomb in cemetery.
West End.
Sir John Soane's Museum, Lincoln's Inn Fields. Private coll. of architect & antiquarian, displayed in house designed by Soane (1812). *Wellington Museum* (Apsley House): Duke of Wellington's trophies, uniforms, paintings, etc.
Westminster.
'Poets' Corner' in south transept of Abbey has tombs & monuments of various literati (e.g. Thomas Gray, P.B. Shelley).

THE THAMES, CHILTERNS & EAST ANGLIA

Ayot St Lawrence, Herts.
Shaw's Corner: house of famous playwright G.B. Shaw, 1906–50.

Bedford, Beds.
Bunyan Meeting Library & Museum. Personal relics of writer John Bunyan.
Bishop's Stortford, Herts.
Rhodes Memorial Museum, birthplace of *Cecil Rhodes*, Victorian statesman & imperialist.
Blenheim Palace, Woodstock, Oxon.
Churchill family home, with personal relics of *Sir Winston Churchill.*
Cambridge, Cambs.
Magdalene College has *Pepys Library*, containing original diary (17th C.). *Scott Polar Research Institute*: relics of Captain R.F. Scott.
Chalfont St Giles, Bucks.
John Milton's cottage: personal relics & 1st editions of poet's work.
Claydon House, Bucks.
Florence Nightingale Museum: objects associated with 19th-C. nursing heroine.
Hughenden Manor, nr High Wycombe, Bucks.
Home of Victorian statesman *Benjamin Disraeli*, 1847–81. Various mementoes.
Sudbury, Suffolk.
House of *Thomas Gainsborough*, painter. Now a museum.
CENTRAL ENGLAND
Broadheath, Heref. & Worcs.
Birthplace of composer *Sir Edward Elgar*, now a museum. Scores, photographs, violin case.
Cheltenham, Glos.
Gustav Holst Museum: birthplace of composer.
Eastwood, Notts.
D.H. Lawrence Museum, in novelist's birthplace, a miner's cottage.
Lichfield, Staffs.
Dr Johnson's birthplace (Breadmarket St). Various pictures & relics.
Newark-on-Trent, Notts.
Cromwell Museum: Oliver Cromwell's school, with portraits & various mementoes.
Newstead Abbey, Notts.
Family home of poet *Lord Byron*. Pictures, furniture, mss, 1st editions.
Nuneaton, Warks.
Museum & Art Gallery contains memorabilia of 19th-C. novelist *George Eliot*.
Shallowford, nr Stafford, Staffs.
Izaak Walton (1593–1683), author of 'The Compleat Angler', lived at Halfhead Farm, preserved as a memorial to him.
Stoke-on-Trent, Staffs.
Novelist *Arnold Bennett*'s family lived at Cobridge from 1880. Museum, with memorabilia.
Stratford-upon-Avon, Warks.
Shakespeare's birthplace (Henley St) contains playwright's school desk. He died in New Place, grave in Church of

Holy Trinity. At nearby Shottery: his wife *Anne Hathaway*'s cottage.
Woolsthorpe Manor, Lincs.
Birthplace of *Sir Isaac Newton* (1642), who formulated laws of motion & gravity here.
YORKSHIRE, HUMBERSIDE & THE NORTH-WEST
Bolton, Gr Manchester.
Hall-i'-th-Wood: house of *Samuel Crompton*, 19th-C. inventor.
Coxwold, N. Yorks.
Shandy Hall, home of 18th-C. novelist *Laurence Sterne.*
Haworth, W. Yorks.
Brontë Parsonage Museum: relics, letters, mss relating to Brontë sisters.
Hull, Humber.
Wilberforce House: birthplace of *William Wilberforce* (1759), campaigner against slavery.
Knutsford, Cheshire.
Elizabeth Gaskell Museum, with relics of 19th-C. novelist.
Whitby, N. Yorks.
Museum has mementoes of 18th-C. circumnavigator *Captain Cook.*
THE NORTH OF ENGLAND
Bamburgh, Northumb.
Grace Darling Museum: memorabilia of lighthouse rescue heroine.
Cockermouth, Cumbria.
William Wordsworth's birthplace (1770), now a Wordsworth museum.
Grasmere, Cumbria.
Dove Cottage & Wordsworth Museum: *William Wordsworth*'s home (from 1799), various mss.
Hill Top, nr Hawkshead, Cumbria.
Farmhouse home of writer & illustrator *Beatrix Potter*. Drawings & pictures.
Marton, Middlesbrough, Cleveland.
Captain Cook Birthplace Museum (Stewarts Park): life & discoveries of 18th-C. navigator.
Rydal Mount, nr Grasmere, Cumbria.
William Wordsworth's home, 1813–50. Furniture, 1st editions, family portraits.
WALES
Criccieth, Gwynedd.
Lloyd George Memorial Museum.
Denbigh, Clwyd.
Castle Museum has mementoes of Victorian explorer *Sir Henry Morton Stanley.*
Laugharne, Dyfed.
Georgian boat house, home of poet *Dylan Thomas* for 16 years. Personal relics, mss.
Merthyr Tydfil, Mid Glam.
Joseph Parry Museum (4 Chapel Row). Relics of 19th-C. Welsh composer.
Monmouth, Gwent.
Museum has items relating to *Admiral Lord Nelson.*
Newton, Powys.
Home (Broad St) of social reformer *Robert Owen*, now an Owen museum.
Rhyd-ddu, Gwynedd.
Birthplace & home of *T.H. Parry-Williams*, Welsh poet (1884–1956).
SOUTHERN SCOTLAND
Abbotsford, Borders.
Country home built for *Sir Walter Scott*. Personal items, incl. coll. of weapons.
Dumfries, Dumf. & Gall.
Burns House. Poet died here, 1796. Many Burns relics.
Ecclefechan, Dumf. & Gall.
Thomas Carlyle's birthplace (1795): mss & personal mementoes of essayist & historian.
Jedburgh, Borders.
Mary Queen of Scots House (Queen St). She supposedly stayed here in 1566. Several relics.
CENTRAL SCOTLAND & STRATHCLYDE
Alloway, Strathclyde.
Burns Cottage & Museum: birthplace of Robert Burns (1759).
Blantyre, Strathclyde.
David Livingstone Centre has relics of 19th-C. missionary & explorer.
Edinburgh, Lothian.
Lady Stair's House has relics of *Robert Burns*, as well as of *Sir Walter Scott & R.L. Stephenson.*
Greenock, Strathclyde.
McLean Museum: tools of Greenock-born inventor *James Watt.*
Kilmarnock, Strathclyde.
Burns Monument & Museum.

FARMING & RURAL LIFE

THE WEST COUNTRY
Avebury, Wilts.
Great Barn Folk Life Museum, in 17th-C. barn.
Bicton Gardens, nr Budleigh Salterton, Devon.
James Countryside Museum has old farm tools.
Bradford-on-Avon, Wilts.
Large medieval *tithe barn.*
Bridgerule, Devon.
Farm implements (with demonstrations) in *Furze Farm Park.*
Bruton, Somerset.
Early 16th-C. monastic *dovecot*, with gables & mullioned windows.
Buckland Abbey, Devon.
Large *tithe barn*, with agricultural machinery inside. Cider press (18th C.).
Camelford, Cornwall.
North Cornwall Museum covers Cornish life, late 19th/early 20th C.
Chulmleigh, Devon.
Ashley Countryside Collection: working farm with rare sheep, historic farm tools, craft demonstrations.
Glastonbury, Somerset.
Somerset Rural Life Museum in 14th-C. abbey barn. Farming history, demonstrations.
Lanreath, nr Looe, Cornwall.
Tithe barn at Lanreath Mill & Museum.
Milton Abbas, Dorset.
Museum of brewing & agriculture.
Shebbear, Devon.
Alscott Farm Agricultural Museum. Implements, tractors, ploughs, dairying.
Stoke sub Hamdon, Somerset.
The Priory: historic farm (various periods).
Tiverton, Devon.
Agricultural exhibits in local *museum.*
Yeovil, Somerset.
Brympton d'Evercy Country Life Museum. Cider-making, etc.
SOUTH-EAST ENGLAND
Breamore, Hants.
Countryside Museum.
Farnham, Surrey.
Old Kiln Agricultural Museum: wagons, hand tools, dairy.
Horsham, W. Sussex.
Museum has forge & wheelwright's & saddler's shops.
Petersfield, Hants.
Butser Ancient Farm in Queen Elizabeth Country Park: working reconstruction of Iron Age farm settlement.
Sedlescombe, E. Sussex.
Norton's Farm Museum.
Singleton, nr Chichester, W. Sussex.
Weald & Downland Open Air Museum. Reconstructed historic buildings incl. aisled barn, Tudor farmhouse, 18th-C. granary, blacksmith's forge.
Upper Dicker, nr Hailsham, E. Sussex.
Michelham Priory: Tudor barn, Sussex wagons, watermill & forge, wheelwright's museum.
Wilminton Priory, E. Sussex.
Agricultural implements, from 18th C.
Wye, Kent.
Agricultural museum (Wye College): timber-framed barn, hop kilns.
GREATER LONDON
Upminster.
Tithe barn of 15th C., contains agricultural & folk *museum.*
THE THAMES, CHILTERNS & EAST ANGLIA
Asthall, nr Burford, Oxon.
Cotswold Folk & Agricultural Museum. Saddler's shop, farm equipment, etc.
Cambridge, Cambs.
Cambridge & County Folk Museum.
Courage Shire Horse Centre, nr Maidenhead, Berks.
Horses, machinery, farrier's shop, cooperage display.
Easton Farm Park, Suffolk.
Model Dairy Farm (1870). Ornate dairy. Farming equipment, livestock, forge.
Great Coxwell, Oxon.
Tithe barn (13th C.), on Beaulieu Abbey estate.
Gressenhall, Norfolk.
Norfolk Rural Life Museum, emphasis on agricultural history.
Holkham Park, Wells-next-the-Sea, Norfolk.
'Bygones at Holkham': craft demonstrations, dairy, harness room, reconstructed brewery.
Martham, Norfolk.
Church Farm: working agricultural museum re-creating 19th-C. village life.
Milton Keynes, Bucks.
Stacey Hill Collection of Industry & Rural Life (Wolverton).
Reading, Berks.
Museum of English Rural Life. Major coll. relating to farming, crafts, village life.
Stowmarket, Suffolk.
Museum of East Anglian Life, in medieval barn. Working machinery, craft demonstrations.
Willington, Beds.
Magnificent 16th-C. *dovecote.*
Witney, Oxon.
Manor Farm Museum (Cogges): Edwardian farm, dairy.
CENTRAL ENGLAND
Acton Scott, nr Church Stretton, Salop.
Working Farm Museum demonstrates farming at turn of century. Craft demonstrations.
Bewdley, Heref. & Worcs.
Museum has reconstructed workshops (coopering, charcoal burning, etc.).
Birmingham, W. Midlands.
Blakesley Hall, Yardley, has craft displays.
Bredon, Heref. & Worcs.
Large 14th-C. *tithe barn.*
Bromsgrove, Heref. & Worcs.
Avoncroft Museum of Buildings has 18th-C. stable & wagon shed & other farm buildings.
Elvaston, Derbys.
Elvaston Castle Museum re-creates rural life *c.* 1910.
Frampton, Lincs.
F.A. Smith Collection: vintage tractors.
Gloucester, Glos.
Folk Museum covers agriculture, crafts.
Hartlebury, Heref. & Worcs.
County Museum has displays on rural life.
Hereford, Heref. & Worcs.
Museum of Cider.
Kemble, Glos.
Smerrill Farm Museum. Wagons, ploughs, dairy equipment, tools.
Laxton, Notts.
Well-preserved *open field system.*

Lincoln, Lincs.
Museum of Lincs. Life. Agricultural tools, machinery, vehicles.
Newark-on-Trent, Notts.
Rufford Craft Centre in Rufford Country Park. Demonstrations.
Northleach, Glos.
Cotswold Countryside Collection. Wagons, horse-drawn implements.

Oakham, Leics.
Rutland County Museum has farm implements.
Shugborough Hall, Great Haywood, Staffs.
Park incl. *Georgian farmstead,* with equipment & rare livestock.
Skegness, Lincs.
Church Farm Museum: 19th-C. farm complex with agricultural & domestic equipment.
YORKSHIRE, HUMBERSIDE & THE NORTH-WEST
Cregneash, Isle of Man.
Folk Museum, with weaver's shed, turner's shop, smithy, farmstead. Manx ways of life.
Douglas, Isle of Man.
Manx Museum has reconstructed Victorian farm buildings.
East Riddlesden Hall, nr Keighley, W. Yorks.
Medieval *tithe barn.*
Golcar, W. Yorks.
Colne Valley Museum. Displays on hand-weaving, clog-making, cobbling.
Halifax, W. Yorks.
W. Yorks. Folk Museum at *Shibden Hall.* Crafts.
Hawes, Wensleydale, N. Yorks.
Upper Dales Folk Museum. Displays on sheep farming, peat cutting, cheese-making.
Hutton-le-Hole, N. Yorks.
Ryedale Folk Museum. Blacksmith's shop, crofter's cottage, barn, etc.
Pickering, N. Yorks.
Beck Isle Museum of Rural Life.
Reeth, N. Yorks.
Swaledale Folk Museum: sheep farming, lead mining.
Ripponden, W. Yorks.
Pennine Farm Museum. Early 19th-C. Pennine farmstead.
THE NORTH OF ENGLAND
Beamish, Durham.
North of England Open Air Museum has farmstead of *c.* 1800, with horse engine house. Harvesting gear, carts.
Coulby Newham, Middlesbrough, Cleveland.
Newham Grange Leisure Farm is working farm with rare animals.
Kendal, Cumbria.
Abbot Hall Museum of Lakeland Life & Industry.
Newton, nr Stocksfield, Northumb.
Hunday National Tractor & Farm Museum has extensive coll: 80 vintage tractors, stationary engines, smithy, harvesting machinery.
WALES
Erddig, nr Wrexham, Clwyd.
17th-C. country house has *agricultural museum* with Victorian exhibits.
Maes Artro, Llanbedr, nr Harlech, Gwynedd.
Craft village, with various demonstrations.
St Fagans, nr Cardiff, S. Glam.
Welsh Folk Museum. Reconstructed buildings incl. barns & 19th-C. corn mill. Working woollen mill & smithy.
Spittal, Dyfed.
Scolton Manor Museum covers rural crafts among other topics.
Usk, Gwent.
Gwent Rural Life Museum.
CENTRAL SCOTLAND & STRATHCLYDE
Auchindrain, Strathclyde.
Museum of rural life, 1790–1914. Barns, farm implements.
Brodick, Isle of Arran.
Rosaburn Heritage Centre has working smithy.
NORTHERN SCOTLAND & THE ISLANDS
Finavon, nr Forfar, Tayside.
Dovecot with over 2,000 nesting boxes, largest in Scotland.
Kingussie, Highland.
Highland Folk Museum incl. agricultural exhibits & craft tools.
Orkney.
Corrigall Farm Museum, Harray.

GARDENS

See also: map of gardens on p 217, & 'Country houses' (p 308).

THE WEST COUNTRY
Abbotsbury Garden, Dorset.
Sub-tropical plants in woodland garden.
Bicton Gardens, nr Budleigh Salterton, Devon.
Famous pinetum, with monkey puzzle avenue. Italian garden, formal lake, early Palm House.
Bowood, nr Calne, Wilts.
'Capability' Brown landscape (1761). Italianate terraces, 1840s.
Castle Drogo, nr Chagford, Devon.
Terraced garden, fine views.
Corsham Court, nr Chippenham, Wilts.
By *'Capability' Brown & Repton*; good trees.
Cotehele House, nr Calstock, Cornwall.
Beautiful stream, waterfall, woodland. Victorian terraces.
Cranborne Manor, Dorset.
Knot garden, mount, superb formal herb garden.
Glendurgan, nr Falmouth, Cornwall.
Semi-wild, trees from Asia & America. Large maze.
Hestercombe, Kingston St Mary, Somerset.
By *Jekyll & Lutyens,* very well restored. Open occasionally.
Knightshayes Court, nr Tiverton, Devon.
Post-war garden, fine wooded area, topiary.
Lanhydrock, nr Bodmin, Cornwall.
Formal, interesting trees. Sycamore avenue.
Longleat House, Wilts.
Great *'Capability' Brown* landscape. Later alterations by *Repton & Russell Page.*
Montacute House, Somerset.
Formal Elizabethan garden, replanted late 19th C. Superb pavilions.
Prior Park, nr Bath, Avon.
18th-C. landscaped park. Palladian bridge.
Stourhead, nr Stourton, Wilts.
Beautiful 18th-C. landscaped park, dotted with lakes & temples.
Tresco Abbey, Isles of Scilly.
Fine sub-tropical gardens founded 1834.
Trewithen, Probus, Cornwall.
Rare plants in wooded, finely landscaped 18th-C. setting.
Wilton House, Wilts.
Classical landscape with Palladian bridge. Italian-style terraces. Water meadows.
SOUTH-EAST ENGLAND
Chilham Castle, Kent.
By *'Capability' Brown,* 1777.
Bedgebury Pinetum, Kent.
National Pinetum since 1924. Over 200 species of conifers.
Great Dixter, Northiam, E. Sussex.
Shows *Jekyll* influence. Rose garden, topiary.
Leonardslee, nr Horsham, W. Sussex.
Woodland garden, famous for rhododendrons.
Nymans, Handcross, W. Sussex.
Collector's garden, with good pinetum.
Scotney Castle, Lamberhurst, Kent.
Romantic landscaped garden. Daffodils, azaleas.
Sheffield Park, nr Uckfield, E. Sussex.
Landscape by *'Capability' Brown,* altered in 19th C. Lakes, rare trees & shrubs. Well known for autumn colour.
Sissinghurst Castle, Kent.
Influential 20th-C. garden, by *Vita Sackville-West* and Sir Harold Nicholson. General effect of luxuriance. Famous rose garden.
Wisley, nr Ripley, Surrey.
Royal Horticultural Society garden. Vast range of plants. Heather garden, island beds, etc.
GREATER LONDON
Central London.
Hyde Park has fine trees, Serpentine lake; adjoins more formal *Kensington Gardens. Regent's Park* landscaped by John Nash, early 19th C.; contains Queen Mary's Garden.
Chiswick House.
Early break with strict formality in 18th C. Work by *William Kent.* Today seems rather formal.
Hampton Court Palace, nr Richmond.
Redesigned in grand French manner by *London & Wise* for William & Mary. Parterres, radiating avenues, canal pool. Tudor knot garden. Famous maze.
Kew Gardens.
Royal Botanic Gardens, in massive park. Lake, rhododendron dell, Chinese pagoda, Great Stove palm house.
Syon Park, Brentford.
By *'Capability' Brown.* Beautiful conservatory (1820s).
THE THAMES, CHILTERNS & EAST ANGLIA
Anglesey Abbey, Lode, Cambs.
20th C. Lovely statuary & trees.
Ascott, Wing, Bucks.
Laid out 19th C. Ilexes, yew hedges.
Blenheim Palace, Woodstock, Oxon.
Superb landscape by *'Capability' Brown,* water paterre formed 1920s.
Blickling Hall, nr Aylsham, Norfolk.
Mixture of styles. Topiary, landscape, woodland, raised terrace.
Bressingham Hall, nr Diss, Norfolk.
Laid out in 1950s by *Alan Bloom,* with alpine plants, heather.
Buscot Park, Oxon.
Formal, Italianate water garden, 1905–10, by *Harold Peto.*
Cambridge, Cambs.
Clare College has fine garden showing 20th-C. ideas. Also: *Botanic Gardens.*
Chiswell Green, St Albans, Herts.
Royal National Rose Society. Over 900 named varieties.
Cliveden, nr Maidenhead, Bucks.
Grand parterre, with R. Thames beyond. Long Garden (clipped box & statues), Japanese garden.
Holkham Hall, Norfolk.
18th-C. garden partly by *'Capability' Brown.* Garden buildings by *William Kent.*
Luton Hoo, Luton, Beds.
By *'Capability' Brown.* Three formal terraces incl. Edwardian rose garden.
Oxford, Oxon.
Botanic Gardens are Britain's oldest.
Rousham House, Oxon.
Most complete of *William Kent's* designs, 18th C. Temples, statues, glades, fine views.

Stowe House, Bucks.
Fine 18th-C. landscape, worked on by *Kent, Brown* & others. Temples, Palladian bridge.
Stratford-upon-Avon, Warks.
Shakespeare Gardens have picturesque knot garden, ancient mulberry.
Windsor Great Park, Berks.
Outstanding *Savill & Valley woodland gardens* (nr Englefield Green).
Wrest Park, nr Silsoe, Beds.
French-style formal garden added to by *'Capability' Brown.* Long canal, statues, urns.
CENTRAL ENGLAND
Alton Towers, nr Alton, Staffs.
Begun 1814 by 15th Earl of Shrewsbury. Many Picturesque fancies, good trees, rock garden.
Burford House, nr Tenbury Wells, Salop.
Made since 1950. Island beds & formal pool.
Chatsworth, nr Bakewell, Derbys.
Water garden by *London & Wise* (17th C.), with cascade. Emperor Fountain by *Paxton.* Modern conservatory. Fine woodland walks.
Compton Wynyates, Tysoe, Warks.
Topiary of 19th C.
Haddon Hall, Rowsley, Derbys.
Terraces, roses, superb setting.
Hardwick Hall, nr Chesterfield, Derbys.
Herb garden, orchards, nut trees; on formal plan.
Hidcote Manor, Mickleton, Glos.
Influential 20th-C. creation, arranged as series of 'rooms'.
Hodnet Hall, nr Market Drayton, Salop.
Made since 1920s, highly colourful in spring & early summer.
Melbourne Hall, nr Derby, Derbys.
Good example of early 18th-C. French-style formality. Ironwork arbour.
Newstead Abbey, Ravenshead, Notts.
Medieval fish pond, Japanese & rock gardens.
Packwood House, Hockley Heath, Warks.
Famous topiary garden said to represent Sermon on The Mount. Also: 17th-C. walled garden.
Sezincote, Moreton-in-the-Marsh, Glos.
19th C., with Indianesque buildings & ornaments.

Shugborough Hall, Great Haywood, Staffs.
18th-C. garden with Picturesque pavilions.
Trentham Gardens, Staffs.
Great variety: Italian, rock gardens, etc.
Westbury Court, Westbury-on-Severn, Glos.
Fine 17th-C. Dutch-style canal garden.
Westonbirt Arboretum, Glos.
Oldest & finest in Britain.
YORKSHIRE, HUMBERSIDE & THE NORTH-WEST
Bramham Park, nr Wetherby, W. Yorks.
One of finest Restoration French-style gardens in Britain, replanted after gale.
Burnby Hall, Pocklington, Humber.
Outstanding water lilies.
Castle Howard, N. Yorks.
Originally formal, landscaped early 18th C. Temple of Four Winds, bridge, mausoleum.
Duncombe Park, Helmsley, N. Yorks.
Early landscaped garden. Parterres, terraces.
Harewood House, W. Yorks.
Landscaped by *'Capability' Brown*, 1772. 19th-C. formal terraces.
Liverpool, Merseyside.
University Botanic Gardens at Ness incl. famous heather garden.
Rudding Park, Follifoot, N. Yorks.
Planned by *Repton*. Celebrated woodland garden.
Studley Royal, nr Ripon, N. Yorks.
18th-C. ornamental gardens by river, with ponds, temple, statues. Attractive walk to Fountains Abbey.
Tatton Park, nr Knutsford, Cheshire.
Various styles. Fernery established *c.* 1850. Sunken Victorian parterre. Japanese garden.
THE NORTH OF ENGLAND
Levens Hall, nr Kendal, Cumbria.
Famous topiary garden, laid out 1692.
Sizergh Castle, Kendal, Cumbria.
Lakes, pools, rock garden with waterfalls.
Wallington Hall, Cambo, Northumb.
Walled garden, magnificent fuschias in conservatory.
WALES
Bodnant, Tal-y-Cfn, Gwynedd.
Finest garden in Wales, early 20th C. Terraces climb hillside, views of Snowdonia.
Powis Castle, Welshpool, Powys.
Late 18th-C. 'hanging' garden, in terraces. Italian baroque influence.
SOUTHERN SCOTLAND
Castle Kennedy, Stranraer, Dumf. & Gall.
Formal (18th C.) with terraces. Restored 19th C., French-style avenues added.
CENTRAL SCOTLAND & STRATHCLYDE
Benmore, Dunoon, Strathclyde.
Woodland garden, annexe of Royal Botanic Garden, Edinburgh.
Brodick Castle, Arran, Strathclyde.
Formal walled garden (from 1710) with sub-tropical shrubs; 'wild' garden with superb rhododendrons.
Crarae Lodge, Strathclyde.
'Natural' garden with exotic trees, conifers, rhododendrons.
Edinburgh, Lothian.
Royal Botanic Garden has superb glasshouses, glorious rock garden.
Glasgow, Strathclyde.
Botanic Garden: public park with Victorian greenhouses, incl. fernery.
NORTHERN SCOTLAND & THE ISLANDS
Aberdeen, Grampian.
Botanic Gardens: 2 large rock gardens.
Crathes Castle, nr Banchory, Grampian.
Well-integrated garden 'rooms', incl. blue garden.
Drummond Castle, nr Crieff, Tayside.
Massive, intricate parterre, 19th C.
Dunrobin Castle, Golspie, Highland.
Formal, 3 parterres.
Edzell Castle, Tayside.
Walled garden dates back to 17th C.
Inverewe, Poolewe, Highland.
Famous woodland garden, founded 1862. Fine exotic plants.
Pitmeddon House, Grampian.
Fine 17th-C. garden, restored 1950s.

THE INDUSTRIAL PAST

See also: 'Canals' (p 305), 'Mining & quarrying' (p 315), 'Railways' (p 317), 'Steam engines' (p 312), 'Textiles & costume' (p 322), 'Watermills & waterwheels' (p 317).

THE WEST COUNTRY
Bristol, Avon.
Industrial Museum.
Sticklepath, Devon.
Finch Foundry (19th C.), where hand tools were made, remains operational as an industrial museum.
SOUTH-EAST ENGLAND
Amberley, W. Sussex.
Chalk Pits Museum covers industrial history of the region. Limeburning, iron founding, brick manufacture.
Fareham, Hants.
Remains of Henry Cort's *reverberatory furnace*, late 18th C.
GREATER LONDON
Kensington.
Science Museum has many industrial relics & working models. Stationary engines, mining, transport, cotton machinery, etc.
South London.
World of Brewing Museum, nr London Bridge.
CENTRAL ENGLAND
Ashby-de-la-Zouche, Leics.
Moira Ironworks. Blast furnace & adjoining foundry date from 1800.
Belper, Derbys.
Town developed by Jedediah Strutt around cotton mills in late 18th C. William Strutt's 'fireproof' *North Mill* (1804) still stands.
Birmingham, W. Midlands.
Museum of Science & Industry has heavy engineering exhibits: steam engines, machine tools, etc.
Burton upon Trent, Staffs.
Bass Museum: restored 19th-C. brewery.
Coalbrookdale, Salop.
See Telford.
Cromford, Derbys.
Richard Arkwright's *Old Mill* (1771) was world's first successful cotton-spinning mill. Nearby: Arkwright's *Masson Mill* (1783). (*See* map, p 144.)
Derby, Derbys.
Industrial Museum. Also: Lombe's *silk mill* (1717), on island in R. Derwent, was first ever factory.
Dudley, W. Midlands.
Black Country Museum. Reconstructed Black Country village of early 19th C. Demonstrations of chain-making. Transport relics, steam machinery.
Hanley, Staffs.
Etruscan Bone & Flint Mill (1857) on Trent & Mersey Canal. Contains small beam engine.
Heyford, Northants.
Remains of 19th-C. iron ore *furnaces*.
Ironbridge, Salop.
See Telford.
Leicester, Leics.
Museum of Technology has power gallery, transport items, steam shovel, beam engines.
Longton, Stoke-on-Trent, Staffs.
Gladstone Pottery Museum has comprehensive 'living' exhibition. Early Victorian potbank with original bottle ovens; restored workshops.
Northampton, Northants.
Grandest of Victorian factories is Renaissance-style *Mansfield Factory*, 1857.
Nottingham, Notts.
Industrial Museum at Wollaton Park. Exhibits on hosiery, lace making, engineering, etc.
Shrewsbury, Salop.
Flax mill of 1797 was world's first iron-framed building. Now a grain warehouse.
Stoke-on-Trent, Staffs.
City Museum has displays on social history of Potteries & technical developments in ceramics.
Telford, Salop.
Ironbridge Gorge Museum: vast complex spread over some 6 miles of Severn Gorge. *Blists Hill Open Air Museum* features reconstructed buildings & working exhibits (steam colliery winding engine, printing shop, blast furnace, Hay Inclined Plane, sawmill). *Coalbrookdale Museum of Iron*, beside Abraham Darby's blast furnaces, tells story of iron & steel, & history of region. Also in Gorge: *Severn Wharf & Warehouse*; *Iron Bridge*; *Coalport China Works Museum*; *Tar Tunnel* (from which natural bitumen was extracted); *Jackfield Tile Works*. (*See* map, p 146.)
Wolverhampton, W. Midlands.
Bilston Museum & Art Gallery. Local industries.
Worcester, Heref. & Worcs.
Dyson Perrins Museum traces history of Worcester porcelain (from 1751).
YORKSHIRE, HUMBERSIDE & THE NORTH-WEST
Abbeydale, nr Sheffield, S. Yorks.
Abbeydale Industrial Hamlet: an 18th-C. scytheworks, with crucible steel furnace, tilt hammers, forges.
Bradford, W. Yorks.
Industrial Museum, in 19th-C. spinning mill, houses items from Bradford's industrial past. Also at Bradford: Manningham Mills (1873).
Leeds, W. Yorks.
Industrial Museum, housed in Armley Mills (by Benjamin Gott, 1805). Incl. historic film footage of Leeds at turn of century. Also in Leeds: *Marshall's flax mill* (19th C.), with magnificent Egyptian-style façade.
Macclesfield, Cheshire.
Major 18th-C. silk-weaving centre. Surviving mills of period incl. *Frost's Mill* (1785) & *Chester Rd Mills*.
Manchester, Gr Manchester.
North Western Museum of Science & Technology. Machines, working models. *National Paper Museum*: exhibits on history of paper-making. Warehouses incl.: *Cooks & Watts Warehouse* (1851).
Salford, Gr Manchester.
Monks Hall Museum, Eccles. Naysmyth machinery.
Saltaire, nr Bradford, W. Yorks.
Sir Titus Salt's model *industrial settlement*. His large alpaca mill (1853), on Leeds & Liverpool Canal, is still in use. Workers' houses can still be seen.
Sheffield, S. Yorks.
Industrial Museum.
Stamford, Lancs.
Brewery Museum, housed in 19th-C. steam brewery.
Stockport, Lancs.
6-storey *Orrell's Mill*, Travis St, Heaton, built mid-1830s.
Styal, Cheshire.
Quarry Bank Mill (1784) & village: one of best surviving examples of an early cotton community. Manager's office, textile machinery.
Wortley, S. Yorks.
Wortley Top Forge. Restored ironworks, with waterwheel, hammers, grindstones, etc.
THE NORTH OF ENGLAND
Beamish, Durham.
North of England Open Air Museum: industrial & social history of north-east England.
Duddon Bridge, Cumbria.
Remains of *blast furnace*.
Newcastle upon Tyne, Tyne & Wear.
Museum of Science & Engineering.
WALES
Bersham, Clwyd.
Ironmaking centre, whose heyday was 1780s. Relics incl. *Octagonal Building*, which may have been a cannon foundry.
Blaenavon, Gwent.
Relics of late 18th-C. *ironworks*, & ruins of ironworkers' houses. *Forgeside Works*, nearby, has a Nasmyth-type steam hammer.
Cardiff, S. Glam.
Welsh Industrial & Maritime Museum has working displays of Welsh industrial heritage.
Furnace, Dyfed.
Dyfi Furnace, built 1755, one of best-preserved examples in Wales.
Gilwern, nr Abergavenny, Gwent.
Llanelly Furnace: charcoal-fired furnace of late 17th C. Keeper's House (1693) nearby.
Llandogo, nr Tintern, Gwent.
Remains of *Coed Ithel Furnace* (17th C.)
Llanelli, Dyfed.
Parc Howard Museum has tinplating display.
Merthyr Tydfil, Mid Glam.
Iron-manufacturing relics incl. *Ynysfach Ironworks* (with early 19th-C. engine house). *Cyfarthfa Castle* (1 m. NW), built by one of Merthyr iron masters, is museum with some relics of the industry.
Neath, W. Glam.
Remains of huge *Neath Abbey Furnaces*.
Pontypool, Gwent.
Industrial museum at Pontypool House.
Swansea, S. Glam.
Royal Institution of South Wales houses small industrial museum.
CENTRAL SCOTLAND & STRATHCLYDE
Blantyre, nr Hamilton, Strathclyde.
Livingstone National Memorial contains industrial relics.

Bonawe, Strathclyde.
Restored iron-smelting *furnace* (18th C.), with workers' houses.
Edinburgh, Lothian.
Royal Scottish Museum. Engineering, transport, mining.
Kirkaldy, Fife.
Local *industrial museum*, with relics of linoleum production.
New Lanark, Strathclyde.
Robert Owen's model *industrial settlement* of early 19th C.
NORTHERN SCOTLAND & THE ISLANDS
Perth, Tayside.
Fine *waterworks* (1830–32), with domed cast-iron storage tank & columnar stone chimney.

MARITIME BRITAIN

See also: 'Military history' (below).

THE WEST COUNTRY
Appledore, Devon.
North Devon Maritime Museum covers local shipbuilding, fishing, navigation.
Bristol, Avon.
SS *Great Britain*, iron ship by Brunel, launched 1843. Museum aboard. *Bristol Museum & Art Gallery* has exhibits on shipping, rope-making,anchors, & Port of Bristol Gallery.
Brixham, Devon.
Museum (Bolton Cross) illustrating fishing industry. Incl. HM Coastguard Museum.
Buckland Abbey, Devon.
Model ships, relics of Sir Francis Drake.
Dartmouth, Devon.
Butterwalk Museum.
Exeter, Devon.
Maritime Museum: large display of craft. Incl. steam dredger (1844) by Brunel.
Penzance, Cornwall.
Museum of Nautical Art, incl. full-size section of 1730 warship.
Poole, Dorset.
Maritime Museum, covers Spanish Armada, mutiny on the Bounty, Newfoundland trade.
Tresco Abbey, Isles of Scilly.
Valhalla Museum: figureheads from wrecked ships.
SOUTH-EAST ENGLAND
Buckler's Hard, nr Beaulieu, Hants.
Maritime Museum has exhibits relating to ships built here for Nelson's fleet.
Eastbourne, E. Sussex.
Lifeboat Museum.
Hastings, E. Sussex.
Fisherman's Museum incl. Enterprise sailing lugger.
Portsmouth, Hants.
HM Submarine *Alliance* open to visitors. Museum illustrates submarine history. *See also* 'Military history'.
Sittingbourne, Kent.
Dolphin Yard Sailing Barge Museum.
Southampton, Hants.
Maritime Museum, large model of Queen Mary liner.
GREATER LONDON
City.
St Katharine's Dock. Maritime Trust coll. of historic ships, incl. schooner, herring drifter. *Museum of London* also has shipping exhibits.
Greenwich.
Cutty Sark in dry dock: last of clipper ships, launched 1869. *National Maritime Museum* has boats, models, navigational equipment, charts, pictures, barge house, etc., in $3\frac{1}{2}$ m. of galleries.
Kensington.
Science Museum: models of ships & docks, exhibits on marine engineering & navigation.
Symon's Wharf, Pool of London.
Cruiser HMS *Belfast*, now a naval museum.
THE THAMES, CHILTERNS & EAST ANGLIA
Canvey Island, Essex.
Dutch Cottage Museum has items connected with Thames shipping.
Great Yarmouth, Norfolk.
Maritime Museum for East Anglia.
Lowestoft, Suffolk.
Maritime Museum, incl. fishing exhibits.
YORKSHIRE, HUMBERSIDE & THE NORTH-WEST
Castletown, Isle of Man.
Nautical Museum, incl. armed yacht built 1791, & sailmaker's loft.
Fleetwood, Lancs.
Local *museum*, emphasis on fishing.
Goole, Humber.
Museum demonstrates growth of Goole. as major port.
Hull, Humber.
Town Docks Museum. Trawling, whaling, shipbuilding.
Liverpool, Merseyside.
Merseyside Maritime Museum, Pier Head. Quayside trail around restored Canning Graving Docks. Large boat hall (with demonstrations), exhibits on liners, etc. Also: *Albert Dock*, masterpiece by Jesse Hartley. (*See* map, p 230.)
THE NORTH OF ENGLAND
Barrow-in-Furness, Cumbria.
Museum, with Vickers-Armstrong coll. of model ships.
Hartlepool, Cleveland.
Maritime Museum covers fishing, shipbuilding, marine engineering.
Marton, Cleveland.
Captain Cook's Birthplace Museum.
Newcastle upon Tyne, Tyne & Wear.
Science Museum has maritime exhibits. Also in Newcastle: *Turbinia Hall*, Exhibition Park, with world's first turbine ship.
Redcar, Cleveland.
Zetland Lifeboat Museum: lifeboat of 1800, fishing relics.
Sunderland, Tyne & Wear.
Museum has shipbuilding exhibits.
Whitehaven, Cumbria.
Old coaling wharves, *museum* featuring maritime history of port.
WALES
Cardiff, S. Glam.
Welsh Industrial & Maritime Museum. Working exhibits.
Cenarth, nr Cardigan, Dyfed.
Fishing Museum has superb coll. of equipment.
Porthmadog, Gwynedd.
Gwynedd Maritime Museum, incl. sailing ketch of 1909.
Swansea, W. Glam.
Maritime & Industrial Museum.
CENTRAL SCOTLAND & STRATHCLYDE
Anstruther, Fife.
Scottish Fisheries Museum.
Glasgow, Strathclyde.
Museum of Transport has fine coll. of model ships.
NORTHERN SCOTLAND & THE ISLANDS
Buckie, Grampian.
Maritime Museum: fishing, lifeboats.
Dundee, Tayside.
Sailing frigate *Unicorn* (1824) in Victoria Dock. *Broughty Castle Museum* has whaling exhibits.
Nairn, Grampian.
Fishertown Museum, relating to herring industry.
Stromness, Orkney.
Museum has maritime display.

MILITARY HISTORY

See also: 'Maritime Britain' (above).

THE WEST COUNTRY
Bovington Camp, Dorset.
Royal Armoured Corps *Tank Museum*, with over 40 armoured vehicles.
Dorchester, Dorset.
Dorset Military Museum. Relics of county regiments.
Yeovilton, Somerset.
Fleet Air Arm Museum: history of naval aviation.
SOUTH-EAST ENGLAND
Aldershot, Hants.
Airborne Forces Museum. Paratroop exhibits.
Ashford, Kent.
Intelligence Corps Museum: exhibits on military intelligence from Elizabethan times.
Canterbury, Kent.
Queen's Regiment Museum (Howe Barracks).
Clandon Park, Guildford, Surrey.
Queen's Royal Surrey Regiment Museum.
Lewes, E. Sussex.
Military Heritage Museum has uniforms, weapons & other items from period 1660–1914.
Portsmouth, Hants.
HMS *Victory* (Nelson's flagship, launched 1765) in dockyard. *Royal Naval Museum* covers naval history from Nelson onwards. Incl. panoramic paintings of Battle of Trafalgar.
Southsea, Hants.
Royal Marines Museum.
Warnham, nr Horsham, W. Sussex.
War Museum, with large coll. of Second World War vehicles, uniforms, medals, etc.
Winchester, Hants.
Royal Green Jackets' Museum (Peninsula Barracks).
GREATER LONDON
Chelsea.
National Army Museum (Royal Hospital) has weapons, uniform gallery, military paintings.
City.
Tower of London has national coll. of arms & armour (medieval to First World War). Royal Fusiliers Museum in Tower has uniforms & campaign medals.

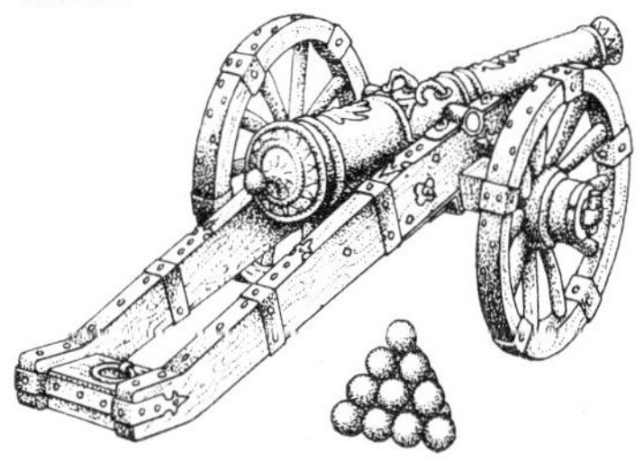

Greenwich.
National Maritime Museum has relics of distinguished sailors (notably Nelson), navigational aids, dioramas, paintings.
Hendon.
Royal Air Force Museum: over 50 historic aircraft; Battle of Britain Museum.
Lambeth.
Imperial War Museum covers all aspects of 20th-C. warfare. Tanks, Spitfire, etc.
West End.
Apsley House, Hyde Park Corner: *Duke of Wellington Museum* has uniforms & trophies.
Woolwich.
Rotunda Museum of Artillery, with exhibits from 12th C. to modern times.
THE THAMES, CHILTERNS & EAST ANGLIA
Duxford, Cambs.
Duxford Airfield (former Battle of Britain station) has large military exhibits. Aircraft, tanks, naval vessels. (Part of Imperial War Museum.)
Salisbury Hall, nr St Albans, Herts.
Mosquito Aircraft Museum contains prototype of de Havilland Mosquito designed here during Second World War.
Windsor, Berks.
Household Cavalry Museum (Combermere Barracks): uniforms, weapons, armour dating from 1685 onwards.
CENTRAL ENGLAND
Belvoir Castle, nr Grantham, Lincs.
Museum of 17th/21st Lancers. Coll. incl. relics of Charge of the Light Brigade.
Copthorne, nr Shrewsbury, Salop.
Light Infantry Museum.
Cosford, nr Wolverhampton, W. Midlands.
RAF Aerospace Museum has over 50 aircraft.
Stoke-on-Trent, Staffs.
Spitfire Museum has 1944 Spitfire & other aeronautical items.
YORKSHIRE, HUMBERSIDE & THE NORTH-WEST
Leconfield, Humber.
Army Transport Museum.
THE NORTH OF ENGLAND
Alnwick Castle, Northumb.
Regimental Museum of the Royal Northumbrian Fusiliers.
Durham, Durham.
Durham Light Infantry Museum: history of regiment, 1758–1968.
WALES
Brecon, Powys.
South Wales Borderers Regimental Museum. Examples of almost every weapon used by regiment since 1800.
Caernarfon, Gwynedd.
Royal Welsh Fusiliers Museum in Castle.
Holywell, Clwyd.
Grange Cavern Military Museum. Coll. incl. over 40 military vehicles & other militaria.
Monmouth, Gwent.
Nelson Museum. Memorabilia incl. swords, naval equipment, model ships.
Plas Newydd, Anglesey.
Military Museum, with uniforms & helmets.
CENTRAL SCOTLAND & STRATHCLYDE
Edinburgh, Lothian.
Scottish United Services Museum (in Castle): uniforms & equipment.

MINING & QUARRYING

Visitors should take special care while visiting old mine sites. Beware of concealed shafts.

THE WEST COUNTRY
Botallack, nr St Just, Cornwall.
Cliff-edge *tin mines*, with engine house & stack. *Levant Mine* at nearby Pendeen has preserved pumping engine (1840).
Camborne, Cornwall.
At *East Pool* are 2 Cornish engines (for winding & pumping in tin mines), both complete in their houses. Also, *Holman Museum* has mining relics.
Carthew, nr St Austell, Cornwall.
Wheal Martyn Museum, devoted to china clay industry. Centred on one of original pits, dug 1820s.
Delabole, Cornwall.
Slate quarry & museum.

Morwellham, Devon.
A Victorian copper port. Ancient *copper mine* may be visited.
Porthtowan, Cornwall.
Remains of *copper mines* incl. 3 engine houses.
Redruth, Cornwall.
Tolgus tin streaming works 1 m. north of town. Guided tours.
Wendron, nr Helstow, Cornwall.
Poldark Mining Company: partly accessible workings of *Wheal Roots tin mine.*
GREATER LONDON
Chislehurst Caves.
Chalk mines, used in 19th C. in connection with lime kilns.
CENTRAL ENGLAND
Castleton, Derbys.
Speedwell Cavern is an 18th-C. lead mining sough. Boat trips. *Treak Cliff Cavern* originally a lead mine, later valued for Blue John (semi-precious stone).
Haughton, Notts.
National Mining Museum, Lound Hall. Coal mining machinery, simulated galleries.
Matlock Bath, Derbys.
Old *lead mines* in Heights of Abraham area. *Peak District Mining Museum* has excellent display, with photographs, models, relics.
Middleton-by-Wirksworth, Derbys.
Goodluck lead mine, open by appt.
Nottingham, Notts.
Wollaton Hall Industrial Museum has mining machinery, incl. horse gin.
Over Haddon, Derbys.
Mandale lead mine. Buildings on site date from *c.* 1800.
Sheldon, Derbys.
Magpie lead mine has extensive surface remains, dating from 18th C. (*See* map on p 152.)
Snailbeach, Salop.
Lead mine remains incl. engine house (1856).
Stoke-on-Trent, Staffs.
Chatterley Whitfield Mining Museum, Tunstall, has tours of old colliery.
Telford, Salop.
Blists Hill Open Air Museum has reconstructed pitheads and coal mining machinery.
Wirksworth, Derbys.
Story of lead mining in local *museum*. *Moot Hall* contains 15th-C. miners' measuring dish.

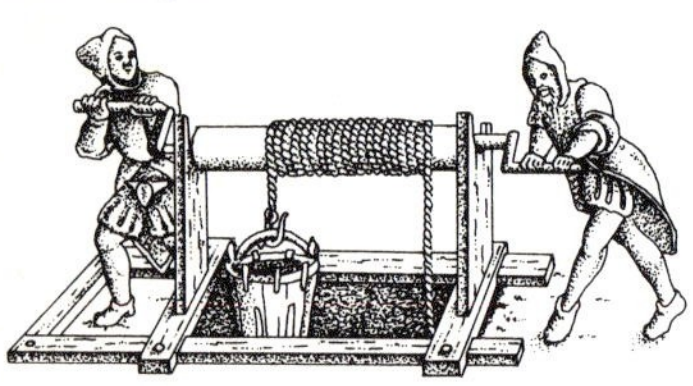

YORKSHIRE, HUMBERSIDE & THE NORTH-WEST
Kirklees, W. Yorks.
Bagshaw Museum has coal mining relics.
Northwich, Cheshire.
Salt Museum, with tools, models, slide show.
Preston-under-Scar, N. Yorks.
Lead-smelting flue, north of village.
Salford, Gr Manchester.
Museum of Mining: extensive coal mining display with underground mine & drift mine.
THE NORTH OF ENGLAND
Beamish, Durham.
North of England Open Air Museum has reconstructed Victorian colliery.
Millom, Cumbria.
Folk Museum contains full-scale replica of old Hodbarrow iron ore mine.
Newcastle upon Tyne, Tyne & Wear.
University has *Museum* of the Dept. of Mining & Engineering, with coll. of safety lamps & other items.
Washington, Tyne & Wear.
Restored colliery, with *industrial museum* in old engine house.
WALES
Aberystwyth, Dyfed.
Lead mining exhibits in *Ceredigion Museum.*
Amlwch, Anglesey.
Parys Copper Mountain, now abandoned.
Blaen-nant, W. Glam.
Blaen-nant Colliery: winding engines & pithead gear.
Blaenau Ffestiniog, Gwynedd.
At *Llechwedd Slate Caverns* are 16 tunnels, which can be visited by railway; one cavern demonstrates mining conditions. Gloddfa Ganol has *museum* with restored machinery.
Blaenafon, Gwent.
Big Pit Museum of Coalmining.
Bontddu, nr Dolgellau, Gwynedd.
Clogair Gold Mine, worked well into this century. Riverside trail. Gold mining exhibition nearby at *Maesgwm*, Coed-y-Brenin.
Carmarthen, Dyfed.
County Museum, Abergwili, with display on Dolaucothi mines.
Cymmer, W. Glam.
Welsh Miners' Museum (Afan Argoed Country Park). Simulated coal faces; miners' equipment.
Dolaucothi, nr Pumsaint, Dyfed.
Roman gold mines: 'waymarked' trail.
Llanberis, Gwynedd.
North Wales Quarrying Museum: history of slate industry. Machinery, audio-visual displays. Vivian Quarry Trail.
Llanfair, nr Harlech, Gwynedd.
Disused 19th-C. *slate quarry*, open to visitors.
Ponterwyd, nr Aberystwyth, Dyfed.
Llywernog Silver-Lead Mine: museum of gold, silver, lead & slate mining.
SOUTHERN SCOTLAND
Wanlockhead, Dumf. & Gall.
Museum of lead industry.
CENTRAL SCOTLAND & STRATHCLYDE
Prestonpans, Lothian.
Prestongrange Museum: history of Scottish coal mining. Beam engine.

MUSICAL INSTRUMENTS

THE WEST COUNTRY
St Keyne, nr Liskeard, Cornwall.
Paul Corin Musical Collection: fair & dance organs, still working.
Thornby, Devon.
Devon Museum of Mechanical Music has barrel pianos, polyphons, etc.
SOUTH-EAST ENGLAND
Brighton, E. Sussex.
Brighton Museum & Art Gallery has small coll. of musical instruments.
Carisbrooke Castle, Isle of Wight.
Castle Museum has oldest organ in country, still in playing order.
Goudhurst, Kent.
Finchcocks has magnificent coll. of early pianos.
Hailsham, E. Sussex.
Mummery Collection of musical instruments, at Michelham Priory.
GREATER LONDON
Bloomsbury.
Thomas Coram Foundation for Children (Brunswick Square): fine coll. of Handel's scores & other relics.
Brentford.
National Piano Museum: outstanding coll. of keyboard instruments, incl. cinema organs.
City.
St Paul's Cathedral has original late 17th-C. organ case by Wren.
Hampstead.
Fenton House has coll. of early instruments.
Kensington.
Royal College of Music: teaching institute with museum of instruments. *Victoria & Albert Museum*. Large coll. of musical instruments incl. virginals played by Elizabeth I.
South London.
Horniman Museum (London Rd): large coll. of instruments, British & foreign. *St Mary's, Rotherhithe*: largely unaltered organ of 1764.
Westminster.
Westminster Abbey has impressive 19th-C. organ cases.
THE THAMES, CHILTERNS & EAST ENGLIA
Cambridge, Cambs.
King's College Chapel has rare & beautiful pre-Civil War organ case by Dallam (organ-builder to Elizabeth I).
Oxford, Oxon.
Ashmolean Museum contains Hill Collection (mostly stringed instruments). *Bate Collection, University Music Faculty*, has wind & brass instruments. *Cathedral* has fine late 17th-C. organ case by Father Smith. European and non-European instruments in *Pitt-Rivers Museum.*
St Albans, Herts.
Organ Museum: colourful coll. of mechanical organs & other instruments.
CENTRAL ENGLAND
Broadheath, nr Worcester, Heref. & Worcs.
Elgar's birthplace (1857) houses composer's scores, photographs, memorabilia.
Cheltenham, Glos.
Gustav Holst Museum (Clarence Rd).
Gloucester, Glos.
Cathedral has impressive late 17th-C. organ case by Harris.
Leicester, Leics.
Small coll. of musical instruments in *Newarke Houses Museum.*
Tewkesbury, Glos.
Abbey church has Milton Organ, a 16th-C. case from Magdalen College, Oxford, purloined by Thomas Cromwell.
Warwick, Warks.
St John's House: modest coll. of instruments.
THE NORTH OF ENGLAND
Newcastle upon Tyne, Tyne & Wear.
Bagpipe Museum.
Rusland Hall, Cumbria.
Contains coll. of *mechanical musical devices.*
York, N. Yorks.
Music Gallery in *Castle Museum* incl. 17th-C. virginals & a barrel organ.
WALES
St Fagans, nr Cardiff, S. Glam.
Welsh Folk Museum has musical section, with Welsh harps.
CENTRAL SCOTLAND & STRATHCLYDE
Edinburgh, Lothian.
St Cecilia's Hall (Cowgate) contains Russell Collection of early keyboard instruments.
Kilmarnock, Strathclyde.
Dean Castle has coll. of over 200 lutes, viols & clavichords.

PREHISTORIC BRITAIN

See also: map on p 193.

THE WEST COUNTRY
Avebury, Wilts.
Stone circle is one of largest in Europe: almost a mile in circumference. Surrounded by bank & ditch. In use *c.* 3000–1500 BC. *Alexander Keiller Museum* has Neolithic & Bronze Age finds from Avebury & Windmill Hill.
Badbury Rings, Dorset.
Iron Age *hillfort.*
Barbury Castle, nr Swindon, Wilts.
Iron Age *earthworks.*
Cadbury Castle, nr Wincanton, Somerset.
Large Iron Age *hillfort*, traditionally the Arthurian Camelot. Refortified against Saxons in 5th & 6th C.
Carn Brae, nr Redruth, Cornwall.
Neolithic *hillfort*, enlarged in Iron Age.
Carn Euni, Cornwall.
Iron Age *village*: traces of several houses.
Castle an Dinas, nr St Columb Major, Cornwall.
Iron Age *hillfort.*
Castle Dore, nr Fowey, Cornwall.
Iron Age *hillfort*, palace of King Mark in Arthurian legend.
Cerne Abbas, Dorset.
Cerne Abbas Giant: outline of naked man carved in chalk hillside, probably 2nd C. AD.
Cheddar, Somerset.
Palaeolithic remains in *Cheddar Caves Museum* incl. almost complete human skeleton.
Chysauster, Cornwall.
Well-preserved Iron Age *hut village*, *c.* 100 BC.
Gough's Cave, nr Wells, Somerset.
Inhabited in Stone Age.
Grimspound, nr Ashburton, Devon.
Late *Bronze Age village*, remains of 20–30 granite huts.
Hambledon Hill, Dorset.
Impressive Iron Age *hillfort*, triple defences.
Hembury Castle, nr Buckfast Abbey, Devon.
Iron Age *camp.*
Hengistbury Head, nr Christchurch, Dorset.
Iron Age *coastal settlement.*
Hod Hill, nr Blandford Forum, Dorset.
Iron Age *hillfort*, used by Romans as garrison.
Knowlton Circles, nr Cranborne, Dorset.
Henge monument, 4,000 yrs old. Ruined Norman church in centre.
Maiden Castle, Dorset.
Celebrated Iron Age *hillfort*, of vast extent, begun *c.* 300 BC, later remodelled.
Normanton Down, nr Salisbury, Wilts.
Bronze Age cemetery, about 24 earth barrows.
Old Sarum, Wilts.
Iron Age *fort* & Saxon settlement; later, site of Norman cathedral.
Salisbury, Wilts.
Salisbury & S. Wilts. Museum: relics from Stonehenge & Old Sarum.
Silbury Hill, Wilts.
Largest *artificial hill* in Europe, an archaeological puzzle. Late Neolithic.
Spinsters' Rock, nr Okehampton, Devon.
Neolithic *burial chamber.*
Stanton Drew, Avon.
Stone circles of early Bronze Age.

Largest of 3 has 27 stones.
Stonehenge, Wilts.
Famous *henge monument*, built between *c.* 2750 & 1300 BC. Contains 'bluestones' brought from south-west Wales. May have been astronomical observatory.

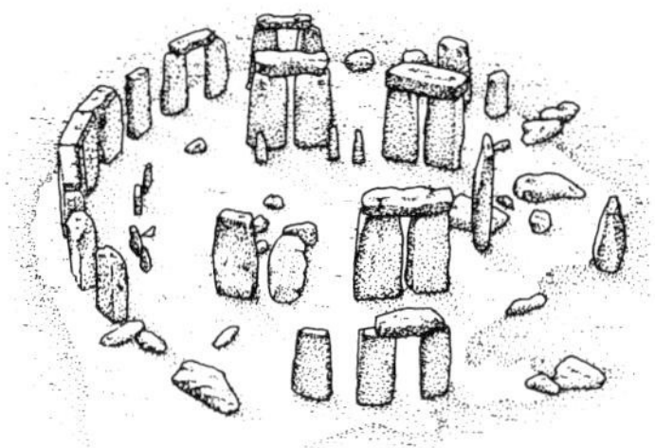

Stony Littleton, nr Bath, Avon.
Long barrow is one of best-preserved Stone Age burial grounds in Britain.
Torquay, Devon.
Kent's Cavern, occupied by Neolithic hunters. Human & animal remains from site exhibited in *Torquay Museum*.
West Kennet, Wilts.
Long barrow, may date from 3250 BC.
Windmill Hill, nr Avebury, Wilts.
Ritual *causewayed enclosure*, *c.* 3250 BC.
Winterbourne Stoke, nr Stonehenge, Wilts.
Group of *burial mounds*, most made by Beaker People (who came from Continent, *c.* 2000 BC).
Woodhenge, nr Amesbury, Wilts.
Concrete stumps mark former location of wooden posts, which were once part of *ceremonial hall* older than Stonehenge.
Worlebury Camp, nr Weston-Super-Mare, Avon.
Cliff-top *fort*; Iron Age pottery found here in storage pits.
Yarnbury Castle, nr Amesbury, Wilts.
Iron Age *hillfort*, with complex outworks commanding entrances.

SOUTH-EAST ENGLAND
Cissbury, nr Worthing, W. Sussex.
Iron Age *hillfort*.
Danebury, Hants.
Hillfort, probably dating to 4th C. BC, enlarged 2nd C. BC.
Wilmington, E. Sussex.
Long Man cut into chalk of Downs, may be pre-Roman in origin.

GREATER LONDON
Kensington.
Natural History Museum: fossils; models & remains of prehistoric animals.

THE THAMES, CHILTERNS & EAST ANGLIA
Cambridge, Cambs.
University Museum of Archaeology & Anthropology.
Grime's Graves, Norfolk.
Prehistoric *flint mines*, in use *c.* 2600–1600 BC.
Lambourn, Berks.
Seven Barrows: Bronze Age cemetery.
Uffington, Oxon.
White horse cut in chalk hillside, probably 1st C. BC.
Warham Camp, nr Wells-next-the-Sea, Norfolk.
Circular *fort* built by Iceni tribe, 1st C. AD.
Wayland's Smithy, Oxon.
Megalithic tomb, with roof stone over ante-chamber. Dates from *c.* 3500 BC. Built over earlier barrow.

CENTRAL ENGLAND
Arbor Law, Derbys.
Stone circle, perhaps built by Beaker People. Surrounding area has many Bronze Age burial mounds.
Belas Knap, nr Cheltenham, Glos.
Neolithic barrow (*c.* 2000 BC) containing 4 small chambers.
Birmingham, W. Midlands.
City Museum has Fossil Gallery, with skull of dinosaur.
Creswell Crags, Derbys.
Caves occupied by Neanderthal men.
Hereford Beacon, nr Great Malvern, Heref. & Worcs.
Iron Age *hillfort*.
Hetty Pegler's Tump, nr Stroud, Glos.
Long barrow, with burial chambers at east end. Major burial here *c.* 3000 BC.
Honington Camp, nr Grantham, Lincs.
Iron Age *fort*; bank & ditch defences.
Mam Tor, nr Whaley Bridge, Derbys.
Possibly one of earliest *hillforts* in country (*c.* 1200 BC).
Stanton Moor, Derbys.
Nine Ladies stone circle, Bronze Age (*c.* 1600 BC). Many standing stones & cairns in this region.

YORKSHIRE, HUMBERSIDE & THE NORTH-WEST
Boroughbridge, N. Yorks.
3 *standing stones*, possibly a Bronze Age sacred site.
Cashtal-yn-Ard, nr Ramsey, Isle of Man.
Neolithic *burial chamber*.
Duggleby Howe, N. Yorks.
Round barrow, one of largest in England. Neolithic. Bone pins, etc., found here now in Hull Museum.
Ingleborough, N. Yorks.
Iron Age *hillfort* on summit, part of walls extant.
Loose Howe, N. Yorks.
Burial mound, *c.* 1600 BC.
Meayll Circle, nr Port Erin, Isle of Man.
Chambered *tombs* in large circle.
Rudston, Humber.
Tallest *standing stone* in Britain in village churchyard. Stone Age.
Stanwick, N. Yorks.
Fortifications built *c.* AD 60, by Brigantes.
Star Carr, N. Yorks.
Mesolithic *hunters' settlement*.

THE NORTH OF ENGLAND
Castlerigg, nr Keswick, Cumbria.
Finest Cumbrian *stone circle*.
Eskdale Moor, Cumbria.
5 *stone circles*, all containing stone cairns. Built *c.* 1500 BC.
Lordenshaws, Hesleyhurst, Northumb.
Hillfort, contains remains of circular Romano-British houses.
Yeavering, Northumb.
Iron Age *fort*, with remains of some 150 stone huts (1st C. BC).

WALES
Barclodiad-y-Gawres, Anglesey.
Small *chambered grave* with entrance passage, *c.* 2000 BC.
Bryn Celli Ddu, Anglesey.
Large *chambered tomb*, *c.* 2000 BC. Built on site of ritual henge.
Carreg Samson Cromlech, nr Fishguard, Dyfed.
Impressive Neolithic *cromlech*, with 7 uprights supporting capstone.
Dinas Dinlle, nr Caernarfon, Gwynedd.
Cliff-top *hillfort*, late Iron Age.
Din Lligwy, Anglesey.
Neolithic *burial chamber*, with massive capstone.
Holyhead Mountain, Anglesey.
Hut circles, probably occupied in late Iron Age and Roman period. Low stone walls & hearths remain.
Pentre Ifan Cromlech, nr Newport, Dyfed.
Megalithic *burial chamber*, 3 uprights with large capstone.
St Lythan's Cromlech, nr Barry, S. Glam.
Neolithic *burial chamber*.
Tre'r Ceiri, nr Pwllheli, Gwynedd.
Hillfort, with remains of some 150 stone huts. Drystone outer wall.

SOUTHERN SCOTLAND
Cairnholy, nr Newton Stewart, Dumf. & Gall.
Impressive *megalithic tombs*, 2 burial mounds (*c.* 3000 BC).

CENTRAL SCOTLAND & STRATHCLYDE
Cairnpapple Hill, nr Bathgate, Lothian.
Stone circle & cairn (latter *c.* 1500 BC).
White Castle, nr Haddington, Lothian.
Spectacularly sited *hillfort*: 3 main ramparts, traces of huts.

NORTHERN SCOTLAND & THE ISLANDS
Callanish, Lewis, Western Isles.
Stone circle, sometimes said to be 2nd in importance to Stonehenge. Neolithic & Bronze Age.
Carn Liath, nr Brora, Highland.
Remains of *broch*.
The Caterthuns, nr Brechin, Tayside.
Ruined stone walls of 2 Iron Age *hillforts*.
Clickhimin, nr Lerwick, Shetland.
Fortified settlement, partly Iron Age. Substantial ruins of broch.
Corrimony Cairn, Glen Urquhart, Highland.
Neolithic *chambered cairn*, encircled by standing stones.
Craig Phadrig, nr Inverness, Highland.
Vitrified fort, now surrounded by forest.
Dun Carloway, Lewis, Western Isles.
Well-preserved Pictish *broch*, *c.* 1st C. BC
Dun Telve, nr Kyle of Lochalsh, Highland.
Well preserved Pictish *broch*. Nearby: Dun Troddan.
Gurness, Orkney.
Iron Age *broch*, with surrounding stone huts.
Holm of Papa Westray, Orkney.
Megalithic *tomb* on islet.
Jarlshof, Sumburgh Head, Shetland.
Ancient village, begun 1st C. BC, occupied for 2 millennia. Extensive remains, with 'wheel-houses'.
Knockfarrel, nr Dingwall, Highland.
Fine *vitrified fort*.
Maes Howe, Orkney.
Chambered burial mound, *c.* 2000 BC. Ransacked by Vikings.
Midhowe, Rousay, Orkney.
Iron Age *broch*, megalithic *chambered tombs*.
Mousa, Shetland.
Best-preserved Iron Age *broch* in Scotland. (On island off Sandwick.)
Ring of Brodgar, Stromness, Orkney.
Henge & magnificent *stone circle*.
Skara Brae, nr Stromness, Orkney.
Superb *Neolithic village*. 10 houses, complete with stone furniture.

RAILWAYS

See also: map on p 266.

THE WEST COUNTRY
Box Tunnel, nr Chippenham, Wilts.
Brunel's Great Western Railway tunnel, completed 1841.
Bristol, Avon.
Industrial Museum has steam loco & other rlwy exhibits. Also in Bristol: trainshed of *Temple Meads Station* by Brunel, 1841.
Buckfastleigh, Devon.
Dart Valley Rlwy, to Totnes (7 m.). Steam locos.
Cranmore, nr Shepton Mallet, Somerset.
East Somerset Rlwy, numerous locos, restored station.
Dawlish Warren, Devon.
South Devon Rlwy Museum & Model Rlwy.
Minehead, Somerset.
West Somerset Rlwy.
Newlyn East, Cornwall.
Lappa Valley Rlwy. Narrow-gauge miners' line.
Paignton, Devon.
Torbay & Dartmouth Steam Rlwy, operates $6\frac{3}{4}$ m. to Kingswear.
Swindon, Wilts.
Great Western Rlwy Museum has historic locos & other GWR relics. Also in Swindon: *Rlwy Village Museum*, with restored foreman's house.

SOUTH-EAST ENGLAND
Alresford, Hants.
Mid-Hants. Rlwy ('Watercress Line'), 3 m. Variety of steam locos.
Brighton, E. Sussex.
Station has fine curved trainshed, 1882.
Brockham, nr Betchworth, Surrey.
Depot with steam locos.
Haven Street, nr Ryde, Isle of Wight.
Steam rlwy with museum.
Liphook, Hants.
Hollycombe Steam Collection.
New Romney, Kent.
Romney, Hythe & Dymchurch Rlwy. Blythe to Dungeness, $13\frac{3}{4}$ m. Gauge 15 in. Exhibition at New Romney station.
Sittingbourne, Kent.
Sittingbourne & Kemsley Light Rlwy, narrow gauge, 2 m.
Southampton, Hants.
Fine Italianate *terminus* by William Tite, 1840.
Tenterden, Kent.
Kent & E. Sussex Rlwy. Various exhibits at Tenterden & Rolvenden stations.
Sheffield Park, E. Sussex.
Bluebell Rlwy. Steam rides to Horsted Keynes, 5 m. Vintage locos & coaches.

GREATER LONDON
Kensington.
Kensington Science Museum has Puffing Billy (1813), Stephenson's Rocket & other exhibits.
West End.
London Transport Museum, Covent Garden: unique coll. incl. underground train, signals, rolling stock.
Notable stations.
Among London's many historic stations are: *King's Cross* (frontage remains as it was in 1852); *Liverpool St* (opened 1875, still has neo-Gothic trainsheds); *Paddington* (terminus of GWR, by Brunel & his associate Digby Wyatt, opened 1854); *St Pancras* (famous for massive neo-Gothic Midland Hotel by Sir Giles Gilbert Scott, late 1860s); *Victoria* (originally 2 stations).

THE THAMES, CHILTERNS & EAST ANGLIA.
Bressingham, nr Diss, Norfolk.
Live Steam Museum. 40 engines incl. large express locos. Steam-hauled rides (narrow gauge).
Cambridge, Cambs.
Attractive *station*, 1847. Inspired by Italian Renaissance style.
Castle Hedingham, nr Halstead, Essex.
Colne Valley Rlwy.

Chappel, Essex.
Stour Valley Rlwy Preservation Society. Some 10 locos, regular steamings.
King's Lynn, Norfolk.
Wolferton Station Museum has small rlwy curios.
Leighton Buzzard, Beds.
Narrow-gauge rlwy.
Quainton, nr Aylesbury, Bucks.
Working *rlwy museum.* Steam locos, rolling stock.
Sheringham, Norfolk.
North Norfolk Rlwy, standard gauge, 3 m. Signal box of 1880s.
Wansford, nr Peterborough, Cambs.
Nene Valley Rlwy, 6 m. Historic locos.
CENTRAL ENGLAND
Ashchurch, Glos.
Dowty Rlwy Preservation Society. Museum with steam locos, rolling stock, signalling gear.
Bewdley, Heref. & Worcs.
Severn Valley Rlwy, to Bridgnorth (12¾ m.). Over 30 steam locos.
Birmingham, W. Midlands.
Rlwy Museum (Tyseley) has steam days. 11 steam locos.
Burton upon Trent, Staffs.
Bass Museum has steam loco & director's coach.
Chasewater Pleasure Park, nr Brownhills, Staffs.
Chasewater Light Rlwy. Steam locos, vintage coaches. Museum.
Cheddleton, Staffs.
N. Staffs. Rlwy Co. Steam line from Leeds to Stoke.
Derby, Derbys.
Rlwy relics in *Derby Museum.*
Dilhorne, nr Cheadle, Staffs.
Foxfield Light Rlwy. Regular steam rides, over 10 steam locos.
Glossop, Derbys.
Dinting Rlwy Centre. Steam locos, large exhibition hall.
Hereford, Heref. & Worcs.
'Steam in Hereford', incl. GWR 6000 King George V. Static displays, steam days.
Loughborough, Leics.
Great Central Rlwy, to Rothley. Museum.
Lydney, Glos.
Norchard Steam Centre (Dean Forest Rlwy): working museum. GWR & industrial engines.
Oswestry, Salop.
Cambrian Rlwy Society, 5 locos.
Ripley, Derbys.
Midland Rlwy Centre (Butterley Station).
Shackerstone, nr Market Bosworth, Leics.
Light rlwy, with museum.
Winchcombe, Glos.
Rlwy museum.
YORKSHIRE, HUMBERSIDE & THE NORTH-WEST
Carnforth, Lancs.
Steamtown Rlwy Museum. Over 25 locos, incl. Flying Scotsman. Main line excursions.
Douglas, Isle of Man.
Narrow-gauge rlwy, to Port Erin (which has large museum).
Haworth, W. Yorks.
Worth Valley Rlwy. Keighley to Oxenhope (5 m.). Some 30 locos.
Leeds, W. Yorks.
Middleton Rlwy, follows route of 18th-c. horse-drawn rlwy (2 m.).
Pickering, N. Yorks.
N. Yorks. Moors Rlwy, very scenic. Information centre.
Skipton, W. Yorks.
Yorks. Dales Rlwy at Embsay. Museum.
Southport, Merseyside.
Steamport Southport Ltd, 5 steam locos.
York, N. Yorks.
National Rlwy Museum covers whole spectrum of rlwy heritage (technical, social, economic). Many full-sized locos, incl. Mallard.

THE NORTH OF ENGLAND
Beamish, Durham.
North of England Open Air Museum has locos in steam.
Darlington, Durham.
North Road Station (terminus of Stockton-Darlington rlwy, built 1842) is now a rlwy museum, with engines & rolling stock from 1825.
Haverthwaite, nr Ulverston, Cumbria.
Lakeside & Haverthwaite Rlwy, originally opened 1869. Connects with steamboats on Lake Windermere.
Newcastle upon Tyne, Tyne & Wear.
Central Station: classical terminus (1865) with curved trainshed.
Ravenglass, Cumbria.
Ravenglass & Eskdale Rlwy, rides to Dalegarth (7 m.). Narrow gauge.
Shildon, Durham.
Stockton & Darlington Rlwy Works partly restored. Replica of early loco. Workers' cottages.
Springwell, Tyne & Wear.
Bowes Rlwy, opened 1826 to carry coal. Demonstrations of rope-worked trains.
Sunderland, Tyne & Wear.
Monkwearmouth Station Museum. Station (1848) with restored booking office, rolling stock exhibits.
WALES
Aberystwyth, Dyfed.
Vale of Rheidol Rlwy, 11¾ m., narrow gauge. Magnificent scenery.
Betws-y-Coed, Gwynedd.
Conwy Valley Rlwy Museum.
Carmarthen, Dyfed.
Gwili Rlwy, 2 m. north of town.
Fairbourne, nr Barmouth, Gwynedd.
Fairbourne Rlwy, runs across sand dunes (2 m.). Narrow gauge.
Porthmadog, Gwynedd.
Ffestiniog Rlwy, world's first narrow-gauge passenger route. Some 10 locos. Museum.
Llanberis, Gwynedd.
Lake Rlwy, built for slate industry, 2 m. *Snowdon Mountain Rlwy* goes to summit, fine views.
Llanfair Caereinion, nr Welshpool, Powys.
Welshpool & Llanfair Light Rlwy, former colliery line.
Llangollen, Clwyd.
Restored station, with static display of locos & rolling stock.
Llanuwchllyn, Gwynedd.
Bala Lake Rlwy, along old GWR route.
Penrhyn Castle, nr Bangor, Gwynedd.
Coll. of old locos in park.
Tywyn, Gwynedd.
Talyllyn Rlwy, built for slate industry. Narrow gauge museum.
CENTRAL SCOTLAND & STRATHCLYDE
Falkirk, Central.
Scottish Rlwy Preservation Society, regular steamings on ½ m. track.
Lochty, nr St Andrews, Fife.
Lochty Private Rlwy, standard gauge. Regular steam days.
Glasgow, Strathclyde.
Museum of Transport has locos from Scottish lines.
NORTHERN SCOTLAND & THE ISLANDS
Boat of Garten, Highland.
Strathspey Rlwy, to Aviemore. 10 locos.

ROAD VEHICLES

THE WEST COUNTRY
Bristol, Avon.
Industrial Museum has various transport items, incl. steam carriage & Wanderer caravan (1880).
Buckland Abbey, Devon.
Carriages, carts & early fire engines (all in tithe barn).
Cheddar, Somerset.
Motor Museum has some 25 cars & 15 motorcycles, dating until early 1950s.
Dodington House, Avon.
Carriage Museum. More than 30 types on display, incl. phaeton, stagecoach, hansom cab. Rides available.
Totnes, Devon.
Motor Museum: vintage & racing cars, motorcycles.
SOUTH-EAST ENGLAND
Beaulieu, Hants.
National Motor Museum has over 200 vehicles, dating from 1895. Private & military cars, motorcycles.

Breamore, Hants.
Carriage Museum has last stagecoach to run between London & Southampton.
Maidstone, Kent.
Tyrwhitt-Drake Museum has horse-drawn vehicles & displays on coach building.
GREATER LONDON
East London.
Vestry House Museum, Walthamstow, has first British motor car.
West End.
London Transport Museum (Covent Garden) has trams, trolley buses, etc.
THE THAMES, CHILTERNS & EAST ANGLIA
Carlton Colville, nr Lowestoft, Suffolk.
East Anglia Transport Museum.
High Wycombe, Bucks.
West Wycombe Motor Museum: racing & luxury cars.
Holkham Park, Wells-next-the-Sea, Norfolk.
'Bygones at Holkham': incl. fire engines, motor cars.
Old Warden, Beds.
Shuttleworth Collection incl. historic cars, carriages, bicycles.
CENTRAL ENGLAND
Bourton-on-the-Water, Glos.
Motor Museum: more than 30 cars & motorcycles from 1903, incl. racing cars.
Bridgnorth, Salop.
Midland Motor Museum.
Coventry, W. Midlands.
Museum of British Road Transport. Over 120 cars & commercial vehicles, 50 motorcycles, 200 cycles.
Crich, Derbys.
National Tramway Museum. Restored horse, steam & electric trams (many operational).
Leicester, Leics.
Museum of Technology has various items, incl. horse-drawn vehicles.
Shugborough, Staffs.
Staffs. County Museum & Mansion House has coll. of horse-drawn vehicles.
Stanford Hall, Leics.
Vintage Motor Cycle & Car Museum.
Stratford-upon-Avon, Warks.
Motor Museum: vintage cars, motorcycles, bicycles.
YORKSHIRE, HUMBERSIDE & THE NORTH-WEST
Aysgarth Falls, N. Yorks.
Yorks. Museum of Horse-drawn Vehicles.
Bradford, W. Yorks.
Vintage cars in *Industrial Museum.*
Bury, Gr Manchester.
Transport Museum has buses, steam roller & other vehicles.
Hull, Humber.
Transport & Archaeology Museum: horse-drawn vehicles & early cars.
Liverpool, Merseyside.
Merseyside County Museum has horse-drawn & steam-powered road vehicles.
Manchester, Gr Manchester.
Museum of Transport has major coll. of vintage buses.
Sandtoft, Humber.
Large coll. of trollybuses & motorbuses.
Southport, Merseyside.
Steamport Transport Museum has tramcars & commercial vehicles as well as locos.
Tatton Park, Cheshire.
Museum contains veteran cars, Victorian fire engine.
Nostell Priory, nr Wakefield, N. Yorks.
Coll. of historic cars & motorcycles.
THE NORTH OF ENGLAND
Cark-in-Cartmel, Cumbria.
Lakeland Motor Museum (Holker Hall).
WALES
Pembroke, Dyfed.
Motor Museum has cars, motorcycles, bicycles. Early motoring costumes.
Swansea, W. Glam.
Maritime & Industrial Museum has numerous transport exhibits.
CENTRAL SCOTLAND & STRATHCLYDE
Edinburgh, Lothian.
Transport Museum.
Glasgow, Strathclyde.
Museum of Transport has trams, horse-drawn vehicles, cars, bicycles.
NORTHERN SCOTLAND & THE ISLANDS
Doune, Tayside.
Motor Museum incl. world's second oldest Rolls-Royce. Some 40 cars.

ROCKS & CAVES

THE WEST COUNTRY
Camborne, Cornwall.
Geological Museum.
Cheddar, Somerset.
Limestone caves with spectacular stalagmites & stalactites. Fine formations in *Gough's & Cox's Caves.* Museum.
Dartmoor, Devon & Cornwall.
Notable tors (outcrops of weathered granite) incl. Haytor & Chinkwell Tor.
Golden Cap, Dorset.
Fossiliferous cliffs (National Trust).
Kent's Cavern, Torquay, Devon.
Vast limestone cave system, occupied in prehistoric times. Stalagmites & stalactites. Guided tours.
Kimmeridge Bay, Dorset.
Fossiliferous cliffs. (Beware of falling rocks.)

Kynance Cove, Cornwall.
Caves in spectacular cliffs with serpentine veins.
Lulworth Cove, Dorset.
Fine cliffs, with folded strata. Nearby: *Durdle Door*, a natural limestone arch.
Portland Bill, Dorset.
Projection from limestone Isle of Portland. Source of famous Portland stone, for building.
Truro, Cornwall.
County Museum contains Cornish minerals.
Wookey Hole, Somerset.
Prehistoric dwelling place. *Great Cave* has massive 'Witch of Wookey' stalagmite. Museum, with displays of geology & archaeology.

SOUTH-EAST ENGLAND

Alum Bay, Isle of Wight.
Coloured Bagshot sands obtained from cliffs.
The Needles, Isle of Wight.
Line of jagged chalk stacks, remains of eroded ridge from Isle of Wight towards Dorset coast.
Seven Sisters, nr Eastbourne, E. Sussex.
Spectacular chalk cliffs, a continuation of S. Downs. Good footpaths.

GREATER LONDON

Kensington.
Geological Museum (Exhibition Rd) has exhibits on British regional geology. Rocks, fossils, minerals, gemstones. *Natural History Museum* has fossils & superb mineral gallery.

THE THAMES, CHILTERNS & EAST ANGLIA

Cambridge, Cambs.
Sedgwick Museum of Geology. Fossils, rocks, ornamental marbles.
West Wycombe, Bucks.
Hell Fire Caves. Labyrinth of caves cut into chalk hillside in 18th C. Meeting place of infamous Hell Fire Club.

CENTRAL ENGLAND

Birmingham, W. Midlands.
University Geology Museum at Edgbaston. By appt.
Buxton, Derbys.
Poole's Cavern: large limestone cavern with stalactites & stalagmites. Audio-visual display.
Castleton, Derbys.
Blue John Caverns: vast range of caverns, with stunning crystal formations & stalactites. Blue John mineral mined here. *Peak Cavern* has largest entrance of any British cave, with vast interior chambers. *Speedwell Cavern*: boat trips along old lead-mining tunnel. *Treak Cliff Cavern*: Blue John, fine stalactites.
Creswell Crags, Derbys.
Limestone caves once inhabited by Stone Age hunters.
Hartlebury, Heref. & Worcs.
Hereford & Worcester County Museum has geological displays.

YORKSHIRE, HUMBERSIDE & THE NORTH-WEST

Brimham Rocks, nr Ripon, N. Yorks.
Fantastic weathered outcrop of millstone grit.
Ingleborough, W. Yorks.
Great limestone cave. Guided tours. Nearby is *Gaping Gill*, largest limestone cave in Britain.
Malham, nr Skipton, N. Yorks.
Dramatic limestone formations, with *limestone pavements*.
Ravenscar, nr Scarborough, N. Yorks.
Geological trail through quarry, ends at Robin Hood's Bay cliffs.

THE NORTH OF ENGLAND

St Bees Head, Cumbria.
Red sandstone cliffs, fine coastal path.

WALES

Bwlchgwyn, Clwyd.
Milestone Museum illustrates development of N. Wales over 600 million years.
Cemaes Head, Dyfed.
High cliffs with folded rock strata.
Dan-yr-Ogog Caves, nr Abercraf, Powys.
Caves with displays on prehistoric inhabitants.

CENTRAL SCOTLAND & STRATHCLYDE

Carsaig, South Mull, Strathclyde.
Sea-carved tunnels in basaltic rock. Also: Nun's Cave.
Drumadoon Bay, Arran, Strathclyde.
Cliffs with veins of quartz, porphyry & occasional semi-precious stones.
Fingal's Cave, Staffa, Strathclyde.
Extraordinary basalt formations & huge cliff-base cave. By boat from Oban.
Glasgow, Strathclyde.
University of Glasgow Hunterian Museum has major geological coll.

NORTHERN SCOTLAND & THE ISLANDS

Bullers of Buchan, nr Peterhead, Grampian.
Spectacular chasm in high cliffs.
Cape Wrath, Highland.
Highest sea cliffs in Britain. *Smoo Cave* nearby, with subterranean waterfall.
Cullen Bay, Cullen, Grampian.
Bay with impressive rock forms, notably *Bow Fiddle Rock*.
Old Man of Hoy, Orkney.
One of best-known sea stacks in Britain, vertical column of granite detached from cliff.

ROMAN BRITAIN

See also: maps on p 194.

THE WEST COUNTRY

Ackling Dyke, Dorset.
Fine stretch of *Roman road* (13 m. SW of Salisbury).
Bath, Avon.
Extensive remains of *Roman Baths*, with adjoining museum. Carved pediment with Gorgon head, lead-lined bath, etc.
Bristol, Avon.
City Museum has relics.
Dorchester, Dorset.
Roman relics in *County Museum*. Remains of 4th-C. town house in Colliton Park.
Exeter, Devon.
Royal Albert Memorial Museum has Roman relics.
Kingsweston, nr Avonmouth, Avon.
Roman *villa*, with hypocausts, 2 mosaics.
Taunton, Somerset.
Relics in *County Museum*.

SOUTH-EAST ENGLAND

Bignor, W. Sussex.
Large *villa* built round a courtyard, famous for 4th-C. mosaics.
Brading, Isle of Wight.
Villa, with unusual pavements.
Canterbury, Kent.
Numerous finds in *Royal Museum*. Also: *Roman Pavement* (Butchery Lane), with 2 mosaics & hypocaust.
Chichester, W. Sussex.
Small *amphitheatre* to east. *Museum* in Little London.
Dover, Kent.
Lighthouse on cliff, remains of painted house & Saxon shore fort.
Fishbourne, W. Sussex.
Largest Roman *villa* complex in Britain. 12 mosaic floors in situ.
Lullingstone, Kent.
Roman *villa*, famous for 4th-C. Christian chapel.
Newport, Isle of Wight.
Small *villa* of 3rd C.
Pevensey, E. Sussex.
Shore fort, with fine Roman gate.
Portchester, Hants.
Late Roman *shore fort*.
Richborough, Kent.
Supply depot, triumphal arch, shore fort. Museum.
Rockbourne, nr Fordingbridge, Hants.
Roman *villa*, museum.
Silchester, Hants.
Calleva Museum devoted to Roman Silchester.
Winchester, Hants.
City Museum has fine Roman items.

GREATER LONDON

Bloomsbury.
Relics in *British Museum* incl. mosaic from Leadenhall St.
City.
Museum of London (Barbican) has fine Roman coll. Also in City: *All Hallows by the Tower* (pavements & other relics in crypt). Best-preserved section of *City Wall* is nr Tower of London.

THE THAMES, CHILTERNS & EAST ANGLIA

Aylesbury, Bucks.
County Museum.
Cambridge, Cambs.
University Museum of Archaeology & Anthropology.
Colchester, Essex.
Most of *Roman Wall* still extant (incl. Balkerne Gate). *Castle Museum* (built over Temple of Claudius) has outstanding relics, incl. jewellery, glass, statues.
Mersea Island, Essex.
Roman *burial mound*, can be entered.
North Leigh, nr Witney, Oxon.
Remains of 2nd-C. *villa*, with mosaic.
Reading, Berks.
Museum has coll. from Silchester.
St Albans, Herts.
Verulamium Museum incl. some of finest mosaics in country.
Welwyn, Herts.
Small *bath house*, containing Roman finds.

CENTRAL ENGLAND

Chedworth, Glos.
Villa remains incl. bath house, dining room. Small museum.
Cirencester, Glos.
Corinium Museum. Roman antiquities.
Coventry, W. Midlands.
Lunt Roman Fort (Baginton): reconstruction. Relics in *Herbert Art Gallery & Museum*.
Gloucester, Glos.
Part of Roman defences in *Kings Walk*. Relics in *City Museum*.
Hereford, Heref. & Worcs.
City Museum has discoveries made at Roman town of Magna (Kentchester).
Leicester, Leics.
Jewry Wall Museum, on site of public baths.
Lincoln, Lincs.
Roman defences incl. *Newport Arch*. City & County *Museum* has Roman relics.
Shrewsbury, Salop.
Rowley's House Museum: coll. of Roman material from Wroxeter.
Wall, Staffs.
Letocetum Museum: finds from excavated Roman station. Bath house.
Woodchester, Glos.
Villa, occasionally uncovered.
Wroxeter, nr Shrewsbury, Salop.
Baths still extant. *Viroconium Museum* has objects found on site.

YORKSHIRE, HUMBERSIDE & THE NORTH-WEST

Aldborough, N. Yorks.
Aldborough Roman Museum: pottery, glass, metalwork, coins.
Blackstone Edge, nr Rochdale, Gr Manchester.
Fine stretch of *Roman road* over Pennines.
Chester, Cheshire.
Roman *wall, amphitheatre*. *Grosvenor Museum* has finds from legionary fort.
Malton, N. Yorks.
Museum has extensive Roman coll.
Oxford, Oxon.
Ashmolean Museum has Roman antiquities in Leeds Room.
Ribchester, Lancs.
Fort on R. Ribble, part of buildings exposed. Small *museum*.
Wheeldale Moor, nr Goathland, N. Yorks.
Foundations of *Roman road*.
York, N. Yorks.
Yorkshire Museum gardens contain Roman ruins; Hospitium houses large Roman coll.
Binchester Fort, nr Bishop Auckland, Durham
Roman cavalry *fort*.
Birdoswald, Northumb.
Hadrian's Wall *fort* in dramatic position.
Carrawburgh, Northumb.
Hadrianic *fort*. Well-preserved small Mithraeum temple.
Chesterholm, Northumb.
Hadrianic Wall *fort* of Vindolanda, with reconstructed defences. Excellent *museum*.
Chesters, Northumb.
Hadrian's Wall *fort* in fine surroundings. *Museum* has sculptures & inscriptions.
Corbridge, Northumb.
Supply depot for Hadrian's Wall, with various remains. Good *museum* on site.
Hardknot, Cumbria.
Mountain *fort*, with bath house.
Housesteads, Northumb.
Impressive remains of Hadrian's Wall *fort*. Well-preserved defences, latrine. *Museum*, granaries, etc.
Newcastle upon Tyne, Tyne & Wear.
Museum of Antiquities, incl. reconstructed temple of Mithras.
Ravenglass, Cumbria.
Well-preserved *bath house*, with windows.
South Shields, Tyne & Wear.
Fort at east end of Hadrian's Wall, converted to supply depot.

WALES

Caerleon, nr Newport, Gwent.
Major *fortress*. Barracks & magnificent *amphitheatre*. Small museum in village.
Caernarfon, Gwynedd.
Roman *fort* of Segontium; museum.
Caerwent, nr Chepstow, Gwent.
Remains of Roman tribal centre incl. fine stretch of *walls* (4th C.).
Cardiff, S. Glam.
City centre has Victorian reconstruction of 4th-C. fort. *National Museum of Wales* incl. relics from Caerleon.
Carmarthen, Dyfed.
Amphitheatre. Large Roman display at *Carmarthen Museum*, Abergwili.

Holyhead, Anglesey.
Coastal *fort* of 4th C.
Newport, Gwent.
Gwent Museum has relics from Caerwent.
SOUTHERN SCOTLAND
Burnswark, Dumf. & Gall.
Roman *camps & hillfort.*
CENTRAL SCOTLAND & STRATHCLYDE
Edinburgh, Lothian.
National Museum of Antiquities has numerous Roman objects.
Glasgow, Strathclyde.
Hunterian Museum has relics of Roman Scotland, model of Antonine wall.
Rough Castle, nr Falkirk, Strathclyde.
Best-preserved Antonine Wall *fort.*
NORTHERN SCOTLAND & THE ISLANDS
Braco, Tayside.
Ardroch Fort: outpost north of Antonine Wall. Earth rampart & multiple ditches.

SCHOOLS, UNIVERSITIES, COLLEGES & LIBRARIES

THE WEST COUNTRY
Wimborne, Dorset.
Minster has chained library of 240 books, from 1686.
Tiverton, Devon.
Blundell's School, founded 1604. Original building survives.
SOUTH-EAST ENGLAND
Brighton, E. Sussex.
Sussex University designed by Sir Basil Spence, founded 1961.
Canterbury, Kent.
King's School, one of the oldest in England. Buildings incl. Norman stairway.
Horsham, W. Sussex.
Christ's Hospital, 16-C. foundation. Boys wear famous blue coats.
Winchester, Hants.
Winchester College, founded by William of Wykeham, 1394.
GREATER LONDON
North London.
British Library, currently being rehoused in Euston Rd. Mss incl. 2 copies of Magna Carta & log of Nelson's 'Victory'. Many rare books.
Westminster.
Blewcoat School, once a charitable institute for educating children of poor. Early 18th-C. school hall.
THE THAMES, CHILTERNS & EAST ANGLIA
Cambridge, Cambs.
Clare College: riverside college founded in 1326, with stately 17th-C. buildings & classical bridge over river.
Emmanuel College has chapel & colonnade designed by Wren, 1666.
History Faculty Library: impressive glass & steel block by James Stirling, 1968.
King's College: outstanding Perpendicular chapel (1446–1515) with fine 16th-C. stained glass, richly carved choir stalls. Magnificent site.
Pembroke College, founded 1347. Chapel by Wren, 1666; enlarged 1880.
Peterhouse College, oldest Cambridge foundation (1284).
Queen's College has Tudor quad (Second Court) with cloisters & fine half-timbered President's Lodge. Erasmus stayed here in 1511.
St John's College has massive Tudor gateway & 19th-C. 'Bridge of Sighs' over R. Cam. Hall has Tudor roof.
Trinity College, founded 1546 by Henry VIII. Massive Great Court. Splendid library in Nevile's Court is by Wren, with Grinling Gibbons carvings.
University Library by Sir Giles Gilbert Scott, 1934.
Eton College, nr Windsor, Berks.
Most famous *public school* in England. Parts open to the public incl. chapel & cloisters.
Mildenhall, Suffolk.
Parvis Chamber over porch of St Mary's Church was schoolroom in Middle Ages.
Norwich, Norfolk.
University of East Anglia, founded in 1961. Campus buildings by Denys Lasdun.
Oxford, Oxon.
(*See* aerial diagram, p 254.)
All Souls College for post-grads, founded 1438. Codrington Library has outstanding coll. of legal works.
Balliol College has mostly Victorian buildings, with restored gates of 1288.
Bodleian Library, one of largest in world. Founded 1444, remodelled 1603. Incl. *Duke Humfrey's Library* (only part open to public) & superb *Radcliffe Camera* (circular building by James Gibbs, 1737).
Christ Church, founded by Cardinal Wolsey, 1525. Spacious Tom Quad is named after bell in Wren's octagonal Tom Tower (built 1682), above entrance gate.
Keble College, built to commemorate Oxford Movement leader, John Keble. Polychrome buildings by William Butterfield, 1867–83; fine chapel.
Magdalen College, retains 15th-C. buildings. Deer park, fine cloisters, restored 15th-C. tower, Addison's Walk (named after Joseph Addison).
Merton College, oldest chartered Oxford foundation (1264). Fine medieval chapel with 13th- & 14th-C. stained glass. Library 1373–8. Oldest part of college is Treasury (1274), adjacent to picturesque 'Mob Quad'.
New College, founded 1380 by William of Wykeham. Much of original architecture survives, notably bell-tower & cloister of splendid chapel.
Pembroke College, founded 1624. Chapel has rich classical interior.
Queen's College, founded 1341. Fine 17th-C. buildings, double quad.
Sheldonian Theatre, used for degree ceremonies. By Wren, 1669.
Trinity College, founded 1555, has 17th-C. Garden Quadrangle by Wren & chapel of 1691.
CENTRAL ENGLAND
Rugby, Warks.
Public school founded as Free Grammar School in Tudor times. Became famous in 19th C under headmaster Thomas Arnold.
Sudbury, Derbys.
Museum of Childhood has reconstructed 19th-C. schoolroom.
Warwick, Warks.
St John's House has Victorian classroom.
YORKSHIRE, HUMBERSIDE & THE NORTH-WEST
Heptonstall, W. Yorks.
Former *grammar school*, founded 1642, closed 1889. Desks & benches preserved. Textbooks of 18th & 19th C.
Lancaster, Lancs.
Reconstructed Victorian schoolroom in *Museum of Childhood* (Judges Lodging).
Leeds, W. Yorks.
Victorian *Mechanics Institute*, now School of Art.
Manchester, Gr Manchester.
Chetham's Library: first free library in Europe, founded 1653.
Manchester Grammar School, founded 1515, has outstanding academic record.
John Rylands University Library (opened 1900) has Gutenberg Bible & 60 books printed by Caxton. *University* buildings, begun 1870, are in French neo-Gothic style.
Preston, Lancs.
Harris Library, by James Hibbert, 1882. Exceptional Greek Revival design.
York, N. Yorks.
University has modern campus buildings at Heslington . Finely landscaped grounds, with lakes.
WALES
Aberystwyth, Dyfed.
National Library of Wales has large coll. of books & documents, incl. Black Book of Carmarthen (oldest surviving ms in Welsh).
CENTRAL SCOTLAND & STRATHCLYDE
Dunblane, Central.
Leighton Library, 1687. Books bequeathed to town's clergy.
Edinburgh, Lothian.
National Library of Scotland, founded 1682. One of 4 largest libraries in Britain. *Royal High School* has monumental Greek Revival design by Thomas Hamilton (1825). Now an assembly building.
Glasgow, Strathclyde.
Mitchell Library, Scotland's largest public reference library, founded 1874.
School of Art by C.R. Mackintosh, begun 1896. Outstanding Art Nouveau architecture. *Glasgow University*: by George Gilbert Scott in neo-Gothic style, completed 1871.
Leadhills, Strathclyde.
Allan Ramsay Library, set up by lead miners, 1741.
St Andrews, Fife.
Ancient college buildings incl. *Divinity College* (St Mary's, founded 1537), & 15th-C. *chapel* of St Salvator.
Stirling, Central.
University has fine modern campus, blending well with landscape.
NORTHERN SCOTLAND & THE ISLANDS
Aberdeen, Grampian.
King's College Chapel, 1505.
Marischal College has fine granite buildings of 19th & early 20th C., notably neo-Perpendicular Broad St façade.
Innerpeffray, nr Crieff, Tayside.
First *public library* in Scotland, 1691. Rare Bibles.

SCIENCE

THE WEST COUNTRY
Bournemouth, Dorset.
Natural Science Society Museum: coll. relating to astronomy, chemistry, geography, geology & physics. Visiting by appt.
Taunton, Somerset.
Post Office Telecommunications Museum.
GREATER LONDON
Greenwich.
Flamstead House, former Royal Observatory, established 1675. Major coll. of astronomical instruments, incl. quadrants & telescopes.
National Maritime Museum has Department of Astronomy.
Harrow.
Kodak Museum: history of photography; audio-visual display.
Kensington.
Science Museum. Wide-ranging coll. of working models & apparatus of scientific research. George III's coll. of items relating to study of physics. Applied science covered in great detail. Incl. *Wellcome Institute of the History of Medicine*.
West End.
Planetarium, Marylebone Rd. Displays on astronomy & astronomers. Domed auditorium with dramatic audio-visual shows on many aspects of universe.
Royal Institution, Albemarle St. Davy-Faraday Research Laboratory commemorates 2 distinguished scientists. Faraday's laboratory of 1845, restored. Adjacent museum has original apparatus used in major discoveries.
THE THAMES, CHILTERNS & EAST ANGLIA
Cambridge, Cambs.
Whipple Museum of the History of Science: coll. of precision scientific instruments (16th, 17th & 18th C.).
Oxford, Oxon.
Museum of the History of Science. Early scientific apparatus, notably astrolabes & early microscopes. Early X-ray apparatus.
CENTRAL ENGLAND
Birmingham, W. Midlands.
Dolland & Aitchison Museum has optical instruments. *Museum of Science & Industry* has model atomic reactor, early motors & electrical apparatus.
Leicester, Leics.
Leics. Museum of Science & Technology. Coll. incl. optical instruments.
Warley, W. Midlands.
Avery Historical Museum: machines, weights & other items relating to history of weighing.
YORKSHIRE, HUMBERSIDE & THE NORTH-WEST
Bradford, W. Yorks.
Colour Museum of the Society of Dyers & Colourists. Exhibits relating to development of colouring & dying technology.
Manchester, Gr Manchester
North Western Museum of Science & Industry. Scientific equipment, esp. optical instruments. Exhibits relating to thermodynamics and to John Dalton's work on atomic theory.
Whitby, N. Yorks.
Museum has equipment used in magnetism experiments.
York, N. Yorks.
Castle Museum has small coll. of scientific instruments & display on horology.
THE NORTH OF ENGLAND
Newcastle upon Tyne, Tyne & Wear
Museum of Science & Engineering.
Rothbury, Northumb.
At *Cragside*: coll. of scientific apparatus. First house ever to be lit by water-generated electricity.
WALES
Machynlleth, Powys.
Centre for Alternative Technology. Experiments in solar, wind & water power.
CENTRAL SCOTLAND & STRATHCLYDE
Edinburgh, Lothian.
Royal Scottish Museum. Playfair Collection of rare 18th-C. chemical glassware. Franks Collection of microscopes. Science gallery covers astronomy, electricity & horology.
Royal College of Surgeons Museum may be seen by appt.
NORTHERN SCOTLAND & THE ISLANDS
Thurso, Highland.
Dounreay Exhibition & Observation Room at England's first fast breeder reactor. Guided tours available.

SPAS & SEASIDE RESORTS

THE WEST COUNTRY
Bath, Avon.
Ancient resort based on hot springs. *Roman Baths.* Outstanding Georgian spa buildings incl. *Pump Room* (1799) & *Assembly Rooms* (1771). Magnificent 18th-C. terraces. *Royal Crescent* (1769) is a masterpiece by John Wood the Younger. No. 1 has been restored & furnished in Georgian style. Elegant neoclassical *Circus* nearby.
Bournemouth, Dorset.
Popular holiday resort since *c.* 1810. *Winter Gardens* built 1875, *Pavilion* 1929. Fragrant pinewoods. Sandy shores, fine *pier.*

Exmouth, Devon.
18th-C. resort. Town houses incl. those in the *Beacon* (18th-C. street), & *A La Ronde*, a curious circular house.
Falmouth, Cornwall.
Yachting & bathing resort. Old town has part of Tudor mansion in *Arwennack House*, Grove Place.
Looe, Cornwall.
Twin resorts, East & West Looe, beside R. Looe. East Looe has *Old Guildhall*, West Looe has *Jolly Sailor Inn* (both 16th C.).
Lyme Regis, Dorset.
Popular seaside resort with celebrated curved breakwater, the *Cobb*, where Duke of Monmouth landed in 1685.
Paignton, Devon.
19th-C. resort with fine sands. Some splendid houses, incl. *Oldway Mansion.*
St Ives, Cornwall.
Old fishing town with picturesque harbour & sandy beach, now a popular resort & haunt of artists.
Penzance, Cornwall.
Capital of 'Cornish Riviera'.
Torquay, Devon.
Popular holiday resort since time of Napoleonic Wars. Elegant houses, palm trees encircling bay.
Weston-Super-Mare, Avon.
Victorian resort around old fishing village. *Grand Pier, Winter Gardens* & *Pavilion.* Woodspring Museum has relics of Victorian seaside life.
Weymouth, Dorset.
Sedate resort town where George III bathed. Esplanade, pleasure *pier*, Regency & Victorian houses.
SOUTH-EAST ENGLAND
Bognor Regis, W. Sussex.
Became popular as resort in 1790s. *Hotham House*, where visiting royalty stayed, is 18th-C. *Pier*, esplanade.
Brighton, E. Sussex.
Popular seaside resort, formerly a fishing village. 17th-C. fishermans' cottages in the *Lanes.* Regency streets & squares (notably Regency Sq.). Old Chain Pier, first of its kind, collapsed in 1896. *West Pier* (1866), now closed, may be restored. *Palace Pier* offers amusements. *Royal Pavilion*: seaside palace of George IV rebuilt by Nash from 1816 in magnificent oriental style. Extravagant chinoiserie interior.
Broadstairs, Kent.
Fashionable Regency & Victorian watering place, miles of sand. *Bleak House* is a Dickens museum.
Cowes, Isle of Wight.
Port & great yachting centre, notable as packet station in days of sailing ships.
Eastbourne, E. Sussex.
Popular resort retaining some of its 19th-C. elegance. Beautifully situated beside *Beachy Head.*
Hastings, E. Sussex.
Former medieval port, now a seaside resort with 2-tier promenade above shingle beach. East end of town has old houses & tall net storage sheds.
Herne Bay, Kent.
Esplanade of 1830. Pier wrecked by storm in 1978.
Hove, E. Sussex.
Seaside resort developed in Regency period. Bow-fronted terraced houses, notably in *Brunswick Sq.*
Margate, Kent.
Popular resort for London day-trippers, developed from 1750s.
Ramsgate, Kent.
Largely Victorian seaside resort, but Queen's Court is 17th-C. mansion. 2 piers curve round Royal Harbour.
Southampton, Hants.
Royal Pier opened 1833, originally had concert hall & horse-drawn tramway. *Wool House* (14th C.) testifies to medieval export trade.
Tunbridge Wells, Kent.
Health-giving waters discovered 1606. Colonnaded street, the *Pantiles*, laid out 1638. Spa designated 'Royal' by Edward VII.
Worthing, W. Sussex.
Resort developed after visit by George III's daughter, 1798. Fine gardens, *pier.*
THE THAMES, CHILTERNS & EAST ANGLIA
Great Yarmouth, Norfolk.
Main resort on Norfolk coast, fine sandy beaches. 2 piers. Fine old houses in the *Rows* district, behind South Quay.
Hunstanton, Norfolk.
Sandy beaches, large Victorian turreted houses. Old village has 15th-C. moated hall.
Lowestoft, Suffolk.
Major seaside resort with fishing harbour. Sandy beaches. Old town has lovely cobbled lanes (the *Scores*).
Southend-on-Sea, Essex.
Holiday resort, formed of an amalgamation of villages on the Thames estuary. *Pier* is $1\frac{1}{3}$ m. long.
CENTRAL ENGLAND
Bakewell, Derbys.
Warm springs known to Romans. *Bath House* of 1697.
Buxton, Derbys.
Warm mineral waters known to Romans. Fine *crescent* (1779-84) by John Carr. Natural Warm Baths, St Ann's Well.
Cheltenham, Glos.
Medicinal spring discovered in early 18th C. Duke of Wellington benefited from waters in 1816. Regency features incl. *Pittville Pump Room* (1825-30), statue-lined *Montpellier Walk*, & *Rotunda.*
Leamington Spa, Warks.
First bath opened 1786, but main period of fame began *c.* 1840. *Royal Pump Room & Baths.* Fine Georgian, Regency & Victorian houses on north bank of R. Leam.
Malvern, Heref. & Worcs.
Great Malvern was famous Victorian spa, at its height *c.* 1840–70. Large 19th-C. hotels.
Matlock Bath, Derbys.
Famous Victorian spa in fine setting. Pavilion is now an entertainments centre. Petrifying wells.
YORKSHIRE, HUMBERSIDE & THE NORTH-WEST
Blackpool, Lancs.
Has been a popular holiday resort for 200 years. Famous *tower* built 1891–94, in imitation of Eiffel Tower, Paris. 3 *piers*, theatre, Winter Gardens, Opera House, *Golden Mile* with electric trams. Illuminations (Sept.–Oct.).
Harrogate, N. Yorks.
Victorian spa par excellence, but well known for waters since 16th C. *Royal Baths* open 1897–1969. Magnificent Victorian hotels. Fine gardens.
Morecambe, Lancs.
Large seaside resort, spectacular coastline. Funfairs, arcades, theatres. Promenade illuminated Aug.–Oct.
Scarborough, N. Yorks.
Famous seaside spa town since 1649. Old Town has splendid Georgian houses. Monumental Victorian hotels.
Whitby, N. Yorks.
Picturesque red-tiled fishing port & Victorian resort.
WALES
Aberystwyth, Dyfed.
Leading seaside resort of west Wales. Stone pier, fine promenade, Victorian villas.
Llandrindod Wells, Powys.
Spa with fine avenues of 19th-C. buildings. *Spa Baths, Pump Room* & *Pavilion.*
Tenby, Dyfed.
Town has harbour for yachts & good beaches. Also Georgian houses & medieval town walls.
SOUTHERN SCOTLAND
Moffat, Dumf. & Gall.
Former spa town with gardened villas, bath house (1827) & *Pump Room.*
CENTRAL SCOTLAND & STRATHCLYDE
Bridge of Allan, Central.
Early 19th-C. spa resort, close to mineral springs at Airthrey.
NORTHERN SCOTLAND & THE ISLANDS
Strathpeffer, Highland.
Popular 19th-C. spa. *Pump Room* (1909) & Edwardian *Pavilion.*

SPORTING HISTORY

SOUTH-EAST ENGLAND
Hambledon, Hants.
Village famous for cricket club, whose heyday was 1760–90. Ground was on *Broadhalfpenny Common*, opposite Bat & Ball Inn.

GREATER LONDON
Hampton Court Palace, nr Richmond.
Tudor 'real' *tennis court*, rebuilt by William III. Still used.
North London.
Famous *Lord's* cricket ground (St John's Wood) has Cricket Memorial Gallery with display on all aspects of cricket history.
South London.
Wimbledon Lawn Tennis Museum: display on tennis & its antecedants.
CENTRAL ENGLAND
Castle Donington, Derbys.
Donington Collection is world's largest coll. of Grand Prix racing cars. Traces history of motor sport
YORKSHIRE, HUMBERSIDE & THE NORTH-WEST
York, N. Yorks.
Castle Museum has small coll. of sporting items, incl. equipment for 'knur & spell' (ball game) & sporting guns.
CENTRAL SCOTLAND & STRATHCLYDE
Falkland Palace, Fife.
Renaissance-style palace has *Royal Tennis Court* of 1539, still used.

STEAM ENGINES

See also: 'The industrial past' (p 314).

THE WEST COUNTRY
Crofton, nr Marlborough, Wilts.
Pumping station with 1812 beam engine still pumping water from Kennet & Avon Canal. Also: beam engine of 1845.
Dartmouth, Devon.
Newcomen Engine House, contains original Newcomen atmospheric engine (*c.* 1725). Still in working order.
Pool, nr Camborne, Cornwall.
Cornish *winding engine* (1887) & *pumping engine* (1892), both standing complete, in stone engine house.
SOUTH-EAST ENGLAND
Hollycombe, W. Sussex.
Working *steam museum*, with steam fairground, agricultural machinery, etc.
Hove, E. Sussex.
Brighton & Hove Engineerium has 1876 Eastons & Anderson beam pumping engine, & many other steam relics.
Portsmouth, Hants.
Eastney pumping station has restored engines of 1887.
GREATER LONDON
Brentford.
Kew Bridge Engines & Water Supply Museum (north of Kew Bridge) has 2 giant beam engines under steam, as well as rotative engines.
Kensington.
Science Museum has several beam engines of 1777–1810, as well as atmospheric engines.
Wandsworth, S. London.
Ram Brewery still uses 2 beam engines of 1835 & 1867.
THE THAMES, CHILTERNS & EAST ANGLIA
Bressingham, Norfolk.
Steam Museum has steam roundabouts & organs, as well as locos.
Holkham Park, Wells-next-the-Sea, Norfolk.
Steam engines at '*Bygones at Holkham*'.
Thursford, nr Fakenham, Norfolk.
Thursford Collection: many steam engines, incl. traction engines, agricultural engines, etc.
CENTRAL ENGLAND
Birmingham, W. Midlands.
Museum of Science & Technology has numerous steam engines.
Hereford, Heref. & Worcs.
Triple-expansion steam engine in *Waterworks Museum.*
Leicester, Leics.
Museum of Technology based on Abbey Pumping Station, with 4 massive beam engines of 1891 (one restored).
Middleton-by-Wirksworth, Derbys.
Middleton Top Engine House: restored

steam engine, originally used for hauling wagons up slope.

Papplewick, Notts.
Pumping station opened 1884, elaborate décor. Pair of handsome beam engines, occasionally steamed.

YORKSHIRE, HUMBERSIDE & THE NORTH-WEST

Gisburn, Lancs.
Todber Museum of Steam has showmen's engines, fairground organ, rare steam wagons.

THE NORTH OF ENGLAND

Kendal, Cumbria.
Levens Hall Steam Collection: working model steam engines; full-size engines regularly in steam.

Newton, nr Stocksfield, Northumb.
Hunday National Tractor & Farm Museum has stationary engines.

Ryhope, Tyne & Wear.
Pumping station (1868) has 2 beam engines in working order.

Shaw, Lancs.
Horizontal mill engine (1907) at *Dee Mill*, operated occasionally.

TEXTILES & COSTUME

See also: 'The industrial past' (p 314).

THE WEST COUNTRY

Bath, Avon.
Museum of Costume (Assembly Rooms): fashion from 17th C. onwards.

Honiton, Devon.
Allhallows Museum has Honiton lace display.

Totnes, Devon.
Devonshire Collection of Period Costume.

SOUTH-EAST ENGLAND

Bexhill, E. Sussex.
Bexhill Manor Costume Museum.

Canterbury, Kent.
Old Weavers' House: weaving demonstrations.

Whitchurch, Hants.
Silk mill (1815). Visitors may see weaving.

GREATER LONDON

Kensington.
Science Museum has textile machinery, incl. Arkwright's water frame. *Victoria & Albert Museum* has fine costume coll.

THE THAMES, CHILTERNS & EAST ANGLIA

Chipping Norton, Oxon.
Bliss Tweed Mill (built 1872). Modern tweed-making viewable by appt.

Lavenham, Suffolk.
Guildhall (1529), first used as centre of wool trade, contains weaving exhibition.

CENTRAL ENGLAND

Calverton, Notts.
Museum of frame knitting.

Hereford, Heref. & Worcs.
Churchill Gardens Museum has extensive costume coll.

Leicester, Leics.
Museum of Technology has knitting gallery. Also in Leicester: *Wygston's House*, a museum of costume (1769–1924).

Northampton, Northants.
Central Museum has footwear coll.

Nottingham, Notts.
Museum of Costumes & Textiles incl. lace room. *Wollaton Hall Industrial Museum* has lace & hosiery machinery.

YORKSHIRE, HUMBERSIDE & THE NORTH-WEST

Blackburn, Lancs.
Lewis Textile Museum: inventions by Kay, Hargreaves, Arkwright, Crompton, displayed in action.

Bolton, Gr Manchester.
Hall-i'-th'-Wood Museum, in Samuel Crompton's house; Crompton relics. Also at Bolton: *Tonge Moor Textile Machine Museum.*

Bradford, W. Yorks.
Relics of woollen & worsted industry in *Industrial Museum.*

Burnley, Lancs.
Canal Toll House & The Weavers' Triangle: textile heritage displays.

Castle Howard, N. Yorks.
Coll. of period costume (18th–20th C.).

Halifax, W. Yorks.
Piece Hall (18th-C. wool trading centre) contains industrial & textile museum.

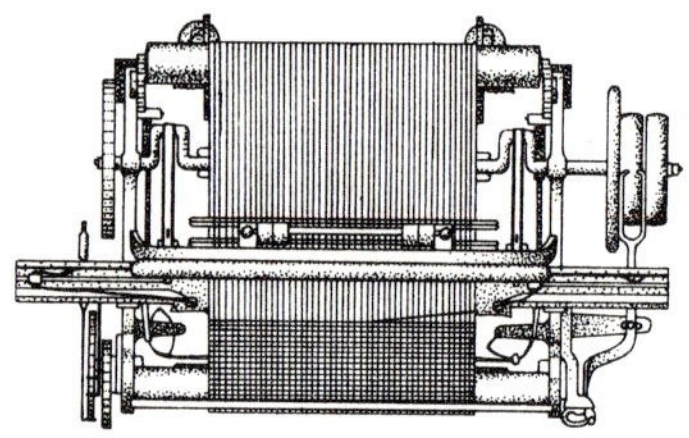

Helmshore, Lancs.
Higher Hill Museum: fulling mill (1789) with waterwheel. Early textile machinery.

Manchester, Gr Manchester.
Gallery of English Costume (Platt Hall), extensive coll. *North-Western Museum of Science & Industry* covers cotton spinning, weaving, dyeing.

Styal, Cheshire.
Quarry Bank Mill: large working museum of cotton industry.

WALES

Ambleston, Haverfordwest, Dyfed.
Wallis Mill (founded *c.* 1800) has 6 looms still in use.

Cynwyl Elfed, nr Carmarthen, Dyfed.
Cwmduad Mill has small working museum.

Dre-fach Felindre, nr Llandyssul, Dyfed.
Museum of the Woollen Industry, occupying part of working mill (founded *c.* 1840).

Maesllyn, nr Llandyssul, Dyfed.
Maesllyn Mill Museum has late 19th-C. machinery still operational.

Newton, Powys.
Textile Museum. Former weaving workshop housing mill machinery.

Penmachno, nr Betws-y-coed, Gwynedd.
Historic *woollen mill*, still operational.

St Fagans, nr Cardiff, S. Glam.
Reconstructed woollen mill in *Welsh Folk Museum.*

Swansea, W. Glam.
Maritime & Industrial Museum has complete working woollen mill.

Tanygrisiau, nr Blaenau Ffestiniog, Gwynedd.
Moelwyn Mill, restored 18th-C. fulling mill.

Trefriw, nr Llanrwst, Gwynedd.
Woollen mill founded 1859. All processes can be seen.

SOUTHERN SCOTLAND

New Abbey, Dumf. & Gall.
Shambellie House has costume museum.

Walkerburn, Borders.
Scottish Museum of Woollen Textiles illustrates history of industry.

CENTRAL SCOTLAND & STRATHCLYDE

Clydebank, Strathclyde.
Clydebank District Museum has coll. of over 500 sewing machines.

Edinburgh, Lothian.
Canongate Tolbooth: Highland dress & tartans.

Kilbarchan, Strathclyde.
Weaving exhibition in 18th-C. craftsman's cottage.

Paisley, Strathclyde.
Paisley Museum: vast shawl exhibition & looms.

NORTHERN SCOTLAND & THE ISLANDS

Comrie, Tayside.
Museum of Scottish Tartans, incl. 18th-C. Highland weaving shed.

THEATRES & CONCERT HALLS

THE WEST COUNTRY

Bristol, Avon.
Theatre Royal: Britain's oldest working theatre, opened 1766.

SOUTH-EAST ENGLAND

Brighton, E. Sussex.
Theatre Royal, established 1807.

Chichester, W. Sussex.
Festival Theatre (1962). Hexagonal design, fine interior.

Glyndebourne, nr Lewes, W. Sussex.
Venue for famous summer opera season.

Margate, Kent.
Theatre Royal, founded 1784, redesigned from 1874 by J.T. Robinson. Now a bingo hall.

Portsmouth, Hants.
Theatre Royal: grand but intimate theatre by C.J. Phipps & Frank Matcham (1884 & 1900). Auditorium preserved.

GREATER LONDON

City.
Barbican Arts Centre contains fine theatre opened 1982. London home of Royal Shakespeare Company.

Islington.
Saddler's Wells, Rosebery Ave. Modern theatre (1931) on site of 17th-C. 'musick house'.

Kensington.
Royal Albert Hall: vast circular concert hall, completed 1871. Famous for Promenade concerts.

South London.
Bear Gardens Museum, Southwark: replica of Elizabethan playhouse, used for performances. Close to site of Shakespearian Globe Theatre.
Grand Theatre, Clapham, is Britain's only remaining chinoiserie-style theatre, dating from 1900. Now a bingo hall.
National Theatre has 3 auditoria (Olivier, Lyttelton & Cottesloe) within impressive concrete complex by Sir Denys Lasdun (1970). Daily tours. Nearby *Royal Festival Hall* (1965) has superb auditorium seating 3,000.
Old Vic, Waterloo Rd. Former Victorian bawdy house renovated by Lilian Baylis. Under restoration.

West End.
(*See* map on p 303.)
Albery Theatre, St Martin's Lane. Unaltered Edwardian theatre, elegant Louis XVI-style décor.
Aldwych Theatre, Aldwych, Royal Shakespeare Company's former home. Georgian-style structure of 1905.
Apollo, Shaftesbury Ave. Built 1901, ornate French Renaissance interior.
Coliseum, St Martin's Lane. Neo-Baroque theatre by Frank Matcham, opened 1904. Home of English National Opera since 1968.
Criterion, Piccadilly Circus, has enchanting underground auditorium (opened 1874). Original Victorian tile work & other wall decorations.
Drury Lane Theatre has longer theatrical tradition than any other theatre in Britain. Opened as Theatre Royal, 1663. Present building 1812.
Her Majesty's, Haymarket. Present theatre commissioned by actor-manager Beerbohm Tree & opened 1897 is 4th on site.
Lyceum, Strand. Victorian theatre (rebuilt 1904). Highly successful under actor-manager Henry Irving & Ellen Terry. Now a ballroom.
Palace, Cambridge Circus. Massive Edwardian theatre of terracotta & brick, fine ornamental design. Former Royal English Opera House.
Playhouse, Charing Cross Rd. 1882 façade with superb Parisian rococo auditorium (1907).
Royal Court, Sloane Sq. Victorian theatre renovated by London Theatre Guild in 1952.
Royal Opera House, Covent Garden. Present theatre (1858) on site of Duke of York, which was granted a royal patent & opened 1732.
Theatre Royal, Haymarket. Handsome building by John Nash (1821), just south of late 18th-C. predecessor. Interior redesigned *c.* 1879.

CENTRAL ENGLAND

Buxton, Derbys.
Opera House, a restored Frank Matcham design (1903).

Nottingham, Notts.
Attractive modern *playhouse.*

Stratford-upon-Avon, Warks.
Shakespeare Memorial Theatre was replaced by present *Royal Shakespeare Theatre* in 1932. Picture Gallery & Museum, with costumes, & portraits of famous players.

YORKSHIRE, HUMBERSIDE & THE NORTH-WEST

Blackpool, Lancs.
Grand Theatre, by Frank Matcham, 1894. Ornate interior.

Leeds, W. Yorks.
City Varieties Music Hall, 1850: one of last remaining music halls still used as such.

Manchester, Gr Manchester.
Free Trade Hall (1856, rebuilt 1951) is home of famous Hallé concerts.
Hulme Hippodrome (now a bingo hall) was one of Britain's most sumptuous music halls.
Royal Exchange Theatre (opened 1976) has highly original design, encased by former cotton exchange.

Liverpool, Merseyside.
Olympia: rare example of circus/variety house, by Frank Matcham, 1905. Now a bingo hall.

Richmond, N. Yorks.
Best-preserved *Georgian theatre* in country, 1788.

THE NORTH OF ENGLAND

Middlesbrough, Tyne & Wear.
Empire (1899, now a bingo hall). Terracotta façade, fine interior.

Newcastle upon Tyne, Tyne & Wear.
Tyne Theatre: restored 19th-C. building, with elegant blue & gold auditorium. Working set of Victorian stage machinery.

WALES

Craig-y-nos, Powys.
Adelina Patti's private theatre. Sloping floor of auditorium may be adjusted to make elegant baroque ballroom.

CENTRAL SCOTLAND & STRATHCLYDE

Edinburgh, Lothian.
Royal Lyceum: fine Victorian theatre, extensively renovated.
Traverse Theatre Club (Grassmarket): celebrated experimental theatre, in late 18th-C. building.

Glasgow, Strathclyde.
Citizens' Theatre (Gorbals). Fine Victorian music hall, opened 1878. Now an experimental theatre.
King's Theatre. Huge Edwardian theatre, sensitively modernized.
Theatre Royal: grand Victorian theatre, elegantly restored. Now home of Scottish Opera.

TOWN ARCHITECTURE

See also: 'Spas & seaside resorts' (p 321), 'Schools, universities, colleges & libraries' (p 320), 'Theatres & concert halls' (p 322).

THE WEST COUNTRY
Barnstaple, Devon.
Largely Georgian town centre. *Queen Anne's Walk*, a colonnade of 1796–8.
Blandford Forum, Dorset.
Market town largely rebuilt in Georgian style after 1731. *Town Hall* (1730s) by William Bastard.
Bridgwater, Somerset.
Georgian architecture on Castle St. *Market Hall*, 1834.
Bradford-on-Avon, Wilts.
Jacobean *Clothier's Hall* in Woolley St.
Bristol, Avon.
Red Lodge: 16th C. altered in 19th. Fine 18th-C. civic buildings incl. the *Exchange* (by John Wood of Bath). Interesting streets incl. King St & Christmas Steps (1669). *Georgian House* has 18th-C. fittings & furniture. Victorian *Bank of England*, by Cockerell. Georgian & Regency terraces in suburb of *Clifton*.
Chippenham, Wilts.
Yelde Hall (15th C.).
Dorchester, Dorset.
County town largely rebuilt in 17th & 18th C. Earlier buildings incl. *Hangman's Cottage* (16th C.).
Exeter, Devon.
Guildhall (on present site since 12th C.) may be oldest municipal building in Britain. Georgian streets incl. graceful *Colleton Cres.*
Marlborough, Wilts.
High St has arcaded Georgian shops with tile-hung façades.
St Austell, Cornwall.
Hillside town. Some Georgian buildings. Fine granite *Town & Market Hall*, 1844.
Salisbury, Wilts.
House of John A'Port (15th C.) & *Joiners' Hall* (16th C.). Fine houses in Cathedral Close incl. *Mompesson House* (1701), with exquisite interior decoration. *Poultry Cross* is 15th-C.
Swindon, Wilts.
Great 19th-C. railway town, mainly built by the Great Western Railway.
Truro, Cornwall.
18th-C. buildings incl. *Assembly Rooms.*
Wells, Somerset.
Well-preserved medieval street.

SOUTH-EAST ENGLAND
Arundel, W. Sussex.
Mainly Victorian, but with numerous 18th-C. houses.
Canterbury, Kent.
Old Weavers' House (1507).
Chichester, W. Sussex.
Town centre has fine Georgian houses, especially in *North St.* Ornate market cross (1501, with cupola of 1724).
Godalming, Surrey.
Historic *High St* (16th–18th C.). Octagonal *Market Hall* of 1814.
Guildford, Surrey.
Abbot's Hospital, built as almshouse, 1619. Georgian High St. *Guildhall* (17th-C. façade, Tudor core).
Rochester, Kent.
Royal Victoria & Bull Hotel (16th C.), *Corn Exchange* (1706), *Guildhall* (1687).
Rye, E. Sussex.
Many Elizabethan buildings, some with Georgian frontages.
Tonbridge, Kent.
Chequers Inn (16th C.), *House of the Portreeve* (15th C.)

GREATER LONDON
(*See* maps on pp 242–51.)
Bloomsbury.
Bedford Sq., Bloomsbury (*c.* 1776): best preserved of late 18th-C. squares. *British Museum* by Robert Smirke, 1820s; neo-classical colonnade built in 1840s.
Chelsea.
Crosby Hall, 15th C. *Cheyne Walk* has attractive red-brick 18th-C. houses, many with fine wrought-iron railings. *Royal Hospital* by Wren, 1683–92; fine chapel, with oak carvings.
City.
Barbican: vast concrete complex begun 1962, with offices, residential blocks, arts buildings. *Goldsmith's Hall* (1835), with classical exterior. *Guildhall*: exterior owes much to George Dance (late 18th C.). *Mansion House* (1739–53): Palladian-style mayoral residence. *National Westminster Bank* by Richard Seifert, begun 1977, is tallest occupied building in Europe. *Tower of London*: *see* 'Castles & forts' (p 306).
Hampstead.
Church Row (18th-C. red-brick houses). *Fenton House* (brick mansion of 1693, with Regency loggia). *Hampstead Garden Suburb*, fine early 20th-C. villas.
Holborn.
Staple Inn, with timbered façade of 1586.
Kensington.
Kensington Palace. Residence of William III & Mary, built 1605, enlarged by Wren. Magnificent interior, wood carvings, painted ceilings. State apartments open to public.
Natural History Museum, neo-Romanesque, by Alfred Waterhouse, 1873–80. *Royal Albert Hall* (1867–70), inspired by Roman architecture in Provence. *Albert Memorial* nearby.
St James's.
Buckingham Palace, a royal residence since 1837. Old palace by Nash (1762) much enlarged. *Marlborough House* begun 1709–11, additions by Sir William Chambers. *Pall Mall* has fine buildings by Sir Charles Barry – Travellers' Club (1829–32) & Reform Club (1837–41). *St James's Palace.* Official Royal residence 1698–1837. Tudor architecture.
South London.
Greenwich has a rich architectural heritage: Royal Navy College (Greenwich Hospital) by Wren (begun 1696), with superb painted baroque ceiling (1708–27) by Thornhill in Painted Hall; Queen's House by Inigo Jones (completed 1635), marking introduction of Palladian style to England. *South Bank arts complex* incl. Royal Festival Hall (completed 1965) & Denys Lasdun's National Theatre in rough-textured concrete.
West End.
Covent Garden shopping complex by Denys Lasdun (1981) incorporates old market hall. *Home House* (no.20), Portman Sq., by Robert Adam, 1770s. Imposing domed oval stairwell. *Piccadilly* has Ritz Hotel (1904–06) & Burlington Arcade (1818). At Hyde Park Corner end is Apsley House, built 1771–8 by Robert Adam; now Wellington Museum. *Regent's Park* & surrounding terraces (incl. Cumberland Terrace) by John Nash, from 1811. *Regent St*: handsome curved boulevard designed by John Nash but largely rebuilt. Architectural highlight of *Regent's Park Zoo* is Berthold Lubetkin's Penguin Pool (1933–5). *Royal Courts of Justice* (Strand), built 1870s by G.E. Street in neo-Gothic style. *Somerset House*, a monumental classical design by Sir William Chambers, 1776–86.
Western suburbs.
Hoover Building, Perivale, on Great West Rd: superb example of Art Deco factory architecture (1932–3).
Westminster.
Banqueting House, Whitehall. Superb Palladian structure by Inigo Jones, 1625; fine Rubens ceiling paintings. Also in Whitehall: William Kent's Horse Guards (1749–59).
Houses of Parliament by Sir Charles Barry in neo-Gothic idiom (1840–50). *Westminster Hall*, built by William I, embellished by William II. Fine hammerbeam roof.

THE THAMES, CHILTERNS & EAST ANGLIA
Abingdon, Berks.
Handsome Renaissance-style *Town Hall*, 1677–80.
Aldeburgh, Suffolk.
Timber-framed *moot hall*, 15th C.
Aylesbury, Bucks.
King's Head (14th C.) has medieval gateway. *Church St* has 17th- & 18th-C. houses. *Prebendal House* (18th C.) was home of MP John Wilkes. *County Hall* (in main square) dates from 1720.
Bury St Edmunds, Suffolk
Moyses Hall (Jew's House) is 12th-C. *Assembly Hall* of 18th C.
Cambridge, Cambs.
Fitzwilliam Museum (1834–45) deploys theme of extended portico. See also 'Schools, universities, colleges & libraries' (p 320).
Chelmsford, Essex.
County town with 18th-C. neoclassical *Shire Hall.*
Colchester, Essex.
'Dutch Quarter' in Stockwell St has houses older than 16th C. *Holly Trees Museum* housed in impressive early 18th-C. house, *Town Hall* of 1902.
Henley-on-Thames, Oxon.
Listed buildings incl. 17th-C. *Speaker's House.* Many Georgian dwellings.
Ipswich, Suffolk.
Ancient House: 15th C., with ornate plasterwork.
King's Lynn, Norfolk.
Guildhall, 1421. *Custom House*, 1683.
Letchworth, Herts.
Britain's first garden city, planned 1903, by Ebenezer Howard.
Norwich, Norfolk.
Strangers' Hall (Charing Cross): earliest parts date to 1320.
Oxford, Oxon.
Semi-circular *Sheldonian Theatre* by Wren, 1669. *Taylorian Insitute* (part of Ashmolean Museum) is a masterpiece by C.R. Cockerell, 1839–45. *See also* 'Schools, universities, colleges & libraries' (p 320).
Peterborough, Cambs.
Precious nucleus of historic buildings, incl. *Butter Cross* (Guildhall), 1671.
St Albans, Herts.
French Row is a medieval street, *Hollywell Hill* a fine Georgian Street. *Pemberton Almshouses*, 1627. *Marlborough Almshouses*, 1736.
Thetford, Norfolk.
Ancient House, 15th C.
Welwyn Garden City, Herts.
Garden city founded by Ebenezer Howard, 1920.
Windsor, Berks.
17th-C. *Guildhall* (by Wren) is now a museum. Many 17th- & 18th-C. buildings in area between Castle Hill & Church Lane. Regency architecture in Adelaide Sq., Victorian in Queen's Terrace.
Wisbech, Cambs.
North Brink & *South Brink*, flanking R. Nene, are fine Georgian streets.
Wymondham, Norfolk.
Market Cross: timbered building of 1616.

CENTRAL ENGLAND
Bimingham, W. Midlands.
Blakesley Hall, Yardley: 16th-C. yeoman's house. *Town Hall* (1834) by Joseph Hansom based on Roman temple. Southern suburb of *Bournville* founded 1879 for Cadbury cocoa workers.
Boston, Lincs.
15th-C. *Guildhall* (now Borough Museum).
Bridgnorth, Salop.
Market town with 17th-C. *Town Hall.* Also: *Bishop Percy's House*, 1580.
Bromsgrove, Heref. & Worcs.
Avoncroft Museum of Buildings has 15th-C. merchant's house.
Chipping Campden, Glos.
Arcaded stone *Market Hall*, 1627.
Cirencester, Glos.
Delightful marketplace has Victorian *Corn Hall*, & inn (King's Head) with 18th-C. frontage.
Gainsborough, Lincs.
Old Hall, late 15th C.
Hereford, Heref. & Worcs.
Jacobean *Old House*, containing Museum.

Ledbury, Heref. & Worcs.
Splendid 17th-C. *Market Hall* & 16th-C. *Feathers Inn.*
Leicester, Leics.
14th-C. *Guildhall.* Georgian houses in Friar Lane & New St. *New Walk* laid out late 18th C.
Lincoln, Lincs.
Castle Sq. has fine 16th-C. merchant's

house. *Aaron the Jew's House* was built at end of 12th C.
Lichfield, Staffs.
Well-preserved medieval, Tudor & Elizabethan houses nr Cathedral.
Loughborough, Leics.
Old Rectory, 13th & 14th C. Victorian *Town Hall*, impressively Italianate.
Ludlow, Salop.
Butter Cross (1743), by William Baker, houses museum. On Broad St, Georgian brick architecture jostles with Tudor half-timbered. *Feathers Inn*, 1603.
Nottingham, Notts.
Ye Olde Trip to Jerusalem: oldest inn in England (12th C.). Spacious market square with classical *Council House* (1928). Many Victorian buildings.
Shrewsbury, Salop.
15th-C. *Henry Tudor House*. Superb Tudor houses on *Butcher Row*.
Stafford, Staffs.
Many-gabled *High House*, 16th–17th C.
Stamford, Lincs.
Elegant 17th- & 18th-C. buildings in local grey stone. *Browne's Hospital* is 15th-C.
Stourport-on-Severn, Heref. & Worcs.
The 'Venice of the Midlands'. Attractive canal town, several fine red-brick Georgian houses.
Stratford-upon-Avon, Warks.
Guildhall & *Nash's House*.
Warwick, Warks.
Tudor buildings incl. *Oken's House*. *Market Hall*, 1670. Pleasing 18th-C. buildings in *Northgate St*.
Worcester, Heref. & Worcs.
Tudor House, now a folk museum. *Guildhall* (1721), by Thomas White, a pupil of Wren.

YORKSHIRE, HUMBERSIDE & THE NORTH-WEST
Bradford, W. Yorks.
Bolling Hall: rooms from 14th C. & after, furnished in appropriate styles. Grandiose *City Hall* (1873) in neo-Gothic idiom. *St George's Hall* (1851) also imposing.
Chester, Cheshire.
The *Rows*, with shops opening on to balustraded walkways, date from 14th C. Medieval city walls.
Crewe, Cheshire.
Earliest of great railway towns, expanded rapidly after 1837.
Doncaster, S. Yorks.
Mansion House, 1745–8, only extant public building by James Paine.
Halifax, W. Yorks.
Piece Hall, rebuilt 1770s, a centre for wool traders. *Halifax Building Society's* headquarters is glass-and-concrete block, opened 1974. Iron & glass *Borough Market* (1895). Nearby: *Shibden Hall* (15th C.).
Huddersfield, W. Yorks.
Victorian neo-Gothic buildings incl. *Market Hall* (1870) & *Clock Tower* (1902).
Lancaster, Lancs.
Fine Georgian houses. *Old Custom House* (1764), splendid *Shire Hall* (1796). Domed *Ashton Memorial* (1909), the 'Taj Mahal of the North'.
Leeds, W. Yorks.
Disturbingly proportioned, domed *Town Hall* by Cuthbert Brodrick, opened 1858. Same architect designed *Corn Exchange* (1861) & *Mechanics' Institute* (1865).
Liverpool, Merseyside.
Wellington Inn, 14th C. *Town Hall* (completed 1754) designed by John Wood of Bath. *St George's Hall* (1840s) is one of Britain's most grandiose 19th-C. classical buildings. *Royal Liver Building* (1910) on R. Mersey has twin towers topped by famous 'Liver' birds.
Kingston upon Hull, Humber.
Historic buildings incl. *White Harte Inn* & 18th-C. *Trinity House*.
Manchester, Gr Manchester.
Gothic *Town Hall* by Alfred Waterhouse, begun 1868, faces Albert Sq.; statues of famous Mancunians inside. Circular *Central Library* opened 1834. *Free Trade Hall* built 1843. Also: Victorian *Barton Arcade* & *Royal Exchange*. (*See* map on p 252.)
Nantwich, Cheshire.
Elizabethan houses.
Port Sunlight, Merseyside.
Model town for Lord Lever's soapworks employees, founded 1888.
Richmond, N. Yorks.
Market town, several pleasant Georgian houses. 18th-C. obelisk in square.
Ripon, N. Yorks.
Wakeman's House, 14th C.
Saltaire, nr Bradford, W. Yorks.
Manufacturing town founded by Sir Titus Salt, 1849.
Sheffield, S. Yorks.
Well-designed modern centre, with some historic buildings (e.g. *Cutler's Hall* of 1832). *Paradise Sq.* retains its Georgian elegance. *Town Hall* (opened 1897) has tower surmounted by Vulcan, the divine blacksmith.
York, N. Yorks.
Famous for medieval streets (*Shambles* & *Stonegate*). Merchant Adventurers' Hall (14th C.) has fine timber roof. Also of note are 17th-C. *Treasurer's House*, 18th-C. *Mansion House* & Lord Burlington's Palladian *Assembly Rooms*.

THE NORTH OF ENGLAND
Carlisle, Cumbria.
Old Town Hall is 18th-C. Spacious marketplace has market cross (1682). Georgian houses on *Abbey St*.
Durham, Durham.
Town Hall by P.C. Hardwick, 1851, has hammerbeam roof. 18th-C. suburb of *Elvet* to east. *Courthouse*, 1809–11.
Hexham, Northumb.
Fine 16th- & 17th-C. houses.
Newcastle upon Tyne, Tyne & Wear.
Unusually well-endowed industrial city. *Guildhall* is essentially 17th-C., *Custom House* essentially 18th. Spacious Victorian streets by builder Richard Grainger & architect John Dobson. (*Grey St* is most impressive).

WALES
Brecon, Powys.
Medieval, Tudor & Jacobean architecture in centre.
Cardiff, S. Glam.
Civic centre in Cathays Park, built from 1894, has huge neo-baroque *City Hall* (1905) & stately *Law Courts*.
Conwy, Gwynedd.
Plas Mawr: an Elizabethan town mansion, almost unaltered. Also: Aberconwy, oldest house in Wales (14th C.).

SOUTHERN SCOTLAND
Dumfries, Dumf. & Gall.
Red-sandstone town, Scottish 'Queen of the South'. *Midsteeple* (1707) built as courthouse & prison.
Kelso, Borders.
Stately *Town Hall* in market square. Fine 18th- & 19th-C. houses.
Kirkcudbright, Dumf. & Gall.
Mercat Cross of 1610.

CENTRAL SCOTLAND & STRATHCLYDE
Ayr, Strathclyde.
Loudoun Hall, restored to 16th-C. state. *Town Buildings* (1828) by Thomas Hamilton of Edinburgh.
Edinburgh, Lothian.
Old Town contains *Huntly House* (16th C.), *Gladstone's Land* (1620), a well-preserved multi-storey tenement, & *Lady Stair's House* (17th C.). Also: *John Knox's house* (1490). *Palace of Holyroodhouse* is residence of Queen in Scotland. Building is mainly late 17th-C. Fine state apartments & picture gallery. New Town, a development based on a scheme of 1767 by James Craig, incl. beautiful *Charlotte Sq.* by Robert Adam (planned 1791); no.7 has been furnished in period style. Also by Adam is *Register House*, begun 1774, altered by W.H. Playfair. Playfair, with T. Hamilton, was leading Greek Revival architect in Edinburgh; his best works are *Royal Scottish Academy* (1822), *National Gallery of Scotland* (1850) & *Surgeons' Hall* (begun 1829).
Glasgow, Strathclyde.
Neoclassical buildings include *Royal Exchange* (1775). Centre of city is George Sq. (late 18th C.), flanked by Victorian Renaissance-style *City Chambers*. Polychrome Venetian *carpet factory* (Victorian) adjoins Glasgow Green. C.R. Mackintosh's Art Nouveau *School of Art* (1897–1909) is brilliantly original.
Haddington, Lothian.
Small town of great architectural interest. *Carlyle House* (early 18th C.) & *Town House* (by William Adam, 1748) are notable.
Helensburgh, Strathclyde.
New Town of the 1780s on north bank of R. Clyde. *Hill House* by C.R. Mackintosh.
Inverary, Strathclyde.
Late 18th-C. New Town, with whitewashed architecture. Old *Town House*, 1753.
St Andrews, Fife.
Old Parliament Hall. Early 17th-C. hall, site of Scottish parliament, 1645–6.
Stirling, Central.
Tolbooth is early 18th-C. *Argyll's Ludging* is one of best-preserved 17th-C. Scottish town houses.

NORTHERN SCOTLAND & THE ISLANDS
Aberdeen, Grampian.
'Silver city' of stark granite architecture. *Mercat Cross*, 1686. *Provost Ross's House* (16th C.) in Shiprow.
Crieff, Tayside.
Old Tolbooth, 1665.
Inverness, Highland.
Dour stone architecture. *Abertarff House*, 1590s. Neo-Gothic *Town House* 1878–82.
Perth, Tayside.
'Fair City', predominantly 18th- and 19th-C. buildings.

VILLAGES

THE WEST COUNTRY
Ashmore, nr Shaftesbury, Dorset.
Hilltop village. Duck pond, some Georgian houses.
Blaise Hamlet, Avon.
Picturesque planned village: ornate cottages by *Sir John Nash*, 1809.
Clovelly, Devon.
Attractive coastal village, with steep, stepped, street. Whitewashed cottages.
Dunsford, Devon.
Cottages with low thatched roofs & traditional cob or clay walls.
Dunster, Somerset.
Picturesque village beneath towering castle. *Luttrell Arms Hotel* is 17th-C.
Lacock, Wilts.
Mainly medieval village, with cobbled streets.
Melksham, Wilts.
Former weaving town, prosperous 17th- & 18th-C. houses.
Milton Abbas, Dorset.
18th-C. planned village with thatched cottages around a green, created by *1st Earl of Dorchester*.
Polperro, Cornwall.
Attractive Cornish fishing village, rugged stone cottages.
Shaftesbury, Dorset.
Ancient township with steep cobbled street (*Gold Hill*).
Widecombe in the Moor, Devon.
Moorland village of granite cottages, famous for *historic fair*.

SOUTH-EAST ENGLAND
Amberley, W. Sussex.
Picturesque ensemble of flint-and-brick thatched cottages.
Burwash, E. Sussex.
Attractive ensemble of traditional south-eastern tile-hung houses.
Chiddingstone, Kent.
Tiny manorial village of half-timbered buildings (National Trust).
Rolvenden, Kent.
Typical south-eastern brick & weather-boarded houses.
Wherwell, Hants.
Showpiece village of timbered & thatched cottages.

THE THAMES, CHILTERNS & EAST ANGLIA

Castle Acre, Norfolk.
Flint-and-brick cottages. Village dominated by monastic ruins.
Cavendish, Suffolk.
Regional flint flushwork & thatching. Spacious green.
Clare, Suffolk.
Historic houses with local *pargeting*.
Euston, nr Thetford, Suffolk.
Charming manorial village of whitewashed thatched cottages & flint-and-brick houses.
Finchingfield, Essex.
16th-C. cottages & Georgian houses. Attractive village pond.
Grantchester, Cambs.
Peaceful village of thatched & timbered cottages beside R. Cam. Inspired famous poem by Rupert Brooke.
Great Tew, Oxon.
Landscaped village. Picturesque limestone thatched cottages, some of 16th & 17th C.
Hemingford Grey, Cambs.
Riverside village with ancient moated manor house.
Kersey, Suffolk.
Attractive timber-framed houses & ford.
Lavenham, Suffolk.
Former wool town, outstanding number of timbered houses with *pargeting* & *carving* on exposed woodwork.
Long Melford, Suffolk.
Large village, much visited. Splendid main street of half-timbered houses. Elizabethan *Melford Hall*. Magnificent parish church.
Nuneham Courtenay, Oxon.
Small village of terraced cottages, built by local landowner in mid-18th C.
Old Warden, Beds.
Village rebuilt in 19th C. as model

settlement, with spacious thatched cottages.

Saffron Walden, Essex.
Ancient town with medieval streets, 15th- & 16th-c. timbered houses. Fine pargeting.

CENTRAL ENGLAND

Abbot's Bromley, Staffs.
Former market town. Small 14th-c. *Butter Cross* on green.

Acton Burnell, Salop.
Typical Border country timber-framed cottages, in manorial village.

Bibury, Glos.
Celebrated Cotswold stone village. Delightful group of 17th-c. weavers' cottages (*Arlington Row*).

Bourton-on-the-Water, Glos.
Beautifully preserved ensemble of Cotswold stone on R. Windrush (crossed by 17th-c. stone bridges).

Broadway, Heref. & Worcs.
Exceptionally pretty Cotswold stone houses of 17th c.

Edensor, Derbys.
Picturesque model village of early 19th c., on Chatsworth estate.

Eyam, Derbys.
High moorland settlement, with fine views, some 17th-c. houses.

Hallaton, Leics.
Picturesque village centred on green with cottages of 17th–19th c.

Pembridge, Heref. & Worcs.
Old coaching station with 15th-c. half-timbered inn & several ancient cottages.

Rockingham, Northants.
Thatched & slated terraces of mellow ironstone near former royal castle.

The Slaughters, Glos.
Two villages with lovely Cotswold stone houses: *Upper Slaughter* has Elizabethan manor, *Lower Slaughter* has river along main street.

Stow-on-the-Wold, Glos.
Former wool town with busy market square & picturesque huddled Cotswold houses.

Weobley, Heref. & Worcs.
Timber-framed cottages, some dating from early 1300s. Examples of *cruck-frame* construction.

YORKSHIRE, HUMBERSIDE & THE NORTH-WEST

Aldborough, N. Yorks.
Ancient Celtic settlement, now a village of red-brick cottages with green & maypole.

Almondbury, W. Yorks.
Hamlet of 18th-c. weavers' houses in moorland country.

Hutton-le-Hole, N. Yorks.
Attractive moorland village of grey stone cottages. *Quaker Cottage* is 17th-c.

Prestbury, Cheshire.
Whitewashed brick houses. *Priest's House* has impressive decorative timber-framing, a Cheshire speciality.

THE NORTH OF ENGLAND

Blanchland, Northumb.
Planned 18th-c. village with a square.

Coniston, Cumbria.
Celebrated village, with fine lakeside setting. Characteristic stone buildings.

Grasmere, Cumbria.
Buildings of rough-hewn local stone. *Dove Cottage* belonged to William & Dorothy Wordsworth.

WALES

Butetown, Mid Glam.
Early 19th-c. model village, stone terraces with stone tile roofing.

Llandegai, Gwynedd.
Early 19th-c. model village built by Lord Penrhyn. *Cottages ornés* around medieval parish church.

Llangranog, Dyfed.
Tiny seaside village, 'the Polperro of Wales'.

Portmeirion, Gwynedd.
Extravagant Italian-style village built by Sir Clough Williams-Ellis, 1920s.

CENTRAL SCOTLAND & STRATHCLYDE

Anstruther, Fife.
Large fishing village; stone crow-step gabled cottages in traditional Scottish style.

Dirleton, Lothian.
Fine manorial village with sandstone cottages clustered round a green, dominated by ruins of 13th-c. castle.

Crail, Fife.
Large fishing village, 17th- & 18th-c. crow-step gabled houses, typical of eastern Fife. *Tolbooth* is 16th-c.

Largo, Fife.
Popular coastal village. Typical whitewashed fishermen's cottages, with red-tiled roofs & crow-step gables.

New Lanark, Strathclyde.
Industrial community created by *Robert Owen*, the 19th-c. industrialist.

NORTHERN SCOTLAND & THE ISLANDS

Fochabers, Grampian.
Stately planned village, late 18th c., with fine Georgian buildings.

Grantown, Grampian.
Well-preserved planned village of 1776 with granite houses, now a resort.

Halkirk, nr Thurso, Highland.
Riverside village planned on strict grid basis in late 18th c.

Plockton, Highland.
Summer resort village, rebuilt from 1801. Typical dormer-windowed Highland cottages.

Tomintoul, Grampian.
Highest village in Britain, established in late 18th c.

THE VISUAL ARTS

See also: maps on pp 290 & 293, & 'Country houses' (p 308).

THE WEST COUNTRY

Bristol, Avon.
City Museum & Art Gallery has 15th–17th-c. Italian paintings & Victorian oils. English decorative arts (incl. glass, silver, ceramics).

Plymouth, Devon.
Museum & Art Gallery has portraits by Reynolds.

St Ives, Cornwall.
Barbara Hepworth Museum displays her sculpture in home, studio & workshops.

Truro, Cornwall.
County Museum & Art Gallery (Royal Institution) has fine 17th- & 18th-c. drawings, & decorative arts.

SOUTH-EAST ENGLAND

Bournemouth, Dorset.
Rothesay Museum: Italian ceramics, English porcelain, 17th-c. furniture. *Russell-Cotes Art Gallery & Museum*: paintings (17th–20th c.), oriental coll.

Brighton, E. Sussex.
Royal Pavilion famous for superb chinoiserie of interior, Regency furniture, etc. *Brighton Museum & Art Gallery* contains Willett Collection of English ceramics, Art Nouveau & Art Deco items.

Burghclere, Hants.
War Memorial Chapel has dramatic murals by Stanley Spencer, 1926–34.

Compton, Surrey.
Watts Gallery, devoted to work of G.F. Watts, popular High Victorian painter.

Maidstone, Kent.
Museum & Art Gallery: 17th-c. Dutch & Italian oils.

Southampton, Hants.
Art Gallery has Burne-Jones studies, 20th-c. British paintings.

GREATER LONDON

Bloomsbury.
British Museum: the national coll. of antiquities, prints & drawings. Sutton Hoo treasures, Elgin marbles, superb oriental & Egyptian antiquities. Medieval illuminated mss, incl. Lindisfarne Gospels.

Dulwich.
Dulwich College Picture Gallery has fine Old Masters, incl. Gainsborough, Rubens, Rembrandt, etc.

East End.
Geffrye Museum, Shoreditch: furniture & costumes in period rooms.

Greenwich.
National Maritime Museum (Greenwich Hospital) has world's best coll. of marine paintings. Also: celebrated Painted Hall by Thornhill, *c.* 1708–27.

Kensington.
Leighton House: High Victorian art, incl. paintings (Burne-Jones, Leighton, Millais). *Victoria & Albert Museum*: outstanding wide-ranging coll. Furniture, English & European glass and ceramics, textiles, jewellery, gold & silver, weapons, British miniatures & watercolours, Raphael tapestry cartoons. Huge oriental coll.

North London.
Kenwood House, Iveagh Bequest: English 18th-c. paintings (Gainsborough, Reynolds), Vermeer, Van Dyck, Rembrandt. *William Morris Gallery*, Walthamstow: Pre-Raphaelite paintings, Arts & Crafts furnishings.

Richmond.
Hampton Court Palace has Mantegna's 'Triumphs of Caesar' & works by Van Dyck, Carracci, Lely.

St James's.
Buckingham Palace: Queen's Gallery, paintings from Royal coll.

West End.
Thomas Coram Foundation, Brunswick Square: pictures by Hogarth & contemporaries. *Courtauld Institute Galleries*, Woburn Square. Famous for Impressionist & Post-Impressionist art (Cézanne, Degas, Gauguin, Manet, Seurat, Van Gogh), also Old Masters. *Museum of Mankind*, Burlington Gardens, contains major coll. of tribal art. *National Gallery* has Britain's national coll. of European painting up to 1900, & British painting from Hogarth to Turner (incl. Constables). Botticelli, Claude Lorraine, Van Eyck, Piero della Francesca. Holbein, Leonardo, Poussin, Rembrandt, Rubens. Also: Wilton Diptych (14th c.). *National Portrait Gallery* has fine Elizabethan portraiture, self-portraits by Hogarth & Gainsborough & works by Kneller. *Percival David Foundation of Chinese Art*, Gordon Square. Outstanding Chinese ceramics. *Royal Academy of Arts*: major exhibitions. *Sir John Soane's Museum*, Lincoln's Inn Fields: eccentric coll. of antiquities, & 2 series of paintings by Hogarth. *Wallace Collection*, Manchester Square: French furniture & paintings of 18th c. (Watteau, Boucher, Fragonard), as well as Dutch, Flemish & Spanish 17th-c. paintings. *Wellington Museum, Apsley House*, Hyde Park Corner. Famous for 3 paintings by Velazquez.

Westminster.
Tate Gallery: British painting up to 1900 (Blake, Hogarth, Pre-Raphaelites, Turner) & modern painting & sculpture, British & foreign (Impressionists, Surrealists, abstract & Pop Art). *Whitehall Banqueting House*: Rubens ceiling painting still in situ.

THE THAMES, CHILTERNS & EAST ANGLIA

Bedford, Beds.
Cecil Higgins Art Gallery has outstanding ceramics & glass.

Cambridge, Cambs.
Fitzwilliam Museum has superb paintings, with emphasis on Italian, Dutch, English. Also, ceramics, applied arts, antiquities.

Cookham-on-Thames, Berks.
Stanley Spencer Gallery: coll. of Spencer's work & memorabilia.

Norwich, Norfolk.
Paintings by Norwich School in *Castle Museum*.

Oxford, Oxon.
Ashmolean Museum: Italian Old Masters, fine French canvases of 17th & 18th c., Flemish & Pre-Raphaelite pictures. Decorative arts. Also in Oxford: *Christ Church Picture Gallery* (Italian paintings).

Sudbury, Suffolk.
Gainsborough's House, birthplace of painter. Paintings & furniture.

Windsor Castle, Berks.
Portraits of English kings & queens, outstanding Holbeins, works by Van Dyck, Canaletto. Ceilings by Verrio, Grinling Gibbons carvings.

CENTRAL ENGLAND

Birmingham, W. Midlands.
Barber Institute: 17th-c. paintings of most major schools. *City Museum & Art Gallery*: famous for Pre-Raphaelite paintings. Bellini, Claude & other Europeans also represented.

Cheltenham, Glos.
Art Gallery & Museum has large coll. of English ceramics & furniture.

Derby, Derbys.
Museum & Art Gallery best known for paintings by Joseph Wright of Derby. Also porcelain.

Leicester, Leics.
Museum & Art Gallery has English fine arts, ceramics, silver, & 20th-c. German art. Paintings by Lowry & Stanley Spencer.

Mansfield, Notts.
Museum & Art Gallery. Ceramics.

Nottingham, Notts.
Castle Museum has ceramics, silver, glass, paintings.

Stoke-on-Trent, Staffs.
City Museum & Art Gallery: major coll. of English & foreign ceramics.

YORKSHIRE, HUMBERSIDE & THE NORTH-WEST

Accrington, Lancs.
Haworth Art Gallery has world's finest coll. of Tiffany glass. Also, early English watercolours.

Burnley, Lancs.
Towneley Hall Art Gallery & Museum. Furniture, ivories, glass (18th c.), Chinese ceramics, paintings.

Kingston upon Hull, Humber.
Ferens Art Gallery has Old Masters (esp. Dutch, 17th c.); British portraits & seascapes.

Leeds, W. Yorks.
City Art Gallery: Old Masters, English watercolours, 19th- & 20th-C. British & French paintings, modern sculpture.
Liverpool, Merseyside.
Merseyside County Museums: magnificent coll. of antiquities, Anglo-Saxon jewellery, & decorative arts. *Walker Art Gallery*: notable coll. of European paintings (esp. early Italian & Flemish). Important British paintings incl. Stubbs, Wilson, Constable, Turner, Pre-Raphaelites.
Manchester, Gr Manchester.
City Art Gallery has fine British paintings (17th C. to present), incl. beautiful Pre-Raphaelite works. Also Italian, Flemish, Dutch, French pictures. *Whitworth Art Gallery*: outstanding English watercolours. Modern art, Japanese prints.
Port Sunlight, Merseyside.
Lady Lever Gallery: paintings of 18th & 19th C. Gainsborough, Reynolds. Chinese ceramics, Wedgwood wares, English furniture.
Sheffield, S. Yorks.
City Museum has ceramics, Old Sheffield Plate. *Graves Art Gallery* has good British portraits & watercolours & European painting.
York, N. Yorks.
Art Gallery: fine European & British paintings from 14th C. onwards.

THE NORTH OF ENGLAND

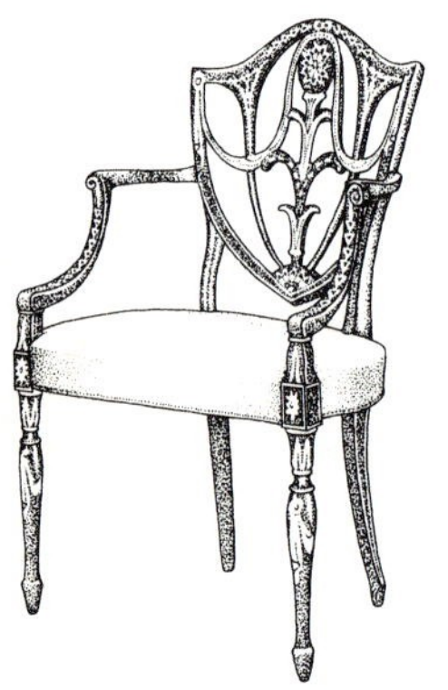

Barnard Castle, Durham.
Bowes Museum has wide-ranging coll. of European arts.
Gateshead, Tyne & Wear.
Shipley Art Gallery: Old Masters.
Newcastle upon Tyne, Tyne & Wear.
Hatton Gallery incl. Old Masters & modern art. *Laing Art Gallery*: British paintings from 17th C., incl. good Pre-Raphaelites.

WALES

Cardiff, S. Glam.
National Museum of Wales, emphasis on 18th- & 20th-C. British schools, esp. Welsh.
Swansea, W. Glam.
Glyn Vivian Art Gallery & Museum: British fine arts, ceramics, glass.

CENTRAL SCOTLAND & STRATHCLYDE

Edinburgh, Lothian.
National Gallery of Scotland. Scottish painting, & 17th–18th-C. English. Raphael, Rubens, Van Eyck, Titian, Poussin, 18th-C. French, Gauguin. Also: *National Portrait Gallery & Royal Scottish Museum*.
Glasgow, Strathclyde.
Art Gallery & Museum is one of richest galleries in Britain. Paintings by Giorgione, Rembrandt, Whistler, Dali, & a superb coll. of French 19th-C. works (Cézanne, Manet, Degas). *Hunterian Art Gallery*: Old Masters (Rembrandt, Chardin), superb Whistlers, works by Mackintosh in reconstruction of his house. *Pollok House*: Spanish paintings, works by William Blake. *Willow Tearooms & Glasgow School of Art* have decorative schemes by their architect, C.R. Mackintosh.

NORTHERN SCOTLAND & THE ISLANDS

Aberdeen, Grampian.
Emphasis of *Art Gallery* coll. is on modern art, incl. sculpture (Rodin, Moore, Hepworth, Epstein).

WATERMILLS & WATERWHEELS

THE WEST COUNTRY

Blaise Hamlet, Avon.
Blaise Castle Folk Museum has reconstruction of Stratford Mill.
Chard, Somerset.
Hornsby Mills. 19th-C. corn mill in working order.
Claverton, nr Bath, Avon.
Wide wheel on R. Avon which powered beam pump used for lifting water to canal.
Cotehele, Cornwall.
Modern Mill on west bank of R. Tamar (National Trust).
Priston Mill, nr Bath, Avon.
Overshot wheel, still grinds flour.
Sticklepath, Devon.
Museum of Rural Industry centred on Finch Foundry, which has 3 working wheels.
Wheal Martyn, Cornwall.
Restored water-powered *beam pump*.

SOUTH-EAST ENGLAND

Burwash, E. Sussex.
Park Mill in grounds of Bateman's restored by National Trust.
Calbourne, Isle of Wight.
Upper Mill has interesting coll. of relics, incl. pair of hand-driven millstones.
Hailsham, E. Sussex.
Michelham Priory, Upper Dicker, has restored flour mill.
Haxted Mill, Surrey.
Coll. of milling relics & 2 working wheels.
Shalford Mill, Surrey.
Dates from 18th C. Wheel & various paraphernalia.

THE THAMES, CHILTERNS & EAST ANGLIA

Bintree Mill, Norfolk.
4-storeyed, on R. Wensum.
Colchester, Essex.
Bourne Mill, built 16th C. Converted to corn-grinding in 19th C. May be seen by permission.
St Albans, Herts.
Kingsbury Watermill Museum.
Woodbridge, Suffolk.
Tidal mill, built *c.* 1793, restored to working order.

CENTRAL ENGLAND

Alcester, Warks.
Great Alne Mill, still grinding flour.
Alvingham Watermill, nr Louth, Lincs.
17th-C. mill, with breast wheel.
Bakewell, Derbys.
Victoria Mill. Water-powered corn mill, built *c.* 1800, operated until 1945.
Balsall Common, Warks.
Berkswell Mill, 4-storey, restored.
Bibury, nr Cirencester, Glos.
Arlington Mill Museum in restored corn mill.
Birmingham, W. Midlands.
Sarehole Mill, Mosely. 18th-C. corn mill (also used for grinding blades) in working order.
Cromford, Derbys.
Arkwright's *Old Mill* has iron overshot wheel.
Leek, Staffs.
Brindley Water Mill, 18th C. Operational. Contains James Brindley Museum. *Cheddleton Flint Mill*. Twin waterwheels operate flint grinders.
Little Billing, Northants.
Billing Mill, early 19th C., restored. Features large iron wheel.
Redditch, Heref. & Worcs.
Forge Mill, a needle mill (1730s).
Rowsely, Derbys.
Caudwell's Mill, built 1874 as a corn mill, later converted to roller milling.
Stamford, Lincs.
Hudd's Mill, 17th C. Has 2 iron waterwheels.
Tealby, Lincs.
Breastshot wheel. Dates from 1790.

YORKSHIRE, HUMBERSIDE & THE NORTH-WEST

Abbeydale, nr Sheffield, S. Yorks.
Abbeydale Industrial Hamlet has 4 waterwheels, associated with scythe-making.
Barnsley, S. Yorks.
Worsbrough Mill Museum. 17th- & 19th-C. corn mills with cast-iron overshot wheel.
Laxey, Isle of Man.
'*Lady Isabella*': giant waterwheel built in 1854 to drain lead mine.
Lothersdale, nr Keighley, N. Yorks.
Dale End Mill has large iron wheel of 1862.
Nether Alderley Mill, Cheshire.
Restored 15th-C. corn mill.
Pately Bridge, N. Yorks.
Foster Beck Mill (hemp) has large external breast wheel.
Sheffield, S. Yorks.
Shepherd Wheel, with restored metalworking machinery.
Skipton, N. Yorks.
High Mill, restored.
Stretton, Cheshire.
Corn mill of 17th C.
Wortley, S. Yorks.
Water-powered *forge*, founded 17th C.

THE NORTH OF ENGLAND

Boot, Cumbria.
Eskdale Watermill. Medieval. 2 wheels, each linked to pair of millstones.
Ford, Northumb.
Heatherslaw Mill has 2 working wheels.
Muncaster, Cumbria.
Restored corn mill.
Otterburn, Northumb.
Woollen mill.
Weardale Forest, Durham.
Huge *overshot wheel* is all that remains of machinery for Killhope Lead Mine.

WALES

Capel Dewi, Llandyssul, Dyfed.
Rock Mills (founded 1890), a woollen mill with 19th-C. wheel still in use.
Carew, nr Pembroke, Dyfed.
French Mill, just below the castle. An interesting tide mill.
Cwm Cou, nr Newcastle Emlyn, Dyfed.
Felin Geri Flour Mill still operates. Rare water-powered saw mill nearby.
Gelligroes, nr Pontllanfraith, Gwent.
Corn mill unaltered since 16th C.
Narberth, Dyfed.
Blackpool Mill, built in 1813 for wheat grinding & flour making. One of Britain's finest corn-grinding mills.
Rossett, nr Wrexham, Clwyd.
Half-timbered corn mill. Dated 1661, but may be 14th-C. in origin. 19th-C. wheel.
St Fagans, Cardiff, S. Glam.
Melin Bompren Corn Mill, in grounds of Welsh Folk Museum. Reconstructed 19th-C. country mill. Also on site: water-powered woollen mill.
Wrexham, Clwyd.
Felin Puleston Corn Mill in use 1620.

SOUTHERN SCOTLAND

Wanlockhead, Dumf. & Gall.
Preserved water-bucket engine, formerly used for draining Straitsheps lead mine.

CENTRAL SCOTLAND & STRATHCLYDE

Edinburgh, Lothian.
Royal Scottish Museum has fine wheel of 'suspension' type, made in 1826.
East Linton, Lothian.
Preston Mill has fine cast-iron wheel (18th C.).

NORTHERN SCOTLAND & THE ISLANDS

Blair Atholl, Tayside.
Meal & flour mill, 18th C.
Dounby, Orkney.
Click Mill: only working example of a traditional Orkney horizontal watermill.

WINDMILLS

THE WEST COUNTRY

Chapel Allerton, Somerset.
Ashton Mill: well-preserved tower mill.
High Ham, Langport, Somerset.
Thatch-roof *tower mill*, 1820s.
Wilton, nr Great Bedwyn, Wilts.
Restored tower mill, 1821.

SOUTH-EAST ENGLAND

Bembridge, Isle of Wight.
Tower mill (early 18th C.).
Margate, Kent.
Draper's Mill: smock mill, mid-19th C.
Mayfield, E. Sussex.
Argos Hill: post mill (*c.* 1835).
Meopham, Kent.
Smock mill of 1801, restored.
Nutley, E. Sussex.
Post Mill (*c.* 1670), not operational.
Polegate, nr Eastbourne, E. Sussex.
Tower mill (early 19th C.); milling exhibits, complete machinery.
Redhill, Surrey.
On Outwood Common:post mill (1665), oldest working windmill in Britain.
Shipley, W. Sussex.
King's Mill: smock mill (1879), once owned by writer Hilaire Belloc.
Singleton, W. Sussex.
Pevensey windpump in *Weald & Downland Open Air Museum*.

THE THAMES, CHILTERNS & EAST ANGLIA

Berney Arms, Norfolk.
Windpump beside R. Yare.
Bocking, Essex.
Post mill, contains milling relics.
Bourn, Cambs.
Typical early *post mill*, 17th C.

Brill, Bucks.
Late 17th-C. *post mill.*
Denver, Norfolk.
Victorian tower mill, with *mill museum.*
Great Bircham, Norfolk.
Victorian *tower mill.*
Holton, Halesworth, Suffolk.
Post mill (1749), little machinery.
Horsey, Norfolk.
Windpump, with view over marshes.
Lacey Green, Bucks.
Oldest *smock mill* in England (*c.* 1650).
Milton Keynes, Bucks.
Bradwell Mill, New Bradwell. Tower mill, *c.* 1815.
Over, Cambs.
Restored 19th-C. *tower mill.* Flour sold.
Pitstone, nr Ivinghoe, Bucks.
Earliest dated English windmill (1627): a *post mill.*

Ramsey, Essex.
Victorian *post mill.*
Rayleigh, Essex.
Late 18th-C. *post mill.*
Saxtead Green, nr Framlingham, Suffolk.
1854 post mill (no longer operational).
Stansted Mountfitchet, Essex.
Tower mill, c. 1785.
Stevington, Beds.
Post mill, 1770.
Sutton, nr Stalham, Norfolk.
Tallest windmill in England: 1789 *tower mill.*
Thaxted, Essex.
Restored *tower mill,* 1804.
Wicken Fen, Cambs.
Drainage *smock mill,* built 1908. Now used to maintain water table of nature reserve.

CENTRAL ENGLAND
Alford, Lincs.
Impressive *tower mill* (1813), still in use.
Balsall Common, W. Midlands.
Berkswell Mill: tower mill (1826), machinery in good order.
Bromsgrove, Heref. & Worcs.
Avoncroft Museum of Buildings has reconstructed post mill.
Burgh-le-Marsh, Lincs.
Restored 5-sailed tower mill (1833), with working machinery.
Chesterton, Warks.
Tower mill, 17th C.
Dale Abbey, Derbys.
Cat & Fiddle Mill: post mill, 1788.
Heage, nr Ambergate, Derbys.
Restored 6-sail *tower mill.*
Heckington, Lincs.
Only 8-sail *tower mill* in England, 1830.

Kibworth Harcourt, Leics.
Restored *post mill,* 1711.
North Leverton, Notts.
Tower mill, 1813.
Sibsey Mill, Lincs.
Restored 6-sail *tower-mill,* 1877.
Wymondham, Leics.
Early 19th-C. *tower mill,* with machinery.
YORKSHIRE, HUMBERSIDE & NORTH-WEST
Wrawby, Humber.
Restored *post mill* (1790s): milling relics.
WALES
Llwyngwern Quarry, nr Machynlleth, Powys.
National Centre for Alternative Technology has experiments in wind-power.

Acknowledgements

CONTRIBUTORS

Page numbers of contributions are given in brackets.
P.J. Banyard (122–7); Professor S.H. Beaver (164–5); Professor E.G. Bowen (46–9, 52–3); Professor Eric Brown 12–29); Professor R.A. Butlin (36–7, 40–41, 134–9, 144–5, 148–51, 206–207, 220–221, 226–7, 234–5, 238–41); Hugh Canning (300 301); Dr Neil Cossons (146–7); Dr Robert A. Dodgshon (42–3, 56–7, 60–65, 128–9, 132–3, 142–3, 152–5, 158–63, 192–5, 222–3, 228–31, 236–7, 256–7); Sarah Eldridge (44–5, 102–3, 200–201, 302–303); Judith Evans (80–81); Shula Fury (86–7, 224–5, 296–9); John Glaves-Smith (288–9); E.H.M. Harris (30–31); Jeanette A. Harris (32–5); R.I. Hodgson (252–3); *the late* Dr Alan J. Lee (120–21); Professor Donal McCartney (66–7); Michael March (272–5); Professor Arthur Marwick (74–5, 90–91, 110–111, 116–19); Dr Richard Pestell (202–205); Colin Read (156–7, 166–83); John A. Roberts (280–87, 290–95); Martin Shreeves (104–105); Frank Sowerby (208–13, 216–19); L.A. Spong (184–7); Dr John Stevenson (68–9, 76–9, 82–5, 88–9, 92–101, 106–109, 112–15); Dr Michael Tracey (276–7); Geoffrey Trease (58–9, 70–73, 196–9, 214–15, 242–51, 254–5); Dr B.J. Turton (260–71); Dr John Waller (50–51, 54–5); Dr J.R. Walton (188–9, 232–3); Dr Mark Wise (140–41).

RESEARCH SOURCES

So many books have been referred to in the course of research for Britain Discovered *that it would be impossible to list them all. The following, however, have proved particularly useful.* John Adair, *The Pilgrim's Way* (1978); Janet and Colin Bord, *A Guide to Ancient Sites in Britain* (1978); Asa Briggs, *Victorian Cities* (1963); Chris Cook and John Stevenson, *Longman Atlas of Modern British History* (1978); R.J. Cootes, *Britain Since 1700* (1968); *The Country Life Book of The Living History of Britain* (1981); David Daiches and John Flower, *Literary Landscapes of the British Isles* (1979); Mark Girouard, *Life in the English Country House* (1978); E.J. Hobsbawm, *Industry and Empire* (1968); W.G. Hoskins, *One Man's England* (1978) and *The Making of the English Landscape* (1977); R.B. Jones, *Economic and Social History of England, 1770–1977* (1979); P.F. Speed, *The Growth of the British Economy, 1700–1850* (1980).

PICTURE CREDITS

The publishers acknowledge the co-operation of photographers, photographic agencies and other organizations as listed below (with page numbers). Abbreviations used are: *t* top; *c* centre; *b* bottom; *l* left; *r* right. BBC HPL BBC Hulton Picture Library; BL The British Library; BM Trustees of the British Museum; CEGB Central Electricity Generating Board; MB Mitchell Beazley; MC The Mansell Collection; MERL University of Reading, Institute of Agricultural History & Museum of English Rural Life; NPG National Portrait Gallery, London; V & A Victoria & Albert Museum.

Jacket front Denis Waugh/Tony Stone Photolibrary. *Front flap* Jon Wyand. *Jacket back tl* S. & C. Mathews; *tr* E.T. Archives; *bl* Ken Hewis Archive; *br* A.F Kersting. *Back flap* The National Maritime Musuem.

1 Chris Forsey. 2–5 Colin Molyneux. 6/7 Anthony Howarth/Susan Griggs Agency. 8/9 Noel Habgood/Derek G. Widdicombe.

NATURE & THE LANDSCAPE
10/11 Cwm-parc, Rhondda Valley, Wales (Colin Molyneux). 12 Fay Godwin's Photo Files. 13*t* Thames Water Authority; *b* Maurice Nimmo; *map* University of Dundee. 15*t* Derek G. Widdicombe; *c* Webster of Oban; *rocks tl, cr* & *br* David Bayliss/Rida; *tr, cl* & *bl* Institute of Geological Sciences. 17*t* Aerofilms; *b* Institute of Geological Sciences. 18*t* P. Morris; *b* Sefton Photo Library, Manchester. 19*t* P. Morris; *b* Cambridge University Collection. 20*t* Bryan & Cherry Alexander; *b* P. Barnes, London Brick. 21*t* Noel Habgood/Derek G. Widdicombe; *cl* Janet & Colin Bord; *br* P. Morris. 22*t* The Ramblers' Association; *b* Handford Photography. 23*t* British Tourist Authority; *b* Sefton Photo Library, Manchester. 24 Aerofilms. 25*l* Rida; *r* Aerofilms. 26*t* Handford Photography; *b* Michael & Pamela Whitehead/Jones. 27*t* S & O Mathews; *b* Institute of Geological Sciences. 29*tl* Airviews (M/c) Ltd.; *tr* John Merrill; *b* Aerofilms. 30*t* William Grant; *cl* S & O Mathews; *cr* A. Horner/Halcyon; *b* Christopher Maguire. 32 C.K. Mylne/Nature Photographers. 33*t* Derek G. Widdicombe; *bl* Bryan Sage; *br* Dr Alan Beaumont. 34*tl* & *tc* Ron & Christine Foord; *tr* Bryan Sage; *b* S & O Mathews. 35*l* Rodger Jackman/Wildlife Picture Agency; *tr* Eric Hosking; *br* Dr Alan Beaumont. 36*tl* Bryan & Cherry Alexander; *tr* & *br* Aerofilms; *bl* Paul Burnham/Ecology Pictures. 37 *t* & *b* Aerofilms; *c* MC.

THE SHAPING OF THE PRESENT
38/9 Sealed Knot Pageant (Spectrum Colour Library). 40 MC. 41*t* MC; *b* Marilyn Clark. 42*t* Chris Forsey; *bl* Homer Sykes; *br* Michael Holford. 43*l* Aerofilms; *r* Pitkin Pictorials Ltd. 44 BBC HPL. 45*tl* GLC Photo Library; *tr* Nicholas Breach; *bl* Mick Gold Archiv; *br* John Sturrock/Network. 46*l* Peter Clayton; *r* Scottish Tourist Board. 47*tl* BL; *tr* & *b* Janet & Colin Bord. 48*t* BL; *cr* MC; *b* BL. 49 Aerofilms; *inserts* MC. 50*tl* & *bl* MC; *tr* BBC HPL; *br* York City Art Gallery. 51*l* NPG; *r* Canon K.W. Coates. 52*l* & *br* MC; *tr* BL. 53*tl* The Museum of London; *tr* Clive Hicks; *bl* Stonyhurst College by kind permission of the Rector/Pye's of Clitheroe; *br* A.F. Kersting. 54*t* Library of the Society of Friends; *bl* engraving from *Wesley, his own biographer*, 1891; *bc* Methodist Church Overseas Division; *br* Colin Molyneux. 55*t* Baptist Union; *b* John Goldblatt. 56*l* Reece Winstone; *r* English Tourist Board. 57*t* City of Manchester Art Galleries; *b* Janet & Colin Bord. 58 By courtesy of Mr Simon Wingfield Digby. Sherborne Castle. 59*t* Society of Antiquaries of London; *c* Camera Press, London; *b* Fox Photos. 60*tl* Master & Fellows of Corpus Christi College, Cambridge; *tr* Clive Hicks; *b* MC. 61*t* & *c* MC; *b* Crown Copyright/The Scottish Development Department. 62*l* Scottish National Portrait Gallery/Tom Scott; *r* P.J. Drinkwater; *map* John Bartholomew & Son Ltd., Edinburgh. 63*t* & *cr* The Museum of Scottish Tartans; *cl* & *c* The Museum of Scottish Tartans/Ph: MB/Angelo Hornak. 64*t* Wales Tourist Board; *b* MC. 65*tl* & *r* Wales Tourist Board; *b* Colin Molyneux. 66*t* National Gallery of Ireland; *bl* The Bridgeman Art Library; *br* Leeds Art Galleries. 67*tl* & *r* MC; *b* Irish Linen Guild. 68*t* & *bl* MC; *br* BL. 69*t* A.F. Kersting; *b* MC. 70*l* Michael Holford; *r* Ghent, University Library, MS 236. 71 British Tourist Authority. 72*tl* NPG; *tr* Fotomas Index; *b* Kevin Brownlow & Andrew Mollo/BFI Production Board. 73*l* BL; *r* MC. 74*t* & *bl* Mary Evans Picture Library; *br* E.T. Archive. 75*tl* John Garrett; *tr* Rugby School/Ph: Midsummer Books; 75*b* Granada Television. 76 MC. 77*tl* MC; *tr* BBC HPL; *b* Fotomas Index. 78*l* The Bridgeman Art Library; *c* & *r* Ken Hewis Archive. 79*tl* Labour Party Library; *tr* Jon Blau/Camera Press, London; *b* Camera Press (The Times), London. 80*t* BBC HPL; *bl* Manchester Public Libraries; *br* Edwin Smith. 81*tl* BBC HPL; *tr* Morning Telegraph, Sheffield; *c* MC; *b* Brian & Sally Shuel. 82 MC. 83*t* & *c* BBC HPL; *b* Topham. 84*tl* & *br* MC; *tr* Trades Union Congress Library; *cr* Labour Party Library; *bl* BBC HPL. 85 John Sturrock/Network. 86*tl* MC; *tc* Courtesy National Museum of Wales (Welsh Folk Museum); *tr* BBC HPL; *b* St Alban's City Museum. 87 Topham. 88*t* National Monuments Record; *b* BBC HPL 89*tl* MC; *tr* & *br* John Sturrock/Network; *bl* BBC HPl. 90*tl* BL; *tr* & *br* MC; *bl* Collection of the Duke of Buccleuch and Queensberry, K.T., Bowhill, Selkirk/Ph: Tom Scott. 91*tl* Harrogate Art Gallery; *tr* John Gorman Collection; *b* Fawcett Library, City of London Polytechnic/Ph: MB/John Goldblatt. 92*tl* MERL; *tr* The Harris Museum & Art Gallery, Preston; *bl* Topham; *br* Richard Perry/Country Life. 92/3*t* MC; *b* Aerofilms. 94 *coins t* Ashmolean Museum, Oxford, *c* & *b* Museum of London; *tr* & *bl* MC; *br* E.T. Archive. 95*tl* & *bl* The Governor and Company of the Bank of England, *tr* Popperfoto; *br* The Stock Exchange. 96*tl* Reproduced by permission of the Trustees, the Wallace Collection, London; *tr* Edwin Smith; *bl* Topham; *br* Loomis Dean/Camera Press, London. 97*tl* Stewart Bale Ltd.; *tr* Frank Herrman/Camera Press, London; *b* Topham. 98 E.T. Archive. 99*tl* Reproduced by permission of the Director of the India Office Library & Records; *tr* National Army Museum; *b* Popperfoto. 100*t* MC; *bl* Bodleian Library; *br* BBC HPL. 101*l* E.T. Archive; *c* MC; *r* Colin Davey/Camera Press, London. 102*tl* MC; *tr* Ironbridge Gorge Museum Trust; *bl* Mary Evans Picture Library; *r* W.H. Smith & Son Ltd. 103*t* Wales Tourist Board; *bl* Freemans PLC; *bc* Unigate PLC; *br* Courtesy of the John Lewis Partnership. 104 *t* & *bl* MC; *c* Fotomas Index; *br* Granada Television. 105 *t* The Scotsman Publications Ltd.; *b* A.F. Kersting. 106*tl* E.T. Archive; *tr* & *b* MC. 107 *l* & *c* Barnaby's Picture Library; *r* Crown Copyright Reserved. 108*t* BL; *b* MC. 109*t* MC; *bl* BBC HPL; *br* Topham; 110*t* The Librarian, Glasgow University Library, MS Hunter 364; *b* St Bartholomew's Hospital, London. 111*t* By courtesy of the Wellcome Trustees; *cl* MC; *cr* St Thomas' Hospital Archives/Greater London Record Office; *b* Papworth Hospital, Cambridge. 112*t* GLC Photo Library; *bl* MC; *br* Crown Copyright Reserved/The Royal Scottish Museum. 113*t* GLC Photo Library; *b* BBC Copyright. 114*tl* British Architectural Library/RIBA; *tr* Thomas Photos, Oxford; *b* University of Saint Andrews. 115*t* University of Sussex;

b Middlesex Polytechnic. 116tl BL; tr Crown Copyright, Science Museum, London; c NPG; b MC. 117t Crown Copyright. Science Museum, London; cl The Tate Gallery, London; cr The National Maritime Museum, London; b MC. 118t MC; c Wimbledon Lawn Tennis Museum/Ph: MB; b The Bridgeman Art Library. 119t Leo Mason; c & b Sporting Pictures (UK) Ltd. 120 tl & b MC; tr BBC HPL; 121t BBC HPL; bl Associated Newspapers Group Ltd.; br Crabtree Vickers. 122tr & br NPG; cl BL; bl Anne Cardale. 123t The Royal Green Jackets Museum; b National Army Museum. 124t & c Imperial War Museum; b BBC HPL. 125t NPG; c Imperial War Museum. 126 Fox Photos. 127t Fox Photos; cl BBC HPL; cr Popperfoto; b Franklin D. Roosevelt Library, NY. 128tl Copyright National Museum of Wales (Welsh Folk Museum); tr The Architects' Journal; b Dean & Chapter of Canterbury Cathedral. 129tl & c National Monuments Record; tr The Landmark Trust; b Aerofilms.

FARMING & INDUSTRY
130/31 Ratcliffe Power Station (CEGB). 132 BL. 133tl Aerofilms; tr BL. 134t Bedfordshire County Council; b R.A. Butlin. 135 MERL. 136t MC; b MERL. 137t MERL; b MC. 138t A.W. Ward/Halcyon; b Daphne Machin Goodall. 139tl David Boag/Halcyon; tr S & O Mathews; cl Midland Marts Group; b Derek G. Widdicombe. 140 Reg Weir. 141l Nik Korda; r MacFisheries Ltd.; b MOD (Navy) Photograph. 142t BL; bl MC; br British Wool Marketing Board. 143tl Clifford Robinson/Halcyon; tr Derek G. Widdicombe; b International Wool Secretariat. 144t Arkwright Collection/Courtauld Institute of Art; c Mary Evans Picture Library; b Crown Copyright. Science Museum, London. 145t & br Ironbridge Gorge Museum Trust; bl MC. 146l Nottingham Industrial Museum; c, r & map Ironbridge Gorge Museum Trust. 147 Ironbridge Gorge Museum Trust. 148t & bl Dr Alan Beaumont; br Bernard Alfieri. 149t Papplewick Pumping Station Trust; bl MC; br Hollycombe Steam Collection, Liphook. 150t Fotomas Index; b MC. 151 National Coal Board. 152tl National Museum of Wales; tr Derbyshire Library Service; b H.M. Parker; map of *Magpie Mine* Peak District Mines Historical Society. 153t Westend Photographic, Redruth; b The National Trust. 154 National Museum of Wales. 154/5 Tarmac Roadstone Holdings Ltd. 155 insert Derek G. Widdicombe; tr The Salt Museum, Northwich (Cheshire Museums); bl R.A. Dodgshon; bc Llechwedd Slate Caverns; br Amey Roadstone Corporation. 156t & b British Gas Corporation; c Lent to Science Museum, London by Drake's Ltd. 157t British Petroleum; b BP Oil Limited. 158t & cr W.K.V. Gale; cl Crown Copyright. Science Museum, London; b Derek G. Widdicombe. 159 British Steel Corporation. 160t Crown Copyright. Science Museum, London; bl MC; br Coats Patons PLC. 161t MC; bl Mick Gold Archiv; br BBC HPL. 162tl The Museum of Costume, Bath; tr Renfrew District Council Museum & Arts Service; b BM. 163t City of Manchester Art Galleries; b Archie Miles. 164l Gladstone Pottery Museum; r MC. 165t Albion Galleries, Stoke-on-Trent; cl & c V & A; cr Gladstone Pottery Museum. 166t BBC HPL; b & map CEGB. 167t Malcolm J. Gilson/Camera Press, London; b Handford Photography. 168t BBC HPL; c UK Atomic Energy Authority; b CEGB. 169tl UK Atomic Energy Authority; tr Michael Abrahams/Network; b CEGB. 170tr The Zoological Society of London; tc The Board of Trinity College, Dublin; bc MC; bl Tim Stephens/The National Trust; bc Jon Wyand; br Timber Research & Development Association. 171l Marjorie Price; r National Westminster Bank PLC. 172tl Malaysian Rubber Producers' Research Association; r Dunlop Ltd.; b Clarks Limited. 173tl Sheffield City Museum; tr MC; b Pilkington Brothers PLC. 174tl Crown Copyright. Science Museum, London; tr Alfred Herbert Ltd; c NPG; bl The Reference Library, Local Studies Dept., Birmingham Public Libraries; br British Rail Western. 175tl This first appeared in 'New Scientist', London; tr Handford Photography; b Hall Automation Ltd. 176t UML Limited; c Keystone Press Agency; b ICI Fibres. 177t Imperial Chemical Industries Ltd.; b Crown Copyright Reserved. 178t Spectrum Colour Library; bl The National Maritime Museum, London; br The National Gallery, London. 179t BBC HPL; cl & cr Anne Cardale; b Archie Miles. 180t Royal Air Force Museum, Hendon; b Rolls-Royce Ltd. 181t Popperfoto; b & diagram British Aerospace. 182tr National Motor Museum, Beaulieu; cl Peter Roberts; b BL Heritage Ltd. 183 Austin Rover. 184t MC; 184/5b Topham. 185t Royal Institution of Cornwall; b Imperial Group Ltd. 186tl & diagram The Distillers Company PLC; cr Hugh Johnson. 187tl H.P. Bulmer; tr S & O Mathews; b John Goldblatt. 188tl MC; tr Edwin Smith; b Kodak Museum/Topham. 189tl Derek G. Widdicombe; tr & bl Fox Photos; br Topham.

BUILDINGS & PLACES
190/91 Nat. West. Tower, London (National Westminster Bank PLC). 192tl Clive Hicks; tr BM; bl Aerofilms; br Janet & Colin Bord. 193t BM; b Janet & Colin Bord. 194t Anne Cardale; b Janet & Colin Bord. 195t Janet & Colin Bord; b Michael Holford. 196t English Tourist Board; b Aerofilms. 197 Scottish Tourist Board. 198t Wales Tourist Board; b Clive Hicks. 199t The National Trust; bl Handford Photography; br Ken Cope/Halcyon. 200 A.F. Kersting. 201tl National Monuments Record; tr & b Edwin Smith. 202tl Sonia Halliday; tr & b A.F. Kersting. 203 A.F. Kersting. 205t A.F. Kersting.; b Edwin Smith. 206 S & O Mathews. 207tl Mount Saint Bernard Abbey; tr & b Saint Michael's Abbey, Farnborough. 208t A.F. Kersting; lc & b MC; rc John Bethell/The National Trust. 209t A.F. Kersting; cr Edwin Smith; b Country Life. 210l Edwin Smith; r A.F. Kersting. 211t Clive Friend/The National Trust; cl A.F. Kersting; cr M.E. Murnane/St Mary's College, Twickenham; b John Bethell/The National Trust. 212t Edwin Smith; c & br A.F. Kersting; bl BBC HPL. 213l A.F. Kersting; r Edwin Smith. 214t Airviews (M/c) Ltd.; b A.F. Kersting. 215t Reproduced by Gracious Permission of Her Majesty the Queen; c BBC HPL; b P. Lichfield/Camera Press, London. 216t from D. Hyll, *The Gardeners' Labyrinth*/Ph: MB/Chris Barker; b Paul Miles. 217t Arthur Hellyer; cl Paul Miles; cr Edwin Smith; b Knyff & Kip, c. 1690/Ph: MB. 218tl Iris Hardwick Library; tr Peter Hayden; b Royal Horticultural Society/Ph: MB/Chris Barker. 219tl from J.E. Smith, *Exot. Bot.*, 1804–5/Ph: MB; tc MC; tr Linda Burgess/Botanical Pictures; bl S & O Mathews; br Royal Botanic Gardens, Edinburgh/Ph: Rich Newton. 220t Topham; b Iris Hardwich Library. 221tl G.A. Jennings/The National Trust; tr Iris Hardwick Library; b Trevor Wood. 222tl Museum of East Anglian Life; bl R.A. Dodgshon; br Clive Hicks. 222/3t Colin Molyneux; tr S & O Mathews; bl Lawrence Clarke; br Aerofilms. 224tl & cl Topham; tr Edwin Smith; cr A.F. Kersting; b BBC HPL. 225t Derek G. Widdicombe; b A.F. Kersting. 226t S & O Mathews; c Angelo Hornak; b MC. 227tl Iris Hardwick Library; tr Clifford Robinson/Halcyon; b The City Engineer, Newcastle. 228tl Fotomas Index; cr & bl BBC HPL. 228/9t UML Limited; tr from E. Howard, *To-Morrow: A Peaceful Path to Real Reform*, 1898. b Cumbernauld Development Corporation. 230t Bristol City Art Gallery/The Bridgeman Art Library; c Westminster Dredging Company. 230/1 Port of London Authority; r Archie Miles; b Ironbridge Gorge Museum Trust. 232tl Edwin Smith; tr Topham; b MERL. 233tl MC; tr Topham; b Godfrey Bell. 234t & b BEAMISH, North of England Open Air Museum; cl BBC HPL; r Wales Tourist Board. 235 Colin Molyneux. 236t MC; c & b BBC HPL. 237tl Topham; tr BBC HPL; b Aerofilms. 238t & cl MC; cr Butlin's Ltd.; b Chris Forsey. 239tl S & O Mathews; tr R. Calbutt/Halycon; b Chris Forsey. 240t & b BBC HPL; cl E.T. Archive; cr London Transport. 241tl BBC HPL; tr & b Topham; cr Robert M. Saxton. 242 The Museum of London. 243tl & b Angelo Hornak; tr BL. 244t MC; cl Guildhall Library, City of London; cr Fotomas Index. 245t Popperfoto; b Crown Copyright reproduced with permission of Her Majesty's Stationery Office. 246t & b Angelo Hornak; c Guildhall Library, City of London. 247t & b The Bridgeman Art Library; c Guildhall Library, City of London. 248l BBC HPL; r MC. 249 MC. 250t Alexander Ramsay; c Brian & Sally Shuel; b The Guildhall, London/The Bridgeman Art Library (detail). 251tl Anne Cardale; tr Will Green; bl Patrick Ward; br Chris Sowe. 252t MC; b Manchester Public Libraries. 253t & c Manchester Public Libraries; b The Royal Exchange Theatre Company; map H.B. Rodgers. 254t Marjorie Price; bl Aerofilms; br Thomas Photos, Oxford. 255tl Billett Potter; tr The Fitzwilliam Museum, Cambridge; b Chris Forsey. 256tl & bl MC; tr BBC HPL; br Robert F. Herrick/Edinburgh Festival Fringe Society. 257t J.M. Mackie; b Scottish Tourist Board.

TRANSPORT & COMMUNICATIONS
258/9 Crossing the River Wansbeck, Northumberland (Mike Esau). 260 BBC HPL. 261tl, b & diagram British Waterways Board; tr Derek Pratt. 262tl Crown Copyright. Science Museum, London; tr MC; b Mike Esau. 263 British Rail, Midland Region. 264tl Unigate PLC; tr & b BBC HPL; c Crown Copyright. National Railway Museum, York. 265tl Mike Esau; tr Crown Copyright. National Railway Museum, York; cl G.J. Biddle, cr London Transport; b BBC HPL. 266tl Crown Copyright. National Railway Museum, York; tr Jarrold, Norwich; b Angelo Hornak. 267t Mike Esau; b British Rail. 268 Aerofilms. 269t MC; b BBC HPL. 270tl BBC HPL; bl & c Topham; br A.R.M. Buist; map Civil Aviation Authority. 270/1 A.R.M. Buist; b Handford Photography. 272tl Post Office; tr & b Crown Copyright. 273t Crown Copyright; others Post Office. 274 British Telecom. 275 British Telecom. 276t The Marconi Company; b BBC HPL. 277tl The Marconi Company; tr & b BBC Copyright.

THE ARTS
278/9 Sir Peter Lely: *An Idyll* ('Lely and his Family'), Courtauld Institute Galleries, London (Lee Collection). 280l BM; r A.F. Kersting. 281tl Dean & Chapter of Winchester/Warburg Institute; tr Edwin Smith; b The National Gallery, London. 282tl The National Gallery, London; tr & b V & A. 283t Reproduced by Gracious Permission of Her Majesty the Queen; bl & c Michael Holford; br Jeremy Whitaker/The National Trust. 284tl & b The National Gallery, London; c A.F. Kersting. 285tl A.F. Kersting; tr City of Manchester Art Galleries; b V & A. 286 Laing Art Gallery & Museum, Newcastle upon Tyne. 287tl The Tate Gallery; tc & tr V & A; cr Birmingham Museums & Art Gallery; bl John Goldblatt; br John Roberts. 288tl Glasgow School of Art; tr & br The Tate Gallery; bl London Transport. 289t Private Collection; c John Goldblatt; b The Tate Gallery. 290t MC; bl BM; br Tony Davison/The National Trust. 291t The National Gallery, London; b Anne Cardale. 292t V & A; cr The National Trust; bl Jeremy Whitaker/The National Trust; br By Permission of the Earl of Harewood. 293t Percival David Foundation of Chinese Art; c BM; b The Royal Pavilion, Art Gallery & Museums, Brighton. 294tl P.J. Drinkwater; tr City of Salford Art Gallery; b Castle Museum, Nottingham. 295tl NPG; tr National Gallery of Scotland/Ph: Tom Scott; bl The National Trust; br BM. 296tl MC; tr Angle Books/Photo: MB/Angelo Hornak; bl Roger Scruton; br Sonia Halliday. 297t & c MC; b British Tourist Authority. 298tl NPG; tr Scottish Tourist Board; cl Robert M. Saxton; bl The Brontë Society/Ph: W. Scott (Bfd.) Ltd.; br The Brontë Society. 299 Colin Molyneux. 300tl British Tourist Authority; tr BBC HPL; b BBC Copyright. 301tl By kind permission of the Whittaker Centenary Fund; tr Guy Gravett/Glyndebourne Festival Opera; b Mick Gold Archiv. 302t & bcl E.T. Archive; bl Gerard Hearne Photography; bcr & br Ken Hewis Archive. 303 Holte Photographics Ltd.; map Ken Hewis.

Index

Page numbers in **bold** indicate that the topic is the subject of an essay, or sequence of essays. *Italic* page numbers refer to illustrations. The index does not cover 'Themes & places' (pp 304–26).